"In these pages are told the simple secrets of love, and Fran's story to uncover and live them. Here are our tears and crises, sudden moments of joy, simple human experiences combined with the taste of a deeper truth. This is the most precious offering we can make to life, to live this story, just as Fran has lived hers."
—From the foreword by Llewellyn Vaughan-Lee, The Golden Sufi Center

"More than eighty years after Paul Brunton's famed *Search in Secret India*, we are blessed to have before us just such a book for our times, Fran Grace's splendid and moving *The Power of Love*. It is full of gifts for the reader: visits with some of the most memorable spiritual figures of the past fifty years; Grace's story of the journey of her own soul as scholar, practitioner, and graced human being; and for all of us, a narrative of love's deep running and overflowing currents in today's thirsting world. This is a book for a wide audience of seekers, travelers, and scholars. It promises to feed the heart and soul, even as it awakens the mind again and again."
—Francis X. Clooney, SJ, Parkman Professor of Divinity, Harvard University

"This book is a masterpiece. Fran Grace takes us on an intimate journey revealing Love in all its facets, from the most sublime peaks of humankind's aspirations, to Love's omnipresence in the most wretched circumstances."
—Nisha Manek, M.D., Fellow of the American College of Physicians

"What matters is here!"
—Fr. Richard Rohr, OFM, Founder, Center for Action and Contemplation

"This book is wonderful. It gives me hope. It's such a good look at what people from all walks of life go through on a spiritual path. 'Doc' is still teaching...."
—Susan J. Hawkins, President, The Institute for Spiritual Research (founded by Dr. David R. "Doc" Hawkins, author of bestsellers *Power vs. Force* and *Letting Go*)

"This book really pulls one in. It's a fascinating look at the all-important subject of 'Love,' written from both a personal and an objective point of view—this is a rare combination!"
—Margaret Johnson, Ph.D., Co-Chief Editor of *Psychological Perspectives*; Board of Directors, C. G. Jung Study Center of Southern California

"This spiritual autobiography is very timely for a fractured world that needs to be reminded of the One in whom we all—regardless of religious affiliation—live and move and have our being. Love, truly, is the underlying path for all of us."
—Wilkie Au, Ph.D., Emeritus Professor of Theological Studies, Loyola Marymount University, Editorial Board of *Presence: An International Journal of Spiritual Direction*

"In her beautifully written and embracing book, Fran Grace gifts her readers the opportunity to 'listen in' on her direct, personal interviews of spiritual leaders from around the world and many spiritual traditions. Grace's sharing of her own life experiences of love alongside the lessons she learned from these spiritual masters invites her readers to reflect on the power of love in their own lives. The world needs this book now!"

—Karen Derris, Ph.D., Professor of Religious Studies at University of Redlands; co-editor of *The Heart is Noble* and *Interconnected* by His Holiness the 17th Karmapa

"What a beautiful gift Fran has given so us, sharing her journey both toward and through love. She reminds us that this is the only journey worth making!"

—Lorne Ladner, Ph.D., Clinical Psychologist, author of *The Lost Art of Compassion: Discovering the Practice of Happiness in the Meeting of Buddhism and Psychology*

"In this deeply honest and moving book, Fran Grace provides a kaleidoscope of images, experiences, and signs—all invitations into the greatest power in the universe. Readers from all walks of life will find what they need in these pages if they are looking for love."

—Hilary Hart, author of *The Unknown She: Eight Faces of an Emerging Consciousness* and *Body of Wisdom: Women's Spiritual Power and How It Serves.*

"*The Power of Love* is not just another monograph written by some expert detached from the real world; it's a look at the universal emotion of love as seen through the minds and hearts of people from all over the world and all walks of life, interwoven with the author's own learning on the journey of love. Each chapter is a book unto itself, with thoughtful and engaging content about different facets of love, while the totality of the book weaves a deep and comprehensive story of love. A decade ago when Fran Grace began her research, almost no one could have predicted the polemic times we are currently experiencing, and thus the timing of the book is perfect, even as *The Power of Love* will surely be timeless in its influence."

—David Taggart, creator of the global platform Republic of Humanity (www.republicofhumanity.org)

"This book gives us an opportunity to think about who we are, where we come from, our identity, and how we have a connection to all of our relatives, our ancestry and the teachings on love and peace that the elders passed onto us.... it shares teachings about the relationship that we have with one another and with people of different religions and different nations. The people who contributed all have a very special relationship not only with humankind but also with all of our relatives, other life forms, so it makes us think about, How do I relate to animal life—the four-legged, the winged, the water life? How are we going to love one another?"

—Mona Polacca, Havasupai-Hopi-Tewa charter member of The International Council of the Thirteen Indigenous Grandmothers, speaking at the 125th Parliament of the World's Religions in Toronto, November 2018

# THE POWER OF LOVE

## A TRANSFORMED HEART
## CHANGES THE WORLD

Fran Grace, Ph.D.

*Inner Pathway*

For information please contact:

The Institute for Contemplative Life
Attn: Inner Pathway Publishing
PO Box 1435
Redlands, CA 92373
Email: info@innerpathway.com
www.innerpathway.com
877 478-7284

Cover and book design by Cypress House/Kiersten Hanna

Publisher's Cataloging-in-Publication Data

Names: Grace, Fran, author.
Title: The power of love : a transformed heart changes the world / Fran Grace.
Description: First edition. | Redlands, CA : Innter Pathway, [2019] | Includes
        bibliographical references.
Identifiers: ISBN: 978-1-7323185-0-2 | 978-1-7323185-1-9 (ebook) |
        LCCN: 2018957377
Subjects: LCSH: Love. | Interpersonal relations. | Kindness. | Compassion. |
Self-realization. | Enlightenment. | Spiritual life. | Conduct of life.
Classification: LCC: BF575.L8 G73 2019 | DDC: 158.2--dc23

Printed in The United States of America

2 4 6 8 9 7 5 3 1

First edition

*Dedicated to my Teacher:*
*Love that is impersonal*
*in its essence,*
*Yet profoundly personal*
*in its effect*

*Out of gratitude for the gifts that were given, and to serve as a channel of love, any profits from the sale of this book will go to the nonprofit organizations of the people who contributed to the book. Through their works of love, they do much to reduce the suffering in our world.*

*Love changed the world each time it replaced non-love. The entire scheme of civilization could be profoundly altered by focusing this power of love at a very specific point. Whenever this happened, history bifurcated down new roads.*

—David R. Hawkins, Power vs. Force

# PERMISSIONS

The writings and recordings by Viktor Frankl, reprinted with permission of the Viktor Frankl Estate, 1 Mariannengasse, A-1090, Vienna, Austria, EU.

From *Long Walk to Freedom* by Nelson Mandela, copyright ©1994, 1995. Reprinted by permission of Little, Brown, and Company, an imprint of Hachette Book Group, Inc.

Heartfelt thanks to Elizabeth M. Cheatham, Fr. William Petrie, Ann and Jeanette Petrie of Petrie Productions, Daniel Liebert, Helen Luke, the Nelson Mandela Foundation, Joseph McMoneagle, O *Magazine*, Marilyn Peck, Ethel Spector Person, M.D., Howard Storm, Heartmath Institute, and Bloomsbury Publishing, Inc., New Directions Publishing, and Bishop Michael Curry.

# TABLE OF CONTENTS

# CAVEAT

The teachers encountered in these pages come from diverse backgrounds, pathways, and traditions. As such, they hold a variety of views on karma, scripture, theology, eschatology, sexuality, gender, and language, yet they all honor Love as a quality of Divinity/Reality and as a goal of spiritual life. At a time when human beings continue to harm and even kill others in the name of God, this book affirms that love is the heartbeat of all true religion and the expression of a truly noble heart.

# FOREWORD

When a spiritual path comes into your life, one question you can ask is "Does this path lead to love?" If it does, follow it. Love is the most mysterious and yet essential substance in our lives, the indefinable oxygen of the soul, which nourishes us in so many unseen ways. It is the most powerful force in creation, and yet expresses itself in the smallest, simplest ways: a glance in the eye, a kiss, a touch, and for the mystic an all-embracing feeling that starts as a sweet sorrow or tenderness within the heart and leads us back to God. Love takes us back to love, to the deepest core of our being where we are one with God, where love and Beloved merge, unite in their essential oneness—*unio mystica*.

*The Power of Love* is a lover's story, a spiritual story of the soul's journey in this world. Fran takes us on her own pilgrimage through life, in which a thread of divine love is woven into the texture of her days. This is the thread she follows, at times invisible, at times confusing and bewildering, painful but always present. It takes her from a fundamentalist sect to the house of her teacher, and then on his death back into the world, on the unexpected journey that for each lover is unique. She learns the lessons of love, openness, vulnerability, patience, and heartbreak, which all lead her deeper to this mystery within.

Fran first came to my door those years ago, wanting to hear my own story of divine love, how love had taken and turned me, given me a glimpse of its hidden face, its light and dazzling darkness. At that time I felt the sincerity of her heart, but I knew little of her own story, her searching and struggles. Through this book I have come to understand more of the longing and the challenges, the very human face of how this divine drama unfolded into her life. And more and more I feel the importance of our own unique story of love, how we journey with our faults and desires, failings and hidden wholeness. This is what we have to offer to our heart's beloved. There, deep within the heart, the mystery is so great, the vistas of divine love so vast, there are few words, just an infinite silence that beckons to the wayfarer, love's pilgrim. But our story, our struggles, are the footsteps we leave behind as we walk toward this infinite ocean. Here are our tears and crises, sudden moments of joy, simple human experiences combined with the taste of a deeper truth. This is the most precious offering we can make to life, to live this story, just as Fran has lived hers. Here the song of the soul is made holy.

Her story of love begins when, as a teenager, silently, unexpectedly, heaven opened and love and light were present. This is the gift that is given. But as every traveler knows, the work is then to live it, the pain is to make it present. And because our culture is starved from a deep understanding of mysticism and grace, there was no outer container, no wise man or woman to guide Fran, just an ignorant church pastor who told her the light and the love were the devil. So she closed a steel door on its unconditional wonder, and began the journey of separation from love that lasted many years.

The Sufis say that there are three journeys: the journey from God, the journey to God, and the journey in God. For Fran, as for many who have been touched unexpectedly by the divine, there were years of struggle, pain, and alienation until the journey to God began. Hers was a path that led through the confines of organized religion, its rules and creeds, where love's all-embracing nature and mystical dimension was veiled. Her struggles with her self and soul will resonate with all those whose path has followed a similar pattern. She was a missionary and a minister's wife, often contrasting "doing good works" with being "a loving person." Finally love takes her by the hand and draws her on a different path. Falling in love with a woman, she breaks free of the patriarchal confines of her church, and begins to experience the depth of her own feminine wisdom, her relationship to nature and to her own body.

Though personal love helped her on this journey, it was meeting the "living fire" of a spiritual teacher that was to finally turn her heart, her soul, her body, on the journey back to God. Here is the moment when the light of love that came to her in her teenage years is realized as the power of divine love. A little old man, who wore ordinary clothes, told jokes and drank espresso, became the most powerful bond of love she had ever experienced. She had found the guide who would take her Home.

The meeting with a real teacher is one of the great moments and mysteries of soul. Fran's whole book speaks to the power of this meeting, in which for the first time in her life she is recognized for her real self. And although this is a most traditional moment, reenacted over the centuries, it is also unique for each of us. It is our heart that is touched, our soul that comes fully alive. Here the story in her book takes on a deeper passion as the fire of love reaches into the core of her being. She leaves behind her identity as a woman wounded by a patriarchal society, fighting for injustice, recognizing that "there is only one change, really, and that is the change to love." Her spectrum of consciousness shifts as she begins to see with the eye of the heart, hear with the ear of the heart, reaching beyond the constrictions of any religious ideology, or even the patterns of personal relationship. And it is through this awakening consciousness that the reader encounters the other teachers Fran meets, hears the different qualities of their loving. She becomes a witness to the different ways of divine love.

It is this weaving together of different threads of love that makes her story sing. Each teacher has his or her own relationship to this divine substance, their own way of uncovering and living this essential power, its beauty and wonder, and Fran does not deny the presence of darkness in these stories. Her own journey had taken her through the struggles of organized religion that separated light and dark, that did not speak to a greater wholeness. But in her stories we hear of Mother Teresa's selfless service to all those in need in the name of love, as well as the despair of our own feelings of being separate from God; and Viktor Frankl's journey that took him through the horrors of the Holocaust as he lived his truth and discovered how love brings meaning. While Fran's experience of the church had been a struggle with their rigid rules and doctrine of excluding those who did not follow their creed, she hears the simple wisdom of Huston Smith who valued the joy at the heart of all religions, and how for him "love meant listening to others."

The stories and sayings of love continue through the pages of this book, told by those who have lived this mystery. Jetsunma Tenzin Palmo, who spent twelve years in a cave in the Himalayas in intensive retreat following direction from her Tibetan lama, speaks of the simple wisdom of loving kindness, "Until you love yourself you cannot love others." While in the forest of northern California, Sunlight, an ordinary person who had discovered the secret of love and its unconditional nature, says "Love people from your heart. That's what heals." The 17th Karmapa, head of a major Buddhist lineage, echoes this when he says, "Pure Love allows us to see the other as a part of ourselves, and we feel ourselves to be a part of the other." Oneness is an essential aspect of love, which always seeks to unite rather than divide.

These teachers of love point to what is most sacred within life. Love is the heartbeat of life, giving a primary color to our human experience. It is simple, essential and yet sadly often overlooked due to the ceaseless demands of our daily life, hidden beneath the noise and clutter of our culture. It cannot be bought or sold, because it belongs to God, and is our most direct experience of the divine. In these pages are told the simple secrets of love, and Fran's story to uncover and live them. It is always a gift—just as the light that descended that day in the classroom was a gift for Fran—but it is a gift that costs us heartache, sorrow and tears, even as it opens us in ways we could never imagine. God is love, and the journey to love is our deepest calling. In the words of Rūmī, love's greatest poet:

in the end
a person tires of everything
except heart's desiring,
soul's journeying

sultan, saint, pickpocket;
love has everyone by the ear
dragging us to God
by secret ways

—Llewellyn Vaughan-Lee,
The Golden Sufi Center

# PREFACE

I met my spiritual teacher when I was thirty-nine. At the time, I was a fiery feminist fighting the patriarchy. An old male sage was the last person I expected to "sit at the feet of"![1] But when the heart opens, there's no defense against the power of love. For me, he was the one place of Pure Love on the planet so I moved to be near him. When he died, my heart split wide-open with a painful longing I'd never felt before. Five days after his death, I had a dream that presaged the journey I would have to make in order to return to that Love.

> I arrive at the place where my teacher used to live. It's where he had his Realization. Everywhere I look, I see lush green. The atmosphere is misty and otherworldly—serene, silent, timeless. There's nothing manmade: No houses, no skyline, no people, no traffic, no noise, no roads. All is quiet; peace prevails. Looking around, I see no path and wonder: *How will I find my teacher's house?*
>
> An old woman sits in front of her hut on the banks of a wide, gently moving river. She appears to be a shopkeeper, but there's no one around to buy her goods. I realize she's there as a signpost, a guide. As in the legend of the Holy Grail, she reveals the answer only to those who ask the right question. To all others, she's just a shopkeeper sitting in front of her hut.

The old woman knows exactly what I mean when I ask, "How do I find the way to his house?" She points across the river and says, "Use the stepping-stones to cross over. Once you reach the other side, you'll see the lane that leads to his house."

Following this guidance, I cross the water and arrive at the other side. Through the mist, I see a narrow lane. Grass grows from the center of it and fir trees line the sides. It's a picturesque scene. I stand there, mesmerized by the simple beauty. This is the path that leads to my teacher's house.

It seems few people have been here. Who would even know it exists? It's not on any map or in any book. The atmosphere is mystical—totally ordinary yet totally rarefied. It's the feeling of being on my own journey now, poised on the path that leads to Love.

This is the journey of every lover—to discover that the love we seek is within. My teacher often said: "The Self of the teacher and that of the student are one and the same." Two years before he died, this book was conceived. Now I see it was a gift to me, to help me find my way back to him from the sea of separation. As in the dream, each encounter in this book was a steppingstone that helped me cross the waters of grief, doubt, and loneliness. I had to trust an inner guidance, imaged as the old woman in the hut. It took me years to arrive at the right question. Without the right question, there can be no right answer. I asked: How do I find my teacher's house?

The answer was to go inward. As depicted in my dream, the inner world is lush green, serene, a paradise so familiar, yet invisible to those with no eyes to see it. The lane hidden in the heart of the forest leads to the house of the Teacher. The Teacher is "featureless and form-less," says the Sufi. The outer teacher points us to the Teacher, which is not a person but the Self. A place within, the essence of Pure Love, That which we truly are, the "face before we were born." As Jesus said, "The kingdom of God is within you." One night, about a year after my teacher's death, I couldn't sleep and took my pain into prayer. Inside myself I heard him say, in his Zen-like style, "It's time to get over it. You have grieved long enough. I never left you. What I AM—you ARE! THAT never dies!"

His lineage is an inner pathway, he often said. "Love is both the means and the end." Before his passing, we went over the people to be interviewed for this book and he verified their capacity to transmit love through these pages. They have lived the message of the book. As in the dream, each of them is a steppingstone for anyone who wishes to understand and embody love. "Love is not what you do. Love is what you are," said Sadhguru. These guides *are* their message. My teacher confirmed them to be so. In their diversity, we see that love comes in many forms, walks of life, and spiritual expressions.

Over the years, I journeyed to meet them and tried my best to live according to the teachings they imparted. In the end, I am solely responsible for the sense I made of what was given to me, and the place I ended up might surprise them. Any errors surely lie with the student and not her guides. Love has taken me to places that others may deem mistaken, but I was told to be true to the light I knew and more would be given. "I follow the religion of Love: whatever way Love's camels take, that is my religion and my faith," wrote the 13th-century Sufi mystic Ibn al-Arabi, and that's the religion I have followed to the best of my ability.

Often the visits with those I interviewed were painful because their lovingness rekindled the longing for my teacher's physical presence. When I visited their meditation meetings or attended their retreats, I would weep. As loving and gracious as they were, these guides could not replace what I had lost. I had to find That within myself. My teacher taught me that it's possible to survive the loss of what we love because its Source is within us.

Love is a substance that purifies everything in its path, much like volcanic lava that melts every obstacle as it rolls relentlessly down the mountain. Love melted much of what I thought I was. It didn't allow me, for example, to stay in the beautiful little town where my teacher lived. When I moved there to be near him, I thought: *Finally I have moved to the place where I will die. I can be settled for the first time in my life. I will always be close to his house and remains.* As someone who had moved thirty-five times in forty-three years, I was relieved to be putting down roots. Yet as soon as he passed, I had to leave. He appeared to me in a dream and showed my soul at a crossroads:

> My teacher has come back to life and guided me to a crossroads. I am sitting in the center, the place where four roads intersect, and I am weeping. The paved road to the right goes to his house and his remains. To the left is a dusty path to the unknown. I know I have to go left, into the unknown. The words are crystal clear: "It's time for you to leave here and become the teachings that you've been given."

Waking from this dream, I knew I had to go left. In esoteric terms, "left" means inward, into the unconscious, the depths. In other words, to unite with my teacher's Spirit, I had to go in the opposite direction from his physical remains. I had wanted to hang onto his relics, his home, his wife, his animals, everything associated with him, but I had to let go of what felt most dear to me and drop into my own depths. I had to give up the attachment to what he is not—his physical attributes—to realize the truth of what he is, a Universal Spirit. The only way I would ever truly be with him was to connect to the eternal part of myself that was the state he inhabited… Love.

His death taught me that the Teacher is not a body but the energy of Love itself. Love requires the letting go of attachment to all external objects, substances, and landmarks. People, places, and things are the avenues of experiencing love, not its Source. My teacher wrote:

> The high state which people seek, by whatever means, is in fact the experience field of their own consciousness (Self). If they are spiritually unsophisticated and lack a context with which to comprehend the experience, they believe it is created from something "out there" (such as a guru, music, drugs, lover,

and so forth). All that has actually happened is that, under special circumstances, they have experienced their own inner reality.... That this joyous, peaceful, fulfilling state is really one's own inner essence has been the basic tenet of every great spiritual teacher (for example, "The kingdom of God is within you").[2]

By vocation, I am a professor. By necessity, I became a student. Unexpectedly, this life became a training in love. It's not a course I remember signing up for, but it's the course life required of me. The only thing I had to do was say yes to the love that came my way. Saying yes wasn't always easy. Each "yes" led to an unraveling of my life as I knew it, for love presented itself in ways I didn't expect or want. This has been the cosmic trick of my life. Whatever I rejected, love came to me in that form, forcing me to leave behind limits in my loving and to embrace what I had thought unlovable.

I'm a traveler on the path of love, not an expert. What traveler arrives at her destination without making a few wrong turns? I feel strange writing a book about love when I'm a struggling and imperfect example of it, but I wasn't allowed to not write this book. My teacher told me, "What you've been given is not for yourself alone. Pass it on."

Many times I wanted to give up, but devotion to my teacher and the support of loving friends kept the book alive. Especially, I didn't want to write about my mistakes on the path of Love. But walking in the woods one day, I heard: "Sometimes a wound serves Me better than a resolution of it. Your mistakes opened your heart to Love."

It was not an audible voice. It was more like an inner dialogue with the Higher Self, or Love Itself. I heard: "I need you to write your story of longing, of making mistakes and of finding your way again— back to Me. Readers will see that I make good use of mistakes."

The dialogue went on:

I asked: "Isn't it enough for the book to contain the wisdom of great teachers?"

"It's best for the book to include many different notes of love. A beautiful symphony requires the lower tones as well as the higher. The teachers you interview are no longer caught, like you are, in the pain and struggles of their ego life. They serve Me in their way, you serve Me in your way."

I protested: "I don't like writing about my mistakes and doubts."

"Readers need something they can relate to. They need to hear from someone who loses a job, falls in love with the wrong person, struggles with doubts, selfishness, addiction, and grief—and who, nonetheless, knows that Love is Real and keeps saying yes to love."

I resisted: "But my Light is not very bright."

"I have given you enough Light so that your Light recognizes those who serve Me. The world needs many different degrees of Light, including yours."

I said yes.

Rūmī wrote, "The wound is the place where the Light enters in." The same principle reverberates throughout many spiritual traditions. In Native American beadwork and weaving, the artist makes an intentional flaw to acknowledge that all human effort is imperfect. As one Navajo weaver told me, pointing to the flaw in the blanket, "This is the gate where the Great Spirit enters."

That weaver's words have stayed with me. Whenever I sleep under the Navajo blanket my father gave me, I hold the corner with the flaw next to my cheek so I can feel it in the night and remember, "The Creator is with me." My father also gave me a hand-woven antique Persian rug made in Iran. Often, when I walk on it, I'm reminded of the Persian weavers who purposefully make an imperfect stitch out of respect for Divinity. "Only Allah is perfect," they say. In Japan, *kintsugi* artists use gold to fill in the cracks of broken pottery, thus transforming brokenness into wholeness. In all these ways, human imperfection is viewed not as a sin or impediment but as a gateway for Grace. My teacher said, "Every defect contains a hidden treasure, and all supposed defects are doorways."

The book you hold in your hands was written by an individual forced by certain life events to travel the path of love. She made mistakes along the way, but over and over again the broken pieces were put back together by gold. She had the Grace to encounter those whom we call enlightened, self-realized, highly conscious, spiritual teachers, visionaries, and exemplars of unconditional love. They differ from us not because they possess more inner Light but because they *live from It.* Love resides in the hearts of all, yet few are those who live in alignment with its power. It is the power of love—and it alone—that has the capacity to heal the wounds in our world.

So here we are. We stand before a little lane hidden in the heart of a misty forest. It is autumn, and the leaves are about to turn.

# ACKNOWLEDGMENTS

Dedicated to my teacher, David R. "Doc" Hawkins, forever in the heart of hearts; and to his wife Susan J. Hawkins.

For companionship, wise counsel, depth of soul, humor, hearth, and the daily experience of love while writing about it—for Diane, joy unspeakable.

My deep gratitude to all the people featured in this book and their communities of followers. They shine the Light of the Real in this world.

Particular thanks to Llewellyn Vaughan-Lee and the friends of that Sufi path for spiritual support after my teacher died. In their company I learned: "Take one step away from yourself and—behold!—the Path!"

For nurturing this book from the very start, sharing her poetry, editing drafts, and traveling with me to the Grandmothers' fire, loving gratitude to Elizabeth M. Cheatham.

For their friendship and vital contribution of diverse energies to this project over the years, heartfelt gratitude to: Sylvia Simpson, Donna Robinson, Arvind and Shashi Kumar, Rita Kumar, Annabella Gupta, Bobbie Sumner, Carol Phelps, Carol Lynne Eyster, Sunlight, Jean Mountaingrove, Marsha Webb, Carol Davis, Nisha Manek, Jack and Vicki Jenkins, Nicole and Tom Tanquary, Shari Hassen, Rebekah and Mark Dillingham, Lester Banh, Urmila More, Mina Jain, Gabe Valencia, Sunny Wallich, Cheryl Simone, Judy Field, and the spiritual community of Hawkins Study Groups, and members of St. Andrews Episcopal Church in Sedona.

For the gift of family love, I'm grateful to Diane, Nala, Luke, Russell E., Sven, David, Elizabeth, Russell C., Walker, Katie, Lance, Kairos, Peter, Maria, Madelynn, Nicolaus, and Athena.

For their contributions of transcription, art, and insights, thanks to: college students Keziah Baltz, Courtney Fichthorn, Amber Rose Bauer, Julian Adame, Kobi Lee, Meggan Austin, Courtney Mera, Katie Bozner, Shapari Samimi, Cade Lawson, and the thousands of students who have been in my classes on Compassion and Meditation since 2004.

For their personal encouragement and institutional support, thanks to my colleagues and administrators at the University of Redlands: Bill Huntley, John Walsh, Karen Derris, Julius Bailey, Lillian Larsen, Sana Tayyen, Larry Gross, Amy Moff-Hudec, Bill Maury-Holmes, Leela MadhavRau, Lorenzo Garbo, Patricia Geary, Teresa Area, Lisa Olson, Celine Ko, Tony Mueller, Nancy Carrick, Kathy Ogren, Kendrick Brown, Ralph and Nancy Kuncl, Denise Spencer, and Tricia Garcia.

For their expert work as translators, I thank two nuns: Sister Joanna of Sinai (Father Pavlos) and Venerable Damchö Diana Finnegan (H.H. the 17th Karmapa).

For expertise in all areas of publishing, helping to make the dream a reality, thanks to Cynthia Frank, Belvie Rooks, and Joe Shaw.

Thanks to these organizations that provided support for academic research: University of Redlands, Trust for the Meditation Process, Lens Fellowship in Spatial Learning, and the Luce Fellowship in Comparative Theology and Theology of Religious Pluralism (awarded by the American Academy of Religion).

# INTRODUCTION

This year, 2018, marks the 125th anniversary of the first Parliament of the World's Religions held in Chicago in 1893. Forward-thinking individuals saw that great good could come by gathering the leaders of various faiths to discuss matters of global significance. Swami Vivekananda, the only Hindu from India on the program, stood out from the crowd with his penetrating eyes, brown skin, and monastic robe. His opening address encapsulated the spirit of the entire gathering; it is deemed one of the greatest speeches ever delivered on US soil. Upon hearing his greeting—"Sisters and Brothers of America"— the 7,000 attendees jumped to their feet in thunderous applause that lasted for three minutes. Swami Vivekananda continued:

> It fills my heart with joy unspeakable to rise in response to the warm and cordial welcome that you have given us.... I am proud to belong to a religion that has taught the world both tolerance and universal acceptance. We believe not only in universal toleration but we accept all religions as true. I am proud to belong to a nation that has sheltered the persecuted and the refugees of all religions and all nations of the earth.... The present convention, which is one of the most august assemblies ever held, is in itself a vindication, a declaration to the world of the wonderful doctrine preached in the Gita: "Whosoever comes to Me, through whatsoever form, I reach him;

all men are struggling through paths which in the end lead to Me." Sectarianism, bigotry, and its horrible descendant, fanaticism, have long possessed this beautiful earth…. But their time is come; and I fervently hope that the bell that tolled this morning in honor of this convention may be the death knell of all fanaticism, of all persecutions with the sword or with the pen, and of all uncharitable feelings between persons wending their way to the same goal.

In the days that followed, Swami Vivekananda laid out the spiritual laws that govern the universe, which he summed up as "the doctrine of love." He made two main points. First, the highest form of love seeks no personal reward. Though love is good even when it seeks a reward (such as heaven), the highest expression of love, he said, is to "love unselfishly for love's sake." His second point was that no single religion is the exclusive holder of the holy, as holiness and devotion take many forms. He used the analogy of the rose. Its fragrance is distinct and would be recognizable even if it were called by a name other than "rose." The same is true for love, he said. Those two points are the foundation of this book: the supremacy of selfless love, and the expression of love in many forms.

Synchronously, *The Power of Love* is published in the year of the 125th Parliament of the World's Religions and its theme, "The Power of Love."

The first task is to define what we mean by "love." Though spoken about everywhere, real love is rare. We come to know what love is only by experiencing it. By analogy, how would we know the fragrance of a rose without having smelled it?

I came to know Pure Love by being near my teacher. His love was self-giving and unconditional, so different from my past experiences of "love." It was like tasting delicious and pristine water for the first time, after a lifetime of drinking murky and metallic water. His love was fresh from the Source, crystal clear and freely given; not tainted with dependencies or muddied by hidden agendas. His love was pure, unwavering, and all-pervading. After my teacher's death, I continued to learn about love from my encounters with the people in this book. Here is a taste of what they taught me.

Love is self-respecting and self-giving. Love is humble and open-hearted. Love is unconditional and nonselective. Love endures all things. Love moves from an inner strength and walks by way of an inner light. Love knows that whatever is done to another is done to oneself; that whatever is given returns to the giver. Love is determined; it finds the opportunity in every obstacle. Love augments the positive; it believes the best. Love is swayed neither by praise nor blame; it treats them as one and the same. Love transcends time; its present moment is forever. Love emerges each instant as both creation and evolution. Love lives in the land of "win/win" and "both/and." Love sees with the eyes of the heart; it knows the whole and values each part.

Like the dog's wagging tail, love responds instantly, without artifice. Like the fruit tree, it gives succor and shelter to all without distinction. Like the sun, it radiates without effort and shines equally on all.

Some of the qualities of love are: generosity, gratitude, joy, faith, forgiveness, patience, compassion, devotion, beauty, synchronicity, surrender, vision, ecstasy, completion, kindness, openness, humor, and *joie de vivre*.

During my visit in India with the 17th Karmapa, head of a major Buddhist lineage, he gave this definition of love: "Love allows us to see the other as a part of ourselves, and we feel ourselves to be a part of the other.... When we witness their pain or their happiness, we experience it as our own pain and our own happiness.... then naturally their pain becomes unbearable for us to witness and we must act to do something about it."

Once we know what real love feels like, we can distinguish it from false substitutes. We begin to recognize it all around us.

"Once you have tasted that beauty in one Master, that unconditional love, that presence and glow of the Supreme in walking and talking, you see it on others," says Swami Chidatmananda, a Hindu monk from India. Similar to Vivekananda, he is a teacher of Vedanta and the ancient scriptures of India. He first experienced Pure Love in his Guru. "There was nothing else like it."

There is indeed no greater power in the universe than love. As Sufi teacher Llewellyn Vaughan-Lee says: "Love is the very fabric of creation. Love is the substance and the center of everything. Without love, the Universe would fall apart...."

"There's power in love.... Real power—power to change the world." Bishop Michael Curry spoke these words in rhythmic beat during his sermon at the recent royal wedding of Prince Harry and Meghan Markle. Love is the source of life, he said, and we are all brothers and sisters made out of love for the purpose of love. Our love is greatest when we put our lives in service for the good of others without seeking reward. When love is not selfish or self-centered, Curry said, it becomes redemptive: "Unselfish, sacrificial, redemptive love can change lives and it can change this world."

Curry's sermon was heard by 29 million viewers in the U.S. alone. He is the first African American presiding bishop of the Episcopal Church, hailing from Chicago, home to the first Parliament of World Religions, where Vivekananda gave his spellbinding speech to 7,000 people. A lot has changed in those 125 years. Within seconds we can tune in to an event that used to take months of planning to attend. Twenty-nine million vs. 7,000 is a huge difference, but what hasn't changed is the message and our need for it: Love is the source of our life, and when we live it unselfishly, love can redeem the world. What is redemptive love?

We find the answer in the sermons of Dr. Martin Luther King, Jr., as quoted by Curry. Dr. King drew on the teachings of Jesus and also the scriptures of India that pulsed Vivekananda's message of universal tolerance. King enacted the redemptive power of *agape* love.

Those with agape in their soul, he said, refuse to mete out hate for hate, for they know that what is given returns to the giver. By choosing to love their enemy, they cut the chain of hate. King was clear: agape is not sentimentalism or passivity. It's not about feeling affection for the enemy, or liking them, but rather seeing them as God sees them, loved and created in the image of God. In the spirit of redemptive goodwill, agape looks for the best in other persons and doesn't define them on the basis of their belief or behavior in one area of life; it sees them in their wholeness. Even as he was imprisoned time and again for his efforts to end segregation, King urged his followers to love the segregationist, for love alone has the power to create a common ground. Love is redemptive, he taught, because it holds the vision that another's heart can be transformed through love, kindness, and respect.[3] "Anything we love can be saved," is how Alice Walker put it.[4]

"My brother – my sister" is the spirit of agape love. This is the greeting used by Mother Teresa, whether she was receiving the Nobel Peace Prize or touching those with leprosy. Bishop Curry, Dr. King, and Swami Vivekananda also said, "My brother, my sister." "All my relations" is an Indigenous way of expressing this love. As the Indigenous Grandmothers state in *The Power of Love*, "all my relations" is a translation of the Lakota phrase *mitakuye oyasin*, and recognizes that the entire universe is present inside all of us. We are not separate from anything that has ever lived, is living now, or will ever live. When we walk with love, we're aware of the next generations, we sanctify our every word and action into an offering, we don't take more than we need, and we reverence the sacredness of life. Selflessness is not that we stop living; it's that we live from our heart. It's that we shift from "me" to "we."

This kind of love—selfless, redemptive, inclusive—is not common, but there is hope that it could be. If we can learn to hate, we can learn to love. First, we have to know what real love is. Many people spend a lifetime enmeshed in dynamics of dependency, thinking it is love to expect another to meet their needs, possessing, controlling, and bargaining: "I did that for you, so now I'd like this from you." Or they are taught a political or religious belief system that limits love. Earlier in life, I belonged to a religious group that believed Vivekananda and even the saintly Mother Teresa were going to hell because they weren't members of my church. This was ignorance. Simply put, I believed in the limiting views of love that had been poured into me. At age thirty-nine, I met my teacher and he opened my heart to real, limitless, unconditional love. In that moment, I discovered the ancient truth that Curry repeated in his sermon: "Wherever true love is found, God himself is there."

When I went to India and visited the room where Swami Vivekananda died in 1902, I felt the unmistakable aura of pure love and holiness. Perhaps that's what the audience sensed at the 1893 Parliament when they jumped to their feet in applause. Standing in his room, I felt the truth of the scripture he had quoted, the words of Divinity : "I am in every religion as the thread through a string of pearls. Wherever you see extraordinary holiness and extraordinary power raising and purifying humanity, know that I am there."

And that is the beauty of *The Power of Love*. It gives the reader an intimate communion with people of different paths who are extraordinary in the purity of their love. Through their life stories, dialogues, and teachings, readers receive a transmission of authentic love and are given many ways to tap into and live the power of love.

Humankind has looked high and low for a power source that can ease planetary problems. We drill and mine the earth in search of energies that will solve our energy crisis, but we have yet to tap into the most plentiful source of power available. This power lies within us.

## The Nature of Power

Now that we've looked at love and how it is approached in this book, it's time to explore what's meant by "power." The statement of Jesus Christ, "The kingdom of God is within you," gives a hint of the inner realm from which true power comes. True power has nothing to do with things such as money, weapons, positions, or status. Mahatma Gandhi brought British imperialism to its knees without any of these things. Where did his power come from?

This question is answered in the book *Power vs. Force*. Originally published in 1995, the book has sold a million copies and been translated into twenty-five languages. It has influenced governments, universities, businesses, hospitals, and religious communities. Recently, Dr. Azza Karam, a coordinator for the United Nations Task Force on Religion referred to *Power vs. Force* as the foundation for how religions should conduct themselves—using power, not force.[5]

The author of *Power vs. Force*, Dr. David R. Hawkins, was a scientist who underwent a profound transformation of consciousness in which the personal self and its suffering dissolved; Infinite Love was all that remained. It took him thirty years to learn to live in such an unusual state and to develop a framework that could communicate its revelation in a meaningful way. He said: "This book was written to comprehend my own subjective experience, to integrate it with scientific discovery, and to put it in a format that was comprehensible to the left brain. This book is the realm of the mystic communicated to the left brain."[6]

The book says there are two basic ways that energy is expressed—positive or negative. "Power" is the term given to positive energy. It is supportive of life in all its expressions. Power energizes. It empowers and uplifts. "Force," on the other hand, weakens. It is coercive, attacking, negating, and draining. The difference is hinted at in the title of a well-known book, *The Chalice and The Blade*.[7]

*Power vs. Force* illustrates the difference between power and force in the case of Mahatma Gandhi and the British Empire. How could a mere ninety-pound man, wearing only his *dhoti*, bring down the largest empire of the time, which ruled two thirds of the world? It defies logic. The source of Gandhi's power lay in his alignment to universal principles of Truth, such as the innate dignity of all people, endowed by Divinity with the right to self-determination. His was not a power *over* but a power from *within*. It was the *power of love*—selfless and redemptive.

Inner alignment of this caliber is much more powerful than mechanisms of force (pride, pomp, coercion, weapons, etc.). Hawkins, writing in *Power vs. Force*, explains why power is more effective than force:

> [P]ower arises from meaning. It has to do with motive, and it has to do with principle. Power is always associated with that which supports the significance of life itself. It appeals to that in human nature that we call noble, in contrast to force, which appeals to that which we call crass. Power appeals to that which uplifts, dignifies, and ennobles. Force must always be justified, whereas power requires no justification. Force is associated with the partial, power with the whole.
>
> If we analyze the nature of force, it becomes readily apparent why it must always succumb to power; this is in accordance with one of the basic laws of physics. Because force automatically creates counterforce, its effect is limited by definition. We could say that force is a movement. It goes from here to there (or tries to) against opposition. Conversely, power stands still, like a standing field that does not move. Gravity itself, for instance, doesn't move against anything. Its power moves all objects within its field, but the gravity field itself does not move.

Force is intrinsically incomplete, says Hawkins, and therefore must constantly be fed energy. Power, on the other hand, is complete within itself. It needs nothing and makes no demands. Whereas force is insatiable and constantly consumes, power energizes, nurtures, gives, and inspires. Power is a positive energy that makes us feel positive about ourselves. Force is a negative energy and tends to make us feel bad about ourselves. Power is associated with compassion; force with judgmentalism. Power unifies, whereas force polarizes. Polarization leads to conflict and a win/lose outcome. Because there is always a losing side, enemies are created and defenses are required. This is what comes from force: conflict, enemies, defenses. Power, on the other hand, sees beyond "us vs. them" and produces a win/win resolution.[8]

Intuitively, the distinction between power and force makes sense, for we are aware in ordinary life of the difference between a positive person (kind, genuine, trustworthy) and a negative person (bitter, deceitful, rigid). It is obvious that the energy of Mother Teresa is different from that of Adolf Hitler, and that nearly everyone's energy lies somewhere between those two examples. Committed above all to communicate pragmatically, Hawkins put his findings on a chart that he called the Map of Consciousness.®

## LEVELS OF CONSCIOUSNESS

Everyone and everything radiates energy. As Dr. William Tiller, Emeritus Professor of Materials Science from Stanford University, told me: "We radiate what we are." The energy might be negative (force) or positive (power). Our overall "energy field" determines how we see the world and respond to others. Different energy fields respond differently to the same situation; this is obvious in everyday life.

Let's take the common example of walking my dog in the neighborhood. The same dog receives different responses. One person is scornful, another is accepting. The inevitable sometimes happens: my dog relieves herself on a neighbor's lawn. One time, the person living across the street from this lawn scolded me, "Don't you think that's rude? What about all the money they spend on their lawn? Your dog is ruining the neighborhood!" She walked away in a huff, leaving the impression that I'd done something unpardonable. I could have told her that I knew the owner didn't mind, that I do my best to guide my dog to patches of dirt anyway, and that I always pick up after my dog; but the neighbor had already judged me a moral failure and wasn't open to hearing any evidence to the contrary. Her opinion of me was set. The next day, of course, my dog did the same thing, only this time the actual owner of the lawn was there, pulling her garbage cans off the street. When I apologized for my dog, she laughed and said, "Oh goodness, that's nature! We can't sweat the small stuff, now can we?"

She smiled appreciatively at my dog's wagging tail, and I felt happy to live near such a kind person.

That is the wonderful and harmonious energy field of Acceptance found on Hawkins's Map of Consciousness. People on that level radiate "power." They are accepting of life on life's terms; we enjoy being around them because they're accepting and easygoing. In contrast, I avoid the critical neighbor; scorn and rigidity are no fun to be around. That's the energy field of Pride: superiority, fault-finding, opinionation, and shaming. As "force," it is draining and has a negative impact on oneself and others.

Acceptance and Pride are two of the energy fields on the Map of Consciousness, which lays out the whole spectrum of consciousness from the lower energy fields of Shame, Guilt, Fear, Desire, Anger, Pride (i.e., levels of force dominated by egotistical drives) to the median energy fields of Courage, Willingness, Acceptance, Reason (i.e., levels of power dominated by personal integrity) to the more expanded energy fields of Love, Unconditional Love/Joy/Healing, Ecstasy, Peace, and Enlightenment. These higher energy fields express great spiritual power. They are increasingly free of personal agendas and are the domain of saints, mystics, *arhats*, and avatars.

**Note:** "Higher" and "lower" are terms of convenience for the linear mind and do not express actual reality. In Reality, there is no such thing as higher or lower, for all of life serves the whole by virtue of what it is. As Hawkins writes:

> Everything reveals the miracle of existence and, therefore, everything, without exception, is equal to everything else by virtue of its existence. The miracle of existence is a quality that supersedes all others. The holiness of the Allness of Creation stands forth as self-evident, and the manifestation of the capacity to exist demonstrates its innate divinity. When presumptions are no longer projected onto the observed, the radiance of Divinity shines forth from the world....[9]

Hawkins found that each of us has a "composite" energy field, and that's the level we "live at." We all have better or worse moments, and we may be more evolved in one area of life than another. A person may have a lot of integrity at work but be addicted to a negative habit in private life. When we let go of any negativity (resentment, fear, shame, etc.), our overall energy field rises and our level of happiness increases.

Each increase in energy is significant. The Map of Consciousness shows the spectrum of energy fields on a logarithmic scale of energetic power ranging from 1 to 1,000. It could have been 1 to 10, or A to Z, or any other symbol. Hawkins chose a scale that would be easy to work with. On the scale, for example, Hitler calibrated at 30 and Mother Teresa at 710. The British Empire calibrated at 190 (Pride) and Gandhi at 760 (Self-Realization). Using the method of muscle testing, Hawkins discovered that calibrations of different energy fields were possible. One gift of his research for humankind is that he verified the pristine state of true mystics, saints, and sages and their benefit to the world. Through their radiation of universal compassion, the world is saved from self-destruction. The level of Acceptance (350), that of my kind-hearted, dog-loving neighbor, is a state of harmony and does wonders to ease the suffering of the world.

The chart is of pragmatic use, as it allows us to see the energy of something relative to the Absolute. For instance, Shame at 20 or Guilt at 30 are not nearly as much energy as Anger at 150, Courage at 200, Reason at 400, or Love at 500. Serial killers calibrate at 20, while saints and mystics calibrate from 540 and up. The level of Courage at 200 is the critical point. It is the dividing line between *power* and *force*. At this level, integrity prevails as one tells the truth about oneself and one's life; the energy now has power and points in a positive direction. As one's level of consciousness increases, the energy grows stronger and magnifies intellectual and creative capacities. Finally, in the higher levels of Love (Joy, Healing, Unconditional Love, Ecstasy), the energy can have a spontaneously healing effect on those within its sphere.

Here is a basic description of the levels of consciousness adapted from Hawkins's books *Power vs. Force* and *Letting Go*. I had the privilege to work closely with him on both the revised edition of *Power vs. Force* and the first edition of *Letting Go*. The descriptions below are therefore not mere words to me—rather, they carry the living memory of being in the presence of my teacher who was the author of this body of work. The descriptions below are my paraphrases and no substitute for studying the original work.[10]

**Shame (20):**   Humiliation, feeling discredited, slinking away, as in "hanging your head in shame" or "losing face." Traditionally accompanied by banishment, often resulting in death. Can be destructive to health, lead to cruelty toward self and others. Suicide may be consciously chosen or passively consented to by self-neglect, overdose, and "accidents."

**Guilt (30):**   Desire to punish and be punished. Leads to self-rejection, masochism, feeling "bad," self-sabotage, and a preoccupation with sin. Religious demagogues and authoritarian personalities easily exploit the unconscious guilt of guilt-ridden people. Accident proneness, suicidal behavior, and projection of self-hatred onto "evil" others as in so-called honor killings. Unconscious guilt, with its self-punishing element, is the basis of many psychosomatic illnesses.

**Apathy (50):**   Hopelessness, helplessness, paralysis, and incapacity. Apathy is an energy that says, "I can't" and "Who cares?" The world and the future look bleak and bleaker. Those in apathy are unable to help themselves and will die unless external caregivers or humanitarian aid pours energy into them. Few are those who have the courage to really look Apathy in the face or be with those in its energy field. Most of the world turns away from Apathy. Mother Teresa (710) and her Missionaries of Charity are a glorious exception.

**Grief (75):**   Despondency, despair, loss, unremitting regret, and the feeling, "If only I had…" Separation. Depression. Chronic sadness. Mournful, as in "I can't go on." The loss of a beloved person, pet, or object is equated with the loss of love itself and therefore feels unbearable and unhealable. Grief sees a sad world and sad people everywhere. As painful as grief is, it is more hopeful than apathy, for tears are a sign of life.

**Fear (100):** "Danger is everywhere." Caution against danger is healthy; however, Fear is different—obsessive anxieties, phobias, avoidance, defensiveness, holding back, constriction, preoccupation with security, and possessiveness of others (due to fear of loss). Religious and other doomsayers play on the fear (and wallets) of the masses with predictions of apocalypse and the end of the world. Totalitarian regimes take advantage of the insecurities of citizens who fear the unknown. Fear limits individual growth by keeping people stuck in chains, closets, abusive relationships, and unfulfilling jobs.

**Desire (125):** A motivating energy for many. Whereas Fear holds us back, Desire drives us forward into achievement of prestige, money, or power over others. "Wanting" obviously has more energy in it than the previous levels. If a person starts to desire a better life, then there's energy to move out of apathy, grief, or fear. Desire can become a springboard to higher levels of consciousness. As a predominant energy field, however, Desire is insatiable and leads to entrapment in the cycle of addiction, consumerism, and compulsion for pleasure. It sees the source of contentment outside of itself, thus the perpetual drive to acquire. "I have to have it."

**Anger (150):** Leads to either constructive or destructive action. Constructively, Anger gives the energy necessary for individuals and groups who suffer injustice or abuse to say, "We've had enough!" Having overcome hopelessness, sadness, and fear, such oppressed people begin to want what others have. When the desire leads to frustration, then Anger comes to the fore and fuels the movements to end inequality. Most often, however, Anger is a destructive force in the form of revenge-seeking, bitter resentment, hatred, insults, attacks, and threats. Those immersed in Anger as a lifestyle are irritable, explosive, volatile, oversensitive to being slighted, and litigious. They are injustice collectors and chronic protestors.

**Pride (175):**   People feel positive in the level of Pride because of increased self-esteem. "Look at what I've made of myself!" The pain and despair of lower levels has been overcome. Pride struts its stuff for all to see. It's the jump from the dead end of poverty into the U.S. Marine Corps. It's leaving shame behind and living "proud to be me!" While Pride may be a step toward self-empowerment, it remains below the critical level of Courage. Pride is weak due to the inner attitudes of superiority, narcissism, and ego-inflation. "My way is the best way," says this level, and can be a prevalent attitude in academic, religious, and political environments. On the individual level, denial prevents people from seeking help and blocks maturation. Fueled by righteousness, Pride on a collective level is the basis of factionalism, nationalism, and zealotry.

**Courage (200):**   Courage is the first level where we find true power. This energy says, "I can do it. I'm up for the challenge." There is genuine empowerment, determination, and a capacity to learn new skills and ideas. This energy is excited about life, productive, and able to take effective action even if there's fear. People in the level of Courage value growth, industriousness, and self-betterment. They put back into the world as much energy as they take, in contrast with the lower levels, which drain energy.

**Neutrality (250):**   Until they reach this energy field, people tend to hold positions that are black and white, right vs. wrong, us vs. them. On the level of Neutrality, rigidity gives way to flexibility about life; like the willow tree, it can bend in the wind so as not to break. "It's okay either way." Neutrality is free of dogmatism and judgmental attitudes. It rolls with the punches. As an energy, it is nonconflicting, noncompetitive, unemotional, and generally unattached to a specific outcome. "Well, if this person doesn't want to go out with me, I'll ask someone else."

**Willingness (310):** This level signals a positive attitude and openness to life. It is friendly, helpful, wants to assist, and seeks to be of service. It's warmer, more caring, more responsive to others, and more dedicated than Neutrality. The job is now not just done but done well. Willingness may be seen as the gateway to the higher levels, which is why people in Twelve Step groups are advised to "pray for the willingness to be willing." People on this level are open-minded and optimistic. They have the capacity to rise above difficulties and make lemonade out of lemons. They are teachable and don't mind hard work. In the field of Willingness, there is the capacity to look at one's own weaknesses and admit mistakes.

**Acceptance (350):** This level reflects an enormous leap. People now take responsibility for what happens in their lives. They meet life on life's terms and don't blame life or other people for what they experience. If someone breaks up with them, they know they haven't lost love itself. Love and happiness are inner capacities that don't depend on anything "out there." Not moralistic, they accept the human condition, with its drives, instincts, difficulties, and diverse expressions. Those at this level seek balance and harmony; they are easygoing and tolerant of life's diversity. As citizens and colleagues, they embrace a plurality of viewpoints and life expressions ("different strokes for different folks"), and they work toward healthy resolutions of conflict.

**Reason (400):** The rational capacity differentiates humans from the animal world. Once the emotionalism of the lower energy levels is transcended, Reason seeks truth for its own sake. It has the ability to see things in the abstract, to conceptualize, to solve problems, and to be objective. Rationality, education, and knowledge are highly valued. Excellence in all of its forms is appreciated. Science, philosophy, theology, medicine, literature, and logic are expressions of this level, as are the truly great thinkers, humorists, literary masters, statesmen, Supreme Court justices, and Nobel Prize winners in science and literature. According to Hawkins's research, Reason is the level of 8 percent of the global population. As impressive as it is, this level becomes an obstacle to spiritual evolution. In its focus on theories and details,

Reason often loses sight of the forest for the trees. All philosophic arguments sound convincing to those who believe them. A rational understanding of phenomena falls short of Reality, which is non-linear, noncausal, nonlocal, nondualistic, and all-inclusive.

**Love (500):**   In contrast to popular depictions of love as dependency, infatuation, attachment, possessiveness, addiction, control, sentimentalism, emotionality, and eroticism, the actual energy field of Love is healing, forgiving, nurturing, peaceful, self-fulfilling, patient, long-suffering, and reverential toward all of life. There may be temporary annoyances but the overall dedication is to be forgiving. Subjective and experiential, Love is a way of being. Since it comes from within, it doesn't fluctuate due to outer conditions. Love emanates from the heart, not the mind. Bypassing the sequential mentalization that characterizes Reason, Love goes quickly to the essence of a situation via intuition, which is instantaneous. The heart deals with wholes, not particulars. Love takes no position; it sees the intrinsic value and lovability of all that exists. Rather than attack the negative, it focuses on the positive. According to Hawkins's research, only 4 percent of the world's population is at this level of consciousness, and only 0.4 percent is at the level of Unconditional Love (540).

**Unconditional Love and Joy (540):**   This love is unchanging, despite circumstances or the actions of others. Inner joy overflows from within. The world is illuminated by exquisite beauty, and the perfection of all creation is self-evident. There is compassion for all, enormous patience, and a capacity to endure suffering. A sense of self-completion prevails. Spiritual groups that operate on this level have a healing and catalytic effect. Works of art and music at this level (e.g., Michelangelo, Mozart, Handel, Beethoven) have an uplifting impact. People at this level have a notable effect on others. Through their presence, joy, and beneficent visage, the energy induces a state of well-being in those around them. There is the desire to use this state of consciousness for the benefit of life itself rather than for oneself or one's familiars. Many near-death experiences, notable for their transformative impact, reveal a glimpse into the energy levels between 540 and 600. Devotion is an energy that calibrates at 550–565; Agape, universal love, is at 570; 575 is a level of love seen in both religious and nonreligious expressions such as the classic texts, Viktor Frankl's *Man's Search for Meaning* and Brother Lawrence's *Practice of the Presence of God*. Ecstasy is at 575–590, the level of such ecstatic saints as Padre Pio and the Baal Shem Tov.

**Peace (600):**   Bliss, illumination, and a state of nonduality. The distinction between subject and object disappears. Those in this level frequently withdraw from worldly activity, as nonduality makes it difficult to relate to the game board of interacting egos. The level is extremely rare in the human realm, and such beings are often designated as saints or viewed as illumined spiritual teachers. They see that everything is alive and radiant, continuously flowing and emerging. Great works of art, music, and architecture (e.g., Taj Mahal, Chartres Cathedral) that calibrate between 600 and 800 can transport us temporarily to higher levels of consciousness. The state of the mystic begins at 600. Those in the 600s include famous mystics such as St. Francis of Assisi, Ibn 'Arabi, Rābi'a, Marguerite Porete, and Swami Vivekananda.

**Self-Realization and Enlightenment (700–1,000):**   This is the level of the great scriptures (e.g., Quran, Bhagavad Gita, Zohar, Upanishads, Heart Sutra), spiritual lineages (e.g., Sufism, Mahayana Buddhism, Karma-Jnana-Bhakti-Raja Yogas), and those we call the Founders of the great religions. Centuries of art portray the individuals at this level with raised palm, bestowing their blessing upon the world. The spiritual patterns that have elevated humanity for centuries originate through these great beings. They speak of the state of Realization as a gift of Grace, which is beyond description. The sense of identity is no longer with the "me" but rather with all of existence, which is realized to be divine. The level that calibrates at 1000 represents the most powerful energy in the human realm; protoplasm cannot handle higher energies than that. It is the energy field of the great teachers such as Jesus Christ, the Buddha, and Krishna; their accounts of "sweating blood" and "bones crushing" suggest the intensity of spiritual power when a physical body reaches its maximum capacity.

Love pervades the entire spectrum, yet only at level 500 does Love become predominant within consciousness.
Evolution of Love:

> Below 200: Narcissistic self-love ("it's all about me");

> 200–499: Healthy self-love, self-respect, plus love for others;

> 500–600: Selfless service out of love for Divinity/ Reality and the whole of creation;

> Over 600: The Self - Oneness - Love Itself

All of life is revealed to be a pulsating symphony of interplaying energy fields. *Power vs. Force* illumines the Oneness of all creation by revealing the energy essence of everything that exists. With each expansion in the level of consciousness, the radiation of energy increases and has a beneficial and healing effect on the world.

The stages of inner evolution outlined by Hawkins are not new; the Map of Consciousness correlates with the levels of initiation and spiritual stations outlined through the centuries by Christian, Sufi, Hindu, Buddhist, Indigenous, Jewish sages and mystics. The beauty of Hawkins's work is simplicity. He uses common clinical terms, not archaic or religious ones. Seekers of whatever faith, religious or non-religious, can find their path of love illumined by this Map.

I found the scale eye opening. For one thing, much of religious history has preached a distorted doctrine of guilt, self-punishment, and fear as the way to God. It can be relieving and a major course correction to see that Guilt and Fear are at the bottom of the scale and Love and Joy at the top. Truth is Love, and thus the way to Truth is in love and through love.

Also informative is to see that Reason, the most highly touted virtue in Western culture, is indeed refined energy, but it pales in comparison to the energy of the heart. Mental knowledge is theoretical and therefore provisional for the same reason that a recipe is. Only after the ingredients have been cooked and the meal tasted is there actualized knowledge of a recipe. This means our life experiences teach us more than any theory or book. "Experience is the only way you internalize anything, and what you internalize becomes part of your spiritual essence," Betty Eadie told me. True knowledge is that which we've internalized into our heart and actualized in real life. Otherwise, we say, "They're just a talking head." This validates the intuitive experience of many seekers who find that purely rational answers to pressing inner questions don't satisfy. The longing is for love, which heals. The explanation of a problem is not the same thing as the healing of it. As Hawkins writes: "The pathway of the heart then bypasses the intellect and puts its faith in the perfection of love rather than the pursuit of the intellect and reason."[11]

## "Changing the World Happens One Heart at a Time—Start With Your Own"

When the heart *chakra* (505) opens within a human being, this is a profound moment not only for that person but also for the world because of the capacity of inner love to heal all of life. Since the power of love is much greater than any negativity, and since we are all connected on the energetic level, *Power vs. Force* states that "the energy of a single individual who calibrates at 500 counterbalances 750,000 individuals below 200."

This statement was so stunning to me that it has taken ten years and the writing of an entire book on *The Power of Love* to explore it from all the necessary angles. When I first came upon the statement, I balked. From my rational, logical standpoint, it sounded farfetched. Where were the cold, hard facts? I was steeped in Ivy League academic training that deconstructed anything that sounded like warm and fuzzy optimism. In terms of critical thinking, it was more satisfying to point out the faults of humankind than its inspiring potentials. Yet, when I encountered that statement—*the energy of a single individual who calibrates at 500 counterbalances 750,000 individuals below 200*—I asked myself, "What would human history have been like without its great thinkers and leaders in the higher energy fields (e.g., Socrates, St. Teresa of Avila, Ibn 'Arabi, Abraham Lincoln, Nelson Mandela, Dr. Martin Luther King, Jr., Gandhi, the Karmapas, Rūmī, Yeshe Tsogyal, Rābi'a, Marguerite Porete, Moses, Mother Teresa, Lao Tzu, the great Native American chiefs and medicine men and women), the Buddha, and Jesus Christ? How would the world be different if these people and others like them hadn't been in it? That question has an easy answer: more war, more poverty, more violence, and possibly the human destruction of the planet.

I concluded that love is what has held the world together. If love is the greatest power in the universe, then how do we tap into it? How do we become a loving presence on the planet? This question inspired a journey to meet living exemplars of love. As my teacher, Hawkins verified that the people included in this book can speak about love in a way that transmits the power of love and thereby touch the heart of the reader. As the heart is transformed, we become a gift to the world: "The power of love emanated by the consciousness of only a fraction of mankind actually totally counterbalances the negativity of the whole mass of humanity.... We change the world not by what we say or do but as a consequence of what we have become. Thus, every spiritual aspirant serves the world."[12]

The more loving a person becomes, the greater is the impact on those nearby and the world at large. Here's how it works: *Power vs. Force* likens Love to a limitless electromagnetic field of infinite power. This power can be transmitted only in amounts suitable to the voltage that each instrument, or level of consciousness, can handle. By analogy, too much electricity can break a circumscribed circuit, but a circuit with wide voltage capacity can handle more power.

The Dalai Lama, for example, has an energy field or level of consciousness that is expansive enough to handle immense amounts of the power of love, and so he radiates high levels of "healing voltage," we might say. His inner states of joy and love bubble over with humor, laughter, kindness, and compassion. Pope Francis is another well-known example.

Most people, however, don't have this same capacity to channel healing energy to others or to the world because their inner attention is focused on their own opinions, needs, feelings, and agendas. They have repressed attitudes and self-expressions, and all of these unconscious fragments take energy to keep hidden from view. Even a single lie takes a lot of energy to keep hidden. Most people's inner circuitry is constricted by self-preservation; as such, they are incapable of unconditional love. Some people, in fact, are almost solely self-absorbed.

At the level of Guilt (30), a person is punitive of self and others. At the level of Fear (100), a person is obsessed with anxiety and survival. There is no energy available to care for others. At the level of Desire (125), people want what they want; they're driven by greed and addiction for something outside themselves, and use any means to get it, even the people close to them. At the level of Pride (175), people are arrogant and mainly interested in proving themselves right, not in listening or learning. At the level of Courage (200), a person has the capacity to be honest and trustworthy for the first time. This is the level, for example, in Alcoholics Anonymous where the addict/alcoholic admits being powerless over a substance.

At the level of Willingness (310), a person is friendly and service-oriented, interested to "make a positive difference in the world." At the level of Acceptance (350), we see the capacity to value diversity, transcend moralism, and take responsibility for one's energies and experience in life. At the level of Reason (400), we see the capacity to transcend emotional motives, to acquire and understand information, and to seek truth for its own sake. At the level of Love (500), there is a major shift from head to heart, linear to nonlinear, logic to intuition, sequence to synchronicity. Purified of self-seeking, one's energy no longer serves the ego but all of life.

Love is a way of being: "Make a gift of your life and lift all mankind by being kind, considerate, forgiving, and compassionate at all times, in all places, and under all conditions, with everyone as well as yourself." When the heart chakra opens (505), the activation of love has enormous potential to heal a suffering world. The level of Unconditional Love (540) denotes the person who loves everything and everyone truly without condition, and the love is not personal: "There is a desire to use one's state of consciousness for the benefit of life itself rather than for particular individuals."[13]

When we grasp how powerful love really is, naturally we want to know, "How can I become more loving?" A first step is to put oneself in beneficial energy fields. As they say in Twelve Step groups, "You get it by osmosis." If we stay close to the fire, eventually we will be warmed. Our own inner light brightens when we're in the company of those who are loving, kind, nonjudgmental, and wise. *Power vs. Force* affirms that the presence of even a small group of loving people outweighs the negativity operating in the world at large. A second step is to commit to a path of inner transformation. As we are changed, we change the world. To let go of even one resentment releases a benefit. Each positive, life-giving step we make comes back to bless us because we too are part of that life. Much like the rising level of the sea lifts all ships, so the radiance of unconditional love within a human heart lifts all of life.

Having spent nearly my entire life in academia, it hasn't been easy for me to drop from head to heart. The motivation came from meeting those whose hearts are fully open. Being in the company of those who contributed to this book was transformative. Simply by being what they are, they uplift the world.

## HOMO SPIRITUS

According to many of the people I interviewed, humanity is at a crossroads. There is a quickening of consciousness as spiritual truth is more available than ever, notable in the fact that millions viewed Curry's sermon on the power of love. For the first time in history, we have the means to come together and imagine creative solutions to the problems that threaten to destroy us. This book itself is an expression of that possibility within the collective consciousness. It gives readers a direct encounter with the spiritual teachers, scientists, activists, and artists who are the voices of a new vision for the world. From diverse faiths and fields of work, they reveal the power of love to be the next frontier of global consciousness. On the surface, we see the end of an era. Yet, the evolution of consciousness marches on. We have no guarantee that the world will continue as we know it. Civilizations come and go. Societies rise and fall. Calendars begin and end. Consciousness, however, evolves. Life emerges in new forms.

In works subsequent to *Power vs. Force*, Hawkins spoke of the emergence of a new kind of human being: *Homo spiritus*, an evolutionary leap from *Homo sapiens*, which, as we know, is capable of walking upright, abstract reasoning, and sub-serving animal instincts to greater concerns. *Homo sapiens* has done wonders in the fields of science and technology, business and government. But as wise as the "sapiens" may be, it lacks knowledge of the spiritual laws that Vivekananda illumined at the Parliament. "Love is the ultimate law of the universe" is one way to put it.[14] Evolved human beings have always known this and sought to align their lives with the law of Love.

To be aligned with Love as a universal law is the wisdom wired into *Homo spiritus*, a "new evolutionary branch of mankind" in which the qualities of the heart (compassion, forgiveness, love) have become innate to the brain structure. It is the "awakened man who has bridged the evolutionary leap from physical to spiritual, from form to non-form, from linear to nonlinear."[15] Nelson Mandela is perhaps an example from recent history. He drew upon *ubuntu*, embodied in the African proverb, "We are people through other people." This consciousness respects the interconnectedness and interdependence of life. It's a consciousness of the heart and of oneness. It's aware of what Indigenous Wisdom calls the original instructions, described by the

Grandmothers in *The Power of Love* as respect for the sacredness of all creation.

There are solutions to the world's problems that await a shift in our collective consciousness from the head to the heart. Those who are aligned with Love have already begun to implement this intelligence of the heart. This is the gift of the interviewees in this book. In the arena of societal healing of racial divides, Belvie Rooks and Dedan Gills have created a vision called Growing a Global Heart that carries forward the teachings of Dr. Martin Luther King on agape love. In the domain of science, Dr. William A. Tiller has pioneered a new paradigm of physics at the interface of science and spirit, demonstrating that loving human intention influences the material world. In the field of psychology, Dr. Viktor Frankl, renowned Holocaust survivor and founder of logotherapy, stands as a timeless example of fortitude in the face of suffering. His grandson, Alexander Vesely, together with Mary Cimiluca, apply Frankl's principles of love and meaningfulness to the arenas of art and business. In the realm of academic study, Dr. Huston Smith exemplifies that one's work and intellectual life can be a path of joy and love. The spiritual teachers of diverse traditions reveal multiple ways that hearts and communities are transformed: Sadhguru Jaggi Vasudev; His Holiness the 17th Karmapa; Llewellyn Vaughan-Lee; Jetsunma Tenzin Palmo; Mother Teresa; Father Pavlos of Sinai; Swami Chidatmananda; Betty Eadie; David R. Hawkins; Mona Polacca, and the Indigenous Grandmothers.

Whole storehouses of new technologies and options for peaceful resolutions await human receptivity. When enlightened by love, the mind can receive breakthrough solutions to longstanding problems. These solutions already exist within consciousness but await the right receptiveness before they can manifest in the human domain. How can anything new come into our lives unless there's a space for it to enter? Humanity doesn't lack for ideas for our pressing global problems. If ideas were enough, the problems would have resolved. What's needed is the inner transformation within the heart of humanity that opens us to the goldmine we're sitting on, the untapped energy of love and the infrastructure it's capable of emerging.

An ancient story from India gives the secret: A beggar lived under a tree. For his whole life, he sat under the tree, his hand out, begging for money and food from passersby. When the beggar died, there was no money for a burial or cremation, so the villagers dug a hole for his grave right where he had sat. To their amazement, they found a trove of diamonds and gold. All along, the beggar had been sitting on a treasure and didn't know it. This is our predicament, the sages tell us. We're sitting on a goldmine and don't know it. The challenge is to shift our consciousness from the beggar to the inner gold.[16]

The beggar is our small self. It feels incomplete. Oriented toward the external world, it begs for attention, information, money, accolades, philosophies, gadgets, security, etc. The gold is our inner wisdom, our heart, our true Self. What if, instead of reaching out a hand for crumbs and coins, the beggar had dug into the ground he sat upon? What if, instead of reaching outward, he had reached inward? If only he had dug a little bit, he would have found an inner completion, an ever-present joy. He would have discovered the innate dignity, beauty, and lovingness of his own higher Self.

Love is the treasure hidden in every heart. Whoever makes the journey will find the treasure. It is free and available to anyone who truly seeks it. Since few do, we call love a miracle.

As we will see, Nelson Mandela is a well-known example of this very process. He went to prison an angry man, bitter at the racist apartheid government for its oppression of his people, but something opened up in Mandela, and he made a journey to the innermost part of himself. His anger at apartheid was transformed into love for his country. After twenty-seven years, he walked out of prison and forged a partnership with apartheid leaders to achieve the first democratically elected government in South Africa. He created something that had never been done before. It all started from a single individual who was willing to look within his heart. "Changing the world happens one heart at a time—start with your own." This is the axiom from Sunlight, a wise woman encountered in the pages of this book.

Love transcends dualistic thinking of win/lose, us/them. Love works for the whole. Love enables life to regenerate itself, for love is the substance of life. Love is holistic, able to envision a future inclusive of the needs of all. Love has the power to heal longstanding conflicts, noted with Gandhi's *soul force* and King's *agape*. Selfless and principled, this level of consciousness is redemptive and victorious.

Love is activated and refined by the spiritual practices described herein. Practices such as the Jesus Prayer, Sufi *zikr* (repetition of the Divine name), Buddhist *tonglen* and loving-kindness meditations, communal tree-planting ceremonies, and prayers that honor the Sacred in creation generate a subtle energy that transforms not only the people doing them but also the world at large. Though simple, they have a certain alchemical potency. Of the simple practice "recollecting of kindness," The Karmapa tells how the remembering of kindnesses can build a momentum of gratitude that extends far and wide. Havasupai-Hopi-Tewa Grandmother Mona speaks of forgiving our mother, she who gave us life, and how that can help to heal our relationship with Mother Earth. Mother Teresa says that even a smile is the beginning of love, and lightens the load of everyone around us. One of the first practices I learned from my teacher is found in *The Practice of the Presence of God*, the book by Brother Lawrence,[17] who focused his attention on the presence of God's love inside and all around him, even while sweeping the kitchen floor in his monastery. These are simple things, but they have the power to open the human heart.

When the heart opens, the world benefits. Love has a healing effect on body and mind because the energy of the heart is more powerful than mental and physical systems. In scientific terms, this is what the HeartMath Institute has found in its research for the last twenty years:

> Our and others' research indicates the heart is far more than a simple pump. It is, in fact, a highly complex information-processing center with its own functional brain, commonly called the heart brain,

which communicates with and influences the cranial brain via the nervous system, hormonal system, and other pathways. These influences affect brain function and most of the body's major organs, and play an important role in mental and emotional experience and the quality of our lives.

The scientists at HeartMath, Dr. William Tiller among them, found that when people direct their attention with sincere appreciation and loving care on someone or something (place, nature, painting, etc.), heart-rate variability and other cardiac indicators shift in a positive direction, stimulating a pro-health response throughout the entire body-mind. The effect is not limited to the health of the practitioner. The researchers found that the heart's magnetic field, radiating beyond the body, affects the people, places, and animals in the immediate surroundings. Their most recent research, Global Coherence Initiative, explores the possible connectivity between human inner coherence and the Earth's magnetic field.[18]

This finding corresponds, as we will see, to Dr. Tiller's experiments, which demonstrate that loving-kindness and compassion are subtle energies with a high level of coherence (a state of harmony and symmetry); they alter the thermodynamics of a space and have a healing effect.

Here is the gist: Love is the greatest power available to us and it resides in the human heart, expressed in qualities such as kindness, compassion, forgiveness, appreciation, gratitude, patience, beauty, friendship, caring, joy, and nobility. When tapped into through simple methods of attention, the energy of love heals our inner and outer divides. It increases regenerative likelihoods and makes possible new expressions of life.

This book carries forward a great truth from Swami Vivekananda's speeches to the 1893 Parliament of the World's Religions. To move with the power of love, agreement on specific points of doctrine is not necessary. Hearts can move in tandem, even as minds evolve their differing viewpoints. This certainly seems to be the spirit of the Global Ethic, a document written in 1993 on the 100th anniversary of the 1893 Parliament and signed by leaders of wide-ranging faiths. It illustrates that whether religious or political, differences of belief do not have to divide people committed to love. To use the phrase of the Indigenous Grandmothers, "We all walk with a different medicine, but we accept each other's ways." This book also gives the example of Father Pavlos, a Greek Orthodox ascetic living in the Sinai desert among Muslim neighbors, and shows that one can hold fast to the tenets of one's own faith and at the same time enjoy harmony with those of other faiths. There are simple truths about love found in this book that are suggested here as a path of living from the heart.

## Simple Truths about Love

All expressions of love, however small, benefit oneself and the world. Anything offered from the heart blesses life—a kind word, a meal cooked with love, a smile, walking with gratitude on the earth, doing "small things with great love" (Mother Teresa).

The more one loves, the more one can love. Love in any form, such as loving one's pet or family or plants, increases one's capacity to love.

To love any single piece of life is to love all of life, for all of life is interconnected.

Prayer is an expression of love often overlooked yet very influential, especially when offered out of love for others and the world.

Love is present everywhere; it needs only to be realized. To look for and affirm love in everyday life increases its occurrence.

To receive love is a form of giving love.

Love seeks nothing and needs nothing in return, for it is self-rewarding. To share what we have become with others is its own reward. The love we give to others always comes back to us.

There is no limit to love.

Romantic love is one of the many forms of Love.

The source of love is within. It requires no object.

Love works for the whole; it is not against anything or anyone. Standing for peace is different than protesting against war.

Love sees the hidden beauty of all that exists. It reverences the sacredness of life. It sees the innate lovability of others and nurtures what is best in them.

Spiritual work is a form of love that blesses the world.

Love comes through us, not from us. By grace we are given love, by grace we express love.

Love is self-respecting but not self-interested.

Love is present in all experiences, in pain as well as joy. "There is as much love in the mother crying for her dying child as in a couple walking to the altar" (Llewellyn Vaughan-Lee).

Love is a way of being. When we become a loving person, everything we do is an expression of love.

Love resides in every heart. Love is our true nature, not just to love one person but to be love itself.

And now the journey begins, to travel the path of love.

# Part One

# Searching for Love

Love,
what do I know of love?

I only know longing,
the yearning of my needs
and emptiness in my soul

Yet, once, I wandered up on
a blood root bloom, an herb
opening upon the forest floor,
of white so pure it startled
and life so brief
I could only gasp

Innocence itself,
giving for its own sake

Then
I was struck
by love

simply lived

—Elizabeth M. Cheatham

# The Journey Begins

*The journey of love begins uniquely for each of us. Somewhere along the way, we awaken to love. It was always there, but we weren't aware of it. The heart is touched, joy is stirred, an inner light clicks on. We feel happy, hopeful, generous, in awe of life, and even ecstatic. Now we know that love exists. The catalysts are as many as the breaths of beings. Perhaps it is the loving arms of a grandmother, a teacher or coach who believes in us, a beloved family pet, the first stirring of romantic feelings during adolescence, the birth of a child, a sudden break-through of creativity, the fulfillment of an inner calling or outer work. In some cases, trauma is the catalyst that awakens us to the existence of love. At age eleven, in the wake of a car accident and loss of his leg, psychologist Robert Johnson had a near-death experience in which he entered a realm of Love that he called the Golden World. He gave the rest of his life to tracing the "slender threads" of this Golden World throughout culture, mythology, and the human psyche. In my case, the discovery of love came by way of Light.*

*The experience of love has a singular effect, unmistakable in its qualities of joy, healing, and wholeness. But perhaps for most of us that initial experience doesn't last. The loving grandmother or family pet dies. The teenage romance ends in heartbreak. We graduate from school and move on from the special teacher or coach. Our baby grows up. The creative piece or outer work we felt so happy about gets mixed reviews. The mystical experience is misunderstood by others, and we end up in a strange solitude, unable to articulate the ineffable and longing for its reoccurrence. In all such cases, we assumed that something outside of ourselves was the source of love when, actually, it was the catalyst. And thus begins the great drama of love—our search for something as if it were outside of ourselves. That search takes us through the valleys of fear, shame, sorrow, anger, and doubt as we face the inner and outer forces that would deny and distort love. Then, seemingly out of nowhere, the clouds part and we find ourselves able to bear more and more of the power of love.*

*"When the clouds are removed, the sun shines forth," my teacher often said.*

## Chapter One

# Light Upon Light

My first experience with love happened in tenth-grade English class. I remember it vividly. My desk was in the middle of the room, directly facing the teacher as she lectured on *The Scarlet Letter*. I was a good student, but I was only half-listening to the story. The rest of my attention was pondering the more pressing problems of teenage life: a crush, tennis tournaments, an upcoming exam. And then it happened:

Suddenly, a Light engulfs me.

It comes from above, as if through the ceiling. A wide pillar of Light encompasses me. I've never seen such Light before. It casts no shadow. It has an intelligence. It is luminous and soft, yet powerful and autonomous. Like nothing I've ever experienced before—totally silent, totally undeniable, totally peaceful.

Within the Light, time stands still. In fact, there is no time. My mental chatter ceases; teenage worries vanish. The Light holds, or rather transmutes, all of me into Itself. I have no memory of thoughts, only the memory of no thoughts. No thought, no sound, no time, no movement. Total stillness. The peace is stunning.

The Light loves. It is Love unlike anything I've ever experienced, because it needs nothing from me. It takes nothing from me. It has dissolved me, yet, in some strange way, it *is* me. The *real* me. The Light radiates over me, around me, through me, and in me. It is a timeless embrace of all I have ever been or will be. It is an infusion of Love.

The Light disappeared just as suddenly as it had appeared. It had come out of nowhere and left on Its own. I—the personal I—had done nothing to cause it. I had been *done to*. The power of the Light was immense and obliterating.

I was astonished. I looked around the classroom in shock. What was *that?* To my amazement, I saw that everyone remained as before. The teacher talked on; the students, half-attending, stared straight ahead. I wanted to jump up and down: "Oh! Wow! Did you *see* that?" How could they have missed the Light? It had been so real. As far as they were concerned, nothing had happened. As far as I was concerned, Something Big had happened, but what?

## The Aftermath

For many months, I told no one. I was a private young person who kept things to myself. The Light was the most intimate and stunning encounter of my life. What could be said about it? The moment had come out of nowhere and passed quickly, yet I felt changed forever.

My parents were conventional, Protestant Christians, born and raised in the Deep South. Everything was done "decently and in order," as they liked to say. My mother was a homemaker and tended toward biblical literalism. My father, a businessman, was a committed rationalist who believed in religion according to the dictates of reason. "Let's be reasonable," I heard him say, "God doesn't violate natural law." Whenever television preachers loudly testified to gifts of the Holy Spirit, he grumbled, "Nutty in the head! Charlatans!" Neither of my parents had ever mentioned spiritual experience and certainly not beams of light coming out of a ceiling! Yet the Light had been more real than anything I'd ever seen. I felt strangely and wondrously altered by it.

The Light had transmitted something to me, but what? I didn't know. "Noetic" is the word used by William James in his classic book,

*Varieties of Religious Experience*, to describe revelational knowledge as opposed to book knowledge.

When I considered the utter spontaneity of it, I became afraid. Whatever it was, the Light was something I had no control over. It had come and gone of its own. It had overtaken me, encompassed me into Itself. The sheer autonomy of it struck me with awe. My temperament was such that I liked to know ahead of time what was coming at me. Before school started, I liked to go the day before and make sure I knew where the classrooms were located. I didn't like leaving things to chance. Growing up in an alcoholic family—Dad's cocktail hour lasted many hours—I had a need for structure and predictability. "Be prepared" was my motto.

The aftermath of the Light became unsettling. There were odd feelings and sensations. A devotionally oriented youth, I had been in the habit of praying to God the Father behind closed doors and felt a level of communion I couldn't explain. After the Light, my prayers brought on a new feeling, especially at night when I was alone. It was an incredible melting sweetness that scared me because it felt like I was dissolving into Something Greater. There would be a warm feeling that ignited near my heart. The closer I felt to God, the more intense the warmth. I would start to feel as if I were dissolving into the warmth completely, into a soft timeless space. I wondered, *what's happening to me? Am I going to dissolve?* I would jump out of bed and shake myself back to reality, as I called it. At other times, my body would start to vibrate and a loud humming would rack inside my head like a train was railing through it. Still, at other times, my body would feel paralyzed, like I wasn't quite in it. I became afraid to go to sleep, as if I had to keep watch over my soul so it wouldn't disappear. This private struggle went on for months.

My mother noticed that I wasn't acting like myself. Worried about me, she kept asking, "What's going on with you?" Maybe she thought I was having trouble at school or some other kind of typical teenage problem, but I wasn't accustomed to sharing my feelings with her. Our relationship had shut down when I hit puberty and my body had become a zone of conflict between us. She'd tried her best to mold me into a Southern belle, but I was more interested in nature and books than make-up and fashion.

Mother persisted, so I finally told her about the Light. Concerned, she took me to the elderly Protestant pastor for our small church in the conservative South. This congregation had been an affirming place for me as a young person with a devotional bent. I sang solos in the church service, and my mother served as an elder (a lay officer of the congregation). We were active in Sunday school and fellowship. I had recently been confirmed in the church; yet, as we drove to the appointment, I had a sinking feeling that the Light was in a different category from religion and that the pastor might take a dim view of it—and of me.

I had never been to the pastor's office before. It felt overly solemn to me. As in a funeral home, it seemed appropriate only to whisper, but the air felt heavy with all that needed to be shouted. I told him the story of the Light, dissolving feeling, sleepless nights, and the fear that I would be dissolved into Something Greater.

We awaited his verdict.

Finally, after what seemed an eternal silence, he pronounced: "It's the *devil!*"

Oh, no! At worst, I had thought he might say I was abnormal in a psychological sense. But—a dwelling place for the devil? I hadn't even considered the possibility! I wasn't even sure what the devil was, but I knew it was the worst of the worst.

Mother shifted awkwardly in her seat but remained quiet. Her silence suggested agreement: it *was* the devil. I felt utterly alone, abandoned, confused. How could it be the devil? This made no sense! It had been such a beautiful experience of Love—something not of this world, yet in it. With no way to understand or articulate what had happened, and having no advocate to support me, I succumbed to the pastor's pronouncement. My mother and I looked up to him as the religious authority in our lives. He was an expert on matters of the spirit, wasn't he?

His declaration "It's the devil" separated me from the truest part of myself; it activated an inner inquisition that attacked everything related to the Light. All the warm feelings of love, the inner stirrings within my heart, the devotion—they were now seen as the devil and had to be rejected. Quashed. Expunged. I became more of a battle-ground than a person.

## The Steel Door

My soul had loved the Light. It was my first encounter with Pure Love, and who ever forgets such love? The exquisite feeling of it stayed with me, even during the many years of darkness that followed the pastor's pronouncement. As Rūmī said, Love had me by the ear, dragging me in secret ways, in both joy and pain…

When I was fifteen, the religious authority had condemned the Love from the Light, and now my unconscious erupted with shame, doubt, and fear. Day and night, I became overwhelmed by arche-typal images of pitchforks and a lethal inner voice that taunted, "I will destroy you." I was caught in a battle of inner forces that can only be worded as good vs. evil. The Love transmitted through the Light was beyond all words to describe its exquisite Far-Nearness. And the violent imagery that condemned it was beyond all words to describe its horror. The ordinarily safe places—school, church, my room—no longer felt safe, as I was haunted and taunted from within. I had nowhere to turn for help, not even inwardly. The sweet inner commu-nion with God that had secretly nourished me as a devout teenager was now fraught with fears of annihilation.

Desperate for psychological survival, I left the Protestant denom-ination of my upbringing and joined a fundamentalist sect that saw itself as *the* original church described in the New Testament. They held to a literalistic view of the Bible, believing themselves to be the one true church. Their denial of spiritual experience brought relief to me because it shut the door on an inner realm that seemed too terri-fyingly potent to handle.

"Trust in the Word of God, not personal experience."

"Follow your head, not your heart."

"The Holy Spirit is dead. We have the Bible now."

"We speak where the Bible speaks and are silent where the Bible is silent."

"Women must keep silent in the church."

"Dancing is a sin."

"We are the one true church."

"Be ye not unequally yoked together with unbelievers."

*Just as I Am* was the invitation hymn as I went forward to make my public confession at the Sunday evening service. Wrapped in white baptismal garments, I was immersed in water as the scattered congregation looked on. When I rejoined the members afterward, I happily noticed their language of family now included me: "*Sister Fran...* "She is in *the* church...." I declared myself a servant of this church and the vision of humanity it presented—which was very different from the Light.

I served the church for nearly twenty years. Its doctrines and rules functioned as a steel door that kept the energies of love at bay. Of course, the steel door didn't eliminate the energies of love that I feared; it merely pushed them from conscious view—a tsunami of emotion stuffed into the closet, raging to roar out. What little ego can hold back a tsunami? The suppression created a buildup of pressure, and I began to suffer daily panic attacks. When in the grip of panic, I would sit as if curled up in a ball, head hung down, eyes fixed on the floor. This was how I got through the three weekly church services and the other settings that activated my panic. It was especially intense when I sat in the fundamentalist church services, because my unconscious picked up on the church's rejection of anything mystical and heartfelt. Palms sweating, heart racing, thoughts escalating—I felt powerless. I tried to hold it together, to appear normal, but I'm sure I looked strange: a young woman hunched over, in a state of lockdown.

During full-blown panic attacks, I had only one relief button: I would silently say the name of my boyfriend over and over again, like a mantra, repeating the name of my beloved and picturing him in my mind's eye. In this odd way, I intuitively discovered a mechanism at the root of many meditative, prayer, and *zikr* practices—the use of a loving word or image that shifts attention from head to heart. The method infused a few seconds of safety into the swirl of panic. As soon as the service was over, and sometimes in the middle of the sermon, I ran out of the church, sweating, my heart racing like the deer fleeing the lion.

The repression of love had fragmented my psyche. I had cut off a part of myself, and that part insisted to be known. It was coming after me, as in a nightmare. This kind of fragmentation is symbolized in the fairytales in which the unwanted child is locked in the basement for years or the princess is imprisoned in the tower to preserve her purity. Eventually the closeted character breaks free because the soul wants to live its wholeness.

I didn't break free until my early thirties when an experience of tender human love opened the steel door. My panic disorder dissolved spontaneously, and I experienced the power of love to heal my inner divides.

"If you are not loved for yourself, then you are split into parts. Spiritual life is about wholeness. You can only go back to God as your whole self." When I heard these words from Sufi teacher, Llewellyn Vaughan-Lee, I felt the poignancy of the steel door and how it had cut me off from the power of love. My visit with him and his wife Anat helped me understand the immensity of the Light and why it had been too much to bear.

Llewellyn Vaughan-Lee
(courtesy of The Golden Sufi Center).

Anat Vaughan-Lee
(courtesy of The Golden Sufi Center).

# Chapter Two

## LONGING FOR LOVE

### Encounter with Llewellyn and Anat Vaughan-Lee

*Light upon Light!*
*Allah guides*
*Whom Allah will*
*To His Light*

—THE LIGHT *SURA*
(QURAN 24:35)

There are lights that ascend and lights that descend. The ascending lights are the lights of the heart; the descending lights are those of the Throne. The lower self (the ego) is the veil between the Throne and the heart. When this veil is rent and a door opens in the heart, like springs toward like. Light rises toward light, and light comes down upon light, and it is light upon light.

Each time a light rises up from you, a light comes down toward you.… This is the secret of the mystical journey.…

—NAJM AL-DÎN KUBRÂ,
13TH-CENTURY SUFI[19]

# ENTERING THE HOUSE OF THE SHEIKH

The Vaughan-Lee home is up a steep hill and down a one-lane gravel road, nestled in a forest of ferns and fir trees. As I approach the front door, I smell incense. According to many spiritual traditions, sweet or sage fragrances repel negativity. Llewellyn opens the door, and I feel the peace of the place. I remove my shoes and step onto a Turkish rug. Anat asks kindly, "Would you like slippers?" They welcome me as a fellow traveler. I would later learn that on the Sufi path this warmhearted courtesy is called *adab*. Inwardly, the Sufi is bowed down to the Divine within oneself and others. It is different from outward piety. Inner adab is a quality of the heart, "the attitude of the soul before God."[20]

Llewellyn is wearing a plain blue pullover sweater, not the white garment he wears when in his public teaching role as a *sheikh*. His eyes are blue—like the ocean, and just as vast. Though he has lived in the United States for three decades, his British accent is evident. Anat speaks softly with an Israeli accent. I am struck by her natural beauty and depth of listening.

They walk me into the kitchen. It's furnished comfortably, no clutter. Sufis follow an ethic to buy only what they need and give away what they don't use. The table has been prepared with a teapot, three cups, and a plate with the most exquisite-looking sweet breads. I sense the unusual harmony of simplicity and generosity.

We are at their kitchen table nearly three hours. The attention is undivided and total. How rare in this modern era that strangers meet around a table and lose track of time in the deeper layers of love and longing of the human heart. Similar to the Light, their love is unconditional. They take nothing from me; they give everything they have to give me in the moment, clean and pure, no strings attached. The atmosphere is transparent and free flowing, and I'm aware of the stark contrast with my meeting three decades earlier with the minister who proclaimed the Light to be the devil. What a difference it makes when a spiritual guide is surrendered to Love rather than afraid of it.

## BACKGROUND

They met as young adults forty years earlier at a Sufi group in London. Llewellyn grew up in a middle-class English home void of affection, and was sent to boarding school at age seven. At sixteen, he had a spiritual awakening while reading a book about Zen Buddhism on the London tube train. This single Zen saying ignited him: "The wild geese do not intend to cast their reflection. The water has no mind to receive their image."

He said the saying was like a key that opened a door inside of him that he didn't know existed:

> I felt a joy that I had never before experienced, a moment of intense exhilaration. For weeks afterwards I inwardly laughed and laughed, as if I saw the secret joke within creation. A world that had been gray began to sparkle and dance. I started to meditate and have experiences.[21]

Sufis call this moment *tauba*, when the heart turns toward God and the soul begins its journey of return to the Source. The journey is unique to each person yet the same for each. According to Sufism, every person is born with a spark of Divine Love in the heart, but it remains covered over until the moment is right and the Beloved ignites the mystery of *light upon light*, the awakening of divine remembrance. The light of the heart rises to God with longing, and this longing in turn attracts the Divine Light. The light within our heart is the same as the Divine Light we long for. Llewellyn explains, "There is only one path, there is only one pilgrim; it is just the Light of God realizing its own nature. And we share that all together and yet we are so alone. Love does with us what it will. This is the closed circle of love…. You look for love because you are love."[22] Sufis call it a mystery because the relationship of lover and Beloved unfolds in the innermost chamber of the heart—"the heart of hearts"—where nothing human enters except the Grace of one's teacher.

When Llewellyn was nineteen, he met his teacher, Irina Tweedie, at a lecture on the esoteric dimension of math. He was sitting behind an elderly lady with striking white hair wrapped up in a bun. After the lecture, a friend took Llewellyn to meet her. She looked at him with piercing blue eyes. "In that instant, I had the physical experience of becoming just a speck of dust on the ground. Then she turned and walked away and I was left utterly bewildered." Many years later he heard the Sufi saying, to become "less than dust at the feet of the teacher." Only after the ego has been ground down to dust can there be a surrender to Divine Love. Over the years to come, this was Llewellyn's experience—to be annihilated by Love, made into a servant of the Beloved, "In the name of He who has no name." He explains:

> I never knew what it meant to love—it was not part of my understanding. And then love came and love did the most strange and crazy things to me; love turned everything upside down; from being an English middle-class school boy to sitting at the feet of this Russian lady whose eyes were intoxicated with God…. She just spoke about her Sheikh with love. Not the love that wants something, not the love full of desires, but love that puts its head to the ground, the love in which you forget yourself. If you really love, you forget yourself; you are lost in love. You want nothing for yourself because you are given everything. And this was the love to which I was introduced—this was the love that changed my mind, that changed my heart.[23]

After his encounter with Irina Tweedie, Llewellyn joined the small group that met for meditation and discussion in Tweedie's studio apartment. She had returned from India after years of intense training by the Sufi master Radha Mohan Lal, known by his disciples as Bhai Sahib (elder brother). Bhai Sahib was a sheikh in the Naqshbandiyya-Mujaddidiyya lineage of Sufis, an Indian branch of the Naqshbandi order, named after the 14th-century master Baha ad-Din Naqshband. They are known as the Silent Sufis, for their *dhikr* (repetition of the Divine Name) is silent, inward. They dress in everyday clothing so as not to set themselves apart from ordinary people. They meet together in private groups for meditation, dream-work, and discussion. The sheikh is the center pole of a group, yet his physical presence isn't always required, as the energy field transcends time and location.

Central to the Naqshbandi path is *rabita*, the bond of love between master and disciple through which the Grace of the tradition is transmitted. Bhai Sahib asked Mrs. Tweedie to give an account of their bond by keeping a diary of her experiences with him. The 829-page book, *Daughter of Fire: Diary of a Spiritual Training with a Sufi Master*, is one of the most detailed descriptions of the teacher-disciple relationship and spiritual transformation in the 20th century. Tweedie was the first Western woman to be trained in this ancient Sufi lineage, and she was the last person to see Bhai Sahib alive. When she returned to England after his death in 1966, she carried with her his transmission of love and brought this Naqshbandiyya-Mujaddidiyya path to the West.

Llewellyn and Anat met in Mrs. Tweedie's group, married, had two children, and bought a house in London. Mrs. Tweedie moved into the lower apartment and opened up the space as a meeting place for pilgrims who came from all over the world to meet her, often as a result of reading *Daughter of Fire*. The book intensifies a seeker's longing for Self-realization. Here is the account of one friend who read it and ended up traveling from the U.S. to be with Mrs. Tweedie. She thought she was just passing through, but...

> As soon as I walked in, it felt like home. I was accepted completely as I was. The search was over. I'd found what I was looking for. But that's not to say it was easy! There's a saying on this Sufi path, "Things

are said to the door so the window can hear," and that's what she did as a teacher to break me open. For example, one time she went on and on about my story in the group for two months, mentioning my name and all that I'd gone through—"Poor girl, she lost her husband at a young age to cancer..." I didn't budge. I was very stoic, never showed my feelings, never cried in front of anyone. I grew up in a large family, so I'd learned to live with a stiff upper lip. But then one day she got me through the *backdoor*. She told a person right in front of me—the energy of it came at me like a knife—"Your poor wife can't show her feelings... please give her my love...." I got out of there as fast as I could. The floodgates opened and the tears started to flow. Somehow I managed to pull myself together for the ride home with a friend in the group. This has been the path for me—the old ego that wants to be strong and in charge has to be broken down to nothing.[24]

"To die before you die" is the aspiration of the Sufi. In numerous talks and writings, Llewellyn describes the process he underwent of *fanâ* (annihilation) and *baqâ* (abiding in God)—the classic Sufi journey from separation to union. He is a mystic, totally surrendered to God. He uses the metaphor of being wood in the fire of Love where all personal striving, identities and desires are burnt to ash. Many years before her death in 1999, Irina Tweedie designated Llewellyn the successor of the lineage, and sent him to America where he founded The Golden Sufi Center (1990) as a vehicle for the teachings of this order.

As a sheikh, Llewellyn is more of a space than a person. In the Sufi tradition, the teacher is traditionally "without a face and without a name," for it is the teaching that matters, not the personhood of the teacher. The real teacher is understood to be the light of the Higher

Self within the heart of the disciple. For Sufis, life itself is the greatest teacher, as the Higher Self attracts the circumstances needed for spiritual evolution.

The work of the Sufis is to "keep watch on the world and for the world." They do so quietly, following the Naqshbandi principle "Solitude in the Crowd," that is, to be "outwardly with people, inwardly with God." Their Higher Self, hidden within the heart of hearts, is the source of their inner light, activated by the teacher. As the heart is polished by the practices of the path, the true self shines forth. Difficulties and inner struggles are welcomed, for friction sparks transformation of the "shadow," which is C. G. Jung's term for whatever we don't want to see in ourselves. Hence the Sufi teaching, "Give your enemy a place in your garden." Llewellyn puts it this way: "The Path begins with what you don't like."

Sufis submit to being transformed by this Fire of Love, and learn to use their light selflessly for the sake of the world. Through their ordinary jobs, family life, inner devotions, and silent prayers, they give light to the world. The light of human love nourishes the light of the world soul. Sufis know that to love any single piece of life is to increase the light within all of creation. Llewellyn explains, "Everything comes into existence through love. Sufis learn to breathe with this love."

A unique dimension of his teaching is the emphasis on the feminine. What began for him as a personal psychological healing of the feminine, recounted beautifully in his autobiography, expanded to become a body of work for the collective.[25] In the West, he notes, things are out of balance because the feminine is devalued and repressed into the cultural shadow. Though the West has the appearance of sexual equality, masculine values of competition, extraversion, logic, action, ego drives, personal goals, and rationalism dominate nearly every area of society. They "even dominate our spiritual quest; we seek to be better, to improve ourself, to get somewhere."[26] We have forgotten the feminine qualities of stillness, receptivity, intuition, feeling, listening, beingness, devotion, intuition, love, interiority, and interrelatedness.

Along with others featured in this book, Llewellyn has been a major leader in the current shift of consciousness to recover the voice and value of the feminine for our time, often worded as a shift from doing to being, from head to heart, from me to we. His book, *The Return of the Feminine and the World Soul*, has received acclaim from spiritual leaders of diverse traditions.[27] His body of work called Spiritual Ecology emerged as a field related to the feminine, and has generated widespread attention to the spiritual basis of our current global ecological crises.[28] Green technology and carbon-reduction policies alone will not heal the planet. There is a cry from the Earth for us to respond to her real need and heal the underlying problems within our collective consciousness—greed, despair, isolation, a lack of love, and especially the loss of our connection with the Sacred within creation.

At a global gathering of women in India, Anat spoke of the responsibility to reclaim our ultimate purpose of honoring the sacredness of life, the "original YES" of creation, and to remember "that we are a soul" and "that the earth is a living being." She called upon men and women to live the "feeling values of the heart" and Mother Teresa's teaching that we "serve life not because it is broken but because it is Holy."[29] It's not common to meet people of any gender who have integrated the feminine into their everyday consciousness. Being at the kitchen table with Llewellyn and Anat was one of the few experiences I've ever had of that wholeness and the selfless love that flows from it.[30]

# CONVERSATION WITH LLEWELLYN AND ANAT VAUGHAN-LEE

## Love and Light within Creation

Q:   As a Sufi teacher, you teach that love is the greatest power of the universe. You've written, for example, that beneath everything "there are connections of pure love that link creation with Creator." Can you speak to that?

LVL:    As far as I know from my experience, love is the very fabric of creation. Love is the substance and the center of everything. You can describe it as Light, and say that it's the One Light that becomes scattered into the many as if through a prism. The One Light of Creation becomes scattered into the many colors of existence.

Without love, the universe would fall apart. Love is the primal relationship between the Creator and the creation. This bond of love is also reflected in the Quranic saying "He loves them and they love Him." And from a mystical point of view the energy coming into manifestation is the energy of love that flows from the uncreated into the created. From that single note of pure love is born the whole flowering of the created world in many different outer forms and also many inner planes of existence. The angels are also made of love.

In order to make the journey from creation back to the Creator, or from multiplicity back to oneness, or from the human being back to God, you need an energy. The Sufis use the energy of love. In particular they work with the longing of the heart, which is the feminine side of love. Love has a masculine side, "I love you," and a feminine side, "I am longing for you, I am waiting for you." Saint Augustine called this *divine discontent*. So Sufis have used the pure energy of love as the most direct connection and most direct access back to God, whom the Sufis call the Beloved. Sufism is a way of working with love.

I often think that in the West we use the word "love" in so many contexts. Many people, when they use the word, are really talking about an emotion, or even sexual passion. It's why I like this poem by Rūmī:

> subtle degrees
> of domination and servitude
> are what you know as love.
> but love is different.
> it arrives complete
> just there

like the moon in the window

.....

desire only that
of which you have no hope.
seek only that
of which you have no clue.

.....

this is not the Oxus River
or some little creek
this is the shoreless sea;
here swimming ends
always in drowning

The Sufis have learned how to use this primal energy of love as a way to make the journey back to God. I think you'll find that different mystical or spiritual traditions use different energies. For example, in my practice of Zen the focus was on empty mind, a certain quality of consciousness, attention. In Sufism, the focus is on love, and it developed an understanding of love, which we do not have in the West. There are the Christian mystics such as St. John of the Cross and St. Teresa of Avila, mystics who have ecstatic states of love—one of my favorites is the Blessed John Ruysbroeck. He talks about the dark silence in which all lovers lose themselves. But Western mysticism has not developed the techniques of love, the "science of love," to such a degree that the Sufis have.[31]

In particular, there's a Sufi understanding of the mystical chambers of the heart. Sufi techniques teach how to use the energy of love together with sacred words or breathing to activate the heart, to go deeper and deeper into the chambers of the heart. I'm often reminded of Coleman Barks when he said that, at one time, Hallmark Card Company requested to use his translations of Rūmī's poems. And he said to them, "I don't think this is the love you are interested in! This love is about annihilation."

There are two things: the personal and the spiritual experiences of love. And one needs to distinguish, as Rūmī does, between them.

Divine Love is different from what most people understand as love, which usually has to do with the field of personal relationships and falling in love and our whole culture that has developed around a certain image of love. We often first learn to love through personal relationship, with our parents or our partners.

And then there is Divine Love. Experiences of Divine Love are often so intimate that most people are not prepared to talk about them. We don't generally share in public the secrets of our love affair, and for the Sufis the love affair is between lover and Beloved. It's a tremendously intimate and sometimes erotic relationship of your soul to God. It's not a relationship of the ego or personality, but of the soul to God. The soul is impregnated with Divine Love—made pregnant with love. This is the mystery of the soul because mystical life has to do with the drama of the soul.

I think the most beautiful expression of Divine Love in the Western canon is the *Song of Songs:* "He brought me to the banqueting house and his banner over me was love." The church said it was to do with the relationship between the Church and God, rather than the soul and God, because they were frightened of mysticism. But Divine Love is this very intimate inner experience of what happens to the heart, what happens *within* the heart.

In every other relationship you can protect yourself or distance yourself. You can create a barrier, or turn away, because the person is outside of you. But in this love affair with God, it happens within your heart. It happens from the inside, from within. You have images from the saints or mystics of being a victim of God's love, taken by love. You are vulnerable. So there is this very intimate individual experience that mystics have. You can read it in the poems of Rūmī and many other Sufi poets who write about their own experience of the heartache and heartbreak—the tears that come.

It's a very painful business because your heart has to be broken. There is the *hadîth* "I am with those whose hearts are broken for My sake." The Sufis say, "Heaven and earth cannot contain Me, but the heart of My devoted servant can." This is because when it is broken open our spiritual heart center can be big as the universe. This is a very painful, intimate, ecstatic, demanding love affair, which is mainly described in the Sufi tradition in poetry. In addition to Sufi poetry, there are the manuals of the tradition to help you make this journey through love. So the people who have gone before have described the stages of the heart or the path, what you go through to purify the heart, and the different levels of experience you can have. Most of those manuals haven't been translated into English.

I remember I once asked my teacher, "Can one increase the love that one has?" And she said, "Of course you can!" There are ways to increase love, to give love to others, to infuse love into the souls of people. This belongs to the esoteric tradition of Sufism. It means working with love with other human beings.

Everybody wants to be loved. Everybody longs to be loved. But mystics or Sufis are those who give themselves completely to this experience. As Rūmī said, "this is the shoreless sea/ here swimming ends/ always in drowning"—be prepared to drown in love! It's not easy. There are no sure results. It is intoxicating, beautiful, and heartbreaking.

The important thing for me at the beginning when I first came to Sufism was to know it was a system, a well-tried method of working with love. I grew up in an English middle-class family. I didn't know what love was. My mother was alcoholic, and my father was very distant. I was sent to boarding school at seven. I never experienced love. I didn't know it existed. It wasn't something that we spoke about. Then I began to experience this incredible love.

Q: You write about a moment where the love of God felt like "butterfly wings in your heart"— in that moment your whole life changed with the completeness and totality of that love.

LVL: Yes. It surprised me. I'd had inklings of this love before. I'd had glimpses of it. But this was a completely unprecedented experience because I was just lying down in meditation and this energy like butterfly wings on the edge of my heart came into me from within and it went throughout all of me. Throughout the whole body, the whole of my being—everything was loved and everything was suffused in love. This is something one can never forget.

I have had many other experiences since that one, because the love can grow, it goes deeper and deeper—there is no limit to love. It's the same as the Sufi Dhû'l Nûn who stood on the shore of the sea and said, "What is the end of love?" And a woman said to him, 'Love has no end because the Beloved has no end.' So the love grows, it gets deeper, sometimes more demanding, sometimes more intoxicating, more gentle sometimes, more tender, more sweet. It has many facets. Sometimes it's like a cold knife that cuts.

But that first experience was a hallmark because it was an experience in my body, soul, and very being of a love that was complete in every way. It is given. It is a gift. You can do all the purification you like, all the practices you like. But those experiences are given—they are a gift given through grace.

## The Light

Q:  What about light and love? You've written about "points of light," that there is a web of light in the outer and inner planes. Traditionally mystics have said that the Love of God radiates as a Light.

LVL:  Yes, one manifestation or one expression of Divine Love is Light. There is also a mystical love that appears to be a darkness. It's called the dazzling darkness. Carl Jung talks about "the dark light of the *Deus absconditus*," the dark light that is beyond any image of God. But there is also this pure light that is a quality of love, a light that belongs to love. It is a light that has no color, fragrance or quality because it is completely pure. It comes into manifestation, through this prism, into the many colors of existence and interacts with people and creation and creates many experiences. Mystical life takes you from the many to the One, back to the core of the experience, and within every human being there is this light that belongs to God.

This quality of Divine Light also has intelligence in it. It is not just a ray of light. In the light itself there is intelligence, there is knowing, understanding, and part of mystical training is to purify oneself to become fine enough to be able to access this light. And also to become strong enough to be able to bear this light. Because it is immensely powerful and immensely brilliant. If you are not ready, it can make the mind crazy, it can send you into a mental hospital.

AVL:   It's a vibration.

LVL:   Yes, this light is a vibration. Mystical life is learning how to access the light, how to live with the light, work with the light. For example, you can give light to human beings, and help them to realize their own light, to be with their own light. There is a whole ancient Taoist tradition that perhaps you know, *The Secret of the Golden Flower*. In it, you create a spiritual body of light. And you need that in order to give birth to your spiritual self. Some Sufis have written a lot about light, for example the 12th-century master Suhrawaradî. And I've been prompted to write a certain amount about light and how there is intelligence and love in light and how one can link together through light—creating a web of light. And this Divine Light is present through all creation.

Q:   So everything radiates light?

LVL:   Everything is suffused with light. The English mystical poet Gerard Manley Hopkins said, "The world is charged with the grandeur of God. It will flame out, like shining from shook foil." I love that image. Silver foil in the sun, you shake it and all the light glitters.

## Light and Love in a Suffering World

Q:   What would you say to people who may be skeptical, who only see the suffering of the world—not the light? They see starving children, they are heartbroken from life, they have perhaps lost a child, been disabled, suffered genocide. They ask, "Where is love in the suffering of the world? How can there be light when there is so much darkness?"

LVL: First, I encourage them to value their experience. Love is beyond good and bad. It is not duality. There is as much love in the mother crying for her dying child as in a couple walking to the altar. Love doesn't differentiate. In fact, St. Paul said, "Love bears *all* things." Love is not good or bad; it is not happiness as opposed to sorrow. Love includes everything. Love embraces everything. If you go deep within any human experience, you'll find a quality of love there because human beings are made in the image of God. We are made out of love. The mystic aspires to experience the very depths of love, which often means incredible suffering. The mystic aspires to the heartbreak of love, and to take it raw, not to try to package it, or make it artificially sweet.

So I would say first to value the experience that you have. Don't judge it. Shakespeare said, "There is nothing either good or bad, but thinking makes it so." Sufi training is not to judge the experience but to say, "Everything comes from God." It is how to *live* with the experience that life gives you. For example, suffering can contract you. It can draw you back into ego, into resentment, into bitterness. Or it can open you—make you aware of a deeper dimension of love.

Love is not about what you want; it is about what love wants. Yes, there is suffering in the world. Some of it is human ignorance. Some of it is a deep teaching. Some of it is easily traced back to love. I suppose that is the difference. The mystic is the one prepared to go beneath the surface. In Christianity, you have the sublime image of love as crucifixion. In Sufism, there is the prince of lovers, the first martyr of love, al-Hallâj, who was also crucified for love. In public, he spoke the truth *anâ'l-Haqq*, that is, "I am the Absolute Truth." He made public what Sufis had always known in secret and kept private: the union of the human and God, the truth that there is only God, only oneness. And he was martyred for this truth.

There have been these great human beings—Nelson Mandela, for example, who lived his suffering with tremendous dignity out of which he helped a nation. Or figures like Christ whose passion was a passion of suffering. He knew he would be betrayed and he lived it, died it. That is an icon of love. He was supposedly one of the first great masters of love. Sadly, the church was more interested in worldly power than in love.

Does knowing this make it easy when one encounters the suffering, the pain? No. But maybe one can have compassion, understanding, and one can practice what the Buddhists call loving-kindness. For the Sufi, it is a recognition that everything comes from God. There is nothing other than God. It is our ignorance, our forgetfulness of that basic truth, that keeps us caught in the illusions of life rather than using them as a thread to discover the hidden secret of life, which for the Sufis is "Everything is God." "Wheresoever you turn, there is the Face of God." And everything is made of love. The anguished cry of the child, at its root, is love.

As far as I can understand, the greatest pain the human being can suffer is not physical or emotional suffering. In physical suffering, when the body can't take any more you become unconscious. The deepest suffering is really that of the heart and soul. And the root of that suffering is the pain of experiencing separation from God. It is the pain and longing of the heart. There is no more potent pain because once you become conscious of that, once it is awakened in you, you can't push it aside. It ruins you. Destroys you. It tears apart every fabric of your existence.

Sufis know about this dark side of love. In fact, they use the pain of love to go back to God…. Sufis say, "Take one sip of Divine Love and you are lost forever." It is addictive. Like main-lining heroin to the soul. It's real. It does things to you that nothing else can. Sufis say, "You will give anything for just another sip of wine." That's why the Sufis talk about the "tavern of ruin." It destroys you. That is the primal sorrow of love, which is a primal sorrow of separation. This is the greatest sorrow the human being can experience: that we are separate from God. It is a cry in the heart. For the Sufi, it is immortalized in the lament of the reed flute that Rūmī talks about in the beginning of the *Mathnawî*: "The lament of the reed torn from the reed-bed." That is the cry in the heart. There is a great description by one of the early Sufis, Abû Sa'id, "Sufism was first heartache, only later it became something to write about." Sufism is for those who are prepared to live that heartache. To pay that price. Yes you can say the rewards are overwhelming because you get to experience what love can do to a human being and what it reveals in the heart. Sufism is for those who want to live their life as a love affair, of lover and Beloved.

## Human Love as a Facet of Divine Love

Q:   Do Sufis see human love as an analog or opening to Divine Love? How does human love relate to Divine Love?

LVL:   The Sufi poet Jâmî said, "Never turn away from love, even love in a human form because love alone will free you from yourself." Our teacher Mrs. Tweedie used to say, "Human love is like playing with dolls." It prepares you. Personally I think it's much easier to love God than it is on the human stage because love for God is very simple. You love God. There are none of the difficulties of the human drama, projection and personal problems.

Q:   What's your view, Anat?

AVL:   I think the danger is that you have a feeling of longing in your heart, to God, to the Divine, but you do not know or understand what that feeling is and then you project it onto another human being, or into a relationship, thinking ignorantly that the other can answer such feelings. That can create great confusion in the relationship. Many people are unconscious. They are not aware that the other cannot give them what they are looking for. Either this leads to a great drama in the relationship, or it can take one into a deeper understanding of the mystery of love.

LVL:   The love relationship is a facet of Infinite Love. You can't divorce it. That's why I feel it's sad that the two have become divorced in the West. I studied cultural history, looking at the troubadours and courtly love. The idea of romantic love didn't really exist in Western consciousness until courtly love introduced it during the Middle Ages. Courtly love was the adoration of the woman that was practiced by the knights. It was a completely unfulfilled love because the woman was the Lady, wife of the Lord. There was no way that the knight could consummate that relationship. It was an idealized romantic love. But it actually came to the West by the troubadours who learned about it from the Sufi poets in Andalusia, which was a cultural and spiritual center of Europe at the time. The troubadours who traveled there came across the Sufi tradition of love.

In Sufi love poetry there is the symbolism of feminine beauty and love of the woman. But it's all an allegory of Divine Love. The Sufis used the image of the woman as a symbol of Divine Love. The mole on the cheek means one aspect of Divine Love, for example, her eyebrow another aspect, her bewitching tresses yet another. The troubadours came across this poetry of the adoration of the woman, but they didn't know or weren't taught the symbolism that was behind it. They thought, it's about women! They didn't know it was an allegory of Divine Love. Rūmī said, 'A woman is God shining through subtle veils.' The troubadours brought back this image of romantic love without understanding its roots in Divine Love.

In Western culture, we have this whole theme of romantic love, which is in every pop song and every Hollywood movie. It's what most people identify with as love. But we have lost its roots in the Sacred. We've lost an essential dimension of romantic love, which is part of the mystery of Divine Love. And of course in the West, we identify it often with sexuality and passion. We are in secular culture dealing with something that has always been understood as a sacred mystery, without the context in which to understand it. It is very difficult for people.

AVL: Romantic love is often associated with self-gratification rather than sharing oneself with another or simply being with another. Self-gratification has seeped into the culture to such a degree that people don't even notice it. There is the unconscious question always, "What can I get out of it? What can you give me?"

## Love Transmitted by the Teacher

LVL:   From a spiritual point of view, the way it works is that most people have never been loved for themselves. They've been loved if they do this, or if they behave like that. They will be loved if they are the person their parents want them to be, successful at school, etc. It's not really love but they get what they take as love. In the Sufi tradition, one of the things that happens when you come to a spiritual teacher is that you are unconditionally loved for yourself, warts and all. That's the only way the path is going to work. If you are not loved for yourself, then you are split into parts. Spiritual life is about wholeness. You can only go back to God as your whole self. Your real self. Most people have never experienced anything like that. It's completely unconditional. The teacher doesn't want anything from you. And I'm sure you've experienced that yourself with your teacher.

Q:   Exactly so. It is extraordinary to be loved exactly as I am.

LVL:   It is a gift that is given. It can be quite startling. It is incredibly healing because it gives you permission to be yourself.... It gives you a container, and in that container of unconditional love given by the teacher, you can discover who you really are. The change happens *within*. You lose the false self to discover the true self. The true self has a direct relationship of love to God. In the Sufi tradition, things fall away. The false coverings of the self fall away because they are not nourished by this love. In fact, they are dissolved by love. You can dissolve things through love. What is revealed underneath is your true nature.

The spiritual teacher is, really, creating the space where love can work its magic. Most people have a little glimpse of this if they fall in love with somebody who really loves them and it gives them permission to discover parts of themselves that they hadn't discovered before. But most human love is conditional. That's the love we've been brought up with—unless you were the rare human being who was loved unconditionally by your parents.

Spiritual love, by its very nature, is unconditional. If it's not unconditional, then it's not love because love is free, without condition, given as a gift. It is very powerful, and it changes you. Completely. It reveals who you really are. Rūmī says, "You return to the root of the root of your real self."

## Our Real Self

LVL:   Human beings are incredibly beautiful. It's what we cover ourselves with that hides this from ourselves. Sufism is a process of unveiling through love. You unveil to discover the real nature of the human being, and all human beings are incredibly beautiful because we are made through love, made in the image of God. The tragedy, of course, is that we can't see it. The great human mystery is not that we are God or that we are love; it's that it's hidden from us. Hopefully, as one walks a spiritual path, that mystery becomes revealed a little bit and you get to experience your divine nature, to see what you were before you were.

Q:   You've seen that divine nature in others. You write about the moment in which you were looking out across the street at a park, and there were schoolchildren walking on the sidewalk. All of a sudden you saw a radiance of Light shining brilliantly from each of their hearts. Each heart radiated like a Sun.

LVL:   That was one of the first experiences I was given of the true nature of the human being. I've only seen it once in my life like that.

Q:   And then you were later at an airport when suddenly a veil lifted and you saw that everyone was filled with Light, yet they had no idea that they were filled with Light. That seems a tragedy—to be so clueless about our true nature.

LVL:   It's a mystery.

Q:  I see, not a tragedy but a mystery. There is a divine timing in which God unveils this love in each being?

LVL:  That's why Ibn 'Arabî says, "The great mystery is that the secrets, the knowledge of all things, are hidden within us and veiled from us." The secrets of life are hidden within our own hearts, veiled from us. That is the trial of incarnation. It is the experience of life to uncover them if you can. Some people uncover them and some people cover them up even more.

AVL:  Some cultures have this mystery at their source. While some cultures, like ours, do not. Then from my understanding it can be very lonely, yet people do not know that they are lonely— they hunger for something but they don't know what it is....

LVL:  One more thing to say about love: whoever comes and asks about love, one of the most basic things that they need to know is that love is about *giving* rather than getting. Because we live, sadly, in a culture that focuses on "What can I get?" The first thing you learn about love is that love is about giving. It's not about you; it's about love and to learn to love is to forget yourself. That is why the Sufis say at the very beginning of the journey: "Take one step away from yourself and behold the path."

In Western culture, love became caught up in self-gratification—"What can I get? What is owed to me? What about *my* dreams?" The first thing you learn about love, especially the Sufi experience of love, is that it is not about you. This point is so central and is something that really separates the core of the spiritual traditions from the core of this Western collective ideology, which says, "My life is about what I can get"—either emotionally or materially, or even spiritually.

Love is about the other, either with a small "o" or finally the Other with a big "O" ... until you realize there is no "Other." You and the Other are One, and always were One. And that is the secret of love. The deepest secret of love is the secret of Oneness. The greatest mystery of the human being is that we are one with God.

From what I can understand, my experience of the Light was a glimpse of the oneness of *light upon light*. But as a teenager, I was not like Llewellyn who, at nineteen, was ready to give up everything for the Beloved. I was not like Anat, who left her homeland in search of spiritual truth. My destiny was different. As a teenager, I couldn't bear the Light or surrender to the Fire of Love. The steel door protected me from what I was unable to handle. Opening to the Light was postponed until my thirties, when I would have the presence of human tenderness to mediate it.

As a teenager, terrified of love, I found refuge in a rigid religious system that repressed the heart's longing. Thus compartmentalized, I developed as a normal person in the eyes of society. I was born with a bookish bent, and so I went off to college and commenced my studies in higher education, which lasted fifteen years, produced six degrees, and landed me in the professoriate. Yet there were cracks in the steel door that I had closed against the inner realms, and the Light occasionally found its way through those cracks.

Author (second from left) with missionary
church in Florence, Italy (author's collection).

The Birth of Venus, painting by Sandro Botticelli,
Uffizi Gallery, Florence, Italy (Wikimedia Commons).

*Chapter Three*

# CRACKS ARE HOW THE LIGHT GETS IN

## COLLEGE YEARS

A t age eighteen, my world was limited to the religious group I had joined. It was an insulated and regimented system. I went to college at one of its schools where 95 percent of professors, staff, and students were members of *the* church. I had the good fortune for my intellectual life to study under several wise male professors (there were no female professors in my course of study). One of them assigned Viktor Frankl's book *Man's Search for Meaning*, and it taught me more about the power of love than any of the 800 sermons I heard in college. As a Holocaust survivor, Frankl testified to the power of love to sustain the human spirit no matter how horrendous the circumstances, even in the Nazi concentration camps. Frankl taught me that, whatever I would have to go through in life, it could never degrade the dignity of my spirit. The light of that truth got through a crack in the steel door of dogma, and it stayed with me. Three decades later, it led me to meet Viktor Frankl's grandson, Alexander Vesely, and the Frankl family representative, Mary Cimiluca, for this book.

Such highlights kept the Light alive during my college years when church dogma might have snuffed it out. I thrived academically under the tutelege of two professors whose views were vaster than the system they lived in, but sectarian doctrines dominated college life overall. The church met in bleak buildings, stripped of beauty and feeling. Legalistic doctrines prevailed: no stained glass, no musical instruments, no women's voices. The church's motto was "If it's not in the Bible, we don't allow it." I was told that ours was *the* New Testament church, the only church in existence based solely on the Bible.

The college had strict moral rules. No dancing. No heavy petting. No visits to opposite-sex dorm rooms. We had to be in our rooms before curfew. Sensuality was forbidden. Males and females could not attend the same hours at the swimming pool, as what they called mixed bathing was prohibited. Women's skirt lines had to be an inch below the knee. I was a good tennis player in high school and looked forward to playing on a team in college. What a surprise to hear the tennis coach there say, "We don't have a women's tennis team here because we can't allow women to wear shorts or tennis skirts."

I said, "But the men tennis players wear shorts."

He replied, "Yes, but, we have to cover the women so that the men won't lust."

I was quite sure the men lusted anyway.

Of course, things went on in secret. When natural instincts are barred from the light of day, they become hidden in the shadows. I had three boyfriends in college, and we found secret places to make out—in his car or in the shaded alley behind the art building. I was careful to stop his hands if they wandered anywhere close to what I imagined "heavy petting" referred to, though the term had never been precisely defined. I learned little about sexuality except to fear it.

Sometimes on a Monday morning, I'd hear of a friend who was expelled for "inappropriate behavior"—that is, caught dancing. It was rumored that our matronly Dean of Women, in her tailored suit, her hair pulled into a tight bun, went to the nightclubs an hour away in the capital city to catch students on the dance floor and expel them. Expelled for dancing! I made sure to steer clear of the dean's policing eye. Perhaps some people were just as afraid to see me coming as I was to see her, for I was also a strict moralist and faultfinder. A hardworking high achiever, I was emotionally cut off and had little mercy for those who struggled. Perfectionism was a lonely place. Even though I had a lot of friends, there was no one to whom I could reveal my true feelings—not even to myself.

The Light had infused me with tremendous life energy, but it was pushed down out of fear, and I cut myself off from nature, instinct, intuition, curiosity, creativity, feeling, and more. These energies have to go *somewhere*. Gasoline, if not used for constructive motion, is dangerously flammable. Since I could not own the energies in myself, I projected them onto the world around me and saw sin everywhere. I was judgmental of what I viewed as self-indulgence, laziness, infatuation, and worldliness. I sermonized my college friends for drinking alcohol, and scolded them for allowing women to lead a prayer in the home Bible study. I had a close friend who was sexually active, and I thought her a horribly immoral person. I was prideful in my prudery, no different from the Puritans who punished Hester Prynne with the scarlet letter. The Light had descended on me during a teacher's lecture about *The Scarlet Letter*, and one day I would learn to walk in the love from the Light, but as a college student…

I lived in the light of the ego. Unlike the Light, the ego cast a shadow. As the saying goes, "The brightest light casts the darkest shadow." The more I tried to be morally perfect, the more rejecting I became. I judged even the most mundane mistakes as morally bad and cast them into the shadow. Psychiatrist C. G. Jung originated the term "shadow"—a hidden yet active part of the personality, made up of everything we refuse to acknowledge about ourselves. Into the shadow I cast my secret sins: cheat sheets for an exam; sexual fantasies; a shirt stolen from the tennis shop where I worked; bottles of alcohol hidden under my mattress. One day, I would have to own these castoff parts and bring them into the light of loving acceptance.

Fortunately, the rules of the church had a certain positive effect on my ego development. They helped me navigate the difficult teenage years and not lose myself to potentially addictive drives. I had a genetic predisposition to alcoholism, the effect of which was delayed because of the teenage abstinence pledge. But my addictive drives weren't resolved—they were merely postponed through suppression.

The church denied the actual pleasure of alcohol, sexuality, and other ecstatic aspects of life, and so I was unprepared to handle the hugeness of those experiences when I encountered them in my thirties. The rules of the church—no mixed swimming, no women's skirts above the knee, no heavy petting and the like—inculcated fear of my physical nature rather than the maturation of love.

A certain strictness is needed when we are children and have little concept of harm. For example, crossing a busy street is dangerous, so we are told, "Stay out of the street." But at some point, we learn that it isn't bad to cross a street; it's simply necessary to look both ways and make sure that we're not harming ourselves or others when we cross. As we become adults, we are taught to trust the inner light of "conscience" (as Viktor Frankl called it). This personal story from a friend reveals the learning process:

> My mother taught me to think for myself. In 1940, when I was five, she took my hand and we walked to the corner of a busy street in the center of town. Suddenly, she let go of my hand and said, "Now, I want you to find your own way home from here," and she turned around and left. I figured it out. I went the opposite direction from her, walked a few blocks, made a turn or two, and I was back home! She was sitting on the front steps waiting for me, a proud smile on her face. She was training me to move from an inner center.

I didn't go through this normal maturation into adult consciousness. Rather than grow to trust my own conscience, I trusted and obeyed the truths of others. Even as an adult, I remained a child who believed that even ordinary things such as dancing were morally bad.

I graduated with two degrees (pre-law), *summa cum laude*. I was the "good girl," a poster child for the church. I remember how self-righteous I felt when I tattled on some friends for drinking beer at a slumber party. In my own mind, I was a superior member of the one true church. My virginity was intact. Trophies and awards ornamented my shelves. I was never caught in the dance club—because I never went.

## MISSIONARY WORK IN FLORENCE, ITALY

After graduating from the religious college, I lived in Florence for two years as a missionary for the church. Unexpectedly, the Renaissance city had an artistic splendor that felt akin to the Light; its beauty touched my soul and softened me.

I had been to Florence for a college semester and had fallen in love with the city, so I jumped at the chance to return. I believed the church leaders when they said: "We must save the lost. We are the one true church, outside of which there is no salvation. Italy is a Catholic country, a land of apostates." A congregation in Tennessee funded me and I promised to send them a monthly newsletter of my efforts to save "the lost."

After language training near Assisi, I settled into missionary work at a Bible School in Florence, established decades before by members of my church. The director of our program encouraged us to stand at the entrance to the University of Florence and pass out biblical literature to Italian students. We were told to strike up conversation and invite them to free English classes. This "friendship evangelism" felt far too forced for me, so I came up with my own approach, which was accepted. I put up signs in grocery stores around the Bible School neighborhood offering FREE ENGLISH CLASSES FOR HOUSEWIVES. The room was full on the first session, and the turnout stayed strong over the two years I taught the class. I used the Bible as our conversation text so that I could point out the "errors" of the Catholic Church. I had memorized the verses that I was told proved the papacy and other Catholic doctrines wrong.

There was not a single convert from my effort, except for the one teaching it. The Catholic women in my class taught me the essence of faith, which is compassion and caring for others. They kindly overlooked the arrogance of a young American coming to their country to undermine their lives. One of the students, Tosca, told me about the death of her mother—how "peaceful and sacred" the passing had been. As Tosca spoke, I felt the reality and truth of her faith. She went to Mass every day. Her life was a prayer. She was truly the salt of the earth. In her fifties, she carried a maturity of faith that I had rarely seen.

It didn't take me long to have a crisis of faith. The missionary agenda seemed based on a terrible falsehood—that I could put myself in the position of God to judge someone as faithful as Tosca to be an apostate.

# Beauty is a Path to God

Living in Florence for two years shed light on some of the shadow elements within me. I had never lived in a big city before, and it was a dramatic change from the small-town college campus. That passionate Italian city breathed life into castoff parts of my psyche— naturalness, creativity, embodiment—and initiated a return to wholeness. There were the warm-blooded dramatics of Italian street life: endless honking in congested, chaotic streets; raised voices and effusive gestures; and, of course, the proverbial pinching. Amidst this human naturalness, there were historic sculptures on every street corner, praising the Divine. The place was resplendent with love in all its many forms.

On my occasional day off, I took the crowded bus into the heart of the city, slipped into the grand Cathedral of Santa Maria del Fiore— the third largest church in the world—and emptied myself into its vastness. Though my church leaders called the cathedral a godless monument, I sensed a timeless Presence that felt akin to the Light, with its total silence and peace. I stood under the majestic dome and stared upward into its vortex of ethereal paintings. When I felt myself begin to dissolve into the circle of light at the very top, I would hurry out to the noisy street and pull myself together. I feared being absorbed into the all-encompassing Silence.

I learned that the cathedral's dome, built 600 years ago, is the largest mason-built dome in the world, but that its construction remains a mystery to modern engineers. How did Brunelleschi, a goldsmith with no architectural training, accomplish the amazing feat of suspending into thin air 37,000 tons, 4 million bricks—with no cranes, no center structure, and no flying buttress support? This defies reason and was my first hint that the power of devotional love accomplishes the seemingly impossible. The Gothic and Renaissance masters were aware of a mystical knowledge ("sacred geometry") that enabled them to create art and architecture that draws down the Divine Light into the light of the human heart, as in the scriptural saying, "Light upon light." To sit in one of the great cathedrals or stand in front of a great painting—this was, momentarily, to exist as a tiny point within the circle of paradise. It was to experience "on earth as it is in heaven."

The 12th-century architects of sacred geometry followed the esoteric law "As above, so below." They were well versed in the mystical vision of Dionysius the Areopagite's *Celestial Hierarchy*, in which the Supreme Principle emanates, with no diminishment to Itself, throughout all things, from the highest celestial realms to the most corporeal elements. As a doctoral student in Princeton years later, I read Dionysius' mystical texts and remembered what it was like to sit in the cathedrals built in accord with his mystical vision of The Supreme. Even later, in my meeting with scientist Dr. William Tiller, I wasn't surprised to learn that human devotion actually alters the thermodynamics of a space, for I had stood in the places where devotion continues to reverberate, century after century. Whatever is made with love exudes the power of love. "There is no art without love," my teacher wrote. "Beauty is an attribute of God."[32]

The art and architecture of Renaissance Florence subtly lit a spiritual renaissance within me. The *feeling* side of me, repressed by church literalism, was rekindled. Looking at Sandro Botticelli's painting *The Birth of Venus* and Michelangelo's sculpture *David*, I was enraptured by their expression of the naked human body. The artists had been inspired by a divine vision of beauty; they presented the human being as *imago Dei*, made in the image of God. I knew it was sacred art, even though the church elders called it carnal.

We all stand naked before God. This is what I felt to be true. As I looked at these Renaissance figures, I longed to be naked as they were, in my own true nature, and stand before God without barriers of fear or shame. To me, nakedness was the ultimate surrender, as one has let go of all outer enhancements. One is bare, for all to see, nothing to hide. Standing with dignity, just exactly as one is created to be. To be naked in a dream is a sign of self-acceptance, without any self-posturing of a persona (clothing). Though I was beginning to admire nakedness, I stayed covered.

Viewing *The Birth of Venus* undid years of dogma. The church made the naked body out to be sinful and lascivious. I had seen church leaders scrunch their faces at "scantily clad" women (their term), or quickly click the channel from a scene of tender kissing, as if these things were evil. Such negative reactions said more about their attitude of scorn than any judgment from the Creator. This is what I decided. Surely it was not God but the ego that made the naked body evil.

My Puritan fastidiousness began to feel out of place in the presence of beauty. As depicted by Botticelli, Venus emerges from the sea, born whole. Celestial winds blow her to the shore on a scallop shell, a medieval Christian symbol of spiritual pilgrimage. She is the epitome of feminine maturity and grace, evoking the loving aura of the Holy Mother. Her long, flowing hair wisps across her nakedness in delicate modesty. This single image stirred both earthly and heavenly dimensions within me. It spoke to me.

The painter of *The Birth of Venus* had, however, fought an inner battle similar to mine. In midlife, Botticelli joined the moral purity crusade of a fundamentalist Dominican friar named Savonarola, who outlawed all "immorality" in 15th-century Florence. Perhaps Savonarola was correct to preach reform in the church. Things were out of balance—money, politics, sexual abuses—but he swung the pendulum to the opposite extreme when he made it a punishable sin to have jewelry, non-religious art, wealth, books by Dante and Ovid, and extra body weight. He launched policing crusades that encouraged citizens to spy on each other and report any sign of immorality.

*The Birth of Venus*, which had stirred my soul to the core, was viewed as especially offensive. In the grip of puritanical pressure, Botticelli is said to have thrown his pagan paintings into Savonarola's public bonfire of vanities. He was never to paint them again, and the world lost the heart of one of its greatest artists.

The historic battle between judgment and love, head and heart, fear and freedom, had torn up the city of Florence during the time of Savonarola. The same battle raged on in my own psyche, but I wasn't fully conscious of it. My panic disorder was the symptom of an inner battle, but I was too ashamed of panic attacks to tell anyone. Whenever I could, I avoided the places that triggered them. Over the coming years, the triggers multiplied, and my life shrunk to the verge of agoraphobia. Some of the phobias were: flying in an airplane, sitting in class or other public places, hiking in the woods, and speaking. Only when the dogmatist Savonarola was put to death did the city recover its flowering of culture and beauty. Psychologically, the same would be true for me. Years later the power of love healed me of my inner battle. As the scripture says, "Perfect love casts out fear."

# DANTE AND THE SECRET CHAMBER OF THE HEART

Italy is a place for lovers, and I imbibed that amorous atmosphere as much as the rigid worldview allowed. "Florence" means "flourishing" and "flowering," and I vaguely sensed that something wanted to blossom in me. I rode my bicycle over the cobblestone streets, passing by lovers embracing freely as they walked in and out of churches and cafés, strolling across the medieval arched bridge, the Ponte Vecchio. I looked over that bridge, staring for long periods into the Arno River, feeling a kinship with the joy of lovers and the flow of the river. In such moments, I felt free. I stood still and let my spirit secretly soar.

I was standing in a place that carried the imprint of one of the greatest encounters of love in Western civilization. Many centuries earlier, in the mid-1200s, this was the place where the poet Dante is said to have first seen Beatrice, his doorway to the Infinite. In *The Divine Comedy*, his literary masterpiece, Dante immortalized Beatrice as the figure of Pure Love who guided him into Paradise where he saw that Love was the greatest power in the universe, moving *everything* from human will to the sun and stars.

At this first sight of Beatrice, Dante recounts in *Vita Nuova* ("New Life"), he was nine years old, as was she. Likely more symbolic than literal, "nine" carries the hint of perfect love, as it is the number of hierarchies in the mystic Dionysius' *Celestial Hierarchy*. Though Dante was soon to be engaged to another woman through an arrangement of the families, his encounter with Beatrice was catalytic. "Here begins a new life," he wrote. "At that moment, the vital spirit, the one that dwells in the most secret chamber of the heart, began to tremble so violently that even the least pulses of my body were strangely affected; and trembling, it spoke these words: 'Here is a God stronger than I, who shall come to rule over me.'"[33]

Dante surrendered to the reign of the "Lord of Love" who came to him in visions after the encounter with Beatrice. His soul became "readily betrothed" to the Lord of Love, such that "from that time on, Love governed [his] soul."[34] But it was not an impetuous romantic infatuation; it was a Divine Love that annihilated every ounce of his separateness. In one vision, the Lord of Love took Dante's burning heart, aflame with Love, and put it into Beatrice's mouth. "Many times without warning, [Love] attacked me so violently that no part of me remained alive except one thought that spoke of this lady.... This is the dark condition Love bestows on me."[35] He became a servant of Love.

Dante's description reminded me of the experience, years before, in the aftermath of the Light, when I lay in bed at night and felt strangely affected by an intense energy coming from the "secret chamber of the heart." But instead of surrendering to its lordship over me, as Dante had done, I became terrified of losing myself. When my mother took me to the minister and he denounced it as the devil, my terror became insurmountable, and a surrender felt impossible.

In Dante's vision of the spiritual journey, the mind gives way to the heart. His first guide in *The Divine Comedy*, Virgil the philosopher, represents the analytical mind and can take him only so far. Then Beatrice—the feminine wisdom of the heart—takes charge and leads him to the realm of Love. Dante's Beatrice remains timeless as an imprint of love within human consciousness. Even Hitler's military honored the purity and potency of that love. In World War II, when the German forces were marching across Italy, they wanted to prevent the Allied forces from coming after them, so they bombed every bridge across the Arno—except the one where Dante had first glimpsed Beatrice. They are said to have told the Allies, "We will not blow up the Ponte Vecchio if you promise not to cross it."[36] This is the power of love. The famous bridge was left intact because it was the one Beatrice had stood upon.

# MOTHER TERESA
# – MISSIONARY OF CHARITY

One day, at Boboli Gardens, I met a group of Italian young people—*ragazzi*—who were curious to talk to an American. "You're a missionary?" they asked. "Why here, in Italy? This is one of the most Christian countries in the world!"

I said, "Catholicism doesn't follow the Bible. Without that, there is no salvation."

The young people balked: "Of course we follow the Bible. The Bible came from Italy!"

Parroting church leaders, I said: "A lot of Catholic beliefs and practices are contrary to the Bible." As part of missionary training, I had been taught the Bible verses that allegedly proved the "errors" of Catholic doctrines such as the papacy, the perpetual virginity of Mary, infant baptism, priesthood, etc. I mentioned a few. Even though my inner world had been letting in some of the Light, the dogmatism was still running on autopilot.

They asked, "What about Mother Teresa? She is Catholic. Are you saying that she isn't going to Heaven?"

"Well…," I said, "the Bible *does* lay out specific steps of salvation, and if a person hasn't taken those steps, then…" I had memorized the "five steps to salvation," the last being full-body-immersion baptism by a man (it could not be a woman) from my sect. A baptism didn't count unless it was done in *the* church.

"That's ridiculous!" The Italian young people stared at me, incredulous. "Mother Teresa is the love of Christ in action, and you say she must join your sect to go to Heaven?!"

Suddenly I felt embarrassed. Ashamed. How preposterous! Who was I to stand in judgment of the beliefs of others, to condemn a whole country to hell? I had mindlessly repeated the dogma I'd heard from others. Suddenly it no longer rang true. Such harsh judgment had to come from my ego, not the All-Merciful One. I saw my own arrogance for the first time and it frightened me. What had I become? "'Judgment is mine,' sayeth the Lord." Indeed. I had memorized biblical verses to point out the supposed errors of others, yet completely overlooked the teaching of Jesus Christ, "Do not judge, or you too will be judged. For in the same way you judge others, you will be judged, and with the measure you use, it will be measured to you (MATTHEW 7:1–2)."

I remained in the church—after all, it was the only community I knew—but Florence softened me. The inner Light had been rekindled. A love for beauty awakened. A creative spark ignited. The glaring brightness of ego dimmed just a bit, and, for the first time, I saw the dark shadows cast by its arrogance and fear. I ended up not being a very successful missionary. Instead of a long roster of new converts, I came home with a poster of Botticelli's *The Birth of Venus*. I would not return to Italy until thirty years later, paradoxically, to attend the canonization of Mother Teresa for sainthood. I was invited by her Missionaries of Charity.

Be only all for
Jesus
through Mary
God Bless you
M. Teresa mc

Rome, 10. Dez. 1975

Mother Teresa, St. Teresa of Kolkata
(courtesy of Mother Teresa Center).

*Chapter Four*

# The Miracle of Love

Encounter with Mother Teresa
and the Missionaries of Charity

*Let us not use religion to divide us.*
*In all the holy books, we see how God calls us to love.*

*If I ever become a saint — I will surely be one of darkness.*
*I will continually be absent from heaven —*
*to light the light of those in darkness on Earth*

—Mother Teresa

## My Complicated Journey to Mother's Simple Path

The miracle of love is this: simply loving people changes the world, for love has the power to heal our inner and outer divides. As Mother Teresa said, "Every act of love is a work of peace, no matter how small."[37]

In 2016, I traveled back to Italy for the first time since my missionary work, one of 120,000 people to attend the canonization of

Mother Teresa in St. Peter's Square in Rome. Her works of love have touched millions worldwide from all religions and none. Of the many people I've met in thirty years of traveling the path of Mother's mission, here are three examples of the universality of her impact: A Hindu in India opened his wallet to show me a picture of Mother Teresa—larger than the photos of his own children—saying, "I respect Mother Teresa more than any other person." A Buddhist nun and scholar I met at a conference ended her study of Mother Teresa's life by wondering if she might well have been a *bodhisattva* who chose to manifest in Christian form to reach the greatest number of people with her compassion.[38] After our study of Mother Teresa in class, an avowedly nonreligious college student wrote, "I've never encountered a love this pure."

"Love one another as I have loved you (JOHN 15:12)." This commandment of Jesus is engraved on the tomb of Mother Teresa at the Motherhouse of the Missionaries of Charity in Calcutta, India. I went there in 2013. I had written to request an interview with Mother Teresa's successor, but was told that Missionaries of Charity do not talk about their work. "Come and see" is what the Missionaries of Charity say. And so I did—Calcutta where her work started; Tijuana, home to the Mother Teresa of Calcutta Center; Rome, site of the canonization, Missionaries of Charity convent and Home for the Poor; San Francisco convent, novitiate site for sisters in the Americas. I have been to places where she walked and served. I've met people who worked with Mother Teresa. I've also witnessed for two decades the impact of her "simple path" on the lives of hundreds of college students who put her teachings into practice in service sites worldwide. The firsthand accounts from all of these sources, together with Mother Teresa's own words, are the basis for this chapter.

At twenty-two, a fundamentalist missionary in Italy, I viewed Mother Teresa as an apostate because she was not a member of my Christian sect. At thirty-two, proud holder of an Ivy League Ph.D., I dismissed her works of love as irrelevant to the struggles of women and other oppressed groups. I was an agnostic scholar-activist who judged Mother Teresa's views on women and family life as behind the times. My thinking was political and critical: "What good is it to love the poor while they are dying? We must uproot the systems of injustice." But Mother focused her compassion on the immediate hunger, homeless, disease, and loneliness of the people right in front of her. "Love is for today; programs are for the future.... Somebody is thirsty for water for today, hungry for food for today. Tomorrow we will not have them if we don't feed them today."

Mother Teresa did not judge the activists and academics that criticized her; she encouraged them to do the work they felt called to do: "You can do what I can't do. I can do what you can't do. Together we can do something beautiful for God." And she was right. I never came across any critic of hers who wanted to do as she did: touch and commune with lepers, clean latrines, go into war zones to retrieve crippled children of another belief system, serve the sick and dying for fifty years smilingly around the clock with no vacation.

At thirty-nine, a spiritual teacher opened my heart and set me on a path of Love. My criticism of saints melted into humble aspiration. The time I spent in Calcutta left me with this sobering fact: I was incapable of her level of love, not even for a day. Though I was not Catholic, Mother Teresa became a patron saint of my path. I didn't have to agree on points of doctrine to take her as a guide in the way of loving.

I learned recently that Mother Teresa blessed the book *Power vs. Force* that brought me to my teacher. In 1991, she wrote him saying, "Continue to use your beautiful gift of writing to the full, so that people may read the good news and glorify the Father." Published in 1995, the book has sold over a million copies and has been translated into over twenty-five languages. People of all religions and no religion say it helps them experience the healing power of love. In Mother Teresa's letter, she told him, "spread, joy, love, and compassion through what you write. The fruit of these three is peace, as you know, the peace that comes from loving and caring and respecting every person as a child of God—my brother—my sister."[39] My teacher wasn't Catholic, yet perhaps Mother's blessing of his writing helped carry it into the world and into the hands of people who, like me, were looking for love. In his and her own way, each was *light upon light* to this seeker struggling to find her way out of the darkness of dogma and despair.

## Rome: Witnessing Sainthood

When I went to Rome for the canonization, I carried a court-certified relic of Mother Teresa—a tiny piece of her hair. I wanted to give it to the Missionaries of Charity, as I figured it belonged to them. In Catholic tradition, this was a first-order relic and wasn't easy to part with; however, Mother Teresa taught to "love until it hurts," and I was willing. I heard this teaching from many people who knew her, including a Hindu lawyer in Calcutta. After Mother Teresa touched and healed his sister of an oozing ear infection, he asked her about giving his spare money to the poor. She replied, "Don't give 'spare' money to the poor—*share* with the poor. Give with compassion, not pity. Love until it hurts."

It hurt to give this relic away. To donate money was much easier. For years, I'd slept with it near my bedside. It brought me comfort and peace. The relic was given to me by a dear friend who knew of my devotion to Mother Teresa's path of Love. I felt blessed and favored to have it. In many religions, the relics of saints and mystics are said to transmit a healing benefit to devotees. A priest that traveled with Catholic relics told me, "God is the cause of healing; relics are the means." He told me of several healings that had occurred as a result of the relic exhibit he traveled with.

As an academic, I was dubious of devotees' claims that special effects emanated from human remains; that is, until I met Dr. William Tiller, physicist and Stanford University Professor Emeritus. He found that the relics of spiritual masters, when activated by human intention, alter the thermodynamics of the spaces they are in and have a healing influence on material objects in the room, including the human body. The authentic relics of genuine masters are more than mere ash or bone—they radiate the healing power of love.

On my first day in Rome, I took the Mother Teresa relic to the Missionaries of Charity convent where I was scheduled to see Sister C, the nun who invited me to the canonization. I had met her two years earlier in California through an odd synchronicity. A friend who spoke Hindi happened to spot a blue- and-white sari in our local drugstore parking lot. Knowing of my interest in Mother Teresa, she got the sister's phone number, and I called. Sister C. opened many doors for me. She grew up in India, was called to the order at age eighteen, and trained under Mother in Calcutta. Whenever she spoke of Mother Teresa, all who listened felt that energy field of joy and unconditional love.

Sister C told us that Mother's main teaching was the Gospel on five fingers: "You - Did - It - To - Me." Whatever they do for the poor, sick, prisoner, dying, or leper, they do it to Jesus. This was the verse from Matthew 25: "Whatever you have done to one of the least of these brothers and sisters of mine, you have done it to me." She said, "Truly every person we see is God, so whatever we do to that person, we have done it to God." Mother Teresa taught her to have "total understanding love" and never to judge drug addicts or the poor or those dying of AIDS, for they needed and deserved to be loved and to die in dignity. The greatest disease, Mother often said, was not leprosy but loneliness—feeling unwanted, uncared for, and shunned by others. When Mother Teresa repeated the words of Jesus in Matthew 25—"I was hungry, and you gave me something to eat; I was naked and you clothed me; I was homeless, and you took me in"—she was quick to add:

Hungry not only for bread—but hungry for love.

Naked not only for clothing—but naked of human dignity and respect.

Homeless not only for want of a home of bricks—but homeless because of rejection.

When my friends and I arrived at the convent in Rome, all was quiet. I wasn't sure where to find Sister C. We walked around the garden path, wandered into the church courtyard, looked up and down the sidewalks. No one in sight. Then, I caught sight of a small open door hidden behind some bushes. I walked over and peeked inside. The sisters were kneeling on the bare stone floor, praying in front of a crucifix marked with the words "I Thirst." Jesus thirsts for the love of souls, and the sisters are the carriers of that love. Every day they have four hours of prayer, including meditation on the Word of God, Holy Mass where they receive the Eucharist, and a Holy Hour where they adore Jesus in the Blessed Sacrament. Their lives are woven with the Eucharist, and this is the fuel for their work. When I asked the sisters, "How do you have the energy for this work?" They said, "Prayer," explaining that Mother at first didn't think they could take time away from serving the poor to do the Daily Hour of Adoration (Blessed Sacrament). In 1973, however, the Society made the unanimous decision to have the Adoration every day, as it infused their work with the Presence of God and the love of Jesus in the poor they serve. Without their hours of prayer and the Eucharist, they explained, it "is just ourselves we give to the poor, not God."

Seeing they were in prayer, we sat in the garden and waited for Sister C, who emerged smiling. Though she and the other sisters had been up since 4:40 a.m.—the sisters begin every day with prayer, Mass, Holy Communion—we were greeted joyously as old friends. Sister apologized for the wait and made a jolly joke about how busy they had been the last few days getting ready for the influx of canonization visitors, services, and exhibits: "At this point it might be easier for you to meet the President of Italy than this little sister from the Mother Teresa Center!"

The sisters were, I'm sure, exhausted from recent events. Not only did they have the usual daily work of caring for the residents in their "Home for the Poor" next to the convent but just a few days prior, when the Missionaries of Charity in Rome were flooded with people and plans for the canonization events, an earthquake hit a nearby town. The sisters went to care for those who were injured and homeless from the quake. The sisters even gave them the tents that had been set up on their convent grounds for the upcoming canonization.

The earthquake victims needed the tents *now*; the canonization was a few days away. Trained by Mother Teresa to ask for nothing and trust in God's providence, they told us, "We are sure the Lord will provide something for us and take care of this."

The sisters are taught to focus on the needs of the moment and give whatever they can to others, not worry for their own welfare. Per Mother Teresa's instruction, they do not fundraise or ask for things but wait for others to give freely in spontaneous collaboration. Whenever Mother was asked about the future of her order or material needs, she said simply that it was His concern and He would provide. Those close to her knew she was a talented organizer who cut through the thickness of government bureaucracies, speaking multiple languages without a script in her efforts to procure the resources needed for her mission. Nonetheless, her focus was always riveted on the present. The sisters told us that she taught them to view their work with the poor as a gift—"We have an opportunity to be twenty-four hours a day with Jesus." They love whomever is in front of them as if it were Jesus himself.

Despite their workload, the sisters were serene and smiling as they took us around the convent, with its historic church and Home for the Poor. They told us that Mother Teresa had taught them to be full of joy and cheerfulness and to smile when in the presence of others, especially the poor and suffering, and always to make sure people left feeling happier and better than when they came. Those who suffer need to be loved, their load lightened; smiling with them eases their pain. One time in Calcutta, they recalled, there was a nun who was long-faced. Mother told her, "Go to bed for the day. The poor already have so many troubles. They do not need to see yours."

At the convent in Rome, smiles and humor flowed easily. In the midst of explaining how to arrive early to the events and avoid the pushing and shoving of pilgrims into St. Peter's Square, the sisters started to laugh at themselves: "Mother must be laughing at all of this—that we are making such a fuss over her! We just pray there will be no stampede of pilgrims!"

They took us through a gate into the monastery hallway to Mother Teresa's room where she had slept. It was nothing special—yet wasn't it? In outer appearance, it was so simple, yet there was something about this very fact that made it stand out. A Nobel Prize winner, honored with over 700 awards during her life, Mother was the founder and, for five decades, superior of the pioneering religious order of Missionaries of Charity, with outposts on every continent. She was a world leader in terms of the human spirit. Presidents, prime ministers, kings, and queens requested to meet with her. Indeed Princess Diana of Wales first met her here in Rome, having flown in for that specific purpose. Mother Teresa was on magazine covers across the globe, was bestowed an honorary degree of Divinity from the University of Cambridge, and endured daily visitors prostrating to touch her feet. And this was where she had slept, in a small room on a cot with a single mattress so thin it could hardly be called a mattress.

Mother's room in Rome looked the same as her room in Calcutta at the Motherhouse, which I had visited a few years earlier. Though both places are hot and humid, she had no fan because the poor they served had no fan. Her calling was to live among the poorest of the poor—to eat what they ate, sleep as they slept, labor as they labored. This set her work apart from other religious and civic outreach programs *to* the poor. She and her missionaries lived *with* the poor, without carpet or washing machine or dishwasher or entertainment or television, nothing to call their own. When convents and other buildings were donated to their cause, Mother stripped them of these common comforts. Bradley James, the musician Mother Teresa chose to put her prayers to music in the album *Gift of Love* and to create hymns for the Missionaries of Charity sung worldwide, gave this firsthand account of her "renovation" of a convent into a Missionaries of Charity house:

> This was a convent where nuns had lived for many years so you can imagine the condition inside was immaculate. But when we get in there, Mother put

us all to work by taking everything out—the beds, chairs, refrigerator, dishwasher, water heater, garbage disposal, carpet, curtains. And I kept saying, 'Aren't you going to need this stuff?' and she said, 'God will provide.' I thought: *But God already provided what's in the house! Why take it out?* It was hard work, tearing this stuff out. I didn't understand their vow of poverty. I'm watching Mother—she didn't ask anyone to do anything that she didn't do first.

So, after a week, the house was completely empty. We got Mother Teresa to the airport and she had two cardboard boxes wrapped in twine—that's her luggage after many months of travel. She blessed all of the sisters and people gathered around at the airport, and then she came over to me and said, 'They are your sisters. You are their brother. And God is your Father.' I wondered: *What does that mean?* I took the four sisters in my little car back to the convent where there had been crowds of people and there's nobody there. I said, 'Where did everybody go?' They said, 'Oh, they only come to see Mother.' I said, 'Well, who's going to take care of you?' Because I knew what was in this house—nothing—and they didn't have a car. They said, 'God will provide.' As I drove away, I was horrified by the reality that they had taken this extreme vow of poverty.

Bradley visited the sisters often and volunteered his time to help them in their service. He continued to be shocked at their level of surrender when it came to the vow of poverty. He told of one night when he delivered a large spread of leftover food from a lush dinner party he'd attended at the home of a wealthy friend in Beverly Hills. It was the middle of the night and dangerous to drive into South-Central L.A. where the nuns lived, but he went anyway. Surprised to see the lights on, he asked them, "Sisters, did something happen here tonight?" They said, "Brother, we were in the chapel tonight praying for those who are hungry because we haven't eaten in three days." He recounted:

> As she said this, I looked over her shoulder and saw a crucifix on the wall and I remembered what Mother said to me: 'They are your sisters. You are their brother. And God is your Father.' And then I knew what Jesus meant when He said, 'I was hungry and you gave me bread.' That's a very real statement. Hungry means that person right in front of us who is hungry, who is thirsty, who is alone, who is forgotten, and we don't have to go anywhere except where we are—if we look, we see them. Not long after that, I was in the house scrubbing the floor, and I heard Mother Teresa coming. I stood up to greet her. She got real close to me, looked me straight in the eye and said, 'Now you understand.'[40]

To voluntarily give up all material comforts and security to serve total strangers rejected by society—as I stood at Mother's room, I wept at the purity of this depth of love. Her life was her message, even down to the bed she slept in. Rarely had I been in someone's home and seen with my own eyes such a total concordance of stated ideal and actual living. No wonder she told people, "Come and see." Who among us can say this so freely? Who is happy for strangers to visit our workplace, not to mention our bedroom, and behold our integrity or lack of it? Yes, I was aware that her critics said she was unrelenting, out of sync with the times, and too strict with her nuns, but it seemed obvious to me (and most of the world) that she emanated a purity of love rare on the planet.

The sisters told us that Mother Teresa always did the most unpleasant tasks herself—cleaning toilets and latrines, wiping the maggots from sick bodies in the streets, stroking the lepers. Her humility was spotless. She refused all credit and accolades for the work, saying she was only "a pencil in God's hand." She accepted the

Nobel Peace Prize because it put attention on the suffering of the poor, and she received it in the name of all those who are hungry, naked, poor, lonely, and uncared for. She spoke to the august assembly in her usual manner, straight from the heart and without notes, surprising many with her request that they join her in the Prayer of St. Francis of Assisi: "Lord make me an instrument of Thy peace...." At her insistence, the banquet that usually accompanied the Nobel event was cancelled and the funds given to the poor. The $7,000 budgeted to feed 135 at the Nobel banquet could feed 400 people for a year.

Sister C took us into the San Gregorio church, originally an old family home belonging to Pope Gregory, and turned into a monastery 1,400 years ago. While waiting for Sister C, we had walked around its courtyard, but had no idea how majestic it was inside. On the outside, it looks old and tattered, but when you enter, it is magnificent. This is not so different from Mother's teaching about human beings. No matter how wretched the outer condition, she saw the goodness of the inner being—"Christ in his distressing disguise" she said.

Last, the sisters took us into their Home for the Poor. My friend remarked as we left, "This is the most meaningful part of our entire trip, even grander than the Sistine chapel and the Vatican Museum." Our tour of the Vatican that morning had been wall-to-wall people pushing to see the historical treasures on display. Here, in the Home for the Poor, we felt an environment of openhearted ease, the love of Christ in action, not a display of ancients but a haven of loving.

The serenity of the Home for the Poor is what amazes, and this peace I attribute to the power of love that motivates the sisters' endeavors. There was not a single person or object or attitude that was un-peaceful. Nothing was rigid, yet everything was in order. In this mini global village, the Missionary of Charity nuns were from Kenya, India, Europe, and the U.S. The male residents were mainly immigrants from Bangladesh, China, Algeria, and Peru who had come to Europe to work and ended up on the streets. One young man was dying of cancer, another was severely crippled, and several were elderly. Without family to take them in, this home was their family. And to be clear, it was a "home" not a shelter.

It could have been chaos with a group of men accustomed to surviving on the streets. In several decades of volunteering at small and large shelters for the homeless and Christian rescue missions on L.A.'s skid row, I had often seen chaos—security guards and scenes of aggression, the stench of urine, trash on the floor, and impatient staff or volunteers bossing the poor around like they were lesser people. In contrast, at the Home for the Poor, there were sixty-five men off the streets watched over by only four nuns, and everything was spotlessly clean, calm, and friendly. The residents are touched with compassion and treated with dignity. A large poster of Mother Teresa in the hallway sets the tone: "The greatest problem is indifference." Nearly all of society is indifferent to the poorest of the poor, but she and her sisters see Christ in them. Mother explained to her sisters that theirs was a calling different from other religious orders: "We must be living holocausts, for the world needs us as such. For by giving the little we possess, we give all—that there is no limit to the love that prompts us to give."

In his homily at the Rite of Canonization, Pope Francis praised Mother Teresa for her "mission to the urban and existential peripheries" as "a tireless worker of mercy" who "helps us to increasingly understand that our only criterion for action is gratuitous love, free from every ideology and all obligations, offered freely to everyone without distinction of language, culture, race, or religion."

Her life was devoted to the work of universal love for all people no matter their race, religion, background or condition. "Each person is a child of God, created to love and to be loved," she said. "All of us have been created by the same loving hand, and we belong to the same loving family." No one is here in the world just to be a number. We are here for the greater purpose of loving and serving, joy and compassion. Mother Teresa and her missionaries are singular in their vows to live among the poorest of the poor and bring to them this unconditional love through "wholehearted and free service." In 2018, I was blessed to attend the Profession of Vows for novices at St. Paul's

Catholic Church in San Francisco. The novices offered their lives as a living sacrifice of love. Their final hymn was a prayer to become the "Silent Bread" of the Sacrament: "Transform me into yourself, that I be bread like you/ Bless me and break me, give me to my thirsting brothers."

A testimony from Yemen, told in St. Peter's Square during the canonization weekend, reveals their selfless service. Yemen is rampant with starvation and trauma in the wake of civil war fueled by Shia-Sunni Muslim tensions and terrorist factions that target Christians among others. The Missionaries of Charity went there in 1973 and are among a few thousand Christians in the Muslim state of 27 million. Sister Sally, a Missionary of Charity, gave this firsthand account:

> Mother lived in total dependence on God for her own needs and for those of the poor and their health care…. We sisters pray daily, to know the designs of Divine Providence, resigning ourselves entirely to Your Will. 25th of March, 2015, in Yemen, the surrounding community was attacked by terrorists, in midst of civil war, shooting and bombing everywhere. We had 64 residents, 14 helpers, and 5 sisters. And we had no food. We found ourselves in an utterly helpless situation. 30th of March, 2015, at 7:30 p.m., there was no electricity, it was pitch-dark, and there was a knock at the door. All of us ran to the door in fear and anxiety. The good news was announced to us: someone brought fruits and vegetables. The situation became worse. It was difficult for us. Gas, diesel, water, other necessities, were no longer available. We cut down some of the trees for firewood. We baked the last flour. Our helpers asked for one loaf of bread to share with their families. We emptied what we had and shared it with them. The next day, at 5:30 a.m., there was a knock. A man brought fresh bread, which was just enough for everybody. For 10 days he never

failed to bring the bread. On the 10th day, he brought flour and wheat.

In the midst of this dangerous situation, our dear Sister Prema, M.C. General Superior, called us from Calcutta and spoke to us individually. She gave us a choice to remain or leave the place. All of us had one answer. 'We choose to stay. To live or die with our poor.' That afternoon, a man brought the very medicines that our poor needed. But then we had only one tank of water left, and our neighbors and other people came with their empty bottles asking for drinking water. With the scourging heat and dangerous situation, who can deny drinking water to a thirsty person or family? We gave even to the last drop. We remembered our dearest Mother's words, 'Thirst is not just for water, but also for understanding love, justice and peace.' Again the providence of God—a truck loaded with bottles of water arrived at our compound. We were filled to the brim with water and gratitude to God.[41]

On March 4, 2016, one year after the episode Sister Sally describes, she witnessed the horrific massacre of her sisters and twelve other people at this care home for impoverished elderly. In midmorning, gunmen entered and shot them execution-style. Sister Sally survived by hiding behind a door. She concluded her story in St. Peter's Square saying: "With our hearts filled with greater love and enthusiasm, we beg God to continue using our nothingness to make the church present in the world of today through the mission invested to us by our Mother Teresa." The archbishop said that Sister Sally begs to go back and serve in Yemen.

# LOVING THE LONELY AND UNWANTED – THE POOREST OF THE POOR

What is the origin of this mission, so selfless that it defies com-prehension?[42] It first appeared to thirty-six-year-old Sister Teresa of the Loreto convent on a train to Darjeeling for her annual retreat. It was September 10, 1946, a day referred to as Inspiration Day. Teresa had been a nun for almost twenty years, working mainly as a teacher of well-to-do girls in the convent's school.

On the train, Jesus gave her a "call within a call." During the fol-lowing months, through interior locutions and visions, Jesus revealed to her His pain at the neglect of the poor and told her He wanted her to dress in simple clothes and go radiate His love among them. "My little one—come, come, carry Me into the holes of the poor. Come, be My light."

Sister Teresa did not reveal the mystical nature of her inspira-tion—after her death it came to light in her private letters—but those who knew her noticed a profound change as this call within a call became the driving force for the rest of her life. It took two years of persistent requests to convince the church hierarchy to let her leave the relative comfort and safety of the Loreto Sisters convent and go into the slums by herself. Outside the convent walls, Muslim-Hindu violence racked the streets, refugees were spilling into Calcutta, and starvation and disease were rampant. How could one woman do any-thing to address the suffering of impoverished millions?

She began one person at a time. In December 1948, she went for the first time to the slums, dressed in a plain white sari with a blue border and carrying the rosary. Her first act of charity was to pick up a man, starved and covered with worms, abandoned and dying alone in the streets. She cared for him as if he were Jesus. When he asked her why she was taking care of him, she said, "Because I love you."[43] She nursed a woman dying of starvation and tuberculosis. She cleaned the wounds of a child. This was her method—to care for the poorest of the poor, one at a time. "I believe in person-to-person contact. Every person is Christ for me, and since there is only one Jesus, the person I am meeting is the one person in the world at that moment."

Her ministry to the dying poor grew quickly. In 1952 she rented a former pilgrims' hostel at the temple for Kali and this hospice home came to be called Nirmal Hriday ("Home of Pure Heart"). When I went into the Kalighat neighborhood of Calcutta where she started her work, I was overwhelmed by the poverty: Garbage piled in public areas; beggars with various deformities lined the sidewalks; mothers with nearly naked children sat on the ground eating rice. At Nirmal Hriday three people with legs as thin as broomsticks lay on the steps looking nearly dead. I was told that the destitute arrive at the home's entrance eaten by maggots, incontinent, starved, and infected with gangrene and other diseases in late stages. I thought: *Only a saint could see Christ in these suffering beings.* One of the patients told Mother early in her mission that he felt like he'd lived as an animal on the street but would die like an angel, totally loved and cared for. As many spiritual traditions teach, to die in a state of love sanctifies the person's life no matter how wretched it has been.

The home for the dying poor was a great public service to the city, yet initially it caused an uproar among Hindu leaders, who threatened to kill Mother Teresa for violating the caste system. They were appalled that the elite-born Indian women who had joined her order were touching the bodies of the dying. Cleaning latrines and tending to dead bodies was deemed "unclean" and relegated to the lowest caste. Even in our own time, disregard for caste rules can lead to shunning and even killing family members. Like Gandhi before her, Mother Teresa openly loved the "untouchables" as those near and dear to God himself. A volunteer who witnessed her bedside manner at Nirmal Hriday likened it to the way priests handled the consecrated host on the altar; that is, both were handling the Presence of Jesus, touching the Body of Christ.

In 1950, the congregation called Missionaries of Charity received official recognition. Unique among religious orders, the intense nature of their service became evident in 1957 when Mother Teresa began to care for the medical and emotional needs of society's most unwanted—lepers. She wanted them to know that they were loved as children of God. Her work began with a mobile medical dispensary. Two years later, she opened the leprosy center at Titagarh, providing medicine, surgery, communal support, and work projects such as weaving. In 1969, she opened a self-supporting community of lepers, Shanti Nagar ("City of Peace"). The papacy provided funds to construct the Shanti Nagar Leprosy Rehabilitation Center on land given by the government. The dry, desolate location was over twenty miles from the closest city, electricity, running water, and transportation. Nonetheless, within a few years the village was home to eight sisters, 200 patients, and seventy children—another example of how the power of love can create something beautiful out of nothing. Here is the account of a layman who went with Mother Teresa to the leper communities:

> In the 1990s, while serving as a missionary in India, I spent time with Mother Teresa in Calcutta. We worked alongside her and various missionaries to reach out to the people she referred to as the 'poorest of the poor.' One morning, during prayer time at the Mother House for the Missionaries of Charity, as we prepared to visit a leper colony, Mother Teresa addressed our fears of being with and/or touching those affected by leprosy. She reminded us of how much they needed touch and love. She went further by saying, 'The answer to all of your fears and their needs lies in the palm of your hand. Five points on five fingers: Just - Let - Him - Do - It.'
>
> At the chapel located in a place set aside for the dying and destitute, including those with leprosy, I was surprised to see walls covered by images and symbols of various gods and faiths. I understood from her that while she believed Jesus to be The Door, she saw all faiths as leading toward God and her task was to love. Any conversion would be an act

of the Holy Spirit and not of her doing. I knew then she was most committed to loving all. The love God put in her heart transcended everything else.[44]

Love was the critical factor in Mother's ministry to the lepers, according to Father William Petrie who spent twenty-five years with Mother Teresa in India: "We were on the mobile clinic for Hansen's Disease (leprosy) patients. A week had been skipped because of the delayed arrival of medical supplies. Mother informed them of why, but one patient stated, 'You should have come anyway.'" In other words, Mother Teresa's loving presence was just as significant as the medicine or food she gave. He called it a "sacred presence" and "charism of positive spiritual energy given to another in a spirit of love."[45] Others called it *darshan* (an occasion of seeing a holy person). Mother Teresa taught that any small act of love given to others, even a simple smile, increases and strengthens the presence of loving energy and has a healing effect. Fr. Petrie wrote of an experiment he witnessed in which scientists found that people listening to Mother Teresa went into the alpha-brainwave state; they became calm, receptive, and relaxed.

When Bradley James first met her, he was moved to tears. He noted the similarity between her presence and the elevation of the elements at Mass. He was a young dancer and singer in Los Angeles who heard she was in town that day, and he made it his mission to meet her. He called several times to the Missionaries of Charity house where Mother was staying, but they said she was unavailable. Finally a priest told him to go to a certain church that evening; he did, and was taken into a room and told to wait. After a while the door swung open and in walked Mother Teresa. Here is James's account:

> Catholics perhaps would call it an aura or a presence. In India, it's called *darshan*. It was so powerful that instantly I couldn't speak and had tears coming down my face. She took her handkerchief, wiped my tears, and said, "Your tears are tears of love that you never expressed." She took my hand to go into the church, which was packed. Now, when the priest picked up

the host for the elevation, the energy I felt coming from her when she walked into that room was the exact same energy I felt when he picked up that host. The very same energy.[46]

His description matches my own experience at Mother Teresa's tomb in Calcutta. As soon as I knelt at the foot of the tomb, I began to weep out of control. The tears came from the core of me and not for any reason that I knew about. It was as if I had come to a place of such vast love and inner safety that all the longing of a lifetime poured out. "Your tears are tears of love that you never expressed," she told Bradley. Love is the greatest medicine, for it heals our inner wounds, deeper than any physical wound.

After establishing her ministries to lepers, the dying, the elderly, and orphans, Mother Teresa spread her work beyond India with the establishment of Missionaries of Charity houses in Venezuela (1965) and eventually to every continent. In 1971 she became a global sensation when Malcolm Muggeridge produced a documentary film about her work and published the book *Something Beautiful for God*. Countless awards, gold medals, and honorary degrees poured in. Mother said they meant nothing to her except an opportunity to speak about the love of Jesus in the poorest of the poor. In 1979, her work was honored with the Nobel Peace Prize. Thus within thirty-one years from the beginning of her mission in 1948, her one-to-one method had miraculously reached millions, and her blue-bordered white sari had become a universal symbol of compassion. *This is the miracle of love.* When she died in 1997, the Missionaries of Charity were spread throughout the world, on all seven continents: 4,000 members, 610 foundations in 123 countries, and over a million lay workers.

# THE DARKNESS: LONGING AND LONELINESS

Hidden from public view was Mother Teresa's interior service to the poor, revealed only after her death. Unknown even to those closest to her, she suffered an existential "darkness" for nearly fifty years. After her mystical union with Jesus—the call within a call that led to the founding of the Missionaries of Charity—the feeling of inner communion with His presence disappeared. From the writings of spiritual masters such as St. John of the Cross, who penned the phrase "Dark Night of the Soul," we know that saints and mystics often go through periods of feeling abandoned by God; the blissful consolations of intimate communion with God suddenly vanish and one no longer feels God's Presence. *Is God still there? Have I been abandoned?* The challenge is to remain faithful despite the desolation, to love God for the sake of God and not for any inner reward. Spiritual life feels arid, cold, and empty. Mother Teresa poured out her painful longing in confidential letters to her spiritual directors:

> Within me everything is icy cold. ... It is only that blind faith that carries me through.
>
> This terrible sense of loss - this untold darkness - this loneliness - this continual longing for God - which gives me that pain deep down in my heart. I just long & long for God - and then it is that I feel - He does not want me - He is not there.... The torture and pain I cannot explain.

For the first eleven years of this inner darkness, Mother Teresa felt bewildered and lost—had God rejected her?—but through her own intuition and the guidance of her confessors, she came to see a greater purpose to her suffering and thus she embraced her anguish as a way to share in the suffering of the poor and the Passion of Jesus:

"I have come to love the darkness - for I believe now that it is a part, a very, very small part of Jesus' darkness and pain on earth.... a 'spiritual side of [the] work.'"

Her private struggles were published by the church after her death and caused a major stir. "She was a fraud. She didn't even believe in God!"—a close friend of mine called me in an upset. My friend's response was not unusual. Critics of Mother Teresa wasted no time in calling her an atheist and hypocrite, but believers found the revelation of her inner struggles to be another confirmation of her sainthood. Indeed, the totality and authenticity of her surrender is obvious in her writings, such as this one included in the exhibit of her life—a handwritten letter to Jesus in 1959:

> Don't mind my feelings. Don't mind even my pain. If my separation from you brings others to you and in their love and company you find pleasure, Why, my Jesus, I am willing to suffer with all my heart to suffer all that I suffer - not only now but for all eternity if this was possible. Your happiness is all that I want - for the rest please do not take the trouble - even if you see me faint with pain - all this is my will - I want to satiate your thirst with every single drop of blood that you can find in me. Don't allow me to do you wrong in any way. Take from me the power of hurting You. Heart and soul I will work for the Sisters - because they are Yours each and everyone - are Yours.
>
> I beg of You only one thing - please do not take the trouble to return soon - I am ready to wait for You for all eternity - your little one

Who can understand this level of surrender, so utterly selfless? When I asked my teacher about it—he was a mystic and knew of such things—he said:

> People think that over a certain level of consciousness, you won't have inner questions. On the contrary. Now you have inner questions but on a different level of comprehension…. Your questions are expressed at the level you are. Mother Teresa was questioning things at a very high level. What she meant at her level is not the same as what others think she meant, reading it from their level of consciousness. Mother Teresa initially experienced Jesus Christ as a Presence, a literal Presence, and when

that miraculous occurrence was not permanent, she felt abandoned and longed for the return of that Presence. Her faith survived despite the loss of the feeling of the Presence, and she offered her suffering for the propitiation of sins of herself and others. The full meaning of her experience is knowable only to God.[47]

And here is the most shocking fact about her inner suffering: No one who lived with her knew about it. I asked Sister C, "Did you or any of the sisters know that Mother suffered like this?" She said, "She never told us anything, no one knew." Even those closest to Mother Teresa had no hint of her affliction. In Catholic tradition, a hallmark of sainthood is consciously to accept one's suffering in silence and bear it with ardent love as a gift to God for the benefit of others. Saints forego the usual human consolation of complaining or telling others what they are going through, for a gift is no longer a gift when it has been unwrapped with others. Mother Teresa taught her nuns that when borne in secret between them and God, their suffering was transformed into a gift of love.

Out of her peerless and saintly love, Mother Teresa kept her suffering to herself so that it could be an offering to the Beloved for her beloved poor. The Mother Teresa of Calcutta Center gives this compelling summary of her interior agony: "It led Mother Teresa to an ever more profound union with God. Through the darkness she mystically participated in the thirst of Jesus, in His painful and burning longing for love, and she shared in the interior desolation of the poor."

Brian Kolodiejchuk, Missionary of Charity, directs the Mother Teresa Center in Tijuana and has done much to evolve an understanding of the anguish she endured. I met him there in 2015 when I visited, invited by Sister C. Father Brian, associated with Mother Teresa from 1977 to 1997, was tasked by the church to edit her private writings for publication, assess thousands of testimonies about her impact and intercessions, and serve as postulator of the cause of canonization for her sainthood. As described in the book he edited of Mother's letters, *Come Be My Light*, Father Brian views her inner darkness not as the dark night of soul in the classical sense of spiritual purification but as an "apostolic darkness" that helped her transmit God's love and increase her solidarity with the poor.

# Learning About Love in a College Class

When the college students in my Compassion course hear that Mother Teresa gave her life in service to others while going through decades of inner suffering without complaining to her sisters, they are dumbfounded. They have just finished a month-long take-home exam that requires them to probe their inner motivations for service. Their realization goes something like this:

> I never realized how much I do things for others out of wanting something in return—approval, friendship, feeling good about myself, or at least a thank-you. Even with family members and those I care about, I want something back. My love isn't freely given. And people I don't even know, strangers who are sick, mutilated and dying? I'm a long way from that kind of selflessness.

Mother Teresa's faith in the midst of darkness gave hope to Amelia Boyle, a student going through a personal crisis:

> Reflecting on Mother Teresa's life gives me hope in dark moments. Even if everything feels purposeless and empty and painful, there is still good that I can do every day. Even if it's just smiling at someone I pass on the street, or eating a meal with a friend, or walking my dog, I can do good every day and have a smidge of faith that I may have more faith tomorrow.

Few students begin the Compassion course excited to study a Catholic saint, but Mother wins their hearts through her purity of motive and practical spirituality. In one of their applied inquiry home-work assignments, students are asked to try a contemplative exercise based on her teaching: "For a day, see 'Christ in his distressing dis-guise' within every person you encounter or observe. That is, look for their innate goodness and lovability, no matter their physical or emo-tional condition."

Students say this simple instruction changes how they interact with people. They see that everyone longs to be loved and is lovable. They take more time to listen. They are more giving, patient, and accepting. Instead of looking down on others, they look into them. When students try Mother Teresa's methods in their community ser-vice sites, they practice cheerful smiling, compassionate touch, and doing "small things with great love"—as these examples reveal:[48]

> I served with suicidal youth at a safe house for home-less teenagers. Mother Teresa taught me that the greatest disease is loneliness and feeling unwanted. Among the teens, loneliness is one of the largest risk factors for suicide. They feel like no one is going to miss them. I always tried to smile, as Mother Teresa taught, and it was amazing how this small change lightened the atmosphere. When I smiled, others smiled back. And often I was assigned to do office work, which was mundane, but when I saw it as 'doing small things with great love,' it became very meaningful.
>
> —SYDNEY BENNETT

> I served a woman dying in hospice who was unable to talk and had Alzheimer's. Every time I came into her room smiling, she would get this big smile on her face, and when I held her hand, she squeezed tight and didn't want to let go. I learned from Mother

Teresa to smile because everyone has their own pain, and by smiling and touching her I was letting her know that someone cares about her. I gave my love wholeheartedly to her and I got to be the one person at that moment who really loved her. And it wasn't based on anything external. We knew nothing about each other's lives. Loving doesn't require us to know somebody. It just asks us to reach out.

—Sidney Finkbohner

Mother Teresa knew the importance of person-to-person contact, and we saw in the *Mother Teresa* film that she wasn't afraid to hold the sick and frail, to love them through touch. I took this idea with me to the children's hospital, where the babies were surrounded by wires and tubes and many of them were unable to move or speak. At first I was scared of holding one of the babies or even getting near them. But I learned from Mother Teresa not to be afraid to love. Once I began touching the babies, it was the joy of loving just as she said.

—Alexis Jimenez-Maldonado

I served at a group home for boys between seven and thirteen years old. A majority have brain damage from prenatal substance abuse and were born addicted to drugs. Some are mentally ill. They are in limbo between foster homes or waiting for their parents to take court-mandated action to become better parents. They feel abandoned and crave love and affection. Every day, I tried to practice Mother Teresa's methods of 'doing small things with great love' and compassionate touch. She said, 'It's not what we do but how much love we put into it,' and that's what I focused on. Every little act of kindness made an impact—a hug, smile, laughter, homework tip, listening ear. I couldn't fix their situation, but I could love them in that moment.

—CLAIRE MCKEEFREY

Mother Teresa did not let her internal struggle prevent her from making the world a better place. This makes me realize how our internal struggles do not have to determine our actions. In my volunteering in Juvenile Hall, sometimes I felt worried that I wasn't capable for a certain task; I saw myself in a negative light. However, I remembered that Mother Teresa dealt with incredible internal struggles too, and I reminded myself that in each situation, I have the ability to choose love and to help others rather than solely focus on my own problems.

—CATHERINE WEBER

I had wanted to take students from my Compassion class to visit the Missionaries of Charity in Tijuana as part of our study of Mother Teresa, but the university deemed it too dangerous for a college field trip. The sisters serve there smilingly. The Missionaries of Charity go where others fear to tread, into the places of poverty, insanity, disease, refuse, starvation, despair, and even civil war and bombing. This fact is undeniable when one watches the documentary film *Mother Teresa* (1986), produced and directed by Ann and Jeanette Petrie.[49] Singular in its inspirational impact, the film features five years' worth of Mother Teresa's unstoppable relief work in ten countries on four continents. In the film, her works of compassion transcend political and religious barriers as she rescues Muslim children from a bombed area of Beirut's civil war, speaks of Americans' "terrible hunger for love" in a commencement address at Harvard University, and gives relief to earthquake victims in Guatemala.

The film shows a saint's unflinching commitment to her calling, sometimes in contrast to that of Catholic leaders. In Beirut, civic and religious authorities try to dissuade her from entering gunfire to rescue crippled Arab children. Undeterred, she prays to Mary for a ceasefire, and when it occurs (as she says it would), she crosses the battle line and rescues the children. In San Francisco, when a Catholic bishop is proud to hand over to her a newly renovated building, she and her sisters immediately remove the carpet, mattresses, washing machines, pews, piano, and water heater. The priest in charge is heard to say, "All of a sudden the vow they took of poverty and the vow I took of poverty began to impress itself upon my mind. Theirs is far more than mine." Mother Teresa explains that it's normal to want such amenities, but the Missionaries of Charity have taken a vow to serve the poorest of the poor and so they live as the poorest of the poor live.

Though it may sound boring—following a saint through slums and rubble—the film is spellbinding, even to younger generations who have only an eight-minute attention span. I have witnessed the potent effect on college students for fifteen years. As the film ends, they're silent, as if in a meditative state. They share how different they feel after watching the film: "I feel hope for the world." "Even my body is calmer." "My anxiety is gone." "I see how powerful just simple loving can be."

In one recent case, a student's migraine headache went away. The response reported by my students matches the study conducted by Harvard Medical School professor Dr. David McClellan, who discovered through a saliva test that students who watched this documentary about Mother Teresa experienced enhanced levels of immunoglobin-A, the body's first order of defense against flu and cold. Dr. McClellan named this life-enhancing impact the "Mother Teresa Effect."[50] Unconditional love benefits not only our spiritual lives but also our physical health.

## PRINCESS DIANA AND MOTHER TERESA

The film astonishes viewers with scenes of Mother Teresa and her sisters stroking and embracing the bodies of the diseased, spastic, starved, and mutilated. The only other image of human touch of the so-called untouchables in the 1980s that seared into the collective psyche was of Princess Diana touching—without gloves—those suffering from AIDS and leprosy. Together the two women revolutionized the world's view of these diseases. They broke the barrier of stigma and isolation by openly loving those suffering from leprosy and AIDS. Two years after Mother Teresa established the first hospice home for people dying of AIDS in the U.S., Diana opened Britain's first hospital unit, at London Middlesex Hospital, for patients infected with HIV/AIDS. The story of their friendship reveals that the power of love is expressed as effectively in the streets as from palaces. For Mother Teresa, location or vocation did not matter. What mattered was to surrender to the place God puts us, whether in the streets or in a palace:

> Total surrender. To be where He wants you to be. If He puts you in the street and everything is taken from you, suddenly you find yourself into the street, to accept to be into the street at that moment. But not for *you* to put yourself in the street, but to accept to be there. This is quite different. To accept if God wants you to be in a palace, alright, to accept to be in a palace as long as *you* are not putting yourself in the palace. This is the difference in total surrender.[51]

Though in her elegance and high heels Princess Diana physically towered over Mother Teresa, she was a spiritual student of the saint. Diana wrote that her encounter with Mother Teresa and the Missionaries of Charity in 1992 gave her the direction she'd been searching for during the troubled years of her marriage and separation from Prince Charles. In her visit to the Motherhouse in Calcutta, Diana said she had an experience while kneeling with the nuns in prayer that made her spirit soar. She struggled to put into words the deep effect of the sisters' love, singing, and compassionate touch. Soon after, she flew to Rome to meet Mother Teresa, who had been too ill to travel to Calcutta. Diana was thirty, Mother Teresa eighty.

She counseled Diana: in times of personal pain, reach out to others who are suffering and they will then reach out in return.

In June 1997, they had their last in-person meeting at Mother Teresa's home in the Bronx, New York. Mother Teresa's doctors warned her not to make the trip to the U.S., but she insisted on going. In a wheelchair and frail, she gave herself to others without complaint. Diana was in New York for a charity event. Here is a first-hand account of their last meeting:

> The convent phone rang and a woman said, 'Princess Diana would like to come see Mother.' Mother was quite sick and was sitting at the top of the steps in a wheelchair. When she heard Diana downstairs, she jumped up and went down to greet her. They went into the chapel. Diana got down on the floor and prayed for Mother. Before Diana left, Mother gave her the *Gift of Love* music album. They walked outside together and lots of people were gathered on the street. Afterward, Mother said, 'Now we must go to the chapel and pray for her—she has a terrible suffering.' So we did the Holy Hour Adoration for Princess Diana.[52]

Within twelve weeks of this final meeting, both women were gone. When Diana was killed in a car accident on August 31, 1997, Mother Teresa sent condolences, noting that their closeness was due to Diana's genuine concern for the poor and unwanted. Diana, who was only thirty-six, was buried holding a rosary that Mother Teresa had given her.

Just a few days later, on September 5 in Calcutta, eighty-seven-year-old Mother Teresa passed away, surrounded by the prayers of her beloved Missionaries of Charity. When her breathing became labored, they called for a breathing machine but couldn't start it because the electricity went out. The entire Motherhouse was in darkness. Quite like a saint to slip out of the world under the cover of darkness when everyone's attention was riveted on the tragic loss of an iconic princess. Mother promised her nuns that she would be available to an even greater degree.

## MIRACULOUS MEDAL

The power of love is available to everyone who asks, but few are those who ask. This was the message of Virgin Mary in her apparition to St. Catherine Laboure, a novice nun at the Chapelle Notre Dame De La Medaille Miraculeuse, in Paris, France, in 1830. In the apparition, Mary's hands extended toward the earth as she stood victorious upon its globe, her foot planted on the head of a serpent. Grace in the form of Light emanated in rays from her fingers—but not from all of them. She explained to St. Catherine that the absent rays represented the Grace that God offers but we refuse. Her parting message to the visionary was that a medal be cast and distributed with a depiction of her Immaculate Conception on the front and a tableau of Calvary on the back. This became the famous "Miraculous Medal."

Mother Teresa gave the Miraculous Medal as a gift of love to the people she encountered. Advanced spiritual beings often give a small object that carries their energy. In India, for example, His Holiness the 17th Karmapa gives a red string to visitors. Such an object is a channel of Grace and reminds devotees that they belong to a spiritual path. The Miraculous Medal became the means by which Mother Teresa touched millions throughout the world—and still does. While alive she handed it to countless numbers, especially the poor. A nun who worked with Mother Teresa told me that Mother always had plenty of the medals with her and instructed the nuns never to visit the poor empty-handed. Mother Teresa kissed the Miraculous Medals and pressed them into the hands of the poor and suffering. She often asked a sick or dying person where they were hurting and she pressed the medal gently in the painful area and prayed to Our Lady to kiss that very place.

Three months before she died, during her last visit to the South Bronx in 1997, Mother Teresa sat in a wheelchair and cradled a basket full of medals on her lap. As the basket emptied, the nuns refilled it.

Mother kissed a handful of the medals and gave them to each priest as they lined up to greet her after Mass.

At this same moment, June 1997, I was in Paris, standing in the very chapel where the vision of the Miraculous Medal had taken place. I had no idea of the vision or the medal or Mother Teresa's use of it. I was in my early thirties, a young professor stuck in a soul-less life. Nothing interested me in Paris except to walk around the corner from our hotel and slip into a little chapel where the Virgin Mary stood radiantly atop the globe, her foot crushing the serpent, hands extended outward, rays of Light emanating from her fingers. My soul had been drawn there, and I went every day and stayed as long as I could, kneeling and asking for help.

Within two months of those prayers in Paris, love came into my life. It unraveled much of what I believed. Perhaps that's why people don't ask for heavenly help! Love undoes who we think we are.

In 2013, I was given a Miraculous Medal when I knelt at Mother Teresa's tomb in Calcutta. To this day, I wear it around my neck. It reminds me to be a carrier of love wherever I am, facing whatever task is in front of me. As Mother Teresa said:

Where God has put you, that is your vocation.

Not all of us can do great things, but we can do small things with great love.

*Pygmalion and Galatea,* painting
by Louis Jean François Lagrenée, 1781
(Wikimedia Commons).

## Chapter Five

# In the Wake of Aphrodite
# – Falling in Love

The feminine face of God was nonexistent in *the* church. There was no Mary to pray to and no female saints to relate to. In fact, such aspects of the Divine Feminine were viewed as heretical. Perhaps that's why, when I came back from the missionary field in Florence, I put *The Birth of Venus* into a place of prominence in my graduate school apartment in Austin, Texas—over the secondhand sofa in the tiny living room. I needed an image that mirrored the sanctity of my feminine soul. She was Aphrodite, the ancient Goddess of Love. (Venus is the Roman goddess of Love, and Aphrodite her Greek counterpart.) Only much later did I come to learn the symbolic significance of Aphrodite. Her legendary work of love wasn't always cuddly. She often required her supplicants to complete exacting tasks or endure banishment. This was no Hollywood version of love, with a sexy wink and sports car! Those who prayed to Aphrodite for help with their love lives were often purified through great sorrows and difficulties before they could be united with the love they longed for. Years later, my teacher affirmed that no struggle in our life is ever wasted as it develops a quality we need on the path.

# Psyche and Eros

In the famous Greek myth of Psyche and Eros, for example, Psyche (Soul) was allowed to marry Eros (Beloved) only after she endured trials that seemed impossible to her. Hearing what Aphrodite required of her before she could unite with her Beloved, Psyche felt hopeless and wanted to throw herself into a river, yet something in her wouldn't let her give up her longing. For every impossible task, help arrived in forms that Psyche didn't expect, and she became a wiser and more conscious woman. Her final test was to go into the Underworld to retrieve a precious box, but in her travels, various people in need asked her for her "coin" or "cake," the gifts she would need to offer to the Gods to secure the box. If Psyche gave these sacred items away to lesser causes, even out of sincere motivation to help others, she would never get the precious box. Therefore she had to say no to many seemingly good opportunities to save others, so that she could complete the journey of her soul and bond with her Beloved. The soul's journey is indeed a razor's edge of discernment between genuine love and its many counterfeits. Psyche had to learn the difference between acts of virtue and real love.

I was unaware of the potency of the symbol hanging over my sofa. We are often lit up by things we don't understand. In Sufi teaching, we are told to follow "the hints," for they reveal a path to our heart. *The Birth of Venus* was exactly this kind of hint for me. It initially brought me back to life—I wrote poetry, composed music, and danced. I felt creative, lit by a Muse I couldn't see. As an archetype, Aphrodite/Venus elicits beauty. Where Her energy touches, beauty is born, as we see in the story of Pygmalion, the sculptor of ancient Greek mythology. According to Ovid's *Metamorphosis*, Pygmalion sculpted his ideal woman out of ivory and named her Galatea. He was so captivated by her beauty that he prayed to Aphrodite to bring him just such a woman in real life. The goddess answered his prayer. When he went home from the temple, he kissed the statue and Galatea was brought to life. Thus we speak of "the Pygmalion effect."

Loving something brings it to life. The power of love sees the potential for beauty and actualizes it. We can look back upon our life and see the magic of the Pygmalion effect as we remember the people and animals who loved us and whose beneficence brought out the best in us. I remembered Mrs. Thomas, who saw something in me that no one else had. In tenth grade, I started out in her English class, but after a month she worked out my transfer into the Advanced Placement class with another teacher. I knew Mrs. Thomas liked having me in class, and she told my parents she hated to see me go. Any teacher knows what a difference it makes to have an eager and affable student in your class. But Mrs. Thomas cared more for my development than for her personal ease. This is what it means to love another person. Her view of me as an advanced student changed my view of myself. Maybe I was intelligent after all! I had been a "B" student, not exactly an academic star. After I was moved to the advanced class, I began making mostly A's and, eighteen years later, was given a full doctoral fellowship at a prestigious graduate school.

For decades, the Pygmalion effect has been studied in educational environments. Students have greater success when teachers are told that their students have high intelligence when, in fact, they might not. If teachers treat them *as if* they are successful, they will likely become so. The same principle applies whenever we treat each other as sacred and lovable. In our own way, we are doing for others what Pygmalion did for Galatea. By loving someone or something, we bring them to life. Seeing the potential for beauty, we help to actualize it.

Coming back to the United States from Florence wasn't easy. There was no outer Pygmalion to help me see the beauty in my life. *The Birth of Venus* hung over my couch, but where was its luminosity? Florence had rekindled my soul, but an apartment in Texas with thrift store furniture felt dull in comparison. The atmosphere of Florence had been magical, as if living in full color, and now I was back to black and white.

I had moved to Texas to be near a boyfriend from college and then floundered, trying on the life designs that others had picked out for me. In the myth, Psyche went to the underworld; she did not give her coin and cake to the energies of seeking approval or wavering self-doubt. By staying faithful to her soul's purpose, she was allowed to bond with her Beloved. But my inner Psyche (soul) wasn't that strong. In order to do *something*, I started a graduate school program in Government. My father wanted me to go to law school, and this was my halfhearted first step. The graduate program in Government held no meaning for me, and the panic attacks were so severe I could barely go to class.

I felt lost and empty. My faith in the church's doctrines had flagged, but I had nowhere else to go. I didn't know that emptiness is a perfect condition for new growth. As a Jungian analyst later told me, feeling flat may suggest depression, but it's also the ideal condition for growth—as in the "flat" in which seeds are planted at a nursery. We see a flat of soil with seeds in it, and we say, "It's empty. Nothing is happening." But the seeds are gestating unseen in the darkness and will soon shoot up into green stems. Souls have long sought empty spaces, where the seeds of contemplation grow. For instance, Father Pavlos and many other lovers of God have taken refuge in the stark emptiness of the Sinai desert in Egypt.

At age twenty-five, the empty space frightened me and it also frightened my parents. They were eager for me to marry and get onto "the right track." It surprised all of us that I fell in love with four men and (of course) married the one most opposite to my parents' middle-class sensibilities.

# AWAKENING TO ROMANTIC LOVE

The energy of love can bring us to our knees. Aphrodite is associated with the sea and known for her sudden and impactful waves of love that, similar to a tsunami or hurricane, will level a house and force a new beginning. Growing up on the Gulf of Mexico in Florida, I experienced the destructive force of the sea. Many times, hurricane warnings forced us to evacuate our house on the shore. Once, we came home from a four-day evacuation and saw that the beach homes in our village had been leveled, their innards scattered for miles across the sand. This was a hint to me of how love would work itself out in my life. It would destroy everything I had built on the sand. The spiritual teacher whom I encountered many years later put it this way: "the inner Self … is quite happy to throw one bodily off a cliff if that's what it takes to awaken and activate the spirit."[53] Sometimes, indeed, it took a catastrophe to wake me up, but back then, at twenty-five, I didn't know that Love would destroy whatever blocked the human heart from the union that it longed for.

I did, however, consciously awaken to the power of romantic love. I longed to merge, to lose myself in the arms of a man. Romantic love followed by marriage was culturally expected and therefore the safest way for me to experience this self-surrender. Aphrodite's energy was activated, and I fell in love simultaneously with four different men.

One was a free-spirited, natural man, a skilled and gentle-hearted psychiatric nurse. It was summertime, and he lived by the ocean. He enjoyed the simple pleasures of life—massage, surfing, drawing, sailing, and lovemaking. One evening after a candlelit dinner at the local Italian restaurant, he invited me into the warm waters of the Gulf to swim naked in the moonlight. I wanted to be naked with him. but I couldn't cross the moral line of "No sex before marriage" and "Be ye not unequally yoked together with unbelievers." He was not a member of the church, and no one knew I was dating him. I had never been naked with a man, and I wasn't ready to be naked with him.

Another was an ardent man from Sicily whom I met at the missionary school in Italy. He would take me in his arms and share his dreams of living in America where he would have great success with his import business. I was spellbound by the attention of such a handsome and charismatic Italian man, but—too risky.

My longtime boyfriend was a literary scholar with a keen intellect. A sensitive man, he wrote me love poems and showered me with artistic presents. We were good friends and intellectual companions, but he was gay and there was little chemistry.

The man I married was an athletic, streetwise man with a sincere calling from God to the ministry. He'd grown up in *the* church, sown his wild oats, and then gone back to college to get a degree in Biblical Studies and enter the ministry. I was attracted to his "blue-collar" background and "checkered past," as my parents characterized him. When I first met him, he seemed aloof, which increased the attraction I felt for him. It was as if he carried a piece of me and this, of course, made him irresistible. We held each other's shadow qualities—he was streetwise and I was book-smart. Climbing on the back of his motorcycle, I loved to wrap my arms around him and feel the wind on my face as he took me to places I'd never been before.

Falling in love is a transcendent experience, as it temporarily disables the ego and allows an experience of oneness with the beloved. It has the power to transport us into places we would never otherwise explore. This was the case with Rev. Arthur Dimmesdale, the young Puritan minister in *The Scarlet Letter* who fell in love with Hester Prynne, the mysterious and passionate woman living on the edge of town, outside the bounds of the Puritan congregation. Their lovechild was named Pearl, an archetypal symbol of love—"the pearl of great price." We often fall in love with people who carry the hidden parts of ourselves, our unlived lives. The inner Self wants to actualize a latent potential—the pearl—and romantic love is often the catalytic condition. Ethel Persons, a Freudian psychiatrist who directed the Columbia University Psychoanalytic Training Center, wrote an extensive study of the effect of romantic love on human psychological transformation; she concluded that romantic love can so realign one's personality and worldview that it is "one of the most significant crucibles for growth" and "resembles the great religious conversion experiences."[54]

Indeed, falling in love with a thirty-three-year-old motorcycle-riding minister realigned my worldview and put me on a path in life I'd never imagined for myself. I threw law school out the window and went to seminary alongside the minister. Marrying him was an act of rebellion against what I perceived to be my parents' acquisitive values. He had no savings and no car, but he did have a big dream. He wanted to minister to the homeless and "disenfranchised," a word I learned from him. In my mind, I was choosing God over mammon.

On a deeper level, falling in love was another longing of my soul for the Light, a primal call within the heart. Romantic love can be a portal to something beyond itself, but I had no awareness that my outer attractions were a longing for self-completion. This caused a deep pain that I didn't understand until much later. I projected a longing for the Infinite that no person could ever fulfill. Only in midlife would I become mature enough to let go of relational drama and enter the mystery of Divine Love. At twenty-five, I fell in love with a man and made him my god.

According to C. G. Jung, when a woman falls in love with a man, it activates the *animus*, an archetypal energy of the masculine spirit, a transpersonal force in her psyche more powerful than her ego. If she is fortunate, she encounters an outer man who is a positive masculine figure, supporting her unique voice and creative life. He does not berate her, criticize her, or seek to possess and control her. This outer masculine helps her access her own masculine spirit, the inner source for her creative life and authentic self. He affirms her soul. It would be many years before I encountered a wholly positive masculine presence in my outer life—and he turned out to be a spiritual teacher rather than a husband or a lover. "You have been a devoted seeker," he told me in our first meeting, speaking to my soul. His statement surprised me. I'd seen the long years prior to him as a waste, but he counted them as part of the path and said I'd been faithful to the quest. That's what love does: it recontextualizes our entire life, turning our lead into gold.

## MARRIAGE AND THE SACRIFICE OF VENUS/ APHRODITE

In my marriage, I experienced the joys of physical intimacy for the first time, as well as the emotional pains of pushing and pulling that often go with young love. Becoming a wife gave meaning to my life. I had a purpose by joining my life to my husband's purpose.

Sometimes the new identity becomes the next prison. Strict moralism prevailed. I threw out all remnants of my artistic and ecstatic tendencies from my Florence era. There had been warning signs. In his first visit to my apartment, he opened the refrigerator and saw a bottle of wine that I had served to friends at dinner earlier in the week. He grabbed the bottle and began marching out of my front door. Obediently, I followed him into the parking lot and watched as he smashed the bottle into the large public trashbin. The sound of glass crashing loudly asserted his authority: "This will not be allowed!"

*The Birth of Venus* was, inevitably, also sacrificed. Early in our dating, provoked by the naked beauty of the Botticelli poster, he asked me for tape, scissors, and paper. I silently looked on as he covered over the nudity of Venus. The poster continued to hang over my couch, but it was botched. It looked ridiculous with crudely cut cardboard pieces taped over her body. When we set up house together as husband and wife, *The Birth of Venus* was discarded—thrown into the trash. Symbolically, the Goddess of Love was thrown back into the ocean of unconsciousness, to reemerge in my life years later, in a very unexpected way.

Even though parts of me were forced underground, marriage gave me the first real lesson in human love. In college, I had read Viktor Frankl's famous words, written about his wife, in his Holocaust memoir, *Man's Search for Meaning*: "Love is the ultimate and the highest goal to which man can aspire." As a college student, I had registered the beauty of those words, but it would be years before I came to Frankl's final realization: "Love goes very far beyond the physical person of the beloved." When I met with Frankl's grandson, Alexander Vesely, and the Frankl family representative, Mary Cimiluca, I heard firsthand accounts of Viktor Frankl's life and the many loves that gave it meaning.

**Dr. Viktor Frankl**
(Imagno/picturedesk.com)

Alexander Vesely,
Frankl's grandson
(courtesy of Noetic Films Inc.).

Mary Cimiluca,
Frankl family representative
(courtesy of Noetic Films Inc.)

*Chapter Six*

# The Meaning of Love

## Encounter with Viktor Frankl, Alexander Vesely, and Mary Cimiluca

*A thought transfixed me: For the first time in my life
I saw the truth as it is set into song by so many poets,
proclaimed as the final wisdom by so many thinkers,
the truth that love is the ultimate and highest goal to
which man can aspire. Then I grasped the meaning of
the greatest secret that human poetry and thought and
belief have to impart: The salvation of man is through
love and in love.*

## Love and the Endurance of Suffering

V iktor Frankl wrote those words shortly after he was liberated from a Nazi concentration camp.[55] He was describing an experience of the power of love that occurred one day in the camp. That day—like countless other days—he was forced to march for miles through the snow in the pitch-black. His feet were swollen with edema, in shoes that were falling apart—"every single step became real torture." "Hurry up, you pigs!" was the constant insult. If anyone slipped on the ice, a guard hit him with a rifle butt.

Though Frankl's existence in that moment seemed pointless, his mind clung to the image of his twenty-four-year-old wife Tilly. He saw her with "an uncanny acuteness." As the sun rose, their work began—pick-axing frozen ground for endless hours—yet he was able to keep his inner eye fixed on the image of his beloved. Was she even alive? He had no idea. They had last seen each other in the selection line at Auschwitz, separated by an unalterable fate. His parting words to her: "Tilly, stay alive at any price. Do you hear? At any price!" For her birthday one year, Frankl had given her a small globe pendant, inscribed, "The world turns on love." Though they were stripped of the pendant and their wedding rings at Auschwitz, somehow this truth remained: "The world turns on love."

As he concentrated on Tilly's image, she became a real presence: "More and more I felt that she was present, that she was with me; I had the feeling that I was able to touch her, able to stretch out my hand and grasp hers. The feeling was very strong; she was *there*." Frankl realized that, in a sense, it didn't matter whether Tilly was alive or not, for "Love goes very far beyond the physical person of the beloved." Frankl's love for Tilly did not depend on her. It found "its deepest meaning in his spiritual being, his inner self." Love is internal to the lover and requires nothing back from the beloved. Love is what enabled his survival in the camps. Love for his wife, love for his mother, and love for his "spiritual child" (the book he wanted to finish) empowered his will to meaning.

Shortly after his liberation, Frankl returned to Vienna and learned that his wife and mother had been killed in the camps. He wrote to close friends that "the best have not returned" and "now I'm all alone."[56]

Mysteriously, a confirmation of love came Viktor's way. He was walking along the road and saw a man with a tiny golden globe pendant in his palm, just like the one he had given Tilly on her birthday many years ago. It said, "The world turns on love." There were only two of these pendants, he had been told. He bought it from the man. "It was dented slightly but the whole world still turned on love."[57]

Frankl experienced many such synchronicities in his life and viewed them with characteristic humility: "I think the only appropriate attitude to such coincidences is to not even try to explain them. Anyway, I am too ignorant to explain them, and too smart to deny them."[58] Frankl wrote those words at age ninety-two, fifty years after his liberation.

Frankl is widely known as the founder of a school of psychotherapy called "Logotherapy/ Existential Analysis." His approach of "healing through meaning" is regarded as the "Third Viennese School of Psychotherapy" (the other two founded by Sigmund Freud and Alfred Adler). At age three, Frankl knew he wanted to be a physician, and it was Freud who influenced him to go into psychiatry. When Frankl was only sixteen, Freud accepted an article written by him for publication in *The International Journal of Psychoanalysis*.

Frankl received M.D. and Ph.D. degrees from the University of Vienna. Suicide prevention became a major thrust of his life's work—to insist on the meaningfulness of human life, no matter how wretched the circumstances. He founded Vienna's first private youth counseling program to help prevent suicide. From 1930–1937, he was in charge of an entire ward at the University Clinic that handled 12,000 women who had attempted suicide. He treated them as fellow human beings, not as problem cases or broken people.

Frankl said he saw his work primarily as "encounter" rather than "technique." To illustrate, he liked to tell the story of a woman who called him at this home at 3 a.m., determined to commit suicide. He gave every argument and used every technique he could think of to dissuade her. After thirty minutes, she had not budged from her plan. Finally, he convinced her to come the next morning to his hospital so they could talk in person. When she arrived, she told him that the only reason she had decided not to take her life was the fact that he had listened to her patiently in the middle of the night instead of being angry with her for disturbing his sleep. The encounter made her believe that "a world in which this can happen must be a world worth living in."[59] Frankl was interested in the spiritual dimension of his patients, and found that they were not fundamentally driven by a "will to pleasure" (Freud) or a "will to power and money" (Adler) but by a "will to meaning."

Frankl's promising medical career took a fateful turn when the Nazis seized Austria. In 1939, they made him the head of neurology at Rothschild, the only Jewish Hospital in Vienna; as a Jew, he was allowed to see only Jewish patients. The position provided temporary protection from deportation for Viktor and his parents, but they witnessed mass deportation of their friends, neighbors, and colleagues. Jews and other targeted groups were forced out of their homes and businesses. Buildings were "Aryanized." Beatings, rapes, theft, and insults were a daily occurrence. Jews were not allowed on public transportation. Suicide was rampant.

As a doctor working under such conditions, Frankl actively sought to spare the lives of mentally ill patients from the Nazis' euthanasia program. With the help of another doctor, Frankl avoided assigning their patients a diagnosis that the Nazis would use as grounds for killing. The other doctor was a member of the Nazi party, yet aided in the obstruction of Nazi goals. Thus Frankl saw the impossibility of "collective guilt"—blaming all Germans for the horrible crimes of the Nazi system. Frankl knew people who'd joined the Nazi Party—perhaps to protect their own families—and risked their lives to save the lives of those the Nazis wanted to exterminate. Frankl refused to judge others: "No man should judge unless he asks himself in absolute honesty whether in a similar situation he might not have done the same."[60]

The day of decision arrived. In 1942, after years of delay, the American Consulate in Vienna sent notice to Viktor Frankl that he could pick up his visa and emigrate to the United States. Freud and Adler had already left Austria for safer lands, but Frankl was torn: Should he leave Austria, escape deportation, and thereby give his life's work a chance to flourish? Or, should he stay to protect his elderly parents and face certain death?

After a walk through the city, he returned home still undecided. On the table, he saw a little piece of marble that his father had picked up in the rubble of a destroyed synagogue. His father said it was a Hebrew letter from one of the Ten Commandments. "Which one?" asked Frankl. His father said, "Honor thy father and thy mother, that thy days may be long upon the land which the Lord thy God giveth thee."

Frankl stayed "upon the land" with his parents, and let the visa lapse.[61] Shortly after, he met and married Tilly; they were one of the last Jewish couples given a wedding permit under the Nazi regime, but the Nazis forced them to abort their unborn child. Frankl, his parents, and Tilly were soon deported. Frankl spent three years in four different camps: Theresienstadt, Auschwitz-Birkenau, Kaufering II, and Türkheim (part of the Dachau system).

Auschwitz, he said, is where "I struck out my former life." He was separated from Tilly, never to see her again. Upon arrival in a cattle car, prisoners were "selected" either for labor or to be gassed to death. Ninety percent of Frankl's transport was sent immediately to the gas chamber to be murdered *en masse*. A person was allowed a bare existence only if useful to the Nazi regime. Tilly, for example, survived initially as slave labor in a munitions plant. Others were used for cruel medical experiments. Once the prisoners were no longer useful, they were gassed or left to starve to death. Frankl describes how they watched their bodies devour themselves to the point of becoming skeletons.

At Auschwitz, Frankl writes, everyone was stripped of their clothes, shaven like sheep for the slaughter—"not a hair was left on our entire bodies." He heard the sound of leather straps hitting naked bodies, followed by screams. "We had nothing now except our bare bodies… all we possessed, literally, was our naked existence."[62]

Tilly had sewn the manuscript for his book on logotherapy inside his coat, but it was taken from him. This was his "spiritual child," his life's work, and now it was gone. As Viktor pondered whether he had anything to live for, he was given an old, torn coat. When he reached into the pocket, he found a scrap of paper with the beloved Jewish prayer, the *Shema Yisrael:* "Hear O Israel, the Lord our God, the Lord is One."

Frankl writes, "How else could I interpret this 'coincidence' than as a challenge to me to *live* what I had written, to practice what I had preached? From that point on, that page stayed with me, hidden in the lining of my coat (as my lost manuscript had been)." Frankl knew he had to *be* the book that he had written, titled *The Doctor and the Soul.* Auschwitz was "the *experimentum crucis,*" the necessary experiment for the testing of logotherapy. His theory was that meaning comes through three avenues, each a path of self-transcendence: 1) a creative work, deed, or vocation; 2) an experience or encounter with beauty, truth, nature, or with another person by loving them in their uniqueness; 3) the attitude taken toward inescapable suffering, to bear it with inner fortitude. Self-actualization eludes us if we seek it as a goal, but when we give ourselves to a cause greater than ourselves, or love someone other than ourselves, happiness and joy are inevitable byproducts.

In the camps, self-giving aided survival, and Frankl himself was an example. When sick with typhus and fellow prisoners were dying all around him, he forced himself to transcend the fatal situation out of resolve to reconstruct his manuscript. For sixteen days, he kept himself awake even in the night to prevent vascular collapse and delirium. He used a pencil stub and some stolen Nazi forms given to him by a friend to scribble the notes for his book. In this way, he did not succumb to the fever and die.[63] In the death camps, Frankl saw firsthand the heroism of self-transcendence, in both the prisoners and the guards. Prisoners gave up their last piece of bread to share with another. Some of the Nazi guards risked their lives to do small acts of mercy for prisoners.

Frankl's theories of life's inherent meaning were put to the ultimate test when he returned to Vienna after the defeat of Hitler. He learned that his mother had been murdered—gassed at Auschwitz. Tilly had died at a women's camp in Bergen-Belsen, the same camp where Anne Frank died. Viktor had clung to the hope of reunion with Tilly and his mother. Now, he wondered, what was the point of his life? He had no one and nothing. He had little will to exist, but decided he would not commit suicide before he had written his book:

> Once I knew that my family was gone except for my sister in Australia, this was the only thing I wanted to do before dying.... Beyond that I didn't want to exist. But I decided not to commit suicide—at least not before I had reconstructed my first book, *The Doctor and the Soul*....[64]

And thus Frankl wrote out his unique theories, called logotherapy, and published the book in German in 1946. In 1955, the book was published in English under the title *The Doctor and The Soul*. Frankl protested the word "soul" because of its religious connotation. Perhaps an apt phrase would be "innermost being," inclusive of both religious and nonreligious persons. Though Frankl was a practicing Jew, he did his daily prayers with the phylacteries in private, and did not assume religion to be the only way to actualize "ultimate meaning."

Friends who read the book on logotherapy asked Frankl to write another book about his experience in the concentration camps. He wrote *Man's Search for Meaning* in nine days, weeping, in an empty room with windows bombed out by the war. He dictated around the clock to three typists. The book is an all-time bestseller. In the United States, it was listed as one of the "ten most influential books in America" according to a survey conducted by the Book of the Month Club and the Library of Congress. It is a standard text in American colleges and treasured around the world. For example, Mother Teresa encouraged her novices to read it as part of their spiritual formation in the Missionaries of Charity order she founded.[65]

# Love Brings Meaning

His books were written—now what? Unexpectedly, romantic love filled the void. Still dispirited from his losses, Frankl's will to meaning was restored through the personal love of a young Catholic dental assistant who worked at the clinic, Elly Schwindt, a strong and heartfelt woman who spoke her mind. Viktor and Elly moved in together and then married once they received the official paperwork confirming Tilly's death. They had a daughter and eventually two grandchildren, one of whom, Alexander, was interviewed for this chapter. Elly became a life partner to Viktor in every way.

Their marital love was unusual for its equality and transparency. It was a fulfillment of the high ideal of human love that Frankl wrote about in *The Doctor and the Soul*. "Love," he explained, is much deeper than "sexual attraction" and "erotic bonding." Frankl was not a moralist regarding sex; he saw its ultimate purpose as an expression of love: "Sex is justified, even sanctified, as soon as, but only as long as, it is a vehicle of love."[66]

Love is one of the three paths of meaning in life, said Frankl. It does not have to be romantic or marital love, though often it is. In the state of love, the lover sees the innermost, "spiritual core" of the beloved:

> Love is living the experience of another person in all his uniqueness and singularity.... In love, the beloved person is comprehended in his very essence, as the unique and singular being that he is; he is comprehended as a Thou.... As a human person, he becomes for the one who loves him indispensable and irreplaceable without having done anything to bring this about..... Love is not deserved, is unmerited—it is simply grace.[67]

Love is a "spiritual act," he wrote, that "apprehends a person not only as he 'is' in his uniqueness and singularity," but also what he "can" and "will be"; in other words, the lover sees and nurtures the "value potentialities" of the beloved. Loving someone brings out the best in them—"Love helps the beloved person to become as the lover sees him."[68] Love is "the only way to grasp another human being in the innermost core of his personality."[69]

Frankl freely acknowledged the crucial presence of Elly for him and logotherapy: "She is the counterpart to me, both quantitatively and qualitatively. What I accomplish with my brain she fulfills with her heart. Jacob Needleman once said, referring to the way in which Elly has been my companion on our lecture tours: 'She is the warmth that accompanies the light.'"[70]

In this environment of familial love, Frankl's professional life flourished—professorships, honorary degrees, thirty-nine books, hundreds of lectures, many awards. His zest for life never faded. He was an avid mountain climber his entire life, and earned his pilot's license at age sixty-seven.

## PERSONAL ENCOUNTER

When I was fifteen (1980), I visited Dachau and Auschwitz with a global education group. Frankl describes being in camps that belonged to the Auschwitz and Dachau complexes. Touring those camps was my first introduction to the Holocaust. I remember the shock that hit me when I learned that the Nazis killed an estimated 15–16 million people between 1933 and 1945. In order to "purify" their state, Hitler's Nazism sought to exterminate Jews, Roma ("gypsies"), Jehovah's Witnesses, people with disabilities, political resistors, and homosexuals.

What I saw seared into me. The displays showed photographs of hundreds of starved corpses, thrown on top of each other as if in a garbage heap. There were rooms full of human hair, artificial limbs, clothes, and shoes—stripped from the prisoners' bodies when they entered the camp or after they had been gassed. Some of the clothing and artifacts had belonged to babies and children. Not before or since have I set foot in such a desolate and eerie place. The cold, mechanistic attitude toward human life was incomprehensible.

Frankl viewed Nazism and the Holocaust as the consequence of a nihilistic philosophical and scientific reductionism of the human being to "nothing but" a mechanical process determined by biological drives and reactions. His warning strikes a chord in our own time, when mass consumerism and scientific-technological advances carry the risk of dehumanization:

> If we present man with a concept of man which is not true, we may well corrupt him. When we present man as an automaton of reflexes, as a mind-machine, as a bundle of instincts, as a pawn of drives and reactions, as a mere product of instinct, heredity, and environment, we feed the nihilism to which modern man is, in any case, prone.
>
> I became acquainted with the last stage of that corruption in my second concentration camp, Auschwitz. The gas chambers of Auschwitz were the ultimate consequence of the theory that man is nothing but the product of heredity and environment—as the Nazi liked to say, of "Blood and Soil." I am absolutely convinced that the gas chambers... were ultimately prepared not in some Ministry or other in Berlin, but rather at the desks and in the lecture halls of nihilistic scientists and philosophers.[71]

As I stood on the eerie ground of those camps, I could not have agreed more. Evil is not the opposite of love but its absence. If humans are reducible to mechanics, to "usefulness," to "good" genetics, then there is an absence of love and no capacity to endure for a noble purpose. "Unfortunates" can be gotten rid of "for the good of society," and others can even decide to kill them out of "mercy," as in, "Who would want to live like that?" Thereby, soullessness is projected onto "unfortunates." Frankl tells the story of a mother who tried to kill herself and her young son who had genetic disabilities, but the boy stopped her. He did not want to die. He liked this life, even with severe disabilities.

Love knows the value of life per se. This was the great teaching of Mother Teresa, who rescued the rejected—unwanted babies, abandoned elderly, diseased poor—and treated them as divine. In my own experience, I saw in my mother that meaning is present even in the case of dementia and severe disability. In the last eight years of her life, she lost all physical functioning and mental cognition. She no longer recognized us; what she said made no logical sense. Somebody observing would have said, "How tragic. She's just a vegetable. She might as well die." But influenced by Viktor Frankl and Mother Teresa, I looked beneath the outer condition of disease and deformity and found an inner essence that became more and more vivid. Perhaps this is what Frankl referred to as "the soul."

As a professor, I have assigned *Man's Search for Meaning* to my college students for over twenty years. They read it alongside *My Land, My People: The Original Autobiography of His Holiness the Dalai Lama of Tibet*. Both books are firsthand accounts of genocide in the mid-20th century—one written by a Jewish doctor, the other a Tibetan Buddhist monk. Though from widely different backgrounds, both men affirm the power of love to sanctify life with meaning. No matter how wretched the circumstances, they say that life calls us to refuse the seduction of blame, despair, and "collective guilt." Yes, there are biological, psychological, and sociological conditions that bear upon us; however, these outer conditions never take away our inner freedom to decide how we face the circumstances of our life. Frankl insisted that by endeavoring to extract the meaning out of the inescapable fate, we turn our predicament into an inner triumph: "... everything can be taken from a man but one thing: the last of the human freedoms—to choose one's attitude in any given set of circumstances, to choose one's own way."[72]

Over the years, I have seen Frankl's book save the lives of students. Those who are haunted by a temptation to kill themselves (the numbers are surprisingly high) decide instead to choose life. Many students are in patterns of "passive suicide," putting themselves in harm's way through reckless sex, drunk driving, drug abuse, degrading relationships, self-harming, and various "accidents." Frankl's bold treatise on meaningfulness helps them decide to see that their lives are worth caring for. One young woman came to my office. She was in a long-standing relationship with a man who abused her. She knew it was a bad situation but felt trapped. "Where else can I go? At least I have a roof over my head." Her life had barely begun and she had already succumbed to what Frankl called give-up-itis—a form of passive suicide. By the end of the term, however, she had left the abusive situation. After reading Frankl's book, she felt she had a responsibility for her life, which she likened to "a precious jewel." She said, "I had to pull the jewel out of the dump and make it shine. Who else will do it but me?" She quoted a sentence of Frankl's that had become her life motto: "When we are no longer able to change a situation, we are challenged to change ourselves."

Frankl wrote *Man's Search for Meaning* because he "thought it might be helpful to people who are prone to despair." He reaffirmed Nietzsche's words, "He who has a *why* to live for can bear with almost any *how*."[73] The primary existential questions are: Does my life have meaning? What does life ask of me?

# CONVERSATION WITH ALEXANDER VESELY AND MARY CIMILUCA

In 2015, I invited Frankl's grandson, Alexander Vesely, and the Frankl family representative, Mary Cimiluca, to the university to share their experience with students who had studied Frankl's *Man's Search for Meaning*. They are co-founders of Noetic Films, Inc., and their first project was the film *Viktor & I*, directed by Alex and produced by Mary. They visited courses in English literature, psychology, and religious studies. They talked with students, faculty, staff, and community members. They screened *Viktor & I* before a large audience of appreciative viewers. During their visit, I interviewed them about Frankl. They give an intimate portrayal of Viktor—his life, love, and work—and his impact on their lives.

## Recollections on Viktor Frankl

Q:   Alex, what stands out to you about your grandfather?

AV:   He cared about finding and speaking the truth. This was his quest in every situation, and he didn't care about gaining societal approval. He cared about the people in his presence. He gave you that same loving presence and attention whether you were a family member or a patient coming into his office or hospital or a young woman working the microphone....

MC:   That's how I first met Viktor Frankl. It was 1987. At the time, I owned a recording company, and the American Psychiatric Association was a client. Dr. Frankl was the keynote speaker at their annual meeting that year because he was receiving the Oskar Pfister Award. I had to put the microphone on him for the event, and I was nervous. He was larger than life, even though he was physically a small man. I went up to the stage as he was talking to a bunch of smart people, and I said quietly, "Excuse me, Dr. Frankl...." He stopped what he was doing and turned to look at me. "Young lady, what can I do for you?" He made me feel comfortable when I was supposed to make him feel comfortable. He had a great ability to speak to the common man or woman as well as to Mother Teresa or Nelson Mandela. It didn't matter who was in front of him. He met us all on the same level. He had the ability to talk to you and look at you as if you were the only person in the room, the only thing that mattered to him. This was in a huge auditorium with ten thousand people. I could feel that he was genuinely interested in who I was and the work I was doing.

Q:   Frankl gave his full love and attention to whomever he was with. Was that your experience, Alex, as his grandchild?

AV:   He was a big child on some level! As a child, I felt a connection with him because he was so playful. He was very serious about his work, and highly intelligent, yet he had a childlike joy and fun in him.

People ask me, "What was he like to be around?" They are usually surprised to hear he was goofy, especially with the kids. For example, he liked to impersonate people and draw caricatures. He also loved to tell jokes and stories. He could tell the same joke a hundred times, but you still laughed every time because of his joy in it. He knew hundreds of jokes, and each one would fit the situation. Now, however, if I tell those same jokes, they're not funny and no one laughs! Some of the jokes were actually not that funny, but when *he* told them, we all laughed. He would make you feel good. He had a therapeutic quality in his very nature. He was genuinely interested in you to be the best version of yourself and to make you feel good about who you are.

Q: How did he affirm the "best version" of you, Alex?

AV: Perhaps the biggest impact he had on me was not by the things he said but by the things he didn't say. When you are close or related to someone of that stature, people ask you, "What did he pass on to you? Did he give you the secret formula to live a great life?" And the answer is no. In fact, one of the strongest influences he had on me was that he never said, "Let me tell you how to do that." He never assumed the position of, "I'll tell you how you should live your life." He respected you and how you chose to live. He lived his life in his way, and, by virtue of his example, I could learn by witnessing.

Q: Yes, I noticed in his writing and speeches, he never presumed to be an authority on someone else's life, even as a psychiatrist with his patients. And as his grandson, you felt free to become yourself?

AV: I remember one instance in particular. We were talking about religion. I felt an urge to tell him that I had decided to believe in certain things. He hadn't asked me about it. He never probed me about my beliefs. It simply came up in the discussion. His response was, "I believe you." And it wasn't about the content of being religious or not. He didn't praise me or question me. It was simply an acknowledgment of me as a person who had thought through an important question—for myself. I think he appreciated that I was making a decision there.

Q:   Your film *Viktor & I* reveals that he himself was devoted to God as "ultimate meaning."

AV:   This is something he kept very much to himself. He prayed every morning—behind closed doors. He was religious, but didn't see it as his job as a psychiatrist to initiate the topic of religion. It was up to the individual patient whether or not to include God in their personal search for meaning, or as he put it, to believe in a task-giver behind each meaningful task.

Q:   He didn't try to change or persuade you?

AV:   I think that was his greatest gift. One felt completely accepted in his presence. Perhaps because he had accepted everything within himself, he knew and accepted that people had the best and worst in them. He was most interested in the best in people.

Q:   And he encouraged people to think for themselves?

AV:   He was something of a prophet; he saw things before they happened. He said, "I don't see myself as such a great thinker, I just think things through to the end." And he did. For example, there's that nice saying "You're not dead as long people remember you." He said, "That's no consolation at all! Think it through, Alex. If I died tomorrow, you will remember me until you die, and then after that, I'm dead. What difference will a few decades make? I don't need anybody to remember me—life is valued whether or not it's remembered!"

I think that having his work, logotherapy, remembered was more important to him than being remembered as a person. He wanted his work to be out there, to be accessible, and for people to be able to benefit from it long after he was gone. And I think he has reached that goal. Logotherapy is helping people all over the world. The interest is growing despite the fact that he has been gone for almost twenty years. There are conferences, congresses, institutes, training programs, and of course, all the books.

Q: Through your film we see the transformative power of a person who lived his message. What happened when he died?

AV: It was a huge loss. We were all close as a family. Growing up, I spent a lot of time with him. It was hard to lose him. My grandfather found a lot of grounding in family. And, of course, his wife, my grandmother, is a strong personality who kept him grounded. They were equals and he needed that. They were good for each other. They did the work of logotherapy *together*.

## Marriage and Love for a Beloved Person

Q: In fact, the excellent biography by Klingberg is a book on both of them, not just Viktor. It would be impossible to separate the man from his marriage. One thing that may surprise people is how transparent Viktor and Elly were with each other. They freely spoke their feelings and ideas in the moment. Visitors were shocked that they openly disagreed with one another, sometimes in raised voices![74]

AV: That is true. If there was a disagreement, you knew it. They took no prisoners!
(*Laughing....*)

Q: When you think about your grandparents' marriage, what does it tell us about love?

AV: I will say that it wasn't easy for my grandmother. Perhaps it's always hard when you're the second wife, and the first one died so young. You know, in *Man's Search for Meaning*, it's all about Tilly. This was his first wife, whom he loved very much, and she died in the camps. One of Elly's friends, Marianne Gruber, whom I interviewed in *Viktor & I*, knew both of my grandparents well. She saw the dynamic between them up close. She told me, "Elly, though she was very young when they married, grew up fast." Elly was only twenty, he was forty. "She lived through the war, and people grew up faster in that generation." Elly was tough, and that's what he needed. Someone who could stand up for herself and stand up to him, yet be unconditionally beside him.

My grandmother made the very conscious decision to sacrifice a lot not only to be Viktor Frankl's wife but also to do the work of logotherapy. She took care of every book (over thirty of them), every letter (usually about twenty-four letters a day). In those days, it wasn't email. They answered every letter on the typewriter. She did all of the typing of correspondence, all the books, and she was at his side for fifty years. They did the work of logotherapy every day. That was their focus. They had visitors constantly. They made ninety-two trips to the U.S. for lectures. They went to every continent. She was with him, helping him behind the scenes. They were a team. She devoted her life to him and logotherapy. Elly is ninety now, and still she is working for logotherapy. Since she can read his handwriting, it's primarily up to her to sort the archives.

Q:   I also liked learning in the biography that Elly had a room of her own, a space where she went for quiet and time with herself. Somehow her love for him was totally self-giving yet not self-depleting. She gave out of her own wholeness as an individual.

AV:   And here's the point about the power of love: She did all this work with him and for him. You would think that this devotion could diminish a person, make her become less and less herself, and take her away from being who *she* can be. But their friend whom I interviewed said, "It was the opposite—Elly grew from it, she stepped into her own." It was *her* life's calling as much as his.

Q:   Love by definition requires freedom and personal choice. It seems that Elly chose logotherapy as a path of meaning and love.

AV:  Love was the foundation of that decision to be his partner in his work as well as life. This love was a path of meaning for her. She was the secretary, the person who answered the phone, and was also the caretaker. She was everything to him. We wouldn't be sitting here talking about Viktor Frankl if it weren't for Elly Frankl.

Q:  Love is one of Frankl's three paths of meaning, and Elly lived it. She told their biographer, Don Klingberg, that it was their deep love that made it possible for her to bear the demands of their life together:
    "Without a very deep love, we never could have done it. It would have been impossible for me. Viktor was not a bad man, but he was out of touch and did his work with little understanding of practical things. To change a light bulb was almost too much."[75]
    Elly's love actually saved his life, didn't it?

AV:  He was suicidal just after the war. In 1945, he came back to Vienna and learned the horrible news that his mother was killed in the gas chambers, and Tilly had also died in the camps. He knew what Elly had done for him. He was very grateful. Their love was meaningful for both of them.

Q:  I wept at the scene in your film when Elly received the honorary doctorate in Chicago in 1993. Your grandfather had received so many honorary degrees in the United States, but she only this one. They gave her a lengthy standing ovation. North Park University had wanted to confer the honor on both of them, but Dr. Frankl wrote to say he would not accept it, for he wanted to make the honor only hers:
    "While I appreciate it, I cannot accept it. As I see it, the more exclusively Elly is to be honored the more conspicuous it will be in making the occasion of special significance for her."[76]

AV:  If there hadn't been this deep love that was the foundation and that made them real equals, then it would not have worked.

Q:   And they will not be together in the same burial ground, because he is Jewish and she is Catholic?

AV:   The city of Vienna offered him a special, honored gravesite, but he declined. He wanted to be buried in the simple Jewish section of the cemetery. She'll be buried in her family cemetery on the other side of the city. It didn't bother them to be buried in different places. What mattered to them was the life they shared. They loved each other, and their love served something beyond themselves. That can never be taken away.

## "Falling Apart" and "Friends for Life"

Q:   It often takes people of two different typologies to birth something. Yin and yang. Seems like you two have that kind of connection.

MC:   That's why we work so well together. We are opposites.

Q:   Mary, how did you get involved with Alex's films, and now serve as the Frankl family representative?

MC:   I read *Man's Search for Meaning* in college in the 1960s and then I met Viktor in 1987, but it was in 2008 that I really "got" Frankl. My life fell out from under me. I lost my entire family. One after the other, every member of my family died. When I thought it couldn't get any worse, my best friend was brutally murdered and I had to go identify the body. I lost my mind and landed in a psych ward in D.C. Some neighbors found me on my kitchen floor and called 911. I woke up strapped to a bed in a straightjacket, looking around a white room. I had no memory of how I got there. I thought: "I've died and this is either purgatory or the first stage of hell!" Later I realized I had become clinically depressed, with what they call complicated grief. I would lose one person dear to me and before I could grieve that loss, there would be another loss. This went on and on.

I was mandated to stay for twenty-one days and be in the care of a psychiatrist. When I got there, he asked me, "How many people are still alive who are in the pictures at your house?" I said, "No one." I had lost everyone close to me. He came in one morning and said, "I want you to read this book, *Man's Search for Meaning.*" I said, "Get out of here with that book—I know all about that book, it's not going to save me now. Everyone I love and care for is lying in the cemetery under a bed of roses; I need something more than Viktor Frankl!" But he told me, "Your life parallels his, and someday you'll realize it." That was true.

He came back a week later and said, "The good news is you survived. The bad news is you survived. Here's how you can break out of here. Create a business plan for your new life, write it up, and give it to me." He let me out when I wrote up my business plan for a new life. At that point, I was safe from suicide. At fifty-eight, I wasn't fond of change, but, six weeks later, I had sold my house, moved to a sunny place across the country, knowing no one, sight unseen, to retire at the beach. My feeling of being settled lasted three months. I started to deteriorate, sitting at home crying. It's what Frankl calls an "existential vacuum." I decided to go back to work in a business I owned that did recording for conferences all over the world. I was recording the proceedings at a psychotherapy conference in 2008, and that's how I met Alex.

Some people are friends for a season, and some for a lifetime. He's for a lifetime. We have a close bond. There are so many different kinds of love in the world. When you encounter another person at a heart-to-heart level and you just click, it's magical. When Alex told me he was Frankl's grandson, I was stunned. It's hard for me to get speechless, but in that moment I was stunned to silence. He told me he was working on a video project for the Frankl archives. I said, "This work needs to go to the world." He said, "I don't think anyone will be interested in a movie about a dead psychiatrist from Vienna." But I knew the world *would* want to see it. So, now it is a film—*Viktor & I.* We are yin and yang, director and producer. I stay out of the creative part. To me, business is fun, like a jigsaw puzzle.

We decided to form a company together (Noetic Films, Inc.) to make films that change people's lives for the better. We're not interested in the next Hollywood dollar. We are interested in doing things that make an impact and can help people. As Dr. Frankl said: "Ever more people have the means to live, but no meaning to live *for*." That is one of my favorite quotes. The work of Frankl for me is personal. His work saved my life. He taught that regardless of our circumstances, we can find meaning in every moment. This is a meaningful moment, here, as we talk about it—the power of love is here.

AV: The film would not have happened without Mary. Hers is one of the stories where my grandfather would have said, "This is exactly those things that I teach—lived out." To overcome these kinds of tragedies, of suffering, and move forward to do meaningful things.

Q: Mary, what did you discover from your breakdown experience?

MC: We all have to face suffering, and we have to realize that ours may be different from another's. People would say to Frankl, "I can't compare my suffering to yours." He would say, "Never compare suffering. Everyone has their own Auschwitz." He always put himself on the same level as those he encountered. Also, I found that if you live your life from the inside out, most of your days will be wonderful. You don't need "stuff." You need to develop your heart and find others to give it to. What matters is to work, love, and speak from your heart. I'm here to serve, not take. To bend, not break. To love, not hate.

Frankl gave us three ways to uncover meaning, and that's what I did. "Creative" way—write a book, make a movie, create a business, etc. "Experiential" way—encounter another person, love them in their uniqueness, or go somewhere that changes your life, like your students do in the Meditation Room. "Attitudinal" way—this is the path for those who face unavoidable suffering such as an incurable illness or the death camps. It involves choosing your attitude. You can't escape the condition, but you can choose your attitude toward it and fill it with meaning. All three of these ways helped me to uncover the meaning in my life.

## Logotherapy/Existential analysis

Q:    What is logotherapy?

AV:    Logos comes from the Greek word for *meaning*. Therapy is *healing*. "Healing through meaning." He created the term before he went to the concentration camps. We are meaning-oriented beings, and we long for meaning. If you struggle, you will become better if you find something meaningful that fills what he called the "existential vacuum."

Q:    Another key aspect of logotherapy is to focus on the positive potential in a person, not on "pathology." It's a kind of Pygmalion effect. How did Frankl exemplify this?

AV:    He brought out the best out in you and he would communicate with the best version of you. People still did things that disappointed him, and he might discontinue his interactions with them, but he would rarely hold grudges. He would just let go of it. He would not waste time to take revenge. I think if you are filled with such a deep love within yourself and for life, there's no place for revenge. He wouldn't let anything negative get to him. I would have understood if he had been hateful, vengeful, and bitter. Having gone through what he went through—he lost everyone he loved. But he did not lose his faith in humankind. Although he struggled to have faith in humankind after the war, he ended up, in logotherapy, affirming a theory of humanity that seeks to elicit the potential for good and for meaning.

Q:    What about the people who criticized him?

AV:    He was not very fond of some people, but he gave those people the benefit of the doubt. He had humility. He would always assume the best in others, even those who assumed the worst about him. This is a basis in his theory of logotherapy—to look for the best in people. As you mentioned, he would say, "If you take a man as he *is*, you make him worse. If you take a man as he *can* be, you help him become who he can be, the best version of who he is." Of course he meant women too—he used the language of the time.

He was not interested in the worst version of anyone and how we can analyze that. For example, in the film, there is the story of how, after the war, my grandfather gave friendship to Gustav Baumhackl, a former Nazi doctor. He knew that Baumhackl had joined the Nazi Party like many people at the time, but he also knew that Baumhackl was not a Nazi in his heart. Baumhackl struggled with the fact that he had joined the Party and he regretted that decision. After the war, he was unemployed, and my grandfather gave him a place to see patients at the clinic. Grandfather focused on the "best version" of you and acted as if you were already there. This had an uplifting effect on people.

Still, he wasn't stupid or one-sided. I want to be clear that he didn't deny the horrors of humanity. How could he? He had come out of the worst savagery. He would say: "After all, man is that being who invented the gas chambers of Auschwitz; however, he is also that being who entered those gas chambers upright, with the Lord's Prayer or the Shema Yisrael on his lips." How he went from this experience and then to say, "Here I am a psychiatrist and I will meet everybody who comes through my door as a potentially good person"—this could not have been easy.

I think it was a choice that he struggled with. He had to wrestle and come to a conclusion, and he did. It's a decision. There is a Hitler and there is a Mother Teresa in all of us, he would say. And it's a personal decision to decide which version of the two we're going to let ourselves become.

Q:   What was the impact of the Holocaust on you, Alex? You must have heard a lot of the stories.

AV:   I only learned about the Holocaust like you did, secondhand information. Maybe I know a little more because my grandfather was a survivor of the camps. He would tell you stories only if you wanted to hear them. Later in his life, he was not fond to talk about the Holocaust. He wrote *Man's Search for Meaning* to get it off his chest, but he didn't see it as defining him. When he met my grand-mother, he told her all the stories and then said, "Now I'm not going to talk about it anymore." You can't forget the past, but you have to move on. Otherwise you waste the opportunities that life presents you in the here and now.

His work was contrary to psychoanalysis at the time, which focused on the problems, going back into one's past and reliving it over and over again. He saw that method as not necessarily helpful because you can re-traumatize someone and make it worse. People then feel desperate, like they'll never be in control of their present life, as if they are determined by what happened to them in the past. He represented the opposite model—you are not determined by what happened to you. You can determine your own fate by the way you deal with what happened to you. Death, suffering, and guilt— he called this the "tragic triad" that we cannot avoid. All of us will encounter these three things in one form or another. He tried to help people restructure their lives, like Mary did when she made a busi-ness plan for a new life. A reorientation. You don't forget what hap-pened to you, but what are you going to do now? What are you still here for? What can you still give to the world?

Q:   What was Frankl's take on Maslow's "hierarchy of needs"?

AV:   Abraham Maslow, in his "hierarchy of needs," said that once basic needs (food, shelter) are met, then the intangibles such as love, meaning and self-actualization can be fulfilled. But my grandfather disagreed. He told Maslow how people did not have their "basic" needs met in the concentration camps, but it was the "higher" needs (i.e., meanings, love, and values) that proved to be much more relevant to their chance of survival. Maslow revised his ideas and said, "Frankl is right." My grandfather emphasized that it's not about "having what you need to live" but asking yourself, "What am I living *for*?" The most affluent societies have all their basic needs met, but they lack some-thing to live *for*, and neurotic disorders tend to increase.

Q: Mary, how did logotherapy help you to get through all of your loss?

MC: With each successive loss, I had a pain in my heart that wouldn't go away. And disorientation. Especially when my father died. He was my bedrock; when I lost him, I went into a black hole and didn't leave the house for a long time. When I woke up in the hospital, it felt like I was in a vat of mud. I couldn't stop wailing. Then, when wailing became more pain than pleasure, I confronted my situation. What am I going to do to change this? At that point, I was ready to look at the meaning of my life. For me, it was to create a business and to experience a place like Southern California. I've always wanted to live in sunshine by the ocean.

Q: Is there a method you use now to avoid sinking back into depression?

MC: Absolutely. I have rules for myself. I will not let myself go back down that black hole. I created a list of ten principles. Here are a few of them. I don't allow people to interrupt my sleep. Sleep is critical for me. I have a visualization method to remove what I call "ANTs"— automatic negative thoughts. For anything out of my control, I write it down on paper and put it in what I call a "Something for God to Do" box. I've learned to let go of things I can't control and be responsible for the things I *can* control, like my inner thoughts. I am pretty disciplined with this. Also, I don't allow angry or negative people in my life—it's not unkindness but survival.

## Individual Conscience and Decency

Q: As I was reading Frankl on conscience, I appreciated that he said "conscience is intuitive and creative" and "has the power to discover meanings that contradict accepted values." As universal values are waning, he said, we have the responsibility to forge "unique meanings."[77] He gave the example of how he told Tilly—as they were forced to part at Auschwitz—to disobey one of the Ten Commandments

("Thou shalt not commit adultery") if she could foster her survival by doing so. He didn't want to be co-responsible for her death by insisting on a moral legalism. In that sense, love trumps legalism. His writings contain many examples of how conscience works differently than commandments or moralism or popular belief.

His conscience made him say things such as, "Decent people are in a minority and always will be." This was from his commemoration speech on the anniversary of Hitler's invasion of Vienna. That was not popular, was it? He was saying that there are two types of people in the world—the "decent" and the "indecent"—and they are found in all nations, races, and groups (even in the Nazi party of his time). This is very different from the victim-perpetrator dichotomy.

AV:   That statement of his gets a lot of reaction. When a reporter asked him about it, he said that he did not mean it "in a pessimistic or optimistic manner, but in an activistic manner." He meant, let's make sure we are not so comfortable as to be certain we are among the "decent." Let's keep our eye on the ball so that we strengthen the decent minority.

Q:   People also criticize Frankl for saying there is meaning to be found in the concentration camp. Is that what he said?

AV:   No. That's a misunderstanding. He wrote very concisely. He wanted to make his books as simple as possible so that anybody could read them. But then people take an already boiled-down statement and remove a key phrase and say something like, "Your grandfather said Auschwitz had a meaning too!" That is of course an absolute distortion. He said, "If you are confronted with unavoidable suffering, what can you learn from the situation? How do we respond to apparently meaningless suffering? What will we do with that now, for we cannot change it? What meaning can we squeeze out of this seemingly meaningless situation?" He did not say the situation itself was meaningful, but maybe a meaning can be derived by understanding what led to the Holocaust, so we have a chance to prevent it from ever happening again. In that commemoration speech, he gave a clear warning: no nation is immune to a holocaust.

No nation, Frankl warned, is immune to a holocaust. "The end justifies the means," he said, is the operative principle of indecent leaders who would take us down a road of destruction. History's sobering lesson is that the majority of citizens silently follow their indecent leaders, even to the point of mass delusion and genocide.

I knew I was not exempt from such silent compliance. As I listened to Alex and Mary describe Frankl's commitment to love others unconditionally and to honor their inner freedom to choose their own meaning, I knew how difficult this was in real life. I thought back to my years in the church and my compliance with leaders who excluded others from religious fellowship, saying, "The end justifies the means." The "end" was purity, and the "means" was exclusion, shaming, or shunning (all modes of *force*, not power).

In that same commemoration speech on the anniversary of Hitler's invasion, Frankl referred to the Milgram Experiment as evidence for the latent tendency toward compulsive obedience to the point of violence. In the study by Stanley Milgram at Yale University during the 1960s, a majority of the citizen sample chose to obey an authority figure when told to administer the "maximum-level" electric shock to another person for giving incorrect answers. In some cases, the other person (a researcher) was clearly showing signs of being tortured by the shocks—yelling, banging on a wall, begging for it to stop, or falling silent as if near death. Ignoring these distress signals, ordinary citizens chose to apply the maximum voltage against their suffering fellow when ordered to do so.[78] The experiment suggests that individuals with no background in abusive behavior will—in an institutional setting that encourages obedience—be cruel to innocents. For Frankl it was no mere experiment; he had seen firsthand the devolution into sadism. The rise of Nazism could only have occurred because large groups of educated and ethical people did not register its cruelty, or, if they registered it, they looked the other way.

In studying Frankl, I saw in my own life how an ordinarily decent human being will act indecently out of obedience to leaders. For example, I remembered the church announcements as a teenager, when the elders took the pulpit at a worship service and read a list of names of fellow congregants who were being "dis-fellowshipped." The names included those who had been divorced and had remarried other people, as well as those who had supported their decision. The divorced individuals would no longer be welcome in the church unless they returned to their former spouses. In some cases, people had been remarried for years and formed new families with children. I tried to imagine what it would be like to be a child and have my parents torn asunder by command of the church. It seemed cruel. Was there no allowance for changes in life? No room for mistakes? No space for grace? While not ideal, divorce happens. In my heart of hearts, I didn't like this punitive exclusion. It seemed to go against the principle of Christian love and Jesus' teaching, "Do unto others as you would have them do unto you." Besides, who among us is a hundred percent pure and can put ourselves in the place of God to judge another? But I too followed along. Our legalism had no love in it. The church proclaimed "sinner" without stopping to encounter, as Viktor Frankl did, the other person as a unique individual created to love and be loved. He sought to bring out the best in people, and he never presumed to know the will of God for others.

Here is the point: We congregants remained silent in the pews as the names of "sinners" were called one by one. It's the silence of the witnesses that is so disturbing to me now as I remember this scene from an ordinary American church service. Such silence in the face of shaming and banishing others—how is this not the basis for even greater cruelty? Sexual sins were seen as especially punishable. Little attention was ever given to gluttony, bearing false witness, greed, jealousy, judgmentalism, spiritual pride, and other sins more frequently mentioned in the Bible.

Across the board (and this is humbling to admit), I remained obedient to church practices that punished others—even when it went against my inner light (conscience). "To thine own self be true" was a teaching I'd heard, but it would be years before I had the courage to live it in actuality. When I read Dante's *The Divine Comedy*, it didn't surprise me to find the passive souls at the entranceway to the inferno. Dante's guide told him that, during their life on earth, these souls had never taken a stand or followed their heart. Lacking passion, they'd gone along with the crowd or sat on the fence. In evading any real decision to be themselves, they hadn't had Frankl's courage to live from individual conscience.

Frankl advised that people clarify their own heroic potential. Learn to stand in the light of their own conscience. At age twenty-five, the light of conscience was rather dim in me, but it was about to be energized. Soon after my marriage to the minister, I was exposed to a new environment where I heard the message of Divine Love for the first time.

Author at her Ph.D. graduation, standing outside
Princeton University Chapel (author's collection).

## Chapter Seven

## The Veil Thickens

### Seminary – Encounter
### with the Mystics

My husband encouraged me to enter seminary with him, and this opened doors for me that neither of us could have predicted. He was a minister for *the* church, and wanted me to do the three-year Master of Divinity program alongside him. Our image of marriage was that of a "team," and so, a week after our honeymoon, we started our first semester of classes at the local seminary. In our church, women were viewed as a "helpmeet" to men, that is, women were created to support men, since men were the "head of the household." My husband and I held to the same view. He was the minister, and I was the minister's wife. It never occurred to us that I too could be a minister. Women had to be silent in our church—not permitted to make an announcement, read a Bible verse, lead a prayer in the worship service, preach a sermon, or serve in a leadership role such as minister, elder, or deacon.

In truth, being silent—"seen not heard"—suited me. At the time, I was suffering from panic disorder and a phobia of public speaking. I was terrified of opening my mouth for fear of speaking in error. Having been declared a dwelling place of the devil, I mistrusted myself completely; therefore, I wasn't unhappy to be in a church that required me to be silent.

When we started the seminary program, the elders in our church advised my husband, "Don't take courses with feminist professors." In the second year of the program, I asked the elders' permission to take the required Preaching course. Women in our church were prohibited from preaching, but this was a Presbyterian seminary and the course was required of all students. I was miserable with anxiety in the course. I spent endless hours typing out my sermons, memorizing them, and practicing my delivery. Much to my surprise (and secret delight), I got an "A" in the class.

Professor Ellen Babinsky was my favorite professor. One of the world's experts on the 13th-century Christian mystic Marguerite Porete, she was translating Porete's mystical text, *The Mirror of Simple Souls*, from Old French. Porete lived in a "beguine" community—a lay religious order whose members strove to imitate the life of Christ through voluntary poverty, care of the needy, and daily devotions. As Professor Babinsky read from the poetic pages of this devoted beguine, I listened with amazement. Porete declared herself totally free as a soul—"annihilated," she said, by "the power of Love" (ch. 25, 107).[79] For this, she was deemed a "heretic" and the Inquisition burned her at the stake in 1310.

Porete and the other mystics we read in class wrote of their marriage to God. They had merged into the *ground of being* only, not with another human being. They wrote of the soul as a lover led by the Beloved into a union of love.

In Professor Babinsky's class, I started to see the Bible differently—not as a book of rigid rules but as a love story of the soul's return to God. The mystics viewed love as the supreme human quality because "God is Love." Even though I was busy tending to the fire of human love, the mystics' accounts of total surrender to Divine Love, *unio mystica*, illumination, and ecstasy captivated me. I felt deeply happy in Professor Babinsky's class—as if I finally belonged somewhere. My husband didn't enjoy her class; he said she was too "feminist" and "liberal" for his liking. We argued over my adoration of the professor and her mystics. Rather than quarrel, I learned to hide the joy I felt about the class.

# DOING "GOOD WORKS" VS. BEING A LOVING PERSON

As a seminary student, I felt grateful to study material that nourished my soul. The study of mystics was my favorite, but all the classes were interesting to me—Hebrew and Greek languages, world religions, theology, ethics, biblical studies, homiletics (preaching), and pastoral care. Many years later, when I interviewed Huston Smith, one of the great scholars in the study of religion, he articulated the feeling well: "We are blessed because we get to dwell our mind and our soul on lofty matters."

More and more, these "lofty matters" were leading me down the lane of love. From the mystics covered in Professor Babinsky's class, I learned the difference between doing good works and being a loving person. The mystics confirmed what I had intuitively come to see in Florence with people like Tosca. Even though my church told me that she was not "saved" because she was Catholic, I knew her to be a loving person—and that's what mattered most to the mystics.

Marguerite Porete put religious people into two categories: "lost" souls and "sad" souls. The lost souls are those who do all the right things and follow the rules of virtue, yet have no heart. They follow doctrines to a tee. They are content with the letter of the law and yet know little of the spirit of the law. They deny the desires of their instincts and bodies, attend mass faithfully, pray, fast, tithe, refuse worldly honors, "fear all kinds of love," and take great pleasure in doing charitable deeds. Such souls are "lost in their works and are in a country where everyone is one-eyed," trying to walk in the dark with only the eye of human reason as a guide. They do not see with the eyes of the heart. They are lost because they have no idea that there is more to religious life than what they believe to be true. "They are like the owl who thinks there is no more beautiful bird in the wood than the young owl" (ch. 55, 132).

A light went on inside me. I was a lost soul—stuck in a prison of good personhood but unaware of my predicament. I followed all of the rules of the church, went to services three times a week, did all manner of good works, and judged negatively those who didn't follow the same rules. I wanted others to see me as a good person, and I looked for the rewards of reaching Heaven and church approval. What a painful paradox to have been a missionary to save lost souls only to realize that I was the lost soul.

The "sad" souls, Porete said, are those who do the same as the lost souls, yet they know there is more. They know that Love is the greatest master, not virtues for their own sake. They see the spirit of the law—love. The sad souls are sad because they know that, without love, their efforts are futile. As St. Paul writes:

> Though I speak with the tongues of men and angels, and have not love in my heart, I am as sounding brass or a tinkling cymbal.
>
> And though I have the gift of prophecy, and understand all mysteries and all knowledge; and though I have all faith, so that I could move mountains, and have not love in my heart, I am nothing.
>
> And though I bestow all my goods to feed the poor, and though I give my body to be burned, and have not love in my heart, I gain nothing (I CORINTHIANS 13).

The same teaching is found in other traditions. The great Jewish mystic, Baal Shem Tov (d. 1760), saw it in a vision. The Baal Shem Tov ("Besht") asked the question of his heavenly guide, "Who keeps the Sabbath in the right way?" In response, the Besht was taken to two homes. In the first, he was shown the most perfect observance of the Sabbath, and in the second, the worst.

When the carriage pulled up to the first home, the man who lived there opened the door and welcomed him warmly. The Besht discovered to his astonishment that his host didn't dress like a Jew or do Jewish prayers or ritually wash his hands before eating. In fact, he seemed more like a gentile. The Besht thought, *Perhaps his holiness is simply very hidden.* There was no eating of kosher food and no reading of the Torah portion, for no scroll existed in the home. It was all very disappointing for the Besht. Then, in the afternoon, his host opened up the home for a party with gentile friends. Men and women mixed freely together, dancing, and drinking; the men even smoked cigars! After the raucous merriment, the Besht asked his host, "Why did you have this party?"

The man explained, "I'll tell you the truth: I'm a Jew but I know nothing about Judaism. I was orphaned when I was a little boy and was raised by gentiles. I remember only one thing about my parents: Every Saturday afternoon they made a big party for all their neighbors. They were very happy. So, I try to be a good Jew in the one way I know—by rejoicing on the Sabbath and making a party for my neighbors to make them joyful. That's all I know of Judaism, but I do it with all my heart."

The Besht then realized that the man had "a true Jewish heart" and "exalted soul." When the Besht started to tell the man about the Sabbath traditions, heaven pressed down on him and he was not allowed to utter a word. The man didn't need all the Sabbath rules; he was already perfect in his observance because he kept the Sabbath in his heart—with joy.

Then the Besht was taken to the place where Sabbath was kept the worst. The horses led his coach into a Jewish neighborhood bustling with preparation. He could smell the aroma of *challah* and *cholent* as he passed through the streets. The coach came to a house from which he heard the chanting of Torah—the home of the city's rabbi. When the Besht arrived, the rabbi was behind the closed door in his study, reading the Torah and reciting his Sabbath prayers. The Besht was brought into the house and left to wait for thirty minutes. Eventually, the rabbi came out of his study and the family performed its Sabbath ritual precisely according to the law. It was orderly and proper, with all the correct wording and sequence, but the Besht felt miserable. There was no love or joy or warmth. The rabbi was afraid even to stretch out his hand lest he accidentally brush a work implement such as a pen. He kept his arms and legs tucked in, sitting like a prisoner in his chair for the whole day. "Gloom and darkness reigned in the rabbi's house."

When it was over, the Besht opened his mouth to tell the rabbi that he must keep his Sabbath in the spirit of joy, but heaven prevented him from saying so. According to the Jewish sages, "If you know a person will not listen to you, it is a *mitzvah* (good deed) to refrain from correcting him, for you will cause strife." The rabbi was so full of pride and certainty about the rightness of his way that he would never have listened to the correction. Thus the Besht learned: "An excessive fear of sin, which produces worry and anxiety and deprives one of joy, gives no pleasure to God."[80] In the language of Marguerite Porete, this rabbi was a lost soul, far from the land of love. Therefore the mystics teach that one can be very religious yet totally ignorant of love. I saw this in myself. It was not hypocrisy but ignorance.

The lost souls are ignorant of Love, says Porete. The sad souls are at a higher level. They see into the Promised Land of Love, yet suffer with longing because they know they are powerless to arrive there on their own. They see the limitations of their own effort. It is the "power of Love," Porete says, which will take them there, and this requires a total surrender of exertion and thinking through endless points of view. The only way to be freed of this mental bondage and enter the realm of love, according to Porete, was "willing nothing, knowing nothing, wanting nothing."

The description of the sad soul illumined my own sadness. I longed for Something More, but I had so many desires of my own—education, being a good minister's wife, a career, buying a home, making a difference in the world, on and on. How could I give up what I wanted? I was a long way from the annihilated soul who has become melted wax, imprinted only by the stamp of God, who is Love. Many years later, I met a spiritual teacher who incarnated this state of annihilated Love, and the experience opened my heart.

As a twenty-five-year-old seminary student, I held Porete's writing in my hands, knowing it was holy, yet not knowing exactly what it meant for me. I was awestruck that it survived through the centuries. Her small circle of followers had rescued a copy of her manuscript from the pyre and preserved it for posterity. Her writing went over my head but into my heart. It was the first account I'd ever read of Divine Love absorbing a human being into Itself.

Porete had refused to deny this inner truth: "I am dissolved in Him" (ch. 80, 156).

To be "dissolved in Him"—what did this mean? Pondering this frightened me, and yet it frightened me not at all. It was the river losing itself into the Sea.

I knew that *she* knew about the Light.

I longed to learn more. I took the only road that seemed available to me as a woman in my church: a Ph.D. in religion. The academic study of religion shed light, but it also veiled the Light.

## TRAVELER IN TWO WORLDS

During my second year in the Ph.D. program at Princeton Theological Seminary, Professor Jane Dempsey Douglass wrote on one of my papers: "I would like for you to speak up in class. I'm certain your verbal sharing would be as lovely and significant as your writing."

She was an eminent theologian and scholar, president of national and international ecumenical organizations, and professor of Christian history. I was a stellar student on a full doctoral fellowship, yet something wasn't right. I couldn't speak in class. I felt encased in a block of silence, like in a prison cell. Despite the momentary cracks while living in Florence, falling in love, and studying mystics, the steel door had closed tighter during my years of being a minister's wife. Reading Professor Douglass' note, I became aware that I felt paralyzed and muted.

While studying at Princeton, I was a traveler in two worlds but inhabitant of neither. From Wednesday evening to Sunday evening, I was a minister's wife in Texas. I attended all three weekly church services, including the Wednesday night Prayer Meeting. I listened to my husband's Sunday morning lessons at the church, and accompanied him to nursing homes where he led communion services. I went with him on some of his pastoral visits to hospital rooms to comfort the sick and the dying. I helped with the large-scale meals that he frequently organized as part of an urban outreach program to the homeless. I accompanied him on short and long trips for the senior citizens of the church. I helped care for those we took into our home—a homeless pregnant teenager, an elderly man who had no family, an injured dog. I cooked, and maintained a hospitable home environment for him and the church members who came for meals and to visit. Potlucks, baby showers, weddings, and funerals were all part of church life. As wife, I took care of many household chores—laundry, housecleaning, shopping, cooking. Before leaving on my weekly trip to Princeton, New Jersey for school, I cooked meals so my husband had something to eat while I was gone: chicken cacciatore, pasta primavera, lasagna. Definite Italian influence. I labeled each Tupperware container and stacked them in the freezer.

This was my life in Texas as a minister's wife. I felt pleased with the role I had; it fulfilled religious and cultural values that I saw as meaningful. I don't remember it as oppressive; rather, I was living out a role that resonated with an aspect of my cultural heritage and my personality. My husband didn't ask me to make his meals; I prepared them out of my sense of caring and my ideal of being a good wife. Blaming him retroactively would be like burning the toast and blaming the toaster, when I was the one who'd put in the slice of bread, turned the dial, and forgotten to check on it. Later I would become conscious of the underlying collective attitudes and patriarchal beliefs that influenced the dynamic between us.

Every once in a while, I heard Psyche's longing to live more closely to my introverted, earthy, creative nature, to discover my own differentiated path in the world. In mythology, Psyche (Soul) is a human longing for her Beloved, the God Eros (Beloved). Psyche is the feminine archetype of soul, sent on a journey of consciousness by

Aphrodite, the goddess of Love, in order to be ripened for union with the Beloved. The challenge of Psyche's journey is to become her own person, to see her own face as it is, not as "they" say it is or should be. The Christian theologian C. S. Lewis wrote of Psyche's journey in his book *Till We Have Faces*. Psyche has to become her true self before surrendering to the Self.

This longing for self-realization was deeply buried in my unconscious. Occasionally, it burst into conscious life as a strong anger and frustration at others, especially my husband. Anger was the energy of an unlived part of the soul that needed to be acknowledged and given its voice, but as a young minister's wife, I judged anger a sin and worked hard to suppress it; its message went unheard.

On Monday mornings, my husband dropped me off at the airport and I took two flights and a train to arrive in Princeton, New Jersey. It was a long commute across the country, but the time I spent alone was worth it. The school gave me a doctoral fellowship that covered all the costs to commute from Texas and rent a small student apartment in Princeton. For two days each week, I went to class, wrote papers, poured myself into my studies, and contemplated life's ultimate questions. I felt at home in the introverted and rarefied atmosphere. I could explore anything I wanted, inwardly, through books and contemplation, though the commitment to my church kept me from any outward exploration of other religions or lifestyles. I spent hour after hour in the reading rooms of the Firestone Memorial Library, sometimes falling asleep over a pile of books. I was drawn to the refined energy of the place. Walking into the library, with its grand arches and high ceiling, was like entering a basilica. There was an atmosphere of quiet devotion that, as an energy field, was more resonant to my soul than the church life back home. Reluctantly, on Wednesday morning, I left the hallowed halls of advanced theological study, took trains and planes back to Texas, and resumed my role as a minister's wife.

In the summer months, when there were no doctoral seminars at Princeton, I stayed in Texas. In addition to fulfilling my role as minister's wife, I taught myself a reading knowledge of French and German, the modern languages required for theological study. I also worked two jobs: I was a waitress at the local Wagon Wheel steakhouse, and a tour guide at an extensive underground cave. I enjoyed the language study, tolerated the cave job, and dreaded the waitress job.

A chasm was growing in me between the Princeton life of intellect and the Texas life of ministry. I tried my best to be present in the life with my husband, but I was cut off from the root of my own nature and thus incapable of loving another person. I was also changing in ways neither one of us could have foreseen. The river of life sometimes carries people in unexpected directions, and even the best efforts to travel in the same boat are no guarantee of arriving together. I would come to discover that, in human love relationships, inner perseverance is an asset, while permanence of outer form is an illusion. Love, if it's true, endures even as inner growth occurs and outer forms change.

Neither was I fully present to the opportunity of the doctoral program. I did the requirements for the degree, but I kept to myself. After class, peers invited me to the local pub where grad students gathered in friendship, with lively discussions of theology and philosophy late into the night. They mentioned the highlights of their discoveries in class the next day. I was intrigued but always turned down their invitation, "No, thanks, I need to study." My longing for solitude was greater than my need for friendship. I preferred the company of books to people, perhaps because I felt I had more control. If I didn't like a book, if it said something disagreeable to me, I could close it. Put it back on the shelf. What would I do at the pub, with real people? I had become closed off from the world. In my role as a minister's wife, church members were the only people in my social circle. "Be ye not unequally yoked with unbelievers" was the teaching of the church (II Corinthians 6:14). Even though this kind of exclusivity didn't sit well with me, I had nowhere else to stand.

I was in a religious no-man's land. I no longer believed all the teachings of the church, yet, psychologically, I was too paralyzed to leave it.

# PSYCHOLOGICAL PARALYSIS

What had happened? How to explain this descent into psychological paralysis, with its literal muteness? As a child, according to family legend and photo albums, I loved to be center stage in spontaneous performances for neighbors and visitors to our home. As a young teenager, before the minister had confused the Light with the devil and callously dismissed that profound experience, I won awards for public speaking, spelling bees, and singing competitions. I thought nothing of standing in front of large audiences to give a speech or sing solos, but by the time I was twenty-eight, sitting in doctoral seminars with fewer than ten students, I felt petrified, too terrified to open my mouth.

The minister's pronouncement many years previous still haunted me. The church commanded, "Women must be silent in the church." Such inculcations were like tape over my mouth, but the real oppressor was the something inside that kept me from reaching up and tearing off the tape. It was as if my arms were caught in a sticky inner glue and couldn't move. Rationally, it seemed an easy step simply to speak up, but willpower alone was insufficient, as anyone who has suffered stage fright, depression, or addiction knows well. Something can sound reasonable—such as "just stop drinking" or "just speak up"—yet be impossible. For the life of me, I could not reach up and pull the tape off my mouth.

Unable to assimilate the experience of the Light and its aftermath at age fifteen, I had succumbed to fear and the need for security. In all matters of life, I looked to external authorities to tell me how to be and what to do. Psychologically, I was in a dangerous place. I had given up my inner truth, letting others speak for me. Graduate study in theology was planting new seeds in the depths of me—intuitions, questions—and it would take time for them to grow. Just as a gardener doesn't yank up seeds from the soil to see if they're sprouting, so I wasn't able to speak about an inner germination process. My intuitive knowing sounded vague compared to the church's concrete logic. It was easier to defer to my husband and other male leaders in the church. They said and taught things that didn't ring true for me, but I lacked the words to articulate why. After a while, I stopped trying. "You lose what you don't use." By the time I was twenty-eight, I had nearly lost my voice.

As a doctoral student, I was cut off from my heart and Higher Self, my true nature. When people live close to their true nature, we experience relief in their presence. They exude a feeling of naturalness and freedom. Because they've come to peace about themselves, they don't need approval from others and can speak freely from their heart. Those who are self-complete can be self-giving. They move with spontaneous ease. From an inner journey, they have come to know what is truly true. They have nothing to prove or hide, guard or defend, and thus are an open book; all their energy is available to give to others. This is the experience I had of being with the people featured in this book. Though their personalities and backgrounds are very different, they are all transparent and natural.

In contrast, I was severely constricted; those who are insecure are self-absorbed and in need of affirmation and security from others. Professor Douglass encouraged discussion in her seminars, but I couldn't overcome my speaking phobia. As oppressive as the prison of fear was, it was the only safe place I knew. I've since talked with people who are incarcerated and express their fear of leaving prison because, as one man told me, "I wouldn't be able to handle the freedom. Here, I know the rules and routines. I don't have to think for myself. I'm told what to do, what to wear, where to go and when."

Indeed it had been a regressive relief to turn my life over to religious leaders who seemed to know what was best. I hoped they could save me from myself, protect me from the power of Love, the pillar of Light. Giving up individual responsibility for my life, however, turned out to be an illusion. In the end, "every hair is counted," as the Bible says, and I was accountable for my life and its singular potential. One day, I would have to stop putting my life into the hands of others, however benevolent I thought they were. One day, I would have to leave my self-created prison and accept the challenge of conscience and freedom—I would have to say *yes* to the risky business of living. There was help on the horizon.

## GLIMPSING THE SHADOW: CARRY A. NATION

It was a firebrand from Kansas who encouraged me to find my voice. I wrote my doctoral dissertation on Carry Nation (d. 1911), an icon of American social reform and leader of the early prohibition movement. She was America's premier killjoy and booze-buster! In the famous photograph of her, she boasts a Bible in one hand and a hatchet in the other. She justified her destruction of illegal saloons on moral grounds. Carry Nation was my alter ego, my shadow side. Whereas I could barely vocalize my ideas to close family members, she had no problem speaking her opinions loudly to the American public—and backing them up with a hatchet!

In writing about Nation, I learned not only about American history but also about myself. Strong attractions are revealing. It's no accident whom we fall in love with, which books call to us from the library or bookstore shelf, or what places make our hearts sing. Something within is guiding us. I remember walking through the stacks on a deserted floor at the Princeton library and feeling an electric current as my hand reached out and pulled Carry Nation's autobiography from the shelf. I was, in a sense, walking through the stacks in my own unconscious and reaching out for an avenue of self-discovery I didn't know I needed.

In the early 1900s, illegal saloons operated in every town in her home state of Kansas, and Nation viewed them as "dens of vice" run by "swill-faced, beak-nosed, donkey bedmates of Satan." She took the moral ruination of the nation into her own hands and launched a "smashing crusade" against the saloons. Just as Jesus had expelled the moneychangers from the temple, she declared, she was destined to smash "saloonacy." Dubbed Cyclone Carry, she stormed into saloons with rocks hidden in her alpaca dress and a hatchet in hand.

She hurled the rocks into mirrors and laid her hatchet into counter-tops and beer kegs. Beer spewed everywhere, much to the delight of drinkers, who egged her on. She destroyed paintings and statues of naked women, such as *Cleopatra at Bath*. Her "hatchetation" move-ment galvanized law-abiding citizens into temperance vigilantes who descended upon saloons and barrooms all across the Midwest with hatchets and rocks. Even the mild-mannered Charles Sheldon, influ-ential minister and author of the still-popular phrase "What Would Jesus Do?" became "Nation-ized" and joined the ranks of Carry Nation's hatchet brigade in Topeka, Kansas. "Malicious destruction of property" was the charge that landed these anti-alcohol temperance crusaders in jail. Nation was jailed at least thirty-one times. She clev-erly rephrased the offense as "destruction of malicious property." She became a Broadway and Vaudeville celebrity, particularly charismatic when she played herself in the popular temperance drama *Ten Nights in a Barroom*, which reviewers cheekily renamed "Ten Barrooms in a night" due to her decimation of décor.

What drew me to this puritanical vigilante crusader? She was inflated with her religious mission and hyperbolic in her claims to know by divine dictation what was morally right for others. Her cru-sade was coercive and repressive. A hatchet, after all! She marched through the streets at the head of her "Home Defenders Army," blan-dishing her hatchet and waving her Bible.

I had to come face to face with the shadow sides to my own per-sonality that Carry Nation embodied, both negative and positive. It wasn't easy to see my own moral superiority. As is generally true with "do-gooderism," Nation's crusade created more problems than it solved. Force leads to counterforce. This is seen in the polarizing effect of well-intentioned moral crusades on both sides of the polit-ical spectrum. I had to accept that the same judgmental, self-right-eous crusader was also in me. The ego loves to be right and to impose its views on others.

Carry Nation's story showed the shadow side of my own mor-alism: self-righteous judgmentalism. She was not, however, only a "blue-nosed, pinch-faced Puritan," as some journalists called her. She possessed many qualities that endeared her to the public and even to the saloon folks—bartenders, drinkers, prostitutes—who noted her concrete demonstrations of material support for the drinkers' families. Decades earlier, in her twenties, Nation had lost her first husband to alcoholism and suffered a heartbreak that nearly killed her. She never forgot the destitution and sorrow that went along with alcohol abuse, and she gave what she could to those who suffered. Whenever she delivered a public speech, she donated the proceeds to the local poor of that city, including prostitutes working the streets, and the wives of alcoholics. She was not a well-off person, yet was ready to share what she had with others. Her compassion extended to animals. Several accounts exist of her buying overworked donkeys and sick horses and giving them a retirement in green and peaceful pastures. In her last years, she moved to Eureka Springs, Arkansas, and bought a large house that she opened as a home for battered women.

Carry Nation was refreshingly open-minded in certain arenas. In contrast to many Protestant Americans of her time, she genuinely respected the faith and practices of Catholics and Jews and others whose religious beliefs differed from hers. She was one of the first women to practice osteopathy, a branch of medicine that she found compatible with her experience as a midwife. Rain or shine, she rode her horse and carriage all over the trails of Kansas and the Territory of Oklahoma, delivering babies and preaching sermons. In terms of her passionate outspokenness, she was my shadow side. She was no prisoner of inner fear, no captive of people's disapproval. "Women must be silent in the church" was a Bible verse that she decided did not apply to her.

And, so, like us all, Carry Nation had many different dimensions. Her generosity toward the poor existed alongside her rigidity toward alcohol. What she called her divine mission existed alongside her ecumenical spirit. As any biographer comes to realize, we humans are all works in progress, in which both our defects and our greatness coexist in splendid and sometimes uneven harmony. We can keep saying yes to what is most positive and loving in ourselves, and "appreciate that every step forward benefits everyone."[81]

I successfully defended my doctoral dissertation "with honors" and turned it into a book that reviewers lauded as "the landmark biography" of one of America's most memorable figures. In 2001, a call came from Washington, D.C., inviting me there for an hour-long interview on the national broadcast program *Booknotes* hosted by Brian Lamb, founder of C-SPAN. He surprised me by ending the program with a personal question: "Are you religious?" By that point, years after graduation from Princeton, I had left the church. I said, "I am not a member of any organized church or religion or spiritual group."

Seven years earlier, when I had begun research on the biography of Carry Nation, I was a silent, submissive woman whose life revolved around her husband's ministry, too petrified even to speak in a small group of classmates. A cloud of regressive forces veiled the inner Light of love, life, and laughter. It was like sitting alone in a prison cell with no windows. By the time I finished the book and the C-SPAN interview, a transformation had occurred. I found it a joyous experience to speak for an hour on national television with no script or advance notice of the questions. What accounts for such a drastic transformation, which some might even call a "miracle"?

In sum, the risk to leave the prison of the familiar finally seemed less terrifying than staying in it. Love opened a door when I could not. Love gave me the courage to leave the place where I no longer belonged, and I ran—dancing—toward an inner voice that called me by my true name.

"God dignifies us by giving us freedom," Huston Smith told me as I sat with him in his living room. He had followed that inner voice that called to him by his true name. He was ninety-two and finishing his last book, *And Live Rejoicing!* He had paved the road that I was beginning to walk upon. He had lived as a scholar *and* a seeker, and saw no conflict between the two. As I sat with him, his joy was palpable.

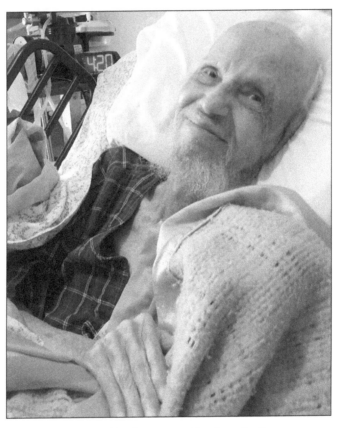

Huston Smith at 97, smiling beatifically
(courtesy of Phil Cousineau, longtime friend and collaborator,
who took the photo shortly before Huston passed).

## Chapter Eight

# OUR WORK AS A PATH OF LOVE

## Encounter with Huston Smith

*At the center of religious life is a particular kind of joy....*
*the human opportunity, the religions tell us,*
*is to transform our flashes of insight into abiding light.*

—HUSTON SMITH

## MEETING A MENTOR

In 2011, I helped arrange for our university to host ten Tibetan
Buddhist monks for a three-day visit to our campus. In their
closing ceremony for the Sand Painting Mandala Exhibition, the
monks performed their multiphonal chanting before a live audience
of hundreds. The sound was ethereal—overtones vibrating from each
set of vocal chords. The chanting of the Tibetan monks was unknown
to Westerners until 1964, when a young religious studies scholar
from America was exploring religion in the Himalayas and heard a
sound he'd never heard before. Enchanted, he followed the sound to a
monastery hidden in the hills, and was astonished at what he saw: a
single monk chanting more than one note at a time.

That adventurer was Huston Smith, and his recording of the monks' "throat singing" became a landmark in musicology. It was precisely during the ceremony of multiphonal chanting at the university that he called and left a voicemail message saying he'd be happy to meet me and be interviewed for this book. Two months later, I pulled up to his home in Berkeley, California, and the first things I noticed were a palette of colors in the flowerbeds and Tibetan prayer flags fluttering in the breeze. The place looked charming. At the front door I saw several pairs of shoes lined along the porch, including those of little children. The door opened and a Tibetan man welcomed me in. "Just one moment," he said and disappeared. I learned later that this man and three generations of his family lived with the Smiths.

I looked around the front room. *Thangkas* (Tibetan Buddhist paintings) graced the walls. Fresh flowers scented the room. It was an atmosphere of devotion and calm. I knew that this home had seen its fair share of human suffering. Huston and Kendra had lost their eldest daughter to cancer, and a granddaughter had died in mysterious circumstances. Huston himself, due to physical decline, had recently spent many months in an assisted care facility and the separation from Kendra had felt like a dark night of loneliness. Yet through these difficulties, his wonder at life did not dim, it deepened. His autobiography, *Tales of Wonder*, inspires with its abiding optimism. Even in the assisted care facility, he woke up each morning with the wish to cheer another human being.

When the goal is to love, every day has meaning. Standing in this home, I felt the contented atmosphere of people who had loved daily and widely.

My spell was broken when a large dog ran up to greet me, wagging his tail with vigor and licking my hand, then rolling over on his back as I reached out to pet him. "Oh, you've met Bobbie!" Huston Smith walked in, a tall man whose dignity was undiminished by his use of a walker. I was taken by his sparkling blue eyes, diffuse with Light. It was as if we'd known each other a long time. "Let's get comfortable," he said, and guided me into the living room where he took a seat in what I gathered was his favorite chair, near a window looking out over the neighborhood street. When I sat at a respectful distance, he motioned me to come closer.

"I am providentially well, but the aging process is coming to me through my hearing." I ended up pulling my chair right in front of him, so close that our knees touched. We held hands for a bit as he looked at me keenly. "You look so familiar—haven't we met before?"

"No but meeting you fulfills a dream I've had my whole career. I want to thank you. Your life and writings have been a major inspiration."

Years previous, when I read his classic bestseller *The World's Religions*—still the standard textbook in college-level comparative religion classes—I thought: *Here is the mentor I've been looking for.* I was just beginning my career in the field of religious studies and was already disheartened by the scorn of spiritual life that I found in the academy. "If these books cannot liberate you from yourself, what is the purpose of them?" That's what the Sufi mystic Shams is said to have asked Rūmī, leading theologian of his time. In our time, perhaps no scholar better exemplified the quest for liberation than Huston Smith.[82]

Huston lived his life as a love affair, and this was a good example for me. When Viktor Frankl visited Harvard University, Huston asked him how to teach values. Frankl answered: "Values cannot be taught; values must be lived. Nor can meaning be given; what a teacher can give to his students is not meaning but rather an *example*, the personal example of his own dedication and devotion to the cause of research, truth, and science...."[83] This is what Huston did—he taught me by example.

Huston's best-selling book, he said, came out of *listening* to each religion expressing itself to the divine. He presented the best of each religion rather than its failings. Huston acknowledged the downside of religions but agreed with Sri Ramakrishna, Hindu saint, that religion was like a cow that both kicks and gives milk; the milk, Huston decided, was worth writing about. In this regard, he was similar to Viktor Frankl and Mother Teresa, who saw the hidden goodness in whatever or whomever was in front of them.

THE POWER OF LOVE

In 2007, when Huston Smith was eighty-eight, the American Academy of Religion recognized his contributions to the field. As I stood there in the packed ballroom adding my little echo to the thundering applause, I sensed we were honoring him not only for his many intellectual achievements—fourteen books, a library of PBS videos, countless articles, keynote lectures, awards and honorary degrees, and a reach of public influence that few scholars before or since enjoy—but also applauding the greatness of a man who had lived the principles he studied. His decades of research had shed light on what he termed the "primordial tradition" or "universal grammar of worldviews," and he daily sought to live its principles of peace, love, humility, self-inquiry, gratitude for life, and understanding of others. Love, he said, meant listening to others.

When I visited Huston in his home, he was ninety-two, a world-renowned figure. He had a hearing aid, but he was still listening—even to a young scholar-cum-seeker unsure of her questions. Physically he was frail, but the radiation of goodness was tangible. In my thirty years in the academic field of religious studies, I had not experienced that energy field coming from a fellow scholar. Call it charisma or aura or love, it was the unmistakable ambience of an opened heart; his towering intellect was in service to the heart's immeasurable graces. In *The World's Religions,* Huston had written that "a particular kind of joy" was at the center of religions. He seemed to have found it.

## TALES OF WONDER

His love affair (as he called it) with religion began in his childhood, growing up in China among Methodist missionaries and surrounded by practitioners of diverse Asian religions. He did his academic training at the University of Chicago Divinity School, and it was also there that he fell in love with the daughter of his favorite professor. Huston and Kendra married in 1943, and for seven decades she joined him in his adventures to study religions around the world and practice them in their home. Intuitive and discerning, she

146

kept his feet on the ground even while accepting him as a "mystic at heart."

Huston remained a Christian his entire life and found that his practice of other traditions enlarged his sense of the Sacred. In 1947, he began a decade of study and practice with Swami Satprakashananda in the Hindu Vedanta tradition. Inspired by the Indian saint Ramakrishna and brought to America by his great disciple, Swami Vivekananda, the Vedanta tradition transmits the message of "One Truth, Many Paths." *The Gospel of Sri Ramakrishna* recounts the inner breakthroughs that led to this realization. Huston, like me, had been lit by reading mystical texts. He referred to mystics like Ramakrishna as "the advance scouts of mankind," for they had attained the goal of human life: direct realization of Truth. When I went on pilgrimage to various Vedanta sites in Calcutta where Ramakrishna and his disciples experienced the Divine, I found it remarkable that Ramakrishna had experienced Universal Truth without leaving the temple he lived in for most of his life. If we surrender our whole being to the Divine, he taught, we can know the universe without going anywhere. "The kingdom of God is within you" Jesus said. The primordial tradition that Huston spent his life uncovering says that Ultimate Reality goes by many names—Absolute, Godhead, Ground of Being, Brahman, Self, the Real—but the Reality is the same.

Different clay vessels are made from the same clay, according to this view. The purpose of spiritual practice is to realize that we are the substance of the clay and not only the form we see. Hence the statement "I am *That*." *That* is the Self, the life force in all things. In the *Kena Upanishad*, the student asks, "What is it that makes my mind to think, my eyes to see, my ears to hear?" The teacher answers, "The Self is the ear of the ear, the eye of the eye, the mind of the mind."

The substrate of existence is the same Self in all that exists, and it is delusion not to see that primal oneness. Huston heard a similar teaching from indigenous Onondaga chief Oren Lyons by way of a story. When he had come back from a short time of college study, Oren's uncle asked him, "Oren, who are you?" Oren answered, "Your nephew," and other outer aspects. The uncle rejected each answer.

Finally, he asked Oren to look around him at the mountain bluff, the pine tree, and the water in the lake. "That's what you are, Oren"— mountain bluff, tree, and water. All of life is sacred, and we are one with that life.

Huston devoted himself to learning the techniques of contemplative prayer, yoga, and meditation laid out by the mystics of various traditions. His process was to learn the texts of a tradition, practice its rituals and techniques, and put himself at the feet of a verified teacher who transmitted the energy of the lineage. Following his decade of Vedanta under the guidance of Swami Satprakashananda, Huston spent a decade of Buddhist practice under a Zen master at a strict monastery in Japan. Reading was not allowed and philosophy not valued. Inner experience was what mattered, and if a meditator dozed off during practice, a stick was used to bring him back to attention. Huston's intellect, brilliant as it was, could not break the riddle of the *koan* he was given. The insight had to come from another dimension of his being. The analytical mind is part and parcel of the ego and cannot be relied upon to transcend itself. If one lets go of ordinary reasoning, there is a noetic way of knowing that is described as revelation because it occurs spontaneously when the effort of thinking is relinquished.

Huston may not have attained *satori* through meditation or yoga, but he glimpsed the Great Reality when he took two tabs of mescaline in Dr. Timothy Leary's home on January 1, 1961. Leary, a professor in Harvard's Center for Personality Research, was testing the effect of non-addictive mind-altering chemicals—mescaline, LSD, psilocybin (all legal at the time)—on human behavior. The phenomena in Leary's living room left Huston in a state of terrifying awe and confirmed the truth of the mystic experience. He saw the levels of reality that he had read about in Vedanta and Plotinus: An unbroken Clear Light with its glorious fracturing into multiple bands and layers of light and emanations of worlds within worlds both timeless and inside of time. Though he eventually decided to stick with his pursuit of enlightenment via religious practice, he remained an advocate for the legalization of ritual peyote in the Native American Church.

Huston's adventures into ecstasy and unitive reality continued with a decade of practice in Sufism. He was initiated into the Sufi Maryamiyya Order under the guidance of Frithjof Schuon, a profound mystical thinker who integrated the living esoteric wisdoms of Native Americans, Marian spirituality, Christian mysticism, Sufism, and Vedanta. When Huston read *Transcendent Unity of Religions*, he felt Schuon to be a sure guide to the Truth he sought. Importantly, Schuon valued the mystical path but advised Huston to keep it private as most people are not interested in esotericism and may find it a stumbling block. Huston was intrigued by this gnostic atmosphere. He danced with dervishes in the secret world of underground Sufism in Iran, made pilgrimage to Rūmī's tomb in Konya, and did the *salat* (five daily Muslim prayers) until back pain made the prostrations impossible.

In Sufi teaching, he found another confirmation of the essential oneness of Reality. Ever since 1947, when he began his friendship with Aldous Huxley, famous philosopher and author of *The Perennial Philosophy*, Huston had probed the idea that while religions have different outer expressions, their essence is the same. Though many academics vehemently criticized him, he insisted on the primordial or universal truths innate to all wisdom traditions. As he liked to say, religions are like a walnut. The shell is the "exoteric" form we see from the outside. From this view, religions are of course very different, but on the inside, the "esoteric" kernel is the same.

When I heard Huston say this, I thought of Meister Eckhart's saying, "If you seek the kernel, you must break the shell." By the time I met Huston in person, many of the shells I'd believed in had broken. Though I hadn't gotten to the kernel, I'd long given up the idea that the shells were all I was looking for.

# CONVERSATION WITH HUSTON SMITH

## Love Affair with Life

Q: Obviously you are a lover of life. When you describe your work—the universal truths found in all the world's religions—you say you are sharing with others what you love.

HS: That's a fair statement. In fact, a chapter in my final book, which is nearly complete, is: "Love Affair with the World."

Q: We read your *Tales of Wonder* last month in a course on religions, and the students were captivated by your life story and how you practiced several different religions even as you remained a Christian.

HS: We do what we can. If it turns out to serve some purpose, all the better. So you are a professor; do you enjoy it?

Q: I love what I do.

HS: Yes, I see that you do. We are blessed because we get to teach and turn our mind and our attention to lofty topics. Some people work at engineering, or how to make a better mousetrap, etc., but we get to dwell our mind and our soul on lofty matters!

## Love and Human Freedom

HS: You asked to discuss love with me. First I would like to know: What are *your* thoughts of love?

Q: You're going to interview me?!

HS: We have to start somewhere, why not with you?
 (*Laughter.*)

Q: That it's everywhere.

HS: Well, now, that takes a little cogitation. Give me a moment. The one that's in the news now. Bin Laden. How do you link love to him—if love is everywhere?

Q: Though hateful of others, perhaps Bin Laden serves love by confronting us with the choice to love or not. Do I return hate with hate, or is there another way? If the world had only loving people in it, then how would I learn to forgive? People like Bin Laden present me with a chance to struggle to choose love in the face of hatred.

HS: Are you saying that love is in all of humanity, throughout all creation?

Q: Perhaps in gradations? In your writings you reference the Great Chain of Being that goes from lowest to highest levels of awareness. In terms of loving, someone like Bin Laden seems only capable of egocentric, narcissistic self-love, but at the other end of the scale, the Dalai Lama is capable of unconditional, compassionate, selfless love. Love is present everywhere, but expressed in different degrees, from total selfishness to self-transcendence.

HS: That could be true.

Q: Now please tell me how *you* put together Divine Love and the existence of a Bin Laden.

HS: I say that God dignifies us by giving us freedom. Being omnipotent, He could have made us like puppets on a string, never making any mistakes. But who wants to be a puppet? He dignified us by endowing us with freedom. That means that we have the power to choose, and from that, it follows that we can make wrong choices. And I think Bin Laden for reasons best known to him has made lots of wrong choices.

Q: Your statement says better with a few words what I couldn't say with many!

(*Laughter…*)

Q: Now, in several of your books, you identify the path of the mystic as your path. For the mystic, it seems, there is a spiritual plane from which all events unfold. Maybe that bears upon our topic of Bin Laden? David Bohm, the quantum physicist, refers to it as the "implicate order." I think in your writing you compare Bohm's idea to Vedanta's Brahman and Meister Eckhart's Ground of Being—that enfolded, timeless, spaceless, unseen Reality, out of which the "explicate" physical world unfolds….

HS: Kendra and I knew David Bohm. In fact I have a true story about him. His wife Saral told us this final anecdote. They had a habit that, when David was about to leave his office at 5 p.m. to go home, he would call her. On this particular day, he said, "Saral, it's been an exciting day! I think I'm onto something!" He hung up, hailed a cab, then died on the ride. I have often wondered whether with his words, "I think I'm onto something," if there was a little prescience there, sort of a foresight into what was happening. Perhaps it shows a link between the "implicate" and "explicate" orders he wrote about. In colloquial terms, "intuition."

(*Peaceful silence.*)

HS: I've spoken. Now it's your turn.

## Lessons from the Dying

Q: Your anecdote about David Bohm brings up the subject of death and dying.

HS: Yes.

Q: People who have near death experiences speak of an "Infinite Love" at death that they enter into—ineffable yet palpable. They often come back from that experience very changed because they learned that the main purpose of earthly life was to love.

HS:   I haven't had a near death experience, but people write to me about theirs. They know that I'm interested in innumerable facets of life in the world. And one of the letters said, "I have just come back to the world from a powerful near-death experience. And I want to write to you about it." He said that he went through three stages. The first stage was just like a tape recorder moving through the major experiences of his life, as if it had all been recorded in detail. Then it went back to the beginning. The second time he went through major experiences of life again, but it was painful because he saw and felt all of the places where he had produced suffering in other people. Then, back to the beginning, and the third stage was going through the same sequence but this time, those incidents or episodes where he had caused suffering to other people was not painful because he saw that he was forgiven. I think there's an adage: "To err is human, to forgive Divine."

Q:   Huston Smith, are you at peace with dying?

HS:   Yes, I am. I will be ninety-two at the end of this month. As far as I'm aware, I am not afraid of dying. If there's physical pain, there are now medications that take care of that. As far as psychological pain, as far as I'm aware, I am at peace with myself. I've had a wonderful life, wonderful family, loving family, loving companions. Currently, we share this big house with loving companions—a Tibetan family. It's a big house and we don't need all of it. So we share it with a Tibetan family, and we have three generations here. We don't charge them rent and they return their gratitude by doing all kinds of things. You may have noticed that our Tibetan friend let you in. He drives me everywhere. And in the morning, when I wake up, I find on my dresser a large container of tea. All I have to do is roll out of bed, go to the bathroom and have my tea.

## Spiritual Devotion

Q:   How do you start your day?

HS:   My day begins with about twenty minutes of what I call my quiet time. I start with a passage from the Bible. Throughout my life, I've read the scriptures of the world's great traditions. Right now, I've worked my way into II Thessalonians. Having refreshed my soul with biblical content, I then pray. I pray first of all that the members of my immediate family may have a rewarding and productive day. Then I pray for associates who are in need. Maybe they're ill or having some kind of family mix-up; I pray for those acquaintances who are in need. Then I pray for myself, because there is an old revival hymn— "Not my preacher, not my brother, but it's me, Oh. Lord, standing in the need of prayer." (*We sing it together.*) Then, when I've done that, I go back to my tea. And what about you? Are you a believer? Do you have a tradition?

Q:   Yes.

HS:   What is it?

Q:   As to religion, I'm a member of the Episcopal Church, though I spent much of my early adult life in a fundamentalist sect. Spiritually, my primary path is with a teacher I met many years ago. He doesn't promote any particular religion per se and respects the core principles of all of them. He teaches a path of direct realization. He opened my heart to Love.

HS:   Good. I'm a Methodist whose father's name was Wesley! What chance did I have? You may know that my parents were Methodist missionaries in China. So I was imprinted with that, and it's fine. I have no complaint, but I am, as I suspect you are, a "universalist" in that there are many paths to God; Christ and Christianity is only one. One of our daughters converted to Judaism, and that was wonderful because while she was still in the area, we would have Seder together. My first one was an eye-opener because I thought religious observances should be solemn. Well, the Seder was certainly serious, but it was not at all solemn! I loved hearing the youngest child ask, "Why is this night different from all other nights?" Then the libations begin to flow—wonderful!

Q: In *Tales of Wonder*, you write about this daughter, Karen, and her dying. You describe a night that you spent in the room with her body after she passed. It was a spiritual experience that was very powerful for you.

HS: I remember that! Powerful. I've written so much and often forget what I wrote. But I remember that very well. Yes, it was a powerful evening. Unforgettable.

Q: Would you say there was a presence of Love there?

HS: Absolutely! So thick you could have cut it. Love and Peace and—this won't surprise *you,* though it would surprise many—Gratitude. There was Gratitude.
   *(Peaceful silence.)*

Q: It can't be spoken?

HS: Such things are hard to describe.

Q: You say it well in the last pages of *Tales of Wonder:* In relation to the Infinite we stand as less than a simple protein in a single cell on a human finger. Though it is alive, that protein cannot know the cell in which it lives ... we are born in mystery, we live in mystery, and we die in mystery.

HS: Yes. I've written many words about That which is unwritable.
   *(Peaceful silence.)*

HS: What do you have in the way of family?

Q: My father died three years ago at ninety, and my mother... Her body is still here in the world, but she has no mental functioning and she can't communicate. She has Parkinson's and dementia. She doesn't recognize any of us.

HS: That's sad.

Q: Well...

HS: That was a wise "Well"! My college roommate was someone with whom we kept in close touch for the rest of his life. His wife had Alzheimer's. So also did the wife of one of my colleagues at Washington University, and he wrote a book about it. In a way, it's good he poured his soul into the book, as it seems to have helped him get through. But when I sent his book to the other friend of mine when his wife developed Alzheimer's, and I asked him what he thought about it, he said, "That man did not understand Alzheimer's at all. It's true that their logical thinking is gone, but their aesthetic sense is still there!" And so, when my friend was not involved in his labors, he spent his time and weekends wheel-chairing his wife to museums and taking her to symphonies and opera.

Q: I found that to be very true about the aesthetic sense. When I visited Mom last week, I sang to her and played music for her. She couldn't talk to me in normal conversation, but she knew the language of love and music. I played familiar songs such as *The Lord's Prayer*, and she sang it; also Nat King Cole songs from her younger years, and she knew all the words. The music took her into a different realm of connection and meaning. I planted flowers outside her window because she likes the color and the beauty of plants.

HS: I think you surfed that very difficult problem superbly. Bringing joy out of the pain for both of you. So, whom are you living with now, or are you alone?

## Marriage vs. Monastic Life

Q: I have a wonderful family life. To be truthful, though, I'm inclined to be a hermit. I love solitude.

HS: Are you saying that a part of you feels like you'd be very happy being a hermit, but that's not for this lifetime, and that the companionship is also good?

Q: Yes, you state it perfectly.

HS: Speaking of hermits, I have a little story about Thomas Merton. Would you like to hear it?

Q: Of course!

HS: I was invited to an ecumenical interfaith conference in Calcutta.[84] I sent my regrets, "Thanks for thinking of me, but it's a long way and I've been to many such conferences." Then I got another mailing and it listed the people who had accepted. Merton was on the list, so I quickly reversed myself: "I made a mistake! I'm coming!" The conference was to begin at a hotel in Calcutta; the convening time was 5 p.m. the day before the conference officially opened. So promptly at 5, I went down to the lawn, and I saw a man sipping a soft drink alone at a table. I went up and said, "Excuse me, I'm Huston Smith. Are you Thomas Merton?" He had a lovely smile. "Yes." I'd been lying in wait for him! He was the most famous person at the conference and would be under great demand, so I thought I'd talk to him while I had the chance. We quickly fell into first names: "Tom, I could never be a monk. The man-woman thing is just too strong in me. But I do have a monastic streak. Really, they're both so strong I could have two lives. What's it like to be a monk?"

"Well, it's very nice," he said. That surprised me!

"But what about those three vows?" I asked.

"Oh, those... poverty is a snap, chastity is a little harder, but it's manageable. Obedience... obedience is a booger!"

We spent a surprising amount of time together. The closing event was to be televised and so they asked him to give the closing homily in clerical garb. He said, "I feel like I'm in costume in this garb! Usually I wear dungarees and a flannel shirt." Then he went on to give a letter-perfect, twelve-minute homily. He said, "I am here to represent the people who don't count"—the poor, the poets, and a third group I can't remember. He ended by saying, "And I want to offer you a small message of hope." To paraphrase, he said that, as long as there are people on the margins who are selfless and faithful to their calling, even in the face of great sacrifice and risk, then life will go on and unity will be possible. When the conference was over, we left on a plane to New Delhi and sat together as planned. We were slap-happy and had a lot of fun! Then the plane landed. We embraced and wished each other a safe journey. I headed north to the Tibetans. And he headed to Bangkok and to his imminent death... electrocuted by a live wire. His objective, as you know, was to build bridges to monks in other traditions.

Q: You weren't a monk this lifetime—you were married over sixty years—so I want to ask you about marital love. In addition to different temperaments and life callings, you and Kendra survived a lot of difficulty: financial struggles, different backgrounds, the loss of a daughter and granddaughter, your own aging process... what can you share about this personal dimension of love?

HS: We've been married sixty-seven years. Here is my response to your question. Warren Harding was not a great president, but he had a way with words. In his autobiography, when he came to his marriage, he said, "So much drivel has been written on this subject that it will pay to be brief. We thought we were made for each other. And for forty years, she has born my infirmities and I have rejoiced in her graces."

Q: Yes, I imagine that only grace, one toward another, makes such a long marriage possible. You've written that personal love is a window to Divine Love. How is that the case in your experience?

HS:   Well, we were made in the image of the Divine, and God is Love, and He has created loving creatures whose natural tendency is to be drawn into loving relation. It's simply a misfiring when that doesn't happen.

Q:   You and Kendra were successful in a way that most people aren't.

HS:   We were blessed. One of our daughters was in Germany, and a friend took her to a very highly regarded psychic. He told her, "The first thing you should know is that your parents love each other." She said, "So?" And he said, "You'd be surprised at how rare that is." I don't know whether I believe it's rare or not, but it's certainly true of us.

Q:   I agree with the psychic!

As I was leaving, Huston said, "When the eagle leaves the other eagle in the nest, they say, Fare well wherever you fare." He kissed my hand, and I kissed his. This expression of affection was our recognition of each other as fellow travelers on the path of love. In the speech that had touched Huston so profoundly that he remembered it for fifty years, Thomas Merton said that communication at its deepest level was "communion." Even though we talked only for an hour, "communion" is what I sensed with Huston Smith.

Perhaps we touched the spirit of the prayer that Thomas Merton offered at the conference in Calcutta:

"Fill us then with love, and let us be bound together with love as we go our diverse ways, united in this one spirit which makes You present in the world, and which makes You witness to the ultimate reality that is love. Love has overcome. Love is victorious. Amen."

Huston had searched for love and found it. I was on the brink.

# PART TWO

# FINDING LOVE

The Ecstasy of St. Teresa of Avila by Gian Lorenzo Bernini,
Cornaro Chapel, Santa Maria della Vittoria, Rome. St. Teresa
(d. 1582) wrote *Interior Castle*, a masterpiece on the soul's journey
(photo by Napoleon Vier, Wikimedia Commons).

# Chapter Nine

# SPIRITUAL DIRECTION

As I finished my doctoral degree in religion, I found myself at a crossroads. The long years of academic study had exposed me to history, theology, comparative religion, and exegesis, yet it had veiled the Light. I longed for "flashes of insight" to be transformed into "abiding light," as Huston Smith said. Just as a monk had helped him make a necessary step, so too was it a monastic who helped me. I met a Jesuit priest who affirmed the Light.

The priest, Wilkie Au, was my spiritual director. I told him about my Light experience at age fifteen and the minister's pronouncement back then. He said, "That Light was the Presence of God, not the devil." I described all the panic, anxiety, and repression that ensued, and the feeling of being encased in a prison cell of silence. His heart was open to me, and I felt his compassion. He seemed to understand my dilemma. By outer measures, my life appeared successful, yet inside a strange darkness had swallowed me.

I'd made the appointment because the three-year training program in Spiritual Direction required it. My husband and I were among several Protestants in this program led by Catholic nuns. Ten years earlier, I was a missionary in Italy trying to convert Catholics, whom I considered apostates. Now I sought to learn about spiritual life from Catholics. The program was my first conscious exploration into spiritual life beyond the sectarian walls that had been my home since age seventeen. It wasn't an academic class but a spiritual community.

The monthly sessions at Mount St. Mary were like water in the desert to me. We read and learned about the Catholic mystics such as St. John of the Cross, St. Teresa of Avila, Meister Eckhart, and *The Cloud of Unknowing*, an anonymous work of Christian mysticism written in the latter half of the 14th century. We were asked to do a contemplative practice, and I chose the Jesus Prayer from Greek Orthodox tradition as one of my primary practices. "Lord Jesus Christ, have mercy on me." It is an inner prayer of the heart, reverberating silently on the rhythm of the breath. This prayer is said to have the power to bring peace, both within and among us. In the words of Father Pavlos, senior ascetic at St. Catherine's Monastery in Sinai, Egypt, where monks have practiced the Jesus Prayer for centuries: "The person who has *inner* peace will also have peace with those around him." When I interviewed him, I felt the truth of his words.

The Spiritual Direction program was based on this foundation: Inner peace leads to outer peace. It had been years since I'd felt inner peace. The sisters' lovingness was genuine and nonjudgmental, and I felt cared for as a soul. The teachings on contemplative prayer gave me a way to reconnect with the inner realm I'd known as a youth—before the steel door. Still, on the inside, I felt empty. The sisters explained: "Sometimes God sends consolations; other times, aridity."

"Arid"—the word did indeed describe my interior. I felt nothing when I prayed in the way taught by my church—petitionary prayer. This form of prayer involved talking to God, often giving a to-do list: "Help me with this, heal this, give me this," and so on. The traditions of my church felt dry. I was bored by the Bible studies and worship services. Every time I sat in church, I had a panic attack. I sat curled up, defeated by fear. I dreaded being in church but felt obligated to go. What was wrong with me? I was finishing a Ph.D. in religion, but had I lost my faith in the process? The sisters at the Spiritual Direction classes weren't concerned or surprised about the fact that I felt dead in my spiritual life. They seemed to nod in understanding, as if the malaise were something to be expected, and they kept saying the word "arid."

As I went through the program, I did occasionally touch into the peace of what the sisters called contemplative prayer. They taught us an apophatic mode of prayer that entailed dropping all names for and ideas about God. This sparseness was a relief. After eight years of graduate study in religion, I was tired of all the labels, names, and talking about God. All that we say of God cannot, finally, be what God is. The medieval prayer manual, *The Cloud of Unknowing*, recommended letting go of all concepts and dogma about God—even the holiest. We were told to gather our "naked intent" and "whole being" onto a single word such as "Love." This wordlessness was a relief from the mentalization of academia.

Still, the silence wasn't easy. My early religious indoctrination made me terrified to sit still; I'd been taught, "Sloth is the devil's gateway." This religious fear covered over a deep existential dread of silence, noted by 17th-century philosopher René Descartes, famous for his dictum "I think, therefore I am." After a series of mental experiments, he decided that the certainty of his existence depended upon his thoughts: "For it might possibly be the case that if I ceased entirely to think, that I should likewise cease altogether to exist."[85] So there it was. My fear was not only the child's fear of a devil but also the adult's terror of nonexistence. If I am not the thinker, what am I? If not thoughts, what is there? I feared having no thoughts, as thoughts are what kept the lid on. It would be several years before I met my teacher, who embodied the fourth state of consciousness—called *turiya* in Sanskrit. This pure consciousness is the state of awareness in which no thoughts impede, in contrast to the other states: waking, dreaming, and sleeping. There was indeed existence without thoughts, as sages throughout history have declared. "We exist in spite of the thoughts, not because of them," my teacher explained. Existence precedes thinkingness. "I *am*, therefore I think," was his modification of Descartes.

Apprehensively, I made my first appointment for spiritual direction with Wilkie Au. Would this Jesuit priest and theology professor find *anything* of God's movement within me? I had become well versed in facts, theories, and theologies, but my soul felt dried-up. When I arrived at his doorstep, I was a pilgrim without a path, a seeker who had lost hope. He welcomed me anyway. It's not what Wilkie said but how, without a word, he welcomed my brokenness and brought my heart forward. He saw and nurtured the signs of life in my flatness. He brought a feminine capacity to listen, to hold my soul, to see the light hidden within the darkness.

My Light experience at fifteen, he told me, was the Presence of God. It was Grace. "You were greatly blessed." Wilkie was the first person ever to validate the reality of the pillar of Light that had descended on me. "Regretfully," he said, "religious history is full of examples like yours, when experiences of God's Grace are judged to be from the devil. The Church has often feared the mystical. It has distrusted the feminine."

I was suddenly aware that my experience was not singular. When we realize we're not alone with a particular struggle of existence, some of the angst is relieved. In my mind's eye, I saw how many lives throughout history had hung in the balance as a clergyman rendered judgment on their inner experience. (Recall Marguerite Porete, burned at the stake as a heretic for declaring her soul to be "dissolved in God.") The priest told me about various female mystics who had suffered self-doubt at the hands of clergy who feared and disparaged their unusual experiences.

"Have you heard of St. Teresa of Avila?"

"Yes, but I haven't read her books."

"I think you might like them. She knew the devil couldn't harm her but that a priest who feared the devil might harm her a great deal! She said, 'I'm more afraid of the people who fear the devil than of the devil himself.'"

What a refreshing attitude! I immediately set out to read the works of this 16th-century Spanish mystic and Doctor of the Catholic Church. Her masterpiece, *Interior Castle*, remains one of the most influential descriptions of the inner journey ever written, and I relished it. Her seven stages ("mansions") of the inner journey made much more sense to me than the "five steps to salvation" taught by my church. Whereas its doctrines focused on outer steps, St. Teresa's manual described an inward mystical union within the chambers of the heart. The innermost part of me, I learned, belonged to the Beloved, not to the church. Still, in her lengthy spiritual autobiography, St. Teresa was obviously under the gun to prove that her raptures and visions were of divine origin and not the work of the devil. She was living in the time of the Inquisition and knew how precarious was the fate of the mystic. Her close spiritual brother and fellow Carmelite reformer, St. John of the Cross, was imprisoned and beaten three times a week by church authorities who felt threatened by his spiritual visions. In his prison cell, he was given inner experiences of Divine Love that he poured into volumes of mystical poetry. At one of our Spiritual Direction training sessions, the sisters read passages from his "Dark Night of the Soul." For the first time, it dawned on me that my "darkness" might have a purpose.

The Jesuit priest, my spiritual director, affirmed that my experience at age fifteen was of Divine Light. Upon hearing this, a healing process began in my psyche. It was a redemption of the feminine; that is, a healing and reclamation of my heart and soul, which had been judged evil. He affirmed my innate goodness. All the Love from the Light did not have to be pushed down anymore. I dared to have hope for my spiritual life.

He would soon no longer be a priest. Shortly after our meetings, he left the Society of Jesus in order to marry a Jungian analyst whose office was next to his. He had spent his whole adult life in the safety of a community of priests, and now he would leave it for a new life. I saw that he was brave, at midlife, to suddenly begin anew. I tried to imagine what his life would now entail—learning to shop for his own clothes, set up a bank account and write checks, be intimate with a woman. He showed me his official letter of dispensation from the Vatican.

How could I have known that a similar fate awaited me, that I too would fall in love with a forbidden someone and need to leave everything? I felt an unexpected rapport with this Jesuit priest. He seemed to know something of the real nature of God. He was kind and humble. He asked, "No one ever told you that God is Love?"

I shook my head. I felt a lump in my throat and tried hard to fight back tears. As I was getting ready to leave his office, he pulled a piece of paper out of his file cabinet and handed it to me: "Work with this passage. See if you can trust the Lord." It was the Gospel of Matthew 14: 25.

Jesus spoke to them at once, "Have courage; it is I; do not be afraid."

And Peter answered, saying, "My Lord, if it is you, command me to come to you on the water."

Jesus said to him, "Come...."

But when he saw that the wind was strong, Peter was afraid, and began to sink, and he raised his voice, "My Lord, save me!"

And our Lord immediately stretched out his hand and grasped him. "Oh you of little faith, why did you doubt?"

When they got into the boat, the wind quieted down. And they who were in the boat came and worshipped him, "Truly you are the Son of God."

Walking to the car, I thought: *I feel witnessed as a soul for the first time in my life.* Wilkie was the first man of God I had ever met who radiated God's compassion and mercy. He didn't have an agenda with me. He wasn't frightened by what I shared. He didn't judge me. His compassion was like a gentle rainfall upon my inner aridity, and I wondered what would grow from it. He knew from his own experience that the soul goes through many dark nights of the soul, because there are endless attachments to relinquish: emotional dependencies, personal beliefs, social and family conditioning, fears, self-concepts, desires for worldly gain, harmful behaviors, resentments, and even attachment to spiritual identities, goals, and communities. He knew what it was like to surrender these attachments and step into the Unknown. He was certain that God is Love.

Unbeknownst to me, an entire lineage of Christians had been breathing the Love of God for centuries in the Sinai desert of Egypt. Meeting Father Pavlos gave a whole new meaning to the word "arid." He had found the Presence of God in one of the driest, most remote places on the planet.

Father Pavlos of Sinai speaking at the University of Redlands on "The Mystery of the Simplicity of Soul," 2011 (author's collection).

## Chapter Ten

# LIVING GOD'S LOVE IN THE DESERT

### Encounter with Father Pavlos of Sinai

*We believe that, within the Orthodox Church,*
*the truth of the Gospel is preserved*
*exactly as Christ taught us it.*
*But we love everybody.*
*Our teaching is simply to love everybody.*
*We don't ask what he is or what he believes.*
*When someone knocks on our door,*
*we show him hospitality.*
*For us, to love God means that*
*you have to love your brother*
*no matter who or what he is.*

—FATHER PAVLOS

## LIFE IN THE SINAI DESERT

Father Pavlos is the senior ascetic priestmonk of Saint Catherine's Monastery[86] at Mount Sinai, Egypt, the oldest continuously functioning Christian monastery in the world. The monastery is singular in its collection of artifacts such as Byzantine icons, mosaics, ancient manuscripts, and other priceless spiritual treasures. Father Pavlos has lived at the monastery over four decades. When asked what led him to the desert, he said:

> I myself cannot explain it. The desire entered into me to go live as a monk in the desert, even though I'd never been there before. And having arrived there, I didn't leave. I loved this area from the first moment. I loved not only the monks of the monastery but also the Bedouins. These things are mysteries that the person himself cannot explain.

When asked how he views the Bedouins, his Muslim neighbors, Father Pavlos said simply, "Our only obligation is to love them because they are created by God." I found his love for the Bedouins to be a refreshing example of how a person can be devoutly committed to his own faith tradition while also loving those outside of it.

Mount Sinai—sacred to all three of the world's monotheistic religions—offers a paradigm for our global society on how to achieve respectful coexistence with those of differing faith through genuine love and caring. As the Monastery Abbot, His Eminence Archbishop Damianos of Sinai has said, "Without any need to compromise the distinctions that characterize its own confession of faith, the Sinai monastery has lived in unbroken peace with its non-Christian neighbors for close to two millennia." Stressing the sanctity of personal freedom, noted His Eminence, the Sinai monks have enjoyed a relationship of mutual respect with the Bedouin tribes with whom they have lived and worked since the centuries predating the dawn of Islam, as well as with the Israelis who have occupied the Sinai Peninsula. The lives of the monks thus bear witness to Mother Teresa's teaching mentioned earlier, "Acts of love are works of peace." As the monastery's website describes:

> The members of the community are Christians, celibate, and Greek speaking. The Bedouin are Moslems, with families, and Arabic speaking. In spite of

differences of religion, language, and culture, there exists an amazing reciprocity between the monks and the Bedouin, extending beyond simple respect, to mutual support. This is one of the messages of Sinai, that peoples of differing creeds and cultures can still manage to live in harmony.

The monastery was built at the foot of Mount Sinai where Moses received the revelation of the Ten Commandments. As far back as the third century, Christian ascetics went to live at the site of the Burning Bush, for it was the place where God spoke. According to the Book of Exodus, the Bush flamed with Fire but was not consumed. God told Moses to take his shoes off—"The place where you stand is holy ground"—and Christian ascetics have tended the holiness of the place now for over 1,700 years. They enter the arid landscape to purify all loves through the transcendent love of Christ, to surrender the "passions" of the ego's "I am something" to the Great "I Am That I Am." Sister Joanna of Sinai, the nun who translated for Father Pavlos, explains what this means for the monks in light of the Orthodox pursuit of *theosis*, or mystical union with God:

> Contrary to the West's philosophical theology in which personality would fail to evolve with contemplation of the divine essence,[87] participation in God for the Orthodox East means the fulfillment of personhood; creativity is not diminished but enhanced when the will, no longer deceived into according substance to the nothingness of evil, is filled with light. The ineffable fire of the Bush proves to Moses that the unknowable God is knowable—not in His essence but in His fiery divine energies—by anyone who strives for purity of soul.[88]

In fact, she says, it is *only* through this unknowability that God may be known, according to the negative theology of the Orthodox tradition. Having removed his sandals before the Burning Bush, Moses approaches God "with the footstep of his mind bare, completely free of human thought." *No one may see My face and live* (Exodus 33.20), yet after forty days with God in the "luminous darkness" on Sinai, Moses has to cover his own face with a veil, for no one can bear its brilliance. Whilst the divine *essence* remains eternally hidden from our gaze, as affirmed in the New Testament (I Tim. 6.16), the divine *energies*— which are God Himself—become our own, says Elder Pavlos, and the conduit of His measureless love for all creation. Living in *mountains and caves and in holes of the earth* (Heb. 11:38), the early hermits and ascetics thus attained a rare wisdom that was not theoretical but living and personal. Pilgrims and disciples sought them out for their saintly presence and wise teachings. The sayings and teachings of the desert fathers and mothers were recorded in an unbroken written tradition of spiritual wisdom and practice that guides Christians both in the monasteries and in the world. Father Pavlos is a living embodiment of this tradition, not only through his knowledge of its writings but also through the illumination of his personal experience.

When asked about a typical day at the monastery, Father Pavlos smiles and says,

> There is never a typical day. Generally, we get up at 3:30–4 a.m. Worship starts at 4:15 a.m. This communal prayer is required for all. Divine Liturgy takes place every day, during which we pray for the many people whose names pilgrims leave for us to read in the service. By 7–8 a.m., we are finished with the morning service and then we rest. At 9 a.m., the monastery opens its doors to visitors who come in masses to see the spiritual treasures. The monastery has a large collection of ancient icons and manuscripts. So at 9 a.m. the monks go to work, as we don't have our bread without working for it. Some go to the library, some to the church to monitor the crowds, some to the Bedouins to see what they need, some to steward the supplies, to cook, to work in the garden. At noon,

the bells ring for quiet and a short church service. We then share our common meal and the door is closed to visitors. We rest until 4 p.m., when we have Vespers and Compline. Some monks are then free for reading and private prayer, while others return to work. The archbishop's office is always in operation. But the chief work of the monk is prayer.

Father Pavlos emphasizes that love is a verb: "Love, for us, must exist as action, not words." During his speaking tours in the United States, he was touched by the loving actions of Americans. Usually they are criticized for selfishness, but Father Pavlos noted their generosity:

> When a person arrives here for the first time, he has the impression that God gathered all the material blessings on earth and tossed them into America! Personally, what moves me is that I find the people to be simple and humble, which is the goal of us monastics. Two students offered me hospitality at their apartment at California Polytechnic Institute. I hadn't realized that this was their own home, when one of them showed me to a room with a nice bed. I was shocked the next morning to find the student sleeping on the floor when I woke up! Even we monks don't practice such hospitality. We have guests stay in the guestroom. We do not give up our bed for the guests.

The Sinai desert tradition was codified in the manual written by St. John Climacus, *The Ladder of Divine Ascent*, which teaches the sovereignty of authentic love as both the means to success and the ultimate crown of all spiritual endeavor. For Father Pavlos, the quintessential Sinaite virtue is the refusal to judge others. Monks take great care to keep the commandment of Jesus given in his Sermon on the Mount: *Judge not, that you not be judged.* Scripture is clear to say that only God may judge. Sister Joanna explains: "As God reserves judgment to Himself, the one who usurps this prerogative makes of himself a false god, say the patristic saints. And what has ever been more destructive to this planet than the worship of its false gods?"

# PERSONAL ENCOUNTER

When I first saw Father Pavlos, his long gray beard and stark black robe stopped me. He looked every bit the austere environment he hailed from. I could almost hear the howling winds of the desert as he walked into the room, but in greeting me, his eyes shone that inner light of unmistakable welcome, and I instantly felt his warmth and kindness. One would think that a person who has spent forty years in the desert would be dry as sand; however, the opposite was true. Father Pavlos was completely natural and open. Being with those who have been with God is a refuge for the heart. Though he was foreign to me—different country, different language, different religious beliefs, different lifestyles—he was entirely relatable. We laughed aplenty, as he and Sister Joanna were full of joy and good humor.

I was aware that the doctrines of his Greek Orthodox Church viewed me as walking a misguided path, yet I felt he wouldn't judge me even if he knew the details of my life. And this, I take it, is the beauty of his Sinaite tradition—he holds fast to the tenets of his Orthodoxy while at the same time refuses to judge others for the way they go. Only God can know the yearning of the human heart. Only God sees the struggle a soul makes to live into the light it has been given.

In our personal conversation and a public Q & A, Father Pavlos shared the Sinai teaching on authentic love and how we can apply it to many life situations. As he related to each of us, he *was* the teaching of authentic love he spoke about.

## Conversation with Father Pavlos

Q:    Father, you make a distinction between authentic, genuine love and inauthentic love. What is genuine, authentic love?

FP:    Love, as portrayed by St. John of Sinai, forms the last rung, the summit of *The Ladder of Divine Ascent*. A monk achieves the other virtues and gradually ascends until he reaches the last step, which is love. Therefore the person who wishes to speak about love and to live the experience of love must first succeed in the other virtues. The first step on this ladder is humility, for a person to become "simple" and humble. In this way he has set the foundation of a house whose roof is love. For us, love is like the roof of a house. You cannot have a roof without a house. But neither can you have a house without a roof. You can put down foundations, you can put up walls, but until the roof is on, it's not a house.

For us, love is the great premise. Love begins in God. First, we love God, for genuine love begins in God. And then, love reaches ourselves. And from that point on, [we love] everybody and everything. And for this very reason, to us, self-destruction, suicide, that is, is the worst sin, because a person who does this act hates his own self. This is the beginning of genuine love—to love in these three ways. A person can never say, "Yes, it's true that I love people, but God whom I have never seen, how can I love Him?" Neither is the opposite possible or conceivable. A person cannot say, "I love God but I don't care about people." So love passes through these three stages: with God first, then ourselves, then everybody and everything.

Furthermore, true love is living experience. It's not theory and words. An ascetic who lived in the desert and who had much love in his heart said, "I want to find a person who has the illness of leprosy." In those days, leprosy was the worst illness. "I want to give him my healthy body and take his leprous one." Chiefly, for us, love is not a matter of words. It's a matter of works.

Q:    What is another example of genuine love in action?

FP:    Somebody might come to you and knock on your door, seeking assistance. One person might react and say, "Go on your way and God will help you." But that's not real love. You need to find a way to help him. Even just to offer him a glass of water with love is important. After a psychology student completed his studies in Greece, one of his professors wanted to test his practical knowledge of the science, so he introduced him to a woman who had psychological problems, in order to see how he would behave toward her. After they were introduced, the graduate took the woman out into a garden. Having nothing else to offer her, as they were walking, he saw a rose and he cut it off and gave it to her. This simple act gave the woman courage, and she was benefited by it. And the professor praised him that he did well.

So, genuine love must find a practical method by which to help another. For us, genuine love as Christ taught it, and He himself lived it, means that we don't just love those who love us but also those who hate us. On the cross, our Christ prayed for those who crucified Him and this is the point we also must reach. It is easy to love those who love you. But the one who doesn't love you and hates you—it requires great effort to love him. For us monks, and since we often don't have material assistance to offer, in this case we take refuge in another gift, that of prayer, and we pray for the other. This is a very great help— to pray.

Q:    You have said that the chief work of the monk is to pray and that you pray for the person who hates you. What is that prayer?

FP:    We say a short prayer, which is easy. "Lord Jesus Christ, have mercy on your servant, _____ (the person's name)."

Q:    Is it the Jesus Prayer for another?

FP:    The Jesus Prayer is the prayer that we say both for ourselves and for others. There is a difference, however. When we say the prayer for ourselves, we say, "Lord Jesus Christ, have mercy on me, the sinner." When we pray for another, we do not say "the sinner" because we don't know if he is a sinner![89] And so the highest expression of genuine love is to love the one who doesn't love you, but hates you. The road is long and uphill… but this is the road of authentic love. In the prayers one reads before receiving Holy Communion, there's an instruction that says: "Be reconciled with those who have offended you." Of course, you have to be reconciled with those you have offended—but even in cases where you are not at fault, love must find a way to reconciliation.

There is an incident in the life of St. John the Merciful who was Patriarch of Alexandria. This great hierarch went to a church to celebrate the Divine Liturgy and was received with much love. He found everything ready upon his arrival, but instead of proceeding with the Liturgy, he told the people assembled there, "Wait." He left to search out a certain deacon upon whom he had placed a disciplinary measure. The deacon had not accepted it well, had fallen into despair and stopped coming to church. Not finding him, St. John asked the people, "Where is he?" And so they told him, "He doesn't come to church anymore." The patriarch said again, "Wait," and he went and found the deacon. He showed him love and was reconciled with him. And afterward, he went to celebrate the Divine Liturgy. This is genuine love in action.

(*A young man enters the room from the hallway where he had seen Father Pavlos. He kneels deeply, receives a blessing.*)

We must not forget what the Apostle Paul said: Even if I have many spiritual gifts, even if I'm wise, even if I am a great author and orator and speak with the tongues of angels, even if I do miracles… but do not have love, then I'm nothing.

Q: What are the monastery's relations with the Bedouins who live in the desert?

FP: They are not Christians unless of course any happen to be Christian in secret. Nonetheless they love the monastery as their own home. Not only do they refrain from doing harm to it, but they also love it as their own home. Recently in the news you've seen political turmoil in our area. From the first moment, the Bedouins remained true to their friendly relationship with the monastery. Their chieftains came to the monastery at the onset and said, "We are arming our tribesmen and sending them up into the mountain passes to guard the monastery; they will make sure no one from afar gets through with any negative intent." A friend shows his true colors in times of stress.

(*Smiling.*) Sometimes the other monks criticize me that I give charity indiscriminately to the Bedouins, because I give them whatever I can to help them. Whatever they need— the doctor, food, supplies. Sometimes the monks tell me I'm not careful enough to make sure I concentrate my giving where the most serious need exists. But after what happened recently, when they went out to protect us without even being asked, I think I will just continue giving them anything I can! There is an incident with a Bedouin woman who received bread from the monastery but didn't have teeth to eat it.[90] And so we gave her money to have dentures made. Now the woman can eat. One of the Bedouin workers we are close to told us that every morning when she wakes up she turns toward the monastery and says, "I thank you, St. Catherine, that now I have teeth and can eat!" If we continue to recount all the details that have taken place there, we will never finish, because so much has happened in the very long history of this blessed place.

Q: In *The Ladder of Divine Ascent* there is this sentence in the chapter on Love: "In its activity, Love is inebriation of the soul." What is your experience of that?

FP: The saint is speaking there chiefly of the love that the soul has for God. He is speaking about divine eros. "Eros" is a word for love that has its origin in the human heart, whereas the word "Agape" has its origin in God, because God is Love. You can understand human "eros" in the love between two young people, a man and a woman. Divine eros, the divine fire of Agape, is something infinitely greater.

Q: So the soul becomes completely intoxicated by Agape love for God?

FP: Yes, this is the love of which St. John is speaking.

Q:   Does the soul dissolve into God?

FP:   No, that never happens, it is only purified. The purified soul is filled with Light and becomes more radiant. The idea of the soul being erased that exists in other religions does not exist with us in the Orthodox Church. We see this in the apostles who were enlightened and wrote the Holy Scriptures, the Gospels. We believe that these writings are God-inspired, that God inspired what they wrote. But amongst each other, they are different. The evangelist John discusses the love of God, he theologizes about God, whereas the evangelist Matthew writes more about the miracles that Christ did, that is, he shows Christ's power. So we see here that while all four evangelists are enlightened by the Holy Spirit, they don't write the exact same things. In other words, God respects this freedom. God enlightens a person but does not erase his personality; on the contrary, He preserves its freedom. This is the basic point.

Q:   Moses, according to the monastery's video, "dwelt for 40 days in Uncreated Light." This Uncreated Light—is that the Love of God?

FP:   This cannot be described. We can only describe that which is created. For that which is Uncreated, we do not have forms of expression. A person can only experience this. He cannot describe it. It's dangerous to talk about love, because God is Love, and when you talk about love, you are talking about God Himself—and it's dangerous to talk about God.

Q:   That is what St. John Climacus says, "The man who wants to talk about love is undertaking to speak about God, but it is risky to talk about God and could be dangerous for the unwary."

FP:   You know that book well.

Q:   No, I am only learning it, thanks to you. Father, you have said that, in genuine love, there is no place for judgment. So, the person who loves never judges?

FP:   Yes, that's true. But we'll make a distinction here. Sometimes it is constructive to counsel a person directly; to explain to him, "You've taken a wrong path, what you're doing is not good—do rather what is good." This is not judgment, it's an expression of love. Again, we observe the element of freedom here, in that one's personality is not compromised when he sees that another person is not doing what is right. Not wishing to see the wrong, he focuses instead on the good in the other person. If we look at this with absoluteness, then yes, he's making a judgment in his mind, but he doesn't pay attention to the bad, choosing to see only the good in the other.

Q:   What has been the response in people of America to these teachings of love and non-judgment?

FP:   I think it's been very positive. The people here have simplicity. This says much to us, because this is what we struggle toward as monastics—to become simple. And so, they are teaching me. I will be benefited very much by this trip.

Q:   Thank you for answering the questions so clearly.

FP:   (*Smiling*) Now, I want to show a little love, a very small amount.
    (*He pulls out a beautiful print of a watercolor of his monastery, as a gift.*)
    This is the best engraving of all. This shows what it really looks like there. The monastery, and above, Mount Moses, the Holy Summit of Sinai. It's the best engraving and it has to go to you.

Q:   Father, this is a perfect example of what you were saying earlier—that genuine love is kindness in action. I am touched by your kindness and generosity.

## Questions and Answers with Father Pavlos

At the University of Redlands, Father Pavlos addressed an audience of 200 local Orthodox Church members, townspeople, and college students. He gave a presentation on "The Mystery of the Simplicity of Soul," with beautiful photographs and sounds from St. Catherine's Monastery in Sinai, Egypt, followed by Q & A.

Q: To what degree is Agape sacrificial? The ultimate expression of that was God sacrificing Himself on the cross.

FP: Yes, that's part of it. But God, from love, does not seek that from us. Not everybody can do that. Therefore, the love that God seeks from us, the measure of love that Christ gives us is made clear when He says, "ἀγαπήσεις τὸν πλησίον σου ὡς σεαυτόν," that is: "Love your neighbor *as yourself*." He doesn't ask us to love our neighbor more than we love ourselves.

Q: What are the writings of the great ascetics who lived at Sinai?

FP: St. John Climacus wrote the profoundly spiritual *Ladder of Divine Ascent*. Amidst a crowd of other holy saints and ascetics, St. Nilus of Sinai, St. Anastasius of Sinai, and St. Gregory of Sinai (who lived in more recent times) left behind powerful writings on the spiritual life. If one studies just one of these works, *The Ladder of Divine Ascent*, this alone will be enough to give him a very clear picture of what sort of people passed through this area. The book describes a ladder with its base on the earth that reaches to heaven. Every rung on this ladder is the subject of a chapter in the book, beginning with the first rung, which is the person's withdrawal from sin, turning from evil to God—to become humble, simple in soul as a child. Gradually ascending this ladder, a person acquires the other virtues in order to reach the highest rung, which is called Love. When a person arrives at this Love, which is genuine love, he has arrived at God Himself, because God is Love. The book describes the struggle that a person wages in order to acquire virtue, whether he lives here in the world, in the desert, or in a monastery. And we also read about the wiles that the enemy, the devil, employs to throw a person into evil, to prevent him from reaching this goal.

Q:   What is an example of "evil" that a person will confront in the ascent to God?

FP:   The most important thing is for a person never, ever, to reach the point of hopelessness. This is the very worst thing. If he fell spiritually, which happens, he must rise up again. This happened, for example, when a young monk confessed to his spiritual elder, "I fell into sin." The elder said, "Get up." Before long, the monk returned to say, "I fell down again." The reply was, "Get up again!" Finally, the young monk asked, "How long can this go on? How many times do I get up?" The elder replied, "Up until the moment that death finds you either fallen in sin or standing in virtue." So, a person must never, ever, open the door to despair because the greatest evil that can touch a person's life is hopelessness. In their works, these saints describe many other details about the struggle one wages in order to live honorably according to God. And they stress that it is not necessary for a person to go live in the desert—that great spiritual feats can be achieved anywhere, here in the turmoil of city life, or wherever one happens to live. It simply requires vigilance (*nepsis*).[91]

Q:   In our country, we are sliding more and more into hedonism and there is despair about how to regain virtue. How do we show it in our lives without becoming like the Pharisees, where we show we're fasting and say our prayers where others can hear?

FP:   Unfortunately, this same germ attacks us also who live in the desert and in the monastery. Nonetheless, if we are vigilant, we can avoid slipping. As a deeply spiritual person has said, "The matter of the salvation of our soul is neither difficult nor easy—it's simply a matter of vigilance (nepsis). It requires carefulness only. In his *Ladder*, St. John mentions that, in all they did, the desert ascetics greatly emphasized the importance of not condemning others, insisting that the person who desires to go closer to God and live with Him must never judge others. When a person is careful and does not judge, he easily reaches the point of humility to achieve the simplicity of soul of a child. It's not that difficult when you are careful not to judge your brother. It's an easy thing.

(*Audience laughter... not judging is anything but easy!*)

(*The elder smiles.*) It seems difficult to you but it's not difficult—it just requires a great deal of vigilance (nepsis)! Another ascetic writer, Abba Dorotheos, recounts that a monk who never judged others stopped by the cell of another monk and found it in a state of great disarray (as occurs, not infrequently, with men's cells). And what did he say? "Look here, this brother spends all his time on spiritual matters, so much so that he has no time left over for material concerns like housekeeping." And, continuing on his way, the ascetic happened to visit the cell of another monk, which he found in that rare condition for a male cell (though not unheard of): clean and orderly, with everything in its place. What did he say then? "Look here, just as this brother maintains his inner world, the interior of his soul, in purity, so does he maintain his outer environment." And he didn't judge anyone! This person has much "agape" within himself, genuine love through which he closes all people, the whole world, inside his heart. Out of this love, he does not endure to judge another.

Q:   In the Bible, St. Paul talks about the body of Christ as the corporate community, but the patristic writings seem to focus more on individual spirituality.

FP:   It may seem that way, but it's actually not the case. From the earliest centuries in which ascetics lived in the desert, the center of their lives was always Christ. You cannot begin to measure the mystical effect of the Jesus Prayer, which we say continually, *Lord Jesus Christ have mercy on me.* For us, no matter what asceticism a person practices, if it does not take place in the name of Christ, it has no value. This means that the person who has abandoned himself to prayer experiences the love of God for the world more intensely than others; he lives the corporate community of Christ more so than those in society, for his whole existence is bound up in Christ.

Q:   I was recently called to be a juror in a criminal case. How should Christians approach that?

FP:   This is a function that you are required to perform by the state. It is a holy work and you are required to do it. Just don't forget what the ancient Greeks said, "Extreme justice is extreme injustice." Fulfill the duty with love because the point of the matter is not to put a person behind bars but to do what will bring him to recognition of the error of his path. It's necessary to exhaust all limits of love for others that you have at your disposal. So what you've been called to do, to sit on the jury, is your duty and actually God wishes it.

Q:   Recently there was a film on the "Mysteries of the Jesus Prayer."[92] You were in it as one of the monks. Did you see it and do you recommend it?

FP:   Yes, I have seen it. If it's beneficial, why not watch it?

Q:   Do you have any advice for how to confront the hopelessness and despair you were talking about earlier?

FP:   A person under *no* circumstances must *ever* open this door. I'll tell you something from my own life. While working in Athens as a young man, I was going to night school to get an education with which to serve God, something daring in those years, to seek an education. At the same time, I was working construction sites, and it would happen that friends would pass by. And when they saw me in my work clothes amidst the dust and heavy labor, I could see they pitied me. Nonetheless, having made it all the way through to the end of high school, I told myself, "And what do I have to lose by applying to the university?" In those days, you had to pass through a sieve to be admitted to university in Greece; the exams were extremely difficult. And I passed, in tenth place, to enter the University's School of Theology. As I sit before you now, I remember those days in construction. Others looked at me and felt sorry for me. But I had my gaze fixed on my dream. And that dream did become reality. And with the money I got from construction, I was also able to help my family. Therefore, no matter what situation you find yourself in, no matter what dire straits, you must never lose this hope. The Greek philosopher Epictetus said, "When things don't come the way we want them, let us want them the way they come." A thinking person will never open the door to hopelessness.

Q:   You talk about avoiding hopelessness and not judging, but how can I apply it myself?

FP:   There is a great spiritual connection. When a person doesn't judge others, he becomes humble and simple as a child in soul. Have you ever seen a child fallen into hopelessness? You won't see that. We were very happy as children. Let's not misunderstand this though; we're not saying a person must cease using his own logic. The mind of the person who believes in Christ correctly is purified. His logic does not cease to function but becomes purified. A local ascetic went into the city and the bishop wanted to ordain him to the priesthood. Great ascetics at that time avoided the priesthood because they considered themselves unworthy of it. The bishop had much love and persuaded the ascetic to become a priest. And then he asked the ascetic about his young disciple monk—"Is he also worthy of the priesthood?" The ascetic who was afraid of the sin of condemnation of others replied, "There is no question that he is a better person than me. But whether or not he is worthy of the priesthood, you will have to examine him yourself." Of course, for someone to enter the priesthood, certain conditions must be satisfied.

  This is how a person who fears to judge another speaks with wisdom. So, refraining from judging others doesn't mean that a person loses his ability to discern or to think. In other religions, there may be an objective for the individual personality to be dissolved. But that does not exist with us. With us, the conscience becomes purified and more radiant. And then we begin to understand our own selves and who we are. As our mind is purified, we gain a clearer image of who we are and then we realize how little we know of the inner world of others. The great ascetic writer Abba Dorotheos of Gaza said, do not judge even the person who actually fell into sin – why? Because you don't see the struggle he waged beforehand to *not* fall into sin. God is Love. And God who is Love sees what we do not see. Naturally, when a person falls into sin God will examine *how* he came to fall; this is consistent with the love of God. He will look at the past life of this person, and how he struggled before finally succumbing to the sin. God will place a great deal of emphasis on this struggle, and judge him according to the struggle, not just on what we saw. Indeed, it's possible that God may count that struggle to him as an achievement and not judge him at all, and neither do we! For we saw only the outcome, the last stage, and nothing that went on beforehand.

Q:   What do you say to someone who has been dealt a difficult life and because of that blames God and rejects God?

FP:   We remember what the great Russian author Dostoevsky said, "When a person tells you that he doesn't believe in God, don't believe him." The person who says he doesn't believe in God is actually trying to tell you something else.

Q:   What does it mean to judge?

FP:   Abba Dorotheos analyzes this matter and says there are three different stages: disparaging someone; condemning him; and finally, writing him off. If you say that a person stole, or fell into a rage, you judge his act; having simply spoken of another's sins, you have already disparaged him. But by saying, "he is a thief, or an angry person, or a liar," then you condemn not only his act but his will, and judge the very disposition of his soul. You have judged his whole being based on one sin. Finally, when you reach the point of writing the person off as "totally worthless," at this point you have decimated his character and this is the worst yet. Each stage is worse than the one before it. So may God preserve us from this sin of judging another, which, although it seems small, is very heavy.

Q:   In raising children, I find it difficult because we live in an age where we want them to seek Christ first. Sometimes we worry about this friend or this influence in their life. This is a struggle within me as a mother. How do you say, "This is not a good influence for you" without judgment?

FP:   There's an example from history. Several years ago in Cyprus, Archbishop Makarios took on the political office of the presidency of Cyprus. This was not in accordance with the canons of the Church, but in conflict with them. In Orthodoxy, the same person cannot be head of Church and also head of state. And even though Archbishop Makarios took on the presidency of the democracy for a good reason, in order to save Cyprus from being partitioned, he was lambasted in the press. In this situation, a person who doesn't judge would have justified him saying, "He actually did this for a good cause [and this is true], in order to save Cyprus from being split in two." But this person would also say the truth, that according to the historical canons of the Church, ecclesiastical and political office cannot be held simultaneously by the same person. In this way a person both speaks the truth and avoids judging another—someone who, in this case, sacrificed to save his country. This is the person who doesn't judge, but also uses his intellect.

After everyone left, I witnessed something unforgettable. It was 10 p.m., the end of a very long day. In his seventies, I imagined he must have been tired. Yet Father Pavlos noticed that there were three college students who had come in to clean the large room and stack 200 chairs. He reached into his bag, pulled out three silver rings, and went to each one saying, "Thank you for your work. I would like to give you something sacred from Mount Sinai, where I live. It is a ring of St. Catherine; it is blessed in our sanctuary and carries the prayers of the monks." They looked astonished. Perhaps no speaker had ever noticed them before.

Seeing the effect on three strangers of this tender and simple act of love, I thought: *Perhaps the path to peace is really quite simple. Attention to the goodness of others. Kindness to everyone we meet. Sharing something that we feel is precious, no matter how small.* Such genuine love seems simple but it can revolutionize a person's life.

Walking an unpaved path… (author's collection).

## Chapter Eleven

# THE ARMS OF LOVE

F or many weeks, I contemplated the Gospel passage that my spiritual director had given me. I imagined myself in the shoes of St. Peter, leaving the boat and walking toward Christ on the Sea. I felt scared. I didn't want to lose my life as I knew it. Yet I had to be willing to leave the "boat" behind and step out onto the Sea toward the figure of Christ, who represented Love. I was desperate for a deeper spirituality but terrified of the unknown. I wondered: How will I do it? Does God really exist? Will His arms of Love be there to catch me if I fall into the Sea?

The arms of love were not the ones I expected. It happened so quickly. One moment I was a faithful minister's wife, submissive church member, Sunday school teacher, missionary for the church, and well-respected teacher in a Christian university. The next moment I was the "worst of sinners."

"You are a heretic. You have followed direct experience over scripture."

"Disloyal female!"

"You are an abomination."

"God will unleash his wrath upon you."

I had done what the spiritual director asked of me: "See if you can trust the Lord." I had opened my heart and let love stir again. The love stirred whenever I was with her. The gentleness felt akin to the Light. At any rate, the closest I'd ever come to it in a human form.

I said yes to this human love for the same reason that the flower turns toward the sunlight.

Panic disorder—gone. Years of terrified silence—over. The heavy pall over my existence for sixteen years—dispelled.

# "You Don't Have to Be Afraid Anymore"

It was the last thing I expected—a human love affair—yet love in whatever form has the power to awaken, to heal, to transform a human being. To this day, it amazes me that the panic disorder that had dominated my life for sixteen years was completely resolved, almost overnight. Love peeked in through the cracks to where my heart was hiding and said, "You don't have to be afraid anymore." Love brought happiness, affection, healing, and hope into a seemingly loveless life. The steel door swung open. What had been pushed into the shadows for so long now burst forth as irrepressible joy. I discovered long-lost or never-known parts of myself. Experiencing them, finally, was to feel more whole. Love set me free, as in the words of the Sufi saint Jâmî: "Never turn away from love, not even love in a human form, for love alone will free you from yourself."[93]

The arms of love seemed to come out of nowhere, yet there had been hints. Others saw it coming long before I did. The wise know the signs on the horizon. The day before my Ph.D. graduation at Princeton, Professor Douglass asked me to come by her office. Silver-white hair, piercing eyes, a wise woman who knew the journey of women. This was the last time I would see her before she and her husband retired and moved away.

Professor Douglass had been my mentor during the four-year doctoral program, but I hadn't been very open to mentoring, for I was too afraid to hear anything that would contradict my beliefs—not so much because I still viewed them as infallible truth, but because they held my small world in place. I feared that if I pulled out even one brick to examine it, the whole wall would collapse.

The elders of my church had warned, "Stay away from anything that smacks of feminism." Professor Douglass was an ordained minister in her denomination; therefore I assumed she was a feminist and kept my guard. Over time I realized she was nothing of the fear-inducing negative stereotype that the elders had played upon. Yes, she was a feminist *and* she was the epitome of grace, calm, rationality, good sense, and wise counsel. When she called me into her office, I had no idea that her question would turn out to be prophetic. She asked, "Fran, how long can you stay in a church that silences you and rejects the gifts you have?"

I took the side of my church. "But they *do* value me. They offered me a job at one of their colleges. I'm the first woman to be a full-time professor in the religion department."

I was proud to be a "pioneer." I was overly optimistic and grandiose. Professor Douglass knew the suffering inherent in being a minority groundbreaker. One of the first women to graduate from Harvard's doctoral program in religion, she had lived out her career in a field dominated by men. It hadn't been easy.

She said, "Time will tell whether they truly want what you will bring. Sometimes institutions want a token, not real change. And you are isolated, the only woman in a large department, the new kid on the block. Who will be your friend?"

This had never occurred to me. A friend? I had little appreciation or need of women as friends. I was self-sufficient, accustomed to succeeding in a man's world.

"I will look into that," I said halfheartedly.

Her eyes narrowed into mine. The sharp look cut through the casing of my denial. She said, "Listen. You have a Ph.D. in religion. You're a gifted and intelligent woman. How will it be for you to sit there, disallowed from uttering a prayer, while twelve-year-old boys can stand up and lead the service?"

What she said was true. Women were not allowed to read scripture, say a prayer, administer communion or baptism, preach a sermon, lead a song, or even make an announcement. Despite being trained in homiletics and exegesis, I wasn't permitted to give a homily. Yet I had never seen the division of gender roles as oppressive. Because of my speaking phobia, the last thing I wanted was to stand up and speak in front of a congregation.

"Professor Douglass, it doesn't really bother me to be silent. Women can do other things—they have their place. Besides, this church is my whole world. It's all I know."

Her tone was firm: "No, Fran, it's not 'all you know.' As much as you've tried to keep yourself closed off to anything that calls your beliefs into question, you've encountered other viewpoints and have uncovered parts of yourself that might not fit easily into your belief system. These new ways of seeing the world, of being yourself, have gone into you somewhere, and one day you will face an inner conflict of major proportion. Either you'll cut off and reject the new parts of yourself in order to fit in or you'll find a way of life that integrates your new growth. You are an expansive person living in a closed system. A human being can withstand the dissonance only so long."

I asked nervously, "And then what?"

"If a change has not been chosen consciously to integrate the new parts of oneself, then a catalyst comes along that *forces a change and demands a decision*."

## FEMINIST AWAKENING

The professor was aware—as I was not—that extreme weather lay ahead in the forecast of my life. A tidal wave in my unconscious had been building for nearly twenty years. By joining *the* church, I had closed a heavy door on the energy of the Light and all the parts of myself that rejoiced in Its Melting Love. The tidal wave contained all the unexpressed feeling and unlived potential of a spirited individual who had been directly infused with the Light. Its ecstatic quality had activated the Infinite within me. If the vital forces of life are pushed down into the sea of the unconscious, they will eventually rise. My day of reckoning was on the horizon.

After the meeting with Professor Douglass, I graduated with my Ph.D. and began my third year of teaching. Finally, I was free of the pressure of finishing a degree! It had been nine years of non-stop, intense graduate study to finish three master's degrees and a Ph.D. In the middle of my doctoral program, a church-related college offered me a teaching position, and my husband and I decided to move from Texas to California. It was the most "liberal" college in our denomination, and I was the first woman ever to be hired as a full-time faculty member in the religion department. The workload was overwhelming. I had to write my dissertation while also beginning my first full-time teaching job. Nonetheless, I completed the Ph.D. in record time.

The summer after graduation, the college asked me to take a group of students to Paris, England, Israel, and Greece—a travel course in Christian history. On the plane, I decided to read the books about feminist theology that the church elders had discouraged. I asked myself, "Am I not willing to see things from another angle?" If my beliefs couldn't withstand some basic inquiry, then perhaps they were unworthy of my allegiance after all. Truth, if it's true, passes the tests we put to it.

So, I read my first book on women and religion by a Christian feminist theologian. It had already been in print for fifteen years, yet I'd never come across it. I'd been sheltered from the cultural changes that had influenced my generation, such as the civil rights and feminist movements. The author peeled back the patriarchal layers of Christian institutional history. She noted the systematic barring of women from education and leadership. She challenged the view that women's bodies, sexuality, and menstrual cycles are impure and unclean. The presumption that female minds are inferior. The doctrines and practices of the church that deem women as untrustworthy, second-class souls. The status of women as property. The distorted theology behind the witchcraze that projected the devil into (mostly) women and led to the execution of untold thousands.

I was devastated to learn that male religious leaders had twisted scripture to secure their power over others, and to realize that patriarchy is deeply embedded in women's psyches, leading women to oppress other women. Often, it was a woman who accused another woman of witchcraft.

For the first time, I was willing to view the dynamics of my life in terms of Professor Douglass's question: "How long can you stay in a church that silences you and rejects the gifts you have?" I had defended the church's position that women were to be submissive to male authority, that women "have *their* roles." Internally, however, I wasn't fully convinced of my own argument. I was aware of my secret; that is, the *real* reason submission didn't bother me was because of my panic disorder and terror of public speaking. Dogma was a cover for my worst fears.

On the trip, I started to notice my fear-based pattern of deference. Here is one telling example: The college paid for my husband to accompany me. When we arrived in Greece, our host walked right past me and mistakenly greeted my husband as "Professor" and "Dr." This was a turning point. Why? Because we did not correct him. My husband didn't point the host toward me and say, "Actually, *she* is the Professor with the Ph.D., not I." And what did I do? I stood there, mute. I feared shaming my husband. I feared being discourteous to the host. I feared their disapproval. I feared being seen as outspoken and too full of myself. Why didn't I fear disowning and disrespecting myself instead? The discourtesy of lying to the host? The pretense? I stood there, silent and confused. These men weren't consciously mal-intentioned. We were all interacting as usual, according to the style of a system that had relegated women to the shadows.

It seemed a minor interaction. Often, it isn't the thing itself that unsettles, but the ubiquity of it—so common as to be hardly noticeable. Day in and day out, the same message: "*This* is where you belong." And if the demeaning treatment is pointed out, the common response is, "You're being silly. It's just sour grapes. Don't make a big deal out of nothing." This is what I heard from church leaders and my inner self-negator. So I stayed in the shadows.

My silent compliance, however, was about to end.

As I read the book, my rose-colored glasses fell off. The traditions of the church that prohibited women from speaking and serving in the worship service no longer made sense to me. Boys could be baptized at age twelve, the "age of accountability," and begin to serve in the worship service, but adult women who had been members of the church for decades weren't even allowed to make an announcement. Church leaders, all male, insisted that this practice was biblical and therefore inviolable, but to me it seemed more of a cultural practice from another era and therefore not essential; indeed their *letter of the law* seemed to go against the *spirit* of the scripture. Hadn't many churches used the same strain of literalism to justify slavery and the prohibition of interracial marriage?

The oppressive environment began to anger me. When we awaken to a new understanding of ourselves, we no longer feel at home in the environments that negate it. As Jesus taught, if we "pour new wine into old wineskins," they "burst" and "spill out" (Matthew 9:17). The old wineskins were about to burst.

Professor Douglass had said, "If a change hasn't been consciously chosen to integrate the new parts of oneself, then a catalyst comes along that *forces* a change." Even given this warning, I was unprepared. The professor had urged me to reach out for a friend, so I did. After returning home from the graduation ceremony and the travel course, I contacted a colleague on campus who had been teaching there for a long time. I'd heard of her from other colleagues who characterized her as "one of our best teachers, innovative, committed to community service, an outspoken and passionate feminist." The word "feminist" no longer scared me. I realized that I'd been taught to put negative labels on things I feared, and I didn't want to live in fear anymore. I was curious to hear from someone who had studied the various viewpoints and had reflected on her experiences as a woman.

I particularly saw my need to talk to a woman who was outspoken because I suffered so deeply from the speech phobia. Imagine the hellish nightmare of being a college professor with a fear of public speaking! The anxiety was so severe that I typed every word of my lectures and read the types pages to the students in class. I was too terrified to look up, for I knew I would see faces bored and etched with resentment. Teaching was to be my career, but speaking was the my most humiliating weakness. Years later, I studied the life of Gandhi and was comforted to learn that, as a young lawyer, he floundered in his first courtroom address. He stood there, petrified, and then fled the courtroom. That same man who had fled in shame later became India's "Mahatma," fearlessly speaking to millions. Humans are capable of miraculous transformations by the power of love, and I was about to experience it for myself.

# THE HEALING EFFECT OF LOVE

The colleague suggested we take a walk at lunchtime. Our campus was high on a hill and had the atmosphere of "enclave" and "living in a bubble"—cut off from the world. It was a close-knit religious community where faculty lived in campus condos with little privacy, like a fishbowl. Symbolically, therefore, it was significant that we went down the hill and out of the university bubble to walk along the Pacific shore in the warm sunlight. It was, literally, another world. The coastal air was refreshing. The sight and sound of the seabirds reminded me of the wild bird refuge in Florida where I had walked as a youth. My colleague and I saw dolphins playing in the sun-stippled waves. Everything seemed to dance and sparkle, as if to say, "Creation is alive."

I had lived on this college campus for over two years and had never been to the beach, though it was only minutes from the campus. A newly arrived faculty member, I'd told myself I was too busy to take a walk, enjoy the ocean view, listen to the cry of the seagull. My head was always in a book. I had a career to launch—"all work, no play" was the recipe for success, wasn't it? Looking back, I feel sad for myself, a young woman in the grip of an inner taskmaster who denied her even the smallest of pleasures.

By driving me down to the shore for our walk, this new friend initiated me into a new dimension of life—or, rather, a *return* to the root of myself. Of course, neither of us had any idea. We were just two colleagues meeting on our lunch break. She probably felt compassion for me, the first and only woman in my department. The resonance was immediate; our souls ignited each other. Once we started talking, we didn't stop for ten years!

Where I was terrified, she seemed fearless. Psychologically, our relationship was irresistible to me because of the growth it encouraged. She honored and nurtured my potential, as in the statement, "A human being is not a problem to solve but a mystery to behold." Our relationship was a mythic secret garden in which long-neglected seeds of my spirit saw sunlight for the first time and were tended with loving care. Like a wilted plant that's moved to an ideal spot in the garden, I began to blossom. Every gardener knows that seeds put into hostile soil don't sprout, and different seeds need different kinds of soil. Perhaps the soil of *the* church was perfect for others, but it lacked the nutrients I needed and was slowly killing me. In the light of love, new life was born in me.

"The end is present at the beginning" is a Sufi saying. Looking back, I see that our first walk on the beach—with dolphins swimming freely in the sunlit sea—presaged the future of our relationship. In that symbolic environment, the message of rebirth was obvious. The dolphin, from ancient Greek times, has been symbolic of rebirth and the advent of a new year. In Christian art, the dolphin stands for Christ and the coming up out of the dark sea into the light of day; it is linked to the Solstice, baptism, and rebirth. The ocean is symbolic of the feminine, the unconscious, the depths. The scenery portended that parts of myself, hidden in the depths, would rise to the light of day and be reborn.

This relationship gave my psyche a safe haven in which long-standing psychic divides began to heal. "Feminine energy is essentially relational, and transforms through love, not knowledge."[94] For many years, I had lived almost exclusively in the academic world of the left-brain intellect—logic, facts, critical analysis, dualities, differentiation.

It was a relief to reconnect to the intuitive and feeling side of life; to move from head to heart; to honor my right-brain awareness of wholes, oneness, and compassion. The world's spiritual traditions emphasize the need to balance the feminine and masculine—Shakti and Shiva, Yin and Yang, Grandmother Earth and Grandfather Sky, and what C. G. Jung described as the two principles of Logos (masculine mind) and Eros (feminine relatedness). I had been living almost completely in the realm of masculine mind, and now love was reconnecting me to my feminine side.

Love returned me to my inner core. It recovered an internal wisdom that had been shelved in my pursuit of an academic career. I had read scholarly books and taken notes from the Ivy League experts, but what about the intelligence of the heart? What about the oneness of creation? What about nature and my own body? In this relationship, I re-collected the feminine ways of interconnection, tenderness, intuition, mutuality, and heart. I had become skilled in the yang (masculine) modes: pursue, act, accomplish. Now I was learning the yin (feminine) modes: surrender, trust, nurture.

In our time together, she took me to nearby places in nature. We hiked to waterfalls that spilled out from high mountain crevices, green with hanging gardens. We napped in sun-warmed meadows. Sitting high up on the cliffs overlooking the Pacific, we watched whales make their migratory journey. In the safety of this love relationship, I embraced the mystery and beauty of my own body. In mountain lakes I swam naked and unashamed. In my youth, I had been a tennis player, swimmer, runner, hiker, and backpacker. As an athlete, I had enjoyed the capabilities of the body, but feminine acceptance gave me a whole new experience of my body as one with Creation. I lay on Mother Earth as a prayer, feeling her as the mother of all. One time, lying under some sycamore trees, we were surrounded by thousands of monarch butterflies.

(Years later, I gratefully came across Franciscan Father Richard Rohr's statement that Creation is the *Body of God*, our *First Bible*, and I remembered that sense of awe at the holiness of God's Creation as I lay upon the earth.)

We prayed inside of caves formed by large rock boulders and listened to the rain as it fell into a stream just outside the cave opening. The cave is a symbol of rebirth that dates back to earlier historical periods when the Great Mother, the Divine Feminine, was duly honored, and women were respected rather than demonized for their unique spiritual and creative powers. In the cave, an archetypal womb of the Great Mother, I experienced the healing of a mother wound. I had always fought against my Southern mother's ideal of womanhood, partly because I lacked the traits to fulfill it. I had neither her same calling for maternity and social affairs, nor her talent in the feminine arts of fashion and domestic life. I had resented her, but as I began to connect to my own authentic feminine side, I felt gratitude for my mother and respect for what she had gone through. We were both women, yet with different paths in life. I didn't need to denigrate her path in order to honor my own.

As Havasupai-Hopi-Tewa Grandmother Mona Polacca told me: "All of us must make peace with our mother. She who gave us our life. Not only Mother Earth, but our own mother of birth. If you can be peaceful with your own mother, then you should be able to have peace with other women as well as our own Mother Earth." Now that I was being loved in my essence, I could love my mother in hers.

I joined other women who had been meeting together for many years. I had been taught to distrust and devalue the way of women, so this sisterhood was a totally new experience for me. In the safety of this circle of prayer and ceremony, I learned to speak again. We studied books related to women's experience and shared the learning with each other and how it applied to our lives. We held each other and wept for the grief of our historic debasement. Dancing and laughing in a circle of women, I reconnected to the holistic, lunar, relational, instinctive, and reflective dimensions of my being. This joy hinted that the oneness of life isn't only the teaching of scripture and the finding of science but, most important, is the ineffable Reality of existence.

It was a relieving balm to be cared for and to have my fundamental female nature respected. Genuine love, in whatever form, heals. As is common in our culture, my body had been objectified, scrutinized, and judged harshly. To feel, finally, a deep acceptance of my own body just as it was created by a loving Creator—this gave me a greater capacity to love.

Love is not possible if we're at war with ourselves. The self-conscious person is very self-centered. The woman who hates herself or rejects her body is so self-absorbed that she can offer little love to anyone. The same is true for any gender. Dedan Gills, civil rights activist and (with his wife Belvie Rooks) the cofounder of Growing a Global Heart, put it well:

> When I wake up in the morning, I look at myself in the mirror. If my stomach is sticking out too much, I need to make peace with that. If my hair's not the way I want it to be—it's turning gray and I'm getting bald in the back—I have to be at peace with that. As I make peace with the first thing I encounter, which is my own body, and I walk out that door, I bring that peace with me into the world. I'm not walking out at war with myself.

Love mirrored back an acceptance of my basic nature, freeing me to see and love the world around me in a new way. For the first time in my life, I noticed daffodils coming up and knew it was a sign of spring. I heard a Lakota elder say, "When we see the meadowlark, we know it's spring. When the cranes leave, it's winter. We don't need a calendar to tell us when a season begins or ends." Being close to the rhythms of nature healed something within my own human nature. Perhaps the relationship was so powerful because she had a more developed feminine side than I had—not in terms of a conventional feminine role but rather the *real* feminine: heartfelt, intuitive, creative, and knowledgeable of the earth and its medicines.

# FALLING

The psyche seeks wholeness, and romantic love often comes to our aid. We often fall in love with people who embody qualities that we ourselves have not yet owned. Wholeness is the natural expression of re-member-ing the lost and rejected parts of ourselves and bringing them into conscious life. Just as a society thrives when all of its members are recognized and given dignity, so the individual thrives when all parts of psychic life are recognized and given dignity. But this inner process is difficult and few people even begin it. Bravery is required because many of the rejected aspects don't fit easily into respectable society. That's why they were cast aside in the first place.

After that first walk along the ocean, seeing the dolphins leaping out of the water, we became very close in the sharing of our souls. Much to my surprise, I fell in love. "Falling" is an apt metaphor. I fell from the pedestal of moral perfectionism—as if I somehow had been above others. This relationship nourished my heart and soul more deeply than any previous connection. It was irresistible because it felt akin to the Light, at least as close as any relationship had ever come to it.

But of course it was very difficult, even torturous, because the soul is one thing, and beliefs are another. As Betty Eadie told me, "God is not what you believe Him to be. Are you willing to surrender your beliefs about God in order to *experience* God?" The soul is nonphysical and knows this simple truth: We are here for love. When Betty Eadie had her near-death experience and was embraced by the Light of Jesus Christ, she saw people in their spiritual essence. In the spirit world, she said, there are no divisions according to race, sexual orientation, class, etc. The soul is not gay or straight, black or white, rich or poor, American, African, or Korean. What I took from her sharing is that these are the physical and material conditions of earthly life that our souls take on in order to learn the crucial lesson of unconditional love. Gay people serve the world, she said, by bringing a gender balance to it and by helping humanity evolve to greater unconditional love.[95]

I was learning that a person's sexual orientation is not primarily about sex but about *a love potential* for bonding, companionship, family support, and the great human task of loving and being loved. Many people's only experience of loving and self-transcendence comes from their bonding with a lovemate and the sharing of life with a lover/partner/spouse. Whatever the sexual orientation, partner and family relationships carry similar challenges. This is how I came to see it. After the initial hormonal flush—Sadhguru Vasudev calls it chemical hijack—the real work of love begins, evident in the true-to-life documentary *Edie & Thea: A Very Long Engagement.* This story touched me deeply for it affirmed that what matters most is the quality and depth of love, not the outer form.

Thea and Edie met during the 1950s when gay people were fired from jobs, barred from churches, subjected to surgeries and change "treatments," and arrested as they gathered for fellowship and dancing. They rejoiced to find each other. Thea had a Ph.D. in clinical psychology and was a leader in her field, but all this changed in her forties when she was struck with MS and slowly became an invalid. In the film, we see Edie's daily loving care of Thea, feeding her, using a pulley to get her in and out of bed, and exercising with her in the pool. Thea had to surrender control over her helpless condition and learn how to receive caring and love. Watching the film, I was reminded of the teaching of Viktor Frankl that loving another person is a hallowed path of meaning. Thea and Edie's partnership lasted over five decades, but was legally recognized only at the very end, just before Thea died. Though rejected by religious institutions, the couple dignified the realm of human love with their example of sustained caring in the face of great difficulties.

I felt my heart break for those whose precious potential for love had been nullified by religious beliefs such as *evil and perverse,* interposing a barrier of fear and shame between their heart and their Creator. How can this not be damaging to a person's spiritual life?

Love is the means of self-transcendence. Love is what heals. Love is what unites. Love is what makes something meaningful. Love is what gives color to the world. Places void of love are literally gray and dull; according to Dr. William Tiller, the thermodynamics are different in places that lack human love. When he told me this, I recalled my first glimpse of a colorless atmosphere when I traveled with my high school to what were then known as the Eastern Bloc countries behind the Berlin Wall. It was 1980. The atmosphere felt heavy and despairing. There was no color. People appeared lifeless, as if the flame of life had been snuffed out by the Iron Curtain ideology that prohibited individual expression.

I came to see this dynamic as psychologically similar for humans. If a wall is built around a person's heart with views such as "That's wrong, sinful, perverted, and the devil," then that person is cut off from their life energy, colorful essence, and innate love potential, thus resulting in a reduced existence.[96] I came to see this as a tragedy not just for the individual but also for society as a whole because love is the source of life. When LGBT people are cut off from their hearts and souls, the world loses a vital resource—the creativity and love potential of untold millions.[97]

Alas, this form of love was not acceptable to *the* church, and I had to make a choice between my heart and the church's belief systems. Divinity does not force us to love. We have to say yes to the risk of losing our self at each moment that true love presents itself. When love comes in forms we don't like, *so much the better*, because we're compelled to sacrifice something the ego clings to.

# THE UNPAVED ROAD

I returned to the place where I'd walked with my friend that very first day we met. I stopped for a moment at the point where the pavement ended, then continued onto the sand and found a spot near the water's edge to watch the sunset. It certainly was the end of the road of my life as I'd known it. My path would continue, but no longer on a paved road.

In the symbolic world of dreams, a paved road represents the conventional road that most people travel upon, the lifestyle C. G. Jung refers to as *collective*. He observed that most people never depart from the security of this paved road, laid out by the traditions and conventions of society. In the dream world, an unpaved road or dirt path signals the beginning of making one's own journey, or as Robert Frost said, "The one less traveled by." Jung coined the word "individuation"—a lifelong process of owning our repressed shadow elements, having the courage to integrate them, and then living as a whole individual, distinct from the herd. Relationships with others are invaluable, he said, because they mirror back our inner aspects. What we thought was a part of them is actually a part of our self. If we are brave enough to make this inner journey, Jung said, we make a contribution forged out of our true self, and it is through this avenue that the collective consciousness evolves.

Sitting there alone on the sand, watching the sun go down on the Pacific, I faced a choice between fear and love. It was a major turning point. In the past, I had chosen the pseudo-security of fear. I had cut myself off from the Light and all of its potent inner energies of lovingness and ecstasy. A religious authority had demonized my experience of the Light, and I had internalized his fear of love. At fifteen, to surrender to love was utterly impossible, but at thirty-three, I had more capacity and courage.

This love was nothing I could understand or define or explain—like the Light, it had come completely out of seeming nowhere—yet my heart *knew* it was good. The love relationship had opened the steel door to my inner realm of innate joy, generosity, and awe. The Light coming in and going out through that doorway brought me such hope that I couldn't bear to shut it again. It was as if the sun had risen inside me. If I chose fear, the sun would set again; I would lose my connection to the Light, which had been reignited by feminine love. I couldn't bear the thought of going back into that inner prison of isolation and panic.

If I chose this form of love, I would lose my job, my marriage, my church, my friends, the approval of all who were important to me, and of society in general. I would lose my self-concepts and the sense of meaning I'd made of my personhood—but I would heal and grow and be true to the power of love. It was a rare gift, and I was not going to give it back to God unopened.

After nearly ten years of marriage, I filed for divorce. Church members had sometimes been "dis-fellowshipped" for divorce, so it was a decision I didn't make lightly. The divorce process was painful, in large part because of my inability to be open and honest. Seeing my mistakes and limitations was humbling. I had learned patterns of self-protection and blaming others that caused me to hide my inner truths. When some of those truths erupted into the light of day, they were shocking to me and to the people I loved. Suddenly I had turned into a completely different person—or so it seemed. The once passive woman, muted by fear and silenced by church tradition, was now an author speaking on national television and an advocate for women's empowerment. The once morally rigid church member who had castigated others for divorce and "sexual sins" was now owning her sexual nature and making life decisions to include it as an expression of her own wholeness.

It seemed a shockingly abrupt transformation, yet seeds of rebirth had been growing for a long time in the womb of my unconscious before they broke through to the light of day. Years before, when I had thrown that magnificent archetype of love—*The Birth of Venus*—into the trashbin, pods of potential growth had been germinating in my depths and when lit and watered by love, they burst to the surface. This very growth process happens in nature every spring and delights us, but when we see sudden growth in a human life, we're shocked. We may even call it a breakdown when it's actually a *breakthrough*. For example, some people said to me, "You're not yourself anymore! Are you having a breakdown?"

As liberating as the experience was, some of my actions were fraught with ignorance and caused suffering. Archetypal forces are much more powerful than the ego, and they can possess a person's consciousness unawares. Only in hindsight did I see my mistakes. At their core was the illusion that a human lover could complete me.

When we see someone else as the source of our happiness and fulfillment, then we *have* to have him or her—and chaos ensues. It's a projection of God onto a human, as if they could fulfill us.

The unraveling of a marriage gave me compassion for the whole endeavor of relational loving. Truly fulfilling relationships are possible only with unconditional love, but where are we ever taught unconditional love? We enter relationships untrained, and have to learn on the job. We do the best we can with what we have learned from our earlier life, but rarely does this background contain a sustained example of unconditional love. Instead, we learn to hide parts of ourselves, fight for our rights, and hone our separateness—"my" life, "my" opinions, "my" needs, "my" career and the like. It's a miracle that any love is given or received at all! Compassion for oneself and the other person is needed when a relationship ends, for we truly did the best we could with what we knew at the time. Our culture may pronounce the ending a failure, but where the journey for love is concerned, how can there be failure?

# From Wounds to Windows

The pain of life is, paradoxically, the path of healing. The divorce knocked me off a pedestal and showed me that I was imperfect, like everyone else, and this became the means of a deeper connection with humanity. I'd always wanted to be better than others, and my moral purity was the ground on which this presumed superiority staked its claim. Divorce was something I said I'd never do, yet here I was, filing for divorce. I lost nearly everything of my former life—except the loving care of three close friends who stood by me when others called me a sinner and a disgrace.

When a relationship ends, it's hard to see the wounds as a path to healing. Slowly, I came to trust that there is a larger mystery of love at work within all relationships, wherein the pain of heartbreak and the joy of loving are two verses of the same song. As Helen Luke, Jungian analyst and founder of Apple Farm Community, says of the ending of her marriage, "I dare to think that the 'injuries' mutually inflicted by my husband and myself on each other carried this mysterious power. That which wounds and that which heals are one."[98]

It took several years for me to see these wounds as windows. "Wounds - Windows" is a poem by Marilyn Peck, a bright and loving eighty-five-year-old student in the intergenerational Compassion course I teach at the university. One day, Marilyn asked if she could say something to the class. I noticed the Light shining through her eyes and felt happy that she was going to share something of that Light with the other students. Little did I know that her story would take me back twenty years to that turning point in my own life when I decided to walk an unpaved path and file for divorce.

Marilyn addressed the students:

> When I was your age, I sat in this very classroom, more than sixty years ago. I was sheltered and knew nothing of sex. I fell in love with a man I met here in college, and we married. He was a talented photographer and I was his main subject matter. I came to embrace my body, to see it as beautiful.

She passed around a photo album. Some of the photographs showed her posing nude in nature. The students' eyes widened with shock and then admiration. One young woman said, "I wish *I* could feel that comfortable in my body!"

Marilyn continued:

> My husband and I lived in a nudist colony. That was a far stretch for two Baptists! Sexually, we were well matched. I experienced bodily things I'd never heard about or imagined possible. I'd sometimes have twenty or thirty orgasms!
>
> But there was something missing. Good sex isn't everything. Don't get me wrong—(she smiled widely)—I'm so happy I learned to enjoy the sexual part of life! It was liberating!

She grew quiet. The students waited, eager to hear what came next. She continued:

> My soul suffered in this relationship. It was an abusive dynamic in many ways. I was free to be sexual but not to be creative. I was seen as 'beautiful' in appearance, but not allowed to grow in my spirit. You see, I am a poet. I have always expressed my soul through my poetry. He would destroy my poems, which was like ripping up my soul. I kept thinking there was something wrong with me. He would say that my poems were worthless, silly. It took me many years to see the cruelty for what it was.
>
> When somebody denigrates your creative work, they are denigrating the divine within you. Love does not denigrate. When you love someone, you encourage them. You nurture their dreams. You support their self-discoveries. I thought I was going crazy. To the outside world, we seemed an evolved couple. But inside the home, I felt put down. I wasn't allowed to be myself.

Some of the students nodded, as if they knew this dynamic of abuse—showing one side of the family to the outside world while hiding cruelty behind closed doors. Marilyn went on:

> He would lock me out of the house and then laugh at me when I slept in the car. I—the real me—wasn't welcomed in that home. The real me *was* locked out. My husband attacked the *imago Dei* in me. I am Christian, and I believe that I am 'created in the image of God.' My poetry expresses this divine part of me.

It was hard to believe that Marilyn hadn't always shone her divine Light. How could such a vital person ever allowed herself to be put down?

Marilyn continued:

> One day, I made the difficult decision to leave—out
> of love for my own soul. Each one of us is respon-
> sible for our own life. We can't blame another person
> for our unhappiness. Yes, things happen to us that
> we can't change or control. Sometimes we are abused,
> and it's not right. When we're young, and abuse hap-
> pens to us, we can't fight back. But as adults, we can
> fight the abuse in our spirits by healing ourselves on
> the inside. We do this by believing in ourselves and in
> the gifts we've been given, and by sharing our journey
> with others so they can wake up to *their* gifts.

Marilyn exemplifies the radiance of a soul that chose love over
fear to the very end. At eighty-five, she chose to leave her comfort
zone and participate in an intensive course with college students.
It was prompted by love. One of her adult children had married a
person of another ethnicity and religious background (Chinese
Buddhist), and she wanted to learn about his religion. She was a lifelong member of the Baptist church and had for many years been married to a Baptist minister (her second husband). It wasn't easy for her
to climb stairs to the classroom and sit for hours. Her hearing was
poor, so she missed a lot of what was said. Yet each day, she was open
to a new discovery. She nurtured the potential and the goodness in
the students. She asked them about their lives and enlarged her heart
to accept whatever they told her. When they shared stories of suicide
attempts, abandonment, and abuse, she wept. Having lived the truth
of her heart, Marilyn could hold the heartache of others.

> For our wounds become our windows
> bridges of compassion
> of understanding
> joining islands of loneliness, of isolation into
> communities of caring.

From wounds to windows—this wisdom eventually came to me, but at the time of my own divorce I was facing the loss of nearly everything. Saying yes to love meant saying goodbye to everything else: the only religious community I'd ever known, my job, security, self-image, belief systems, reputation, friends, family, furnishings, photo albums and the entire style of living they depicted. Love answers to the heart, not dogma or the bottom line.

People lose a lot when a fire consumes their house, but the Fire of Love burns more than physical things. It incinerates what you thought you were. How else to be released from judgmentalism than to become the very "sinner" one has judged? Because my ego was so strongly identified as holier than thou, it was imperative for me, like Hester Prynne in *The Scarlet Letter*, to be cast out of the fold and receive the mercy of the fallen. As Jesus taught, I could no longer cast the first stone or point my finger at "those" people, for I was now one of them.

If in the journey of love we are brave, we can expect to be criticized, and perhaps thrown out, for dancing to the beat of a different drum. We're told that our love has crossed a line when we include people the majority rejects. For example, at a New York temple, when Viktor Frankl expressed a forgiving attitude toward some of the Viennese citizens who had joined the Nazi party—perhaps in order to save their or family members' lives—he was booed off stage and taunted with death threats.[99] Frankl was bitterly criticized for going too far.

Belvie Rooks, cofounder of Growing a Global Heart, speaks of the critical moment in her journey when she knew she had to include the Confederate soldiers—those who fought to keep her African ancestors enslaved—within the sphere of the global heart. She told me:

> We had envisioned that we'd be planting trees along
> the Underground Railroad to honor all of the enslaved
> people who had died. And then, in the heart of the
> Confederacy, I awoke one morning with this ques-
> tion: "What about the Confederate soldier?" It was

a question from my heart that came out of nowhere, and to be honest with you, I wasn't happy about that question. I thought: *If the Confederacy had won, we'd still be enslaved! How can we plant trees for them?!* But an inner voice nudged me, "We're not talking about them—this is about *you*. If you are who you say you're trying to become, then what about the Confederate soldier?" We ended up including the Confederate soldier in the vision of tree planting. Trees breathe for *everybody*. The soil receives *everybody*.

It takes bravery to go beyond conventional limits, to transcend "us vs. them." Many travelers on the path of love go to the edge but do not jump. The ego has a survival instinct and clings to its beliefs and feelings. It's one thing to preach about love but quite another to live the power of love when, inevitably, it leads one over the cliff of social acceptability.

At some point on the path of love, we come face to face with something that seems impossible to include within the sphere of love. That moment is a critical test. In my case, I had to embrace my love for a woman even though it was despicable to my parents, culture, and religion, and was considered a crime in seventy-two countries (punishable by death in eight of them). To deny such a healing love would have been to deny the God that had created me for love.

A Sufi story that I heard along the way brings the point home: A disciple who longed for truth heard there was a master in the forest. He left his house and belongings and went into the forest to find the master. When he saw the master, he knelt and said, "Please take me as your disciple. I have studied all the scriptures and now I need a genuine master to guide me."

The master said, "You are not ready."

The disciple was shocked. "But how can I not be ready? I have left everything behind to come sit at your feet."

The master repeated, "You are not ready to be my disciple."

"But I have fasted faithfully, I do all the prayers, I give to the poor, and I have impeccable ethics! Please take me! I want to learn the way to Truth and I have nowhere else to go!"

The master said, "Okay, then. Go now and buy a jug of fine wine and we will sit on the street corner in Baghdad and drink it!"

The disciple was horrified. "But I can't do that! That's a sin! What would people think?"

The master said, "Exactly as I said, you are not ready. As long as you cannot surrender the opinions of mere humans, how will you surrender to God?"

Without knowing it at the time, I had passed a test. By saying yes to love when it appeared in a "detestable" form, Somewhere a door opened to even greater love.

The journey had been similar to that of the caterpillar. Havasupai-Hopi-Tewa Grandmother Mona Polacca told me:

> In the Hopi language, my name, 'Polacca,' means *but-terfly*, and is a symbol of spiritual transformation. The process begins with the caterpillar that crawls on the ground. It sees nothing but what is right under its nose. Then, it enters a dark cocoon and undergoes a major change into a butterfly. Darkness can be a time for the old ways to break down and something new to develop. The butterfly remains in its cocoon until it is fully ready to break out of its shell and flutter its wings. Now it can fly. It can see things from a vaster viewpoint.

My encounter with the Indigenous Grandmothers revealed the vaster viewpoint. They taught me emphatically: "Everyone and everything is our 'relative.'"

The original Thirteen Indigenous Grandmothers,
New York, 2004 (Marisol Villaneuva, courtesy of The
International Council of the Thirteen Grandmothers).

## Chapter Twelve

# Love As Kindness –
# "All My Relations"

Encounter with Grandmother Mona Polacca
and The International Council of the Thirteen
Indigenous Grandmothers

*We have been brought together by a common vision
to form a new global alliance. Ours is an alliance of
prayer, education, and healing for our Mother Earth,
all of her inhabitants, all of the children, and for the
next seven generations to come.*

—Mission Statement,
Thirteen Indigenous Grandmothers

## Grandmothers' Gathering

In 2014, I traveled to the Black Hills of South Dakota and went to the Grandmothers' Gathering called The Sacred Hoop of Peace and Compassion. It was hosted by Lakota Grandmother Rita Long Visitor Holy Dance, and lasted several days. The program included prayer, ceremony, music, group dialogue, teachings on

Native medicines, and the sharing of life wisdoms from every continent. In Native traditions, you rise before the sun. The opening ceremony began at 5:45 a.m.

I heard the rattles as soon as I got out of the car. I looked around for an event but all I saw were flames dancing in the distance. I headed up a hill, arrived at the ceremony, and huddled next to strangers around the small fire. Grandmother Mona told me later, "Natives build a small fire so that everyone has to come closer. This is in contrast to the big bonfires that non-natives build, which force people outward and away from each other."

Prayers pierced the atmosphere—cries from the heart of the Grandmothers. Each one stepped into the center of the circle and made her prayer to the Creator on behalf of humanity and Mother Earth. Though they spoke and sang in languages I didn't understand, an intensity of love reverberated. After two hours, I was so cold I couldn't feel my toes anymore, but there was that unmistakable feeling—the kindling of an inner flame.

After the opening ceremony, the gathering shifted indoors, and the Grandmothers sat in a semicircle in front of us. Each made a greeting, sometimes through an interpreter. They spoke of their hope to "unite the hearts of the world." They pointed out that we humans are already united in our sharing of the sun and the moon and our common need of water, air, fire, and earth. Why not the heart? Can we not see that we belong to each other? Their emphatic message was, "We must learn to love one another again. The people who will survive are those who love and affirm life in every way." Everyone and everything is our relative.

Sitting there, I thought of all the grandmothers, past and present, unnumbered and unnamed. Their selfless love has fostered our survival as a species. My biological grandmothers died before I had the chance to know them, but I treasured the stories I heard about their fortitude and faith in the face of poverty, war, natural disasters, illness, heartbreak, and the deaths of their children.

When I was in my forties, Elizabeth came into my life as a surrogate grandmother. One night, I had a dream in which she gave me a gift—a Native American storyteller sculpture in the shape of a woman seated with children around her. In the dream, as Elizabeth handed the sculpture to me, she said: "The Grandmothers of the world are the storytellers. Their stories and prayers are what will save us—not the legacy of material wealth from the fathers." According to Native American spirituality, our prayers align us with the Creator, the Great Spirit. Our stories remind us of who and what we are; they create heartstrings in us that connect us to other people, animals, and the land.[100] Shortly after this dream, I found myself at the Grandmothers' gathering.

The International Council of the Thirteen Indigenous Grandmothers is a circle of wise women from around the world.[101] In their own countries, they're known as tribal elders, medicine women, shamans, and *curanderas*. They live in deserts, rainforests, badlands, and city apartments. Coming from five continents and the four directions, they met together for the first time in Phoenicia, New York, in October 2004. Some of the Grandmothers were in their eighties and had never been on a plane or spoken in public, yet they said yes to a demanding work of love that would take them to far-flung places. Since that first meeting, they've traveled to remote villages in the rainforests of the Amazon and Africa. They've planted their prayers in places such as Nagasaki, Japan, where an atomic bomb destroyed masses of people. They've spoken at United Nations conferences, international inter-religious congresses, and Ivy League university lecture platforms. They have received many awards and recognitions for their humanitarian efforts.

"They are not women of politics. They are women of prayer"— says Jyoti, whose vision of a Grandmothers Council was a major catalyst for the initial gathering of the Grandmothers in 2004.[102] The Grandmothers speak with the inner authority that comes from lived experience. They carry the valiant spirit of those who have endured personal heartache and communal devastation. They walk and talk the power of love. This is a power *within*, not a power *over*. They speak from the heart, not from the head or with the fist. They use humor, not sarcasm. Theirs is an inner knowledge. As the spiritual axiom goes, "Simplicity is a hallmark of truth."

When the Grandmothers opened a talk at Wellesley College, in Massachusetts, they held eagle feathers in their hands, not lecture notes. Grandmother Mona Polacca began with a Native song—without fanfare or orchestra. Her strong, singular voice pierced the atmosphere of the auditorium like an arrowhead. In the silence that followed, people noted that they felt "a recognition" of each other. Communal prayer and silence have a way of uniting us. The Grandmothers spoke in plain language about the wisdom they know from living close to the land: preservers of seeds; cultivators of sacred medicine; survivors of genocide; health workers with the ill, the dying, and those suffering from addiction. They didn't quote from books or experts. They sat and shared as living encyclopedias of a forgotten wisdom.

Their mission statement: "We have been brought together by a common vision to form a new global alliance. Ours is an alliance of prayer, education, and healing for our Mother Earth, all of her inhabitants, all of the children, and for the next seven generations to come." These are the original Thirteen Indigenous Grandmothers:

Margaret Behan Arapaho, Cheyenne of Montana, USA;

Rita Pitka Blumenstein, Yup'ik from Alaska, USA;

Aama Bombo (Buddhi Maya Lama), Tamang from Nepal;

Julieta Casimiro, Mazatec from Huautla de Jimenez, Mexico;

Flordemayo, Mayan from the Highlands of Central America and New Mexico;

Maria Alice Campos Freire from the Amazonian Rainforest, Brazil;

Bernadette Rebienot, Omyene of Gabon, Africa;

Tsering Dolma Gyaltong from Tibet;

Beatrice Long Visitor Holy Dance, Oglala Lakota from the Black Hills of South Dakota, USA;

Rita Long Visitor Holy Dance, Oglala Lakota from the Black Hills, South Dakota, USA;

Agnes Baker Pilgrim, Takelma Siletz of Grants Pass, Oregon, USA;

Mona Polacca, Havasupai-Hopi-Tewa from Arizona, USA;

Clara Shinobu Iura of the Amazonian Rainforest, Brazil.

"We must be warriors with the power of love," the Grandmothers said at the gathering in the Black Hills of South Dakota. Havasupai-Hopi-Tewa Grandmother Mona Polacca spoke about their origins:

> When we came together and met each other for the first time, we recognized that there was something we all shared. We recognized that we are all relatives, even though we come from the four directions. We realized we had a sacred responsibility as Grandmothers to take a stand, to step forward and speak through our prayers, songs, dances, and instruments. We recognized that we carried that wisdom not just for ourselves. We recognized that if we joined in an alliance with each other, we had more strength. It's like the story that says if you have one stick it breaks easily, but the more sticks you add to it, the stronger it becomes. We join our prayers, thoughts, feelings, dreams, hopes, wishes so that we can fulfill the sacred responsibility that our ancestors carried for us, and the prayers they made that said, 'Bless our future generations,' the ones we will not see. It's not all about us. We must think beyond ourselves.

Sitting there, I thought: *What a different world from the academic one!* The Grandmothers spoke freely from their hearts, not from prepared papers or PowerPoint presentations. Their ideas weren't disconnected from their bodies, hearts, and souls; all was shared from an integrated whole. Their comments were free of jargon, theory, and argument. They didn't imitate others or quote the experiences of others. They spoke with inner authority of their own Native traditions and life experience. They offered prayers around the fire circle, each in her own way. They said, "We all walk with a different medicine, but we accept each other's ways."

The Grandmothers spoke the truth that we all know unconsciously but are reluctant to speak aloud: our greed-driven consumer culture is not sustainable. They see with their own eyes the loss of young people to suicide and addiction, the wars for potable water, yet they spoke with *hope*, not fear and not denial. Fear is what we hear from religious pundits who preach punishment and apocalypse. Denial is what we hear from politicians who promise that *their* policies will assure us a secure future.

In contrast to authorities and politicos, the Grandmothers spoke of the power of love to unite us as we face a time of transition. As I listened, I recalled my teacher telling me that there is no guarantee that the world will continue as we know it. Civilizations come and go. *Love*, however, is timeless. Grandmother Maria Alice from Brazil said, "We are not on the planet only to suffer. We are here to blossom." Nature affirms that life is ever opening. Grandmother Mona Polacca told us a recent story from Hopi Mesa in Arizona:

> Not long ago, I went up to Hopi land to meet with my Hopi elders. They were all men. They said that the solar calendar has been complete. The solar is the calendar of the masculine. They said we are now in the time of the lunar calendar, the time of the feminine. The feminine has been degraded for so long. In order for us to make peace with Mother Earth, we

must make peace with our mother. She who gave us life. Then we will be able to understand something.

Coming to peace about our mother, she who gave us life, is something we all can do to bring the spirit of peace to life itself. For those with a mother wound—abandonment, abuse, neglect—Grandmother Mona said to start working on it within our self, to heal the feeling, and seek counseling if necessary. "It is a deep pain and it hurts not only ourselves but also life itself." The mother doesn't need to be present for us to heal a mother wound. "It would be letting go of wanting some kind of revenge on your mother. Letting go of resentment against her. Revenge doesn't do you any good. It only hurts you more. Healing that mother wound heals something fundamental in the fabric of life."

## FEMININE CONSCIOUSNESS

The work of the council is "the reawakening of having good relationships," Grandmother Mona told me. "I call it the basic call to consciousness, which is something I've heard from my elders. It has to start with the foundation of the elements—water, air, fire, earth—and expand from there to include everything and everyone."

The oldest Grandmother, in her nineties, Agnes Baker Pilgrim from Oregon, embodies this paradigm of "all my relations." She has been a barber, singer, logger, truck driver, and stock-car racer. A Takelma-Siletz spiritual leader of the Federated Tribes of Siletz, she is called a treasure among her people. "Grandma Aggie" is the matriarch of five generations in her family, and sees herself as a "Grandmother to the world." She told us:

> Love is all there is. Love and compassion are all there is. And this is why we're here today. We are all one. We are all one family. I pray to the beloved Creator. My prayer today is: 'Dearly Beloved, when you take me from this world, I pray that I have walked and

225

done everything I was meant to do; that when I'm gone, you'll take care of those I've left behind.' I believe we Grandmothers are living the feminine in all of its true power. The men in this room—don't forget that it took a woman's body to get you here! Men need feminine consciousness in them and to be balanced.

I thought of the many men I know who express feminine consciousness. As Vandana Shiva says, "The feminine is a principle, not a sex."[103] In the office next to mine at the university, Professor Larry Gross sits every day, ready to lend a hand and foster what he calls "heart-to-heart connection." He is an Indigenous man who embodies the Anishinaabe practice of kindness. If a student is looking for a classroom, he points the way. If someone needs help with the copier, he's there. Whenever I'm moving tables or equipment, Larry comes out of his office: "Here, let me give you a hand." Whatever our gender—and it is mysteriously diverse how consciousness inhabits a physical body—the challenge is to integrate the cosmic energies called masculine and feminine, yin and yang, Shakti and Shiva, solar and lunar, right brain and left brain.

Grandmother Julieta Casimiro, a Mazatec elder from Mexico, prays ceaselessly to the Virgin of Guadalupe, the Divine Feminine. Speaking through an interpreter, she gave this passionate statement:

God listens to us because the Virgin of Guadalupe is always present and She is the Mother who always listens to us. So that the Mother listens to us, put your hands together and pray to Her. Bless the water to drink and to bathe, so it can continue to give us life in the spirit. I pray with my rosary every day. Mother maintains us, gives us water to drink and food to eat. She represents all the good in the world. We love Her so much because she is the Mother of God and the whole world. We are so accustomed in our daily life to pray to Her with red roses and incense, so She

hears our prayers for everything. This is our custom
in Oaxaca today.

Being with the Grandmothers gave me an experience of women
with an integrated masculine and feminine consciousness. Their
feminine is potent. It has nothing to do with the traditional wom-
en's role I'd grown up with—the constriction of women into a carica-
ture of femininity based on servitude. The Grandmothers' feminine
is instinctual, close with the earth and its medicines, tapped into the
power of the heart, and intuitive; it knows the way of reconciliation
and reciprocity. Their masculine is creative, original in its thinking,
plainspoken, discerning, and in service to the whole of life, not the
personal ego. At the gathering, Grandmother Agnes told us where
to start:

> If you want peace, love, compassion, and joy, then
> create it where you are and give it away. Love is an
> inside job. I told my children, 'I can't give you all those
> good things. That's your own inside job.' Every day,
> I'm still a student. I learn from the little people. We
> pray for all children everywhere. We pray for the ani-
> mals too. We are their voice. We are the voice for the
> one legged, the tree people. We are the voice of all
> living things, little and big. We are the only voice they
> have. And it's our job to take care of their environ-
> ment, their habitat. Without them, we cannot live.
> Did you know that? You know it now. Without them,
> we cannot live.

The Grandmothers hold their Council in a circle, which is traditional among Indigenous peoples. When I met with Grandmother
Mona, she explained:

> The circle symbolizes interrelationship. The circle
> has no beginning and no end. And the other part of it
> is that we are all equal, no one higher or below. We're

all equal. We sit in a circle and shoulder to shoulder, supporting one another. Things in a circle have power. Like the wind. The world. A hurricane. A bird's nest. The trees. The greatest power is in a circle.

# THE POWER OF PRAYER

With her background among the Hopi, Grandmother Mona knows the power of prayer. The Hopi live in the High Desert with no rivers or lakes. She said they survive because they maintain their connection with the Sacred:

> The Hopi remember and follow what we call the 'original instructions' about how to care for life. They know where the water comes from. They know where the water flows. They know where to plant their gardens. The main thing is prayer. The Hopi rely on prayer for their whole existence. All Indigenous people, they rely on prayer. Their spiritual practices. Their spiritual beliefs. If you look at where they live, they can only exist there through prayer. Look at the people of the Arctic. The people in South America and the jungles. The people out in Africa and Kenya and out there in the desert lands. They've maintained that connection with the Sacred. They make offerings. It's give and take. Reciprocity.

My teacher also taught that, in times of difficulty, *sincere, heartfelt prayer* is greatly effective. "Rattle the Gates of Heaven," he said, "because God cannot refuse a sincere cry for help." He gave this example from the Hopi Mesa. In the 1970s, during a severe drought, a tribal leader invited him there to observe the Snake Dance ceremony. It was held in old Oraibi, on top of Third Mesa, considered the oldest continuously inhabited settlement in North America (est.

AD 1100). The corn plants were struggling to survive. Before the ceremony, there was no sign of rain. Here is his account of what occurred:

> People crowded the rooftops and then, just prior to
> the start of the Antelope Dances, the elders arrived
> and took their seats of honor. Even though it had not
> rained in many months, they all carried umbrellas!
> The reason soon became apparent—as the Antelope
> Dancers began, clouds formed in the sky, which later
> darkened rapidly when the Snake Dancers began to
> circle about, holding live rattlesnakes in their mouths.
> They sprinkled cornmeal on the ground, and, one by
> one, let the snakes go to crawl through it and then
> into the crowd of onlookers. The snakes approached
> very closely and then slithered away. Calm prevailed.
> And then after the prolonged, relentless, scorching
> drought, rain began to fall—-but not on the gath-
> ered celebrants, only just past the nearby cliff, pre-
> cisely onto the cornfields far below. It did not rain
> elsewhere but only on the acres of corn plants. It was
> the last Snake Dance to which white people were
> admitted, since some of them had been disrespectful
> in the past.[104]

He taught me that when we align with Love and surrender our
will, the seemingly impossible can happen, for "Love is the ultimate
law of the universe."

The Grandmothers express the kind of love that can draw down
the rain. Grandmother Mona Polacca told me, "We Indigenous
know from our experience that prayers bring water. And also stop it.
One of the greatest moments of prayer was when we were in Japan
and a typhoon dissipated." The Grandmothers were there to speak
at a United Nations Conference on Biodiversity. Just after a beautiful ceremony with Japanese spiritual elders, a rainbow, and a fire lit
from the Atomic Flame brought by a Buddhist nun, they got news

that the largest typhoon of the season was going to hit right there. Grandmother Mona recounted:

> We got our best tobacco for the offerings and gathered around the fire and started praying as hard as we could, to turn that typhoon away from us. 'Take it back out there where it's not going to hurt anybody or better yet make it disappear. You can do that. We believe you can do that. We're here trying to do something good.' We ate dinner and went to sleep. Next morning, we all sat down at our round table to have our circle. Somebody walked in and told us, "The typhoon stopped and turned away, then all of a sudden it just dissipated." We didn't even get any rain. It was sunny the whole time we were there.

## SACRED MEDICINE AND HEALING

The Grandmothers are not only warriors of prayer but also keepers of sacred medicine. In their Native communities, they work with plant medicines to heal tuberculosis, cancer, headaches, skin diseases, memory problems, and other ailments. The energy field of reverence is what makes the plant sacred. Grandmother Rita Pitka Blumenstein from Alaska—the first traditional doctor certified in the state of Alaska—described her process with white birch and how she uses it to treat cancer. She harvests the substance underneath the bark at a precise time of year and then makes it into a tea—all by hand and with prayer. "Talk to the medicine. Sometimes it will say not to use it for that person." As she gives the physical treatment, she also addresses mental and spiritual healing. In the Yup'ik worldview, the mind is very powerful in its effect on the material world.[105] "Cancer is a hidden problem. It comes from our mind and what we worry about," she says, and asks her patients, "Are you willing to change how you are thinking? Let go of your worries?"

Deep within the Amazon rainforest, Grandmother Maria Alice lives in a small religious community whose central ritual is the drinking of Santo Daime (a tea made of ayahuasca—both its vine and bush—representing a union of masculine and feminine principles). Drinking this tea is said to take the communicant back to the reality of oneness and to heal the inner spirit. Grandmother Maria Alice specializes in herbal medicines from the rainforest. She told us: "In the forest, all of creation—trees, vines, nests, birds, animals—they all live together in peace and harmony. That's the teaching I carry in my heart—to be in harmony with all of creation and be a sister to all living things."

As she described the healing effects of ayahuasca on mind, body, and spirit, I thought of a cowboy I know. Just before arriving to the Grandmothers Gathering in South Dakota, I spent a week with him and a group of horse people on the plains of Wyoming. One night, around the campfire, he told us of this experience:

> I've struggled my whole life with severe depression. It's genetic. I tried everything that Western medicine had to offer. My wife and I researched all possible modes to help me. Finally, we decided on ayahuasca. We found a place in Peru that seemed to be the most authentic setting for my experience. You have to be careful—many places are run by spiritual con artists. I prepared months before going. I was highly moti-vated. I gave up coffee and did everything they told me to do to prepare for my twelve-day treatment. Everything went well, even logistics. Frankly, I was so desperate that I didn't care if the plane crashed or if I was eaten by a snake. Either this treatment worked for me or it was the end. It was a long flight, then an hour-long boat ride down an offshoot of the Amazon.
>
> The first class session was on vomiting. It's called *La Purga.* Purgation. They gave us a tea and then most people vomited. I vomited some but not much. The ceremony was from 8 p.m. to 3 a.m. in a round

temple structure made of native materials. There were three grandmother shamans and two male shamans. They sang chants in the candlelight. It was all very moving and sacred. They called each person up to get their glass of the 'medicine.' The doses were different for each person.

Within the first hour, I had an experience in which I was given the answer to my depression. I was also given an understanding about relationships, how they are eternal and everyone is connected and there are unique roles for men and women. It was magical. Way beyond my expectation and hopes. The shamans used a natural humor that made us all laugh, even though we spoke different languages. It was a universal humor that we all somehow understood. They emphasized the Divine Feminine, and I felt that presence of love and compassion.

I came back a changed man. My wife says I'm different. I have a better outlook and more energy. I grew up here in Wyoming. I'm a cowboy through and through. Going off to Peru to drink tea with shamans is not something I ever thought I'd do. But the fact is it helped me.[106]

The Western mind tends to be reductionist. It hears the cowboy's story and thinks that a certain molecule in this plant "caused" the healing. This misconception leads naive seekers to chase after the chemical itself, or pharmaceutical companies to strip the forest in an effort to extract the molecule and make it into a pill. This mindset reduces sacred medicine to a drug. For Indigenous communities, healing doesn't come from a chemical but from the whole ritual experience set by the communal energy field of reverence, devotion, and respect. The ritual is guided by medicine men and women who steward a sacred knowledge received through a process of transmission and verified through their own experience. If the chemical is stripped from this ritual context of love, it loses its *magic*. Medicine used in the wrong way is poison.

With the Grandmothers, I was learning that most things are not bad in themselves (substances, sexuality, spears, money) but in how they're used—the need, the intention, the setting, the reverence. Grandmother Rita from the Pine Ridge Reservation in South Dakota talked about the Lakota ways of medicine. "Mother Nature placed all of the medicine for us. We walk all over it. We abuse it." She explained that there is a precise way to harvest tobacco and use it. "You have to have a purpose to dig it up. Pray to the medicine. If you don't do it right, it will go against you." Substances in nature, such as tobacco, are not innately the problem. They are given by the Creator as medicine. The problem lies in the human tendency to use them in a poisonous way.[107]

Spiritual principles and practices are often misused. The spiritual marketplace has no end of appeals to the ego's desire for shortcuts to bliss—psychic powers, money, fame, foretelling of one's future, lust, exotica, and specialness. Books abound as to how to use spiritual power for our own ends, to "manifest" a new car, a perfect partner, a good investment. Sufi teacher Llewellyn Vaughan-Lee uses the term "grey magic" to refer to the distorted use of spiritual power for egoistic gain. Black magic is the use of spiritual power to hurt others, and white magic to help others. Grey magic is "all about me."[108]

The sweat lodge is an authentic Native American spiritual practice that has a healing effect. Sometimes the healing is spiritual, sometimes physical, but sometimes it's misused. I was living in Sedona, Arizona, at the time of a so-called sweat lodge there that led to the deaths of three people. The three were among fifty participants who each paid $10,000 to be in a five-day "Spiritual Warrior" seminar with a popular new-age guru. The seminar was designed to push their limits, as in an endurance test. The culmination was a sauna-like ceremony that mimicked the Native American sweat lodge. Three people died of heatstroke and organ failure. A jury found the "sweat lodge guru" guilty of negligent homicide and sentenced him to two years in prison.

As the trial was ending, I read the newspaper article about it to my teacher. He was in his eighties and liked to keep an eye on the world, despite his declining vision. After finishing the article, I felt upset and asked him, "What went wrong here?"

He said, "Spiritual practices taken out of context lose their energy, especially if commercialized, as in this case." I took from his statement that when spiritual knowledge is misused for personal gain, then the Light of that knowledge—its energy—is taken away. The light bulb may still be there, but there's *no live current*. At the Grandmothers' gathering in the Black Hills, I certainly felt the live current of spiritual energy. Humility is key. Grandmother Rita from Alaska put it this way: "If you know an elder, listen. If you have a good answer, ask a question."

## Grandmothers Around the World

The International Council of Thirteen Indigenous Grandmothers is part of a larger shift in consciousness. Worldwide, grandmothers and wise women who know the power of love are nurturing a new vision for humanity. Men who have integrated their feminine side are standing with them and supporting this shift. This statement from Sufi teacher Llewellyn Vaughan-Lee, in the introduction to the book *Spiritual Ecology: The Cry of the Earth*, sums up the shift precisely:

> The world is not a problem to be solved; it is a living being to which we belong. The world is part of our own self and we are a part of its suffering wholeness. Until we go to the root of our image of separateness, there can be no healing. And the deepest part of our separateness from creation lies in our forgetfulness of its sacred nature, which is also our own sacred nature.[109]

Betty J. Eadie had a vision of this shift in consciousness over forty years ago. Born to a Lakota mother and raised in Indian boarding schools, Betty reconnected with her Native American spiritual roots after a profound near-death experience at age thirty-one. Now in her seventies, she is the mother of eight children and many grandchildren. Her best-selling book, *Embraced by the Light* (1992), gives an account of her near-death experience. Her second book, also a bestseller, *The Awakening Heart: My Continuing Journey to Love*, published in 1996, describes some of what she was shown of the world situation.[110] In a sort of slide show, Eadie saw a devastation of the earth, the effect of human greed. The soul of the earth had been desecrated. One thinks of the *anima mundi*—the world soul—spoken of by Plato and medieval alchemists. The sacredness of creation had been disregarded. Betty saw mountain peaks that were melting. Brown fog filled the atmosphere. People wandered aimlessly, like empty shells. I thought of the "hungry ghosts" spoken of in Buddhism.

When I met with her, Betty told me she was hopeful because she was shown a spiritual awakening led by those who have preserved a pure knowledge of the Creator and a way of life grounded in love and respect. Especially important were Native American concepts and practices: 1) reverence for the spirit of God in everything; 2) humble attitude toward the Creator; 3) avoidance of ego-driven and man-made religion; and 4) respect for family and self-sacrifice. "It all goes back to love," she told me, and the "Grandmothers of the world are the carriers of that love." She said their triumph will come not by political or legal force but by their wisdom to insist that society act out of concern and care. "God is not going to destroy the world. God created the earth and loves it. But I do believe we are coming to the end of an era." Grandmothers—"wise women" (not only biological grandmothers)—are "blessed and prepared" to bring the energy of healing and love that is needed at this time. "These women are already in place," she said. "Many of them know who they are because they feel compelled." Eadie's vision is indeed unfolding. The International Council of the Thirteen Indigenous Grandmothers is one of the most visible and influential expressions of it.

Grandmother Mona, as well as many of the people interviewed for this book, say that we are in an era of global transition in which *small groups with a spiritual center* have a key role in the nurturance of loving-kindness, remembrance of the sacred, and basic care for each other. We might not see our small circles of love as significant, but they actually keep the world from total self-destruction. In Jewish tradition, for instance, it is said that the preservation of the world depends on the presence of the *Lamed Vav*—thirty-six righteous people. Though their identities are not known, their just ways and pure hearts bless the world. Other spiritual traditions affirm the same truth: small groups of people aligned with Love outweigh the negativity operating in the world at large. If you are reading this book, you are probably in that minority and contribute more than you think.

Grandmother Mona Polacca tending the fire
(courtesy of Mona Polacca).

# Conversation with Grandmother Mona Polacca

For this interview, Grandmother Mona asked me to meet her at a picturesque organic farm, called The Farm, on the outskirts of Phoenix. A pecan orchard graces the grounds, and hundreds of birds fill the air with song. The café serves homemade food, fresh from their garden. It's an oasis of nature amidst urban sprawl.

## The Power of Simple Kindness

Q:  The significance of your name, "Polacca," tells me there is a purpose to darkness and this relates to some of your published articles on addiction. What is the role of spirituality in overcoming addiction or other dark periods?

GMP:   We call it *recognizing yourself.* To be able to recognize yourself as being a life form. As having a life. You have a life, your life is *sacred,* and your life starts from the very basic things like water, air, fire, earth. We call these the basic foundations. You have to start there, to see that your life is sacred. The sacred is the connection that you have to life itself. Going back to the beginning. The first moment you entered this world. That's what we call your sacred beginning. Of course the first step they take is to say, "I need help." *Humility* has to be there. And then to talk about their spiritual life. Many Native Americans were cut off from their spiritual roots. When they reconnect to their spiritual roots, then there is hope for them. That's the approach I see as being effective. I've seen a lot of Native Americans sustain their sobriety through the first step of recognizing themselves in the spiritual meaning of that term. That's what I have seen all the years I've done this work. I've tried to do something else, but I can't.

Q:  You tried to quit your work with addiction recovery, but you couldn't—what happened?

GMP:   I wanted to get skilled for some kind of eight-to-five job. When I had my children, I wanted to stay home and take care of the kids. But life is happening around you. You can't shut it all out and act like it doesn't matter. It matters, because your kids live in it. My kids lived in the community. They were being exposed to some of the woes of life. The people I cared about were suffering. I wanted my children to care about them also. I taught my children to care for others. So I continued to help those in my community while at the same time to raise my children. I had to teach the people I was bringing into my home how to be a good person, how to be someone who was healthy to be around my kids. I had to make sure it was safe for my kids. I engaged some of the people suffering in my life, made them a part of my family. It was a different environment from the alcohol, drugs, and violent television they were used to. We created a different environment inside our home.

Q:   When you invited people with addiction problems into your home, how did it go?

GMP:   I will tell you about one of them—a man who was an alcoholic and spent time in prison. He got out of prison and came into the community where I was working with the Alcoholic and Drug Recovery Program. I told my father, "Everybody calls him a name, a certain name, which isn't very complimentary, rather than his given name. He's really, really mean. He's angry all the time. He doesn't talk nice." And my father said, "You still have to be kind to him. He doesn't know what kindness is like. He has to learn. He doesn't know kindness, and he doesn't know how to treat people nice. It's life experience. How he grew up. The way he was raised. He doesn't know how to be treated nice or to treat people nice. He doesn't know how to be friendly. He's always on guard and ready to fight." My mother said, "He's like a puppy. If you have a puppy and you treat it really mean, if you pick on it, if you hit it, that puppy's going to grow up to be a mean dog."

Q:   We become what we're taught—as children we're innocent?

GMP: That's what my parents taught me—"Treat him nice because he can't help the way he is." So then my parents would go out for coffee and cake or pie or something at a coffee shop. And if he came in, they'd wave at him, call him over, and invite him to sit down for a visit. Eventually, I worked with him so he could come over to my house for dinner and be around my children. I had to teach people like him how to be around them. And when he'd get there, my kids would run to him and hug him. One was hanging on his leg. They got it. My children were kind to him. In public when they'd see him, they'd hug him. Call him by his real name, not the nickname. He told me, "You and your family, you're the only ones that call me by my real name. And your kids, they always act like they're happy to see me." I said, "Well, they *are* happy to see you!"

So, I taught him how to be around family. Then I taught him to drive. He wanted to learn how. He got into the car and put it in reverse and hit the gas pedal and almost crashed. I said, "Stop! Hit the brake!" It was a close call. I told him, "You always have to look and see what's behind you."

One day I said, "Let's go over to Dairy Queen and get an ice cream." I took the kids and him. When we got there, he stood way back. We picked out what we wanted. I asked him, "What do you want?" He said, 'I don't know. I don't know.' He'd never been to Dairy Queen. He'd never ordered ice cream anywhere. He didn't know what to do. Part of it was he didn't know how to read. We picked out something for him.

We got him into an adult basic education class. He learned how to read and write. And then he got his GED. He told me, "I'm clean and sober for years, I have my GED, but everybody still calls me by that bad name and they still treat me like they used to." He still dressed the same old way—jeans and white Tshirts with the sleeves rolled up. That was his uniform. So my colleague took him out shopping and bought him slacks and polo shirts and some new shoes and got him dressed up. It made a big difference. He felt good about his appearance. After that, nobody called him that bad name any more. They called him by his real name.

I gave him his first job, in a halfway house. He was a resident and worked part-time there. Then he finished his program and started working for me as a manager. He was eventually certified by the state of Arizona to be a chemical dependency counselor. He's the only one on our whole reservation who accomplished that.

Q: What a stunning story! And it all started with basic human kindness.

GMP: Basic kindness! He was someone who didn't know what kindness was. Had never been treated nice. Had never been kind to others. And kindness changed his whole life.

## Non-Possessiveness

Q: What does the water element feel like?

GMP: It's one of the elements of life. The water. The air. The fire. The earth. Look around us. These trees. The birds. It's beautiful. The elements of life are not separate. They are all connected. And just to be here, you are part of that connection. I can be sitting at my place, which is a small apartment in Tucson, and I can pray. I'm still practicing my spirituality. But to be in it, to be in what I'm praying about, that's important. In this day and age, the society we live in, there's a lot of consumerism and possessiveness. People want to possess. They want to own it. They think, "I have to have it." No! We don't have to own something in order to enjoy it. I don't own this place, but I can be part of it and have it at special moments. I don't have to own it. I don't have to grab it and take it. I don't have to try to take it home with me or pull up the trees! They have the garden. I can enjoy its beauty. If I wanted to take something home with me, I could go get something from the garden. Or I could save the food we're eating right now and take it with me. It's good energy. But I don't have to possess it. People think they have to own things, but they don't.

One time I met a young man who went to a ceremony using the sacred medicine. A couple days later, he asked me, "What do I need to do to get that medicine?" I said, "You want to possess it?" He said, "Yeah, what do I need to do to get it?" I said, "You don't have to do anything. You partook of it. You already have it in you. That's all. You don't have to have it and carry it around with you and show it off. You don't have to walk around and say, 'I have this in my possession.' You don't have to do that." Same thing with all other sacred ways. The instruments used in Tibetan Buddhism. In Christianity, the Eucharist. Whatever the world religions, they have certain things that are sacred medicine, sacred items. Just like Native Americans have sacred medicine and sacred herbs. We use them, but they do not belong to us.

People think they have to possess something in order to practice spirituality, but respect is the key. Hold the medicine, the ceremony, the path, with respect. Look at it and speak about it with respect. If you have the opportunity to be in the ceremony, be respectful, right in your heart, and be humble. That's the number one thing— be respectful. Don't grab something for yourself. If it's offered to you, receive it with respect. Those are some of the thoughts I would share with young people. I think about these things, but I haven't had a chance to talk about them.

## "All My Relations"

Q:   One phrase that the younger generations really connect with is "All my relations." What does that mean?

GMP:   It refers to interconnectedness with all of life. Everything. We're all related. We are here for *all* our relations. I'm not just talking about my relatives, my immediate family or husband or children. I'm talking about everything from within Mother Earth to the surface of the Earth, up to the Sky—all the way to the universe and beyond. That's our "relations." That's our existence. Whatever we do to another, it's the same as if done to us.

Q:   If we were taught that the other person is "me," that the water is "me," we wouldn't harm them. Instead, we are instilled with "It's all about me!"

GMP:    I was instilled with "It's *not* all about me!" When I was thirteen or fourteen, my mother told me, "You're not in this world for nothing. You have a purpose in life. What you do affects everything else—your parents, your siblings, your whole family, the family name, the community, the town, the state, the country, the world. Everything you do has a connection with everything else." That's interconnectedness. That's what "all my relations" means. That's having a relationship with life and understanding that we are all related. My mother is Havasupai from down in the Grand Canyon. *Havasu* means "the water." *Havasupai* means "people of the blue water." So, she'd say, "The fish in the water, they're your relatives." When we approached the waterfall, she said, "Let the water know you are here, that you'd like to be in it. Give it respect." This understanding is universal with Indigenous people. We say red, yellow, black, and white. That's the people. We're the people. Even whites are indigenous. I was told that we're all indigenous people to Mother Earth. We were all given the instructions on how to live here and to honor this relationship. But some have forgotten.

## The Basic Foundation: Creation and the Four Elements

Q:    I—and the white people I know—don't seem to remember the "original instructions" of caring for the Earth. I was taught from books, not from nature. But you had a different upbringing. You're emphatic that we must see what we all have in common.

GMP:    Do you know what it is?

Q:    Please tell me.

GMP:    I already told you.

Q:    You already told me?

GMP:    You're not listening yet. We are *all* dependent on the basic elements of life. None of us can do without any one of them. Water. Fire. Air. Earth. Water is the first foundation of life because we live in water in the womb, and we follow the water out of the mother. Air is the second foundation as we take our first breath as soon as we arrive in the world. We open our mouth and fill our lungs with air. When we let it out, we make our first cry and let the world know we are here. We express ourselves and what we need in life. We give our song. Fire is the third element as we are taken into the warmth of our mother's arms and our caretakers build up a fire for us that is warm and welcoming. They take us outside and the Sun sees us. Then, the fourth foundation is the earth, as we are laid on Mother Earth. Finally, we are made to stand up on our feet. With our feet planted on Mother Earth, we experience balance for the first time. We take our first steps on the earth, and we walk our path, which has brought us to this point. Every person has a primal connection to these four elements and all of Creation. Awareness of life means to awaken with gratitude for the Creator who is in water, fire, air, earth. And who also lives inside of us.

Q:   But most of the world has forgotten this primal connection to creation and the four elements. What will it take for humans to change the way we relate to the earth?

GMP:   There's a saying: "Only when all of the waters are polluted, only when we cannot breathe, only when the plants no longer grow, only when the sun is covered by pollution and there is no sunlight— only then will we realize that we cannot live on money alone." That's where we're heading. It shouldn't have to take that. It shouldn't take a crisis. It should take anybody to look at a little child, their newborn baby, and say, "My little child, I'm going to make sure that this, your life, is going to be strong and healthy. You're going to have good clean water to drink, whether you have money or not." But many people do not care about others. They have no understanding of "all my relations." If we viewed the Earth as a living being, which it is, would we treat it like this? No.

Q:   Is there anything ordinary people can do in their daily life to bring more balance and care to this situation?

GMP:   The word that comes up for me is "preservation." To think about preservation. What does it mean? Preservation of the existence of the ones that are yet to come. It's really pretty simple. What are the steps you're willing to take to preserve water, for example? Out of love for life, are you willing not to waste? Getting conscious of your own usage. Realizing it's *not* "all about me." One of the instructions I was given when I was growing up was to "know your water." Where is your good clean drinking water? Where's your source of water? And you have to take care of it and protect it. Keep it clean.

## Forgiveness, Respect for All People, Human Rights

Q:   You and your people have been through horrific suffering. How do you relate to the atrocities of the past?

GMP:   We are not defined by our past and what has been done to us. This is not to say that we forget it. But I was raised to have a good nature and to have good relations. I was taught by my elders always to be kind.

Q:   Even with the people who are the enemy, those who have harmed you?

GMP:   My father specifically said to me, "Be kind to your enemies. Treat them with kindness. Greet them." There was a person who offended me, who did and said some mean things. I was at a community event and saw him. People were greeting me. I was greeting everybody and hugs and smiling and all that. And he was standing there. I walked right past him, totally ignoring him. I observed him after that, and I saw how hurt he was. I don't like to inflict that kind of hurt. The same thing with my words. I don't want to speak unkindly either. I was taught that it's bad medicine to treat others unkindly. It's like stabbing someone. It's hurting them. It's like you could say something to somebody and it could cut them. You could even look at somebody in a mean way and hurt them. Even walking by them with that energy, you could hurt them. That's what I was taught.

Q:   At the gathering, I was shocked to learn that the Catholic Church still has papal bulls that call for the forcible conversion and conquest of Indigenous peoples.[111]

GMP:   We are beseeching Pope Francis to rescind the bulls that call for the use of force against Indigenous peoples. These bulls remain the spiritual, legal, and moral foundation for exercising jurisdiction over tribal people. When we went to the Vatican, we did not plant our flags; we planted our prayers. The Vatican is a place of prayer. It's considered sacred. Anytime we go to a sacred place, we plant our prayer and make our offering. It could be a mountain. It could be a river. It could be a lake. It could be anyplace. When we went there, we had planned on being at one of Pope Benedict's public audiences, but he cancelled his public audience. We went there anyway because it really isn't about him per se. It's about what the Vatican represents.

We were planting a prayer. When we were there, praying, an American man walked up and yelled at us, "Stop this! What you're doing is antiCatholicism and I'm calling the police!" We just looked at him and we kept praying. He stood there and watched us in a hostile sort of way. The police came and shouted at us. We still kept on praying while some of our helpers spoke with them.

When Beatrice, the Lakota Grandmother in her eighties, stepped up to the chief of the pope's security, I saw a little, tiny butterfly fly in, touch her moccasin, and then fly up and over the basilica. And you know what she did? Grandmother Beatrice told the officer, 'What's the matter here? We're just little old grandmas praying here. That's all we're doing.' She put her hand on his heart and said, 'You have a grandmother, don't you?' 'Yes.' 'Now, tell me, would you forcibly stop your grandmother from praying?' He shook his head. And then he turned to his officers and said, 'Well, looks like everything's okay here. They're not doing anything wrong.' He looked at us and said, 'Grandmas, you go ahead and finish your prayer. And then when you're through, I'll have this security officer escort you straight into the basilica. You can continue your prayer in there or you can sit and relax and have a drink of water and cool down.'

Q: That's a great example of how love can diffuse conflict. Grandmother Beatrice didn't attack him or get angry and defensive. She spoke to his heart and made a connection.

GMP: It was powerful.

## Living in Alignment

Q: The Grandmothers have formed a council to address the problems of the world, spread compassion, share their wisdom. What do you recommend for others to do?

GMP: We all want something good in our lives, but at the same time, there are teachings to follow in order to be in alignment. Basic teachings. For one, I was taught to be up by the time the sun rises. At dawn, be awake. Stand up. Be ready to go out to receive the opportunities that the day has to give you. I was told, "If you're lying down when the sun comes up and the sun sees you lying there, it might think you're dead!" Rise with the sun. Travel with the sun all day long. Another teaching is not to be lazy. Keep yourself clean. Take care of the things around you. Take care of yourself, your parents, your animals. Before we could go anywhere, we had to clean. We couldn't go anywhere unless the house was clean. Even if the parents had to be somewhere, they wouldn't leave until we finished cleaning. Anyway, there were certain things about how to greet the day.

Q: What are the prayers each day?

GMP: We thank everything—all the basic elements in life from the time you first meet the day. You just acknowledge them and give thanks for them. The prayer has been made. We say it "makes a way for you." The prayer creates the clearing of your path for you to go forward in the day. Prayer in the morning. Every morning. This reminds me of Grandmother Beatrice, one of our Lakota grandmas. She is almost ninety. I shared a room with her when we went to an event. At night, she gets in bed and lies down, then closes her eyes and starts praying. And she prays and she prays and she prays till she goes to sleep. And I do that now sometimes. To rise in prayer and go to sleep in prayer. And then Grandmother Tsering, the Tibetan grandmother, I shared a room with her. Early in the morning, she's got her little altar with her and the sun's not even up yet. I wake up and see her. She's sitting there on her bed with her Tibetan altar. It looks like a little house. She's saying her prayers. How beautiful that I was able to see these elders and how they pray. Even in their own private moments, praying.

Q:   In terms of ordinary people wanting to help the world, where's a good place to start?

GMP:   Small circles. That's a good way to start because the important thing is connection. In huge corporations and organizations, there's no sense of that connection. We have to rebuild our knowledge of interconnectedness in small ways. If you start in your small circle, you build understanding of each other, a relationship of caring and sharing. They don't have to be blood relatives. They're like chosen family. Create a small circle and start there. And everybody has their gifts, knowledge, and experience to bring to the circle. If you build the relationship of trust and caring, then you are prepared to help each other. When the shelves in the grocery store are empty, what are you going to eat? When the electricity goes out, how are you going to stay warm? Those are very real things, and it's not a matter of being a "Debbie Downer." It's a matter of realizing that we are interconnected. It's the basic need for kindness and caring. It's a time of transition, and we don't know what lies ahead. I never thought I would live to see the day when that calendar could be completed, as my elders prophesied. So, we are being aware and listening and preparing our minds and hearts. At the same time, it's important to know that we have this opportunity to live our life in joy and surround ourselves with beauty. To enjoy—truly enjoy—our life. Just listen to those birds!

Grandmother Mona opened my eyes to the beauty of life all around me. Even though we talked about the world's difficulties, I felt more hope. I saw more clearly the power of love to transform a difficult situation—an addiction, a typhoon, an argument. I heard that to bless or appreciate something gives it life. To show people genuine kindness lifts them to a higher plane. Simply to be thankful for water and food makes a positive contribution. As I walked to my car, I was newly aware of all four elements—the air, the water, the sun, and the Earth—the basic foundations of life we cannot live without. The trees, grasses, passersby, dogs, squirrels—I had a new appreciation for my "relatives." Creation is alive. We are never alone.

The Grandmothers helped me remember what I'd forgotten. Spiritual teaching is mainly *remembrance* of the truth we already know because it's inside of us. The "original instructions" are that "All of life is sacred" and "We are all connected."

"All my relations" is a translation of the Lakota phrase *mitakuye oyasin*, and reminds us that we are all connected to each other as relatives in the sacred web of life since the beginning of time and till the end of time, including ancestors who have passed and children yet to be born, and every blade of grass and drop of rain. Rita Long Visitor Holy Dance, a Lakota member of the International Council of the Thirteen Indigenous Grandmothers, told a gathering that "all my relations" functions as a prayer: "You think of everything in your prayers, even the birds and insects. 'All my relations' is a prayer in itself, one that covers the whole world."

What I learned from the Grandmothers is to be authentic to what we are. To pray with heart and soul, to water the seeds of hope and healing. To be stewards of whatever positive teachings we've been given. To be respectful of where and how we walk. To use spiritual medicine wisely. To honor the sacredness of life within us and all around us. To be kind to the life inside and around us. For greatest effect, my teacher would teach me later, our practice of kindness is unconditional, desiring no reward.

Dr. David R. ("Doc") Hawkins
(courtesy of The Institute for Spiritual Research).

*Chapter Thirteen*

## "When the Student Is Ready, the Teacher Appears."

## "You Yourself Are What You're Looking For"

W hen I left *the* church for the sake of love, huge energies of longing, repressed my entire life, were activated before I had the spiritual wisdom to navigate them.

In India, they tell the story of the musk deer, which catches a hint of sweet fragrance and runs after it, not knowing that the fragrance comes from a secretion within its own abdomen. This indeed was my predicament. I was chasing after every hint of love—a "high," a place to call home, an erotic attraction, an adventure—as if love were *elsewhere*. Like the musk deer, I didn't know that the sweetness was inside of the heart of hearts, and so my constant chasing after something else always ended in more longing. Finally, at thirty-nine, life dropped me at the doorstep of a spiritual teacher, and I heard the truth: "You yourself are what you're looking for."

I first encountered him in a book recommended by my psycho-therapist. At the time I entered therapy, I was sinking into what Frankl called an existential vacuum. In outer terms, my life was going well. Love had healed an essential, deep part of me. The panic was gone. I could speak freely, even in front of hundreds of people and to millions on national TV. I was open to life and much more accepting of self and others. My partner and I had left the church and were creating a new life together. It was difficult to do so without the sanction and support of a church community, but the freedom to be authentic was enlivening. I enjoyed new levels of friendship, creativity, and happiness. I was living closer to my heart and truer to my nature. Professionally, I was successful and had received tenure at another university, where I could offer the best parts of myself and was given the freedom to grow.

In sum, in the previous several years, I had come through a major earthquake and rebuilt my life on a new foundation. I had a new family, new friends, a new house, and a new job as a religious studies professor. The outer parts of life seemed solid, but internally, my spirit was restless. Unbeknownst to me, I had rebuilt my life on the same fault line as before—a longing for love, thinking it was outside of myself.

Inner uneasiness gnawed at me. I was drinking too much and gaining a lot of weight. I was in the love relationship that had healed so much for me but, inexplicably, I still felt restless for romance—did I need to be with someone else? I was exhausting myself with over-socializing and overwork. The old desperation for approval hadn't gone away, and the lifelong inferiority made it difficult to be vulnerable. Despite being surrounded by friends, I felt alone—"No one really knows me. If they did, they wouldn't like me." In the academic domain, where skills of logic and argument reigned, I felt inferior due to my feeling and intuitive typology. Like a very short person trying to make it in professional basketball, the rules of engagement did not favor my assets. I dealt with the pain of self-deficiency through various distractions and addictive habits.

I'd had the courage to change my whole life for love. The healing had been profound and necessary. So why the inner longing for *something more?* This period of confusion served a purpose. As my teacher put it, "The mature spiritual aspirant is one who has explored the ego's options and false promises of happiness. The ego's final song, after examination, is represented by a famous singer's poignant song, 'Is That All There Is?'"[112]

Modern physics tells us that vacuum states are dynamic and full of creative forces; this was certainly true of the existential vacuum I found myself in.

An influx of spiritual wisdom came from Buddhist teachers such as Jetsunma Tenzin Palmo, Pema Chödrön, and Joanna Macy. From Buddhism, I learned meditation methods that helped me to sort out out truth from illusion. When I met with her, Palmo told me, "Inherently you have Buddha-nature. That's our true nature… but because of our delusion, we often act more like demons. We create so much suffering for ourselves and for the world around us." Through meditation, I worked to cultivate wholesome habits of thought.

Palmo said, "It's like weeding the garden. You water good plants and you pull out the weeds. That way, gradually, the mind and heart begin to un-pollute." I found loving-kindness meditation (*metta bhavana*) to be especially effective. It reduced my anger at the church leaders for having rejected me. Much to my surprise, Palmo told me that loving-kindness had to start with myself: "Until you love yourself, you cannot love others! It would just be a dependency."

These principles and practices gave me a life raft while I felt lost at sea. Buddhism, as I understood it at the time, did not require a belief in God or transcendent Being, and this fit with my agnosticism. I had left the church in order to say yes to love. I knew that Love was real. The Light had been incredible. But God? I wasn't so sure. The word itself made me uneasy, as I'd seen it used in so many unloving ways. My agnosticism was a humble position that acknowledged the probable existence of Something Greater without calling it God. I was going through a process of partial atheism, in which the God I'd been brought up to believe in was dead to me. That God had been little more than a child's projection of the punitive parent. The child felt guilty for being bad, and feared punishment from the great-big parent in the sky. This childish image of God *had* to die; it had nothing to do with Love. It was infantile ego projection, not the Great Reality. Sigmund Freud was correct to state that such anthropomorphic projections onto God were fallacious, but Freud's final conclusion would not be my own. Just because the negative projections of God weren't true didn't mean that there was no Higher Power at all.

I found hope in Gandhi's description of the Real as "an indefinable mysterious Power that pervades everything." His inner experiences led him to say: "I do dimly perceive that whilst everything around me is ever changing, ever dying, there is, underlying all that change, a Living Power that is changeless, that holds all together, that creates, dissolves, and recreates. That informing Power or Spirit is God." Gandhi asked, "Is this Power benevolent or malevolent?" He saw this Power as purely benevolent based on his observation, "In the midst of death life persists, in the midst of untruth truth persists, in the midst of darkness light persists. Hence, I gather that God is Life, Truth, Light. He is Love. He is the Supreme Good."[113] I was hoping that, one day, I would come to know the God of Light, Truth and Love. For God to be God, He (or She) had to have that same quality of Love infused in the Light I'd experienced at fifteen.

## LIGHT TO LIGHT

A year into psychotherapy, I began to feel more real. Some of my walls had come down. I had lost weight, gotten more honest with myself and with others, and felt much happier. I asked my therapist, "Is there anything I can read about this process?" I wanted to understand what she meant by "levels of consciousness" and "energy fields." She replied, "*Power vs. Force* by David R. Hawkins." I'd never heard of him. When the book arrived, I glanced at the author photo on the back and sighed—another white man? My politics at that time led me to take a dim view of men, so I tossed the book aside. It was the middle of a busy college semester and there were student papers to read.

The day after Christmas, I opened the book to its last section, "About the Author," a brief spiritual autobiography. As I read it, I became unexpectedly magnetized—as if some switch inside of me had been turned off my entire life and now, suddenly, it turned to ON. I heard myself say, "My God! This is the *real deal!*" He was a fire, and I was a moth drawn to the flame. I was faintly aware that my life as I knew it was going to end.

As a scholar, I had studied and taught about mystics for many years—Marguerite Porete, Meister Eckhart, Dogen, Ramakrishna, St. Hildegard, St. Teresa of Avila, Rūmī, and others—but I'd never encountered one in real life. The author's experiences reached out to me from the pages as if I were actually reading about the innermost part of my own Self that had long been forgotten—as if I weren't learning something new but rather remembering something true. Two of his experiences especially electrified me.

One winter day when he was twelve, he was biking his seventeen-mile paper route and a storm hit, with gusting winds at twenty below zero. The wind knocked over his bicycle, and he fell on the frozen ground. He dug out a hollow in the snow bank along the road. Though freezing, he soon experienced a timeless and gentle "Presence" of overwhelming Love:

> Soon the shivering stopped; there was a delicious warmth, and then a state of peace beyond all description. This was accompanied by a suffusion of light and a presence of Infinite Love, which had no beginning and no end and was undifferentiated from my own essence.... The mind grew silent; all thought stopped. An Infinite Presence was all that was or could be, beyond all time and description.[114]

Reading this, I remembered the experience of the Light. I sensed that he had discovered the Source of himself—and that it was also *my* Source.

At sixteen, despite that early experience of Infinite Love, he rejected the idea of God. Walking through the woods one day, he was hit with a sudden revelation of the horrible suffering of human beings throughout all of time, and in that moment he blamed God and became an atheist. Yet he was still driven by an intense quest to reach the truth about existence. Blessed with a good mind, he easily mastered the world of science and the intellect. While other teenage boys played stickball and read comic books, he listened to the weekly opera program and read Shakespeare and Plato. He completed medical school while holding three jobs, and became the head psychiatrist running a large hospital and publishing a plethora of scientific articles. To all appearances, he was successful; he had the largest psychiatric practice in New York State, owned luxurious homes, and enjoyed membership in elite social circles. On the personal level, he'd gone through many years of psychoanalysis with one of the leading Freudians of the time. Yet all of his investigations brought only deeper despair. At the pinnacle of worldly success, he was confronted with a vast and wayless inner darkness.

The crisis culminated in 1965 when he was thirty-eight and at the point of death due to a progressive illness. He likened the agony of his existential despair to Dante's *Inferno* where the sign is posted: ABANDON HOPE ALL YE WHO ENTER HERE. The hopelessness, he said, was "forever." All of his efforts to pursue the meaning of existence via the intellect had failed: "I was *in extremis* and knew I was about to die. I didn't care about the body, but my spirit was in a state of extreme anguish and despair. As the final moment approached, the thought flashed through my mind, What if there is a God?" And with that, he called out a prayer—"If there is a God, I ask Him to help me now"—and surrendered totally to "whatever God there might be." Immediately he went into "oblivion." It took him thirty years to recount the earth-shattering aftermath:

When I awoke, a transformation of such enor-
mity had taken place that I was struck dumb with
awe. The 'person' that I had been no longer existed.
There was no personal self or ego, only an Infinite
Presence of unlimited power that it was all that was.
This Presence had replaced what had been 'me,' and
the body and its actions were controlled solely by
the Infinite Will of the Presence. The world was illuminated by the clarity of an Infinite Oneness that
expressed itself as all things revealed their infinite
beauty and perfection.

In the wake of this transfiguration of consciousness, all of life was
revealed in its timeless beauty and oneness: "The incredible beauty of
all things shone forth, and where the world saw ugliness, there was
only timeless beauty. This spiritual love suffused all perception and
all boundaries between here and there and then and now, and separation disappeared."[115] *Power vs. Force*, the book suggested by my therapist, was published three decades after this Realization, for it took the
author that long to integrate the experience and to present it in a way
that would be helpful to others.

His account was stunning to me. It revealed the pure, eternal
essence of the human being and the Oneness/Allness of Life. He took
no credit. The experience was "given" as a "gift of Grace," he said—not
an achievement. He told me later, "In that state, there is no person left
to 'claim' anything." Oneness, Kingdom of Heaven, Self-Realization,
Buddha-nature—whatever terminology is used, this state of completion is within all of us, he affirmed, saying simply: "When the clouds
are removed, the sun shines forth." What a shock to realize that the
Love I had looked for my entire life had always been around me and
within me.

Still, at that time, a spiritual teacher was the last thing on my
mind. It had never occurred to me to look for one. I had no famili-
arity with gurus; if anything, I viewed them as highly suspect. I still
harbored hurt over how religious authorities had rejected my inner

life and denied my soul's longing for love and experience of the Light. Yet, underneath my hurts, my soul had evidently been searching for a "pillar of Light," as described by Sufi teacher Llewellyn Vaughan-Lee:

> We're looking for a pillar of Light, a place of light in the world. They say, traditionally, it's actually the teacher that looks for the light of the disciple. But it's the same thing. A path or a teacher is a connection of Light. You can see it clearly in the inner world. It is a pillar of Light in the darkness of the world. You are looking somewhere, continually scanning the horizon in your world. It can be years, even decades, and then your attention is taken to a place of Light and there you lock on, your radar locks on. It might not be immediately, but eventually you find your way to that path, to that tradition, to that teacher that is this Light. This is the simplicity of finding the path that's right for you. Because your light resonates with the light of the teacher or the path that is right for you. There is this resonance of light to light.[116]

Indeed, as I read *Power vs. Force*, my radar locked on, as light to light. My light resonated with his. He taught that the Light was the Self, not the person of the teacher: "It is not a person who is the teacher but the Self of the teacher. By analogy, it is not the lighthouse that guides the ships but the light shining from the lighthouse. One is free to pursue the light or not. Neither the light nor the lighthouse has any stake in the matter. Religions tend to deify the lighthouse at the price of the light."[117]

When I finished the book, I said to myself: "Finally, after twenty years, I understand the Light! Finally—to know that God is Love, and that Love is the greatest power in the universe. This changes everything." It was a total paradigm shift, as if I had exited the elevator at a different floor. The world I saw was not the same world as before. The book validated the meaningfulness of my life and the search for Truth, inseparable from Love. It confirmed certain intuitions I'd had most of my life, such as: the world is an interplay of different energies that constellate into "energy fields" or "levels of consciousness." Thus we commonly hear, "Like goes to like" and "birds of a feather flock together."

I recognized the levels of consciousness on his Map of Consciousness® as the classic stages of human inner evolution found in the world's sacred literature and suggested by philosophers, sages, and mystics throughout the centuries. Yet this book was the first time I had read a scientific work that confirmed them as actual, measurable "attractor patterns" and "energy fields." It was a compelling verification of right-brain intuition through the means of left-brain knowledge. He said he'd written the work to comprehend the sudden transformation of consciousness he had undergone, classically termed *enlightenment,* to integrate it with scientific discovery, and then to put it in a format that was understandable to the left brain of Western readers. *Power vs. Force,* he said, "is the realm of the mystic communicated to the left brain."[118]

I immediately read his other books: *The Eye of the I: From Which Nothing is Hidden* and *I: Reality and Subjectivity.* In them, I encountered the realm of the mystic. It was the same essence I'd encountered when reading the mystics of Professor Babinsky's class in seminary and those in the Spiritual Direction program, except that this essence was presented in the language of my own time. Swami Chidatmananda of India, a teacher of Vedanta whom I encountered in my journey for *The Power of Love,* told me that David Hawkins's books were essentially the same as the ancient Upanishads, written in our modern idiom: "There is no difference between what he has experienced and discussed and what was said by the great sages and saints of India."

The restlessness in me felt finally relieved. What I'd been searching for my entire life was somehow given to me in the pages of these books. The search was over. I had found what I'd been longing for. As the story goes—the musk deer finally realized that the fragrance he smelled everywhere around him was actually inside him.

As I read these books, I recalled certain moments of oneness as a young person growing up along the Gulf of Mexico in Florida, where my family lived in the Coffeen Nature Preserve, a wild bird refuge. In that place of pristine nature, the veils were thin between this world and the Self. I recalled my walks on the beach in the company of hundreds of birds. My destination was always the place where the river flowed into the sea. Somehow, I knew that it represented the destiny of my soul. In my teacher's books, it was repeated that the search for Love ends always with the surrender of the self (river) into the Self (Sea).

One time, as I walked the beach, there was no person in sight. At first I passed by him, thinking it was a lump of sea debris, but then I turned back to look. It was a large bird. He sat perfectly still, radiating. Only a slight turning of the head toward me—an invitation? I sat down on the sand, a foot or so away—close yet respectful, as when entering a great cathedral where devoted people kneel in prayer. I saw that he was injured. I sensed he was dying. At first, fantasies of bird rescue, scenes of heroism, of taking the bird home and nursing it back to health. Yet the moment called for witnessing, simply "being with," not action. I sat still. An otherworldly light passed between us across the sand. The bird's serenity settled over me, the serenity of acceptance. For a moment, we became as familiar as lovers enjoying a sunset—nothing to do, nothing to say. We watched another bird, a tiny snowy plover, scamper back and forth across the sheen on twig-like legs, drilling its little beak into the sand as waves rolled back and forth into the sea. The plover was hunting for sand fleas. There we were: eating, dying, sitting, watching. In the silence, all was understood. All was One.

The next morning, I ran back there to see him again. Only a carcass remained. "You can't kill life. It merely changes form. Life goes to life." This was what my teacher told me years later. He had remembered many physical deaths, saying they were not an end to life but rather the letting go of "form."

As a youth, I didn't have the language to articulate the awareness of oneness I experienced in nature—different forms of life breathed by the same Life. I told no one of these moments. In time, this awareness of life's oneness was covered over by a religious conditioning, one-sided in favor of a transcendent God up in Heaven. I was told that it was heresy to say that God was present within creation.

As I read Dr. Hawkins's books, the core of me that had searched for Love was validated. Intuitively, it made sense that certain energy fields are positive while others are negative, and that "Love is the greatest power in the universe." It was obvious that the energy of Mother Teresa was different from the energy of Adolf Hitler, and that most people's energy lay somewhere in-between. *Power vs. Force* delineates two basic categories of energy: "power," which has a positive and life-affirming effect, and "force," which has a negative effect. Dr. Hawkins illustrated the difference between them in the cases of Mahatma Gandhi and Nelson Mandela, both of whom radiated an inner power that brought down long-standing systems of oppression in a short amount of time. How could a prisoner break the system of apartheid, or a ninety-pound devotee wearing only a loincloth bring the British Empire to its knees? What force cannot accomplish with all its might, the power of love does effortlessly.

*Power vs. Force* resonated with common sense. Negativity drains, positivity uplifts. Positive energy fields (courage, willingness, acceptance, reason, love) are more powerful than negative ones (shame, apathy, fear, anger, pride) because they are aligned with what is Real. Love, for example, radiates a beneficial and healing effect, while fear has a constricting and polarizing effect. Love moves us forward; fear holds us back. Each energy field represents a view of life that makes sense to those at that level of consciousness. Endless arguments can go on between people at different levels (even in the same family or workplace) because each person is actually seeing a different world. If one is wearing red-colored glasses, everything will appear red no matter how strong the case presented by those wearing green-colored glasses. Is the world green or red? The world you see depends on the lens you're looking through. A lot of frustration is eased when one realizes that people aren't bad or stupid, they're simply seeing life the way they see it because of the lens they are looking through. That lens is their level of consciousness. The consciousness level of Love is visionary, inclusive, healing, self-giving, and capable of long-lasting changes that uplift millions of people. It's also rare.

*Power vs. Force* confirmed that spiritual practices done with sincerity and devotion have a beneficial effect. This is true, for example, of the Native American sweat lodge, Tibetan prayer wheel, Christian labyrinth walking, Hindu ritual bathing in the Ganges, Jewish prayers at the Wailing Wall, chanting OM, and most other common spiritual practices. The form isn't fundamentally important—and this was a revolutionary point for me, as I'd been taught that the outer form of something determined its purity. The book said, rather, that the healing effect comes from the inner purity of the heart and the intention and overall energy field of the practice—such as devotion and reverence. Moreover, certain places, writings, and pieces of art and music also radiate the energy field of Love and have a beneficial effect; e.g., Stonehenge, Chartres Cathedral, Tibetan Buddhist stupas, the Bhagavad Gita, the Psalms, the Heart Sutra, the United States Declaration of Independence, Mozart, Louis Armstrong, Rembrandt, *Ave Maria,* etc. The Divine is found everywhere. As mystic Marguerite Porete said, "I find Him everywhere, and He is there."

*Power vs. Force* presents an easy-to-grasp Map of Consciousness that shows the arch of spiritual evolution from its basest expression (shame and self-hatred) to its most sublime (Infinite Love, The Real, Christ, Buddhahood, Krishna). On the Map, Guilt, Hate, and Fear are energy fields at the bottom, while the energy field of Love is pinpointed as the gateway to spiritual reality, characterized by the opening of the heart. "Whereas the mind thinks, the heart *knows*." Interestingly, the author found that few people actually live on the level of Love, even though love is much discussed and commercialized. The minority of people who radiate the energy fields of Love sustain humanity as a whole. These are the Mother Teresas, Nelson Mandelas, and Viktor Frankls of the world.

The purer and more selfless the love, the more powerful the effect. The outer form doesn't matter. It could be a simple smile or a home-made meal or a random act of kindness. As Mother Teresa taught, "Do small things with great love," for it's not how much we do, but how much love we put into the doing. Something made or done or given or said with genuine and selfless love—no matter how small—has the greatest impact. This was the take-home message from the book, and it redirected the course of my life. Now that I knew the energy field of Love was the greatest hope for humanity, I made a conscious dec-laration to become more loving. Naively, I thought this meant I had to acquire something I didn't have; instead, it meant removing what I didn't need, that is, the inner obstacles to love. "When the clouds are removed, the sun shines forth."

I wanted to go see the author, Dr. Hawkins. I knew I needed something I couldn't get from a book, a philosophy, or from trying hard. I needed an actual presence, a living fire. From my many years of academic study of the mystics and saints, I remembered that the spiritual seeker was to treasure the opportunity to be in the phys-ical presence of a sage or saint. The aura of the true teacher was said to have a catalytic effect on the openhearted listener, referred to as "Grace of the Guru" and "silent transmission." This is why spiritual aspirants in all traditions throughout history have embarked on long pilgrimages to be in the presence of Gandhi, Ramana Maharshi, the Karmapa, Mother Teresa, the Dalai Lama, Padre Pio, Sadhguru Vasudev, Llewellyn Vaughan-Lee, Ramakrishna, and others. Even after the body of a mystic or saint has expired, the effect is still felt. Hundreds of thousands of devotees, for example, kiss the tombs of Sufi and other saints. When visiting the tomb of Mother Teresa in Calcutta, the energy field of Love is so palpable that people often weep for a long time. Travelers on the path of love go to great lengths to be in the presence of Pure Love.

As I drove to his seminar, I felt hopeful but skeptical. I had tried various spiritual and religious groups over the years, but found they weren't able to give what they advertised: unconditional love. Their love had a limit to it; there was always an "except for…" that excluded me, so I was nervous—would it turn out to be another disappointment? Still, I couldn't not go. I was a log longing for the Fire.

# Bowing Down to the Light

Even now as I write about the moment when I heard him in person for the first time, it's impossible to capture the feeling of being in an environment of total safety for the soul. All of me—whatever I was and would ever become—felt fully received and loved. I was totally free, yet totally looked after. It was the recognition of my own innate wholeness. He explained:

> What people in the world actually want is the recognition of who they really are on the highest level; to see that the same Self radiates forth within everyone; heals their feeling of separation; and brings about a feeling of peace. To bring peace and joy to others is the gift of the benevolence of the Presence.[119]

It was a magnetic moment. On the surface, he was a little old man who lectured and answered questions. He didn't dress or act like the stereotype of a spiritual teacher. He was married, wore ordinary clothes, told jokes, drank Pepsi and espresso, and could talk like a sailor if the occasion called for it. He sought to be ordinary, not "spiritual." There were no robes or rituals, saintly affects, or special incantations, no theatrics or miracles performed onstage. There was no organization to join or dues to pay. The true teacher, he said, has no interest in special clothing, dramatic performances, names or titles, for there is no egotism that would care about such things. Even if by karmic duty a teacher is required to have a certain title and robe (as with Pope Francis or the Karmapa), they carry out the role in a spirit of service, not specialness. "Teaching is a function, not a person," he told us.

Someone described my teacher's personality as a mixture of Einstein, the Buddha, and Mr. Magoo, a personality that interacted with the world in a comical, intelligent, compassionate, unexpected, piercing, and sometimes tough-love way. It was love, he said, that animated the interface with others: "The Self seeks to make a healing contact with the Self of the person in the world who is suffering. This same love, which is a quality of the Self, seeks to contact the Self in everyone in its writing, speaking, or conveying of information that could be useful."[120]

He was the "pole" that set the world aright for me. It was the most powerful bond of love I've ever experienced, and it had nothing to do with romantic or personal feelings.

I learned to not presume that others would find him helpful. As we know from academic education, different students are drawn to different teachers, and it's impossible to decipher the reason for this. Nor do I presume that a teacher in physical form is the answer for others. I've seen people awaken in other ways: music; nature; pilgrimage; support groups; love relationship or loss of one; cancer; near-death experience—the list of catalytic possibilities goes on and on. For reasons I still don't understand, it was an old male sage who opened my heart.

The discovery of this teacher for my inner life was profound, perhaps in a similar way that it would be for an initiate in any field of learning to come upon a coach or mentor or master who had attained the highest degree of excellence in that field: The music composer who meets a Mozart, the physicist who meets an Einstein, the poet who meets a Mary Oliver, the painter who meets a Rembrandt. In the vast literature on the inner sciences, a principal requirement for the spiritual student is the guidance of a realized master. This would be true for any field of endeavor. When I was a competitive tennis player, I sought the best tennis coach I could find. In the realm of spiritual work, I needed instruction and transmission from a realized teacher.

For others, it was different. When we went to a public lecture to hear him, my partner left after the first hour: "This is not for me." This reaction was shocking and disappointing, but gave me a needed lesson in trust and acceptance. Everyone finds what they need. Not all plants thrive in the same soil. This was the point made by Swami Vivekananda, the great disciple of Ramakrishna, at the Parliament of the World's Religions in Chicago in 1893. Divinity knows the hearts of all and receives the love of those who seek Truth. Swami Vivekananda told the audience, "In the heart of everything, the same truth reigns." My teacher embodied the scriptures quoted by Vivekananda, and I became aware that Truth does not belong to any single religion or group of people.

*Jivanmukta* is the Sanskrit term for a being who is liberated while living on Earth, and that was what I knew my teacher to be—a liberated being, free, spontaneous, crystal clear. He never sought followers and had no interest in persuading others. "I'm not interested in big-shot-ism," he said once. He simply shared what he knew to be true. "He who has ears to hear, let him hear," he would say. Though he appeared in the form of a man, he was somehow beyond male and female. He was in the world but not of it. His lectures gave our thinking mind something to pay attention to, but the real teaching unfolded on the plane of the Self, silently, nonverbally. He taught that the high-energy field of the Self is already present within the student and that the presence of the teacher merely activates what's Real within the student, like a tuning fork.

A yearning was activated inside me. As often as I could, I attended his teaching events and *satsangs*. I sat and listened, read the books, and did the practices. In silence, the inner being was transformed. I learned from his words, but mostly it was his presence and way of being that taught me. For three years, I watched people of all ages, faiths, races, and countries go onto the stage and sit across from him. Many of them had a burning question, and some had even crossed the world to ask it. They came from Africa, Korea, Japan, Ireland, India, Argentina, England, Australia, Norway, Egypt, China, Canada, Poland. They were agnostics, Christians, Buddhists, Jews, Hindus, Zoroastrians, Sufis, from all walks of life.

If you could ask a question of a Self-realized being, what would it be? A Hindu woman from India wanted to know how to concentrate her mind on the Divine. A twenty-something rock musician wanted to know how to avoid the seductions of fame, drugs, and money. A local woman who channeled wanted to know whether to trust the entities speaking through her. A Buddhist nun wanted to know why she felt compelled to come all the way from Asia to hear him, even though she understood no English. A Christian man wanted to know if miracles are real. A middle-aged woman wanted to know how to forgive the man who had molested her when she was a child. Every question was answered with rare compassion and skillful insight. Each person was addressed uniquely in their deepest unspoken need. His answers to the same question sometimes differed, depending on the psyche and spiritual level of the person who asked.

Many people simply wanted to say thank you, or "May I look into your eyes? It's the only time I ever experience unconditional love." They asked for blessings. A father took his young son up to the platform and asked, "Will you please touch my son?" A pregnant teenager and her mother: "Please touch her belly." Newly married couples wanted a blessing on their union. People poured gifts into his hands: stuffed animals, baked goods, paintings, hand-carved instruments, and plants. They sang songs and told jokes. They poured out their gifts and they poured out their hearts. He received their loving gestures because people needed to give them, not because he needed to have them.

A Buddhist nun from South Korea quickly ate the food left on his plate. She told me, "In my country, it's a blessing to eat from the plate of a master." I'd never heard or seen such a thing, but I understood this nun's hunger for the energy of Love, which was so palpable in his presence. Hindus from India touched his feet and prostrated. Though I'd never been inclined to such gestures, in this case prostration felt completely correct. As the Sufi says, "To be less than dust at the feet of the teacher." I knew instinctively that this was not submission in the self-effacing way of patriarchal culture; it was a surrender of the heart of the student to the heart of the teacher who abides within the heart of God. Inwardly, I offered my life as a prostration. It was the ultimate yes to Love—not to the person of the teacher but to the core of Love within him.

Once again, love was appearing to me in a specially rejected form. I couldn't explain to others this surge of devotion within my heart. This time, I was breaking not only a religious orthodoxy but a secular orthodoxy as well. Love for a spiritual teacher was nowhere in my background or culture or circle of friends or groups of colleagues—even though our field was religious studies. I wondered if I would perhaps lose my career from the lofty halls of academe where it's orthodox to study a guru with objective distance but heretical to become a devotee. Though I felt alone in my experience, I also felt certain of the truth of it. The teacher's unconditional love had opened my heart, and the experience of my real Self was irresistible.

As Llewellyn Vaughan-Lee told me: "One of the things that happens when you come to a spiritual teacher... is that you are unconditionally loved for yourself, warts and all.... Most people have never experienced anything like that. It's completely unconditional. The teacher doesn't want anything from you." In Sufism, this is the moment of *tauba*, the turning of the heart toward God/ Love, when the soul begins its journey Home. Without a guide, he said, the journey is not possible.

After three years of silently listening in the audience, I longed to express my heart and receive my teacher's blessing. During the Q&A portion at the end of one seminar, I went forward and stood in line, nervous about expressing something so intimate in front of hundreds of people, but the only opportunity to interact with him was in these public gatherings.

When it was my turn, I walked onto the stage and sat in front of him. I felt the melting Love again—that of the Light. The unique quality of Pure Love is that it needs nothing—it only gives. It *radiates*, like the sun. As I looked at him across the small round table, it was unsettling. His eyes looked back at me without the customary veil or hesitation or intent. There was no person looking back at me.

Looking into his eyes—this is impossible to explain—there was no inner agent. Never before had I looked into someone's eyes and not found the inner agent looking back at me, with its feelings, needs, and ideas. He was an empty space, more a presence than a person. "The basic thing about the spiritual teacher is that the spiritual teacher is not there. They are an empty space. They are so surrendered that they are not there."[121]

Sitting there, I could barely hold his gaze for fear of dissolving into the infinite blue of those eyes. I tried to remember why I had gone up there—*Oh, yeah*, I reminded myself: *gratitude; kneeling; blessing.*

I said into the microphone: "For a long time I've wanted to kneel in front of you. Would you please let me do that? I want to acknowledge the gratitude I feel for being able to come here." I yearned to kneel, to bow down and fulfill this act of devotion, yet I didn't understand why. This was nowhere in my upbringing. It certainly went against my feminist politics. For three years, I'd listened while others went up to ask a question. Always my own inner questions were answered in time. When I meditated, I had the image of his hand on the top of my head as I knelt down.

I needed to make this step—to surrender my pride and kneel in front of a genuine guide. My biggest fear was that he would not allow it. I had seen him turn others away with a joke, kindly banter, or a verbal answer to the question they hadn't asked. He didn't see himself as special, but it was hard for us not to see him as special.

"Of course, sweetheart," he said.

Relief washed over me. I walked over to where he sat, and I knelt. I felt his hand touch the top of my head, an infusion of compassion. My eyes filled with tears. I heard him say, "I understand, sweetheart. I understand." My gratitude was immeasurable. Finally, to have found a genuine guide. According to many religions, this is a pivotal point on the path.

Author kneels and receives a blessing from her teacher; given the
surrender of the moment, she is happy to be invisible in the photo.
(Mike Gover / Courtesy, The Institute for Spiritual Research).

Jesus Christ, Matthew 7:13–14:

Straight is the gate and narrow is the way that leads to life, and
few there be that find it.

Shankara (9th-century Hindu sage from India):[122]

Only through God's grace may we obtain those three rarest
advantages—human birth, the longing for liberation, and the disci-
pleship to an illumined teacher.

The 14th Dalai Lama (21st-century Buddhist leader):

The direct introduction to *rigpa* (pure awareness) requires that
we rely upon an authentic guru who already has this experience. It is

when the blessings of the guru infuse our mindstream that this direct introduction is effected. But it is not an easy process ... the role of the master is therefore crucial.[123]

Hafiz (14th-century Persian Sufi poet):
  Do not take a step
  on the path of love without a guide.
  I have tried it
  one hundred times and failed.[124]

By kneeling, I had said yes to Love. Saying yes to the teacher was saying yes to the Light. I surrendered not to the outer person of the teacher but to the Light within him.

Another door would open when, a year later, I met with him at his home and we began several years of working together. The first thing he told me was that such steps of surrender are just that: *steps.* "Devotion to a teacher would be a step. Then, as you become more enlightened, you realize that what you are devoted to is the Self with a capital "S" within the teacher—which is not different than the Self within *you*."

At that time, no one in my life understood my need to kneel and surrender to the Love I felt within the teacher. In fact, I didn't understand it myself. My *heart* bowed down to a Love it knew was true—my mind would never understand.

My partner couldn't understand either. After years of trying to hold onto each other despite this major upheaval, we parted ways. She had been the catalyst to liberate me from an oppressive belief system. We'd been through so much together. It was painful to realize that a romantic love relationship was a necessary doorway but not the destination in my search for love.

In the opening story of his masterpiece *The Mathnawi,* Rūmī shows how painful the limits of romance can be. A young woman, taken into the king's court, has become ill. The king adores her and is distraught. He stops at nothing to get her the necessary help, but she only gets worse. Finally, he arranges for a holy man—a physician of the soul—to diagnose and heal her. As soon as this Saint arrives, he is able to see into the woman's psyche. He tells no one what he has discovered—she is simply heartsick over her separation from the man she loves. The Saint finds the young man in a faraway village and brings him to the king's castle to work as a goldsmith. Finally together, the two lovers are beside themselves with joy, and the woman quickly revives. But their bliss does not last long, for the Saint secretly injects the young man with a poison to shrivel his physical form so that he loses his virility and good looks. Early in his decline, the young woman falls out of love with him, faced with the pain of knowing that her attraction for him was based on his physical form and had nothing to do with his actual essence. It was an attachment, not real love. Though cruel, the Saint's action reveals the truth of Love: our outer attachments to another human being can never completely fulfill our longing for That which is changeless and eternal.

In the Sufi tradition of Rūmī, the "heart of hearts" is a place within us that belongs only to The Real/ The Beloved/ Divinity, not to a romantic lover. The only human who can enter our heart of hearts is the spiritual teacher who holds the key to unlock its door. This is why I say my teacher opened my heart.

My path includes human love, partnership, and family life. Unlike some of the people I interviewed for this book, a celibate monastic life was not the path I was called to. I've had to work through all my illusions about love in the context of an ordinary life. Fully giving myself to a real person in flesh and blood has been a precursor to turning my life over to the Reality I cannot see. A key quality for the devotee is willingness to risk disapproval for the sake of love, and I've learned that critical lesson through personal loving. As the years progressed, my awareness that no person can fill the soul's core longing put the desire for human companionship into better balance.

Though wholesome and beautiful, romantic love wasn't strong enough to bear the heat of a deeper quest in my heart. Years later, I would be blessed with the gift of a companion and the singular joy that comes from sharing one's life with a lovemate. Yet the relationship with the teacher remained primary for the simple fact that it was free from all conditions, inner limitations, emotionalisms, dependencies, and needs. His presence was the same as the Light, with its all-encompassing Love. Twenty-five years previously, I had allowed a minister's condemnation of the Light to put a wedge between me and Love. This time I knew better. I gave my whole heart and hoped always to abide in his.

Devotional love for a spiritual teacher has no parallel in human experience. Jetsunma Tenzin Palmo recognized her Guru the first time she ever saw his name in print. It was on a letter that arrived at the school in India where she was stationed, and she knew that he would be her spiritual master. She told me, it was "a total openness and surrender.... It never happened with anyone else." He became her infallible guide in her commitment to become enlightened no matter how many lifetimes it took.

Jetsunma Tenzin Palmo (courtesy of DGL Nunnery, India).

Chapter Fourteen

# The Inner Cultivation of Love

## Encounter with Jetsunma Tenzin Palmo

*In general, in the West, people are too much in the head
and need to come down into the heart, which is the seat
of our true self.*

—Jetsunma Tenzin Palmo

## Becoming a Buddhist Nun

Tenzin Palmo grew up in London as Diane Perry, the only daughter of a spiritualist mother and fishmonger father. Her father died when Diane was two. At age eighteen, she read a book and realized, "I am a Buddhist." She was especially moved by the story of 11th-century Tibetan Buddhist master Milarepa, a murderer-turned-mystic Yogi who spent much of his life in a Himalayan cave. Reincarnation seemed natural to her: "I always believed in it. I can't remember when I didn't."[125]

With her mother's blessing, Palmo moved to India at twenty, where she taught English at a school for young lamas. She met her root lama, His Eminence the 8th Khamtrul Rinpoche, a great Drukpa Kagyu lama, and took refuge in him. Her lama was the only male to whom she ever committed herself, despite having had several suitors when she was a young woman, and more than one marriage proposal. Selfless and pure, he was the one person she felt she could trust completely. For her (and also me), devotional love for the spiritual teacher has no parallel in human experience.

In 1964, at age twenty-one, her head was shaved and she became one of the first Westerners to be ordained a monastic in the Tibetan Buddhist tradition. She was given the name Drubgyu Tenzin Palmo—"Glorious Lady who Upholds the Doctrine of the Practice Succession." The path wasn't easy. For six years she was the only nun among a hundred monks at the monastery of Khamtrul Rinpoche in Dalhousie (now Tashi Jong). The monks were very discouraging of her spiritual goals. Their view was that only men could realize Buddhahood, so why should she, a woman, be given the advanced teachings? Against these odds, she kept her flame alive. She was going to pursue enlightenment no matter what the men had to say about it.

In 1976, following direction from her lama, Tenzin Palmo began a twelve-year intensive retreat in a cave high in the Himalayas— the first Western woman to carry out such a retreat as a Yogi within Tibetan Buddhism. Just getting to the cave was a life-threatening climb with no path to follow. When she asked the local people to help her with preparations and supplies, they refused. "We don't want the karma of aiding in your certain death!" They didn't expect her to survive. The cave was 13,200 feet above sea level, through Rhotang Pass, known as the Plain of Corpses. One faulty step and she might fall to her death. After she showed them a letter from her lama, some villagers agreed to help her.

The 6 × 6-foot cave was her home from ages thirty-three to forty-five.[126] Snow surrounded her for eight months each year, and temperatures registered below −30° Fahrenheit. She melted snow for water and grew her own food. Her hero Milarepa had survived on nettles, and she on turnips and potatoes! The wild animals and harsh elements were a daily reality. One time, she was completely snowed in. Faced with dwindling oxygen, she wondered if she would be buried alive. She survived by digging out of the packed snow with a pot lid. She didn't sleep much for twelve years, as she viewed sleep as unimportant. Adhering to strict Buddhist instruction, she meditated twelve hours a day in a "meditation box," beginning at 3 a.m. For Palmo, the cave was home. She had the boundless joy of focusing entirely on her practice. No interruptions, no unwanted conversation, no supermarket aisles, no office work, no phone calls, no one and nothing to take care of. All was stunningly quiet and pristine. She missed nothing in the world except her lama.

In 1988, she was forced to come out of the cave because of a problem with her visa. The first human voice she heard after three years of isolation was that of a policeman! Hiking all the way up to her cave, he threatened her with arrest if she didn't come down from the mountain and take care of her paperwork.

How did the retreat affect her? Any major attainments? When asked such questions, she would simply say, "I was never bored." Following tantric protocol, she declined to discuss her spiritual experiences. When asked what she had gained from her years in the cave, she replied: "It's not what you gain but what you lose. The idea that there's somewhere we have to get to, and something we have to attain, is our basic delusion." The point is not ecstatic visions of light and angels, but to see things as they really are. She revealed that while "Bliss is the fuel of retreat, better than anything the world has to offer,"[127] when people *seek* bliss, the goal becomes the obstacle. It's best to let go of concepts of progress and attainment. Was the heart awakened? That's what matters.

In 1998, the publication of her biography, *Cave in the Snow,* by Vicki Mackenzie, brought a wave of interest in Palmo; she began to offer teachings around the world, with the intention to raise funds for the establishment of a nunnery. Her lama had given her the major task of establishing a nunnery and, against many odds, construction began on Dongyu Gatsal Ling Nunnery in 2001. Known as Garden of the Authentic Lineage, it is in the region of the Dalai Lama's residence in Dharamsala and close to Tashi Jong monastery. The DGL nunnery gives women a rare opportunity for traditional training in Buddhist practice, philosophy, and spiritual excellence. The nunnery completed its temple in 2013, a traditional religious space yet pioneering in its splendor of sacred feminine imagery drawn from Buddhist iconography. The temple is the first of its kind—magnificent with depictions of the Divine Feminine and female arhats (Buddhist term for advanced spiritual state). The visuals are a vivid mirror to the nuns of women's divine nature and the path of liberation.

Palmo has become a worldwide leader in the advancement of women's spiritual opportunities. In 1993, at the first conference on Western Buddhism at Dharamsala with His Holiness the Dalai Lama, she spoke candidly of her experience as a nun in the monastery with a hundred monks. She recounted to the Dalai Lama what they had told her—being female is an inferior birth, and her only hope for spiritual realization was to be born male in her next lifetime. Hearing her account, the Dalai Lama wept.

In 2008, Tenzin Palmo was given the rare title "Jetsunma" by the head of the Drukpa Lineage, His Holiness the 12th Gyalwang Drukpa, thus designating her as a senior nun and "Venerable Master." Palmo's initial reaction was to refuse this distinction; however, after hearing from others that it advanced the status of women overall, she realized the title had nothing to do with herself and received it with gratitude on behalf of women. Her message is for women to stand together and support each other and, she told me, to support men rather than compete with them: "We're not taking anything from men. It's not a cake—'if you get a bigger slice, I get less.' No! Giving opportunities to women raises the whole human race. Love brings about a win-win effect. The ego sees only win-lose, but love benefits everyone. When women pursue their own happiness in a spirit of genuine love, it is a win also for men."

The steadfast advocacy for Buddhist nuns by Palmo and others reached fruition in January 2015 when the Karmapa announced the beginning of a three-step process for *bhikshuni*—full ordination for nuns. The announcement was met with resounding applause. He explained that it had nothing to do with pressures about "gender equality" or "to placate anyone." It was, rather, "necessary" in order "to uphold Buddhist teachings," which require "fully ordained nuns as one pillar of the fourfold community needed for Buddhadharma." The Buddha himself, said the Karmapa, ordained women as nuns and "gave them everything they needed in order to practice all the paths and levels in their entirety."[128] As it happened, shortly after making this announcement, the Karmapa came to the University of Redlands where I teach. He shared his joy about this historic step.

## FROM LIFETIME TO LIFETIME

Jetsunma Tenzin Palmo told me: "I took the vow to attain enlightenment in a female body, no matter how many lifetimes it may take." This statement takes the power of love to a whole new level. It suggests that devotion to a path, and loving concern for others, goes from lifetime to lifetime. His Holiness the 17th Karmapa, during a visit to the United States, shared his experience of such connections:

> Love and friendship are very powerful forces that can remain from lifetime to lifetime. The connections and relationships that we make with other people through love and friendship don't just last for one lifetime alone but can endure from lifetime to lifetime and become ever more deepened.[129]

Jetsunma Tenzin Palmo has experienced this kind of heart connection with her root lama, His Eminence the 8th Khamtrul Rinpoche, as well as other Tibetan Buddhist lamas such as the Karmapa. Palmo told me that she was a man in her previous lifetime and took rebirth in her current female body in order to plow a path for Buddhist women in their pursuit of spiritual life. Sufi teacher Llewellyn Vaughan-Lee says that he has encountered women whom he knew as male monastics in other lifetimes in Tibet and China; they've come back as women to do a certain spiritual work for humanity.

Initially, these ideas were strange to me. Raised Christian, I had little exposure to rebirth, reincarnation, multiple lifetimes, and karma; however, on the experiential level, it made perfect sense to me. When, at age thirty-nine, I met my teacher, the recognition was instantaneous. He had always been my teacher, and my heart bowed down to the inner vastness I sensed before me. It felt similar to what Palmo told me about meeting her teacher: "I just knew he was my teacher. An immediate recognition, together with that very strong sense that the innermost part of my being had suddenly taken material form in front of me." In other areas of life, I noted deep resonance with certain people, places, symbols, and themes that couldn't be explained according to the usual childhood analysis. I felt a close connection with particular people—and strong aversions to others—that seemed greater than the known facts about them from this lifetime. Some people just feel instantly familiar.

In the case of such experiences, there's a mystery at work difficult to put into words, yet many people are aware of it on a feeling level. When Betty Eadie told me about her near-death experience, she said that the people we meet may be "related to some sort of mission we have in our life," and we experience them as "soul friends." Also—and harder to grasp—those who oppose us are helpful. As a senior Tibetan Buddhist monk told me when I asked him how to deal with my "enemy": "Be grateful for their service to you. The people and forces that oppose you are vehicles of your own karma. Without enemies, how would you reach your aspiration of compassion?" The point is to embrace circumstances as innately purposeful. Instead of viewing them as "pathological," we may presume them to be our *path*. As my teacher put it, "All persons are born under the most optimal conditions for spiritual evolution, no matter what the appearance seems to be."[130] In other words, what we are, and the situations in which we find ourselves, are not accidental. Being with Tenzin Palmo strengthened my trust in these hints and recognitions, for she had unwavering faith in them.

## PERSONAL ENCOUNTER

When I visited Palmo at her nunnery, the nuns were fun-spirited, and their laughter made me feel welcome and at ease. Palmo and

I had a good laugh about the fact that I tripped coming into her room and nearly stumbled into her. Though I had taken careful attention to carry out what I imagined to be all the proper rituals of meeting an important Buddhist leader, my nervousness got the best of me. This embarrassing moment was met with humor and kindness. Thus I had a firsthand experience of her teaching on humor: "We need to encourage ourselves and our fellow practitioners to lighten up and stop taking ourselves so seriously. Sometimes I think the seventh *paramita* (perfection) should be a sense of humor!"[131]

Being with Jetsunma Tenzin Palmo was more compelling to me than reading a book on Buddhist practice. She *was* the practice. In her presence, the purpose of spiritual practice became clear: It's not to set oneself apart from others but rather to return to one's most natural way of being. The practitioner, then, is relatable and one with others. My visit with Palmo gave me an experience of the freeing realm in which the doingness of spiritual practice has given way to the sheer joy of beingness, with no gap between the *dharma* (teaching) and the person.

# CONVERSATION WITH JETSUNMA TENZIN PALMO

## Love and Loving-kindness

Q:   In the book *Cave in the Snow,* I got the sense that you went into retreat for many years not only for yourself but for all beings. Would you say that our spiritual work is of benefit to the world even if we're alone?

JTP:   Absolutely! In the Mahayana Buddhist tradition, which is not just in Tibet and India but also China, Korea, Japan, and Vietnam, the whole motivation for spiritual work is based on *compassion*. As one begins to see with more clarity, one recognizes what the problem is. All beings want happiness and want to avoid suffering. But, because we are deluded and don't see clearly, we act in ways that are calculated to create suffering for ourselves and others. And we do this in pursuit of what we *think* will bring happiness. Modern-day society is mainly based on what the Buddha described as the three poisons: our *greed* and our *aggression*, both of which are rooted in our *delusion* about an ego. The "self" is right in the middle of everything, and we think this self has to be satisfied and defended. The more we inflate our ego and encourage it, the more we zero in on "me, me, me"—the more desperate we become, hoping that if we just keep going, somehow it's all going to end up in one great bonanza of everlasting joy. But in fact you just end up taking more Valium!

(*Laughter.*)

So, yes, the motivation for the Mahayana Buddhist is based on seeing that we all inherently have Buddha-nature. That's our true nature, not the ephemeral personality we grasp at. By nature we should all be Buddhas, but because of our delusion, we often act more like demons. We create so much suffering for ourselves and for the world around us. When our potential is so incredible—look at what we do with it! This intelligence that we are so proud of—look at what we do with it! So it often becomes demonic. Therefore the aspiration for the spiritual path is rooted in compassion: to attain enlightenment in order to help others also to be liberated. Without masters, how will we break free?

Q:  The most profound experience of love I ever had was with a master, that is, spiritual teacher. But in the West, love is seen mainly as romantic love.

JTP:  Partly, it's the poverty of our language. People say, "I love ice cream, I love my children, I love my partner, I love all sentient beings." These are very different emotions they're talking about, but we have only the one word. When we talk about love in the English language, basically it's meaningless because everyone has their own idea of what they mean by love. In Buddhism, people talk about "loving-kindness" just to get a different feeling. You don't have loving-kindness toward ice cream!

Q:  Where does one begin in terms of cultivating loving-kindness?

JTP:  The Buddha himself taught: When we cultivate loving-kindness and compassion, we start with ourselves. That is very important. At first, we start with giving *ourselves* loving-kindness. We have to give ourselves compassion. We have to befriend ourselves. Even though ultimately the ego is something to be dissolved and recognized for what it is, nonetheless for almost the whole of the path we take our ego along with us. It's our sense of self. Therefore we need to have a healthy sense of self, because that's what we are going to work with as we travel on the path. All spiritual paths deal with how to have a happy, healthy, enthusiastic "me." Even if at the end the "I" dissolves into something greater. In the meantime, if our sense of self is wounded or if we have low self-esteem or self-hatred, we're not going to be able to be the spiritual warrior on the path. We have to heal ourselves.

Q:  When I do loving-kindness meditation with college students, they are resistant to give themselves loving-kindness. What can I tell them?

JTP:  You tell them, "Until you love yourself, you cannot love others!" It would just be a dependency. If you don't have love for yourself, you will look to love someone else in the hope that they will love you back to make you feel complete. That's not love. That's just attachment, fear, and grasping. That's why romantic love is so iffy, because it's based on the fantasy that somebody else can make me feel complete. That's nonsense! We have to make ourselves feel complete. And the only way to do that is to open up to oneself and in appreciation of oneself and encouragement of oneself and to have a healthy sense of ego. Someone whose ego is damaged is always thinking about themselves. But people with a healthy ego don't think about themselves much, because they have the space to think about everybody else. You'll notice that loving people don't take themselves so seriously. They are able to laugh at themselves. Humor is medicine, and they know how to use it.

Q: Some people find it hard to practice loving-kindness for themselves because they associate it with egoism.

JTP: Tell them that it's not selfish or egoistic. Until they are at home with themselves, and friendly toward themselves, how will they be that way with others? One thing I say to people is, "Listen to what you say to yourself, the way you talk with yourself. Would you talk like that to your best friend? Would you have any friends if you talked like that? If you would never talk to a friend like that, then why talk to yourself like that?" We have to have love for all sentient beings. We are also a sentient being. And we are the sentient being we are most responsible for. So, if we don't really love ourselves, where will it come from for another? All our talk about love will be just another form of clinging. It won't be genuine love because genuine love radiates from a light inside that radiates outward. But most people's idea of love is just grasping, just attachment. Inside, they are saying, "I love you because you're going to make me happy." That isn't love at all. It is wantingness and attachment.

## From Romantic Love to Unconditional Love

Q: Do men and women have different attachments to work through?

JTP: Generally, men have to work on controlling sexual desire, and women have to work with attachments to comfort and security because that's what they biologically depend on for raising children. To reach the stage where you love the whole world exactly like your own children—now that's really something! But it's rare. You don't love your own children less—you love the whole world more.

Q: Is there any value to romantic love?

JTP: It keeps the species going!
(*Laughter.*)

Q:   At a spiritual level?

JTP:   If you're attracted to someone and recognize that this is nature's lure to get you together, go beyond that and ask yourself whether you like the person. That's more important! If you truly like the person, then it can carry on. If you start only with romantic ideas, then it's so inflated that you can only come down! Underneath the sexual attraction, if you don't actually like the person, then there's nothing to build on. Sexual attraction is one thing, and love is quite another. Do you really want to be with this person for life? Do you have a lot to talk about? Do you have interests in common? How do they treat other people? Do you have the same values? It might start off as a fairytale, but what happens to the frog and princess in that "happily ever after" when you have to look at each other across the breakfast table?

Q:   One would hope the "falling in love" experience opens a person to caring for someone and perhaps serves as a launching pad for unconditional love.

JTP:   In Buddhism, the model for perfect love is not romantic love; it's a mother with her child. Just as a mother loves her only child, that is how we want to feel toward all beings. The traditional loving-kindness meditation cultivates this kind of unconditional love. As set down by the Buddha, first we direct loving-kindness toward ourselves: "May I be well and happy, May I be peaceful and at my ease, May I be free of suffering, and so forth." Then you think of the people you love, that you care for, such as your parents, partner, children, siblings, and good friends, and you wish them the same goodwill: "May they be well and happy, may they be peaceful and at their ease," etc., really wishing them all of these things. Then you think of people you feel neutral toward, people you see every day but don't have strong feelings about one way or the other, such as the postman or someone in your office whom you don't know well or have any feeling about. You think of that *one* person and really imagine that person being happy and how wonderful it would be for him or her, and for their family, really sending the person goodwill. And then you think of someone you have problems with, called the "enemy," which means someone who pushes your buttons, and you really wish them to be happy and free of their suffering. In this way, love becomes unconditional and totally inclusive.

Q:   When a single human heart develops that kind of extended love, does it help the world at large?

JTP:   Of course! Like His Holiness the Dalai Lama... Whomever he meets, you can see his automatic thought is "May you be well and happy." And he's talking straight to the essence of the person, not to their persona. This radiance of love is very powerful. Generally, people are projecting so much thought pollution, which is far worse than the other pollution everyone is concerned about. If we could see it, we would see that this planet is in very bad shape because of the amount of violence, hate, greed, and envy emanating not only from the individuals but also from movies, television, and newspapers. So, any Light that shines into darkness is bound to be very radiant.... If you go to a holy place, you see the difference. It isn't polluted with hatred and so forth. I lived for several years near Assisi, Italy, where St. Francis lived. Even though it's highly commercialized, still so many people have had profound spiritual experiences without realizing how it could have happened. In contrast, if you go to Auschwitz, you don't even have to know what happened there to know that it was something horrible. It's there. It's tangible. So, yes, anything we can do to radiate Light and Love into the universe is bound to benefit everyone. This is the idea within Catholicism and other religions that have contemplative orders or any group of people coming together quietly to radiate something positive to the universe. It makes a *big* impact.

## Inner Cultivation: Depolluting the Mind and Heart

Q:   What would you say to people who view contemplative practices as impractical? For instance, some parents of the college students who take a meditation class ask them, "Why do you take a class where you sit and do nothing? What good does it serve?"

JTP:   I would say that our actions and our speech, which definitely have an influence on the world, depend upon our mind. Everything depends on the mind and the way we see things. The reason the world is in such a horrible state today is not the world's fault! It's the fault of the beings that inhabit the world—and not the lions and the tigers, but the humans! The world is run by people with polluted minds. This means we can't see correctly.

Q:   How does a person start to unpollute the mind?

JTP:   First of all, by recognizing that there is a pollution. And you can only recognize that by looking at it—going *within*. This is the benefit of meditation or any contemplative practice. So first you get your mind a little calmer, more attentive, and focused, and then you turn your focus inward and observe the thoughts. What kinds of thoughts are there? Not judging the mind but really looking at it. Whoa! What thoughts! And learning how not to identify with the thoughts so much. Most people somehow believe that they *are* their thoughts and emotions and beliefs and memories, but they need to recognize that this is just an ephemeral flow, like a movie projected onto a screen; it isn't reality. And then you get back into contact with the underlying awareness which sees that. That's what we have to go back to—our pure awareness—and stop identifying with the thinking process.

Of course, we can think! But first we need to recognize that we are not our thoughts—only *have* thoughts. We see those thoughts that are wholesome and lead to happiness, and we see those thoughts that are like poison and create problems all around. When we see the difference, then we can encourage the good thoughts and start weeding out the poisonous ones. It's like weeding the garden. You water good plants and you pull out the weeds. That way, gradually, the mind begins to unpollute. Then one's speech will reflect one's thoughts, and one's actions will flow from there—with more skill, more clarity, and based on a good heart instead of a polluted heart. It's obvious. You know this very well, but most people try to change things on the outside. They don't understand that it has to start from *inside!* It's good that you are teaching this knowledge to your students. Even if they just get a taste, they will know that this is something genuine at last.

Q:   You travel and teach in the West. What would you say is something that Westerners are missing on this topic of Love?

JTP:   In general, people in the West are too much in the head and need to come down into the heart, which is the seat of our true self. Inner transformation will only take place when the arena of action is brought down to the heart center. You will notice that when we reference our personhood, we point to the center of our chest, not the head. There is also the problem that we were saying earlier: Most people don't know what love is. They confuse love with attachment. They think the more they are attached to a person, this proves how much they love them. And they think that nonattachment means that you're cold. Sometimes when people ask me "What's the difference between love and attachment?" I say, "Attachment is the thought 'I love you, so therefore I want you to make me happy.' Love says, 'I love you, and I want you to be happy whether it includes me or not.'"

Q:   And your own mother? Wasn't she an example of unconditional love?

JTP:   She was an absolute example of it! She wanted *me* to be happy, and if that did not include her in the picture, she was happy because I was happy.

Q:   Was that hard for her? You were her only daughter and she hardly saw you.

JTP:   Perhaps it was hard for her, but she didn't make it hard for me. She acted as though she were happy. She never wrote, "I miss you—please come back!" Every ten years, she would write to ask, "If I send you a return ticket, will you please come back for a month?" And she told some friends of mine, who told me later, "She always prayed that in the next lifetime she would come back again as your mother because she was afraid that otherwise you wouldn't have parents who would understand that you needed a special sort of life." *That* is real love. She would have been happy to go through it all again, because she wanted me to be happy.

## How to Handle Difficulty and Suffering

Q: Does an understanding of karma help dissolve resentments from childhood and the hardships of life?

JTP: It could, but there's a lot of resistance in the West to accepting responsibility for anything that goes wrong in our lives. We're happy to accept responsibility for anything good. We take credit for the good things as if *we* are the sole reason they occurred! But anything that goes wrong for us, we run from all responsibility! We blame something or someone outside of ourselves. We don't want to admit that we have anything to do with the problems or hardships in our life— let alone that maybe we created the causes and conditions for them in past lives. Usually I say to people, "Look, from a Buddhist perspective, we've had endless lifetimes in all forms, in all genders, in all nationalities, up and down, everywhere. During that time, we have done just about everything—good, bad, and indifferent. We've done it all. You name it, we've done it at some point. So, all those seeds of our intentional actions are buried, and they will come up when causes and conditions are right for them to come up." Therefore bad things happen to good people, and good things happen to bad people. It's futile to ask, "Why me? What did I do to deserve this?" These questions are from a victim viewpoint, of tragic misfortune.

Q: My teacher taught me to say "Forgive the one in me who did this to others" whenever I encounter something that feels like an injustice.

JTP: Yes, that's a recognition of your own part. The fact is that at some point or another we created these causes that are now being purified, and therefore the best thing to do is respond skillfully, which means not being resentful, upset, and angry, but to ask, "In this situation, how can I act in a way that will transform this hardship onto the path?"

Q: We should take advantage of the difficulties in our life?

JTP: Absolutely! If we don't take everything onto the path, then there is no path! As we all know, when we look back on our lives, it's often the most difficult parts where we learned the most! Someone said that life is a gymnasium for the soul. You go to the gym to work out, not lie around on the mattresses. You have this equipment that challenges the body so that you can become strong. In that way, as one lama said to me when I was complaining about obstacles: "If you call it an obstacle, it's an obstacle; if you call it an opportunity, it's an opportunity. It's what you make of it."

Q: Westerners resist seeing any karmic context for physical suffering such as poverty or racism.

JTP: Yes, but if you were a rich landlord and exploited your peasants, where are you going to end up? Who knows? You're not laying blame. All you're saying is that we've all done terrible things and it's going to come up at some point. It doesn't mean that just because you are in a poor abusive relationship you have to remain in that relationship. You may also have a bit of karma to get the help to get out of it. In the meantime, instead of blaming the government or this or that, you can work with it.

Q: If I know someone who is suffering on some level—physically, emotionally, financially—what would be a skillful, compassionate response?

JTP: It depends... I would do *tonglen*. Then you can look at the situation. Is there anything that could be done to alleviate it? If so, then you do it. If there isn't, then you carry on with your tonglen. Because we are all, as the Buddha said, "Heirs to our own karma"—responsible for our past deeds. We cannot take on the karma of others. They have to go through it. Maybe they need to. Sometimes people pray to God, Jesus, Mary, or Tara, "Please let me be free of this suffering." But maybe it's necessary to suffer it, and maybe this is part of the pattern. The point is not to pray to remove anything that's nasty or that I don't like, but to have the courage and wisdom to deal with it skillfully and integrate it on my spiritual path.

This doesn't mean that we don't help where we can. One of the shortcomings of the Buddhist attitude is that so often people just sit on their cushions thinking, "May all beings be well and happy," but then they don't actually get out and do much. This is now being challenged in many Buddhist countries, and certainly in the West where there are a lot of people running hospices, working with street people, addicts, and in prisons. But sometimes nothing can be done. We also have to remember that this is *samsara*, and samsara by its very nature is not satisfactory. We have to accept that since the beginning of time, people have been poor, they have been sick, they have been miserable, and this is not going to change in the near future because we are not creating the causes for it to change. This is the problem. As a race, we humans are creating negative karma. How can we expect peace and well-being when we're not sowing the seeds for peace and well-being? Until we change our whole attitude and actions, things will not get any better. That's why it's important to teach young people to understand the *inner* basis… they realize the change starts *within*. This is a great hope.

## Devotional Love to a Teacher/Guru

Q: What about devotional love to a spiritual teacher?

JTP: It is always tricky, because that kind of devotion is a total openness and surrender. And one has to be very careful in being open and devotional. People were very devoted to Hitler. He was a god to them. People often are attracted like moths to a flame when it comes to charisma, but charismatic people aren't necessarily good. So, the first thing is to have discrimination. In the tantric texts, it says one should examine the guru for up to twelve years. Of course, people don't, but that's the advice. The Dalai Lama says that, if possible, you should spy on your guru. In other words, look at him not when he's sitting on his throne or being the great omniscient teacher, but rather, what is he like behind the scenes with the people who are of no benefit to him? How does he treat ordinary people in private? Is his heart genuinely only for the benefit of helping others, or is it just another big ego trip? Often, people with inflated or shiny egos are very attractive. And it's hard for an ordinary person to discern this sort of thing when they are desperately looking for someone to believe in and trust. That's the first challenge—to have some discrimination and not become a groupie. The whole point of devotion is that it's an absolute openness and total trust, so one has to be discriminating.

But if you do happen to find someone who is worthy of that trust and is able to understand the students better than they understand themselves and to guide them skillfully, then from the point of view of the students, it's good to open to that blessing. It's like if you compared the genuine teacher to the sun—the sun is always shining—but it's up to us whether or not we pull up the blinds to let in the light. If we close all the shutters and then say, "It's dark," that's not the fault of the sun. From our side, what we need to do is trust, when we have understood that this is truly someone whom we can trust.

Q: How did you know that you could trust your Guru?

JTP: I say all this about the need for discrimination and then, with my Guru, just hearing his name was enough. In fact, I asked him to be my teacher and to take refuge with him without even knowing what he looked like! I was too frightened to look at him—I was just looking at the bottom of his robe and brown shoes. I didn't know whether he was old or young, fat or thin, anything about him at all. I just knew that he was my teacher. When I *did* look at him, there was this very strong feeling of meeting someone again whom I had known very well.

Q:  It was a recognition?

JTP:  A recognition, together with that very strong sense that the innermost part of my being had suddenly taken material form in front of me. Only with him did that ever happen, never with anyone else. He was immaculate. He was really a Buddha. So that was fortunate. Nonetheless, having said that, I do not advise people to go around looking for that. I advise people to be very careful, because I so often see people who, inwardly, were badly injured by trusting in someone who was not trustworthy. A lot of books go on about how the student should act toward the guru, but very few books tell how the guru should act—*their* guidelines.

Q:  My teacher said to his students, "Let me tell you what my responsibility is as a teacher." He emphasized the freedom of the student and the karmic accountability of the teacher.

JTP:  Exactly. Very few people think about that.

Q:  How do you handle the people who look to you as a teacher?

JTP:  I'm not a teacher.

Q:  Okay, but they have that devotion toward you.

JTP:  That's their problem!

Q:  How do you handle it?

JTP:  I say very clearly that I am not a teacher. I don't have the qualifications.

Q:  Do you mean enlightenment?

JTP:  Yes, and even an understanding of their needs. I don't have those qualities. I would be fooling them and fooling myself if I pretended to be a teacher when I'm not one. I offer talks that give people some general pointers, and then they can go off and find someone to take them further. And people come here because they are confused, and I try to give them a little clarity for the next step so they can keep going forward. That's all. Mostly my energies are taken up running this nunnery. In the nunnery, I'm not their teacher.

Q:   What are you?

JTP:   An administrator. The nuns have their lamas at Tashi Jong monastery, near here. They have teachers for philosophy who teach them every day, and other teachers. I just kind of keep things going!

To encounter Jetsunma Tenzin Palmo in monastic robes, shaved head, and piercing blue eyes was like meeting my brother, my sister, my father, my mother, my superior, my friend, myself—all in one person. After meeting with her, I felt like I'd been in a meditation hall. I felt calmer, more at peace, and clearer about what life is really all about. In her presence, the mud settled. The time was now. I heard the urgency to go inward: Stop and take a look at yourself, your motive, your attitude, your heart. Before you add something to the water of life, make sure it's not contaminated with confusion, greed, and anger.

Q:   What's the most important thing I can do for the world?

JTP:   Recognize and develop your own innate wisdom. Everything flows from there.

This is the power of practice according to Buddhism—we become the fruition of the seeds we cultivate in our inner garden.

# PART THREE

# TRANSFORMED BY LOVE

Sunlight and her dog Shadow. Sunlight helped the author face her own shadow (courtesy of Meadow/Deep Dish Ranch, pre-1980s).

*Chapter Fifteen*

## "Changing the World One Heart at a Time"

### Start With Your Own

The search for love had unexpectedly landed me at the feet of a spiritual teacher. His presence was the only place where I felt that very same Pure Love that I'd experienced in the Light. It was intoxicating, and I wanted nothing else. The Sufis say, "Stay away, stay away from the lane of Love! It's a Tavern of Ruin!" In other words, once Pure Love is tasted, nothing else will satisfy and the ego's pleasures are "ruined." As my teacher told me, "Anyone who has heard of enlightened truth will never be satisfied with anything less, even though it takes innumerable lifetimes."

I knew I could trust him absolutely. Unlike religious leaders of my past who demanded obedience to their authority and traditions, he told me to give reverence only to God/Truth:

> One's commitment should be to God and Truth only. Teachers are to be respected, but devotion should be restricted to only the Truth. As Buddha said, "Put no head above your own," meaning that one's only true

guru is the Self (the Buddha-nature). The Self of the
teacher and one's own Self are one and the same.[132]

"To thine own Self be true" turned out to be challenging. My
teacher's presence was like a mirror, and I saw myself for the first
time. No judgment came from the mirror; it merely showed me what
I needed to see—both the innate wisdom of the Higher Self and the
patterns of illusion that clouded it. Just being in his loving energy
field made me conscious of the non-love within me. A sorting process
was activated in my consciousness, and I began to go through all of
my attitudes, affiliations, beliefs, behaviors, books in my library, and
so on—to separate the wheat from the chaff.

In the archetypal myths of the inner journey, the seeker faces a
sorting task. It seems impossible until help arrives from unexpected
places—birds, ants, fairies. In the ancient Greek myth, Psyche (soul)
was not allowed to unite with Eros (Beloved) until she fulfilled four
tasks required by Aphrodite (Goddess of Love). Psyche's first task
was to sort a huge pile of mixed seeds within an impossible time
frame. In despair, as she sat weeping, an army of ants came to her
rescue and did the sorting task for her. The ants symbolize her shift
to integrate a quality of consciousness that is disciplined, efficient,
and interdependent.

As I faced the task of sorting through the pile of potentials and
drives in my life, I too had to have a shift of consciousness. My teacher
made it clear that problems can't be solved at the same level of consciousness that created them. Changes in the world depend on a
transformation of the heart. He said, "Begin with who and what you
are. All truth is found within. If you want to improve yourself, start
where you are, with whatever is coming up for you. You don't have to
learn secret codes or ancient mantras. *Life itself* is the best workshop."
He initiated a shift of my consciousness from head to heart, from
changing others to changing myself. By changing myself, I would be
changing the world—for I was part of that world.

*Start where you are* is what I heard. At the time of meeting him, I was a disheartened activist, burned out by trying to tackle social injustices, exhausted from a way of teaching and "doingness" that aimed at changing institutional structures of injustice. I hadn't realized that societal changes had to start from the *inside* of us. As a professor, I was teaching classes on religious violence and oppression. The students reacted to the material on a personal level, and the discussions became polarized—men vs. women, white vs. black, gay vs. straight, etc. They learned to assert their identities, not how to heal their inner divides. They learned about sociopolitical power, not the power within.

Of what ultimate good was knowledge if it didn't relieve suffering? This was my core belief. At the time, my best attempt to enact it was to collaborate with a talented young woman of color, Lily Gomez, to teach a course called "Love and Liberation"; we sought to give a communal space to examine white privilege and other layers of oppression. Student resistance was so strong that Lily and I renamed the course "Love and Frustration."

I was focused on the problems, not the solutions. My classrooms felt like a battleground because the study was based on a victim/perpetrator model that engendered blame. It was a mindset that carried thought forms of anger and condemnation. As in physics, force results in equal and opposite counterforce. It was a perpetual tug-of-war, of attack and counterattack. In sum, I was doing triage, not teaching. No wonder I felt exhausted.

I didn't know how to shift out of this crusade consciousness; I had crusaded for causes for most of my life. It was a lifelong habit of mind, a mindset. I couldn't see how things would change unless I was *against* something.

During my twenties, I had embraced the rightwing political agenda of religious fundamentalism. In college, I gave strident speeches for rightwing causes. I viewed feminism as a threat to the moral order of society and scolded my female friends for wanting to pray in public. After all, hadn't the Bible commanded that women be silent in church? I told a gay family member he was living in sin and wasn't allowed to visit my house. In a letter, I admonished, "You need to do conversion therapy to change yourself into a heterosexual." At the time, I knew nothing about the struggles he faced or the harmful effects of conversion therapy. I was merely repeating what my church elders had told me. "Hate the sin, love the sinner" was the confusing message. It didn't occur to me that "hatred of sin is still just hatred."[133] At the time, I thought of myself as morally superior and in a position to tell others how to live their lives.

Then, in my early thirties, life gave me an experience of being judged and rejected—a taste of my own medicine. The day came when it was *my* name that the church elders read from the pulpit. I had gone against the elders and traditions of the church, among other things, by writing a "Declaration for Women's Inclusion," a public statement that called for the full participation of women in the church's ministries. Even though the document was grounded in biblical principle, my attitude was arrogant and angry. The elders called me a heretic and disloyal to the church. Nearly overnight, I went from being a pillar in the church to being persona non grata.

Still, "holier than thou" was a hard habit to break, and I continued my moral crusade, only this time it was from the left wing. Though the banners I waved were now for the other side, my energy field was the same—being right and feeling superior. I marched in rallies and stood on the street corners with inflammatory signs: ASSES OF EVIL, with a picture of President Bush and his cabinet members; this seemed clever at the time, but it had hate in it. Disagreement with others is one thing, but hostility quite another. In truth, I got a thrill out of protest—grandstanding, acrimony, proving my point! Even though I carried PEACE signs, I was intolerant of the other side. If a religious leader prayed to "God the Father," I walked out of the room. Wasn't it hegemony and sexism? Just as I had been vigilant about moral correctness when I was a religionist, I was now vigilant about politically correct language. As soon as someone opened their mouth, I pigeonholed them either as an ally or an enemy. Where was the goodwill in that?

Whether rightwing or leftwing, mine was a moral crusade to *"make* the world better"—according to *my* opinion of how the world should be. I was stunned when my teacher introduced me to the saying of Indian sage Ramana Maharshi: "The world you see does not exist." Before this, I was certain that the world was exactly as I presumed it to be: a battle between victims and perpetrators, the right and the wrong, the saved and the unsaved. It was going to be an endless task to save the world, and by age thirty-nine I was burned out.

I heard my teacher say, "Just because you love chocolate doesn't mean you have to hate vanilla." It seemed so obvious that fighting *against* something didn't work. I wanted to be done with crusading. But how? The only solution I could think of was to quit my job, move to another state, and pursue a more holistic career—the well-known geographic cure.

I complained to a friend about feeling stuck: "I want to leave my job. I'm tired of academe. Cut off from my heart and soul. It's like living from the neck up—all in my head."

"What do you want to do?" she asked.

"I've been accepted at a massage school in Santa Fe where I can get certified in a new profession—the healing arts—something more holistic."

"You really think you can study your way to a healed life? The problem is not that you don't know enough. The problem is that you don't know *who you are.*"

She was right. I needed to go inward, not fight another cause or get another degree. I ripped up the tuition check to massage school, packed the camper van, and headed north to a forest where I could face myself. Unaware of the irony, I slid a case of wine next to the box of my teacher's audios. Just as Psyche had to sort the pile of seeds and was helped by an unexpected source, I too was going to have to do a major sorting, guided by someone I didn't expect.

# Sunlight

Traveling north, I found myself on the doorstep of a wise old woman known as Sunlight. She was nearly eighty years old and lived down a narrow country lane in the coastal forest of northern California. "Sunlight" was not her birth name; she had chosen it for herself in midlife to mark a new chapter in her life. Several years before, I had met her when I drove through her town on a road trip. Though at that time I'd spent only a few hours with her and then lost touch, the memory of her lovingness never left me. Now, like a sea turtle that returns to its natal shore, I returned to her doorstep. She didn't ask why I'd come. If she had, I wouldn't have known what to tell her. She simply welcomed me as an old friend.

My weeklong visit turned out to be an initiation. Sunlight took me inward—to the heart. Even though I knew and believed my teacher's message that change had to start within, I didn't know how to go about it.

I asked Sunlight, "How can we heal societal wounds?"

She said, "Changing the world happens one heart at a time—start with your own!"

I'd been determined to change other people, often by angry insistence. I pressed her: "But doesn't anger have a place? Don't we need to rise up and be heard? How else will the world learn of injustice?"

Sunlight replied, "Isn't there enough anger in the world? What the world needs is love, not another lashing. If you have anger in your heart, then you put anger into the world."

In truth, I was exhausted from years of anger. I constantly played over in my mind the wounds from being a woman in a patriarchal society. I fought back with angry words, and took offense if a man opened the door for me or used the word "mankind." I got a secret smug satisfaction out of collecting the injustices done me. "See how terrible they are! How intolerant! How ignorant!" Because I saw myself as a victim of injustice, I felt I had the right to stew in my discontent, but the truth was, my years of activism—standing on street corners, protest marches, door-to-door petitions, teaching college courses on oppression—had worn me out. I was trying to save the world but could barely save the only life under my control—my own. Physicist Dr. William Tiller told me, "My first area of work is continued experiential development of Self, because you can't continue to make progress with anything unless you feel it inside."

I set to work on the experiential development of Self, and Sunlight was there to help me.

Sunlight lived in a one-room cabin she built when she was in her sixties. It was off the grid, with solar panels and a greenhouse. She'd had a former life as an activist and research scientist in Paris and New York. Then she left it all and moved to the coastal forest in northern California. Here, her life revolved around planting, writing, and serving her community in simple ways. She lived to love and loved to live. She grew some of her own food. Rhododendron sprinkled reds and pinks all over her woods. The birds sang, the deer grazed. Cats visited daily.

"There is only one change, really, and that is the change to Love. Everything else will follow." That's quoted from Sunlight's book, *Being*.[134] And she lived it. Sunlight de-slugged her garden at night and put the squirmy creatures out to pasture. She was careful not to hurt the worms and ants. I thought: *A quiet life that harms nothing and no one—maybe that kind of life helps the world more than an activist life that creates opposition and deepens the wound of separation.* People want to know what to do; perhaps it's equally helpful to ask what not to do, as in *ahimsa*, non-harming. As Grandmother Mona said, "We are here for all our relations. Whatever we do to another, it's the same as if done to us."

I arrived at Sunlight's cabin with a case of wine in the camper. "Spending time with myself" had become a euphemism for drinking alone. Alcohol was my go-to friend. After leaving the church as persona non grata, I felt bitter, lonely, and unwanted. In its denigration of my love orientation, the church had rejected what felt like the core of me, so I'd turned to another "spirit" for company. Alcohol gave me an escape from the psychic pain. There was a genetic predisposition toward alcoholism in my family, and drinking soon became a physical-emotional addiction. I awoke in the morning thinking of wine, and couldn't get through the day without a bottle or two or more. I hid bottles in my desk drawer at the university and chewed gum to mask the smell. Heavy daily drinking had deteriorated my health, affected my job, and had become a major barrier in relationships. What an irony! I had just published a biography of the best-known prohibitionist in American history. Indeed, I'd written the raucous story of tee-totaling Carry Nation and her saloon-smashing hatchet crusade as I poured one drink after another! I wanted to stop, but felt hopeless I ever could.

Some alcoholics are binge drinkers; others are daily drinkers. I was a daily drinker. I couldn't imagine writing without a drink, making love without a drink, going to a party or watching the sunset or eating dinner or falling asleep without a drink. Drinking was easy to rationalize, as I could always think of someone who drank more than I, but deep inside, I was concerned about myself. What was wrong with me? I'd been raised with the motto "Where there's a will, there's a way!" This implied that I could overcome addiction through sheer ego-will, but I'd never seen it work in the lives of family members. I tried several times to stop drinking through willpower, only to feel more like a failure when the self-coercion didn't work. I was long past the early drinking years when it felt good. I was drinking now because I had to. I didn't understand addiction. Why could some people enjoy a couple of glasses of wine but I had to drink a bottle or two?

On the drive to Sunlight's house, I had listened to audio tracks by my teacher on "Consciousness and Addiction." The teaching was compassionate and eye opening. Addicts and alcoholics aren't bad people, he said. They're not moral failures. There are genetic physiological factors that make it extremely hard for them to stop the substance. Most important, they have a yearning for bliss, which he said is our "birthright." Their reliance on "spirits" is the expression of a deep spiritual longing for joy and boundlessness. He referenced the 1961 letters between Bill Wilson (co-founder of Alcoholics Anonymous) and C. G. Jung, in which Jung said that the alcoholic's craving for alcohol was related to the "spiritual thirst for wholeness" and "union with God" (*Unio mystica*). In other words, addicts and alcoholics have the right goal but not the best method. "*Spiritus contra spiritum*," suggested Jung. In order to recover from addiction to "spirits," one needs a path of the Spirit.

My teacher said, "Never be ashamed of your longing for bliss, for it is your destiny. Change your technique, not your aspiration." This way of holding addiction was revolutionary to me. It wasn't based on fear or punishment of sin but on the power of love. It affirmed my innocence and dignity. Listening to the audio recording, I deeply felt the longing to be free of drinking and experience the real bliss he described. But how? I had tried to quit many times, without success. Pride had gotten in the way; I hadn't been willing to admit I needed help.

"Humility," my teacher said, is the *open sesame*. It unlocks the door to truth and invites in the help of unseen forces waiting for us to ask. He liked to give the famous example of Bill Wilson, whom he'd known in New York. Bill's moment of surrender turned out to be a portal of freedom for millions of people across the world. In 1934, Bill was admitted for the last time to Towns Hospital. Doctors told Bill's wife, Lois, that he was a hopeless case of alcoholism, and advised her to put him into an asylum so he wouldn't hurt himself or her or others. Bill, who was only thirty-five, plunged into despair. He was an agnostic and the idea of a God who could help him seemed ridiculous, but alone in his hospital bed, there was nowhere else to turn. Bill cried out, "I'll do anything, anything at all... If there be a God, let him show himself." The effect of the prayer was instant and dramatic. Suddenly, his room filled with an unbelievably bright white Light. The atmosphere was electric, and he felt an elation beyond description, greater than any joy he'd ever known. In that state of ecstasy, he knew he was finally free. As the Light began to subside, he felt a Presence in the room, the Great Reality, which he thought must be what religious people called God. Bill Wilson never drank again. The Light had transformed him. He co-founded Alcoholics Anonymous, which has become one of the most inclusive and transformative global spiritual movements of the past century.[135]

I listened to this story as I drove. Did our individual breakthroughs really benefit the world? The case of Bill Wilson was one thing, but what about the rest of us? My teacher was emphatic that it was precisely our inner healing that helps the world: "To endeavor to evolve spiritually is the greatest gift one can give."[136]

# POURING OUT THE 'SPIRITS'

I wasn't planning to tell Sunlight about my drinking problem—it just tumbled out of me. It was a winter evening, and we were sitting and warming ourselves in front of her woodstove. The kitty purred. I could hear the whisper of the wind. It felt safe to share my burden.

"Sunlight, I think I have a drinking problem."

"People who don't have a drinking problem don't usually say that."

"Okay. I *know* I have a problem. I want to quit, but I don't know how." There. I had said it. The secret was out. What she said next shocked me.

"It's possible to quit. I can say that because I've been sober over thirty years."

"*What?*" My eyes got big. I couldn't believe I hadn't known about her drinking.

Sunlight ignored my shock and carried on with her story. "One day I hit bottom and reached out for help. I was having blackouts and couldn't remember what I'd done the night before. I'd wake up in strange places. I'd get my phone bill and see I made long expensive calls to Europe, but couldn't remember what I'd said. I saw that I was getting worse and worse and knew that one day I might end up on a sidewalk in the Bowery (New York skid row), left to die alone. I knew I had to ask for help. Someone invited me to a recovery meeting. I was ready. As they say, I was 'sick and tired of being sick and tired.'"

I was stunned! I couldn't imagine *her* being drunk. She definitely didn't fit my image of an alcoholic. (For that matter neither did I.)

Sunlight went on, "They told me at the meeting, 'Just don't pick up that first drink, one hour and one day at a time.' The problem of the alcoholic is that if we take the first drink, we can't stop. So that really was the only way for me—to not have the first drink. That day was the hardest of my life. I was terrified. My hands were trembling. I had a splitting headache. But somehow I made it through the day without a drink. Then it was another hour, another day, and another hour, another day. Now it's been decades. Giving up the drinking was just the beginning. It opened the door to love."

We shared our experiences openly, late into the night. Before going to sleep, I poured out all the alcohol I'd stockpiled in my van. The liquid spirits were gone. With Sunlight's help, that major sorting was accomplished. Later, I learned that her story was published in a book studied daily in group meetings worldwide. When we're ripe for change, life has a way of putting us in the right place at the right time with the right person.

Sometimes the best gift of love is simply to let the other be. Give space. Don't intervene. This was exactly how Sunlight loved me. At a crucial crossroads in my life, she helped me as I sorted out my drinking issue. She didn't lift the weights *for* me, but as soon as I was ready to try, she "spotted" me. She didn't *tell* me I had a drinking problem, but as soon as I said I did, she was there to listen. She didn't *advise* me to stop drinking, but as soon as I said I wanted to, she was there to share her own experience.

In my first few days of not drinking, Sunlight took me along on her community activities. I learned a lot by listening. We went to a church service where there was a man who had lost his wife and was attending a grief group run by the minister. He told Sunlight, "I've not been involved spiritually for forty-five years." I thought: *Yeah, it's good for him to be here, so he can* receive *love.* Sunlight was thinking the opposite and said to him, "You have a lot of love to *give* here, don't you?" Tears came to his eyes. She had seen his soul.

On another occasion, I shared with Sunlight that I was seeing colorful auras around people and wanted to know their meaning. I was feeling special, thinking it was a sign that I'd arrived to a "higher" spiritual level. It had happened spontaneously one day when I was at an academic conference. Bored by the theoretical papers being read, I went inward and melded into a statement from my teacher: "Everything reveals the miracle of existence and therefore is equal to everything else."[137] Meditatively, I looked around the room and registered the equal holiness and preciousness of each person. At that moment, each one lit up and around their head appeared a white light. At first, I thought: *Oh! What's going on with the lighting?* I thought it was a mechanical malfunction, or that something was wrong with my eyes, but then I started to see colors around different parts of their bodies: blue, yellow, green, orange, purple, black. Each person was an energy field made of light and colors. It seemed that each person had the potential to be the full rainbow spectrum, but only if they had owned their wholeness, and no one had. I felt that something of their beautiful nature was being revealed to me—something more essential than their ideas or physical appearance. The conference lasted for several days and the phenomenon continued. I noticed that the colors around people varied, and I wanted to know the reason for this.

I said to Sunlight, "What do the colors mean? If I knew, then maybe I could help people." Sunlight looked at me as if she felt sorry for me—I had missed the whole point. She said, "Can't you just enjoy them? Love people from your heart. *That's* what heals." She saw auras and the Light everywhere, yet didn't seek to gain anything from it or analyze it. Life was illuminated for her, and she kept it to herself.

Sunlight was an ordinary person who had discovered the secret of love. She didn't talk much about it—you just knew it was true. She kept saying, "Love is not something to talk about—it's something you *are*, that you *radiate*." Still, I pressed on with my questions because I felt desperate to understand certain things.

"What about romantic love?" I'd always associated love with romance and coupledom.

She said, "Love is universal energy and gives us our own completion. Love therefore doesn't require an outer partner or a lover. I am completely happy by myself. It's nice to have a partner, but love doesn't depend upon having a partner. Love is who you are. Love is present everywhere." She'd had partners but now lived by herself. She viewed everything as a part of Love. "I see love in everything." The plants in her greenhouse grew in vibrant agreement—tomatoes, green peppers, and flowers. "I see that we all are really one, and I never feel alone."

When I was with Sunlight, I could almost feel the Oneness of Love, but—not wanting a lover, a partner, that special someone to share life with? I couldn't imagine life without romance. Later, as I made this journey of love, I encountered couples—David and Susan Hawkins; Bill and Jean Tiller; Llewellyn and Anat Vaughan-Lee; Viktor and Elly Frankl; Belvie Rooks and Dedan Gills—who showed me that a romantic partnership could be put into service to the power of a greater love.

I met Belvie Rooks and Dedan Gills one day when Sunlight took me for breakfast at Queenie's Roadhouse Cafe in Elk, California, a remote town with a population of 200. In that unlikely location in the middle of nowhere, her friends Belvie and Dedan happened to be there. She hadn't seen them in a long time. She turned to me and said, "There are no accidents. Would you like to meet them?"

Later, as they spoke of their experience as longtime civil rights activists, standing at the Door of No Return at Elmina slave dungeon in Ghana, chills went up my spine. Their anger at racism had been transformed into a vision of healing for the whole. They were no longer stuck in "us vs. them" mindset. I knew they would be my teachers on the path of loving my "enemy." Over the following years, that's exactly what happened as I met with them several times to discuss this book.

As Sunlight and I drove home, I couldn't get Belvie and Dedan out of my mind. How had they made the shift from us vs. them to the global heart?

I asked Sunlight, "How do I get rid of my anger? When I think of all the injustices done to me, I boil inside." She suggested I make an inventory of all my hurts and resentments. Yes! I rolled up my sleeves and wrote through the night. All the terrible things *they* had done to me!

After I read my long list of hurts to Sunlight, she said, "Okay, now, look just as closely at your own motives. What were you expecting from others? What was *your* part in these situations and interactions?"

I'm sure I looked bewildered, but she was matter-of-fact: "You are resentful against others, quick to see their faults, their prejudice, their intolerance, their ignorance, their greed, their egotism. You see them as the enemy. Aren't these things also in you?"

Was she crazy? Hadn't she heard how I'd been mistreated? How obviously terrible those people were? How unfair and unjust the situations? I didn't protest, however. Somewhere in me I knew it was true: whatever I hated in them was also in me; if not, how could I have recognized it? As my teacher had said, "You're always looking in a mirror."

Sunlight told me, "If you can face your own darkness and come to love all that you discover there, then you will be a force for good in this world."

Love all the parts of myself that I've pushed out of view? Sunlight was asking me to know and own all of myself—my self-pity, my arrogance, my egotism, my hypocrisy, my prejudice, my self-hatred, etc. Then I had to come to love all that was found? It seemed impossible. It was easier to be a beggar, always needing something or someone outside of myself to validate and love me. Sunlight finished with this clincher: "One day you'll see that the enemy is not another person or group. It is the *ignorance* inside all of us."

I heard her words but fought against them. I was still attached to a paradigm of polarity, of the oppressed against the oppressor. "Don't you care about equality?" I quipped.

Sunlight spoke slowly and firmly:

> I care more about Oneness. Equality was the battle cry
> of my generation—we all fought for it. But equality
> can never be achieved because it stems from separate-
> ness. Oneness—this is what I care about. This is the

consciousness I choose to live. Oneness carries the knowledge of our wholeness and our interconnectedness with each other. It includes differences, but not adversaries. Those of us that fought against inequality fought for a good cause, but it was still a mentality of us versus them. We were committed to nonviolence, but we used the word 'oppression' as a psychic weapon. If the *end* is Oneness and respect for each other's dignity, then the *means* we use must carry that same respect. There is no place for self-righteousness and blame. Everyone has been hurt by oppression— this is the starting point for any real change.

I challenged Sunlight on one last point: "Okay, then, how did you deal with homophobia?" She grew up in the U.S. at a time when gay people were considered criminals. I knew she had faced a lot of prejudice and hatred. How could she not be angry about this? How could she not feel like a victim of injustice?

Sunlight replied, "Unconditional love—over and over again."

"What do you mean?" I asked.

She said, "Love that is not unconditional is not love. We have to love our self completely, because all of us are created by a loving Creator who loves all of creation. Also, we extend love to those who hate and judge us."

Her reply was resolute, with no room for questions. "Listen to the wind outside, how it moves through the trees." I had to empty myself in order to listen. "Love is like the wind," Sunlight said. "It touches each tree differently. Some rustle, some whisper. Some bend, some break. It's not up to us to ask, 'Why this way, not that way'? Our work is to see—to really know and feel—that Love moves through all and is in all."

She asked me to read some poetry by Mary Oliver, whose poems take a reader into the dimension of Love that moves through all things. "Where Does the Temple Begin, Where Does It End?" is the title of a poem. I read for a while and then we fell into peaceful silence.

The kitty, curled up on the window seat, purred; the fire crackled; the rain gently pattered; the wind blew through the meadow grasses. The trees seemed to sing and sigh in the wind. I listened with empty ears and heard what I'd never heard before.

After perhaps an hour, Sunlight looked up at me. She said, "You've done good work here. Now it's time for you to leave. There are some things that can only be learned in solitude. I've arranged for you to stay at a friend's cabin, a few hours north of here. We call it the Moon Cabin. It's deep in the forest. You can stay there as long as you like."

I noticed that her eyes shone from an inner Light—which made it hard to leave.

Belvie Rooks and Dedan Gills showed me the critical link between inner wholeness and societal healing. It's said, on the path of love, our enemy is the best teacher. I heard the Dalai Lama say at a gathering, "The enemy is our teacher. Without the enemy, how can we learn tolerance and forgiveness? If you want to learn compassion, thank your enemy." Sunlight had said a similar thing. The person who despises us is also a part of us. Unconditional love requires that we find a place in our hearts for those who reject and abuse us. I felt the truth of this, but had no idea how to live it. The story of Belvie Rooks and Dedan Gills showed me how.

Belvie Rooks and Dedan Gills in Redlands, California, 2014
(Larry Rose/courtesy of The Institute of Contemplative Life).

*Chapter Sixteen*

# GROWING A GLOBAL HEART – HEALING OUR SOCIETAL WOUNDS

Encounter with Belvie Rooks and Dedan Gills

*To plant a tree is to plant hope.*
—BELVIE ROOKS AND DEDAN GILLS

B elvie Rooks and Dedan Gills are the founders of Growing a Global Heart, a vision that inspires the ceremonial planting of millions of memorial trees to honor the forgotten souls of our past—victims of urban violence, the Underground Railroad, and the Trans-Atlantic Slave Route in West Africa—as part of a process of collective healing and as a solution to climate change. The Growing a Global Heart motto is: "Healing the wounds of the past—in the present—while creating a sustainable future." The tree-planting ceremonies seed new hope for humanity and the Earth. Here is the story of their vision.

## FROM A BROKEN TO AN OPEN HEART

The "Door of No Return" is in Ghana, West Africa, at the Elmina slave dungeon. After standing in this doorway, Belvie Rooks and

Dedan Gills were never quite the same. The dungeon was the origin site of their African ancestors' enslavement. For over three centuries, African men, women, and children were kidnapped from their villages and their families and thrown into slave dungeons along Africa's west coast. If they survived the horror of the dungeons, they were pushed through the Door of No Return onto the infamous slave ships for transport across the Atlantic Ocean. If they survived that voyage, they arrived in "the New World," to be branded and sold into slavery. As Belvie and Dedan stood at the Door of No Return, their pain was overwhelming, their tears overflowed. It was during that journey—in the depths of despair—that their "global heart" vision was born.

Like the water that breaks to signal the birth of a child, their tears ushered in a new creation. When I first met Belvie Rooks and Dedan Gills, I felt the presence of something that had been born in them. I came to know it as the power of love. Their broken-heartedness had been transformed into openheartedness. I met them at a small roadside cafe in the middle of nowhere. "Synchronicity," we all said. As I heard their story, I felt they'd found a way out of the most lethal prison of our time—not a prison with iron bars but an inner one. It's the mindset of "us vs. them," and I felt that Belvie and Dedan were breaking free from it. Even those who had been enemies to African Americans—Confederate soldiers—came to be included in the sphere of their concern. They recognized that "trees breathe for the whole" and the soil contains the "blood, bone, sweat, and tears" of everyone. I saw a similarity to Nelson Mandela's journey to transcend societal divides and emerge a new vision of truth and reconciliation.

At the time I met Belvie and Dedan, I had been fighting against the forces I viewed as my enemy. Protest against an outer enemy seemed the only viable path to social change. Even though I carried PEACE signs, I saw the world as a battle, "us vs. them." Belvie and Dedan, however, saw the world quite differently—the whole human race was "our family" and the small blue planet was "our common home." As African Americans, they suffered from the history of racial hatred and discrimination endemic to our culture. "Back of the bus." "Whites Only." "Stay in your place." They'd been longtime civil rights activists.

In 2007, they traveled to Ghana to be married in midlife, and while there, a new path of activism opened up for them. It was heart-based. At Elmina, they wept for the African children, men, and women—many ancient ancestors—who had been pushed through that door. Their ancestors' names were erased from history. Belvie and Dedan could find out the names of the ships and their capitalistic investors, but the names of those who'd entered through the Door of No Return were unknown. "Erasure," Belvie said, is "a deep, deep wound." Standing in the dungeon, a place of incomprehensible violence and suffering, they wept. They felt rage. Despair loomed large. What could ever heal this horrific historic wound done by and to humanity? The natural human emotions of rage and despair were alchemized into the power of love by a single question that Dedan posed at that critical point: "What would healing look like?"

This question had a profound impact, and it had a carrier wave of creativity, unity, and hope. As they attempted to live out the impact of the question, Belvie and Dedan found it impossible to see the world solely in terms of "us vs. them." What would it mean to live from a place of embracing the whole human race as family, and this beautiful small blue planet our common home? Once, while Belvie sat in quiet meditation, another powerful question emerged: "What about the Confederate soldier?" This was the ultimate enemy. In the moment, it wasn't a question she was prepared for; in fact, she actively resisted it. In a quest to unravel its mystery, she traveled alone to visit a Confederate cemetery—where she had a profound epiphany.

Belvie explained their quest and approach to a group of college students, speaking of her work in social justice and civil rights. "Yes, it's important to focus on the problem, but it's equally important to focus on the solution." Belvie had a dream experience of embracing children of all different races from around the world. Waves of energy emanated from her heart and she felt a "deep, deep love for the children of every nation." In the wake of the dream, she wondered, *What would the world be like if our love of children inspired our love for all?* "Love is the key healer," she concluded, and "Love is calling through the youth, longing to be protected and nurtured." It reminded me of

Jetsunma Tenzin Palmo's statement "To love all children as if they were one's own—now that is something!"

Belvie's dream showed the power of the heart to heal humanity. Love unifies, anger divides. Similarly, Dedan told of his belief that hearts long to beat in tandem with each other:

> I read somewhere that if you take the heart cells of two different human beings beating at different rates, and you put them in the same petri dish, one of them will pause so that they can beat in synchronicity with one another. I think that's what we want to do. I think that's what we yearn for—to be in synchronicity with other hearts. And that's what Growing a Global Heart is about. To take pause from how you look at the world and try to beat in tandem with the other hearts around you.

Belvie and Dedan taught me to take pause of my beliefs and listen to others. As an activist, I'd been opinionated and oppositional. This kind of attitude was noted by His Holiness the 17th Karmapa during his US tour in 2015: "Activists can often be unwarrantedly aggressive." He emphasized the need for people to approach activism "with compassion, not with arrogance or pride or the mentality that they are somehow better than others."

From the people I interviewed for this book, I learned that when we apply the principles of love to societal problems, it works best to stand for truth (e.g., "All are created equal") rather than fight against something or someone. Blaming gets us nowhere. Force leads to counterforce. Someone who worked with Mother Teresa told me that Mother Teresa might stand at a peace vigil but never at an antiwar protest.

This is what I saw in Belvie and Dedan. They stand for the oneness of being—a oneness of being that includes the natural world, celebrated in one of Dedan's poems, "The Tree and Me."

## The Tree and Me

Morning glow, prelude to flight
Moving shadows, dazzling light
Insect array, melodic sound
Wandering roots, fertile ground
Dying leaf, tender bud
Sun parched earth, winter mud

Sanctuary joy, leafy glade
April shower, summer shade
Carbon loving, oxygen giving
The universe and I, reciprocal living
Hushed in silence, her canopies entrance
Together we live, together we dance.

—DEDAN GILLS[138]

When I met with Belvie and Dedan, I asked why plant trees? They told me that the tree is an inclusive manifestation of unconditional love. When a tree reaches maturity, it bears fruit, provides shade and sanctuary, and can be used to make houses. On a hot day, when you're trying to walk across town, you can get cool and comfortable under a tree. "It unconditionally gives to everyone who comes into its presence. It doesn't say, 'You can't have any of my fruit' to one and 'You can have some' to another. It bears the fruit and it's there for the picking—for the birds, rodents, squirrels, whatever and whoever comes." Dedan explained the unifying symbolism of the tree for societal problems:

> We live at a time in which none of the standard ways of resolving human conflict are working for us. Somehow we have to come up with transcendent models that are beyond Democrat vs. Republican, nation-state vs. nation-state, male vs. female, the old vs. the young. All of these divides and identities put

walls around us and point at other people as being the cause of our misery. The tree transcends these divides. It challenges us to emulate it in its magnificence and its beauty, in its stillness, in its nobility. To plant a tree is an act of love because, depending on the type of tree, it may take many years for it to bear fruit. An olive tree takes twenty-five or thirty years to produce an olive. This means you're not planting it for yourself—you're planting it for the future.

# Growing a Global Heart—The Story

In 2011 and 2014, Belvie and Dedan came to the University of Redlands and shared their story of transformation with groups of college students and community members from all walks of life. Through photographs, poetry, and personal experiences, they told the story of where, when, and how their vision was born. The audience was riveted. Here's what Belvie and Dedan said.

## Experience in Africa

Belvie:    In 2007, we were in Ghana, West Africa, to get married! We're actually celebrating our seventh wedding anniversary this month.

Dedan:    When people like you come out to hear our message, the honor is ours. We feel like what we have to say is important in the world. We know the vision we came up with in Africa is not a solution to all the world's problems, and we're not telling anyone else what to do. In the complexity of life, every segment and every aspect of the living dynamic is necessary and moves us forward. People approach social change a thousand different ways.

Belvie:    With this photo, I've invited into this room my great-great-grandmother—Grandma Martha—who was twelve years old when the Emancipation Proclamation occurred. This means she lived for twelve years as an enslaved child. I like to invite her into spaces like this because these are the spaces she never would have been allowed to enter. We want to use her, also, as a way of inviting all of our ancestors into the room, your ancestors as well, all of our ancestors. In 1957, Ghana was the first African country to get its independence from British Colonial rule. I had met Brother Ishmael Tetteh in Los Angeles at the Agape Spiritual Center. Brother Tetteh is a West African shamanic teacher and wisdom holder from the Akan spiritual tradition. He said, "If you come to Ghana, I'll perform your wedding ceremony."

Dedan:   (Points to a photo of the church in Ghana where they were married.) This was a transformative moment for me because of my background. When I was going to UCLA, I was a college student in the daytime and in the Black Panther Party underground at night. When I stood in that church that day, in Ghana, and they introduced us to that congregation, everybody reached out their hands and started saying—some in different languages, and some in English— "Welcome home, welcome home, this is your home." I was touched so deeply by that experience, I don't think I've been the same since.

Belvie:   While we were preparing for our wedding ceremony in Accra, in northern Ghana, they had a major flood that displaced 400,000 people. We were there just at the time they were having this major disaster. Catastrophic climate change in Africa takes two forms. Sometimes it's flooding, and at other times it's drought. Bishop Desmond Tutu lists twenty-eight countries in the world as most vulnerable to climate change, and twenty-two of them are in Africa, even though Africa has a very small carbon footprint. It was hard for us to ignore that we were there at a critical time, seeing things that made us conscious of the larger environmental context. Immediately following our commitment ceremony in Accra, we left for the Cape Coast of Ghana to visit the Elmina slave dungeon. We wanted to begin our union by paying homage to the countless ancestors who had begun the long journey into slavery from one of the more than a hundred slave dungeons along Africa's west coast.

Dedan:　Right in the center of the dungeon, also called a castle, is the Dutch Reform Church. Above the door is a reference to Psalms 132:13—"The LORD has chosen Zion; he has desired it for his habitation." I couldn't make sense of that; it felt so ironic. It's important to look back and know the history and the lineage of a problem. In academia, they call it the formative context. When you go to a doctor or to the hospital, they ask you, "Did your mother have this, did your father have that, is there a history of this in your family?" They want to know the formative context of your medical condition.

When a dog has been brutalized, he might be vicious if you try to touch him. That's why a person who works with dogs wants to know the formative context. They don't judge the dog on its current manifestations; they want to know how she got like that. And so we need to understand the formative context of how we arrived at the current racial situation in America and in the world. With every other problem, we hear, "You have to face it." A psychologist says, "Go back and look at your life to understand it." It's ironic that when the question of race comes up, most people have a tendency to say, instead, "Get over it. You don't need to look at the past. It has nothing to do with today." They don't say that about a dog, they don't say that about a person who had a mental breakdown, they don't say that about someone who's in a hospital. We felt it was important to visit the slave dungeon and look back as a way of understanding the formative context around race as we experienced and understood it from the perspective of our reality in America.

Belvie:　(Points to a photo at the "Door of No Return.") Earlier, Dedan said Elmina was referred to as both a "castle" and a "dungeon." If you were one of the millions of people who passed through the underground dungeons awaiting shipment, it was a slave dungeon. If, on the other hand, you were the governor and his family living on the floors above and dancing the night away in the lap of luxury, it was a castle. The Door of No Return was the last point of contact with the African continent for the enslaved African people prior to being put onto ships for the long journey across the ocean and into an unknown and uncertain future. It was also the point where many enslaved men and women chose suicide by jumping into the sea rather than depart from Africa's shores.

Dedan:   When we stood at that door, we both had this sensation of actually standing in the past and looking across time into the future. We thought about our children and grandchildren, and we thought about all the people who had left places like Elmina so many years ago. We felt as if we had stepped into the story. We stood there and knew that it was important to share this story and our experience.

Belvie:   I'd like to share with you my journal entry coming out of this experience:

> As I stood looking out at the vast ocean beyond, I tried hard to imagine what reaching this spot, this Door of No Return, must have felt like for some long-ago, unremembered African ancestor as she stood trembling on the precipice of a terrifyingly uncertain future. One of the most horrifying bits of information shared was the fact that at the height of the slave trade, there were so many dead and dying bodies tossed into the sea at this very spot, the frenzied feeding opportunity resulted in the change of the shark migration pattern along this entire bit of coast. My tears flowed uncontrollably. I sobbed as I glanced at the ocean below. It was hard to process the fact that for over 300 years, without interruption, millions of African men, women, and children had begun the journey into slavery from this very spot. The names of the people passing through the Door of No Return have all been erased from our historical memory. The names of the mothers, the fathers, the children, the sisters, the brothers, the babies, the aunts, the potters, weavers, farmers, priests, and healers (most of whom were women). The numerous

slave dungeons (over a hundred along the west coast of Africa in places like Elmina and the Cape Coast in Ghana and Gorée Island in Senegal) are living monuments and stark reminders of our inhumane history. All of our histories, and all of our collective lineages of suffering.

And, now, could we just sit and breathe for a minute?

*(Silence in the hall. A sense of profound respect for the depth of what has been shared.)*

For a long time, I couldn't read this without crying. It was hard to write, it's hard to re-experience even now, and it's hard for people like you, who are so open-hearted, to hear. We sit in silent and heartfelt embrace of all the millions of people forced to endure it.

Dedan:   Belvie wept while we were in that dungeon. I am kind of stoic and held it in, like men tend to do. We men don't want to let people see us cry. We try to be strong. Still, there was a certain place in that building that touched me very deeply. (Points to a photo of a dungeon with *Enfants* inscribed over the doorway.) I was doing really well until I looked in that little room and thought about the infants and children who had been kidnapped from their families. Oftentimes, the kidnappers, to be perfectly honest with you, were people who looked like me. They were harvesting for the Europeans who waited on the coastline to purchase these children for guns, liquor, and trinkets. They did this for 300 years—can you imagine? It broke my heart to think of all those children sleeping on straw mats in that dark, damp, smelly, horrible place.

Belvie:   Afterward, we sat quietly and listened to the crashing waves on the rocks and the howling winds. The wind reminded us of the wails and moans of the people who passed through these dungeons. I believe it's important to go into the depths of darkness. People are excited about what we do now and the current transformation, but my spiritual teachers talk about how important it is to go into the depths of the darkness and despair. This is where the discomfort is, the pain and longing and tears. It is also where the healing occurs. We appreciate your being with us and so present at this stage of the journey, when it was very hard.

It was particularly hard for me because I had heard so much about the women and their suffering. I don't see myself as having a lot of courage, but I had to go back into the women's dungeon alone and just sit and be there. I felt called to honor the spirits of the hundreds and thousands of women who had been forced to live the horror. They were forced to endure it—the least I could do was bear witness, as best I could, to their suffering. I must confess that it was one of the hardest things I've ever done. It's almost as if the energy and spirit of all these women were there in that suffocating space. On our guided tour of the dungeon, we had actually walked up the back stairs to the governor's private bedroom, the back stairs that led down to the court-yard of the enslaved women. Periodically, the governor would order that one of the young women, a virgin, be cleaned up and brought up those stairs to his bedroom. I tried to imagine what it would have been like to be a part of a community of women preparing a young woman to go up those stairs for the governor's pleasure. Since most of the captured didn't speak the same language, I tried to imagine them singing together. What songs did they sing? I felt like I was there in the circle with them so I knew there had to be lots of tears. For me the tears flowed uncontrollably. We were told that often, after the governor had taken his satisfaction, he turned the young girl over to his elite guards to be raped by them before she was returned to the community of women below. I tried to imagine what it was like the next morning to welcome this ravaged spirit of a child back into the community. I wept uncontrollably as I imagined being there, holding this child, this ravaged and broken young woman. I even tried to imagine what it would be like, being the person going up those stairs—I could not go there. I wanted to imagine accompanying her up the stairs but I didn't have the courage.

Something broke deep within me. I became enraged. I went back to the hotel and couldn't stop crying. We didn't know the names of these women, but I felt like they deserved tears. I cried for two days (Belvie chokes up with emotion). I thought I was able to talk about this without being tearful, but I'm still not able to—and that's okay. In that moment of debilitating grief, I forgot everything I thought I knew and believed. I was on the boards of organizations like the Institute of Noetic Sciences; I professed a belief in Oneness; I had spent a lot of time in Quaker circles, but I forgot all the spiritual principles I thought I knew. I had hatred in my heart. I had rage. That's where I was.

After two days of abject despair, Dedan came and knelt by the bed and gently took my hand and asked me, "What hurts so badly?" It's important to name the pain, but you don't always know what to call it. I ended up telling him that what hurt so badly was the erasure. I knew the names of the ships, I knew the name of the ships' captains, I knew the names of the ships' investors, I knew the amount of cargo that was on each ship, I knew the date when the ships left Bristol, Rhode Island, and when they stopped in Jamaica. I knew everything except who the actual people were—the names of the people! They were just called slaves—not mothers, not fathers, aunties, or grand-mothers. They were not even seen as human beings. That's what hurt so badly—the wound of erasure.

Dedan:   I'll say again that the formative context is vitally important. Also, we were on our honeymoon! My wife was crying all day and all night. I wanted to know, out of frustration and out of something deep within me wanting to know if we could ever heal these horrible wounds left upon our souls. It was in the depth of that despair and grief that the question arose: What would healing look like?

## The Transformative Question

Belvie:   That was it. I realized the next morning that Dedan's question was the breakthrough. "What would healing look like?"

Dedan:    I simply asked her, "In the best-case scenario, what would healing look like?"

Belvie:    It was a profound question, but being in the midst of tears, anger, and the wound, my first reaction was one of annoyance: "Healing?" I wasn't even in that universe! To be honest, initially the question was a jarring interruption to the space I was in. What's important about that interruption is that the seed was planted. Dedan's question "What would healing look like?" planted a seed. Yes, we have to be with and attend to the wound. We have to be fully there. We have to feel and go through the range of our emotions, but we don't need to stay there; that's not where we need to live. Embracing the heartache and the tears and the sadness, despair and rage, Dedan's question was from the depth of his soul to the depth of mine as he gently held my hand and asked me to look at him. In order to see him, I had to wipe away the tears. I also felt that all the love he had and that we shared was embodied in that question, "What would healing look like?"

The next morning I got out of bed because I remembered something the African elders had said to us, "When you come out of the slave dungeons, you need to perform a cleansing ritual. You must go to the nearest running water and ceremonially wash your feet, because you don't want to walk with all that sorrow." When I remembered that, I went down to the beach for a ritual washing of my feet.

While doing that, I kept hearing the phrase "Plant a tree." At some point I recognized it as a line from one of Alice Walker's poems, called "Torture." "When they torture your mother, plant a tree. / When they torture your father, plant a tree...." The epiphany in the moment was the awareness that a poem that I'd always thought of as being about hopelessness was in fact a poem of hope. The very act of planting a tree, sowing a seed, showed that there was a commitment and a vision for the future. It was at that moment, alone on the beach, washing my feet of sorrow, my beloved Dedan watching protectively from above, remembering Alice's poem, that one answer to Dedan's question emerged. In retrospect, with the slave dungeon looming in the distance, it seems quite mystical. The idea of ceremonially planting trees in memory of all those unknown, unheralded, and forgotten ancestors. So much came together in that moment! Catastrophic climate change, as we had witnessed, was having a devastating impact on the African continent. the persistence of the phrase "Plant a tree" felt like an act of honoring and modeling, for trees, in their givingness, breathe for the whole! The whole planet—the collective embodiment of all there is! From the depth of despair, a vision of hope and possibility emerged in response to Dedan's question.

Jean Houston's reflections on the sacred wound also came to mind: "The wound becomes sacred when we are willing to let go of our old stories and become the vehicles through which the new story may emerge in time." The question also seemed to speak directly to Thomas Berry's observation that we are "in-between" stories. The old ones no longer serve and the new ones are being birthed.

I just want to underscore the power of art. In that moment of great despair, I remembered a line—"plant a tree"—from a poem that gave rise to a vision of communal healing. Artists clearly have a critical consciousness-shifting role to play as it relates to social change.

Dedan:    I'm from L.A., and we're always talking about the carbon footprint. Carbon was at 350 parts per million when we were in Ghana in 2007. Seven years later, it's now up to 390 and still rising. I don't care whose side you're on, where you stand on this emerging new environmental reality, where you are in the world, if you're rich, white, black, African, Hispanic, Latino, Asian, it makes no difference. If that carbon keeps going up, nobody's going to be able to live on this planet. That puts us all in the same boat, and our boat's sinking. When the boat is sinking, what does the captain yell out? Is it "Abandon ship?" It depends on the captain, and sometimes it's the captain who abandons the ship! The captain is supposed to shout, "All hands on deck!" Everyone has to come and contribute to the well-being of the ship when it's sinking. And this is the time that we live in right now, a time when all hands have to be on deck. Technology has a role in it, but this is about the soul. This is about new relationships.

Belvie:   According to one of my friends and teachers, Angeles Arrien, it's often the questions that we hold that most impact our inner landscape in a way that profoundly shifts our outer world. That's what happened with Dedan's question, "What would healing look like?" In that moment, I didn't want to hear it, but a powerful seed was planted. It was a question I couldn't walk away from. It was a question about the future—our collective future, a sustainable and thriving future for my daughter and my grandson. It was a question that asked, "Can we love all of you young people enough? Can we love you enough to ensure your future and your survival?" I knew I couldn't come out of that slave dungeon and stand before you with only rage, with only anger and despair and a desire to never see another white person. Rage and despair are natural responses, but then what? What was the larger, emerging new story? I had to get to hope.

## The First Tree Plantings

Belvie:   After marrying in Ghana we went to Senegal for three weeks. While there we engaged in a tree-planting project with a group of Senegalese women who had a tree-planting collective. We shared our vision and there was a great deal of synergy. We spent a lot of time with Coumba Toure, a brilliant young Senegalese woman who, at the time, was the West African director of Ashoka, an organization engaging in social entrepreneurship around the world. (Coumba is now the coordinator of Africans Rising.) Two years after our time with her in Senegal, Coumba ended up here in the U.S. and having a baby without family support. Since we'd been incorporated into her family when we were in Senegal, we flew to Tennessee to be with her for the birth. She gave birth at The Farm Midwifery Center in Summertown, which trains people from all over the world to be midwives.

As it turns out, Summertown is in Pulaski County, the very county that gave birth to the Ku Klux Klan in 1865. When we found this out, we thought, "What better place to plant trees?" So our very first tree planting was in the heart of the Confederacy, in the home of the Klan, at a global birthing center that attracted women from all over the world. There were times we were blown away by the syn-chronicity. We have a picture with African, African American, and Euro American hands joined together in a tree-planting ceremony.

Immediately, a question came up for us. We had envisioned that we would be planting trees along the Underground Railroad to honor all the enslaved people who had died in their quest for freedom. And here we were in the heart of the Confederacy and the home of the Klan. One morning, I realized there was this persistent and nag-ging question: "What about the Confederate soldier?" The question, which was disturbingly heartfelt, seemed to come out of nowhere, and to be honest, I wasn't happy about that question and its nagging persistence. I remember mentally talking back: "If the Confederacy had won, we'd still be enslaved! How can we plant trees for them?!" But an inner voice challenged me, "We're not talking about them—this is about you. If you are who you say you're trying to become, then what about the Confederate soldier?" We ended up including the Confederate soldier in our vision of tree planting.

Dedan:   This is what I wrote for the ceremony that day: "We invoke the spirit of the ancestors as we celebrate this firstborn child, Takuma, by planting an endangered tree, the longleaf pine. This is an endan-gered plant that once covered the entire South but is now found only in the southeastern United States and is almost extinct. It's the most carbon-sequestering tree in the United States." We praised the baby's arrival by singing out his name, and we gave thanks to the many ances-tors who had contributed their lives, their dreams, and their hopes to make the miracle of this new birth possible. Our small circle con-sisted of Africans (mother and baby), African Americans, and Euro Americans circling up together as we gently patted the last handful of dirt around the base of the longleaf pine sapling. Our collective wish was that this rich, black soil would bring life-giving nutrients to our young tree as our prayers nurtured a new birth. We also were keenly aware that this fertile soil was enriched with the blood, bone, sweat, and tears of so many."The Choctaw and the Cherokee are here. The remains of the enslaved and the enslavers are here. The soil is drenched with the blood and tears of both Confederate and Union soldiers. The haters and the hated are all here, intermingled in this fertile womb of life-giving earth."

I remember thinking, "What an irony this is. All the horrible things we do to each other, and when we pass over to the other side, our physical bodies, our uniforms, our flags, all symbols of separation, compost back into this soil and give life to the living!" Now what kind of lesson is in that? All these lives in countless and unrecognized ways had been sacrificed to the mystery of this rich Tennessee soil. Although separated in life, they were now united in giving new life and sustenance to our little tree. The words of Shes-his, a late-19th-century Reno Crow shaman, resonated deeply: "The soil you see is not ordinary soil; it is the dust of the blood, the flesh, and the bones of our ancestors.... You will have to dig down through the surface before you can find nature's earth, as the upper portion is Crow. The land, as it is, my blood and my dead; it is consecrated...."[139]

Belvie:   We were deeply honored to have been invited to Selma, Alabama, to plant trees at the foot of the Edmund Pettus Bridge to help commemorate the anniversary of the historic march from Selma to Montgomery where civil rights workers were beaten bloody and not allowed to proceed. That was March 7, 1965. The day would go down in history as "Bloody Sunday." The images of state police violence against the peaceful marchers outraged the world and galvanized the movement and the nation, forcing Congress to eventually pass the historic Voting Rights Act. The footage and the story are relived in the PBS documentary *Eyes on the Prize*. We did a ceremonial tree planting at the foot of the Edmund Pettus bridge, at the place where "Bloody Sunday" had taken place decades earlier. We were joined by a cross-section of people, civil rights legends, activists, and representatives from organizations from around the world, including Congressman John Lewis, Dick Gregory, Janet and Bob Moses, Drew Dellinger, Rev. Sekou, Karlene Griffin, and a daughter of Viola Liuzzo. This tree planting along the Underground Railroad and the Civil Rights Trail was cosponsored by the National Voting Rights

Museum, the Alabama Forestry Commission, the U.S. Forestry Service, the National Wildlife Federation, and the Federation of Southern Cooperatives. People from around the country and the world came to help plant our little trees of healing and remembrance in a place that had caused so much pain and suffering. Many young people joined us in this ceremony. Some of them came from Oakland, California, where we were engaged in intergenerational tree-planting ceremonies focused on combating urban violence.

Dedan:    The young people we've had the privilege of working with and learning from are very talented. Often, they spontaneously create music and song for the occasion. We've done ceremonial plantings in a number of different places including Alabama, Georgia, and Tennessee in the Deep South; along the Underground Railroad in Canada, at one of the last cabins to welcome and conceal hundreds of people escaping slavery in the U.S. The plantings have provided an opportunity to meet and collaborate, and to be surprised by the profound shifts in consciousness we encountered. We did a tree-planting ceremony with someone we viewed as a classic "Southern Belle," but at the end of the ceremony I conducted, she said in a very familiar drawl, "I'm tired of this Southern way of life and how it disrespects certain people. Ya'll need to come down here and plant more trees. We've got to heal this stuff!"

Belvie:    The tree-planting ceremony she participated in was in Colquitt, Georgia and occurred during the 150th anniversary of the beginning of the Civil War (1861–1865). All across the South, the 150th-anniversary commemoration took the form of reenacting various Civil War battles with hundreds of men in gray and blue uniforms running around "shooting" each other. We were deeply honored to provide a different healing and ceremonial experience around such a painful, devastating, and unhealed national wound.

Dedan:    We were also invited to Canada to spend some time in ceremony with Diane Longboat and our Mohawk friends. I was extremely ill at the time, in the midst of cancer treatment. We'd been invited to attend a spiritual ceremony in their lodge, a ceremony they had been holding on my behalf since hearing of my cancer diagnosis some six months earlier. As Belvie said, we planted a tree at one of the last standing cabins along the Canadian portion of the Underground Railroad. While in Canada, I took a handful of soil with me because there had been a man enslaved there named Richard Pierpoint; his last wish was to be sent home. He was not allowed to return home to Africa even though he was a free man. While in Canada, we spent time with an African returning home to Africa. I sent that soil back to Africa so at least some particles of Richard Pierpoint could go where he'd wanted to be.

Belvie:    These stories and others illustrated for us the power and presence of the soil and the wisdom of the trees. How could we plant trees, of all things, along the Underground Railroad for just one group of people? Since trees breathe for everyone, the logic of the very symbol of healing that we had chosen to plant dictated that we include the enslaved and the enslavers, as well as both Confederate and Union soldiers. As Dedan pointed out in his ceremonial offering, the soil receives everybody. The soil and the seeds became a much-needed metaphor for hope and possibility.

Dedan:    And a metaphor for community. The people who come to join our ceremonies come together from all different backgrounds to work hard side by side, digging holes in the ground, getting dirty. By the time we're ready for the tree planting, it's like a lovefest. That's what healing looks and feels like!

Belvie:    In response to the question "What does healing look like?"—you're what healing looks like. (She gestures to the audience of college students and people of all ages from the community.) This is what healing looks like. I know there's a lot in the culture about what's not working, but what's really important, and why we like to share a little about what we do, is to focus on what is working. We often get caught up—particularly those of us who are older activists—on the struggle, the problem. We came of age in the civil rights movement, so it was a struggle. When we were in the Deep South as young people, we had to sit in the back of the bus, and we could only drink from the COLORED public fountain, so struggle is really important, and focusing on the problems is important, but equally important is focusing on the solutions! In spaces like this, that's what you get to do.

We are very hopeful. We come here because of your energy. However strong our energy is, we won't be here forever, but we can see the future through you! And so we thank you.

Shortly after my last meeting with Dedan and Belvie, Dedan's cancer was found to have spread and he entered Zen Hospice of San Francisco. He said he was in a "dance" and not a fight with life. Belvie was at his side. She recounts:

> A shot caller on the streets of L.A. for most of his life and a shot caller to the end. His hospice instructions: 'I know, my love, that there will be tears and sadness and heartache. But try also to remember the journey: the beauty, the laughter, and most important—the love. And especially during the hard times, try to remember all the seeds we have planted. Seeds that will need nurturing now more than ever. Know that I will be there!'
>
> On the Winter Solstice, December 20, 2015, Dedan, surrounded by me and his three wonderful sons, Tranell, Dedan, Jr., and Mansa, took his last breath. Glancing beyond us with a wide-eyed look of awe and wonder at whatever or whomever he was seeing in the distance, he smiled and took his very last breath. Later, we all agreed that his ecstatic, smiling departure was his final gift to us!

## Child of the Middle Passage

I am a descendant of the Middle Passage
My lips are African
My last name is European, not African.
I am a stunning mix of human diversity.
In my centuries of suffering
I embody the whole
I am the ultimate global being.
Despite the tragedy that marred my journey
I have arrived at this moment of clarity.
Whether from passion, kidnap, rape or love
When the sperm embraced the egg
New life was ignited beauty blossomed
in the face of the newborn innocents
reaching out to love and be loved.

—DEDAN GILLS[140]

Moon Cabin in the forest (author's collection).

*Chapter Seventeen*

# Moon Cabin

## Owning the Shadow

It was time to go within, to face my inner darkness. As Belvie and Dedan expressed, the journey takes us into our inner depths, and it's within that dark womb that transformation occurs. I'd run from the shadow my entire life, but now there was nowhere else to go but into it. "You yourself are what you're looking for," my teacher said. *Finally*, I thought, *I'm looking in the right place*. There were parts of myself I needed to reclaim and others I needed to let go. As I was leaving Sunlight's house, she said, "The world you see is a reflection of who you are. When you own your wholeness, the world reveals its oneness."

I traveled north to the cabin in the forest that she had arranged for me to stay in. "The forest is dark in the winter," she said. "It's a good place to see what you need to see." I knew what she meant: Winter meant low outer light, and so I'd have to see into the darkness by way of an inner light.

I was already seeing myself and the world differently. The world wasn't full of enemies out to attack me. The confrontation was now more internal than external. I had read in *Power vs. Force* that any single individual devoted to inner transformation helps to relieve the suffering of the world. "In this interconnected universe, every improvement we make in our private world improves the world at large for everyone."[141] That statement gave me the courage to peer into my "private world," which was much vaster than expected.

In the heart of that darkness lay the buried treasure. "The gold is in the shadow," Jung had written. As described in the *Katha Upanishad*: "That boundless Power, source of every power, manifesting itself as life, entering every heart, living there among the elements, that is Self; that Being no bigger than a thumb, burning like flame without smoke, maker of past and future, the same tomorrow as today, that is Self." The Self: the inner gold; the soul; eternal essence; primordial oneness. I wasn't sure what I'd have to confront to find It, but I was willing.

The cabin was off the grid, several miles into the forest, down an unpaved road. It was called the Moon Cabin. The symbolism of the name wasn't lost on me. "Moon" signified the yin consciousness of solitude and stillness. The cabin was austere—no electricity, no indoor plumbing, no cell phone reception, no computer, no Internet or email. At night, I lit a kerosene lamp to read. Water from a spring was carried by gravity through a little hose to an outdoor sink on the porch. I hiked downhill through snow to get to the compost toilet, and heated the cabin with a woodstove.

I had read *Cave in the Snow*, the book about Jetsunma Tenzin Palmo's twelve-year retreat of solitude in a small cave high in the Himalayas. In her Tibetan Buddhist tradition and many other pathways, periods of retreat are recommended for the spiritual seeker. One leaves the outer world to explore the inner one. The work is done in solitude, yet isn't for oneself alone. Palmo told me that she hadn't gone to the cave just for herself. Whatever clarity she had attained, she said, it had been for all beings.

To be honest, I was far from that level. My initial motives were self-serving. I thought Self-Realization was a goal to be achieved. I imagined blissful states of satori, samadhi, and the like. These fantasies of cosmic spiritual attainments were instantly nipped in the bud by the reality of the stark setting. I had barely unpacked my van and terror crept over me. What hubris to imagine I'd blissfully probe the cosmic darkness when I could barely peer into the coming night!

It was my first night alone since pouring out all of my alcohol. For years my evening habit was to drink myself into a slumber (i.e., blackout) as I engaged in distractions (Internet, socializing, work, etc.). Now there was no way to distract myself. I was miles into the forest, alone in the Moon Cabin with no electricity, phone, or Internet service. As I stood in the starkness and company of my naked self, terror struck. I had nowhere to escape and nothing to drink. I started to panic—*What if I die of a heart attack out here in the boonies? What if negative forces overtake me?* The fearful thoughts compounded. When I was parked on Sunlight's land, sleeping in my camper van, I could go knock on her door. Now it was just I, alone, with all my jagged fear. The mind spun scenes of disaster: "If you stay here, death is certain," it said. I thought, *Maybe I'd better pack up and leave before nightfall.*

From Somewhere in me came my teacher's words, "All fear is illusion. Walk straight ahead no matter what." I decided to stay in the cabin and put his teaching to a test.

The key was to not resist the feelings. He said, "If you let go of resisting the feeling, the energy will dissipate." I was frightened to feel the feelings, and now I was supposed to let them come—even welcome them and ask for more? But I sat down and did it. I felt the energy of fear move through my body—pulse racing, adrenaline pumping, palms sweating. I remembered his teaching to not label the sensations with a concept (e.g., "heart attack"). Rather, he said to let go of all mental ideas, stay on the edge of the moment, and go into the experience of the energy itself by focusing on the sensations in the body—pulse, sweat—while being aware of the breath. I did this to the best of my ability. I stepped back from the panic as if watching it from a distance. I let the wild and catastrophic thoughts run, and shifted attention to the sensations themselves, while aware of my breath. "Legs wanting to run." "Pulse racing." "Forehead sweating." Without resisting, I simply sat there and let the energy run its course through my body. Before nightfall, an inner pressure was released; something had broken free.

It was an inner victory. I had been terrified of something, yet hadn't run away or tried to numb it with a drink or distraction. Inside myself I had found Something that could handle terror. I'd stayed the course and hadn't died from fear. Elation—this was the genuine "high" of trusting the Higher Self. An inner pathway to freedom had revealed itself. Facing that terror was the first of many times during my solitude when I had to work with feelings that I found difficult— grief, guilt, anger, fear, and more fear.

My teacher had been a psychiatrist and taught a clinical approach to inner phenomena. I recalled his statement "You don't have to believe everything you think. You don't have to act on every feeling you have." He said, "No one has to be ruled by the mind with its parade of sub- jects and endless stream of options, all disguised as memories, fanta- sies, fears, concepts, etc.," as it's always a choice whether to believe in the thought stream or not.

This clinical approach made it possible for "forbidden" or repressed shadow elements to surface. We all know that if we feel judged we want to hide. The same is true for the inner parts of our self. They hide from a condemning superego, and then they become the backseat drivers that we never see. As the saying goes, "What you resist, persists." I let go of resisting the shadow elements in myself and faced the truth of Viktor Frankl's point that there's a Mother Teresa and Hitler in all of us. I recognized the Hitler part of me; that it *would* like to destroy the enemy, be adored, and rule over others. The Mother Teresa part of me *would* be capable of giving my whole heart to love, touch the untouchables, and go to great lengths to care for a total stranger.

Owning the inner despot was a turning point. I recalled a story from Dedan Gills. It was the moment when he realized that the very hatred that he despised in his enemy was also inside of him. He'd come across a photograph that showed a lynching. He described his response:

It was an African American man being burned at the stake. A group of white people stood around him in nice clothes, like they had just been to church. The little girls had on nice white dresses. I sat down and looked at that picture for a long time. At some point, it dawned on me that I was actually everybody in that picture. I was the man being burned—the victim. And I had the potential within me to be the perpetrator. When I looked at that picture, seeing those white people standing there in their nice clothes, I was filled with rage and I thought, *I could kill them all, even the children!* I had to be honest with myself and say that there are moments when I have the potential to be the one being lynched and the one that's the lyncher. It wasn't easy for me to say that or accept it in myself.

Having owned the lyncher in himself, Dedan stopped hating his enemy and found a way forward that included *everyone*. As he writes in his poem, "The Middle Passage": "In my centuries of suffering/ I embody the whole." Sunlight's wisdom became apparent: "If you can face your own darkness and come to love all that you discover there, then you will be a force for good in this world." I went deeper into the darkness.

## Seeing the Log in Your Own Eye

It was a long winter in the Moon Cabin. Snow covered the ground most of the time. I rarely saw sunshine through the clouds and trees. The cabin's isolation accentuated the aloneness of the journey. Chilly winds blew through the walls, so I kept close to the woodstove. The fire became a friend. I gave it wood and it gave back warmth. "Love is a Fire"—this mystical saying came to life for me. The fire symbolized the love of my teacher, whose energy was transforming me. When I put a piece of wood into the fire, I imagined that I was surrendering something of myself—opinions, hatreds, self-identities, sorrows, resentments, fears—into the fire of his love, to be transformed.

The exercise was cathartic. Putting one log after another into the fire, I was reminded of Jesus' teaching about the hypocrites who see the speck in the eye of another but don't notice the log in their own eye (Matthew 7:3–5). I had spent most of my life going after the speck in others, oblivious of the log in my own eye. The surrender was gradual, one log at a time. Some of the mental-emotional patterns had carried a lifetime of suffering. Surrendering them to the fire, I watched as the logs popped, caught flame, and burned to ash. The relief was immense.

One of the biggest logs I surrendered into the fire was my blaming of others. "*They* did it to me. *They* are to blame for my misery." This was the victim-perpetrator paradigm, "us vs. them." Sunlight had gotten me to see that the faults I saw in others were also in me—prejudice, intolerance, wanting to control others, etc. In my litanies of what others had done to me, I'd been utterly blind to the log in my own eye. The truth of Sunlight's statement became obvious: "One day you will see that the enemy is not another person or group. It's the ignorance in all of us." I could stop pointing the finger of blame. Ignorance is no one's fault. It's part of the human condition, and no one escapes it. I felt compassion for myself and for humankind. I thought of the minister who told me I had the devil inside me when I was fifteen. How could he have known that the Light was Love? When had he ever been taught to trust such experiences? Out of ignorance, we fear. I put my log of blaming the minister into the fire. And this was just the beginning....

Reviewing my entire life, the idea of karma hit me on a visceral level. As a Westerner, I had not been exposed to karma, yet it was notable in such sayings as "What goes around comes around" and "You reap what you sow." I'd read about karma in my teacher's books, but it didn't sink in till I was alone in the forest listening to the logs crackle in the fire. Karma was not pre-determinism, he said, for there is always free will. Rather, it meant that we have certain karmic propensities that increase the likelihood of what will arise for us. He said that karma was a "shorthand term for the totality of all factors present at birth, both physical and spiritual."[142]

I was confronted with the question: What if all of the negativities I'd experienced in life were actually a reflection of what I had done to others in another time and place?

My teacher said that many human incarnations acquaint us with a range of experiences, and this exposure evolves our consciousness. Unless we walk a mile in their shoes, how can we ever understand? Being with him, I had the feeling that he knew all of humanity from firsthand experience; he had compassion for every situation because, it seemed, he knew what it was like to be that. He spoke of his many lifetimes as chapters in the same book, recounting various lives and deaths that he had experienced in other bodies, eras, and countries. He gave the personal example of slavery, when he was "chained to the oars of a slave ship." Here is his account:

> I remember vividly the exact details of the entire experience. I remember that the pain and suffering reached a point of non-tolerance. The slave master became enraged at me and extremely savage. Not only was it brutal but on that ship there was no sanitary facility. Everyone defecated and urinated right where they sat at the oars. I can remember being at the point of breaking, that I couldn't tolerate it anymore. I suddenly let the body go and went out of body. I realized that I could never be imprisoned. I was free! I validated my spiritual reality! I showed that S.O.B. and died on him! [Joyous push of arm upward, as if to declare, 'Here—take that!'] That was the purpose of that lifetime—they can catch my body but not my spirit![143]

He explained, "Each one of us takes turns being master and slave, being the exploited and the exploiter." He himself had been a pirate who killed others out of greed and he had been a slave exploited by the greed of others. He said that each lifetime served a specific purpose, for us to learn certain lessons and undo any harm we'd done to others. As Tenzin Palmo had told me, "From a Buddhist perspective, we've had endless lifetimes in all forms, genders, nationalities, every-where. During that time, we've done everything—good, bad, and indifferent. You name it, we've done it."

The old paradigm had cast me in the role of self-righteous victim rejected by others who were the perpetrators, but karma put a different frame on the experience. It suggested the possibility that victim and perpetrator are roles we trade from lifetime to lifetime to help each other evolve by presenting the option of forgiveness. Such a view doesn't negate the need to take proper legal action against, or distance oneself from, harmful people. Earlier in life, for instance, I had needed to get a restraining order to protect myself from someone who'd threatened to kill me. Now a karmic view helped me to see that person in a more compassionate light.[144] My teacher taught the prayer *Forgive the one in me who has ever done this to others.*

I didn't need to believe in karma as a religious doctrine in order to apply the karmic principle "We reap what we sow." It seemed to be inherent to nature. If I planted parsley seeds in the soil, I would see parsley plants one day, not pumpkins. It made sense to me that, whatever actions I had sown, I would reap the consequences of those actions somewhere down the line. This view of life cleared out a life-time of resentments and self-pity.

Over the coming years, however, I learned not to suggest karma to others. Matters of belief are precious. I have no business tinkering with the life supports that other people rely on. Whether religious or secular, our belief systems are the rafts that carry us through the voyage of life. They give us the meaning we need to endure the heat and burden of the day. There's no love in criticizing someone's belief or even sharing with others a spiritual principle that they might find dis-agreeable. Though I find it liberating, many people find karma hard to swallow. Having once been a missionary who crossed the world to convert others to my sect, I learned to let people have their own des-tiny. How could I know what was best for others? Neither was karma an excuse for detached indifference to suffering. Rather, it revealed the need for unconditional compassion, for we humans are painfully at the effect of countless causes and conditions that we don't see, and it's understandable that we often feel as if life were unjust. Following in the steps of Belvie and Dedan, I wanted to feel the whole human race as my family.

"Love is the ultimate law of the universe," my teacher said, and "every person has some good karma somewhere," so if we call out for help from the utter depths of our being, we will be heard. He also spoke of the world as a "karmic unity." Even as he encouraged the recognition of individual karmic inheritance, his teaching always went beyond the personal self to the greater Allness of life: "The cause of anything is always the same. It is the totality of all that exists now or ever has existed throughout all of time."[145]

In the forest, I touched into that Allness. I validated for myself the discovery that many meditators make: It wasn't necessary to try to stop thoughts and feelings through force (as if one could), only to shift attention away from them. By means of the breath, a mantra, a visualization, a movement, or the invocation of a Divine Name, the shift occurred.

My teacher taught: "Be the field, not the content of the field." He likened "content" to the clouds and "field" to the blue sky. "Focus on the sky, not the clouds." The clouds come and go, intensify and disperse, yet the sky is not affected. It is the field, the Self—silent, changeless, vast.

My attention shifted to the silence underneath all sounds. The silence was found to be always, everywhere. There was the crackling of the fire. The creaking of the cabin when the wind blew. The pattering of rain on the metal roof. All of these sounds registered into an Infinite Silence, which was the witness that never slept. It was the space in which everything began and ended, and Itself had no beginning or ending.

In the cabin, I noticed the difference. When I took the perspective of the personal "me" (ego), anxiety was common. There was a continuous stream of content (thoughts, emotions, memories, images); contentment was rare. When the locus shifted to the underlying

345

silence of the field, peace prevailed. It was a shift from personhood to Presence. From knower to known. Instead of watching, I was being watched. Instead of hearing, I was being heard. Instead of breathing, I was being breathed. The silence was aware of everything. It rejected nothing.

As winter gave birth to spring, I was still at the Moon Cabin and began to take walks outside. There was the same all-pervading Presence. One day, I walked down the hill to a little creek. I heard myself walk—leaves crunching, body breathing. It wasn't the personal "I" that heard the footsteps, but Something else—impersonal Awareness. Shifting from the "me" to the greater "we" of the forest, I knew that the trees were aware of me. All I did was follow my teacher's instruction to shift from the content (sound, thought, movement) to the field (silence, awareness, space). The silence and space had always been there, as if waiting to be identified with. Life was alive in ways I hadn't known. The water, the trees, the stones, and the air were actually aware of my presence. In fact, all was the Presence.

Over the years to come, these brief moments of awe continued to occur. I experienced them most readily in the presence of my teacher. One time, I was standing with him near a tree. "The tree knows when love walks by," he said. In the oneness of existence, he said, "knower and known are one." All that exists serves all that exists. He would often begin his public lectures by saying: "Nothing causes anything. Everything arises spontaneously by virtue of what it is." Such statements planted a seed of awareness in me that's still growing.

"The Self," Sadhguru Vasudev told me, "is within, awaiting Realization." Self-realization doesn't unfold by way of a fight, personal achievement, or outer discovery. "You can only 'realize' what's already there, inside you."

Sadhguru Jaggi Vasudev (courtesy of Isha Foundation).

# Chapter Eighteen

## YOGA AND THE PATH
## OF SELF-REALIZATION

### Encounter with Sadhguru Jaggi Vasudev

*You don't have to love the whole universe.*
*You can't stand the guy next to you—just change that*
*and your whole life will change.*

—SADHGURU VASUDEV

## SELF-REALIZATION

Yoga classes and yoga products are everywhere, yet few yogis have realized the Self. By definition, Yoga is union with the Divine, and this means total self-transformation, not minor enhancements to your ego. "Union" means you lose who you thought you were because you really are so much more. "Right now," Sadhguru said, "by breathing, you are in unconscious union with existence. We say you are a Yogi when this union with everything has become a conscious union. This is the state of *ananda*, bliss.'" Self-Realization is not an attainment but a *homecoming*, he said, "because now you are home wherever you are." Yoga is not a headstand, cardio workout, or stretch. It's a state and statement of oneness with existence.

As a method, yoga is a time-tested system that harnesses our inner fire—body, mind, emotion, and life energy. It's a comprehensive inner science with physical, mental, ethical, and meditative methods designed to dissolve the dross and free us to live our limitless nature. According to Patanjali's classic manual, *Yoga Sutras*, there are eight branches of yoga, *hatha* yoga (physical postures) being only one of them. *Ha* means sun, *tha* means moon, and ideally this practice balances those basic energies. But, says Sadhguru, "studio yoga" is limited when it sticks merely to the physical level and presents hatha yoga as the end of yoga rather than a preparatory stage.

Yoga is a path of Self-Realization, and only a Self-realized yogi can transmit the fullness of the path. This is the gift of a being like Sadhguru. He spent twenty-one years fine-tuning a certain *kriya* yoga called *Shambhavi Mahamudra* so it could be taught widely to the public without harmful effect. These inner technologies have always been shared with caution, as they can blow out the circuits of an uninitiated practitioner. For the person who is karmically ready, however, the effect can be very positive.

Before meeting Sadhguru, I met one of his students whose life had been transformed. A dedicated seeker, she had encountered various spiritual teachings and teachers over the course of her life, but nothing and no one had satisfied her yearning for the Truth. By midlife, though she'd been very successful in her work in real estate, she wasn't happy and had chronic health problems. Doctors had nothing optimistic to tell her as they had prescribed one pill after another. Her encounter with Sadhguru changed all that. After a few months of *sadhana* (practices), her physical well-being soared. The doctors looked at her lab results with disbelief and took her off the pills. She wrote about her experience in a compelling book, *Midnights with the Mystic*.[146]

Realized teachers are different from other teachers because they're connected to a live current of energy from within. Light infuses them, and they are the teaching they teach. Even if they talk about the weather, they're transmitting the truth of the universe. This is impossible to understand unless you've experienced it. The teacher who is not Self-realized can still be helpful in imparting spiritual information or yoga postures and principles, but to be transformed, you need a transformer, someone who's plugged into the energy system of the universe and can activate the wiring for joy that lies latent inside you. Depicted in literature as a coiled serpent at the base of the spine, this spiritual energy is dormant until a spark of real spirit awakens it.

Here is the difference explained another way: If a lamp in our house is connected to a live current, then it shines a real light and we can see better, but if the lamp is not wired to a source of energy, then it's perhaps pleasant to look at but it doesn't light up the house. The point of a spiritual path is not to be a pretty lamp but one that's lit by a live current. As Jesus said, "You are the light of the world," for he had transmitted a live current.

Sadhguru Jaggi Vasudev is a rare occurrence. Self-realized yogis usually live apart from the world—in a Himalayan cave, for example—because the state of blissful oneness is not easily manageable in ego-driven society. How to get along without a sense of personal self? Such states radiate a great benefit to the world even from a cave. The energy itself is like a magnetic field that uplifts humankind. When, as in the case of Sadhguru, the enlightened mystic walks among us and has the capacity to communicate the Reality of Oneness in a meaningful way to thousands of people in diverse cultures, as well as governments, scientists, businesses, and scholars, then the potential for transforming individual lives has few parallels. Such beings awaken people to their most creative and capable, joyous and free selves. This is because the realized being is merged with Reality and has access to universal truths that can address problems at their root inner causes, not just the outer symptoms.

## PERSONAL ENCOUNTER

That was my experience with Sadhguru. I spent only a few days in his presence, yet an old inner pattern was dissolved that had held me in bondage for years. The release was unexpected and liberating. A true guru by definition dispels darkness and removes obstacles, and that's what happened. It's like taking your car through a high-pressure blower. Old stuck-on cobwebs don't have a chance as the force of the wind blows off all the sticky debris. The car is instantly cleaner through no effort of its own; it was simply driven through the right place. So it was with Sadhguru's energy field. I had gone there with a major attachment, unable to move forward in life even though I wanted to. Self-analysis had identified the problem but not resolved it. After five days of retreat with Sadhguru, the attachment was gone with the wind, and within the year, I had moved into a whole new arena of living.

Liberation from limits, ecstasy, he told us, is our "birthright," but most of us are so tied to self-preservation that we're not willing to trust our natural longing for self-transcendence. If we did, we would touch the Infinite.

The Infinite opened up for Sadhguru when he was twenty-five. He was sitting on a hill in southern India when suddenly a veil lifted and he became one with everything around him. His sense of "me" and "mine" dissolved and he saw himself in the rocks, air, grass, and trees. He was overwhelmed by the joy of seeing the nature of existence as it really is—alive with magnificent oneness. All perception of separation disappeared as the Divine was seen to be vibrating in all of creation. This is Yoga—the Realization of Union. It was perhaps the mystical state of St. Francis of Assisi celebrated in the Catholic world (and garden statues) as "brother sun, sister moon." For Sadhguru, it was intensely blissful, the ultimate high, a dimension beyond time. Before he knew it, over four hours had passed and it had seemed only ten minutes. He got up to leave but never went back to the old way of seeing himself. Over the next years, this awakening to Reality, with its infusion of Light and intelligence—what the world calls "enlightenment"—transformed his body-mind-energy system from the inside out, a state of Self-Realization described in the scriptures of India.[147]

Sadhguru says he is neither ancient nor modern but simply "contemporary" in his endeavor to share this state of awareness with others. He has developed inner technologies of yoga that transmit the process in contemporary language so others might realize the ecstatic joy of who they really are. His Isha Foundation has reached millions all over the world. He is an internationally recognized visionary who brings creative solutions to environmental and economic problems.

After completing the two initial trainings of Inner Engineering and Shambhavi Mahamudra, I traveled to his home base in Tennessee for a retreat of several days at the Isha Institute of Inner-sciences, site of the largest meditation hall in North America, a taste of India transplanted into Middle Tennessee. I had requested an interview for this book but was given no guarantee. I went anyway. There was the book, and then there was my quest. The quest, Sadhguru told us, is our longing to unite with something beyond our self. It may start as a longing for food, romance, sex, a new house, etc., but eventually we turn inward with the longing to unite with the source of life itself.

As I wended my way into the ashram, I felt ready for the next phase of my quest. Hundreds of trees were covered with fall colors ablaze in the last light of day—the turning of a season. A few of the red-yellow-orange leaves spotted the gravel road, but not many. Five days later, as I drove out, it would look quite different.

Crossing the threshold into Isha Institute, I had to leave behind most of what was familiar to me—computer, cell phone, coffee, sugar, and sleep. The retreat volunteers took my gadgets and gave me a ticket so I could retrieve them five days later. It felt strange to have no phone, but I was most concerned about not having coffee. I had already devised a scheme to get around this rule, for I couldn't fathom a day without my brew. I had packed some instant coffee, a mug, and an electric water heater in my carry-on, and thought I'd carry out the deed in the privacy of my room. Imagine my surprise when I was taken to a dorm room full of bunk beds and other retreatants, women and children, all from India. There was no privacy. I instantly hatched plan B. On the first morning, I got up at 3:30, snuck my mug and packet of instant coffee into the shower stall, and made do with the hot water from the showerhead. As I watched myself go to this extreme for a little brown fluid, I had to laugh; "Who are you fooling? Are you really so attached to a physical habit that you can't survive a few days without it?"

So I dropped the farce and did what I was asked to do. I was here to learn yoga; maybe if I were humbly willing, I could learn something, and overcoming a physical compulsion was a good place to start. Yes, I had given up alcohol, but there were still other bonds of attachment to unravel. Sadhguru said it was crucial to let go of physical and emotional compulsions. They keep a person stuck. If you're attached to physical substances or conditions as the basis for your happiness, then what hope is there for any lasting peace? Spiritual work, he said, was mainly to shift from compulsiveness to consciousness. I was willing, but I dreaded withdrawal. In all my past experience without caffeine, I'd suffered terrible headaches.

Amazingly, there was no headache. In fact I felt wonderful, and this was true even though I hardly slept for five days. My dormmates were in and out all during the nights, going to the Mahima (the huge circular meditation hall), and one night we all slept there on mats—hundreds of people sleeping (and snoring) in the Mahima. Surprisingly, I woke up refreshed and vitalized. How to explain my increased energy despite very little sleep and no coffee for days? It certainly was a lesson in Sadhguru's teaching that our life energy comes not from the physical domain but from an inner one. It was an experience, as he promised, of breaking free of mental and physical limits—a real ecstasy, which means to "go beyond" oneself. He said, "Doctors say you must sleep ten hours a day. What's the use? If your car needs to be serviced fifteen days a month, what's the point of having such a car? If you live a hundred years, then you've slept almost forty years!" There are ways other than coffee and sleep to rejuvenate the physical system. This is one of the secrets of yoga.

The Oneness of Reality is another secret, and to realize this truth, said the sages, is finally to experience an end to suffering. Intellectually, I had grasped that we're all interconnected. It was a political, social, environmental reality, hard to deny in the face of globalization and the Worldwide Web. In my grocery store in California, there are avocados from Mexico, pasta from Italy, and coffee beans from Africa. Clothing, household appliances, the car I drive—different parts of them are made in different countries. Each item is an orchestration of global interdependence.

But mental knowledge about interdependence is different from the inner realization of oneness. Sadhguru asked us, "Do you want to be a living being or a thinking being? Most people most of time are just thinking about living and not really living." He told us we had to give up thinking about interdependence and be willing to experience it. All we have to do is look deeply at life itself—any piece of life. "Each particle is a doorway to the Infinite." To see that we are one with everything and everyone, that the source of life itself lives inside us (and everything else with equal magnificence) brings finally an end to the ego striving for survival and its inevitable suffering of fear, grief, resentment, and loneliness. We are then at home anywhere.

Though I didn't experience nirvana at Isha, a little progress was made in the experience of interdependence. In the dialogue below, Sadhguru laid out the necessary shift, and for me, a shift took place in my relationship to Mother Earth. The banana that she yields turns into "me" when I eat it. What I call a banana, a fruit of Mother Earth, is now "Fran." A few hours later, what I called "Fran" is released as waste and returned to Mother Earth. Out of convenience (and illusion), I label things separately as banana, Fran, waste, but they are the same life energy in different forms. I am, truly, one with the Earth.

I did not, however, feel at one with a man sitting next to me. Even though I'd tossed logs of pride and anger into the fire at Moon Cabin, the irritation revealed I had more shadow layers to excavate and release. I was annoyed at the man for talking like a know-it-all. Here I was at the retreat on a quest to learn about love, but I had little love for him. His intellectual superiority (that's how it seemed to me) annoyed and angered me. I'm sure it was a projection of my own shadow—being an academic know-it-all. Facing this fact about myself was not pleasant. I had an ideal of love but not total success applying it to real people around me. Sadhguru made fun of me for

my "hallucination" in the dialogue below, and his humor had the positive effect of humbling me. He redirected my focus from love as a
grandiose cosmic principle to the unglamorous challenge of loving
the stranger right next to me. His answers to my questions revealed
to me my own misconceptions about love. In this way, I unlearned
as much as I learned. "Guru" means, as I said, "remover of obstacles."

Before coming to the retreat, I had studied Sadhguru's teachings
on love, some of which he expressed during the retreat. Love gets a
bad rap in our culture, he said, which looks down upon love as "less
than" the intellect. Spiritual traditions, however, have always honored
devotion as a key to liberation. The devotee may look like a fool to an
intellectual person, but the devotee has experiential knowledge that
an intellectual will never touch. This is because, Sadhguru said, the
intellect knows only pieces of life, while devotion knows its wholeness. Love in its most intense expression is all-inclusive.[148]

Love is unlimited, Sadhguru said, but few are the people who
experience that. Most so-called "love" relationships are in fact bonds
of attachment in which people are dependent on others. Real love has
nothing to do with anyone else. Romantic love can be pleasant but
it certainly isn't necessary. What's very beautiful is to meet a person
in terms of their ultimate nature, not their outer appearance—to
inwardly bow down to the source of creation within them. If your
life becomes woven with the life of another human being, this is
the unique chance to shed your selfish tendencies that cause them
suffering. Love is about surrender of your wants, not getting what
you want.

It's possible to learn selfless love in romantic partnerships, but, he
said, most people never reach that level of loving. They get hijacked
by a rush of hormones, make a bond with the person they "can't live
without," and then, eighteen months later when the hormones have
worn off, they don't "love" the person any more. Was this love to begin
with, or was it a chemical rush? Sexuality is one thing, love is another.

Our culture, he said, has badly confused the two, and religion, with its moralism on sex and its celestial spin on love, hasn't helped.[149]

The five days of the retreat were packed with transformative experiences, and they freed me. I won't spoil it for others by describing the specific exercises and elements. I went there to learn about love, and I got what I needed.

On the second day, one of Sadhguru's assistants found me and said, "Sadhguru would like to know if it's okay for you to interview him at the satsang (group gathering with the teacher)."

I said, "Of course—whatever Sadhguru wishes."

There was no time to prepare because the satsang was thirty minutes away. I watched as a team of volunteers set up blankets, placed cushions in perfect rows, and prepared the space on a lovely lawn overlooking the lake. They positioned Sadhguru's chair next to a table with flowers and a glass of water. The sound and video people set up the lighting behind him and ran lots of cords with microphones and sound equipment everywhere. It was getting cold, the sun disappearing, a fall wind stirring. I shivered, both from nerves and chill. People gathered and sat quietly on the lawn as an air of expectancy settled over the place. At 5:30 p.m., we heard tires roll into the parking lot behind us. Sadhguru got out of the car and went to take his seat in the chair in front. He led a chant and music was played. Then silence.

# SATSANG WITH SADHGURU JAGGI VASUDEV

## What is Realization?

SV:  This is supposed to be an interview. Is it you? (He looks at me.)

Q:  Yes. I have a few questions for you, for a book called *The Power of Love*. In the West, we know a lot about the power of the mind but not about the power of the heart to transform, heal, and evolve consciousness. I'm interviewing living masters to learn what they can teach us about the power of the heart.

SV:   Did you check out whether I am living or not?

(*Laughter.*) He had told us previously that scientists were shocked to discover that by certain physical measurements he should be "dead." The brainwaves of mystics are much slower than other people's.

Q:   The first matter, in fact, is about what you are. Your biography starts with the sentence "He is a realized master, mystic, and yogi." What does it mean to be "realized"? People in the West, we don't really—

SV:   Realize....

Q:   We don't realize much.

SV:   So, "Realization" as a word says it all. It does not mean an achievement. It does not mean a conquest. It does not even mean an attainment. It just means a Realization. You can only realize what's already there. If you realize what is not there, that's called hallucination! So, the whole thing is just to realize what's already there. It's not about reinventing something. Don't you know what is already there? Most human beings know what is there right now only to the extent that it's necessary to their survival. To survive in the world—that's the extent of what they know. Beyond their survival, they don't know anything. Even so-called science and technology and—now I enter dangerous terrain—even many who consider themselves religious, it's only about survival still. Science is always talking about how to use everything for your well-being. We even know how to use an invisible atom. We know how to use everything. But we still don't know how to be well. Is religion any different? If you look at all the prayers on the planet, it's always "Dear God, give me this, give me that, save me, protect me." Does it sound like survival to you, or does it sound like transcendence? Definitely it is survival, just survival rooted through heaven. People seek divine help for survival because they are inefficient with their survival process or they're fearful about their survival process.

Realization is not about survival. Human beings use all their intelligence and even their so-called love affairs, largely for survival. When you're in a survival mode, you do not realize anything beyond that. When somebody's willing for a moment to just look at life, Realization is possible. The instinct of self-preservation that drives our survival is overactive right now. And we're raising our survival bar higher and higher. There was a time when you ate a meal and had a roof over your head, you survived. Today, you must have three homes to survive!

(*Laughter.*)

So, what we are referring to as Realization is the realization of the nature of your existence. Realization is pure science because science is the pure pursuit of knowing. You just want to know, because human intelligence cannot keep quiet. It wants to know. This same longing that drives the scientist also drives the spiritual seeker. The seeker thinks, "No, we're different." Your methods may be different but it's the same human longing: Wanting to know. Maybe you want to know about the bird or insect. Somebody else wants to know about himself. So, this longing to know the nature of who I am beyond the instinct of survival, when this takes root in you, it naturally drives you inward. Because, if you go outward, it's a limitless expanse. You'll get lost.

Experientially, there are only two dimensions: Inward and outward. The rest is just all made up for convenience. When you realize that going outward will get you lost forever, you turn inward. When you turn inward, everything that you want to know about this piece of life (yourself) you will know, because this human being is being manufactured from within. When the simple food put in the form of fruit or bread or whatever goes inside, it becomes a sophisticated mechanism called a human being. There is an intelligence here, a competence, a knowing, which is the very source of creation. If you want to know anything about creation, better consult the source of creation inside of you. If you delve deeply enough into this, you realize the nature of the existence. What is the nature of existence? We say, yoga.

When I say, "Yoga," do not imagine impossible physical postures. Yoga is not a word. It is a statement. We look at the world and say, Yoga. That means it's a Union. Everything is just One. When you look at it only through your sense perception, everything is separate because sense organs can only function with comparison. You know what is light only because of darkness. You know what is small only because there's something called big. You know day only because there is night. You know male only because there is female. Your sense organs cannot perceive anything without comparison. Whatever you perceive in comparison is a distortion of Reality. What you think is big may be very small for somebody else.

Therefore what you perceive in comparison is only useful for survival. And it's a distortion of Reality. It's a limited reality created or perceived only for the sake of survival. When you realize the nature of existence, you say, Yoga. That means you understand it's all in Union. This is not just mental understanding. You experience that it's all in Union.

It is the physical nature that separates us. It divides us into you and me. Because you have a body (points to my body) and I have a body (points to his body), we are different. If you did not have a body—I know it's difficult to imagine—what is you and what is me would not be so distinctly separate. And it is this distinction of physical nature that keeps two things distinctly, uniquely apart. The stronger your identity is with your physical nature, the stronger your distinctions will become. The less identified you are with the body, the less the distinctions are.

Today in the world, if you hear the word "love," people think of a physical relationship—at least in this part of the world—because that's the only way they can drop their identification with their own physicality. The two bodies come together. Now the sense of what is me and what is you has kind of merged. Nothing wrong with it, but it's a very inefficient way of doing it. However hard you try, you don't become one. There are moments when people imagine they are one, but everything is still seen as separate. The distinction between this and that rules. Because they are looking at it through sense perception, everything is still separate. I am separate, you are separate, planet is separate, sun is separate.

But in Reality, it is not like this. The nature of existence is such that it's all happening as One. It's happening as one big happening. Today modern sciences are reaching closer to this reality. They are beginning to say, "Everything is one energy manifesting in a million different ways." If everything is one energy, the only reason you're not experiencing it that way is because you are identified strongly with the boundaries of your physical body. What you call your boundaries of your physical body is a myth. It is not a reality. You had your lunch. Something that is not "you" has become you now in a few hours! What is you right now, by tomorrow morning a part of it will go down the drain!

(*Laughter.*)

Every day this is happening. What is not you (food) is becoming you. What you thought was yours is going away. If you stay here and do three weeks of yoga, you may lose five kilograms. So then these five kilograms of "you" is gone. Where will you go in search of it? It's simply gone. And you'll be happy, yes?

Q:   Yes, I'd be happy to lose five kilos!

SV:   What you thought and imagined as you is gone. Every day this transaction is happening. And a much closer one would be your own breath. Every moment, in and out, it's happening. If this doesn't happen, you won't exist. So what you call a body is actually a process. It is not an absolute thing. To believe this body is me, but the earth I walk on is not me—this is a certain level of ignorance. Realization is experiential transcendence beyond this ignorance that you think you are separate from the rest of the existence. When that goes away, when your illusion that you are a separate existence goes away, we look at you and say, "Ah, Yoga."

## Love – From Pleasant Emotion to Selfless Devotion

Q: How does this relate to love?

SV: The longing to know you are not separate is always happening. It's finding expression in so many ways. If it finds a physical expression, we call it sexuality. This longing to become one with something. If it happens as a psychological or a mental expression, we call this conquest or ambition. You want to include something that is not you as a part of yourself. You want to conquer something, you want to get something, or, we call it shopping!
(*Laughter.*)
It's all the same, isn't it? If it finds an emotional expression, we call it love. If it finds an energy expression—your very energies long to unite and they do—then we say you are in Yoga. So we're not talking about anything different. Whether sexuality, shopping, love, yoga—they are not different. All are longings for union. It's only a question about efficiency. How efficiently will you do it?

Q: Surely love is more efficient than shopping.

SV: Nowadays, many people fall in love, get married, and then all they do is shopping.
(*Laughter.*)

Q: What about love that is a universal—that's what I am asking about, not personal romantic love.

SV: This has become a fashion, particularly in the West. "I love the whole humanity—universal love!" It's very easy to love the universe, because then you don't have to love anybody. If you love one person, it costs your life. If you love the whole universe, you don't have to love anybody! You can do your own thing and keep on talking about it. So, talking about it, thinking about it, keeps people entertained. The word "love" has always been attractive to human beings, because it's the sweetest emotion they can share within themselves. It doesn't matter how intellectual people claim to be, emotion is still the most forceful and intense experience they have. These are the four dimensions that make you who you are: physical body, mind, emotions, and energies. Emotional intensity is a common factor in a large number of people. If they are not capable of love or compassion, they are definitely capable of anger or fear or resentment or something else, in various levels of intensity. You don't have to do much work on it; you just have to transform it. Instead of being fearful, you can be loving. Instead of being angry, you can be loving. Because of the simplicity of this shift, too many people have spoken about it, and because too many have spoken about it and so much marketing about love has happened, now everyone is now talking about it.

How many people are capable of holding on to their emotion—love, compassion, anger, fear, resentment? Ask them to hold it for twenty-four hours and they cannot. If you stay in the intensity of your emotion for twenty-four hours, you will become realized. If you want to be in social circumstances and maintain an intensity of emotion, love is the only option you have. If you are practicing resentment, anger, or fear, nobody wants to be around you, and it's not pleasant for you either. The important thing to know is that it's the intensity we are looking for. If you have emotion, when it becomes intense enough, you say, "I love you." If it becomes very intense, you say, "I've fallen in love." It's the same emotion, getting more and more intense. It's getting intense beyond reason—this means you've fallen in love. Otherwise, you just love and then you're out of love. You're in and out of love. Because it's still operating within the limits of reason. When it turns outside the limits of reason, then we say, "You've fallen in love."

If it crosses all sense of reason, then you cannot be reclaimed. You've gone. Then we say, "You are in devotion." The process of dissolution has started for you. So, you're in devotion. It's the same thing. Getting sweeter and sweeter, more and more intense. Not always a pleasure. But once you've tasted it, you can't live without it. It need not always be pleasant. Love is not always pleasant. It's just a sheer intensity that drives a person. This is because a person wants to know life. He wants to know love. He wants to know life and he finds generally that he touches life easily with love. So love becomes important for him as a device. He could do that with the intensity of his intellect. He could do that with the intensity of his physical nature. He could do that very efficiently with the intensity of his energy. But love comes easy because emotion is already intense.

Q: What is the trajectory of devotion, a student's love for the Guru or God?

SV: Why should everything go somewhere? If you're really in love, you don't want to go anywhere. It's not that you say, "Okay, what's the takeaway from the love affair?" That's not love. That's a transaction. So, as a guru, I never demand love from them, or anybody for that matter. I think it's obscene to tell somebody, "Please love me." Love should always be a helpless thing that you do. It's not that you decided to love somebody. It is that, helplessly, you fall into it. The English term, "falling in love," is significant. You are talking about a "trajectory"; you're talking about rising in love. Nobody rises in love. They only fall in love!

What is it that's falling? If you have to really experience love at a certain level of intensity, something that you call "myself," at least a part of it, has to go. Something in you has to fall. If a part of you falls, you will know a part-time love affair. If all of you falls, you will know a full-time love affair. So if all of you falls completely, if who you are is fallen and disappeared, then you're in a constant love affair. Not with anyone or anything, but with life itself.

## Love is What You Are, Not What You Do

Q: What's an example of love?

SV: Love is not a thing that you *do*—it's something you become. There is substantial medical and scientific evidence that people are at their physical and mental best when their emotions are pleasant. They have always known this by experience, and that's what they are trying to achieve by loving somebody. Now, loving "somebody" is—this is an unpopular thing to say—a kind of a myth, because all human experience happens only within you. You're only using the other person as a key, or as a stimulant to stimulate the love in you. If you love somebody, and that somebody isn't even here right now, you can still sit here and love, because the memory of that person is a stimulant. Suppose the person fell dead somewhere and you didn't know. Still you could be sitting here and loving. You don't really need the person.

Your love is just on push-start right now. I'm talking about putting it on self-start so that you can just be loving. Whether somebody is here or not here, you can share your love with them. If no one is here, you can sit alone and be loving. If you are the only person on this planet, you can still be loving because it's your emotion. It's not somebody else's emotion. Somebody loving you or not is not the important thing. Many people are bothered about whether somebody loves them or not because they are in a certain state of insecurity. If insecurity is not your problem, it doesn't matter whether somebody loves you or not. What matters is whether you're capable of love or not. Somebody standing there at the edge of the forest and loving you is only nice for him, not for you. So you loving is what's important.

(*Silence. Evening birdsong in the background.*)

I didn't give you the answer you wanted. Let's put it this way: For myself, I'm in a constant state of love. With whom? With anybody, whether they are willing or not. I don't care. It's not even about loving them, it's just about being love. That's the nature of your emotion. It's just that if you are a rudimentary machine, you have a bad engine, and you need to be pushed to start in the morning. If you're an efficient engine, you self-start. You will breathe sweet, live sweet, and sleep sweet. You will see that when people are in love, they sleep with a smile on their face. That shows that a certain sweetness has come into everything of their life.

People say, "Love is in the air," because when somebody is really loving, he feels it everywhere and everything is lit up. Everything seems to be brighter. Not that everything *is* brighter, but your body, mind, and chemistry are functioning at their best. When I say "chemistry," today it's a strange thing. In the East, where we come from, I can just tell you, "I love you," simply like that, without wondering how you will take it. But in this part of the world, if I say, "I love you," it could mean so many things because hormone-fire love affairs have been the most prominent thing. It's time that humanity evolved beyond that. We do not have to equate our physical compulsions with the sweetness of the emotion that we can generate without those things. The physical aspects can be dealt with separately. Those things are in everybody's life. But you don't have to raise sex to heaven.

You don't have to raise love to heaven either. Today, if you say "love," people will call it "divine" love. No. It's not about the Divine. Love is a human possibility. Human beings are capable of love if they are in a state of willingness. Love is essentially a certain level of willingness to experience. With everybody else, you are shut off, a closed wall. With one person, you open a small window and there is the "love affair."

What spiritual process means—what Yoga means—is that we want to demolish the walls, and we are not interested in opening just one more window. If you demolish the walls, that is how you will be—you will be love! Love is a way to be, not something you do. Anybody who has experienced this even for a moment, will know that for a single moment, they had become that. They didn't "do" it. You can only become love, you can't *do* it.

(*Silence.*)

Q: Where to start?

SV: Just understand this much: Wherever you are right now and whatever you are right now, consider the limitations... and just see how to go one step further. One step at a time is good enough. Those who try to take ten steps at a time will fall flat on their face. One step is good—always one. That's how you walk, that's how you run, that's how you do anything, one thing at a time. Today, just break one limitation; tomorrow, another one. Don't think of all those big things. Nothing will happen except hallucination. Right now, you can't stand the person who is next to you. Just change that. You don't have to love the whole universe. You can't stand this guy next to you—just change that and your whole life will change. You will try to love the whole universe and nothing will change because you don't know where the damn thing begins and ends. So you can love it, you can hallucinate it, but you can't stand the person sitting next to you. Change that and your life will change phenomenally.

(*Whistle.*)

(*Communal chant.*)

When the chant was over, I looked up and he was gone. All was silent, except for the sound of the evening breeze on his microphone.

Being in the company of advanced beings is disconcerting because they see things in us we can't or don't want to see. Sadhguru called me out for waxing eloquent on "universal love" while having my heart shut to the guy sitting next to me. My questions came from a limited experience, and Sadhguru began dissolving those limits even as he answered the questions. The true guru dispels our fantasies. They are a powerful wind that blows our soul free of illusory debris.

As I drove out of the ashram, I noticed that nearly all the colorful autumn leaves had fallen to the ground. The road was a thick bed of leaves. A whole season had come and gone in just a few days. There had been a fierce wind, not only in the outer landscape but also in my inner world.

During the retreat, we had learned that the wind was an energy of transformation moving through life. Whatever hung by a weak stem was blown off as we did the exercise. Old habits of passive acceptance; not living in accord with our soul; having a limited view of what is possible in life and in the lives of those around us.

One of Sadhguru's last instructions to the group: "Every particle is a doorway to the Infinite. You can open the doorway or not, but be fully with everything you come into contact with." I stopped talking about universal love and opened my heart to each person in front of me. Most of them were college students.

Author with college students in the Rumi Dome at Cal-Earth
Institute, 2017 (Meggan Austin/author's collection).

# Chapter Nineteen

# RETURN TO THE WORLD

On the path of love that I travel, periods of retreat are intermittent, and there is always a return to the world. My teacher told me, "The experiences you've been given are not for yourself alone. Share what you have become."

After the retreat at Moon Cabin, I returned to my work at the university—lighter, clearer, happier—and my teaching took a very different turn. Instead of courses on oppression and violence, I began to teach courses intended to bring about a change of heart. They focused more on the solutions than the problems. I looked around the world for models of people who'd undergone the transformation of their consciousness and who, from that inner foundation, had helped humanity as a whole. They were the pioneers of the power of love, and I made their philosophies and methodologies the basis for my new courses. I wanted to put Sunlight's axiom into practice: "Changing the world happens one heart at a time—start with your own!" Even one college student's inner transformation could uplift the lives of thousands.

# PUTTING THE *HIGHER* BACK INTO HIGHER EDUCATION

With the support of the administration and colleagues at the University of Redlands, we transformed a classroom near my office into a "meditation room," which became one of the first contemplative classrooms in the country. It seeded a program that now has many branches, as described in numerous publications:[150] 1) a growing curriculum of inner education that integrates traditional academic learning with contemplative process; 2) community classes in yoga, dreamwork, contemplative prayer, and meditation, all free to the public; 3) intergenerational courses for college students and older adults from the local community; 4) interdisciplinary research into the benefits of meditation and compassion training for college students;[151] 5) large-scale public events that provide the region with inspirational experiences from different spiritual traditions; and 6) a quiet space for private practice during the day.

Just a year earlier, I had wanted to leave my career in education, as it had seemed hopeless and exhausting, but thanks to the influence of my teacher and the guides in this book, I realized it was an inner change that was needed, not an outer one.

Our pioneering program has become a hub for seekers from all walks of life who are looking for meaningful community and want to learn spiritual practices that can help them deal with the stressors of modern life. When His Holiness the 17th Karmapa visited our classroom, he said he rejoiced that we have people of different backgrounds and age groups learning together and sharing their experiences with each other. He noted that we do not treat yoga or meditation as a commercial enterprise but as a way to share our genuine concern to benefit one another. He said this was quite different from what he'd seen elsewhere of the commercial marketing of spiritual practices. He told us a Tibetan saying: "It's like milk in a crowded market." When farmers come to the market they bring fresh, pure, unadulterated milk. But if they see a lot of people coming, then they start adding water to it so there'll be more to sell.[152] In contrast to this kind of "watering-down," he noted the "genuine" nature of our practice and community.

Our program's mission is "Changing the World from the Inside Out." Whatever field of work the students go into, it matters completely who they are on the inside. Have they learned the inner disarmament of anger, hatred, blame, and greed? Have they uncovered the inner gold of self-knowledge, intuitive wisdom, and compassion? If so, they will live as peaceable beings. The bombs that explode in the world have their origin within our own psyches, and so the detonation begins within. Here's the account of one young man who learned to self-regulate his anger in the introductory meditation course:

> Sometimes the rage inside builds up so much I want to explode. But I've learned now not to act. It takes about ninety seconds for the anger to leave. Every time I feel this way, I sit down, close my eyes, and meditate. I just watch the feelings that make me angry pass by, like each thought is a cloud in the sky floating away. Before learning meditation, if I ever felt this way, I would always have to let it out in a physical way, whether it was hitting a bag or lifting weights or... When I meditate, it feels completely gone. I feel like a new person.

Students learn to access the intelligence of the heart, which holds the key for our future as a global community. Forgiveness, appreciation, gratitude, and compassion are qualities of the heart and can be cultivated. These qualities will be the basis of any real solution to the pressing problems we face, for if we don't feel our connection to others, how can we act to benefit them and the world? It is the feeling of caring for something or someone that leads us to take care of them. If we have a feeling of love and appreciation for Mother Earth, we will take care not to harm her.

Students learn that it's their inner world that determines the quality of their action. Is the mind clear? Is the heart open? If so, then their thought, speech, and action make a positive contribution. If the inner world is "polluted" (Tenzin Palmo's word) by egotism, anger, greed, or delusions, then they may do more harm than good.

The courses teach the students how to be aware of their inner world. They find it challenging to sit still because the Protestant work ethic is deeply ingrained. Most of them associate stillness, meditation, or prayer with doing nothing, a waste of time. This tendency was noted in a fascinating research project done by scientists at the University of Virginia and Harvard (July 2014 issue of *Science*). They asked their subjects to spend fifteen minutes alone in a room—no phone, no gadgets, no book, no companion. The subjects were shown a button that, if pressed, would deliver a negative static shock to their ankle. When left alone with nothing else to do, sixty-seven percent of the men chose to shock themselves, and twenty-five percent of the women did the same. One person pressed the button 190 times! The authors summarized their findings: "Most people seem to prefer to be doing something rather than nothing, even if that something is negative."

This finding concurs with what students in the Compassion course tell me. One of them, an honors student with a double major, admitted, "This is one of the hardest classes I've ever taken, because it asks me to do so much that I've never done before—to see what needs to change inside me, and then do it!" She initially thought the meditation practices were a waste of time. Her attitude changed one day when she was in a panic because she couldn't find her car keys and needed to drive to work. She probed several times inside her purse, looked all around her dorm room, and even dug around in the Dumpster outside. No keys. After thirty minutes of frantic searching, she remembered—"Oh, yeah! I'll try that breath meditation we learned in class." She sat down and focused on the sensation of breath. After ten minutes, she felt considerably calmed. She looked in her purse and found the keys. "Imagine my surprise—I had looked there several times before!" The impact of the stress on her brain function had literally closed her mind and she couldn't see what was right in front of her. This student gained an experience of the centuries-old wisdom of Lao Tzu, who advised seekers to be patient and wait until the mud settles, the water clears, and an answer arises of its own.

Students learn that if they stop long enough for the "mud to settle," they'll see what's really happening. In a state of panic and confusion, they will never find the key to anything. If the mind is in disharmony, one's speech and actions only add to the disharmony at large. Another student in the Compassion class put it well: "My major is Peace Studies. How will I ever be able to negotiate peace among the nations if I'm not at peace within myself?"

This is the consciousness needed in the world, Grandmother Mona Polacca told me. In the Hopi worldview, she explained, humanity has reached a fork in the road. One road veers off and ends in destruction. The people on this road are "out of balance" (*koyaaniskatsi*) with the foundations of life. In Hopi prophecy, they are depicted with their heads disconnected from their bodies, run by greed, materialism, frantic with their self-seeking, with no respect for the sacredness of their own life, the needs of others, or the Great Spirit. This road will end in humanity's self-destruction and depletion of the earth, making it uninhabitable.

The other road stretches long and straight into the future. This road is taken by those who have a consciousness of care and kindness for "all my relations." They honor the sacredness of life, the Creator, and the interconnectedness of all. People who walk this road live according to the "Original Instructions." They recognize their own Higher Self. They remember that the Earth is a living being and enjoy it with gratitude. They live by reciprocity, not greed, taking only what they need and giving something in return. They are aware of the next seven generations. They are humble and know that human beings are only a small part in the cycle of life. The Hopi believe that it's time for each person to decide which road to take.

The students learn and apply this consciousness of care and kindness taught by the Indigenous Grandmothers and other teachers in this book. Kindness to oneself and others is a more effective means of social change than big demonstrations and loud protests. This is because force creates counterforce and leads to gridlock and futility. Hawkins explains:

> Simple kindness to one's self and all that lives is the most powerful transformational force of all. It produces no backlash, has no downside, and never leads to loss or despair. It increases one's own true power without exacting any toll. But to reach maximum power, such kindness can permit no exceptions, nor can it be practiced with the expectation of some selfish gain or reward. And its effect is as far-reaching as it is subtle.

The impact is far greater than we imagine. "In the universe, time is measured in eons. Beyond that it doesn't even exist at all. Every kindness is therefore forever."[153] This is the unconditional kindness that the students and I seek to cultivate in our courses.

## COMPASSION COURSE

Compassion class at the University of Redlands, 2010 (author's collection).

In the Compassion course, we study the compassion teachings of the world's religions, with a focus on such great exemplars as Gandhi, Nelson Mandela, the Dalai Lama, Mother Teresa, Viktor Frankl, and Mary Oliver. Students apply these teachings to everyday life, as well as practice them within a community service site of their choosing. They are required to select a service that is meaningful to them. Past examples include a safe house for homeless teenagers, hospice care for the dying, community garden, tutoring center for children with autism, shelters for abandoned animals, nursing homes, juvenile hall, a support agency for women transitioning out of prison into society, and many others.

Every year some of the students go to a medical facility for children with severe disabilities. Many of these children have never lived in a home because their medical condition requires lifelong hospitalization and medical machinery. In some cases, their families abandoned them at birth and they became wards of the state. When the students go to the facility for the first time, they're nervous. "What if I can't handle it?" "What if they don't like me?" "How do I talk with someone who's had a tracheotomy?" Their thoughts are self-absorbed. After that first visit, they nearly always say, "I can't go back. It's too hard! The children don't respond." I encourage them to go back and see the children through the eyes of compassion.

Seeing the children again, some of the students remember the saying of the Dalai Lama, "I meet every new person as my friend." They follow his method of tonglen meditation, breathing in the suffering of the child and breathing out compassion. They remember Mother Teresa's teaching, "Do small things with great love." They use her method of compassionate touch and looking for the "Christ in distressing disguise"—the innate goodness within each person, underneath the physical condition. These teachings ground the students in their own inner essence of love, which calms their fears and helps them reach out in a caring manner. As one student said, "I learned to look underneath the children's disabilities and love them for who and what they are. Not all of them are able to do the things they want, but that's why I'm there. If they like to play video games but can't use their hands, I am their hands."

The Compassion course is not the "feel good" haven that many students expect. They start the semester thinking that compassion is activism for a cause, a favor they give, or a role they play. They equate compassion with do-goodism; and expect to be admired and thanked for their good deeds. Over the semester, they come to realize that true compassion is void of self-gain and of any personal agenda. As Sadhguru Vasudev puts it, "compassion does not choose." It is nonselective. It has nothing to do with pity for others, rescuing others, or fighting against something.

Sometimes the most compassionate response is not to intervene, and thus students learn that compassion must be skillful and paired with wisdom. Mother Teresa's approach, for example, was to see the inherent dignity of every being just as they were. She went alongside the poor and cared for and loved them. This is what one student learned when he served at the local residential center for people with Alzheimer's. He was initially upset that the residents didn't remember him or thank him for being there. He devised a scheme to "improve" their memory, but this only led to more disappointment. Finally, he realized that compassion asked him simply to be with them as they were, without trying to change them.

Students learn to ask themselves, "Am I seeking any personal gain out of this or am I truly selfless? Is my view of the situation muddy or clear?" In true compassion, the motivation and view are clear. The students learn various meditation techniques to clear their view, beginning with basic breath awareness. I show them a glass jar that has water and a bit of soil in it. When shaken, it becomes opaque. I say, "Most people, most of the time, have an inner state like this—so muddy you can't see through it. During the day, they get churned up often, but never take time to let the mud settle. They just go about their lives, pouring muddy water into their daily interactions. Instead of clarifying matters, they add their own muddy confusion, fear, and anger. Of course, they're not conscious of being churned up. They assume it's normal."

Then I show the students a jar that's lain still for a day. The soil has settled to the bottom and the water is so clear that they can see through it. "When you take time to be still, aware of yourself, focused on the breath, you give the mud a chance to settle. Then you can see things more clearly. Otherwise you're just pouring your muddy water into muddy situations. The world doesn't need more muddy water!"

Before the course, students had no awareness of their muddy "shadow" motives when they did good works. This becomes obvious to them when, in one of their first assignments, they're asked to spend a week simply observing their motives when they help a friend. They're shocked at what they see. One student gave this reflection: "I never realized how much I want people to like me. People say I'm generous, but I think I give a lot of things to my friends because I want them to like me. I'm afraid to say no when they ask for something—like a ride, or to borrow clothes, or help on a project—because if I say no, they won't be my friend." The students see that this is not true compassion but rather an exchange of goods. It's giving something to a friend in order to secure approval. Once they acknowledge their shadow motives, they can choose to come from a more compassionate inner place. The process of self-discovery liberates their loving essence. "When the clouds are removed, the sun shines forth."

One time the muddy jar sat on the shelf all summer. When I returned to my office in September, I was surprised to find that green growth was emerging up out of the brown soil that had settled on the bottom. When I showed the jar to the students, they were delighted by the implication. We often think we'll produce growth by activity and effort, yet perhaps the opposite is just as true: When given time and space, new growth spontaneously emerges from hidden inner potentials.

Compassion is both inward and outward. Self-compassion is the starting point, for we can't give to others what we don't have. When compassion is directed inward, often called self-compassion, we turn the spotlight within to see where our suffering is coming from. Are we willing to renounce the thoughts and actions that cause our suffering? The Karmapa calls this renunciation "a determination to be free." Self-compassion, he says, "needs to begin with an attitude of loving kindness toward oneself and a willingness to take care of oneself and more deeply understand the situation that oneself is in."[154] Self-compassion means that we honestly take stock of the mental, physical, emotional patterns that cause suffering in our life. For example, some of the students notice that they have the habit of overdosing on video games, binge eating, or not getting enough sleep, which makes them feel dull and exhausted all day. Or they notice that due to peer pressure, they'll go to every happy hour in town. Heavy drinking, self-hatred, over-working, compulsive eating, drug abuse, sex with people they don't care for—they begin to see how they're working against their own contentment and well-being.

With self-compassion, students ask, "Why am I doing these things to myself? I'm in college. It's a time to connect, to learn, to explore, to be at my full mental, personal, interpersonal, and creative levels. What is it that causes these obstacles for me?" They look at the underlying conditions and see if they're willing and able to change them. One student with an eating disorder wrote: "Through meditation, I learned that my thoughts don't have to control me. After six years of an eating disorder, I am finally winning. I don't feel like a prisoner anymore." Another wrote of facing alcoholism: "Compassion class transformed the way I view others, as well as the way I view myself. I was forced to look inward and confront truths about myself and take action to be the person I was meant to be. This was the catalyst for the greatest change in my life: getting sober. It motivated my decision to go into the mental health field and helped me find my purpose, which I believe is to help others work through their suffering."

Our desire to alleviate the suffering of others is compassion directed outward. Students learn to neither fear the suffering nor take it on themselves as fixers and rescuers. Not every problem can be "fixed," yet every person can be loved. One student applied this principle at the local animal shelter, which euthanizes animals after a certain number of days of non-adoption:

> I couldn't change the fact that some animals needed to be put down because of aggression or illness, but I could change the way I judged those who were involved. Our study of Mother Teresa had a big impact on my compassion practice. Every time I walked into the shelter, I realized that the animals wanted something very simple—they wanted to be loved. I couldn't give them a home or all of my time, but I could make their day a little brighter. Every second I spent with an animal was a second that they didn't sit in the cage alone.

In their service, some students silently do the tonglen meditation, a Tibetan Buddhist method that we learn from the 14th Dalai Lama and the 17th Karmapa.[155] They breathe in the suffering of animals, Mother Earth, children, and the elderly, and breathe out compassion, hope, and healing. In tonglen, we "exchange" our peace and well-being with the suffering of others. It's not our ego that exchanges its well-being for their suffering, for the ego is full of self-interest. Rather, we give our hearts' essence, which is limitless in its love.

Usually, we are absorbed in our own needs and interests. Tonglen trains us to feel that our interests are no more important than the interests of others, and we may even surrender our own comfort completely. For example, when Jetsunma Tenzin Palmo was nine, her nylon dress caught on fire and her mother spontaneously did tonglen, praying to take upon herself all of her daughter's suffering—"Don't let her suffer, give the pain to me instead." Palmo told me, "This is the intense love that is tonglen. We care more about the healing of the other person than our own comfort. The Buddha said for us to do this for all beings in the same way, just as a mother would for her child."

The students begin tonglen practice with their own pain. Once they learn to breathe their own suffering into their hearts and breathe out compassion, they expand to include others who share their same suffering—stress, depression, poverty, disease, grief, loneliness, heartbreak, etc.—perhaps untold millions of people worldwide who have their same suffering.

Then the students go further and try the Karmapa's suggestion to use the Internet to learn about the people who manufacture the clothing or other personal items they buy.[156] This exercise transforms the usual use of technology from commercialism to compassion, and reveals the interconnectedness of life as the students discover the workers' struggles and view photographs of their environment. They breathe in the struggles and breathe out compassion. It makes them think twice about buying things—*Is this something I really need, or just something I want?* One student said that, to her, tonglen was to become like a tree. Just as a tree oxidizes our physical environment by taking in toxins and giving out oxygen, tonglen oxidizes the emotional environment by inhaling suffering and exhaling compassion.

When I introduce this meditation, students are initially afraid to breathe in the suffering of others because they think it will cause harm to their own body or well-being. They are surprised to discover that tonglen actually has a wholesome effect as they come to feel closer to others. Here is one student's first experience with tonglen:

> This week's meditation was especially powerful for me. Usually I'm wrapped up in my own dramas and problems, but this assignment forced me to think of others. I chose to take in the suffering of my mom because she's been having a particularly rough time lately. She recently found out that she has a terminal illness, and I've seen her spirit drop dramatically. I focused very closely and thought of all the emotional as well as physical suffering that she's been experiencing. I was aware of each breath, and I kept visualizing the black cloud of suffering growing with each of her worries. The practice helped me to come to terms with her illness and feel much more compassion for

her and what she's going through. It was almost as if a weight was being taken off of my shoulders each time I breathed in her suffering and replaced it with pure love.

Another student, working as an Emergency Medical Technician (EMT), discovered the power of tonglen practice one day when he got a 911 call. A woman had suffered a stillbirth in the bathroom of her home. When the ambulance arrived, she was on the floor, traumatized and surrounded by blood. The student silently did tonglen while tending to the mother's medical needs, breathing in her pain and breathing out hope and healing. Until that moment, he said, he hadn't understood the value of inner practices. As a first responder, he was a very action-oriented person, yet the need of the moment went beyond EMT training. There were no words or equipment that could bring the baby back to life. Tonglen meditation gave the student a silent way of connecting with the mother, through the breath. His heart opened to the psychic pain of another.

Over time, tonglen reduces our habitual narcissism and we realize, "Oh! I'm not the only one who suffers." We see that we're not the only ones having a bad day due to stress, breakup, failed exam, illness, or depression. Tonglen opens our hearts to the suffering of others. Students, long after they've graduated, write to me saying it helps them in their work as parents, teachers, therapists, doctors, and environmentalists. One student moved to Berlin and now applies tonglen in her job as a social worker caring for Syrian refugee children traumatized by warfare.

Tonglen is not for everyone. In Buddhism and other spiritual traditions, it is said that each individual's nature, disposition, and level of understanding must be taken into account—different methods of inner cultivation work for different types of people. The Karmapa emphasized this when he visited our meditation classroom. One of the students said she was applying some of the methods from the Compassion course to her work at a health clinic for underprivileged women. She asked, "Why do some forms of meditation work for some people while others don't seem to work?" The Karmapa said that according to Buddhist teachings, all people have their own distinct interests and dispositions, and because of that, some techniques will be beneficial to some and not to others, so therefore it's best to make many techniques available so people can find one that fits them.

I find great truth in this statement and its correlate in Sufi tradition, in which there are many *tariqas* (paths), and in the Quranic verse 24:41, "Each creature has its own mode of prayer and praise, and Allah is aware of all that they do." Some students in the Compassion course resonate with tonglen, while others resonate with walking meditation or breath awareness or the Jesus Prayer or another of the many techniques they learn about.

I'm not evolved enough to know my students' karmic propensities and guide them in a path—that would be the function of a spiritual teacher. Since I'm an educator, my role is to expose them to a variety of basic techniques for inner cultivation, with the idea that they may one day choose to pursue their resonances within a specific path— or not. As my teacher told me, "You are responsible for planting the seeds, not what becomes of them."

The students' compassion practice extends even to micro-moments, like suddenly seeing nature in a whole new way. This was the breakthrough of one student who was always rushing from one place to another, a cup of coffee in hand. The class was studying the nature poetry of Mary Oliver. To get out of our own self-absorbing thoughts, we were learning to pay attention to the life around us. Compassion starts with attention. If we don't know how to pay attention, how can we notice suffering? During our Nature Observation exercise in class, this student had an experience that surprised and delighted him:

> A small green insect landed on my finger. Normally I would immediately crush it or brush it from my finger, but this time I didn't. I looked at it, studying its light-green body and the way its two wings made one when together. I didn't have it in me to kill this insect. I became aware of its existence and it of mine.

I may never share such acute awareness of power and love between two beings in such a way again. In a brief moment that bug was the only thing I felt connected to.

Compassion is about the relief of suffering, so we study the levels of suffering—physical, mental, and spiritual. Physical suffering is the most obvious, and we see it all around us and in the media—disease, homelessness, violence, and natural disasters. Mental suffering is also obvious, but it takes a while for students to see it because they're so accustomed to looking at the outer world. Once they understand mental suffering, they see it is everywhere. Even people who appear to have everything are still vulnerable to misery, anguish, hatred, grief, and fear. From Dr. Lorne Ladner's *The Lost Art of Compassion,* the Buddhist psychology textbook studied in the course, we learn that mental suffering is related to the impermanence of life. Everything is always changing; loss and uncertainty are facts of existence; there's nothing that we can hang on to. As the Sufi saying goes, "Only that which cannot be lost in a shipwreck is yours." This fact creates anxiety, sadness, and efforts to control life and those around us. Spiritual suffering is rooted in the belief that we are separate. We suffer existential loneliness because we've forgotten that we are part of the oneness of life, forgotten that we belong to each other. We long to be loved, to be reminded of our innate lovability and inner essence, but few are the places where we experience unconditional love.

The exemplars we study in the course address all three levels of suffering. This is how their approach differs from the usual political or social justice solutions. Yes, it's important to feed those who hunger for bread, and they address material needs, but humanity's deeper suffering is the hunger for meaning and for love. By way of their teachings and presence, these exemplars light the way out of mental and spiritual suffering, often by pointing us inward. As Sadhguru says, "The way out is in."

Class members share their firsthand experience with all three levels of suffering. Awakening to compassion occurs spontaneously when we deeply listen to each other's difficulties and experiences with suffering. When students share their struggles, we come to see that suffering is inherent in life. It becomes clear that everyone—no matter race, religion, socioeconomic class, gender, or national origin—suffers. Age is said to be the greatest divide in this country, and so the intergenerational aspect of the class is a unique opportunity for participants to realize that people of all ages have suffered loss, oppression, and pain. We are all, truly, as Mother Teresa would say, "my brother, my sister."

The older participants are forty-five to eighty-five years old; they've been through most of life's hardships—poverty, abusive relationships, loss of loved ones, crisis of faith, addiction, racism, caring for a spouse with Alzheimer's, disabilities, and job loss. Many are lifelong Christians, yet they learn new ways of being compassionate. In a closing session, one of them said, "Compassion is a lifetime work, and I'm glad I'm only seventy-five!"

The older adults listen with open hearts to the college students who risk sharing the wounds of their younger generation: suicide, drug overdoses, meaninglessness, depression, and pressure to achieve. At least half of the students have a friend who committed suicide. Some of their angst is lessened when the pain of their hearts is heard and held by community elders.

Each student is like a textbook for the rest of us. On the first day of class, one eighty-year-old man from the local retirement village said, "Each of us is a book waiting to be read." As we share our life stories, we learn something about humanity, and our hearts inevitably enlarge because that facet of humanity is sitting in the room with us. Separated from one's family due to the war in Syria. Being an immigrant from Vietnam. Pressured to conform to unattainable body perfection. Feeling the inner conflict of being biracial and not knowing where to belong. Abandoned by parents who are meth addicts, forced to fend for survival on the streets, alone. Living with a parent who has cancer, Alzheimer's, or MS. Assaulted, molested, raped, or bullied.

What used to be just a quick headline in the news or statistic in science research is now embodied as a human being in front of us. In each story, we bear witness to our common ground of suffering. We honor the courage it takes to share one's experience. When pain is pulled up out of our inner darkness, brought into the light of communal love, it can be transformed. Our so-called pathologies become our path. In that context of being witnessed on all three levels of suffering, some students have a major awakening.

One such student, Courtney, started out the semester in a painful state. When I asked the students to draw a picture of their path, hers depicted an inner war. Two weeks later, she cut her wrists, ended up in the psych ward, and dropped out of school. This crisis became the turning point in her life. A little ray of light shone into the bottom of a dark, dank well of self-hatred. Against all odds, she had faith in that little ray of light, which she felt in the company of her new-found friends in the psych ward. She told me that in "Group," she felt heard, understood, and cared for, as in, "We'll love you until you can love yourself." She couldn't love herself, but she could let herself be loved just a little. When she began to come off of alcohol and drugs, her wounds were laid bare: Feeling rejected by family; feeling used by friends; feeling guilty for all the tricks she played on others to win their love; all the self-harm, manipulations, the loneliness. Now, without drugs and alcohol, there was no numbing or running away. Several times she told me, "I don't think I can do it. I'm gonna have to drink. It's just too painful to look at." But she stayed sober. As she did one "next right thing" after another, her confidence grew. She was discharged from the hospital and continued in an outpatient recovery program. It was slippery ground and she fell a few times. In one of her published creative writings, she wrote: "...God waxed the floor again." She learned to not give up; keep reaching out; let go the "liquid poison" and have faith in "Something Else."

When Courtney reenrolled in school to finish her degree, she took the intergenerational Compassion course that included older adults. She was a bright spot in the class. People expressed admiration for her courage. She allowed herself to be loved by wise older women. They saw her as an adorable person, an easily lovable, kind-hearted, sincere, multitalented, and necessary presence on the planet. Through their eyes, she began to see herself as having unique value.

As a mentor to help others get sober, Courtney is now the carrier of that love for youth who hang on the edge between life and death. She is a sought-after speaker and leader in the community. Because she said yes to a little ray of love that came her way even though she didn't feel it, her life was saved and she is saving the lives of others. Truly, a little love goes a long way.

As they awaken to the power of their hearts, students put compassion to work in their service sites. They not only tend to the dying, feed the homeless, care for unwanted animals, and tutor disadvantaged children but learn to do so with great love, opening their hearts to the inner essence of the other. One student, who did her service in a hospice agency, learned that love is possible between strangers. She was present at the bedside of an eighty-year-old woman who was dying. The student knew nothing of the details of her life—the places she'd lived or her accomplishments—yet, as she held the woman's hand, she became aware of her inner heart. The student said, "I experienced love in a way I never had before. I'd always thought that love had to be personal, but the dying woman was a total stranger to me. I can't explain it. We were with each other in our bare state. It was a revelation to me that we don't have to know people in order to love them."

Another student was serving as Miss Los Angeles during her semester in the Compassion course. She worked with girls in junior high school to heal their body hatred. Because she was a beauty queen, they looked up to her, saying, "I wanna look like you in this picture!" She told them, "Listen, I don't look like that. That's not me—it's Photoshop!" Her obsession with physical appearance ended when she was nineteen, after she nearly died in two car accidents within weeks of each other, making her realize: "When you leave this world, it's the relationships that matter." In her community service, she worked to get girls in middle school to focus on inner beauty: "Your true beauty comes from being confidently beautiful within. It's not the way you look, it's the way you make a difference in other people's lives."

Compassion changes the people who study it. As the axiom goes: "We become what we think about." The Compassion course transforms countless lives, including my own. The course has been taught over twenty times. I'm deeply moved by each experience of studying compassion in the company of young people and older adults. The Light in all of us becomes brighter by our study and being together. The atmosphere in the room has a healing effect. Like other small groups dedicated to an honest and open study of inspirational material, our class often becomes electric with the power of love.

Simply by studying the lives of those who are authentic and compassionate, we become more authentic and compassionate. It becomes experientially evident that love is a more effective path than anger, blame, or us vs. them. Merely to want to become a loving person begins to transform one's life. Through the Compassion course, students become conscious of their inner resources and how to channel them for the benefit of themselves and the world at large. By uncovering the source of peace within themselves, they become avenues of peace for others.

Hardship is not an excuse to hate and blame—this is one of the most challenging lessons that students and I have learned by studying the lives of people like Viktor Frankl, the Dalai Lama, Mother Teresa, Nelson Mandela, Mary Oliver, and Gandhi. Each of the exemplars faced genocide, oppression, or hardship, yet they embraced their circumstances as a path. They chose the high road of self-respect, trust in life, and goodwill toward others. They could have used their suffering as an excuse to be victims, take revenge or be bitter about life. Instead, they embraced it as a training; a fire that could transform them to be of service in the world. It wasn't that they went out and looked for a cause or joined a protest movement; they simply and bravely faced the suffering right where they were, and said yes to being transformed in their specific situations, according to their unique traits.

In the class, we study a range of attitudes about suffering and societal problems. The attitudes accord with the levels of consciousness or energy fields presented on the Map of Consciousness® by David Hawkins. The students and I see that most of us have experienced the entire range of attitudes about oppression in society and in ourselves. In our study of the exemplars, we find convincing evidence that Love is ultimately the most effective energy field for addressing these individual and societal problems. Here is a paraphrased recap of our class discussions.

On the level of Shame (20), people feel worthless, as if they deserve to be ostracized. They have internalized and identified with the collective hatred of their oppressed aspect (disease, body, race, ethnicity, gender, so on) so completely that they view themselves as disgusting, an abomination. When directed outward, people shame, shun, and ostracize others whom they view to be despicable. On the level of Guilt (30), people feel they are sinful and deserve punishment; there is no mercy for themselves or others. They believe the only recourse is to "pay for your sins" through extremes of penance, self-punishment, and even death (killings of so-called sinners). At Apathy (50), people are hopeless. They wonder, "What's the use? Why try? I might as well give up." People have risen out of this numb listlessness to Grief (75) when they start to weep about their life: "My life is so sad. Life has passed me by." At least now there is a feeling, and tears can be healing. At Fear (100), people have a lot more energy, but it is spent on anxiety and keeping themselves hidden in various enclaves, ghettos, closets, dogmas, and islands of isolation. Reaching Desire (125), people want something badly enough (success, relationship, growth, money, etc.) to come out of their shell. At Anger (150), people have enough energy to rise up and say, "This is unfair! I'm not taking it any more!" However, because it attacks, meeting hatred with hatred, this energy widens the wounds instead of healing them;

fuming and raising fists create instant enemies, not lasting break-throughs. People are relieved to arrive at Pride (175) because now they feel they have indeed "arrived." It is liberating to march in parades and strut one's stuff. It feels grand to ascend a pulpit and preach to others. People at Pride feel entitled to make demands on others and tell others how to run their lives; they are in love with their own opin-ions and not able to listen.

Up to this point, the energy fields exert force (regressive or aggres-sive) and result in counterforce, making individual and collective res-olutions impossible to envision or achieve.

Courage (200) is the critical level where the energy can now point in a positive direction. It is the beginning of self-honesty and personal integrity. "To thine own self be true. I have nothing to be ashamed about, and nothing to prove to anyone but myself. I may have been dealt difficult circumstances, but I can rise above them. Sometimes I feel afraid and get angry, but those reactions aren't in the driver's seat of my life." People at this level begin to feel truly free of inner and outer chains. At Neutrality (250), they become flexible and able to go with the flow: "It's a relief not to be rigid. It's okay either way." When people are genuinely warm-hearted and actively helpful toward others, they've reached the level of Willingness (310): "I'm a Good Samaritan. I enjoy helping others and volunteering for good causes. I like to cheer people on." They are willing to see that their views are evolving, and they are willing to learn from hearing the views of others. They are able to collaborate successfully across the various divides, but sometimes they help too much and get over-com-mitted to "all the good causes."

In the energy field of Acceptance (350), people say: "I accept myself and others. We are who we are. All I've been through is what makes me who I am today. Not all of it was pleasant, but I hold no grudges. I'm not out to save the world. Social agreement in a world of multitudinous expressions is unlikely. I don't have a soapbox or a cause. I take responsibility for my own experience of life and have a good sense of humor about life and myself. Forgiveness and harmony are my values."

By the time people have reached the level of Reason (400), emotionally-driven and personalized motivations have been transcended: "Let's be practical. Different measures are needed for different situations. Major social changes take time because there are large segments of a population that are attached to traditional ways. Education is key. Information and knowledge are necessary and sufficient to transform society. It's important to research the formative context of the problem by examining history, psychology, philosophy, science, literature, and religion. The longstanding problem of racism, for example, can be resolved through education and policy. A change of mind is the answer. This comes through conferences, dialogues, policy changes, artistic portrayals, formal statements and declarations, global summits, expert testimonies, and adjudication in the U.S. Supreme Court."

Love (500) is the breakthrough into another realm, for now people are seeing the whole, not only the different parts. They are led by the heart. "Knowledge alone is insufficient. Only a change of heart will work." People at the level of Love have themselves become, through subjective realization, the qualities of love: selflessness, perseverance, mercy, gratitude, and compassion. They have internalized them into their essence. Synchronicities occur continually. They have enormous capacity for patience and vision, which are needed to bring forth golden resolutions that both sides will experience as a win-win. The power of love accomplishes the seemingly impossible. It's what brought down the Berlin Wall. It was the Gettysburg Address by Abraham Lincoln. It was the inspiration of the movements led by Nelson Mandela, Martin Luther King Jr., and Mahatma Gandhi. Love is aligned with universal spiritual truths such as: All are created equal, endowed by their Creator with certain unalienable Rights. Love is holistic and all-inclusive—"all children are my children."

Love is unmistakable. When someone moves from the heart, we feel it. Hardship is no obstacle. His Holiness the 17th Karmapa is a case in point. A teenage refugee from Tibet, in exile from his homeland, he has not had an easy life, yet he radiates tangible compassion.

When he visited our university, people were strongly affected. Perhaps it was their first encounter with true compassion. Students, faculty, and staff lit up when they talked about their interaction with the Karmapa. He had connected with them on the level of the heart; he knew nothing about their personal backgrounds and identities. As one person told me, "It was the feeling that he just knew me—my essence—even though he actually knew nothing about the details of my life." They were surprised at the feeling of a heart connection with someone who knew nothing about the details of their lives.

Rather than the usual focus on outer identities, the Karmapa deeply felt the innate commonalities that exist among all beings— that we all suffer and we all long to be loved and to be happy. On this basis, the Karmapa called everyone a friend. Each group he visited said, "He is one of us"—whether they were white, black, female, male, transgender, student, custodian, president, mayor, or mascot. The department coordinator for our office, a woman of African heritage, asked the Karmapa to comment on the race riots in the U.S. She couldn't get over the compassion she felt in his response: "It was something about the words he spoke and the authenticity of his compassion that struck me. I wanted to weep with relief that someone understood and felt genuine love for everyone."

His Holiness the 17th Karmapa speaking on
"Compassion" at the University of Redlands, March 2015
(Carlos Puma/courtesy of University of Redlands).

# Chapter Twenty

# Compassion

Encounter with His Holiness the 17ᵗʰ Gyalwang
Karmapa, Ogyen Trinley Dorje¹⁵⁷

*We need to let the heart lead.*

—H.H. the 17th Karmapa

I first encountered the Karmapa's radiation of compassion in his
relics before I met him in person. This reiterates an important
point made throughout this book: Love is an energy field that
takes many forms. Just as the fragrance of the rose is unmistakable
in whatever form it takes (rosebush, rose oil, rosewater, etc.), so the
energy of love is recognizable in its countless forms. Great beings and
spiritual masters such as the Karmapa have the capacity to materi-
alize or manifest their love and compassion in ways that go beyond
ordinary understanding. Relics are an example of this.

The Loving Kindness Buddha Relic exhibit (2000–2015), an
international tour of rarely seen relics of Buddhist masters, sponsored by His Holiness the 14th Dalai Lama, included relics of the
16th Karmapa, lineage and incarnation predecessor of the current
Karmapa. I had the privilege to visit this exhibit five times in different
locations and, in 2015, our university hosted one of the last events.

Relics are translucent pearl-like crystals found in the cremation ash of a spiritual master. According to Buddhist belief, the beautiful crystals are deliberately produced by a master at death and embody the master's spiritual qualities of compassion and wisdom.

Like the Dalai Lama, the Karmapa is the head of a Tibetan Buddhist lineage and a spiritual leader with worldwide influence. "A teacher for the world" is how they introduced him at Stanford University when he spoke there in 2015. Buddhists consider the Karmapa an enlightened teacher who chooses his rebirth to carry on the activity of a Buddha in the world for successive generations. This level of compassion exceeds ordinary comprehension in that he keeps coming back, lifetime after lifetime, to serve in this role for the benefit of all sentient beings. He has been doing this for over 900 years, each Karmapa leaving a letter that predicts the details of his next birth. When the 16th Karmapa died in 1981, he left such a letter. The 17th Karmapa was born in 1985. Several years later, a search party discovered him according to details given in the prediction letter.

The Loving Kindness Buddha Relic exhibit displayed the relics of the historical Buddha Shakyamuni (donated by the Dalai Lama), Milarepa, Yeshe Tsogyal, Kasyapa, 16th Karmapa, and many other masters. The presence of their compassion was palpable, and this is not mere fantasy. Dr. William Tiller, Professor Emeritus of Stanford University's Department of Materials Science, has verified through repeated experiments with his colleague Nisha Manek, M.D. (Mayo Clinic) that these relics radiate what he calls the "subtle energy of loving-kindness." Tiller found that this subtle energy measurably changes the thermodynamics of a space, increasing coherence in the environment and even material objects, including the physical body.[158] Coherence is an overall state of clarity, harmony, and symmetry, found to be critical in all experiences of health, healing, contentment, and resolution of conflict. In contrast, states of incoherence (anxiety, hatred, inner conflict) are weak and depleting. Fortunately for all of us, incoherent states yield to the stronger radiation of coherent states (compassion, patience, loving-kindness), which explains why people visiting the relics felt better afterward.

Accounts abound of the benefit of being in the presence of compassion masters. For example, Dr. Paul Ekman, a University of California Medical School (San Francisco) professor, confessed that he experienced an unexpected and profound healing when the 14th Dalai Lama held his hands. Though not a religious believer, he was filled with a sense of goodness and total body sensation that he couldn't define. The encounter had a lasting effect—Dr. Ekman's lifelong struggle with anger left in that moment.[159] This healing event was so provocative to him that he conducted research and a series of dialogues with the Dalai Lama, but his inquiries produced no scientific explanation for his personal transformation. Ekman, an authority on the science of evolutionary psychology, concluded that the "radiance of goodness" he experienced as emanating from the Dalai Lama was real, even if he didn't have the scientific tools to prove it and measure it.[160]

Tiller has developed those tools, and his research confirms that the relics themselves also radiate beneficial subtle energy. This may sound far-fetched, but is it? In everyday life, we're aware that certain places, foods, and persons radiate a "vibe" that we experience as positive or negative. Material substances are made of energy, and if loving intention has been infused into an object or substance, as the Buddhist masters are said to do in their cremated remains, then the energy of that object has a discernible loving quality to it. In ordinary life, we appreciate a lovingly home-cooked meal and say we can "taste the love in it." We appreciate hand-crafted items made with care. Tiller's research is the first scientific demonstration that objects infused with compassion, such as the Buddhist relics, alter the thermodynamics of a space such that the increased coherence has a healing effect.

When we held the Loving Kindness Buddha Relic exhibit at our university, we set it up in a large event room that is often used for faculty meetings and academic presentations. Once the setup was complete and the relics ceremonially laid on the tables, that space became qualitatively different. In Tiller's terminology, the subtle energy of loving-kindness imprinted in the relics conditioned the space. The staff members from our Office of Event Services noticed the difference, calling it "sacred," "peaceful," and "otherworldly"—words never used about a faculty meeting or other gathering in that room! Newspaper reporters commented about the atmosphere, saying there was "a quiet reverence," "feeling of peace," "inspirational and compassionate setting," and "feeling of friendship and love with people from all walks of life coming together to create a truly sacred space."

Relics of Buddhist masters, Maitreya Buddha Loving Kindness exhibit; research by Dr. Bill Tiller and Dr. Nisha Manek found that the exhibit had a profound effect on the thermodynamics of a space (courtesy of University of Redlands).

The exhibit had special significance for Buddhists, but everyone noted the effect, regardless of religious affiliation or none. The compassionate presence of the Buddhist masters, embodied in the relics, turned an ordinary workspace into a zone of healing. According to the Karmapa, this is the "power of the heart," and we ourselves can become this presence to others when we cultivate the qualities of love and compassion.

In the scientific terms of Dr. Tiller, love and compassion are energy fields of high coherence that have the power to reduce the suffering caused by conflicts inside us and around us. We experience this relief in ordinary life when we're in a state of anxiety over something and then feel better after talking to a friend who loves us. It could even be a stranger that helps us feel better, as in the case of a friend of mine who recently felt lifted out of a despairing mood when the attendant at a drive-thru greeted her kindly, took time to listen to her woes, and encouraged her.

Innate to the human heart, says the Karmapa, is this basic goodwill for others. We feel it most easily with people we're personally connected to, but it can also exist for strangers as illustrated in the story above. We are largely, however, unaware of the heart's power. A simple step, he said, is to become conscious of and value our innate capacity to love and feel compassion. Love is an "energy source" we have inside of us, he said, and by valuing this quality within ourselves, we enhance its power and become able to offer it to others. This is similar to what other spiritual teachers in this book have said about where to start: Recognize the love you have inside of you, value it, and consciously cultivate it like you would roses in the garden. As Havasupai-Hopi-Tewa Grandmother Mona Polacca told me: "Start by recognizing your sacred beginning—the sacredness you share with all of life."

Buddhists consciously work with the subtle energies of the heart by training in the Four Immeasurables: equanimity, love, compassion, sympathetic joy. The training begins with equanimity, moving beyond our tendency to categorize beings into those we like (friend), those we dislike (enemy), and those we are indifferent to (stranger). These limited perceptions are easily found to be false when we recall our friends who used to be strangers, our enemies who used to be friends, and so on. Equanimity prevails when we recognize that, underneath these false divides, we are close to everyone in terms of the fundamental reality we all share: wanting to be happy and not wanting to suffer. "We are all family," the Karmapa told me. On the basis of that common ground, love begins to grow in our hearts as we see that each person and animal longs to be happy and content, just like we do.

We seek to feel deeply about them and desire their welfare and happiness—even wanting success and happiness for those we have difficulty with and those we don't know. Why? Because we know we are woven into the web of life, and to love our neighbor is to love our self.

But this inclusive love takes time, the Karmapa emphasized, and loving-kindness has to start with care for oneself. This involves an honest look at one's situation and a willingness to renounce the habits that cause suffering in one's life. "In order to have genuine compassion toward others, we have to have care and love for ourselves." We can't transmit what we haven't got. Those who have done this training say that it can take many years of learning to accept oneself and let go of false self-concepts and negative habits. At the same time that one grows in self-compassion, one can of course practice care for other people, animals, plants, places, and things. Love inward and love outward intensify each other, for love is love, and the more we love the more we can love.

Eventually our love for others grows to the point that we feel great joy for their success as if it were our own. Compassion prevails when the suffering of others is also our own, and we do all we can to relieve it. As the Karmapa told me, "When we witness their pain or happiness, we experience it as our own pain and our own happiness.... This is what true love feels like."

In cases where direct action is not possible, the Karmapa said, "We can hold those people in our heart, make aspirations for them, and dedicate even the smallest positive action that we perform to their welfare, healing, and ease." Performing grand projects is not necessary. Any heartfelt wish, aspiration, or action for others, however small, is of benefit. Speaking at our university, the Karmapa emphasized the importance of practicing compassion in the minutiae of ordinary life:

> A lot of people have exaggerated ideas about what compassion should look like.... grab headlines somewhere... require a lot of money or position of influence.... True compassion, however, is something that doesn't involve those requirements. Being truly

compassionate and responsible means just working with our day-to-day experiences and feelings in a skillful way. We can use all of these normal daily experiences as a basis of benefiting others—physically, verbally, and mentally.... This is the first step in our training, and the foundation of all of our further developments.

Along these lines, in his book, *Interconnected*, the Karmapa tells of a simple practice called "recollecting of kindness."[161] You call to mind a situation in which you've received something beneficial from others. You turn it over and over in your mind, so your awareness of the kindnesses intensifies. Naturally your gratitude and appreciation will magnify and you'll feel grateful and happy. Many people keep gratitude journals for the same reason, and this can be an excellent way to cultivate love.

The Karmapa walking into the classroom building to meet with our meditation community (Carlos Puma/courtesy of University of Redlands).

In his comments to the meditation community on our campus, he warned that compassion training isn't always comfortable; if we expect it to be so, then our compassion will be stunted. Life has many adverse conditions and difficult emotions to work through, and he said to not be discouraged. With our "strength of heart," he told us, we can actually hope for adversity so that our compassion deepens and we will feel closer to other beings by virtue of having endured what they endure.

This is the deep compassion of an advanced being. Even before I met him, the depth of his teachings was discernible in the presence of his relics—not as words but as an emanation.

My second encounter was also unusual: a dream of the 17th Karmapa. Dreams are honored in many spiritual traditions, including Tibetan Buddhism. In the Sufi tradition that guides my understanding of dreamwork, there is a class of dreams called experiences, notable for their numinous and noetic impact. The message from an "experience dream" is not forgotten, and the feeling of it is vivid upon recollection, similar to a catalytic experience in real life. The dream showed me aspects of the Karmapa that were solidly confirmed when I met him in person. Here is the dream:

> The Karmapa has made a simple but substantial veg-
> etarian meal for me with boiled potatoes. I sit down
> with him at a table. I feel relaxed, cared for, and
> unconditionally loved. I marvel at how effortless the
> cooking was for him. He's a world-renowned figure
> with countless responsibilities, yet he cooked this
> meal with single-minded focus. I know he's busy with
> outer activities, but you'd never know it, as he was
> completely content and available.

This dream gave me a direct experience of the Karmapa's state of peace and compassion. It transmitted the truth that, contrary to popular belief, stress is not caused by a busy schedule of outer demands but by an anxious mind. It's possible to be intensely engaged with worldly activities yet be totally peaceful, present, and nourishing to the person right in front of you.

It also reminded me of the teaching from Zen Master Thich Nhat Hanh: We can transform our negative emotion in the same way we boil potatoes. Raw potatoes taste terrible—we would never serve them to anyone. We put them into a pot of water, cover them with a lid, light the fire, and watch them boil. It may take a while but when they are cooked thoroughly, the potatoes are substantial and delicious. Just so with a negative emotion such as anger. Raw anger is unpleasant, but it can be transformed into love and understanding when we put it into the container of our practice, cover it with the lid of our patience, and light the fire of our devotion and persistent mindfulness. The dream impressed upon me this truth: the Karmapa offers the nourishment of a fully transformed heart.

Years later, when the Karmapa spent ninety minutes in the university's Meditation Room to dialogue with community members, I experienced his compassion in real life. A special table of tea and food had been set up for him, as well as a large chair to sit in, but he had little interest in the display of food. Choosing dialogue over delicacies, he moved from the chair to a floor cushion to be completely available, meeting us on the level of the heart, according equal dignity to everyone. As in my dream, he offered real nourishment from the table of his peaceful presence.

After these experiences, I was keen to meet the Karmapa in a living, breathing body. My encounter with him at his home base of Gyuto Monastery in India turned out to be startling for the simple reason that I'd always associated wisdom with old age. Then I met the twenty-eight-year-old whose inner wisdom was so instantaneous and vast that it seemed as if he were, in fact, 900 years old. Like the Karmapa in my dreams, he was playful, free, spontaneous, boundless, warmhearted, nourishing, and completely at peace with himself and his surroundings.

The trip from Delhi north to the Himalayan town of Sidhbari was long and tedious. The flight was cancelled, so we traveled by way of a hired taxi that left Delhi at 4 p.m. We rode all night through chaotic traffic on roads shared with various species of animals and vehicles, pounded by thunderstorms. We arrived in the wee hours of the morning, carsick from the winding, potholed roads.

On this long ride, I imagined the treacherous journey made by His Holiness to Dharamsala at age fourteen, all the way from Tibet, over the Himalayas on foot, train, helicopter, and horseback.[162] My trip had been easy compared to his. Despite the danger and difficulty, he was poetically inspired with a feeling of oneness and joy. On a cold starry night, he heard the Divine Mother singing a celestial melody that strengthened and soothed his heart. This melody was recorded, together with the poem he wrote to accompany it, on an album called *Sweet Melody of Joyful Aspiration*. I listened to it during the long car ride, as I fell in and out of sleep.

The entrance to Gyuto Monastery is right off the streets of Sidbhari, giving the feel of an easy flow between monks and others. Crimson-robed monks of all ages were welcoming of visitors—taking photos, laughing—even as they clearly had a purpose of their own: monastic studies, ritual, and meditation. Little boy monks were seated on cushions around the temple, drawing auspicious symbols in their notebooks. Incense, chanting, and the sound of horns filled the air. In the midst of the monks walking happily about the grounds, I saw a lame donkey lying in the grass near a central area in the monastery. I wondered how it got there. Later, I was told that the Dalai Lama had seen it in the streets, abandoned and decrepit. He told his assistant: "Take it to Gyuto so it can be cared for." And so it was. Treatment of animals says a lot about the level of love in a place.

Before the private audience for the interview, I attended a public audience with the Karmapa, held in the temple at Gyuto. Public audiences occur on a regular basis, so that people from all over the world may come to be in his presence and receive a blessing. About 200 had gathered to pay their respects that day, and all of us had to be processed through the security department and given clearance to enter the temple. Buddhist monks and nuns were seated on the left side of the temple floor; they were called up first to pass by His Holiness. Many bowed and prostrated. To be in his presence is understood to be a karmic event that carries a blessing beyond this lifetime. Then, the lay people were motioned forward. We presented the *khata* (white scarf) and it was placed around our necks. His Holiness gave each person a red string symbolic of the transmission. No words. It all happened in silence.

Several days later, I went to Gyuto for the private audience and had no idea what to expect. Venerable Damchö, the American-born nun who'd helped arrange the interview, had carefully reviewed all of my questions. She warned me there was no guarantee of getting them answered, for it was common for His Holiness to dismiss visitors quickly. As I went through the security process and pat-down where everything was removed—purse, pens, recorder, paper, camera, phone—I did an internal process of removing all expectations. What if he dismissed me after five minutes? What if I never got to ask my questions? I let go needing or wanting anything. After security, we were ushered into a waiting room. There was a group of twenty Buddhist disciples from Canada who had come from a community founded there by the 16th Karmapa. We were all in the waiting room for about an hour, mainly in silence, until the Canadian group was called in to see His Holiness. They didn't stay long, and suddenly it was our turn.

We lined up, shoes off, set our offerings on a tray. I had brought many gifts, most of them related to my teacher, the most treasured of all things to me. It was because of him that I even knew of the Karmapa. He had met the 16th Karmapa and spoke of the significance of that transmission, which he said had been wordless. In standing before the 17th Karmapa, bringing heartfelt gifts related to my teacher, I had the feeling of completing a link in the mystic chain of selfless love.

I was awkward with the protocol, wielding many gifts, but His Holiness was kind and helped ease the situation by taking the gifts from my hands, then putting the khata on me. I had the sense that he tolerated the ritual formalities of his role because they were important to those around him, but he himself didn't need them. As was the custom, he sat in a chair and I sat on the floor. His many male assistants lined the outer edges of the large library room whose windows looked out onto the monastery grounds. He spoke mostly in Tibetan, with occasional comments in English. He asked Venerable Damchö to be the interpreter, a rare role for nuns within the male-oriented Buddhist monastic system and surely a statement about the Karmapa's commitment to gender equality. It all went very smoothly. Toward the end, there was laughter when I asked him about romantic love and he made a joke about his lack of personal experience in that area.

# Private Audience with His Holiness the 17th Karmapa

In the Gyuto Monastery, Sidbhari, India[163] Tibetan horns and chanting in the background, and incense in the air.

## The Power of Love in the World

Q:    Some people view love as weak and naïve, especially in the practical arenas of business, global economy, the environment, and politics. They say love has little practical value in the world, yet Your Holiness says: "If we have a powerful heart full of love, this can change the world in vivid ways." Can you elaborate? What is the practical benefit of love in the world?

HHK:    If you're asking about the power or the potential of a heart full of love, in terms of its effect in the business world, perhaps for a businessman, in terms of what he's able to do, it's difficult to point to a specific power of love. But this certainly does not mean that love doesn't have a beneficial role or power, even in the business environment. For example, a large corporation has many employees, and part of the successful functioning of the business is for the employer to have concern for and to take care of the well-being of employees. There's a recent example that we can look to in China. The factories producing Apple products are subject to very strict rules, and the working environment is so tight and so strictly regulated that many employees have actually come to the point of suicide. So, this makes it clear that there is an obvious need for love and affection to maintain the ongoing operation of a company. This is not just in terms of extracting profit, but in more general terms, there's an absolutely central role for an attitude of altruism, wishing to benefit others.

When we think about human beings, in order for us to be born our parents have to come together. And from the very moment we are born, if our parents don't have love and affection for us, we would not even be able to survive. So, this is a display or result of the power of love. Love is a basic component of our existence. It is a basic power, which I believe is indispensable for human existence.

Q: When pure love expands within a single human heart, how does this inner change benefit the world?

HHK: The inner love or affection we have within us is not something that can be perceived with the naked eye from the outside. It is an inner quality, obviously not subject to perception. But through our actions and activities motivated by the love we have within us, this invisible quality within us is made visible on the outside through our actions. We can see this clearly in the case of Mother Teresa, and there are many other people like this in the world, whose actions display the love they have within them. And in this way love is not just a word; it's not something that just sounds nice and that we pay lip service to. When there is true love within us, the actions that it motivates bring about changes in people's lives that we can actually see. And these actions would not come about without the power or motivating force of love. In this sense, love is an energy source.

Love is certainly not just an idea. For example, with compassion, when we look at the suffering of someone else, if it's on the level of an idea, we might feel pity and say, "Oh, poor thing." This would be an example of an expression of something that is not actually pure love within us. But when the love within us is manifesting outside, we are seeing others, seeing their suffering, seeing the other as a part of ourselves, and we feel ourselves to be a part of the other. For that reason, when we witness their pain or their happiness, we experience it as our own pain and our own happiness. And when this basis is there, the basis that comes from love, then naturally their pain becomes unbearable for us to witness and we must act to do something about it.

There's a verse from Milarepa that says: "When true compassion arises, then it's like you are burning with an inner fire." It is unbearable. You want to get out from inside this fire. This is what true love feels like. It is the urgency to do something about the pain of the other, when the other's pain becomes unbearable.

Q: What does Your Holiness see as the most important work of love in the twenty-first century? Are there particular areas on which we should focus our love for the maximum benefit of all? What should we take more notice of?

HHK: Since the Industrial Revolution, technology has amplified the impact that our behavior can have hundreds of thousands of times. So, when we're acting based on greed compared with previous centuries, the impact of our pursuit of greed has had a much greater negative effect on the natural environment, and the pace of our use of natural resources has increased exponentially. As a result of the impact of our greed and our desires on the environment, we nowadays must be much more careful and pay more attention to the consequences of our actions, and we need to examine the results of our behavior. I think the natural environment itself is an important object for us to direct our love and our concern. The twenty-first century offers us a big lesson in terms of the huge problems that the environment faces as a result of our careless behavior. Also, in terms of wildlife and animal welfare, our increasing use of cars and other forms of technology is infringing on their environment and having a negative impact on their well-being. We can also see great differences between the levels of wealth in different societies. We have countries or societies that are experiencing great levels of poverty. There are also communities that are facing wars.

We do not exist in a vacuum. We do not exist independently of each other. And the fact that we're impacting each other means that we have a mutual responsibility to take care. Also in the area of women's well-being within society—this is still an issue that needs to be addressed. We also have sectarian fighting among religious traditions, which is another area to be addressed.

The world we live in today is, in an important sense, smaller than it was before. There's more information readily available about what's going on elsewhere. There are many situations that previously we were unable to do anything about or to take any responsibility for changing, simply because we were unaware of them. That is no longer the case. We now have a great deal of knowledge about what goes on in other parts of the world. What we need to do now is take this knowledge and allow it to enter into our hearts so that we transform our actions in a way that can have an effect.

## How to Increase Our Love and Compassion

Q:  Your Holiness teaches that love and compassion are innate seeds within all beings. How do we water these seeds? Is there a basic meditation practice that you recommend to awaken and cultivate love?

HHK:  Recently, we've seen scientific studies where research is demonstrating that we are actually hardwired to feel empathy. Empathy is innate in us, but we have developed the ability to switch it off. We see instances of soldiers who have learned how to suppress this basic feeling of empathy. They overcome this natural thought in themselves in order to kill other human beings. There were instances during World War II, and also at the end of the war, of soldiers, maybe American or English, who remained unable to feel love as a result of all the violence they had been through and as a result of this process of switching off their empathy. Similarly, during the Iraqi war, there were soldiers who returned after serving in that war who clearly showed the lasting effects of this process of turning off empathy—including those who even ended up killing their family members out of severe mental distress. So, this is something that we do have, this capacity for empathy within us, but we have also learned to close the door on it.

What to do about this? First we need to recognize that we have this quality, and then we need to recognize that it has innate value. It is valuable and important for you and for others.

A way to train in this—we do this with what we call the Four Immeasurable thoughts: Equanimity, Love, Compassion, and Sympathetic Joy. It helps us to recognize that all sentient beings are the same in terms of wanting to be happy and not wanting to suffer. And when we train in this, we begin with equanimity. Equanimity means that we recognize that we discriminate between friends and enemies, those who are far or near; we discriminate in terms of our own perceptions and in terms of how others relate to us. But in terms of wanting to be happy and not wanting to suffer, there is no such thing as a friend or an enemy. As we recognize this shared humanity and cultivate a wish to serve and benefit humanity, then we can train in the Four Immeasurables. We begin in Equanimity and go on to train in Compassion and Love.

Tragic things happen because too few people take care or have concern for others. For example, malaria is a world killer, but it doesn't have to be. There is no need for so many people to die from this disease, but people ignore the problem and think, "This is not my business." If it isn't happening to them, they think it's okay and not a problem. Having a good heart or feeling empathy is not enough. We can see in the great tragedies of history, such as Hitlerism, that there were not enough goodhearted people who acted from true inner compassion to change something. People need to understand how important compassion is—not just empathy or sympathy—to change the hearts with simple knowledge and action.

Q:   Some people say, "My heart is closed and numb. As much as I try, I feel no love for myself or others." This is the case for some of the college students in the Compassion course. What does Your Holiness recommend?

HHK:   There are some cases where people in this kind of situation need psychiatric care. If it's neurological or a problem with brain chemistry, then it's a physical problem. Something is "broken" and, if you put in the part that's missing, you can get it to function. So, there are cases where you have to take recourse to psychiatric, medical, and pharmaceutical care.

If it's a question of the mind and heart, we can think about it in this way: If you feel you are well off and want to offer yourself to others, but people don't accept the love you're offering or the offering of yourself that you're making, or they don't respond to you, then you may fall into a state of loneliness or self-pity. You may have the feeling "Poor me, nobody cares about me...." You can fall into this state of feeling lonely and then it becomes very difficult.

When the heart is cold or frozen, the first thing you have to do is warm it. One way is to recognize that you have something valuable to give to others. You warm the heart yourself by recognizing the value of what you have, so you enhance the power of what you have by recognizing it yourself. Our capacity to love or feel compassion is really a jewel.

When we recognize that we have a jewel, the first thing is that we ourselves feel happy to have it. So, in this sense, the first step is to value ourselves and what we have, and to cultivate a feeling of closeness with our own quality. Only with acceptance of yourself and your own quality will you then be able to offer it to others, and only then will you be able to feel close to others and have acceptance from others.

## Love for All Beings, Even the "Enemy"

Q: Your Holiness has said that you love all beings. What is that like, to love all beings equally? What are you aware of when you look at people of all races, and at plants, animals, and objects?

(*Silence.*)

HHK: You are asking about something that is hard to express in words. Maybe the time hasn't come yet for me to do so. When you ask about love for all sentient beings, these are big words. Maybe before we get to the point of entering into "all sentient beings," we need to make ourselves ready for it.

One way to think about this comes from Tibet in previous centuries, when there was no geographic knowledge. We had no map of the world that we could refer to. We didn't know where places were. But there was this idea that wherever the sky is, there must be our parents and friends; there must be other sentient beings who are our family, our "relatives," and so we would send love out to them.

This is not a matter of having love for the people you directly see around you. This is a kind of mental preparation that is a prior step to that, in which you just generate the feeling of love for anyone who feels this wish to be happy and not to suffer. Even though Western people think it's sort of strange or alien, they can still generate love and compassion for others because already they see that, similar to themselves, others have pain and suffering and want happiness.

So, anyone you see whom you recognize feels this wish to be happy and who has the capacity to experience pain and suffering and wishes not to, you are ready to accept them and to respect them. In fact, if the opportunity arises, you are preparing yourself to be ready to act to help them. So then this idea of all sentient beings is not some form of artificial—that is, mental, conceptual—knowledge. It's really more the case of something that you're feeling in the heart.

Q: In particular, how does Your Holiness regard those people who have harmed, imprisoned, and acted with hatred toward you and the Tibetan people?

HHK:   Recently, some Tibetans killed one of my friends, a lama. The initial feeling was something you could describe along the lines of anger. It was the feeling of, "Why did this happen? What for? What was the point?" First of all, the way of killing and the circumstances around the death were really terrible, so this first impulse was, "Why? This is so terrible!"

Later, in thinking it over, one thing that occurred to me was: Clearly there is some sort of karmic connection. One hand alone can't clap. Both hands need to come together to perform the action of clapping, and both of those hands through that action of clapping are connected.

And thinking in a broader way, it is possible to see that the person who does the killing is actually an object of greater compassion than the victim of the killing, because it's an action done out of great ignorance. And at the time he did it, he probably had no idea of what he was doing. Clearly, he must have been out of control. If he had just remained in his natural state, this would never have happened. Clearly, there was some sort of emotion that was overwhelming and that he lost control of. There is no other reason to do this sort of action—only lack of control over his own emotional state would make it possible.

Looking at the action, it was clearly wrong, it was a mistake, and there's no way around that fact. There is no excusing the action. But the person himself can be forgiven. Even the government or decision-makers also have great ignorance. We need the space for forgiving and opportunities to forgive—not for the actions but for the person.

In terms of Buddhist understanding, there are many things involved. We are concerned for the person that kills a lama because it will affect his future lives, not just this lifetime. Also, if I am the killer, I have a lot of depression and sadness and regret. Who will forgive me? That's why I say to be more concerned for the person who kills....

Q: For ordinary people, how can we begin to love those who have harmed us?

HHK: That's a difficult one. We all have different kinds of capabilities, and in terms of our ability to forgive, some can do it easily while for others it takes much more work. There's no one-size-fits-all response to this question.

Let's think about what happens when someone else harms us. We respond with feelings of anger and wanting to harm back—revenge and payback. The idea is that our anger and our grudge is a sort of answer to what they've done to us. And the answer we're sending to them is: "I don't like what you did." So, we're sending them back a message. If we really think about it, the hatred we feel and this wish to harm that we're generating is actually harming us at exactly the same time that we direct it at others. And, as we can see from our own experience, as long as we have anger, malevolence toward the other person, and a wish to harm, we do not have peace and happiness. So, we see that as we wish to harm the other, we actually at the very same moment harm ourselves. The question would be: If our anger and wish to harm is meant to be a response to *them*, how do we respond to the fact that we are actually only harming ourselves?

## The Reality of Interdependence— "We Are One Family"

Q: Your Holiness teaches that in Reality, there is no actual boundary between "me" and anything else. How do we, as ordinary human beings, break free from the duality of "me" and "you"?

HHK: Just to clarify: It's not that there's no such thing as me and no such thing as you and no such thing as them. The problem comes because these things don't exist in the way that we normally think. These "I" and "you" and other things don't have a kind of separate and independent existence. You and I and others exist interdependently— and not only interdependently but there is also a certain form of independent existence.

The way to start to understand this correctly is to look at self and other, and look at how many connections there are and see how intimately connected we are. Take the case of your body. Normally when we say "I," the primary point of reference we're thinking of is the body. If we look at our body from head to toe, every single piece of it comes from others, comes from our parents. Not only that, everything that we use with our body, all the things we have, all the things we own physically, all that we eat and drink, all the air we breathe—all of this is coming from others. It makes it very clear that this solid sense of "I" who is the owner of my own experiences does not exist in this way.

Nevertheless, it is permissible to speak of "I" and to speak of "you" and to speak of us having some sort of separate existence. But if you think of yourself as being the owner, or being independent, then the question you need to ask yourself is: Did you make your own body? Did you make your own cloak? Clearly, the answer is no. All the things we have are intimately connected with others. We have a completely mistaken view of how it is that we exist. If we're looking on this physical level, we can say that we are tremendously interrelated with others. If we are speaking about a self that is separate from others, then it's just not valid to do.

When we come to the mental level, maybe there is some slight measure of independence that we can point to, but even so, our mind is based on our bodies and is dependent on the physical level.

We need a middle path. It doesn't mean that there is no distinction between "me" and "you." There is some distinction, but it's not what we think it is. We think we are independent, but this is a mistaken view, and actions based on this view are also mistaken.

Q: Your Holiness creates beautiful poetry, calligraphy, music, and theatrical plays. How are these artistic expressions related to love?

HHK: You have misrepresented things; it's not how you say it is. Forget about me having any artistic expertise! Actually, I can't even do it properly. Here is how I think of it: When I am creating music, for example, my feeling is that the music can bridge the gap that exists between people. It can shrink the gap that keeps us separate. Many kinds of differences separate us—for example, language. These differences create barriers and create a distance. With my work in music, we can all hear it. It becomes like a universal language, and this gives us the opportunity to experience and to recognize that actually we are all the same. It's not like we belong to a different species. We are all very much the same. We are the same species, the same in terms of our feelings of pain or suffering and happiness, and the same in terms of all being part of one family. So, whether it's with painting or music or art, this is what I'm trying to express.

## Romantic Love

Q: Personal, romantic love is the most sought-after form of love in the West. What is the value of this kind of love? What is its limitation?

HHK: If we think about it theoretically in the case of, for example, our ultimate spiritual practitioner, the bodhisattva, a bodhisattva has given everything he has to all others. So, if you have given away everything you had to all others, it isn't really consistent to have personal love, to give it to one person exclusively. It's not clear whether they could really be made compatible. It is a bit doubtful.

But love is a generic term with a universal application. For that reason, there can be different forms of love for different people. Generally speaking, I don't have much to say about romantic love!
(*Laughing.*)
It's complicated—maybe next time!
(*Laughing.*)

I would observe that there is a strong danger for personal romantic love to become selfish. When romantic love becomes selfish, then it's not very healthy. This happens quite often. If one person is alone and is thinking only about his own welfare, then that's one thing, but when you get two people in a relationship and it becomes mutually selfish, then it's complicated. A relationship of romantic love should be for the benefit of two people. If the people in it are seeking their own well-being, this obviously gets very complicated. For something to really be love, it has to be unselfish. And this is the danger with romantic love, because when it starts to become selfish, it is not healthy.

Q:   What is the aspiration prayer of Your Holiness for readers of this book?

HHK:   That through this book, by helping people understand how to offer love and how to enhance their ability to love, and through that—within their own lives, family, community, country, and world— there could be great benefit.

I felt transformed by his presence and teachings, and that he understood me in my essence, that he knew, loved, accepted, and respected me despite my ignorance. He saw my best and overlooked the rest. What he burned off in me was a barrier between myself and those whose suffering I had seen as "none of my business." I learned from him that I had a responsibility for the well-being of all life, no matter the supposed distance. To see the suffering of others is to feel a fire inside that wants to end the suffering. That inner fire is Love Itself.

When the 17th Karmapa was a child in Tibet, another world leader was approaching the end of his twenty-seven-year prison term. Prison, not a monastery, was his training ground for compassion. It was in South Africa, home to a longstanding racist system called apartheid. Nelson Mandela had been convicted of treason for his protests against a government led by the white minority. In his prison cell, Mandela had plenty of time to "cook" his anger in the heat of heartfelt self-examination, and it transformed into compassion. Similar to the Karmapa's teaching, the basis of Mandela's compassion was interdependence—in African terms, *ubuntu*, that is, "I am because we are."

Nelson Mandela revisits his prison cell on Robben Island in
1994 (photo by Jurgen Schadeberg, used with permission).

*Chapter Twenty-One*

# LIVING THE LINK BETWEEN INNER AND OUTER TRANSFORMATION

## NARRATIVE CASE STUDY: NELSON MANDELA

T hanks to a college student, Nelson Mandela came to be included in the Compassion course. The student was struggling in one of my classes, so I called him into my office to talk. He told me he had a learning disability and that it was difficult for him to read. In fact, he had read only one book in its entirety: *Long Walk to Freedom* by Nelson Mandela, over 600 pages. I read the book and found Mandela a compelling example of the energy field of Love. We've studied him in the Compassion class ever since. Mandela's story is a case study from recent history that illumines a key point of this book: when a single heart opens, the world is changed.

Nelson Mandela grew up in South Africa under apartheid, a system of severe racial segregation in which the fifteen percent white minority controlled the government and access to education, land, finance, travel, marriage, voting, and other rights and privileges. Mandela was not a free man; everything about his experience was limited by systemic racism. Overcoming fear and hopelessness, Mandela joined the African National Congress (ANC) to pursue nonviolent political solutions, but after a government massacre that left sixty-nine black Africans dead, he became militant and made an inflammatory statement to support violence as the best course of action. In retaliation, the government banned the ANC and sentenced Mandela to prison for twenty-seven years. Paradoxically, it was in the confines of a seven-by-nine-foot prison cell that Nelson Mandela was liberated from the prison of a militant mindset.

Once, a student in the Compassion class put masking tape on the floor to mark out the space of Mandela's cell. She asked us to stand in that small box and contemplate Mandela's circumstances—confinement in a small and stark environment, derisive attitudes of prison guards, loss of contact with the outside world, loss of friends and family, loss of freedom of movement, loss of control over what to eat and even when to go to the bathroom. She asked us, "How do you view your situation?" No one could say they saw the prison cell as Mandela had—an opportunity for self-development and service to humanity.

But Mandela didn't begin his prison sentence that way. He started out with anger and arrogance. In that cell, he went through a transformation of consciousness. What happened to him? What can we learn?

In his interviews with Oprah Winfrey, Mandela said that the prison term allowed him the opportunity to achieve "the most difficult task in life, which is to change oneself." Before his imprisonment, he explained, he hadn't taken time to look at himself. In the prison cell, he said, "I had time to think. I had a clear view of my past and present, and I found that my past left much to be desired, both in regard to my relations with other humans and in developing personal worth." He realized that he had been ungrateful and thoughtless regarding the family members and other people who had helped him in his life. He had been self-absorbed and arrogant. "In my younger days, I was arrogant—jail helped me to get rid of it. I did nothing but make enemies because of my arrogance."[164]

Mandela said that prison taught him how everything depended upon the support of others, and he experienced ubuntu, the African proverb, "We are people through other people." The proverb underscores the interdependence inherent in life. Mandela also educated himself in prison by reading great literature and the scriptures of the world's religions, and working to develop his "powers of thinking and discipline." Prison took away his arrogance, he told Oprah, but not his dignity.

Mandela emerged from prison a changed man. He had refused self-hatred and had given up the blame game. He had put his effort into learning from others, nurturing their talents, and doing the most menial labors (such as cleaning his cell) with as much care as possible. In his way, he became a free man even while in prison. One story from his book suffices to illustrate this. He asked the prison authorities if he could use a small patch of rocky dirt in the courtyard for a garden. He saw potential in it that no one else saw. They refused many times, but he kept asking. Finally, seeing no harm in it, they relented. Mandela set out to cultivate the rocky soil into a garden. Though everyone made fun of him, he focused on the task and what he could learn from it. He saw it as a metaphor for his life—he needed to cultivate himself, plant good seeds, watch how they grew, and eliminate whatever choked them. Through trial and error, he became an outstanding gardener and shared the harvest of tomatoes and onions with the prison guards.

In his book, Mandela shows us how to transform hatred and despair into the power of love. First, he did not deny the pain of racism or try to cover over the wounds: "The policy of apartheid created a deep and lasting wound in my country and my people."

Second, he did not nurse the wound or cling to the past. Rather, he looked for the hidden gold within the painful history: "The decades of oppression and brutality had another, unintended effect" in that it "produced the great heroes of the struggle for democracy.... Perhaps it requires such depth of oppression to create such heights of character."

Third, he refused the deadly allure of self-pity and resentment. "Resentment is like drinking poison and waiting for the other person to die" is among his well-known quotes.

Fourth, Mandela held onto the belief that "deep down in every human heart, there is mercy and generosity." He kept his eye on the glimmers of goodness in those who were against him. Even in prison, when he was pushed to his limits by the cruelty of certain guards and pointless regimens, he would "see a glimmer of humanity in one of the guards, perhaps just for a second"; that glimmer reassured him that "man's goodness is a flame that can be hidden but never extinguished."

Fifth, he gave up the blame game and focused his attention on hope. He understood that people can't help how they have been conditioned. If they can learn to hate, they can learn also to love: "No one is born hating another person because of the color of his skin, or his background, or his religion. People must learn to hate, and if they can learn to hate, they can be taught to love, for love comes more naturally to the human heart than its opposite."[165]

By 1990, South Africa was ripe for change, and Mandela was internally prepared to be a leader. Due to international pressure, the apartheid government lifted the ban on the ANC and released Mandela and his cohorts in 1990. Government leaders had tried many times to seduce Mandela with special favors for his own release, but he refused all options that offered only personal advantage. He was committed to ubuntu, "We are people through other people," as a matter of ethical principle. He did not fall into the trap of "the end justifies the means" that consumes many activists who naively think they can use hostile means of protest to achieve the goal of peace. Mandela was a tireless advocate of the idea that common principles are more important than individual personalities. A leader should be fearless in the face of difficulty, yet humble in receiving honors. As he told Oprah, "When there is danger, a good leader takes the front line; but when there is celebration, a good leader stays in the back of the room."[166]

Mandela emerged as a leader for all of South Africa. He had been a militant tribal fighter for one side, yet became a leader for all sides. "During those long and lonely years," Mandela explained,

> ...my hunger for the freedom of my own people became a hunger for the freedom of all people, white and black. I knew as well as I knew anything that the oppressor must be liberated just as surely as the oppressed. A man who takes away another man's freedom is a prisoner of hatred, he is locked behind the bars of prejudice and narrow-mindedness.... For to be free is not merely to cast off one's chains, but to live in a way that respects and enhances the freedom of others.[167]

In a remarkable moment, Nelson Mandela and F. W. de Klerk, president of the apartheid government, were honored together with the Nobel Peace Prize in 1993 for their global example of collaborative leadership. In 1994, Mandela was seventy-five years old and voted for the first time in his life. The ANC won the election, and Mandela was inaugurated as South Africa's first democratically elected president.

In a speech shortly after he became President of South Africa, Mandela said that the "hearts of South Africans" had come to "beat as one," and "we rediscovered the human being in all of us."[168] The occurrence hints at a phenomenon that Dedan Gills observed: "Hearts want to beat in tandem with other hearts." "Hearts in tandem"—this is what the pioneers of the power of love know will work to heal societal divides. Mandela chose to serve only one term, and devoted the rest of his life to humanitarian work for the poor, education for children, and the HIV/AIDS crisis.

In his writings and speeches, Mandela presented his "collective leadership" conviction, which expresses qualities of the level of consciousness of Love, referred to earlier on the Map of Consciousness. These qualities characterize a noble and humanistic mindset, and can be practiced in everyday life as a way of becoming a truly effect change agent:

+ Look for what unites instead of what divides.

+ Avoid humiliating others. When you must correct the mistakes of another person, always also point out the positive side to the person, allowing them to save face.

+ Treat everyone with respect and graciousness, and their inherent goodness will become apparent to you.

+ Appeal to the noble qualities within your opponents. Point out how the oppressive system is crippling everyone and will lead to the violent demise of both sides unless forces are joined to save the country.

+ Do not view other individuals as your enemy. They may not even agree with the racist system they are working for. See the system as the common enemy.

+ Give people a chance to voice their standpoint and where it comes from. Listen patiently and ask questions. Do not criticize, even if you think the views are wrong.

+ Cultivate collective leadership by noting the contributions and strengths of others. Do what you can to support others in the expression of their talents.

+ Be humble and others won't feel threatened by you.

+ Use your brain not your emotions when dealing with anger.

In 1997, the Truth and Reconciliation Commission (TRC) was established in South Africa, overseen by Archbishop Desmond Tutu. The TRC was created to carry out Mandela's commitment to heal societal wounds through truth-telling and forgiveness, to serve as "a beacon to future generations that the mistakes of the past will never be repeated."[169]

In the Compassion course, we study one of the stories from the annals of the TRC because it involves a young person who lived close to our university. In 1993, Amy Biehl, a young American white woman from Southern California, was killed in South Africa while on a Fulbright scholarship. After graduation from UC Berkeley, she went to South Africa to join the work to end apartheid. She'd been inspired by reading Nelson Mandela's book in college; in fact she painted his name on her graduation cap. On August 25, 1993, Amy was beaten and stabbed to death in a black township near Cape Town. Four young black men were convicted of her murder. In 1998, after serving five years in prison, they applied to the TRC for amnesty. Amy's parents, Linda and Peter Biehl, attended the hearings, forgave the young men, and supported their amnesty. The Biehls eventually hired Easy Nofemela and Ntobeko Peni, two of the men who killed their daughter, to work for the Amy Biehl Foundation Trust.

At the TRC hearing in 1998, the young men confessed that they had instantly seen Amy, a white woman, as their enemy. That very day, they had witnessed a fellow black youth shot by white officers, and they saw a chance for revenge by killing a white woman. At the hearing, Amy's parents told her killers about her life's work, that she had been devoted to ending apartheid. The young men told the Biehls what it was like to grow up as black youths in Cape Town. Amy's brother visited the depressing area and said, "If I had been raised [in this environment], I could have been a militant myself."[170] The Biehls made a decision to carry Amy's torch, forgive her killers, and establish a foundation in her name that would work to create educational and economic opportunities for black youth in Cape Town.

"Forgiveness was a process," Linda Biehl said. She felt that some of Amy's spirit had gone into the two young men who had killed her. This made it impossible for Linda to reject them, for it would have been to reject her own daughter. Speaking of her decision to join hands with Easy Nofemela and Ntobeko Peni, Linda says:

I've grown fond of these young men. They're like my own kids. It may sound strange, but I tend to think there's a little bit of Amy's spirit in them. I have come to believe passionately in restorative justice. It's what Desmond Tutu calls ubuntu: to choose to forgive rather than demand retribution, a belief that 'my humanity is inextricably caught up in yours.' I can't look at myself as a victim—it diminishes me as a person.[171]

Easy Nofemela told the interviewer:

I'd grown up being taught never to trust a white person. Not until I met Linda and Peter Biehl did I understand that white people are human beings too. I was a member of Azanian People's Liberation Army, the armed wing of the Pan Africanist Congress. Our slogan was 'one settler, one bullet.' The first time I saw them on TV, I hated them. I thought this was the strategy of the whites, to come to South Africa to call for capital punishment. But they didn't even mention wanting to hang us. I was very confused.

At first I didn't want to go to the TRC to give my testimony. I thought it was a sellout, but then I read in the press that Linda and Peter had said that it was not up to them to forgive; it was up to the people in South Africa to learn to forgive each other. I decided to go and tell our story and show remorse. Amnesty wasn't my motivation. I just wanted to ask for forgiveness. I wanted to say in front of Linda and Peter, face to face, 'I am sorry, can you forgive me?' I wanted to be free in my mind and body. It must have been so painful for them to lose their daughter, but by coming to South Africa—not to speak of recrimination, but to speak of the pain of our struggle—they gave me back my freedom.[172]

This is the power of love in action. We see that Nelson Mandela's inner transformation paved the way not only for the ending of apartheid in South Africa but also for the healing of individuals and communities worldwide. Yes, there are still difficulties—racist structures continue to exist in South Africa—but Mandela's inclusive vision imprinted a gold standard in the collective psyche as we struggle with racism. The same is true for Mother Teresa's example. While it did not end poverty, her work among the poor imprinted a new note of love into human consciousness. Racism and poverty will probably always exist, but Mandela and Mother Teresa and others like them show how love reduces their cruel impact and can heal the inner wounds that cause them.

"It has to start from the inside," is what Jetsunma Tenzin Palmo told me: "If we had the eyes to see it, we would see that this planet is in very bad shape because of the amount of violence, hate, greed, and envy. It is emanating not only from the individuals but also from movies, television, and news media. People always try to change things on the outside. They don't understand that it has to start from the inside."

Each student in the Compassion course has a Nelson Mandela within—the seeds of greatness and vision. In fact, we all do. Whatever is beneficial, whatever is loving, whatever is wise, if watered, grows. I see it in the students when suddenly they wake up to the beauty of life or contact something great inside themselves. It might be a moment of oneness with an oak tree during a walking meditation. It might occur when they listen wholeheartedly to a classmate's personal story. It might be at a party when suddenly they see how absurd it is to get "wasted," sick with a hangover, and call this fun. Sometimes it's a reading for class that ignites the spark. I remember a student who came dancing into class after reading a chapter on the Indigenous Grandmothers and their "Life is sacred" teaching. The student was joyous to discover something meaningful to her. I watched as the seed of this truth—"Life is sacred"—took root in her life. Certain negative habits started to recede as she watered this single truth with her attention. One truth—"Life is sacred"—had the power to undo long-standing destructive habits without ever pointing them out. In whatever way, a light suddenly comes on. They see through the cloud of false conditioning and touch something real.

Mandela's breakthrough in that prison cell is an option for all of us when we feel bitter or oppressed. As biologist Rupert Sheldrake has demonstrated, when one person or group does something on the planet that hasn't been done before, then it creates a new collective memory and others can do it more easily. This is the effect of our interconnected consciousness, which is pervasive and nonlocal. Sheldrake found, for example, that as soon one person on the planet solves a crossword puzzle, other people are more likely to solve the puzzle. Such invisible organizing patterns are inherent to all species (e.g., beehives and termite colonies). He uses the term "morphogenetic field (M-field)." Roger Bannister, for example, created a new M-field when he broke the four-minute mile in 1954, setting a record that was soon repeated by many other runners. In a similar way, we might look at Nelson Mandela and those interviewed in this book as having created new M-fields in the realm of human consciousness, breaking open previously unknown pathways of the heart that change the world through the power of love. Of course they didn't set out to change the world or create a new M-field; they simply faced the difficult circumstances of their lives with willingness and inner bravery.

We never know the wider impact of our private inner triumphs. We don't have to be famous or perfect—just willing to say, "Yes, maybe there is hope," instead of giving up in despair or blaming others.

Bill Wilson died decades ago, but his "yes" turned out to be a major breakthrough from addiction that remains a liberating imprint in human consciousness. Here is a story that brings it home: When a friend of mine was nineteen, she almost died of a drug overdose in the bathroom of a cheap motel. Now she's twenty-five years clean and sober, with peace of mind, children who love her, and a job she enjoys. She wanted to go to the cemetery in Vermont where Bill Wilson is buried to pay respect to him. Here is her account:

When I drove into the parking lot, my hopes were dashed. Snow covered the entire grounds of the cemetery. Everywhere I looked, there was white. How was I going to find his grave? I got out of the car and started looking around. Finally, to my amazement, I saw a wide path of footprints in the snow, and they were all going to the same place. I followed the footprints and, sure enough, it was the grave marker for Bill W. I stood there for a long time. I thought of all the countless people who are alive today because of that man.

She was quiet for a few seconds, and then said, "You never know the difference you can make just by saying yes to hope in the most despairing moment of your life."

The journey of transformation begins in myriad ways. Prison cell. Hospital room. Bathroom in a cheap motel. Alcoholic blackout. Forest cabin. College classroom. Himalayan cave. Encounter at a roadside cafe. Weeping in a slave dungeon. Heartbreak. Meeting the teacher. Being given a second chance. A phone call just as you're sitting down to dinner—"We have some bad news...." What we decide in those critical moments affects not only our life but all of life. Do we have the courage to live from the realest part of ourselves—our heart?

From my studies and experiences, I knew the power of love was real, but as an academic I wanted to verify it scientifically. I wondered, *What's the effect of a loving intention on the world we live in? Can the impact of human love be measured?*

## EXPLORING THE SCIENCE OF LOVE

The people in this book hold a spiritual worldview in which human intention—especially pure and unconditional love—is a critical influence in any situation. We saw the worldwide impact of

Nelson Mandela's "change of heart." We saw how the Biehls' forgiveness turned a tragedy into a triumph for Cape Town and beyond. We
saw the communal healing made possible when Belvie and Dedan
enlarged their hearts to include their historic enemy. We saw how the
Indigenous Grandmothers worked with the power of love to influence physical phenomena. Fervent prayers redirected a typhoon. The
Snake Dance brought rain to dying corn plants at Hopi Mesa. We
saw Mother Teresa pray for a ceasefire during the civil war in Beirut,
Lebanon, so she could rescue a group of severely disabled Muslim
children trapped in a bombed-out building—and the ceasefire happened precisely at the time she specified.

Obviously, occurrences such as the ceasefire are multifactorial,
and thus spiritual leaders like Mother Teresa and the Indigenous
Grandmothers do not claim that their intention or prayer sin-
gle-handedly caused something to happen. Rather, the take-home
message is that focused loving intention increases the likelihood of
a certain outcome. The purer the intention the greater the effect; in
other words, the more that an intention is in service to something
greater than oneself the more likely it is to influence an outcome in
the desired direction.

The people featured in this book know how to work with the
unseen subtle powers such as love in a way that potentiates resolution
and healing on the physical plane. Scientists are beginning to depict
the dynamic connection between the subtle and physical dimensions.
As my teacher wrote on the opening page of his book *Power vs. Force*:

> The skillful are not obvious
> They appear to be simpleminded
> Those who know this know the patterns of the Absolute
> To know the patterns is the Subtle Power
> The Subtle Power moves all things and has no name.

The Subtle Power, previously known only to mystics and sages,
is now breaking through to the broader public via scientific discovery.
There are thousands of scientific studies on the physical and emotional benefits of inner practices such as meditation, mindfulness,

loving-kindness, gratitude, and forgiveness. It's not uncommon for ordinary people to experience the axiom "What you hold in mind tends to manifest." Yet, since most people are concerned mainly for their own welfare, they apply the axiom only to personal goals—a job, partner, physical healing, or some other favorable occurrence in their individual lives.

On a more nuanced level, the scientific work of Dr. William A. Tiller suggests that we can radiate beneficial subtle energy *in the world at large* if we refine our consciousness into greater coherence; that through loving and focused attention, we can serve as a doorway between the realm of subtle power and the physical realm. The key is to put our own ego in service to something greater than itself, such as the innate dignity of humankind, the meaningfulness and sacredness of life, Love, Truth, etc. Such principles are the source of real power, as we saw in the example of Nelson Mandela.

The physics of Dr. Tiller demonstrate the powerful effect of such pure intentions. He told me, "People need to come to the place of serving Love, not self." Tiller's physics reveal that love is at its greatest power when it is unconditional, focused, and selfless. The potency of this kind of selflessness is captured in archetypal films such as *Wonder Woman*. At a pivotal point in the film, the superhero focuses with laser-like precision to align her intention to the principle of Love. At that point, her subtle (spiritual) power condenses into a magnificent laser that obliterates an entire era of negativity on the physical plane.

When I spoke with Dr. Tiller, Professor Emeritus of the Stanford University Department of Materials Science, he likened human intention to a laser. In landmark experiments over the past few decades, carried out with rigorous scientific methodology, Tiller and his colleagues have demonstrated the power of loving human intention 1) to change the properties of organic and inorganic matter; 2) to change the thermodynamic qualities of spaces; and 3) to change both matter and space from long distances, even from across the world.[173] On this last point, here are two examples: 1) working with physicists in Berlin, Tiller conducted a successful experiment to "broadcast" an intention from his lab in Arizona to change the pH by 1.5

units in water located in Berlin, in a particular room, on a particular floor, of a particular house, on a particular corner; and 2) Tiller and his colleagues carried out an experiment to broadcast an intention from Arizona to Australia to alleviate the suffering associated with autism—in both children and their parents. All participants in the treatment groups showed immediate and remarkable improvement.

Lastly, Tiller and his colleague Nisha Manek, M.D., (Mayo Clinic), have demonstrated that the subtle energy of loving-kindness, present in the relics of Buddhist Masters, can be imprinted onto a simple electrical device used to hold an intention statement. When the imprinted device is placed into a lab space and activated by human intention, measurable changes occur: 1) thermodynamically, a raised gauge symmetry; 2) biologically, the ordering of the atom molecules into greater coherence; and 3) energetically, the alignment of the physical body's acupuncture-meridian system, which has a healthful effect on cellular function.[174]

The conclusion to be drawn is this: Love is a subtle energy that induces coherence in material environments and physical bodies. In sum, real love heals. Tiller emphasizes that human beings can become channels of healing love in the world: "There is a profound connectivity between any part of nature and another. Any one of us can influence all biological life forms around us."[175]

Like most people, I sensed the truth of the above statement, that we are all interconnected and our intentions affect others. "That place has a good vibe." "That person lights up the room." Such remarks are common; they signal our intuition that people radiate a certain energy and that different places have different energy fields. People with the gift of clairvoyance can see the energy exchanges between people and in group meetings. Even the most ordinary of us know whether or not we feel welcome as soon as we walk into a room. "The place felt creepy. I didn't want to go inside." "It had a friendly feeling. I felt safe."

Despite these everyday intuitions, I had a nagging doubt: "Wait a minute, this sounds woo-woo. Where's the science to prove it?" My life had been transformed by the unconditional love of my teacher. There was something about his energy field that had a healing effect on me; I couldn't deny the resolution of many lifelong physical and emotional problems, including many allergies. A new dimension of clarity, joy, and beauty opened up to me. Even some of the places that had been painful for me became illuminated by the Presence of Light. Here was one experience:

> I went to a Sunday worship service at *the* church. I hadn't set foot in there for years. It was Mother's Day, and we were all home to visit Mom and Dad. I knew it would mean a lot to Mom for me to attend church with the family. I was thinking: *These church people are narrow and unevolved. There's no spirit here.* To my surprise, when the communion was served, something exquisite happened. I saw streams of light rise up from the top of each person's head to the heavens and back again. It was obvious that God loves each and every one. The place was full of thin streams of Light ascending and descending for each person. I may have been an outsider in this group, but the Light was not.

After meeting my teacher, I'd had a handful of such glimpses into the interpenetration of the solid and subtle realms, yet I still couldn't erase decades of academic training overnight, and I wanted some sort of understanding according to criteria of logic and measurement. I wondered, *Where are the scientists who are exploring the interface of the seen and the unseen? Have they found ways to measure the impact of love's subtle power on physical life?*

Once I started looking, I found many scientists who'd undergone profound experiences with the unseen subtle domains. It took them years, even decades, to come to terms with the experience, which led to breakthroughs in their scientific understanding. Their colleagues and family members often took a dim view of their paradigm shifts. At great personal cost, these scientists insisted on the truth of their experience and felt a responsibility to share it publicly. This is how human understanding has always evolved. Certain people are given breakthrough experiences. If they have the courage to probe into the phenomena, integrate the information, and share their discoveries, then our knowledge advances.

For example, physicist Fritjof Capra was sitting on the beach one day and had a mystic experience in which the usual boundaries of separateness dissolved and he saw the oneness of life, with its dance of interacting energies. It took him years to integrate this experience with his understanding of physics and Eastern philosophy, and then he wrote *The Tao of Physics*, which remains a classic after thirty years.

This kind of mystic experience can happen out of nowhere, and to anyone. An academic acquaintance once told me of a moment, three decades prior, when she was a teenager sitting on the grass, and suddenly the blades of grass appeared to dissolve into pure energy. "It was the most magical moment of my life. The grass seemed to be alive with the same energy as my body. The grass was not separate from me." When I was at a retreat with Sadhguru Vasudev, I heard a similar experience. Sadhguru had instructed us, "Go outside and observe a single piece of life." When we came back inside, a woman shared: "In the moonlight, I saw the grass blades vibrating—they appeared to be pure energy. I felt like I was under a spell, and now I'm back to reality." Sadhguru laughed and said, "That was not a spell—that is Reality. Ordinarily you are under the spell of separateness and you do not see the real Reality!"

Sadhguru is a mystic, that is, a human whose baseline everyday awareness is what Capra described. The sense of personal self has dissolved into that which is Universal. Though the mystic appears to be a physical body like other people, the identity is with the Self, not the self. The Self is seen to be in all things, the same substance permeating everything. My teacher once said, "When I look in other people's eyes, there is only one Self."[176]

This phenomenon occurred to Harvard University Medical School brain scientist Dr. Jill Bolte-Taylor. As a stroke erupted in her brain and voided her left-brain cognition, with its sense of separateness, Dr. Bolte-Taylor became "enfolded by a blanket of tranquil euphoria" and "expanding sense of grace"; her "consciousness soared into an all-knowingness, a "being at one" with the universe."[177] She saw that she was more a fluid than a solid, and that her body's molecules were vibrating in a spectacular energy dance with everything around her—water, objects, air, people. Everything was composed of trillions of particles of energy. This awakened perspective revealed the illusion of the ego. Lodged in the analytical left brain, the ego was seen to be a small group of molecules that leads people to believe they exist as an "I," a separate solid in the world. But when that restricted brain circuitry was voided by the stroke, the truth of existence shone forth: "I was simply a being of light radiating in the world."[178] In that state of oneness, it was no longer possible to feel lonely or isolated, and she felt immense gratitude to be given an experience of who she really is—an eternal state of peace and joy. "I'm no authority, but I think Buddhists would say I entered the mode of existence they call Nirvana. In the absence of my left hemisphere's analytical judgment, I was completely entranced by feelings of tranquility, safety, blessedness, euphoria, and omniscience."[179]

Though to outside observers Bolte-Taylor looked tragic, a drooling stroke patient unable to speak or feed herself, on the inside she was experiencing euphoria, in love with her existence. She knew she was perfectly whole and beautiful just as she was. Even in a condition of seeming dementia and mental disability, her soul was vast, joyful, and totally at peace with the universe. The experience was so exquisite that she didn't want to "squeeze" the "enormousness of [her] spirit" back into her body.[180] She chose to do so only out of love for humanity. Since she was a brain scientist, she knew that her account of the experience would be helpful to others and to science. This was truly a heroic choice as it took eight long years of recovery for her to relearn all the left-brain functions of how to walk, talk, and other basic skills. The power of love was a critical factor in her recovery, and it took the form of her mother, who moved to be with her and see after every step of her healing process.

Bolte-Taylor affirms that the timeless, tranquil, loving, and compassionate right-brain consciousness is available to everyone at all times as soon as they choose it. Instead, most people choose to live from their left-brain logical linear mode, which defines them as separate from others according to their physical body. She notes that human beings share 99.9% of identical genetic sequences, and thus all of our hostility hinges on the difference of .01%! Our right-brain consciousness knows that we are all literally one with each other, sharing the same energy, and in that state of awareness, compassion for everything and everyone is a natural occurrence. The Golden Rule is known to be more than a precept; it's an actual fact that what we do to others we do to ourselves.

Everything is "energy," Bolte-Taylor says, and human beings are "concentrated packets of energy" that can be divided into two groups: those that bring energy and those that drain energy.[181] A key point she makes in her book, lectures, and interviews is that people need to "take responsibility for the kind of energy" they bring.[182] Those who take energy are self-absorbed, coercive, anxious, angry, and preoccupied with past or future. Those who give energy are tuned in to others, respectful, positive, caring, accepting, dedicated, and present to the moment. When Bolte-Taylor was in the hospital recovering from the stroke, she turned herself away from negative people and forced herself to rouse for loving, thoughtful, and kind people. She needed every ounce of help, and knew instinctively that the energy of positive people would have a healing effect on her. Reading this makes us more conscious of the energy we bring to all of the circumstances in our lives.

Bolte-Taylor's discovery matches that of my teacher. His book, *Power vs. Force*, proposes that there are two basic categories of energy: power, which has a positive and life-affirming effect, and force, which has a draining effect. As we saw in the examples of Mandela and Gandhi, power is greater than force. Whereas force is *power over*, true power comes from within, sourced from the subtle planes. My teacher and Bolte-Taylor are both scientists who had mind-blowing mystic experiences and then worked hard to articulate what they came to know in a way that would be meaningful to ordinary people. Their research confirms that we all radiate energy, and that loving energy has healing potency. The power of love is real.

This was also the conclusion of Dr. Eben Alexander, neurosurgeon and author of the best-selling book *Proof of Heaven*. Suddenly hit with an extremely rare and acute bacterial meningoencephalitis, Alexander went into a coma that lasted seven days. He was given only a slim chance of survival—and no chance of recovery should he happen to survive. Medical staffers were shocked when, on the seventh day, he opened his eyes and progressed beyond expectation to robust functionality. Even more shocking to them, and to Alexander himself, was his account of a near-death experience. As a neurosurgeon, he had never believed patients when they came back from comas and talked of mystical experiences. He had always held to a conventional scientific "physicalist" view in which there is no room for nonphysical consciousness to see, know, hear, or experience anything. Yet, while in his coma, he made a journey beyond space-time into several different realms where he experienced an atmosphere of Infinite Love, leading him to conclude: "Love is, without a doubt, the basis of everything."[183]

Having read these accounts, I was interested to explore my own nonphysical consciousness. As Dr. Tiller told me, "Experiential development of Self is crucial." Following in the steps of Dr. Alexander and other scientists, I went to The Monroe Institute in Virginia, founded decades ago by Robert Monroe. This is a hub for people interested in exploring subtle domains through various methods. It has been a significant community for scientists like Eben Alexander to further research experiences that fall outside the box of the dominant physicalist scientific paradigm. Monroe pioneered a hemi-synch music technology that creates a state of deep relaxation and inner coherence to facilitate explorations of nonphysical consciousness. As many meditators know, when the physical body completely relaxes, the inner consciousness can expand beyond the body or leave it. At The

Monroe Institute, for example, a friend of mine learned how to go out of body and read what was written on a piece of paper inside of a small box. The training at Monroe is summed up in the statement: You are more than your physical body.

I had some interesting experiences at the institute, and I'll mention here the one that surprised me the most: a training exercise in remote viewing. I'd never been exposed to remote viewing before and it sounded far-fetched. According to Joseph McMoneagle, one of the US government's top remote viewers, remote viewing is "a human ability to produce information about a targeted object, person, place, or event while being completely isolated from the target by space, time, and other forms of shielding."[184] Governments have used remote viewers to locate and draw in detail other countries' military outposts and missile stations. Also, police departments have used remote viewers to find missing persons.

Here's what happened for me in the remote viewing exercise. The workshop facilitator wrote the latitude and longitude of a location on a flip chart. He said, "This location is somewhere on Earth, in the United States. Take just a few minutes and write down or draw whatever comes to you. When the bell rings, stop." I closed my eyes, went into a meditative state, and concentrated on the location specified on the flip chart. "Darkness. Space. Now – white clouds, blue sky. A brightness that would hurt the eyes, shining metal, something heavy." Those are the words I wrote based on what I was "seeing" during those few minutes. When the bell rang, I thought: *This is stupid. What kind of place could this possibly be?* Then we watched a video of the professional remote viewer's description of his process to discover the location. Imagine my shock when the very first scenes matched what I had seen in my mind's eye! White clouds, blue sky, and a heavy metal that glinted in the sun. I was blown away. Out of all the zillions of images that could have come to mind as I was asked to focus on a totally unknown location "somewhere on Earth"! The video reveal went on for about twenty minutes, until the remote viewer, Joe McMoneagle, figured out that the target location was the arch (clad in stainless steel) at St Louis.

At that point in the class, Joe McMoneagle walked into the room. He was one of the best-known remote viewers for the US military, from 1978 to 1995. Unbeknownst to us, he was an instructor at The Monroe Institute and had been asked to make a guest appearance. He explained to our class that remote-viewing protocol requires that no one in the room knows the location. Technically, therefore, I was not remote viewing the St. Louis arch, since the facilitator was in the room and knew the location. It's quite possible that the images came to me not from the target location but from the thought field in the room. Either way, the experience verified for me that information exists outside of space and time, and that humans have the capacity to tap into the nonlocal, timeless subtle realms where all information resides. Tiller's physics is a scientific paradigm that can explain such phenomena.

McMoneagle told us that such intuitive abilities are innate to all of us. In his case, he said, they opened up after a near-death experience at age twenty-four. Stationed in Germany at the time, he was working for the US Armed Forces on a highly classified intelligence mission. He was eating dinner with his wife and a colleague at a restaurant. Suddenly, after a few sips of a cocktail, he felt sick and got up to walk outside. He heard a *pop*, went out of his body, and saw his body lying on the ground, convulsing. He'd been poisoned, and he knew who'd done it. McMoneagle said he watched as his friend put his finger in his mouth to keep him from swallowing his tongue. When the ambulance came and took his body to the hospital, he followed behind it, in his energy body. In medical terms, his body was in a coma for thirty hours and clinically dead for 8–15 minutes. In terms of consciousness, he drifted up to the ceiling of the hospital room as the staff tried to revive him. His consciousness (energy body) then fell into a tunnel and ended up in a space with the brightest light he had ever seen, with an overwhelming joy and comfort. He felt whole and complete, wanting and needing nothing. He was given a review of his life, and saw his impact on others. He felt sorrow for all the times he had acted unkindly, not acted when he could have, and misunderstood what others had needed from him. He said to us, "The

experience was observational, not judgmental." He felt a melting forgiveness wash over him.[185]

After coming back to his body and recovering from the illness,
McMoneagle returned to the military job. Doctors were certain he'd
have brain damage, but he didn't. He was, however, a changed person.
He refused to carry a gun because he didn't want to harm anyone.
And he had psychic capabilities. He began work in the military as a
remote viewer, and he also helped find missing persons. He told us, "A
rule of the psychic universe is that you cannot have a direct influence
on another person without their consent. You can't find those who
don't want to be found." McMoneagle emphasized the importance of
loving intention to be helpful to humanity.

Love and being of service to humanity was also the bottom-line
message from Dr. Elisabeth Kübler-Ross, medical doctor and catalyst
of the hospice movement in the West. Her book, *On Death and Dying*,
is a classic and her "Stages of Grief" have become a core curriculum for
health professionals worldwide. As a doctor, her conversations with
thousands of dying patients of all ages and backgrounds convinced
her of the reality of the unseen world. She subsequently had her own
vivid encounters with what she called Cosmic Consciousness. Like
other scientists, Kübler-Ross went to The Monroe Institute and used
that laboratory to further explore her own nonphysical consciousness. She recounts the full range of experiences in her autobiography,
*The Wheel of Life*. I mention only one here:

> Whatever part of my body I looked at began to vibrate
> with the same fantastic speed. The vibrations broke
> everything down to their most basic structure, so that
> when I stared at anything, my eyes feasted on the bil-
> lions of dancing molecules. I indulged in the peace,
> beauty, and serenity of the vibrating world. Whatever
> my eyes landed on vibrated—walls, ceiling, win-
> dows, trees outside. My vision, which extended for
> miles and miles, caused me to see everything—from
> a blade of grass to a wooden door—in its molecular

structure, in its vibrations. I observed with great awe and respect that everything had a life, a divinity. All the while, I continued to move slowly through the lotus flower, toward the light. Finally, I was merged with it, one with the warmth and love. A million everlasting orgasms cannot describe the sensation of the love, warmth and sense of welcome that I experienced....

After decades of sitting with countless dying people as they left their bodies, Dr. Kübler-Ross concluded that the main purpose of human life is the giving and receiving of unconditional love.

My study of these scientific cases led me to conclude: 1) There is a vast, timeless, dynamic, infinitely loving Reality that is more real than the physical life commonly assumed to be "reality"; 2) the unseen subtle planes are where the real power is, and these realms are infused with unconditional love; 3) Love is the ultimate law of the universe; 4) yet on the physical plane, there are very few access points of real, unconditional love and most people are oblivious to the presence of love; 5) the rare human beings who are aligned with love function as an access point or doorway or channel of this loving energy from the subtle realms to the physical plane; and 6) this subtle energy of love is what touches everyone and everything around them, activating the potential for transformation, healing, and the oneness that lies within every form of life.

This last point is observable in everyday life when genuine caring and kindness often elicit a spark of recognition from a fellow human. It's what Grandmother Mona Polacca referred to as "recognizing your sacred beginning—the sacredness you share with all of life." It's the "imprint of the Absolute" that Sufi teacher Llewellyn Vaughan-Lee said is hidden within every living thing. Christian mystic Meister Eckhart called it the "divine spark" within every person. When this spark is blown upon, it ignites. Given attention, it comes to life.

If consciously nourished with loving intention, it has enormous capacity to transform an individual and, yes, the world. This is why Vaughan-Lee and others teach that "subtle activism" is the most effective means for social transformation.[186]

From these findings, I concluded that activism that stays only on the level of physical and political efforts is similar to moving the furniture on the *Titanic*—it does little to stop a sinking ship. An uptake of new energy is needed to make a real change. The source of that new energy lies hidden within each form of life. For humans, this energy source lies within the heart and remains largely untapped (despite much sentimentalism and talk about "love" in our culture). When the real depth of the heart is touched and awakened, then something dynamic and visionary can occur. At that point, what had seemed impossible becomes possible. New ideas emerge. There is a ray of hope in what had seemed a hopeless situation. Love is the greatest power in the universe, and its most potent access point is the human heart. When hearts move in tandem, then societal healing is especially momentous.

This is what my personal encounters had taught me, and now it had been experientially validated. Next, I wondered, *If the heart has the power, then how do we tap into it?*

## Two Classroom Experiments

A hint of something occurred one day when I was sitting at my desk at the university. I noticed a young man walking into the Meditation Room next door to my office. He looked upset, so I went in to check on him and found that he was hyperventilating. He said, "Can you show me how to meditate? I've heard it helps with anxiety, but I have no idea how to do it. I'm having a panic attack right now, and I need to calm down."

I asked him to lie down on one of the long cushions available for deep relaxation. He closed his eyes. I guided him in a deep-relaxation meditation—tensing and relaxing each muscle, and then shifting attention to the breath. Usually, this process calms a person. The heart rate evens out, muscles relax, and breathing softens; however, it didn't work for him. He continued to breathe in a panicked way.

Then I told him to focus on someone he loved. Instantly, his breathing softened, the tension in his face released, and his body relaxed. I told the young man to drop into his heart and stay with the feeling of love for as long as he wanted. After a long time, he opened his eyes.

I asked, "What happened for you?"

"I thought of my dad. I know he'll love me no matter what. Just before I walked in here, I found out that I didn't make the football team. My whole life went up in flames when I heard that. I panicked—If I don't have an athletic scholarship, I can't afford college, and then my whole life is ruined."

"And when you focused on your dad?"

"It brought me peace. I knew Dad would love me anyway. Just thinking of him gave me what I needed to get through this crisis. Maybe what happened today isn't the worst thing that could have happened. I'm going to look into some other options."

Nothing in the young man's outer life changed, yet he experienced mental clarity and inner peace. He gained a creative outlook on a hopeless situation. New options came into view. Anxiety dissipated and he felt serene and happy. All he did was shift his attention from head to heart. Recollecting his father's love connected this young man to his heart. The example is so useful because of its ordinariness. Clearly, anytime and anywhere, we have the option to go within and think of someone we love. It reminded me of Viktor Frankl's account of focusing on the inner image of his wife Tilly. Though he was in the bleakest and most grueling of situations—a Nazi concentration camp—he suddenly felt solace and joy. The power of love induced by a single recollection of someone we love has the capacity to transform our inner state completely.

"The heart knows," we say. Its knowledge is activated when we recall something or someone we love—a place, person, pet, Divine Being, etc. This is the power of spiritual practices described by the teachers in this book. Practices such as tonglen, the Jesus Prayer, and walking with gratitute open the heart. When the heart opens, the energy of love is released and has a healing effect on body and mind and the world at large. Visionary solutions emerge that are far more effective than what the mind can strategize. Whereas the mind sees parts, the heart knows the whole.

At first, the young man had catastrophized, "If I don't play foot-ball, my life is ruined." After the heart meditation, he said, "Maybe it's not the worst thing that could have happened. I'm going to look into some other options." Just a few minutes of a loving inner environment and he broke free of his limited thought pattern. Under the influence of genuine care and kindness, which can be internally generated, the body relaxes and brain circuitry opens. Love brings a release of vital and creative energy that wasn't there before. What had previously not been possible, with love, becomes so.

The second classroom experiment unfolded one day when a group of students came into my Issues in Modern Religion class and said, "We want to test the power of our intention." They reached into their backpacks and pulled out two empty plastic Gatorade bottles and a container of boiled white rice. "Here's our equipment. We want to make it a class experiment."

I looked at them and then at the bottles and rice. Not wanting to squelch their curiosity, I inquired, "How do you propose to go about this?"

"We want to see if hateful words have a different impact on rice than loving words. We'd like to put the rice into these two bottles and label them: 1) We hate you. We want to kill you; and 2) We love you. We thank you."

"How long do you plan to run this experiment?" I secretly hoped it would be short-lived. The unpleasant image came to mind of two bottles of gross decaying rice.

"Two weeks. And we'd like for the entire class to participate. We thought it would be cool if we vocalized the words to each bottle at the start of every class session."

The whole group lit up with excitement. They looked more enthusiastic about this crazy experiment than they had about our sessions on religious pluralism and modern theologies. Their animated faces tipped me over the edge of skepticism, and I said, "Okay, let's try it."

They taped the words onto the two bottles. At the beginning of every class session, we took each bottle, one by one, and spoke the words on the label to the rice in that bottle. The rest of the time, both bottles sat on a shelf in my office. If I happened to think of it when I was in my office, I vocalized the words on the label to the rice in that bottle. At the end of two weeks, the rice grains in the HATE bottle had decomposed into mush. The rice grains in the LOVE bottle remained mostly intact. When I opened the bottles, the rice in the HATE bottle exploded out and splattered my hand, desk, and chair. The students called this "an explosion of rice guts." When I opened the bottle of LOVE rice, nothing occurred. It was peaceful. Though I had taught the importance of loving intention for years, I was quite surprised by its effect on rice!

Obviously, the experiment wasn't scientific. Nonetheless, it seemed to be a hint of something. It was dramatic to see the change in the HATE rice after two weeks. We spent part of a class session pondering the experience and its implications. One student, a psychology major, applied it to the psyche: "It makes sense to me that if someone is hated, if they're told such horrible things, like if they're bullied by peers or abused by parents, then they would decay or explode with anger." Another student turned the focus inward: "I think that if a person is self-hating, if their thoughts are full of rejection and self-loathing, then their body and health suffer." Another student, a biology major and also a classical musician, pointed us to research being done to study the effect of music on the growth of plants: "Plants thrive when Mozart is continually broadcast. Mozart is beautiful music. It seems to me that beauty is like loving intention and would have a beneficial influence on biological life." A sociology major added, "I just read an article for one of my classes that relates to this. It showed the positive impact of random acts of kindness on the people who witness them. Just seeing someone else be kind to others or the environment—like picking up trash—has a positive effect."

The discussion continued as different students shared their academic and personal knowledge. We ended in general agreement that qualities of love such as kindness, compassion, forgiveness, and artistic beauty have a beneficial impact on health, psychology, and the environment. We didn't know how to prove this scientifically, yet the lack of proof did not mean it wasn't true. It meant that the methods to measure the effect of love were not yet available—or so we thought...

And then I met Dr. William Tiller. He had by that point written several books and hundreds of articles about scientific demonstrations to measure what he called the "subtle energy" of loving-kindness and the power of loving human intention to influence the material world. In some experiments, intention changed the properties of organic and inorganic matter, such as altering the pH balance in water by a significant degree. In other experiments, intention was significantly successful in relieving the suffering of people with depression, anxiety, and autism—even from across the world in the latter case. In still other experiments, intention changed the thermodynamic qualities of spaces, producing high levels of coherence, which in effect conditions the spaces into zones of healing. Love, Tiller found, was the "crucial" element in the intentions.

Bill and Jean Tiller
(courtesy of The William A. Tiller Foundation).

*Chapter Twenty-Two*

# THE POWER OF INTENTION

Encounter with Dr. William A. and Jean Tiller

*There is a profound connectivity between*
*any part of nature and another.*

*Any one of us can influence all*
*biological life forms around us....*

—WILLIAM A. TILLER

A fter many years of probing the interface of the seen and unseen realms, I was ready to encounter Dr. Tiller. "When the student is ready, the teacher appears" is a saying that applies to many areas of life a person might be exploring. Tiller told me that we're not given information until we're ready to receive it. If we give meaning to something—as I had done with the crazy rice experiment—then doors open to relevant experiences that further illumine our search for truth. If we discount the hints by saying, "Oh, that's just silly," then the doors to Reality remain closed, our quest stunted.

My meeting with Bill and Jean Tiller was catalytic for my quest. They confirmed that we have the capacity to change the world by our intention. "Mind over matter" is a concept I'd heard for years, and Tiller's research confirms it as fact. This is a major challenge to the current scientific orthodoxy of materialistic reductionism, which holds that human consciousness does not influence the material world. Tiller told me:

> Decades ago, when I first started this kind of research, I was following my intuition. I wanted to test the assumption of René Descartes in the early 1600s that no qualities of human consciousness, intention, emotion, mind, or spirit could significantly influence a well-designed targeted experiment of physical reality. At that time in history, Descartes' statement was important because people were still stuck in the theocratic perspective. With his assumption, you could separate science from religion, a very useful theoretical move at the time. The problem in today's world is that orthodox science and orthodox medicine still unconsciously hold that assumption—even though it has never been tested in over 400 years! My decision was to go to work and test Descartes' assumption. We started with the first phase—to show that intention could alter different physical materials. Then, in the second phase, we showed that intention could alter or "condition" physical space. The third stage was to show that intention could be broadcast across a long distance.

Tiller's scientific career has followed two parallel tracks. In the conventional one, he's a world-class expert in the science of crystallization—the transition of physical matter from one form to another—with publication of over 450 articles, three books, and several patents. "I've always had a great feeling for crystals, I love crystals, I love looking at them. Obviously somewhere in a previous life I did an awful lot with crystals."

In his avocational track in the science of "psychoenergetics"—his word for the interface of the seen (physical) and unseen (spiritual) dimensions—he has published over 150 articles and four seminal books elucidating the influence of intention on physical matter and environments. His wife, Jean, he told me, has been crucial to his experiments in the realm of intention.

## BACKGROUND

Bill Tiller grew up in a poor family in Toronto, Canada. He said, "One of the things I learned from those circumstances was how to focus, work hard, and get a job done." A high school teacher who saw his genius awakened a love for learning in him and convinced his parents to allow him to go to college, the first in his family to do so. "They said they could afford to feed me and keep me at home, but there was no money for me to go and live on campus." He rode his bike to the University of Toronto to study physics, and joined a naval service to earn the tuition money. "I learned things weren't going to come easy. I almost failed physics during my first year and decided that I really had to apply myself, which I did, and was first or second in my graduating class."

After graduation, he married Jean and did graduate work with a professor in materials science, creating a new model in the science of crystallization. "For my master's degree, I gave the theoretical part of it, and I did the experimental proof part for my Ph.D." Cambridge University Press later published the two books that remain classics in the field. "To be honest, I was a world-class expert in crystallization along with all the physics and mathematics that go into it. You're dealing with the transformation of material from one form into another—liquid to solid, gas to liquid, gas to solid. The transformation issue is important in the making of semiconductor chips and other technologies."

In the mid-1950s, he and Jean moved to the U.S. when Bill took a job at Westinghouse Research Laboratories. "I had a group of people, about a dozen, who worked with me, and most of our work was supported by the government. In the nine years I was there, I published about sixty scientific papers." They wanted to promote him to a higher management position, but he declined because he preferred to focus on his scientific research, and he saw that the company's greatest resource—its people—wasn't being developed. "I thought the real value of any company is its people, and that you should work hard to build the people by giving them opportunities to grow personally as well as do their work." Lack of personal development was the same flaw he saw in the modern education system: "They teach knowledge but no experiential development of Self. Those two things have to go hand in hand."

Bill left Westinghouse when Stanford University offered him a tenured professorship in the department of materials science, and thus began his thirty-five-year career in academe. As he and Jean drove cross-country to begin a new life, she said to him, "Bill, when we get to California, let's pull together the spiritual side of our life." Jean had always been drawn to the intuitive and spiritual. She just "knew" things. Her father was a police officer, and she knew of occasions when a psychic had helped the police force find missing persons. The police didn't reveal their use of psychics because they didn't want it reported in the newspapers. Unlike Bill, who rejected religious institutions at an early age, Jean saw no conflict between her metaphysical side and her religious life: "When we first met, Bill tended to be more agnostic. I always felt that there was more than what I was learning in church, but I never felt that I had to throw religion away." When she and Bill found the writings of American psychic Edgar Cayce, it filled in a missing piece for her: "I found what I wasn't getting from church, especially reincarnation."

In 1964, they joined the A.R.E. (the Association for Research and Enlightenment, founded by Cayce) and then started a study and meditation group in their home. Tiller said, "Meditation was like coming home. I took to it like a fish to water." For him it seemed "a natural thing for a scientist" to study inner workings, "as it involved learning about phenomena of nature." To his surprise, other scientists turned out to be more critical than curious about exploring the inner terrain. Whereas most stayed loyal to their theories, Tiller thought it was "healthy to question inherited dogma."

The meditation technique the Tillers practiced was simple: "First, you sit in a straight-back chair and you focus your intention on something. As your mind drifts, you keep bringing it back to the something. I really learned how to keep a focus. Then, the next ten minutes is where you open yourself and let your mind go wherever it's going to go, and you just track it." Both skills—focusing and witnessing—helped him handle his growing professional responsibilities. He became department chair at Stanford, taught graduate students, continued his research, and served as a consultant for various industries.

Tiller's initiation into psychoenergetics research came in his first sabbatical from Stanford when he received a Guggenheim fellowship and went to Oxford, England. When he, Jean, and their children left for Oxford, he picked up a little book, *The Psychic Discoveries Behind the Iron Curtain* by Ostrander and Schroeder. Bill was confronted with the question that would become his life's most important work: "How might the universe be constructed to allow this crazy-seeming kind of stuff to naturally coexist with the orthodox science I'm doing every day at the Stanford labs with my Ph.D. students?" His challenge was to create a model of physics in which orthodox science and pyschoenergetics could both be true. Unlike other scientists, he wasn't willing to discount psychic phenomena just because the current scientific paradigm couldn't explain them. Over the years, through trial and error, the Tillers gained spiritual discernment in their experiences with psychics. "Psychics are people like anyone else," he told me. "There are the good ones, there are the great ones, and then there are the not so good and the not so great." The not so good ones "do not follow a spiritual path" and "use their gifts as they will."

He put himself to the task of creating a new paradigm, and Jean's role was indeed crucial. "Even though I get most of the credit because I'm the public figure, my work would not have been possible without Jean as a supportive partner. She believed in the truth and importance of what I was doing, and she has a sensitivity to the higher dimensions that strongly nourished the spiritual core of the projects."

Bill and Jean knew they'd been with each other in other lifetimes and had come together in this one to do a certain work. They valued each other's different gifts and temperaments and credited their marital happiness to these basic principles: "To respect the differences, needs, and the strengths of the other. Begin to see yourself in the other. Take risks and be willing to carry your partner along with your own interests. And be willing to go along with their interests too. There's so much to gain by being in double harmony with the other person." They emphasized humor and affection—"So many hugs a day and so many laughs a day," Jean told me.

Their daily one-hour meditation practice was the space out of which Bill's new paradigm of physics emerged:

> As Jean and I did our daily meditation practice, I held the question like a brick in my palm, like a supplicant asking for help with a problem. In doing that, often some measure of light comes, not a clear answer, but in the realm of intuition and feeling about something. After our meditation session, Jean and I would discuss it. She is very intelligent, with a high level of sensitivity in many domains. Then I'd go upstairs and work on it all day in my study. I put all the intuitive ideas to the test. I asked myself, "Does it violate any experimental data?" I didn't care about theories. I wanted to know if it violated any experimental data. And by the end of the day, I'd come up with more questions. The next day, I took those questions into the meditation, and then the next day, the next day, the next day. After six months, I had a reasonable picture as to how a model might be constructed, and it was very clear that no progress would be made unless we could go outside of distance-time. As long as we could expand beyond distance-time, there was a real possibility that the two kinds of stuff could be connected. The barrier was that the orthodox science community and also the medical community think in terms of distance-time only. That's their mindset. At

any rate, after six months, I came up with a working hypothesis model that was multidimensional.

When he returned to Stanford, he resigned from administrative and consulting positions so he could devote as much time as possible to testing his model through experiments. The first area of work, he said, "was continued experiential development of Self, because you can't continue to make progress unless you feel it inside." And for the next decades, he led a dual life as an orthodox scientist and as a pioneering researcher in psychoenergetics. Through rigorous experiments, he produced a new model of physics that demonstrates the significant influence of conscious intention on the material world.

His Stanford colleagues weren't happy with his study of psychoenergies.

> I made the erroneous assumption that, since I had been highly thought of as a 'normal' scientist in my field, surely the scientists who had respected me would be interested to read the new stuff I was doing. But, of course, I was quite wrong. It was a naive assumption on my part. Scientists are like most folks—they like where they are, they follow rather than lead, they don't want to take risks, and they don't want to put their reputation on the line. Fortunately, I had tenure, so as long as I did my day job and did it well, they couldn't just get rid of me.

Though it's increasingly common to hear about psychoenergetic phenomena in public, the orthodox scientific community remains closed to it. In 2004, the film *What the Bleep Do We Know!?* sought to show the link between quantum physics and consciousness, and Dr. Tiller was one of the featured experts. But the film, he said, was outrageous to most scientists: "Quantum mechanics is a second-order partial differential equation solution, whereas the things we're talking about here are higher domains of reality, higher levels of consciousness. They are things that quantum mechanics will grow into, but it's not there." Tiller's paradigm brings "the addition of intention and con-sciousness as very significant experimental variables in the study of nature."

He knows that one day his research "will find its way into quantum mechanics." Therefore he keeps a good record of his exper-iments, and the Tiller Foundation website provides a library of free "White Papers" that show the formulas and findings.

> My task is to keep good records and write up all the experiments and theoretical models that we've worked on for decades. One day, other scientists will be ready for them. Right now, the orthodox sci-entific community is behaving exactly like the the-ocratic community behaved in the days of Galileo, Copernicus, Kepler, and Newton. They have just as much hubris about their assumptions as those who rejected Galileo, et al. But they too will change. They'll open the door and see that it's a remarkable adventure ahead of them, not only in the study of sci-ence but in the awareness of themselves.

## PERSONAL ENCOUNTER

I met Bill Tiller at the Loving Kindness Buddha Relic Tour when it was on exhibit in Arizona. He invited me to come to Scottsdale to sit in on a brainstorming session with him and his laboratory staff. At the lab meeting, they discussed the "broadcasting of intention" to improve the cognitive functioning of children with autism—in Australia! This was astounding, and I understood why he describes his experiments as "mind-boggling." This is what Copernicus also faced; he boggled the minds of his contemporaries when he shared his discovery that the earth revolved around the sun. It took a long time for humankind to integrate that fact, and it's why Tiller refers to his new paradigm of physics as "the second Copernican revolution."

I pondered the magnitude of what I was hearing—long-distance broadcasting of intention from Arizona to treat autistic children in Australia. On the intuitive level, I knew that loving prayers and intentions worked outside space-time. I'd had several personal experiences with nonlocal healing effects, yet there was that nagging doubt: "Can this stuff really be scientifically demonstrated?"

Several months later, full of questions, I arrived at the home of Bill and Jean Tiller. As I crossed the threshold, the atmosphere was noticeably peaceful. During the conversation, I learned why. Spaces are "conditioned" (Tiller's word) by human intention. This is commonly noted in places of a sacred nature like cathedrals, Buddhist stupas, or Indigenous sweat lodge ceremonies. I'd experienced this effect at the Loving Kindness Buddha Relic exhibit held at our university, and an academic meeting room was transfigured into a sacred space.

The Tiller home was a domestic space conditioned by the residents' intention to be channels of love. I learned from the Tillers that everyone can condition a space through loving intention. They emphasized an attitude of service to the larger whole, and told me that this earthly plane is a classroom where love is the lesson and purity of intent the guiding principle. Everyone is here on Earth to learn and evolve. Free will is tantamount. Having compassion for others is important, but we must respect the free will of others to learn and grow from their own choices—including their mistakes.

They taught me that within the unseen subtle dimension there are infinite resources available to expand our awareness when we're ready. If we are internally coherent, then we become channels of these subtle energies into the earthly, physical plane of existence. Thus if we really want to be helpful to humanity, we need to start with the conscious development of our own inner coherence. This is what all the teachers in this book have said. In one way or another they affirm Sunlight's axiom: "Changing the world happens one heart at a time—start with your own."

# Conversation with William and Jean Tiller

## The Intention Host Device (IHD)

First, I asked Dr. Tiller how he conditions an experimental space. He uses a small electronic device that's commercially available from a medical research and development company. The device contains a simple electronic circuit, housed in a 7" × 3" × 1" black plastic box with an ON/OFF switch. It plugs into a standard wall outlet. "Years ago, I found that the device could hold an intention. It became a useful host device for all the intention experiments." He found it necessary to use a device to hold an intention for an experiment because human consciousness fluctuates quite a bit. "For scientific purposes, we needed an intention imprint that was stable and could be used from experiment to experiment. We find it consistently reproducible." The intention host device (IHD) stores a specific intention imprinted by a group of meditators when they're in a highly coherent state, and then the device can be used to condition spaces in different locations. The device objectifies the intention and makes it stable across multiple experiments. Bill explained:

> We actually do two intentions. The first is the intention for the target of the treatment group. The second intention statement is to seal the imprint in the device. This is because it can be lost quickly. It's not equilibrium thermodynamics, in which case what is done would be a change forever. It's called 'meta-stable thermodynamics.' The simplest example of meta-stable thermodynamics for people who don't deal with it every day is the laser. So as long as you keep 'pumping' it with energy, the laser device will keep lasing. But if you stop pumping, then it will stop lasing. That is a meta-stable thermodynamic state. In other words, the lasing process isn't continuous

without pumping the system to a higher free energy state. Our system is the same in the sense that we pump energy into the IHD during the imprinting session. But we discovered that the energy (i.e., information) would leak. The energy we put into the IHD leaked, and so we lost the ability to do an experiment within three to five days. By use of aluminum foil and a grounded Faraday cage, I found that I could keep the intention in the device for three to six months depending on the space.

Tiller writes a specific intention statement for each experiment he conducts. For example, when he did an experiment targeting people with depression and anxiety, he wrote an intention statement to "broadcast significant benefits to the people in the treatment group, mainly to reduce the period, the frequency, and the duration of depression and anxiety events in their life." When he feels that the intention statement is ready to be imprinted onto the IHD, he gathers four serious meditators with decades of practice—Jean, himself, and two people from the lab.

> We sit together and silently settle ourselves around a table where I put the IHD.... We all go into a deep meditative state, connect with each other, and connect with what appear to be unseen colleagues; we can feel them when they come. We focus to cleanse the environment around the device. We cohere with ourselves, we cohere with the unseen, and we cohere with what we need to cohere with in the cosmos in order to treat. Our goal is to be a channel for the unseen to flow through us. My sense is that the unseen [colleagues in other dimension], not us, do the heavy lifting in our cooperative process between dimensions. When there is the feeling of total coherence on all levels, I read the intention statement and each of us holds the intention statement in our own

way. And when the process feels cooked, with all steps of the imprinting process completed, I say, 'So be it. Thy will be done.' That's the way the intention statement for the treatment group is imprinted onto the intention host device.

Once the imprinting of the intention is complete, the IHD is ready to be used in experiments.

## Turning Science on its Head: Three Phases of Intention Research

### Changing the Properties of Physical Materials

Q:  Once you established the intention-imprinting protocol, how did you begin to test the effect of intention on physical matter?

WT:  Starting decades ago, the first phase was to imprint an intention in the IHD to change the properties of materials (living and nonliving), what we call physical reality. My colleagues and I discovered that it's possible to make a significant change in the properties of a material substance by consciously holding a clear intention to do so. We conducted four experiments that demonstrate this. In two of them, the intention was to change the acid/alkaline balance (pH) in a vessel of water—first to increase and then to decrease it by one unit.

Q:  Why use pH in water as the measure?

WT:  It's a standard scientific measure and easy to replicate in other locations.

Q:  As I understand it, to change the pH in water by one point is a significant change in physical matter. Raising pH by one point is like buying a bottled water versus a bottle of −8.0 alkaline water at the store—it's a different liquid now. And you didn't touch the water or add anything to it like magnetic energy or a chemical of any kind. The only intervention was human intention. That sounds like a really big deal.

WT:  Yes, it *is* a really big deal!

Q:  What was next?

WT:  In the third and fourth experiments, we targeted other materials. In the third experiment, we targeted an in-vitro biological molecule, alkaline phosphatase (ALP), a liver enzyme. The intention was to increase the chemical activity of ALP. Again, compared to the controls, it was remarkably successful (p-value less than 0.001). The fourth experiment targeted a living organism, fruit-fly larvae. The intention was to quicken the maturation time of the larvae to adulthood by targeting the ratio of the cell's energy-storage molecule, ATP, to its chemical precursor, ADP. And again, it was remarkably successful (p-value less than 0.001).

Q:  So these four experiments demonstrated that a specific human intention, imprinted into an intention host device and placed in a lab, altered the actual properties of different kinds of physical matter in accordance with the stated intention?

WT:  Yes, and yet there is no framework in orthodox science that can explain the success of these experiments.

## Creating a Space that Heals

Q:  So the first phase was to show that intention could alter physical matter. What was the second phase of your research?

WT:  To see if the imprinting did anything to the actual space, that is, did the IHD, imprinted with an intention, change the space into which it was placed? It became something *very* non-distance-time normal, as I explain in the White Papers. In brief, the intention *does* condition the space. When we used the imprint from the Loving Kindness Buddha Relic Tour, the change was dramatic.

Q:   I'm familiar with the Loving Kindness Buddha Relic exhibit; I can say that it altered the atmosphere of the room and we all noticed it, even our event services staff. It's mind-boggling that we could feel the compassion of Buddhist masters who've been dead for centuries! In itself, this is an example of the power of intentions made from far away in space and time. And now you've found a way to measure it. You placed an IHD at the exhibit?

WT:   One of my colleagues, Nisha Manek, M.D., hosted the three-day exhibit in California. The IHD was placed in the room near the relic table during the exhibit. It was a passive imprint—the IHD just sat there. Then this Relic IHD, imprinted with the Loving Kindness essence of the Relic Tour, was sent to me in Arizona where I put it in an unused room and took measurements for a few weeks. Nothing happened. There was no change in pH or any other measurable space condition. We were puzzled. Then, however, we made an intention statement asking specifically for the energy to be made manifest in a measurable way:"We respectfully request that the excess thermodynamic free energy aspect of this loving kindness essence be made manifest in this space so that we can experimentally measure its thermodynamic magnitude via the active pH, temperature, and magnetic field sensors present in this space." The effect was immediate and dramatic. The pH increased by 2.5 units within two weeks and it kept climbing, so the experiment was stopped. The answer was clear. The Relic IHD was robustly conditioning the room.

Q:   Mind-blowing! The intention statement made all the difference. That's when the space was measurably different?

WT:   Indeed. In thermal energy terms, this number is very large. It would take an increase of about 700 degrees Celsius for it to occur. The measured thermodynamic free energy change was probably due to a large decrease of thermodynamic entropy via an increased coherence in the strongly conditioned space.

Q: My understanding of what you just said is that the IHD imprinted with the intention of Loving Kindness from the relic exhibit dramatically altered the thermodynamics of the room it was placed in. There were measurable fluctuations in pH, conductivity, and air and water temperature. The room became measurably more coherent, with a higher-gauge symmetry state effect correlating to a higher level of consciousness.

WT: Yes—and this finding corresponds to everyday life experience, does it not? We are aware that each space has a certain "feel" to it. Dramatic examples of highly coherent space are the great cathedrals of Europe, conditioned by centuries of devotion and prayer.

Q: I believe you use the term "subtle energy" to distinguish the energy of Love from the forces already established by orthodox science—gravity, nuclear forces, and electromagnetism. In other words, the Loving Kindness Buddha Relic IHD had a huge effect on the room, but the effect can't be explained with reference to standard concepts of energy. Could one say your research demonstrates that those relics have a subtle energy that has a healing effect on the environment and the people in it? It's not going too far to say that?

WT: Yes, it has a healing effect, and no, I don't think it's going too far. And statistically the numbers from our experiment are very big. But not everyone will recognize it. There is freedom of choice. People don't have to accept it, so we let go of being frustrated at people if they're resistant. There will be other opportunities for them.

## Broadcasting the Intention to Heal from a Distance

Q: We've covered the first two phases of your research—to test the effect of intention on physical materials of different kinds, and then on physical space. What was the third phase?

WT:   To learn to broadcast an intention across a great distance, and that started when Cindy Reed approached me to do an experiment to treat depression and anxiety. She was getting a graduate degree and studying under Norm Shealy (founding president of the American Holistic Medical Association). For her thesis, she wanted to see if she could do something to help people with depression and anxiety who lived at a distance. She said, "Maybe we can broadcast it." Speaking from intuition, I said, "Well, I think we can do something like that." I didn't know if it would work, and neither did she. We did an experiment to test the broadcasting of an intention to reduce depression and anxiety in a target population. There were 520 people to start the program. Half were in the control group, and half in the treatment group. To broadcast the intention for the treatment group, we conditioned a space at Norm Shealy's home near Springfield, Missouri. In that space, we had a laptop computer on which we scrolled the names and addresses of the people in the treatment group, who were in Guelph, Canada, 1,500 to 2,000 miles away. And this was the treatment—simply to scroll the names and addresses continuously, in that conditioned space. We had a control site in Cedar Rapids, Iowa, that was about 500 miles from Guelph, and everything was the same for those in the control group—names and addresses were scrolled through a computer—but there was no conditioning of the space in which the names of the control group were scrolled. We gathered the data at three- and eight-month intervals.

Q:   What was the outcome?

WT:   After three months, the data didn't look very promising; however, at eight months, we said, "Wow!" because of the data. The data were based on the Zung self-rating scales for depression and the State-Trait Anxiety Inventory. According to these standard measures, by eight months, nearly all the people in the treatment group had improved. Statistically, it showed that they were really benefiting. The p-values were better than 0.001.

Q:   And what change showed in the control group, those who didn't receive the intention?

WT:   No change at all.

Q:   That *is* a "Wow!" To recap: the experiment showed that a focused and loving intention had the power to broadcast a significant healing effect on people who suffer from depression and anxiety, nearly 2,000 miles away, within eight months. Given that people suffer from depression and anxiety for years—sometimes with self-loathing and suicidal tendencies—all of which has a negative impact on personal, familial, and societal vitality, this is a huge breakthrough, mind-boggling in its implications. Basically, you've found a way to demonstrate, and with repeatable experiments, that human consciousness *does* influence physical matter and psychological health, even from a great distance.

## Autism Experiment

After the initial broadcast experiment to treat depression and anxiety, Tiller and his associates did another, this time with autism in Australia. In 2011, he met Suzy Miller, author of *Awesomism*, a book based on her work with the parents of children diagnosed with autism. Tiller and Miller decided to test the effect of intention on this population, from across the world, from Arizona to Australia. They had a total of forty-four parents of autistic children, and forty-four children. They imprinted two treatment intentions, one for children and one for parents. Tiller saw the children's autism difficulties as due to "the impedance mismatch between their very advanced souls and their bio-body suits in this time and space." Based on that idea, his intention statement for their treatment was: "To support the integration of these children diagnosed with autism so they can become more easily able to function here in space-time according to their soul's purpose for the lifetime's experience."

When he wrote the intention for the children's parents, he was aware that they had "suffered great slings and arrows" from their communities and even from the medical doctors who say, "Look, kids over seven will not advance, and the last thing to happen will be a cognitive function." The doctors' normal charges are $100,000–$200,000 in a two-year program, and it takes years before they even test a child. Tiller knew the parents of autistic children had faced a lot of discouragement. The intention he wrote for them was: "To support the parents of these children so they may readily reduce and/or eliminate their daily stresses related to lovingly parenting these children in this joint adventure." The price for them to participate in Tiller's treatment was $25 for the yearlong program.

Tiller said that the imprinting session for the children and parents was "Glorious. Clearly our unseen colleagues wanted to help with that program." After imprinting, the IHD for each group was placed in a different space with a computer that scrolled the forty-four names and addresses so that each person's name was exposed for one minute per cycle. That was the treatment. The effect was immediate.

WT: The day after the imprint session, a mother called from Australia. She and her three-year-old daughter were in the experiment. The autistic girl had never spoken and was awake most nights. They both suffered from chronic lack of sleep. The mother told us that she had overslept and so had her daughter, and that when she went in and woke her, the child opened her eyes and smiled glowingly. And the most amazing part was that the daughter said twenty words that day—all of them articulate, all with the right sense of things. That was the first day. The child has continued to improve: she sleeps through the night, she sits in the lap, she blows kisses, she talks to her siblings.

Q: That's amazing, given what the medical community had predicted, that cognitive improvement is slow.

WT: We found that cognitive function happened in all the children with autism from the get-go... in all the age groups: birth to three years, four to seven years, thirteen to twenty, and older than

twenty. In this group of forty-four, only twelve of the children participating were between the ages of birth and seven. The other thirty-two
were eight years old and older. The ages are significant because most
medical research suggests that children diagnosed with autism make
limited progress in the area of communication and socialization after
age seven. I wrote White Paper 30 after four months, just showing
trends of the program. We could see by the trends that they were all
doing remarkably well.

Q:    All forty-four children improved?

WT:    At four months, we saw that all of them were getting benefits. At eight months, we gathered data at p-values less than 0.00001.
This means there's a less than 1 in 100,000 chance that we'd have seen
these observations otherwise, so this is very significant. Obviously it's
working. Obviously the unseen are helping. Whoever is helping, and
however it's taking place, it is something significant.

Q:    Again, mind-blowing results! What about the parents? Did
they show reduced stress?

WT:    For a baseline, each parent was required at the beginning to fill out the standardized Zung Self-Rating for Depression
and Anxiety forms and the ATEC (Autism Treatment Evaluation
Checklist) form. Parents were also required to submit monthly Zung
and ATEC forms so we could monitor progress both anecdotally and
statistically. Incidentally, one of the things we found very beneficial
was a Facebook group, where they could talk to each other. Those
who joined the group got greater benefits than those who didn't.

Q:    How do you understand that?

WT:    I think it's because they themselves are working on it; they're
pumping the system by talking to each other. The problem isn't with
the kids; it's with the parents. The parents are hurt and discouraged.

The children are not broken in any way, and they don't need as much juice. After four months, we doubled the juice with the parents.

Q:    What does "double the juice" mean?

WT:    Instead of getting one minute, each parent name is getting two minutes' exposure in the scrolling, which means twice as much energy. In terms of the data, there was immediate benefits in the parents, and then, after we doubled the juice, an even greater change at five months.

## The Power of Love— Everyday Applications of Intention

Q:    This seems to give hope for all kinds of problems in the world. It shows that love is an energy resource that can be harnessed and broadcast across the world to reduce suffering. But there's a catch, isn't there? Unconditional love is not most people's inner state, so won't it take a lot of inner development on the part of human beings in order to have this kind of influence?

WT:    Experiential development of Self is crucial. Here's why: Intention is an act of creation. We're doing this all the time, yet we don't realize it. We couldn't live in this world without intending— to walk across the floor, write a poem, play football, paint a painting, talk to someone… So, the step would be for intention to become a conscious act of creation, and that can't happen without inner development.

Q:    What's your advice to people who want to give serious attention to their ability to consciously improve their own lives and those of others through their intention?

WT:    Try it. Investigate! I would tell them, "Practice—do an experiment—work on yourself. See yourself as an experimental vehicle." In the White Papers, especially White Paper 15, I give people information on how to build the ability to move energy in their own body and strengthen it, then apply it to healing themselves, their animals, their plants.

Q:   And would you encourage them to meditate?

WT:   Meditate first. It's the foundation because it cuts down the noise. We're in a very noisy world. As people learn to meditate, they begin to experience the feel of other levels of nature and dimensions within themselves. And they develop inner self-management. If people want to use the power of intention, they have to become coherent. You might say we were put in this playpen that we call the cosmos in order to grow in coherence, to develop our gifts of intentionality, to become what we we're intended to become. We are amazing souls with absolutely remarkable capabilities that every one of us can develop.

Q:   In your framework, how important is love as a factor in becoming coherent?

WT:   Crucial! Love is the Universal solvent. Our Creator is Love. Love is that which is in everything, and we're encouraged to explore that everything and become it. That's it! And then you keep on keeping on. As we transform ourselves, we transform others, and we help in the process for everyone. In what I term "the ladder of understanding," that's our task ahead, to make every one of those levels solid. To experiment with inner practices and to build into ourselves what I call infrastructure. That's how we grow in consciousness and how we will be able to help evolve humanity.

Q:   Jean, what's your advice to people on how to bring coherence and harmony into their life and home?

JT:   In general what I say to people who believe they're not capable of really doing anything to make this a better, happier world is, "You can at least be kind." I'm very much an advocate of simply being kind.

It's interesting the results one gets. I go out of my way to be kind to waiters and waitresses, people in the grocery store, and I see their surprise—"Oh! Someone is interested in me!" So that's a general approach. The philosophy I live by, as close as I can, every day, minute by minute, comes from Edgar Cayce's little books, *Search for God – Books One and Two.* I say to myself every day, "Not my will but Thine be done, O Lord, in me and through me. Let me ever be a channel of blessings to others, to those I meet in every way, let my coming in and my going out be in accord with that Thou would have me do, and when the time comes, send me, use me." The great commandment is all we need, if people would just practice it! "Love the Lord thy God with all thy heart, with all thy soul, and with all thy mind. And love thy neighbor as thyself."

WT:   Spoken like a true bodhisattva.

Q:   Yes, Jean speaks from the heart. If we do that—refine our consciousness through inner practices such as that prayer—we have the ability to impact our environment?

WT:   David Hawkins gave you a good example.

Q:   He was a radiation of love. But of course he had to make the journey you describe—of a scientist who had profound spiritual experiences and then had the courage to go outside the box of orthodoxy and explore those other domains. Like you, he was criticized, even though he had a highly respected record of orthodox medical publications before he began to explore the interface of consciousness with physical sciences such as medicine, kinesiology, etc.[187]

WT:   We utilize his work. We now have an experimental jewel for measurement of intention. Kinesiology and dowsing, and doing it well, is the only tool we really have meaning for. I address it in White Paper 29. I think highly of David Hawkins.

Q: He's the reason I'm doing this book on the power of love, which I experienced in and through his presence. I'm grateful for the years of close association I had with him.

WT: Yes, a very, very rare opportunity.

Q: It's interesting that both Hawkins's Map of Consciousness and your experiment with the Loving Kindness Buddha Relic IHD indicate that the purer and more coherent the energy of Love the greater its impact. On his scale, one person who calibrates at the basic level of Love (500) counterbalances the negativity of 750,000 people. I think you'd agree that the purer the intention the greater the impact?

WT: Absolutely. Unconditional Love is extremely powerful. In my framework, we are always radiating what we are. It's the subtle energy radiations, outside of space-time. You can begin to see how the lasers work. As you become more coherent, the energy density is greater, more powerful. I think of it as a technology of love. It's important for us to think about it for the future. It means that if you have antagonists, probably the only effective thing to use is love, a technology of love. Which means that love is what you become.

Q: Is that how you dealt with your antagonists in academe?

WT: In the beginning I was angry with them, but then I came to the view that they're similar to children—they're not conscious enough to understand what I'm doing and they fear for their own reputations. Therefore I could be with them and feel free. I wasn't happy with the university, but it is what it is. It gets its money from governments and from people who earned their money in business, and these people might say, "I'm not going to give you any money because you have this kook who does crazy stuff!"

Q: Are you saying that a technology of love presumes an underlying unity?

WT:   Yes, Love means to recognize that we are all one. We are, no matter how much we might think otherwise, connected to the source. All the things that happen to us are for our benefit and greater good, but we don't necessarily see it as greater good until we really can reflect on it. One of the professors wanted me kicked out of the department and wanted to get other people to do it. Then I recognized that I had met him in an earlier life. At the Inquisition, he was the guy on the podium, passing judgment. I learned to let things go. It goes back to the growth of consciousness. We can't change others, but we ourselves can get more conscious, and then we're capable of all sorts of things.

Q:   How can an ordinary person condition a space?

WT:   It's like going into the most marvelous cathedral you've ever experienced. You know that what conditions it to become sacred is the people who've gone there to pray, to become something more, day one, day two, week one, week two, month one, month two, year one, year two, hundreds of years, with hundreds and hundreds of people who have radiated their aspiration.

Q:   Their heart—the higher parts of their humanity?

WT:   Exactly. That's what has conditioned the space. Anyone can do it. If you become more and more conscious, you can't help radiating into your space. Whatever you've become inside of yourself, that's what you radiate. Even if you don't meditate.

Q:   If someone goes to the Loving Kindness Buddha Relic exhibit, and they bring some of the holy water home and put it on their altar, what happens? Or it could be any object that they consider sacred in whatever tradition they follow. Does that sacred object condition the home?

WT:   It depends on their intention. They could pump it or let it decay.

Q: So I'm learning from your work that decay, entropy, is the normal course of things, but if energy is pumped into something, it reduces entropy. So, in terms of a sacred object, we would pump an intention with our devotion, like putting a flower near the sacred object every day, or prostrating before the altar, or inwardly remembering its significance. I don't mean as empty rituals, but meaningful expressions of the heart.

WT: It takes a lot. You have to give meaning to it. If you're conditioned to do these actions, it probably required many lifetimes. Everyone has the capability to condition space, and the probability of them doing it is becoming higher now with more and more people recognizing its significance. Their consciousness has gone over that threshold where it's become meaningful to them. When you give meaning to something, then your unconscious will feed you. Giving meaning to things is really important. Our normal distance-time mind processes less than fifty bits per second, but the unconscious processes at least 50 billion bits! Thus we have within us systems that can help us if we give things meaning—like what's happening for you with the book you're writing. You were open to the experience of seeing certain things. You gave it meaning, and your unconscious is then giving you information that allows you to explore that meaning.

Q: The meaning I gave to seeing auras was that we are more than our bodies—we're made up of energy, different dimensions of energy. This is such an obvious spiritual truth, but I guess I needed to "see" it to really get it. I wasn't trying to see such things.

WT: I would propose that the unseen higher dimensional colleagues saw that you were ready and they expanded and developed your ability to see these things in a transformed way. And so, what do you do with that?

Q:   I've not done really anything.

WT:   Yes, I think you have. The point is that it confirms certain things for you.

Q:   That's true. It was a valuable confirmation of a reality beyond the concepts of my thinking, logical mind. This isn't something I can talk about with my academic colleagues. They'd think I was crazy.

WT:   Of course. It's not the right timing for them.

## The Future: Are We Machines or Creators of Love and Meaning?

Q:   What's your sense of the influence of your work right now?

WT:   I don't think the orthodox scientific community is interested in what I've been doing, but the lay public seems ready to know what it means. My work is to try to do things that will reach them and that will also be there for orthodox science when they're willing to get off the pot. That's how it always happens. It's true also for me that I learn when I'm ready; my colleagues in the unseen domains make me aware of things when I'm ready and when I give them meaning. That meaning thing slips away and most people don't really think about it, but it's incredibly important. It's very much related to consciousness. People aren't conscious enough to see what's right in front of them because they haven't given this stuff any meaning. They can see the experimental data on the table (pointing to the psychoenergetics books on the table), and they can't see it. If we look at a lot of scientists and medical people, they might be 350 or 400 or 450 on Hawkins's scale, yet Unconditional Love begins at 540.

Q:   The level of consciousness called Love is a totally different paradigm, isn't it? As a person rises in levels of consciousness, especially to the level of Love, this affects thermodynamics. In White Paper 25, you and Dr. Nisha Manek say, "As one ascends the levels of consciousness, the greater the power of Love and the higher the gauge symmetry state of the physical vacuum, the more excess thermodynamic free energy is available." Hawkins spoke of the overall evolution of consciousness and emergence of *Homo spiritus*… an awakened humanity in which compassion and love are innate to the brain structure.

WT: I think these are meaningful data points. They should give real hope. It's very important to give hope to others. We're certainly struggling with a lack of hope in our political system. But if we can find a way to give others hope, then we get hope. If you forgive others, then you are forgiven. A lot of these simple things are much more meaningful than people realize. And what's coming to the fore in the lifetime of people now in college is the question "What are you going to do with your life when robots can do everything you know how to do?" Several companies in the U.S. now use factories with simple robots that can do the labor at low cost. It's happening quickly. We'll have to move people a long way so that they give meaning to things and know how to build themselves.

Q: So we need to educate people as to their unique abilities innate to human consciousness, which no robot can replicate?

WT: People need to build themselves to higher dimensional levels. Human consciousness has unique capacities for love and meaning.

Q: I'm reminded of the work of Viktor Frankl, the Jewish psychiatrist who survived the Holocaust and created Logotherapy, "healing through meaning." We study his books in my classes. He warned about the destructiveness of a scientific reduction of the human being to "nothing but" a mechanical process. In his view, this kind of nihilism was the basis for the Holocaust. I think his warning is a good one to heed in the coming robotic age. To remember the importance of love and meaning, and that humans are more than machinery.

WT: Your opportunity to teach meditation and compassion at the university is impressive. I looked for a long time at various universities

475

around the world that would be open to the idea, but they are generally closed-minded. Your university is open-minded and forward thinking.

Q: I feel fortunate to teach at a place where education includes questions of meaning and methods of self-inquiry. Students tap into their own inner resources. How do your experiments relate to this?

WT: We are always radiating what we are, so experiential development of Self is crucial. And we can change material properties, which we have shown in our experiments. College students and people in general need to see themselves as the creators of their environment and develop those capacities. They've given scientists more trust than they should. Ultimately, the people are the vehicle, and they're what's being created here in this process. It's a great adventure, requires a lot of thoughtfulness and a lot of emotion. When we imprint, Jean keeps saying to me, "Bill, you have to give a lot of emotion to this"— Love, primarily. To consciously put in love, support, and the desire for the betterment of whatever we're working on. For example, Jean was in theater, and there you have actors and actresses who are able to project their part in the play to the person in the farthest corner of the room, not by shouting but by getting the signal there. We are transmitters and we can be very powerful. People need to begin to see themselves that way. It's not about egotism or showing off. I think the human ego is important if it is put in service to the larger whole. Right now, the ego is being misused. A healthy, strong ego that's in service to the whole is beneficial. People have to come to the place of serving Love, not self. All of my work is an act of love.

Q: Any closing words for our readers?

WT: I remember one time I asked a numerical question, "What does it mean if just one soul adds to the coherent being of what we call God?" I worked it all out mathematically, and came to the conclusion that it makes a huge difference for a single soul to be aligned with Love.

We radiate what we are. We change the world by virtue of what we have become. Through conscious intention, we can cultivate our innate capacity to love and to broadcast loving intention into the world with great effect. This is the power of a saint like Mother Teresa and a sage such as Gandhi who, because of their purity of love, operated at a higher thermodynamic-gauge symmetry than the masses of impoverished millions and the entire British Empire.

Being in the company of people who are in service to love exponentially facilitates our inner coherence. That's what I experienced during my daylong visit with the Tillers. I felt changed for the better. Clarified. Coherent. Connected. Simply being with them provided the proof I'd been searching for. Focused intention has a powerful effect. This is not only a matter of scientific demonstration for the Tillers but also a living radiation.

When someone asked my teacher what he recommended as a meditation practice, he said, sit with arms slightly raised and palms facing outward in the form of a blessing, as if you are an "antenna of radiance" and a channel of God's unconditional love for the world and humanity. He said to be a laser beam of love. Begin with a prayer like the Prayer of St. Francis: "Lord make me a channel of Thy peace," and give all the love you are capable of giving. By doing this, opening your heart completely, one day, you will awaken to what the world is crying for. "It's simple and direct like a laser," he said. He said it might take years, but eventually the needs of humanity will be revealed to you, and finally the Reality of the world will shine forth as the Self. Out of my longing to become this kind of conduit for love in the world, I moved to Arizona to be closer to my teacher.

PART FOUR

# SURRENDERING TO LOVE

View of Cathedral Rock from Red Rock Loop Road, Sedona,
Arizona. This was the road to the author's cabin, around
the corner from her teacher (author's collection).

## Chapter Twenty-Three

# MOVING CLOSER TO THE FIRE

As meaningful as the university work was to me, I longed to give myself more completely to inner work. I saw that love alone had the power to heal all inner and outer divides. Moving closer to the Fire of my teacher, I hoped to be melted down further and further until, like wax, I could be imprinted with the stamp of love. Without the fire, I knew it wouldn't be possible. Being near a true teacher was a rare opportunity—worth everything I could give it.

I worked out an arrangement with the University of Redlands to reduce my load to part-time, and then I rented a small cabin just around the corner from my teacher's home in Arizona. Over the next five years, I lived near him for half of the year and taught in California for the other half. This arrangement echoed the "retreat and return" rhythm of my life, such that a link was made between the inner transformation and the outer world.

It wasn't always easy to pursue the path of love while continuing a career as an academic. Critics abound in every sector. Travelers on the path of love learn to walk through the hail of bullets and carry on with what they know to be a positive work. My efforts to integrate contemplative methods into higher education got mixed reviews in certain halls of academe, but the gratitude of college students year after year renewed my commitment to the endeavor. Thankfully

I had the support of my department colleagues and the university administrators.

Perhaps I'd committed the ultimate academic heresy: I was not only studying the mystics as a scholar but I had become a devotee. I had moved from objective analysis of the topic and entered into it experientially. Simply put, I could not deny the spiritual realm I was coming to know, any more than travelers to a beautiful place can pretend they never saw it. Academic training had sharpened the dualistic proclivity of mind to classify, dissect, compare, contrast, criticize, analyze, intellectualize, politicize, memorize, and categorize, ad infinitum. And now a spiritual process was melting these mentalisms into the heart.

As I followed in the footsteps of Huston Smith and William Tiller, my academic life came to be guided by a deep spiritual interest, rightly called devotion, and I trusted the intelligence of the heart more and more.

## Teacher and Student

Moving into the rental cabin around the corner from my teacher, I finally felt at home. In previous years, when I had come to Arizona to attend his monthly events, I cried while driving back to California, like I was being ripped from the most essential part of myself. I knew that one day I would come here to be with him. That time had come. As far as I knew, he didn't know me or know that I had moved to be near him.

It took a lot of planning and effort to get there, and then—nothing. I saw him at the monthly events, but otherwise not much happened for the first three months. Day after day, I sat on the couch, staring out the window at the pines and cottonwoods and feeling the last cold of winter. Spring was in process but hidden. In the early morning, I'd walk in the woods along the river. Only the herons were there, and all was silent. At the edge of the river I'd bow in secret to my teacher who lived downstream. I was offering myself into his being, as the river loses itself in the sea. In mystical traditions, there is the saying "the river merges into the Sea." I prayed that my little stream would merge into the vast Sea. To me, he was the infinite shoreless Sea.

The days were empty and I wondered: *Why am I here?*

It seemed that life had played a trick on me, as in the story of "The Man with the Miserable Sack." In Sufi tales from the Middle East, Mulla Nasruddin is an enlightened "trickster." In this story, he is walking on the road and comes upon a man sitting hunched over his tattered sack, desolate.

"What's wrong?" the Mulla asked.

The man pointed to his sack and moaned, "My life is wretched. Poor me. Everything that I own is in this miserable sack. This is all I have in the world."

"Too bad," said the Mulla, and with that, he snatched the sack from the man's hands and ran down the road with it.

The man jumped up to grab his sack, but it was too late. He burst into tears, now more miserable than before. The sack wasn't much, but it was all he had.

The Mulla ran up the hill and around the bend and placed the sack in the middle of the road where he knew the man would see it. Then he hid behind a bush and waited.

The man slowly trudged up the hill, crying out, "Oh, miserable me. My sack is gone." When he came over the hill and rounded the bend, he saw his sack in the road. "Oh—my sack!" Beside himself with joy, he sang and danced and shouted, "My sack! My wonderful sack! Oh, my precious sack, I thought I'd lost you!"

Watching through the bushes, the Mulla chuckled. "Well, that's one way to make someone happy! Show them the value of what they hold in their very own hand!"

The Mulla had taken the man's life and given it back to him—shifted to new ground. What the man had decried as "miserable" he now cherished as precious.

Like Mulla Nasruddin, my teacher had shifted me to new ground, and I could see how precious my life was. Even some of the things in my sack that I'd been ashamed of, like the alcoholism, I now saw as gifts. But for what? As I sat and watched the winter and wondered why I'd moved around the corner from my teacher, I slowly read *Daughter of Fire: Diary of a Spiritual Training with a Sufi Master,* Irina Tweedie's 829-page description of spiritual training. A college student had shown me the book and said she wanted to study it with me for an individualized course the following school year. Though I'd never heard of it, I was strangely drawn to the book. It was the only one I brought with me to Arizona other than those written by my teacher, and I thought it might give me some idea as to what was going to happen to me. I had to look no further than the dedication: "The Path of Love is like a bridge of hair across a chasm of fire—*To the lotus feet of my Revered Teacher.*" I had come to Arizona to be near the Fire, just as Tweedie's Guru told her: "To realize Love is to realize God. If we sit before an open fire it warms us; there is no effort on our part. Those who have realized God are like this fire. Keep in their company."[188]

*Daughter of Fire* transmits a pristine example of love between guru and disciple, the unique bond that can take a person to God / Reality. When Tweedie first went to India in 1961, a middle-aged woman in search of a spiritual teacher, she imagined sitting at the feet of a great guru who would teach her special Yoga practices. What she encountered was a brutal confrontation with her own inner darkness. The Sufi master called Bhai Sahib ("elder brother") wore down her ego. She wrote, "What he did mainly was force me to face the darkness in myself and it almost killed me."[189]

I longed to have Tweedie's depth of surrender. She exemplified the famous verse in the Upanishads, "If you want the Truth as badly as a drowning man wants air, then you'll realize it in a split second." I knew I was a long way from that one-pointed devotion. Irina Tweedie was willing to have her ego ground down to nothing so that only the Infinite would be in her heart. This is the journey of the mystic—it requires the total surrender of a "me."

I was terrified but willing.

Irina Tweedie and her classic book, *Daughter of Fire: A Diary of a Spiritual Training with a Sufi Master*, provided inspiration and guidance to the author (courtesy of The Golden Sufi Center).

Tweedie's Guru told her there were stages. In the beginning, the devotee had to surrender everything to the guru, but later, she had to give up seeing the guru as God because the outer guru points to the inner guru, the Self. This is also what I heard from my teacher—"Devotion to a teacher is a step." Thus even as I moved to live near him, I knew that one day I would have to surrender my projection of the Self onto him. Love requires its own authentic realization, not a vicarious one.[190] In his books and events, my teacher often said, "The Self of the teacher and one's own Self are one and the same." When people expressed appreciation for what he radiated, he said, "It's your own Self reflected back. What you're experiencing is your own Self."

I prayed to surrender as Tweedie surrendered, to be, as the Sufis say, "less than dust at the feet of the Teacher." When I read her Guru's description of disciple and devotee, my heart burned to be a devotee:

A disciple is following the Teacher in order to acquire knowledge. The duality always remains. There are always two of them—the Master and the pupil. Among the disciples are few devotees.... Between the devotee and the Master the duality disappears. Devotees have to sacrifice themselves. Completely. When there is duality, there can be no realization. To surrender all possessions is relatively easy. But to surrender the mind is very difficult. It means one has no mind of one's own. One is like a dead body in the hands of the Teacher. How is the dead body? ... It cannot protest. A disciple can sacrifice himself only to a certain degree. If you want something, the duality will always remain. A devotee wants nothing....[191]

To want nothing and give everything—this felt true to me. When her Guru, Bhai Sahib, died, Tweedie pressed her forehead against his feet. I thought: *Yes, this is how it should be.* The longing was to be completely at the feet of the Master. It was not submission in the self-effacing way of patriarchal culture; it was the surrender to a great Master who receives you into her or his Unconditional Love and thereby gives you an experience of your wholeness. I knew that if I gave my whole heart, I would gain the whole world.

I struggled with how to explain this longing to others. Devotion to a spiritual teacher went against my upbringing, my academic training, and my own personality full of stubbornness, pride, know-it-allism. I felt embarrassed to say to family, friends, and colleagues, "I moved to Arizona to be with my guru." American culture instills distrust, with headline stories about a megalomaniac who killed his followers with cyanide, or the latest "guru" from India who had sex with his followers and ran off with their money.

There are many wolves in sheep's clothing who exploit followers to get sex, money, and power over others. Seekers are vulnerable because they long to be loved. Exploitation can be so subtle that they don't realize they've been had. Unconsciousness prevails on both sides. Those who prematurely set themselves up as teachers often don't realize they're using followers to feed their own need for security or love. They subtly siphon off the light and energy of others because the connection to their own inner light is not complete. A true teacher needs nothing, takes nothing, wants nothing. Like the rose, their beautiful fragrance infuses the air without taking anything from the atmosphere.

I hesitated to use the word "guru" when speaking about my teacher because it had lost its original purity due to misuse. Similarly, we can't say "lawyer" in this country without constellating negative associations, even though we know that not all lawyers are greed mongers who take advantage of unfortunate events for their own gain.

It eased my mind to learn that in many contexts around the world, to serve a master, sheikh, lama, or guru is highly encouraged. When I later went to India to do interviews for this book, I saw pictures of a guru in every home and even in businesses such as banks. I also saw a parallel in Eastern Orthodox Christianity in Greece, Egypt, Russia, and the Middle East, in which devotees prayed with icons that imaged the great saints. There was the example of Mary Magdalene's love for Christ as "an echo of an echo" of the Master-Student relationship.[192] When Jesus spoke her name at the empty tomb, she uttered, "Raboni," which is to say, "Master."

I remembered Rūmī's famed encounter with his Master, Shams-i-Tabrīzī, in the 13th century. According to one account, Rūmī was a professor of theology, walking in the marketplace with an armful of books. Suddenly, out of nowhere, the mystic Shams came up to him and asked, "If these books cannot liberate you from yourself, what is the purpose of them?" The question yanked Rūmī out of his scholarly sobriety. In one story, the books burst into flames, and in another, Shams threw them into a fountain. Shams told Rūmī that his intellect had brought him up to the threshold but it was useless to take him into the house of the Beloved.[193] Rūmī surrendered at the feet of Shams, his "Sun," and gave the rest of his life to the burning love ignited within him. Rūmī's mystical poetry reaches across seven centuries to transmit the Fire of selfless Love that turned his heart and now turns ours.

# TESTING THE TEACHER

Despite these global examples, I found no signposts from my own culture to guide this part of my journey. American society honored the intensity of personal romantic relationships, not the deep bond of devotion between teacher and devotee. To be a devotee at the feet of the teacher therefore required me to trust a light that others couldn't see. I had to rely on the truth of my heart and surrender the fear that I was throwing my life away.

At the time, Tweedie's book was the only outer validation I had. *Daughter of Fire* revealed the essence of a true guru, and I recognized my teacher on every page. When Tweedie asked her Guru how to tell a good from a bad teacher, he replied:

> A bad teacher will always behave as his followers expect him to behave. The conventional idea of a spiritual Teacher is that he is always kind, benevolent, compassionate, dignified, wearing robes or garments which distinguish him from the ordinary mortals, uttering at all times wise, profound sentences. So he will behave accordingly... because he is after personal prestige or worldly possessions, or even money or honors. But a good Teacher obeys a law of which the world has no notion.
>
> Do you know what is *Swadharma?* It is a Sanskrit word and it means a Dharma, a duty that is innate in the thing itself, imbedded in its *Swabhave* (true nature). For instance, the *Swadharma* of the water is to be wet and fluid, that of the fire is to burn and to consume, of the wind to blow. They cannot help it; it is in their nature. So it is with the *Sat Guru;* he just IS. He may do things people don't understand,

or may even condemn. Love does not always conform to the idea people have of it.... Love can appear
in the shape of great cruelty, great injustice, or even
calamity.[194]

The true guru (Sat Guru) is totally natural and does not conform
to worldly convention. Bhai Sahib gave the example of Shams who
was said to be rude and abrupt, sometimes addressing his audience as
"asses." Yet Shams was the great Master who awakened Rūmī. Such
real teachers often don't look or act as the seeker expects. They cultivate mannerisms that discourage rather than entice the spiritual ego. I
saw this in my teacher. He was very down-to-earth, "nothing special,"
as they say in Zen. Being with him, one had the sense that he'd seen
it all, done it all. He drank Diet Pepsi, and this got rid of moralists
who couldn't see beyond their nutritional beliefs. He was the epitome
of compassion and graciousness, yet he did not people-please or promote, as he had no need for people to "follow" or "like" him.

At the beginning of his books, he put a warning to readers, similar to those of mystics in earlier centuries: "Caveat: The traditional
religionist or the spiritually timid are forewarned that the material
presented herein may be disturbing and therefore better bypassed."[195]

True teachers follow the warning of Jesus: "Do not cast your
pearls before swine" (MATTHEW 7:6)—often to prevent harm. When
Paul Brunton made his journey to India, recounted in his 1935 bestseller *The Search for Secret India*, the yoga masters were careful to teach
him only the elementary body postures allowable for non-initiates.
They warned him of the physical and psychic dangers if advanced
yoga teachings were brought to the market for public display. In some
mystical traditions, the seeker must ask for a teaching three times
before it is given.

I learned that true teachers can see into a person's heart. They
will not share advanced teachings until a disciple has been tested and
is ready to receive it. They know the art of deflecting spiritual look-
ie-loos who lack genuine spiritual interest. For example, after completing her training in India, Irina Tweedie returned to Europe and

began to speak about her experiences to various audiences, sometimes "trimming off the fat" right at the beginning. At one seminar, when the room was full of leftwing socialists, she repeatedly complimented conservative political leaders Margaret Thatcher and Ronald Reagan. After a group of attendees left in disgust, she proceeded to transmit her esoteric Sufi teaching.[196] A friend who learned at the feet of Tweedie in London said:

"I learned by watching how she dealt with people. She saw the essence, their intention. One person could bring something like a bouquet of flowers and she'd be delighted by it and put it on her table, while another person brought the same thing and she'd toss it out. She saw where it was coming from. That's how I learned it's not what you do, it's where it comes from."[197]

Only reluctantly did my teacher speak in public and interact with those who called themselves students of his work. "I wasn't happy to discover that people needed the physical presence. I'd just as soon have stayed home!" His research revealed to him, however, that seekers are greatly helped by the physical presence of a realized teacher, so he made himself available through public seminars and satsangs. His teaching function (as he called it) emerged solely in response to people's needs and requests. He followed the principle, "attraction not promotion." When he published *Power vs. Force*, the boxes of books sat around for years and he was fine with that. Then one day, a well-known American spiritual figure named Wayne Dyer asked if he could have the book published through Hay House, one of the largest international publishers of spiritual books. Dyer lauded the book on major media networks and in lectures worldwide. This attention catalyzed a huge work for my teacher, with many more books published and a demanding schedule of seminars and interviews. He was also fine with that. "Whatever *is*, is the will of God," he said.

The Dalai Lama advised to test a teacher, to see how he acts when no one else is there. At the events, I watched my teacher closely—how he dealt with money, how he treated ordinary people, how he handled adulation from followers, and how he processed attacks from critics. He passed every test I put to him: Did he seek admiration, approval, flattery or financial gain? No. Did he take credit for the experiences he had? No. Did he encourage followers to serve and glorify him? No. Did he demand loyalty? No. Did he malign critics? No. Was he controlling? No. Did he pressure people to join or stay? No. All were free to come and go.

I saw that he treated every person and creature with equal regard, had no need for adoration or approval, asked for nothing from anyone, and had no interest in controlling or proselytizing others. He always pointed people inward, to find the Truth within. He repeated the Buddha's saying, "Put no head above your own." In his writings, he pointed people to the teachings, not the personage of the teacher:

> The teachings and not the teacher are what is important. Inasmuch as the teachings do not come from the personage of the teacher at all, it does not make sense to idolize or worship that personage. The information is transmitted as a gift because it was received as such. There is, therefore, nothing to sell, to enforce, to control, or to charge for inasmuch as the information was free and a gift from God. A valid spiritual organization may make nominal charges to cover ordinary expenses in that everyone contributes for the common good.[198]

I could not rely on the experiences of others. Some people worshipped my teacher; others disdained him. My path kept me on a straight edge between adulators and critics. "By their fruits you shall know them," said Jesus. I looked at the effect of his teachings. In my own life and that of others, the effect was transformative. Longstanding patterns of suffering were relieved. One of his books was so effective in helping people recover from heroin and other addictions that it came to be used in treatment centers nationwide. Truth brings peace. Love heals.

Even as I knew him to be a true teacher and felt I had made the right decision to move around the corner from him, I still wondered: *Now what?* I had a nagging intuition that my move to Arizona was for something beyond myself. The bond felt ancient and purposeful, so what was I supposed to do with it?

To find an answer, I traveled to visit a hypnotherapist skilled in past-life regressions. She had never heard of my teacher. I wanted to know "What is the bond with this teacher? Do I have a karmic commitment?"

During the session, I relived snapshots from another lifetime when, as a seeker of Truth, I encountered a Radiance of Light in the desert, around which a large crowd had gathered. This Radiance was featureless and formless, with no visible personhood, yet I knew it was the same energy as my teacher. In that other lifetime, I had approached the Light and been blessed, then gone on my way, happy to have heard the Truth, kept it to myself, and carried out my life as a householder. In the next scene of this experience, I approached the Radiance of Light in the current lifetime. I heard this message: "Hearing the Truth does not obligate you; but if you wish to share My message, you may."

This experience made a strong impact. It was an invitation to share with others what I was going to learn from him. I took it very seriously. Soon afterward, I mailed him a letter saying I felt called to write a biography of him.

Within days the phone rang. "This is Doc Hawkins. We got your letter. It's fine for you to write the book. You can come over now."

I stammered, "I need a couple of weeks to prepare my questions."

"Okay, then call back when you're ready."

This was how it went for several months. I would call to schedule an appointment for our next meeting, and he would say, "Come right now."

I would always slow it down. One time I said, "Oh, but I need to take a shower!"

"Well, come after that."

He was instantaneous, yet never in a rush. He simply took care of things in the moment, as a need arose. I saw that my ego always wanted to rush ahead or hold back, caught between desire and fear, and I saw that he was totally free of this ego dynamic.

The first time I went to his house, my hands shook, my pulse raced. I'd been a student of his teachings for several years, yet we had never talked one on one.

I followed his directions and turned down a narrow gravel lane to find a woodsy little home, nestled in the trees, with animals all round. He opened the door and welcomed me into his small office just off the den. A tree grew in the middle of the room. His wife, Susan, later told me, "Dave can't bear to cut down a tree, so we have a tree growing in the house, right through the roof!"

As soon as I sat down, a large Maine Coon cat came over and rubbed against my leg. "Bootsie" made me feel instantly at home. (Bootsie deserves a credit line in this book for all the love he gave, year after year.) The first thing my teacher told me was not a "spiritual" lesson but the story of how he found Bootsie, who had been caged in a pet store.

> Here is Bootsie—this is such a great kitty! I went overboard with him and paid fifty bucks! (*Laughter.*) All our other kitties come from the woodpile outside. This one was in a pet store in a little cage that was too small for him to stand up in, and everybody was going by, sticking their fingers in at him. He looked at me as if to say, 'Please adopt me and take me home.' He didn't know how to purr. I taught him how to purr. Purrrrrr…. He purrs the way I purr—on the expiration. One of my unseen duties in the world is to teach a cat how to purr! (*Laughter.*) We have three cats, one dog, and an African grey parrot, Broccoli. Broccoli talks up a storm. She knows the dog's name Kelsey and calls her over to the cage. Then Broccoli scolds the dog for being close to the cage! (*Laughter.*) Chickens and goats… I had a mule and horses, even llamas….

Humor and animals have a way of putting someone at ease. "Doc"—this is what we students called him—immediately made me feel connected with him and his life just by sharing a story about his love for animals. Each animal was understood, appreciated, and loved as it was.

I relaxed and pulled out my long list of interview questions. Just as I got to the second one, Bootsie plopped his ample furry mass atop my recorder and the paper with my questions. I didn't want to push him off. I thought: *Well, so much for my list that took me two weeks to prepare!* I had to wing it, which turned out to be better anyway.

I spent a couple of hours there, asking all sorts of questions. In the next four years, hundreds of hours would follow as I developed a close rapport with Doc and Susan. Something in me knew I wasn't there for myself but for future readers and seekers. My role was not to understand all that I heard and experienced—how could I?—but to document it. The feeling reminded me of the statement of Mahendranath Gupta, scholar-devotee who documented his observations of his Master in the book *Gospel of Ramakrishna*: "I am an insignificant person. I live by the side of an ocean and keep with me a few pitchers of seawater." I too felt like I was in the presence of wisdom as vast as the ocean, with only a few pitchers' worth of capacity to hold what I heard.

In that first visit, I experienced the qualities of love that are obvious yet often overlooked. Spontaneity. Simplicity. Humor. Transparency. Naturalness. Graciousness. Putting others at ease. Sharing. Laughter. Appreciation of every form of life as uniquely dear—tree, kitty, dog, couch, paper, parrot, friend, flower, espresso cup. Joy. Recognition. Affection. Honesty. Openness. Nurturing. The love was free and unconditional, just like the Pillar of Light I'd experienced when I was fifteen, the Love took nothing from me; it needed nothing in return. Like the sun, it radiated.

"Beatific vision" was Doc's response when I told him about my experience of the Light. He affirmed the innermost, timeless core of me.

"Doc" Hawkins a few weeks before his passing, 2012
(Fran Grace/courtesy of The Institute for Spiritual Research).

# Chapter Twenty-Four

## LOVE IN EVERYDAY LIFE

### Encounter with Dr. David and Susan Hawkins

*The whole world is a Bodhi tree.*

—DR. DAVID R. HAWKINS

## THE LIGHT

The first day I was with Doc in his little office with the tree growing through it, discussing mystical states, Susan popped in with a hat she'd found at the thrift store. She had been out running errands with Gabe—a tall, strapping soccer star who was their driver and handyman and was like a son. Doc seemed just as interested in Susan's happiness with a hat as speaking to an interviewer about enlightenment. Susan lit up the room with her laughter and tales from the trip into town. I sensed her large heart and spot-on intuition. There was the feeling of instant friendship. The conversation shifted easily between everyday life and mystical revelations. She said that it was the Light that started their sharing with the world:

It was early morning, around four a.m., and Dave and I were lying in bed. All of a sudden I looked at the corner of the room and there was a Light that got bigger and bigger until it came into the whole room. It was the most brilliant Light you could think of. My eyes were wide-open. And if you closed your eyes, you could see and feel this Light. Then suddenly the Light went into me. There was an Energy with that Light. It was engulfing. I asked Dave what it was, and he said, 'Divine Light.' It changed me. After that, I knew we had to start the work, do the lectures. It was 1998. He had already written *Power vs. Force*, but he wasn't speaking at all. People would ask him to speak, and he said, 'No, I'm not going to speak.' After the Light, that's when we decided we better do the lectures.

Doc added, "That's what Bill Wilson experienced. The room lit up. It was lit up by the Presence, which is not different from Light, which is not different from Love."

Following the Light experience, they began fourteen years of events, travel, publication of books, study groups all over the world, radio interviews, audio and video recordings, and interactions with thousands of people. Susan talked about the challenges of going public and the sacrifice of privacy and higher states: "At one point, he lived that divine life. When you're teaching, writing, and trying to put all your thoughts on paper, the high state is always present, but it's in the background. Nothing would get done if he were in that state the whole time. People don't think there's a normal household living here, but there is." Doc added, "Oh, yes the protoplasmic dance...." Listening, I registered the compassion it takes for a sage or mystic to leave the space of infinite peace and squeeze into our linear boxes. Having broken free from prison, who would want to go back? They do so only out of great love, to liberate the rest of us.

When I asked Susan what it was like to deal with a worldwide community that looked to Doc as a teacher, she said, "Don't put so much emphasis on the teacher as much as the work. Just because he's able to write this and put it into words, it's not really the person that matters. It's the body of the work. Maybe Mother Teresa felt the same way. It was a Presence. She really was, I believe, a saint. She didn't write things down as a teaching; it was a hands-on work that she did. Mystics are given different talents. Dave's talent happens to be that he's able to write down all the inner workings. He's bridged the gap between different religions to say they're all looking for the same thing but go about it in a different way."

Then Susan left to take care of household duties. "A storm is coming tomorrow," she said as she went with Gabe to climb up on the roof and clean out the rain gutters.

Thus began my rapport with Doc and Susan Hawkins. Over the coming years, our friendship deepened, and we cared for each other in the pain and joy of everyday life. This very human connection with them existed alongside the singular and unbreakable bond I felt with him as my teacher. That bond was an impersonal power that worked beneath the surface, within the heart of hearts, even as we all ran errands, watched TV, walked Kelsey the dog, went to the doctor, celebrated holidays, and laughed and wept with the vicissitudes of life.

## BIOGRAPHIC SUMMARY

Doc Hawkins was born in Wisconsin in 1927, and knew early on that he wanted to become a doctor, to be on the front lines of suffering. He went into psychiatry because that was the realm of inner suffering, which he saw as the root of the problem. After serving in the U.S. Navy during WWII, he graduated from the Medical College of Wisconsin in 1953. For the next twenty-five years, he lived in New York, where his pioneering work as a psychiatrist brought major clinical breakthroughs, especially in the treatment of schizophrenia and alcoholism. His research findings were published widely in medical, scientific, and psychoanalytic journals. As Medical Director of the North Nassau Mental Health Center and Director of Research at Brunswick Hospital on Long Island, he had the largest practice in New York. He also served as a psychiatric advisor to Catholic, Protestant, and Buddhist monasteries, where he was called upon to distinguish spiritual states such as Samadhi, illumination, dark night of the soul, and Unio mystica from pathological states such as catatonia, depression, grandiosity, and mania. In 1973, he coauthored *Orthomolecular Psychiatry* with double Nobel Laureate chemist Linus Pauling, initiating a new field within psychiatry that incorporated the role of nutrition in brain chemistry. Doc appeared on numerous national broadcasts such as *The Today Show*, *The Barbara Walters Show*, and *The MacNeil/Lehrer News Hour*.

In midlife, an unexpected and shattering realization of the Oneness of All Existence transformed his life. *"Gloria in Excelsis Deo"* is what he could say about it. He eventually moved to rural Arizona where he lived the life of a hermit for several years, sleeping on a thrift-store cot, rarely eating, immersed in Divine consciousness. He was researching the nature of consciousness from the inside out. In 1995, with the publication of *Power vs. Force: The Hidden Determinants of Human Behavior,* he communicated the nonlinear inner revelations via a framework that was linear and thus could be understood by non-mystics. Spiritual traditions say that the thinking mind is one of the greatest obstacles to Realization, yet in the West the thinking mind is the most highly valued asset. His work sought to help humanity overcome this most difficult hurdle, not by devaluing the thinking mind but by putting its limitations into an overall context of spiritual evolution. The book was translated into twenty-five languages, with over a million copies sold, and evoked praise from such notables as Mother Teresa. Many other books followed.

From 1998 to 2011, Doc traveled widely as a lecturer throughout the U.S. and overseas, speaking at the Oxford Forum and Westminster Abbey, as well as universities such as Harvard, the University of Argentina, Notre Dame, the University of California, and Fordham University. Susan was always at his side, and he was not on the stage without her. Documentary films, magazines, and radio interviews (e.g., Oprah Radio) featured him. He received many awards and recognitions for his contributions to humanity. In 2000, a large community of Buddhists in Seoul, South Korea, bestowed upon him the designation "Tae Ryoung Sun Kak Tosa" (Teacher of Enlightenment).

At age eighty-four, in 2011, Doc gave his final public lecture, on the topic of "Love," to an audience of 1,700 people spanning many nationalities and religious backgrounds. I read *Power vs. Force* in 2003. My interviews with him began in 2008. He died in 2012.

Doc and Susan Hawkins onstage, "Love" lecture, Prescott, Arizona, 2011 (Lou Deserio/courtesy of The Institute for Spiritual Research).

# CONVERSATION WITH
# DR. DAVID R. HAWKINS

## Devotion

Q:   I wasn't looking for a spiritual teacher. I had a Ph.D. in religious studies and was skeptical of mystics, but when I read your book, the doubts fell away and there was clarity about the truth of their experience. How can that be?

A:  The energy. You were waiting for that energy to hit your aura and then it all fell together. You learn all kinds of things on the spiritual pathway, and then one day, out of the blue, you suddenly get what it means—might be twenty years later—you see it in greater fullness.

Q:  It was profound for me—and shocking, because devotion to a spiritual teacher was the last thing I expected of myself.

A:  Devotion is actually to the Self, with a capital "S," within the teacher, but it tends to get quite personalized. You look at famous fallen gurus and disasters like that. It got personalized. What is the devotion to? In the Hindu tradition, first it's devotion to the teacher, and this diminishes the personal ego of the student. Then, as you become more enlightened, you realize that what you're devoted to is the Self within the teacher—which is not different than the Self that is within you. That is the final step.

Q:  So you're saying the Self is here within me—it's present in all of us, but the teacher activates our awareness of it?

A:  Yes. So devotion to a teacher would be a step. Then you see it's the reflection of Divinity through the teacher via the Self that is the real Teacher. The naïve teacher thinks that it is they who are the teacher, but it's not. The Knowingness of the response arises spontaneously as a consequence of the Self. The self with a small "s" will have to figure that out. When I give a lecture, I hear the words for the first time just like everyone else!

Q:  When people walk up to you at the seminars and say, "Oh, I feel so wonderful here with you," you always say: "It's your own Self reflected back. What you're experiencing is your own Self." That feeling of love, of joy that we feel around you is really our own Self?

A:  Yes. It's your own Self that's making you feel good. You first see it in the teacher before you realize it's within you. The teacher should reflect that back to you. What is it within you that's being activated by the aura of the teacher? The teacher's aura just activates what's already within you. That's why the aura of the teacher is important. It's an energy field that one would not encounter unless one came directly into contact with it.

Q: And now there is the idea to write a book about you. It can't be an accident to have the academic training about mystics and then to meet one. It's like there's something to share, by whatever means.

A: Yes, it's a perfect setup. You are seeing that your gifts are there just to enable you to share with the world… like my being an M.D., a psychiatrist. I couldn't help a lot of the people unless I had that title. They would listen to me with proper respect, and I could write a prescription or something. But that was all just to be of service to them. That's all. Yes, very often there aren't many people available for a certain task in the world; probably only a couple people like yourself. Divine Will expresses itself in multiple ways. There's speaking about it. And then there's people speaking about your speaking about it to people who never would have heard about it otherwise. So, each one serves a function in communication.

Q: I didn't know I needed a teacher until I met one.

A: You were already on a pathway. You weren't looking for golf lessons when you came here, were you?!

Q: It's crazy what I've believed—I didn't know it was a pathway.

A: Well, we've all been through that. I remember one time going out with a whole bunch of UFO people, with a spokesperson who got direct transmissions from this UFO group and said the UFOs were going to land in the field that evening at eight o'clock. So we went out to the field and at eight o'clock she got a transmission that the fields were not clear for transport at this time. That's a lame excuse: "This is not a propitious time for us to land!" It's such an area of falsehood, all these sects that wander off and form their own compartments…

And how people seem to like someone to tell them what to do, what to believe, what to wear, whom to go to bed with, how to change their name, who can ride in the cars with whom—I mean, how boring to have to tell people what to do all the time. There must be something within people that they want to be ruled.

Q: I saw that in myself for fifteen years as a member of a sectarian group that believed it was the only group going to heaven. I was into specialness and wanting to defer to leaders. Now I look back and wonder how I could've believed that.

A: There's a dominant energy field, and they all come out of that same energy field. There's something within the person that yearns to surrender their will to a higher will. And then you remove all responsibility and just do what you're told. There's a certain relief in it. It's best to avoid putting trust in a teacher who isn't willing to commit to you. Most are interested in you committing to them, controlling you, and squeezing what they can get out of you. They say, "Do what I say, let me control your life, follow my rules, go to bed with me, give me your money, bow and pay respect to me." Spiritual rape is more painful than physical rape; it's devastating. I've treated patients who've been through it. The teacher should make a declaration of intention to students: "I am committed to the highest Truth and will not exploit the student-teacher relationship." The true teacher is complete within himself and needs nothing from a student.

Q: I was in a religious group that was very controlling. Then I left. I thought I was done with religion, and spent a few years as an agnostic, but that didn't mesh with some spiritual experiences I'd had. I've spent my life jumping from one little pond to another, jumping and jumping each time I hit up against their manmade dogma or tradition. I knew Truth was beyond dogma. When I read your book, I thought, "This is it! I'll go to Sedona and see what this is about."

A: So you had a spiritual drivenness as a karmic inheritance. There's a spiritual drivenness to find out what is the Truth and become aligned with it and then eventually it's confirmed experientially. So that is a drivenness. I had the same drivenness. I checked out one thing after another. Growing up I was a religionist, then an atheist and agnostic. I was a Buddhist for years. I was a vegetarian for about ten years. What really counts is the fidelity. It's the building up of fidelity. First you do this, then you do that. And it's not that you were wrong before but you're perfecting the tools you need to go the whole way, which is fidelity, commitment, alignment with and verification of the highest truth you can find. So those are the tools, and we go through all these phases.

Q: When I came here, I felt finally free of all the dogmas and small ponds, like I'd entered an ocean with no limits. I felt completely free and finally "home."

A: You've been a devoted seeker. I get that this group comes in on the planet about the same time, meaning within a century or so. We all tend to swoop into this plane and then we swoop out again, and then we swoop back into it again a hundred years later... to flock together on that particular shore... then take off again and later re-flock. Yes, we come in together and go out together. It helps to eliminate the fear of dying, which is really the fear of being alone. When you realize you're not going to be alone and you in fact can't be alone, you're gonna be with approximately the same group of people. You will not be separated from them.

Seems to be a group dedicated to finding the Truth, having checked out this, checked out that. All destined for enlightenment. They reincarnate to be together because the group goal is enlightenment. Like the goal of an AA group is to stay sober, the destiny of this group is to be enlightened. The group is held together by a shared commitment to enlightenment. That pathway is assisted by sharing holy company of others with the same commitment. So we serve each other by virtue of what we've become, and what we become is by virtue of our own spiritual dedication and decision. It's a very rare intention—practically never happens.

## Love in Everyday Life

Q: What is Love?

A: Love is an energy field that is available everywhere all the time.

Q: Then why do people look for love as if they don't have it?

A: People think of love primarily as affection, as in "honey" and "sweetheart." They tend to think of being "in love" and romantic love. In reality, romance is a minor portion of one's life experience. Yes, a big love affair at age eighteen is overwhelming, but most of life involves other expressions of love: love of family, love of friends, love of pets, love of home, love of possessions, love of health, love of ideals, love of values, love of country, love of purpose, etc. In everyday life, most of our friends and activities are occurring in the field of love, but it isn't romantic love. There is actually an invisible, all-encompassing energy field of Love that surrounds everyone and everything.

Love takes many forms in everyday life: Love as gratitude; Love as enthusiasm; Love as loyalty and friendship; Love as forgiveness; Love as appreciation; Love as beauty; Love as virtue; Love as affection; Love as respect; Love as motivator. Love, in fact, is the motivator behind the majority of our actions. So love is a prevailing energy field. It's a way of being with oneself and others, a way of being in the world, a way of seeing and appreciating life and all of creation. We appreciate our own existence and the existence of others. We also have love of our own commitments and ideals such as love of one's country, fellow man, or military service, which is love as valor. I had a relative who just loved his life in the air force. He thrived in that lifestyle and its values. So, you love what you do, you love who you are, you love whom you're with, and you love the overall environment of your life.

Q: At your birthday gathering, you said, "Love has a certain gravity of its own. Love goes to love. Love attracts love. Love precipitates love. It's because of love that we're here at this moment. Our capacity to love increases simply by recognizing that love already prevails in our life."

A: By recognizing that love prevails in everyday life, the capacity to love increases, but people don't usually recognize the love behind their actions and those of others, so they take them for granted rather than appreciate them. Love in any expression adds to the quality of life. You can live without recognizing the love in your life, but it's grim. Love is a kitty's purr or a dog's wagging tail. We've found that having a dog increases your lifespan by ten years due to the healing effect of love. Just think of all the bizarre things people do to add ten years onto their lives! I'm grateful for the presence of Kelsey in our life.

Q: How did you find Kelsey?

A: There were two dogs in the Humane Society that connected psychically with me. One was a black Dalmatian who jumped up and was very excited. And then there was Kelsey who was in the background, nose to the ground, shy, looking up like this (he demonstrates a forlorn and lonely dog). I knew the Dalmatian had the energy to attract to itself someone to rescue it, but Kelsey would be overlooked. They give the dogs ten days to be adopted, and she was on day 9. I knew the other dog would be all right, so we brought Kelsey home. She's a great doggie. On our Map of Consciousness, the kitty's purr and the dog's wagging tail calibrate at 500. That's the level of Love and the heart.

Q: You've said that dogs and kitties are more benign than some humans.

A: That's true. I'd rather be around Kelsey than around many humans! I think we calibrated her energy at 250. It's an energy of neutrality, so it doesn't take a stand against anything, it's peaceable. A dog's energy field is more benevolent than the energy of many people in the news. On top of that, the dog's wagging tail calibrates at 500, the energy field of love.

Q: I remember you told the story of how a dog's wagging tail stopped a gunman in Canada. He was right on the verge of shooting people at a beach—guns loaded and triggers unlocked—when a dog ran over to him, wagging and wanting to play. The man put down the guns and turned himself in.[199]

A: Love has the power to transfigure a situation like that. People put a lot of stock in reasoning and talking through something. They try to persuade through logic, but love is actually what makes the difference in our lives. Love is the energy that brings a shift in attitude. All of a sudden, because of the presence of love, someone breaks free; they're able to let go of a longstanding grudge or major insecurity. They might say, seemingly out of nowhere, "What's the point of holding on to that?"

As a psychiatrist, I often recommended that patients get a pet. If you love a pet, then the capacity of love will grow. The more you love, the more you can love. You can start with a pet. We love the kitty, we love loving the kitty, the kitty loves being loved, and we love that the kitty loves being loved! See how love grows? Love and our capacity to love compounds, just as hatred would compound in the opposite direction. All love benefits all of life and the whole human race. When we love our pet dog and pet kitties, we benefit all of existence.

Q: You say, "Love is a way of being in the world." Is there anything a person can do to develop this way of being?

A: A place to start is to love that you are, that you exist, and to be grateful for your existence. Your own existence is proof that you are loved.

We bring more love into our lives simply by consciously focusing on its presence as a motivator in everyday life. For example, the love involved in making the family dinner, cleaning the kitty boxes, going to work to pay the bills. Ordinary endeavors, done out of love, carry great power. A dinner made with love makes a difference for the family. The Olympian who runs the race out of love for his country has a more positive experience than the one who runs to win for himself. Love as a motivator has great power to it.

You make a gift of your life by sanctifying all endeavors with love, devotion, and selfless service. I like to say, "Live your life like a prayer." Every movement is a *mudra*, every action a form of worship. Selfless service is paradoxically self-rewarding. What you give to others you are really giving to yourself. Even the smallest acts done with love—a smile, a kind word—benefit the world. They ripple out as a blessing and benefit yourself as well as the world.

During the war, we did things out of love for our shipmates that we wouldn't have done otherwise. That is love as a bond of unity. It is fraternal love. There is also maternal love, which is the willingness of the mother to sacrifice for her child. Lovingness as a way of being expresses itself in all these ways. Lovingness is all-inclusive. It is one with beauty. As a way of being in the world, lovingness is forgiving, nurturing, and supportive. It discerns the essence of things and focuses on the goodness of life in all of its expressions. Eventually, it becomes unconditional.

Q:   Love is all around us but we just don't see it?

A:   We are saying that love prevails throughout society where it's often least suspected. Much can be learned about yourself and life in general by pausing to look at the role that love has in its great variety of expressions. Love prevails in many endeavors where it is given different names: service, honor, nurturance, humor, dedication, respect, affection, protectiveness, admiration, maternal self-sacrifice, and valor. Love in one form or another is an unconscious motivator in the great multitude of human endeavors where it is not accorded conscious importance. These are the hidden forms of love. With intention, you begin to see it more and more.

The world thinks that ambition, hard work, and success are what life is all about, but underneath all of these things is the love one experiences as a consequence of "success." Isn't it the seeking of love that is behind ambition, hard work, self-sacrifice, endeavor, and service to others? In all these pursuits, we are hoping for an experience of love, being loved, and loving.

To do something out of love instead of duty creates a whole different enterprise. For example, the tedium of an assembly-line job becomes bearable when there's a loving relationship with fellow workers. Love prevails throughout the ordinary, but we often don't recognize it as love—phone calls from friends, attention to responsibilities, walking the dog, encouraging a colleague, taking care of one's health, etc. For example, the love of life itself leads us to look after our health. To love life in all of its expressions is a form of appreciation for creation itself.

## How to Help the World and Others

Q:   What to do for world peace?

A:   Become what you are to the best of your ability. If you want to improve yourself, start with whatever is coming up for you. You don't have to learn secret codes or chant ancient mantras. Life itself is the best workshop.

Q:   Our inner work serves the world at large? You've said it's more effective to raise the level of the sea than to bail out individual ships— meaning that if we raise our own level of consciousness, then we raise the whole of humanity.

A:   Realize that every person committed to love, appreciation, and kindness raises the consciousness of all humanity. This makes your daily life important—what you think on the subway makes a difference in the world. One loving thought cancels all the negative thoughts of the week. If you surrender a block to love, then you lift the field, and the field lifts the people. This is more effective than fighting against something. If you play classical music in a parking lot, the graffiti makers leave of their own. The answer is not another anti-crime program but to raise the overall energy field. Love radiates an energy that transforms everything around it. It happens of its own. A loving person doesn't have to *do* anything; they simply *are*. By virtue of their presence, the meeting goes better. A healing is more likely. A peaceful resolution becomes possible. "Miraculous" is a word often used to describe the effect of love, but we don't have to give it that label.

Q: Sometimes I feel guilty for being happy in a world full of suffering. How to work through that? For example, does a parent have a right to be happy if a child is suicidal or an addict?

A: What good would it do if you were unhappy? You can't save someone from hitting the brick wall if that's where they're headed. Don't keep putting a cushion there. Watch them touch the heat and withdraw. Don't hold up their evolution by not surrendering your ego need to save them.

Q: What's the best way to help someone who's struggling? I've heard it said, "Sometimes you have to let the drowning man drown."

A: What you do in any given situation depends on your level of consciousness. Usually it's best not to get involved. You may think that you know what's best for others. This leads to trying to change people or situations "for their own good." This is a vanity of the ego, to think it knows better than God. Intervention may do more harm than good. For example, if you intervene in an addict's recovery, you rob the person of karmic merit. You lower their bottom if you keep helping. In 12-Step language, this is called enabling. It prolongs their suffering. You need to walk away, surrender them to God. You have to be willing to sacrifice your own ego need to save others or get their approval. You do this out of love for them—"tough love." Your do-goodism may sentence somebody to further struggle if they're in the midst of a karmic undoing. Sometimes the best way to help others is to save them from the aggravation of your intervention!

Q: What about sharing with others what we have learned from a spiritual path?

A: People are given what they need for their spiritual evolution when it's the right time for them to encounter it. Timing is often the critical factor, and only the Self is capable of incorporating unknown karmic conditions. Not everything that you've been given should be shared with others, because they may not have the karmic right to it. It may even cause harm. It's like the unwise surgery that kills the patient because he's not ready. People may have spiritual work to do before they can use a certain teaching without harm. Don't give them something just because you're trying to be a good neighbor. It's better simply to share with others what you have become.

Q: Does prayer help?

A: Prayer is a gift we give to others out of our love for them. As a doctor, I've prayed for the recovery of every patient I've ever seen. I don't tell them that—it might make them nervous. My responsibility is to fulfill God's expectation of me and to utilize the gifts God has given me for the betterment of mankind and the good of individual patients. I love each patient and I pray for them. It doubles the rate of recovery if you pray for a patient. Every time you pray for someone, you're actually praying for everyone. Your prayer benefits all mankind.

## Pragmatics of Love

Q: So, being a caring person in everyday life is a form of love?

A: And also recognizing that you yourself are cared for by the life around you. Caringness is an expression of love. What matters in life is that we feel cared for. If we are ill or going through a difficult situation, what really matters is that we feel loved and cared for. If we do, we can bear anything. If you want to help the world, be a caring person. To be a kind and caring person in everyday life is really all that's necessary. The rest reveals itself in due time. People look for a special spiritual technique or secret mantra that will rocket-launch them to Nirvana, but all it takes is to be a kind and caring person in everyday life, to love all of life in all its expressions, without exception, including yourself.

Love and kindness provide a pleasant ambience to many areas of life that would otherwise be onerous. Cleaning out the kitty boxes, sweeping the floor, paying the bills, taking out the garbage —these are all forms of love as caringness. We see caringness in many arenas of life—caring for the environment, caring for the welfare of others, caring for our pets, caring for our appliances, caring for our garden, and caring about the quality of our life. So we try to maximize the quality of our life in all that we do—our cooking, the way we dress, our efforts at work, our home décor, and so on. We do so partly by anticipating and fulfilling other people's expectations. When people come to one of our seminars, for instance, they have certain expectations. I care about their effort to take time and show up, and I try to do the best job I can to be creative, original, and appropriate. We value other people's time and effort in the general field of lovingness.

Q:   Love has pragmatic value?

A:   To be of pragmatic value is a form of love for the more sophisticated! For the unsophisticated, love is merely a smooch and a squeeze. People commonly equate "love" with romance, but romantic love is only a minor portion of one's life. More often, the energy of love is expressed through the pragmatics of everyday life. Love, as expressed through life's pragmatic accomplishments, includes an appreciation of quality—quality of effort, excellence, and expression. Love seeks excellence. If you buy a present for someone you love, you search for what will be most appropriate, pleasing, and valuable to them. If you're making a salad for a loved one, you make it beautiful and delicious.

Q:   How do pragmatics of love in ordinary life relate to spiritual goals?

A:   They're one and the same. By loving our ordinary existence, we are loving God.

Q:   That reminds me of the Bible verse "God is Love."

A:   Divinity flows through our loving, so when you love someone, you radiate Divinity to that person. You bless them with your love. We might say that love is actually the Presence of God. God and Love are the same thing. When you love someone, you are bringing God into their life—but you don't tell them that because it might scare them! Lovingness is the most positive influence in the universe.

## Love in Difficult Situations

Q:   Is it possible to be a loving person but sometimes feel annoyed or angry in our daily interactions?

A:   It's an illusion that spiritually evolved people never have a negative feeling. The higher states come and go. To have a human existence, you can't be in a celestial state all the time and still survive. In a very high state, there's no appetite and no thought of physical survival. This state isn't workable for most people, so they need to have compassion for their human condition and all that goes with it—nervous system, brain function, and the vicissitudes of life. Feeling annoyed and frustrated is part of the human condition. It's best to let go of guilt about being an ordinary human who has ordinary human feelings. Acceptance of your innate humanness brings peace. Compassion for yourself brings equanimity. When spiritually aware people have angelic ambitions, they are bothered by their anger, so they heap guilt about anger on top of the anger! They have to realize that feelings come and go, whereas the commitment to evolve is more significant and is unwavering. This level of commitment is love expressed as devotion.

Q:   When our love becomes unconditional, do we love everyone all the time?

A:   It puts no conditions, no expectations, and no demands on others that they must be a certain way in order to be loved. We love them no matter how they are. We see their innate lovability, even if they're obnoxious! We have no attachment and no hidden agenda with them. They're free to be as they are. We have no conscious or unconscious expectations of them; therefore the state is free of emotional manipulation. In many relationships, people feel a subtle pressure to behave in a manner that will please the other. They fear the loss of relationship. Dependency and attachment have nothing to do with love.

Q: So the level of Unconditional Love means to accept even the people who mistreat us?

A: Love is to not want to change them. You see that everyone is doing the best they can or else they'd do it differently. The same is true for you. Love is accepting and loving everything as it is. Unconditional Love is loving people the way they are, without needing or trying to change them. I like to refer to Socrates who taught that people are always doing whatever they believe will bring the good or happiness. Their problem is ignorance—they don't know what true happiness is—and we can't fault people or our self for ignorance.

Q: Does Unconditional Love mean we have to stay with negative people?

A: We have love of our own self. Sometimes love of oneself means it's best to let certain things alone and avoid certain people. You don't keep petting a dog that bites you, do you? That would be naive. You have compassion for such an aggressive dog, but you wouldn't bring it home to play with your children. You have compassion for negative people, and at the same time avoid interacting with them. You know their shadow side and act accordingly. If a person is greedy for money or esteem, you avoid getting involved with them on your project. You keep your contact to a minimum. We have love of our own self and our own integrity. Love is all-inclusive, which means it includes our own self-respect and love of life itself. We love our own life and choose things that are uplifting for our own consciousness. It's not necessary to feel guilty about protecting the serenity of your own life. Guilt doesn't get you enlightened, only an ulcer!

You might say that one form of love is generally called self-respect. Out of self-respect, you don't allow yourself to be insulted or taken advantage of. There is love of your own integrity. You're not willing to violate your sense of integrity for the emotional gain of pleasing others or trying to get their approval. And often you'll find that you have an attachment to certain people or situations or ideals, and that's why you're staying in an unpleasant environment.

Q: Jesus taught to love our enemies, to do good to those who hate us. How to understand this?

A: Hatred is defeated by love. If you calibrate hatred on our scale, it's at 150. Love calibrates 500 and over. Love is infinitely more powerful.

Q: In a practical situation where someone has been hateful towards me, how does love defeat hatred? Do I just forgive and forget?

A: On our scale, forgiveness is at the level of Acceptance (350). Love calibrates at 500. Acceptance allows us to forgive others. It's obvious they can't be or do otherwise. They're doing the best they can, given what they are. At a certain level of consciousness, it makes perfect sense to rob an old lady. At another level, it would never occur to you, and you'd help the old lady across the street. Each person operates at their own level of consciousness.

Q: How does forgiveness relate to Love?

A: We forgive but we do not forget whom we're dealing with. I accept the alligator and how it kills to eat, but I don't go swimming in a lake full of alligators! In the field of Love, you eventually see there is actually nothing and no one to forgive. Forgiveness implies you had a position that someone did something wrong and you are forgiving them. Love sees it differently—no one can help being exactly as they are. Love knows this truth and takes no position. Love bypasses logic, with its mental processing of an event and all that was done. Love sees the oneness of all things. In the field of Love, spontaneous intuitive knowingness progressively replaces thinkingness. The knowingness is holistic and all-inclusive because the energy of Love is one with the interconnected universe.

Forgiveness allows us to see life events from the viewpoint of mercy. We see the ego as a little pet. It isn't bad; it's merely limited. We don't view the guy who robbed an old lady as bad; we feel compassion for him, that he saw such an action as a good idea. Likewise, we don't beat ourselves up for the errors we made when we were less evolved. We didn't know better. The most we can say about it is that we thought it was a good idea at the time. A key to making love unconditional is this willingness to forgive. With forgiveness comes the humility and willingness to surrender our perception of a past event.

Q: How to go about this? It's hard to let go of seeing it the way I see it.

A: Pray for a miracle to see the truth about the situation or the other person. Let go of your opinions about whatever happened. Let go of the emotional payoffs you get from being wronged, being right, and blaming. Blaming is a choice, and you can choose differently. No matter how justified you may feel, you don't have to blame. You don't have to see it as right versus wrong.

Q: I'm inspired by the examples of Nelson Mandela and Viktor Frankl. They both endured horrific suffering, yet didn't blame the people who persecuted them.

A: That option is open also to you. The energy field of Love has the power to recontextualize even tragedy and trauma into a spiritual gift.

Q: So Viktor Frankl's capacity to see the meaning of his suffering during the Holocaust is what becomes possible in the energy field of Unconditional Love?

A: At that point, you no longer see the person or situation as "wrong" and in need of being forgiven. It is saintly, really. You've surrendered all judgment to God. Since all judgment is really self-judgment, you've liberated yourself in the process and you have become a gift to mankind.

Q: Some Christians teach that if someone hits you, just let them keep hitting you.

A: Christ taught to avoid negativity, not fight it. In a way, it's seeing others as children. You love them even though they're misbehaving because they don't know any better. They have no self-control. You love them even though they're being foolish. Christ said, "Forgive them for they know not what they do." You let them be as they are, without getting involved. His teaching was to avoid negativity. "Straight and narrow is the way. Waste no time."

Q: Where should spiritual seekers look for a community to evolve them in this direction? It seems that many religious groups are not at the level of Love.

A: You want to look for places where Love prevails, where it is the dominant environment and energy field. If some group claims to be a religion but teaches hatred, then how can that be? Why would any religion want to control its members or denigrate the beliefs of others? These are red flags. Some groups are actually hate groups masking as religions so they can claim freedom of religion and legal protection. I think dominating others would be a horrible responsibility. I have enough trouble between the front door and the back door. That keeps me busy all day. The dog, the cats, the birdie, I'm up to my ears in work already!

Q:    Does the potential for love exist within those who are dictators and haters?

A:    They've got self-love. In its lowest form, love is narcissism. Narcissus looks in the water and falls in love with his own image. Whether the love is love of oneself or of others makes the difference between narcissism and lovingness. Some people limit their life to what they can get out of the world and out of others. There are many forms of limited narcissistic love, as in the tendency to love things or ideas because they are "mine." The level of love we call narcissism is really the antithesis of what's commonly referred to as love. It's important to discern the direction of the love. Is it solely narcissistic and egocentric, or is it unselfish and giving?

We speak of the level of Unconditional Love as the ideal. This is the Self versus the self. Its most expanded form is Agape, which is Universal Love. This is the ultimate goal of personal development—to become loving to life in all its expressions, without exception. It's easy to love your own children and grandchildren, and more challenging to love all children. Love expands as you move from loving "mine" to loving "all." Mother Teresa is a great example.

## Seeing the Divine in Everything

Q:    Your description of the state of Unconditional Love is beautiful:

> It is experienced as inner joy, and the joy arises from within each moment of existence rather than from any outer source. The world that one sees is illuminated by exquisite beauty, and the perfection of all creation shines forth. Everything happens effortlessly by synchronicity, and everything in the world is seen to be an expression of Love and Divinity. There is the capacity to love many people simultaneously, as love has no limit. The desire is to use one's state of consciousness for the benefit of life itself, rather than for particular individuals or groups. At this level,

individual will merges into Divine Will. That which the world calls 'miraculous' occurs continuously and without effort. These phenomena happen of their own as a consequence of the power of the energy field, not of the individual person. One has become a channel of Divine Grace.

A: In the beginning, love is seen as dualistic—a *this* loving a *that*. Love starts out as dualistic, as conditional, as a feeling state. Later, it becomes a way of being.

Q: Is there anything people can do to reach this state of Unconditional Love?

A: Practice loving everything with the intention of realizing its Divinity. (He pats the table). You see this beautiful table? It's here for us. It's an expression of God being a table. Everything is God. Real. (He points to different things in the room.) We can't say, "This kitty is real, this table is real, this Kleenex is real, this doggie is not real!" Either they are all real or none of them is real. Nothing exists except Divinity.

Q: You've said, "To understand the nature of God, it is necessary only to know the nature of Love itself." Where to begin?

A: What you do is try to uncover for yourself the awareness of the Divinity of everything that exists. Nothing could exist unless it was Divinity. This (pointing) is God being a table, this is God being Doc Hawkins, this is God being you. A Buddhist would not say God but Buddha-nature, which is the same. The Buddha avoided using the word "God" because of the ignorance that surrounded it. As you become more loving, you see that you're surrounded by nothing but friends. Everything you see is a friend. Everything is a part of God. Everybody's on your side. Many people won't let you love them. Love scares a lot of people. If they're not awake to love, then sometimes you can awaken them to that love and make them realize that love is present.

Q:   How long does it take to reach the state of Unconditional Love?

A:   You can't rush it or make it happen. It's not something to accomplish. You simply surrender the blocks to love and ask to see things differently. You let go of wanting to control life. You let go of wanting something. You do what you can to remove the inner obstacles to love.

Q:   You have said that Unconditional Love is a rare energy field, yet it's possible for people to reach it. What would increase the possibility?

A:   There has to be a time when all your emotional energies pour into that space of Divinity. Nothing can be more important than experiencing and realizing the Divinity of this table, here and now. It's not here by accident; it's here by design. You make it a goal to recognize and experience the Divinity as the essence of all that exists. Everything is God. There is nothing else.

You'll see that everyone contributes something unique. You can't say one thing is better than another. You have a cute little doggie, and his little tail wags. And then you have a cute little kitty, and she purrs and purrs. And you have a wonderful wife, lovely neighbors, and loving friends. How can you say that one thing is better than another? Is a tree better than a house? Is a house better than a rabbit? A rabbit better than a chicken? One person better than another? You can't say that one is better than another. Each is unique, and you learn to love everything and everyone *because* they are unique. There's only one you. No one except you can be you.

Q:   So can loving one's everyday life take one straight to God, without religion?

A:   Yes, so, you love doing what you do. Playing the best game of golf that you know how. Bicycle racing or whatever it is that you love.

Cooking pancakes. Loving what you do. To see that Divinity is the essence of all that exists in all expressions is Agape. Universal loving-ness. Agape is a state of consciousness, not a religion.

## Love is Timeless

Q: So one sees that Love is present everywhere, without beginning and without end?

A: Love is outside of time; it has nothing to do with time or place. Love is caringness. And respect. You respect the trees and the woods. You don't just go around slashing them. Everything that exists is aware. The tree knows when love walks by. The forest is aware of our love. You respect everything because you see the Divinity of everything. Because Divinity is the essence of all that exists, you have a loving respect for all that is. We love God by loving all of exist-ence. Discussing love is tantamount to discussing life itself. "Love is the Ultimate Law of the Universe" is a truthful statement. Most people think that survival is the basic law of the universe, but actu-ally it is Love.

Q: In the snowbank, you melted into Love. You said that as a boy on your seventeen-mile newspaper route in the Wisconsin winter, you fell from your bike in the freezing wind. To get out of the storm, you burrowed into a snowbank. What was the experience?

A: Infinite Love. All negative emotion disappeared—fear, impa-tience, frustration—all disappeared. Instead there was only the Radiance of Infinite, timeless, everlasting, all-encompassing Love, which was not different than the Reality of what I was, what I am. The Infinite Love was not different than the essence of who and what I am. All fear of death disappeared. It has never returned. There is no fear of death, because your reality is outside of time. If you stop iden-tifying with this body, Reality doesn't disappear; it's just not located in this body anymore. It is the Self that radiates as one's Reality instead of the small self. I remember I breathed again, resumed this physicality, because otherwise my father would have felt guilty that I'd died. He had come out in the storm to find me. Out of love for my father, I knew I had to breathe again and resume. So, when he pulled on my leg, I came back to the world to save him a lifetime of guilt. But if it hadn't been for my father, I would have just left and been fine. In the infinite state of foreverness bliss, nothing else compares!

Q: What is your awareness of death right now, at eighty-three?

A: Everything happens spontaneously. What I do is I surrender to God's will all the time. Whether to eat lunch or not, whether to do the seminar on Saturday or not... I let go resisting being in the world. I'd just as soon leave, but everything in due time. When it's time to leave, you leave. There's no need to worry about it. I reenergize being in the world because of Susan. I love her and want her to be happy. I'm interested in fulfilling my service to the world and what makes other people happy—giving lectures or staying here to be with Susan and Kelsey and the kitties. So, actually, I stay for the sake of love. That's what it's about. I want to fulfill all the roles I can, to be of benefit to this world.

Letting go of attachment and possessiveness is a positive step. You can look at everything and everyone in your life as belonging to God, not to you. The ego thinks it owns and can control. It thinks in terms of *mine*, but in Reality, nothing can be owned or be mine. Nothing belongs to you. All your relationships and properties are a matter of stewardship. Even your body belongs not to you but to God.

Q: Does old age bring an opportunity to love in a unique way?

A: It gives you a chance to recontextualize many of life's events, to see them in a different light and just accept them as part of the human experience. Part of the human experience is facing physical decline and accepting it gracefully instead of cursing it all the time! I don't remember being this old before, in other lifetimes. The part I don't like is your physical dependence on others for things you yourself once handled without a second thought. You have to ask for help with things that are so simple because you can't see them. I find this part of old age annoying—to be incompetent in areas in which you once excelled. I suppose incapacities of age are appropriate in that they get you ready to leave the world. If you were still involved in being a star in some area of life, you'd resent leaving the world and wouldn't be very graceful about it. So the decline gives you time to adjust, get used to the fact that you'll be leaving, and do any kind of spiritual work you'll want to have completed by the time you leave here.

Losing vision in the right eye changed my life. I grew up with a Protestant ethic that said you always had to be busy, creating or making or doing something like writing a book, etc. What's left for me is to love. I try to love everything and everyone all the time. I don't have to have vision for that or a piece a paper to write on. I spend most of my time in prayer, to be loving toward all things at all times. All the while I'm talking to you, I'm praying for your happiness, enlightenment, and salvation, grateful for your presence, which is significant and a blessing.

(*Peaceful silence.*)

Q: Doc, what do you recommend as a goal for the readers of this book?

A: A worthy goal is to love what you do, love what you are, and love whom you're with to the best of your ability. Love that which you are and you will love the Source.

He was a teacher I could trust absolutely, so I studied every hint, gesture, and expression. Each interaction with him was a training.

"The whole world is a Bodhi tree," he said when we were watching the news one day. (He said he liked to keep an eye on the world.) To me, the news showed a hopeless and suffering world. To him, each place, each happening of the world held Ultimate Reality within it. Therefore one could wake up to Reality anywhere, at any time. The

Buddha woke up under the Bodhi tree. Doc told me it wasn't the tree that made it happen. Awakening can happen anywhere. It's that the Buddha sat where he was with total surrender—fearing nothing, wanting nothing, knowing nothing.

Author built this altar at the top of Cathedral Rock,
Sedona, in gratitude for the gift of her teacher's love.

# Chapter Twenty-Five

# DEVOTIONAL LIFE

D oc's teachings on Love were a relief to me. "To understand the nature of God, it is necessary only to know the nature of love itself. To truly know love is to know and understand God, and to know God is to understand love."[200] What mattered most was not what I did and not even what I believed, but that genuine love was in my heart. Over time, that lovingness began to intensify and I experienced myself as devoted.

## DEVOTED TO LOVE, NOT BELIEF SYSTEMS

Devotion was different from commitment. Previously, as an activist, religionist, and scholar, I had been committed. I'd finished four graduate degrees in record time with top grades. I'd gone to church three times a week for fifteen years. But these commitments were about getting something—self-fulfillment, approval, status, security, identity, eternal life. In contrast, devotion was about selfless service—wanting nothing for myself.

My teacher pointed to the family dog as an example of devotion. The dog's attention is fixed on the master, and he often waits all day at the door for his master to return home. Doc told me the story of a dog that continued to go to the street corner every day at 5 p.m.

to meet his master coming home from work—even for years after the master had died. A dog's faithfulness is unconditional. His eyes are always on the master, and he returns to his master's doorstep no matter what. Devotion is like this: "I'll do whatever is asked."

And that's how it was. Soon after my first private visit with Doc at his house, a strange and unexpected interaction occurred. A large crowd of people was at a picnic in the park to celebrate his birthday. This annual picnic was one of the few opportunities for local people to be in his presence, aside from the monthly public events. Everyone was joyously gathered around him. I hung back and didn't even say hello. It was enough to be there in his presence. I didn't need or expect to interact with him on a personal level. He knew my essence, and that's all that mattered to me.

When it came time for him to leave, Gabe was by his side, holding his arm to steady him as they walked to the car. Suddenly, Doc turned back to the group and asked loudly, "Where is Fran? I want to see her." Someone called me over. He put himself right in front of me, just two inches between us. He was a short man, and we were eye to eye. His aura encircled me and I entered another dimension. It was absolutely magnetic.

Looking at me intensely, he said, "I want to get a look at you, to see you. I know your energy, but I want to see what you look like. And to tell you to teach about mystics in the churches."

"Yes, sir. I will do that."

And then he walked away to his car. I was stunned. Where did that come from? What a strange directive for him to give me. Speaking on mystics at churches? What churches? When? I hadn't been to a church in years, and I couldn't imagine ever being in one again, yet two years later, that's exactly what happened. I was asked to give several presentations on "The Power of Love" and "Exploring the Mystics" at the Episcopal, Unity, and other churches. Not only that—I had joined one.

Looking back, I see how his directive at the picnic brought completion to the Christian dimension of my life. Years earlier, after leaving *the* church, I had steered clear of all Christian communities.

It made me bristle even to walk into a church. My teacher healed this wound in his embodiment of agape—the unconditional and universal love taught by Jesus. As an infant, I had been christened in the Episcopal Church in line with my father's heritage, but I didn't know that until my thirties. Now as an adult I decided to be confirmed in the Episcopal Church, reentering the communion of Christians from a place of heart. To this day, the church remains a place of fellowship, and I find great joy and meaning in participating in its lineage of Christian love. The Eucharist transmits the Light, a mystical phenomenon that can be seen as each person receives the sacrament. After I became a member, the priest allowed me to serve as a lay Eucharistic minister and to take the consecrated bread and wine to Doc and Susan at their home during the last two years of Doc's life. To share the consecrated Presence of Christ in communion with my teacher and his wife in their home was an experience I have no words for.

"In any way that men love Me, in that same way they find My Love; for many are the paths of men, but they all in the end come to Me." My teacher often quoted that verse from the Bhagavad Gita, just as Swami Vivekananda had at the 1893 Parliament of the World's Religions. "Many are the paths to God," he said. Coming from a fundamentalist background, this took time for me to integrate. During one of my visits to his house, I asked Doc about the words of Jesus in the New Testament (John 14:2–6) that are used as marching orders for missionizing:

> 'In my Father's house are many mansions; if it were not so, I would have told you. I go to prepare a place for you. And if I go and prepare a place for you, I will come again and take you to me, so that where I am you may be also. You know where I am going and you know the way.' Thomas said to him, 'Our Lord, we do not know where you are going, and how can we know the way?' Jesus said to him, 'I am the way and

the truth and the life; no man comes to the Father
but by me.'

When I was a missionary for the church, I believed that Jesus was
saying that only Christians go to heaven. This is a common interpretation by Christians—that only Christians can reach God. Doc said
that this exclusivist interpretation is a misunderstanding, for everyone
is already chosen and loved by God by virtue of their existence. He
pointed me to the beginning of the passage "In my Father's house are
many mansions." He explained that what the world calls heaven has
many dimensions to it, and he used the word "neighborhood" so I
could understand. We might say that each neighborhood has its own
entry gate. For those who hold to an exclusivist belief system, yes,
their experience will be that only those who believe in that doctrine
can enter that neighborhood. Thus, he said, there might be Baptist,
Jehovah's Witness, Mormon, Adventist, Atheist, etc., neighborhoods.
They're not aware that their neighborhood is one of many. Those who
have transcended particular and exclusivist belief systems see that
there are many rooms or mansions on the other side, and they move
freely among and beyond them, just as they do on earth. The liberated person can visit any truly holy place and smell the fragrance of
love. Jesus was speaking to his disciples when he told them that he
was their "way" and that no one could reach the Father but through
him. Interestingly, the Buddha and Krishna said something similar to
their followers.

If both Jesus and Krishna say, "I am the way," then what to
do? Each has its sacred scriptures, each is understood by billions
of people to be an incarnation of Divinity; then is one wrong and
the other right? The polarizing question arises from a limited level
of consciousness that fathoms a God who would create billions of
people and then exclude them from finding their way back to Him.
This would be absurd! It became obvious to me that the "I" or "Me"
in such statements of "I am the way" are not referencing the historical
figure but the Guiding Spirit of Divinity Itself. The important point,
my teacher said, was to follow a truly Great Teacher and commit

your soul into their care, for you need their guidance and energy to take you beyond your ego. No swimmer, however capable, can make it across the Pacific Ocean unaided. Doc also told me that it was no great merit to be "overly sophisticated" by knowing so much about the different religions, as the path of Truth requires only a simple surrender to one Great Teacher. I'd been feeling smug about how much I knew of diverse scriptures and traditions, and his comment was a correction to my intellectual vanity.

Doc was a member of the Episcopal Church from childhood, but he was a Universal Spirit beyond time, place, caste, or religion. His lineage, he said, was "an inner pathway."

Love is "both the means and the end," for it alone has the power to transform life. "Its power sweeps away all obstacles," he said.[201] Love is everywhere, he taught, and doesn't belong to any single religion any more than the sun belongs to one of its rays. He gave respect to the local Episcopal church with his attendance and contributions, yet most members never knew that a living mystic knelt right next to them at the altar. Mystics hadn't fared well in church history, so he never revealed the fullness of his Light except to those who sought him out. He told a group of his students one time, "I stand in front of you a convicted mystic who would have been hanged for what he's going to say today."[202] Although the entire Christian religion was born from the experiences of the early disciples, who had an inner realization of the Presence of God as Christ, churches often condemn direct realizations as heresy. Doc said simply to respect religion, recognize its limitations, give reverence to Truth itself, and have compassion for human fallibility: "We cannot condemn a whole organization for the acts of its weakest or its worst moments. Institutions are run by fallible humans."[203]

"Be passionate for God, not belief systems," he said. "God has no given name; Divinity is not deceived. Those who truly long for God are embraced by that Infinite Presence, which is beyond all religions."[204] He warned that devotion to Truth might require the sacrifice of even our loftiest spiritual ideas. Sufism has a similar teaching: "Love is the fire that burns both belief and nonbelief. Those who practice it have neither religion nor caste," said the 11th-century Sufi master Abû Sa'îd Ibn Abî-L-Khayr. Irina Tweedie discovered this teaching to her dismay. When she was in India with her Guru, Bhai Sahib, he ground down even her religious beliefs. Tweedie wrote:

> Every belief to which we cling gives us a bit of firm ground to stand upon, a security. We give up Religion and become Vegetarians or Theosophists or Agnostics; and each of these new beliefs is a substitute for the old, a new ground where we feel safe. How little we know that we build our castles on sand... Spiritual life is the tearing down of all the castles, of all securities. For only then, and then only, can we reach the Ultimate Security. If I don't give up all beliefs absolutely, the little self, the pride, will never go.[205]

She was right. I could see in myself a lot of pride wrapped up in my beliefs. They were "mine" afterall! Didn't that make them important? My teacher taught me to respect religion, but not to be attached to religious beliefs and rituals. He suggested a simple inner practice: being aware of the Presence of Love. He pointed me to Brother Lawrence's little book *The Practice of the Presence of God*. He said, "It shows the importance of constancy and the most powerful tool at your disposal—devotion." The little book describes Brother Lawrence's practice of continual awareness of the presence of God, whom he considered always with him and inside him. Brother Lawrence did his secret practice of awareness no matter where he was, which was often in the kitchen, sweeping and cooking. He found there was no difference between praying in the kitchen and kneeling at the sacrament.

My teacher saw the face of God in everything. I remember working with him in his office on a book project when suddenly, in the window, he caught a glimpse of Gus, their large orange cat, and went into a state of ecstasy, repeating over and over, "Divine kitty! Divine kitty!" After the ecstasy passed, he said to me, "When you see this Divine kitty, isn't it obvious that God IS? This is God manifest as Orange Kitty." To me, Gus appeared to be just an ordinary cat, but to Doc, everything was illumined by the Light and Glory of God.

I worked hard to appreciate the beauty in all things. Whatever was in front of me to do—walk the dog, listen to a friend, cook a meal, grade papers, sweep the floor—I tried to be aware of the presence of God and the lovability of all creation.

Truthfully, however, my mind was often full of thoughts more related to my human struggles than the Presence of God. I was often distracted by intensely felt reactions to people and situations. I suffered painful self-doubts, was easily triggered by what I thought were the judgments of others, and wondered: *How can I be so close to my teacher yet be so poor at keeping my focus on the presence of God?* In my confusion—I really thought I should be more advanced by then—I asked my teacher, "Why aren't I enlightened by now? I'm in your presence several times a week, yet I have all these doubts and problems." It's embarrassing to admit that I asked such a question, but that's the state I was in at the time.

He said to me, "Everything that exists is perfect as it is. You are perfect and complete just as you are—even with your doubts. You are serving just as you are." He liked to give the example of the rose: "A rosebud is not an imperfect rose but a perfect rosebud. When half open, it is a perfect unfolding flower, and when completely opened, it is a perfect open flower. As it fades, it is a perfect faded flower, and then becomes a perfect withered plant, which then becomes perfectly dormant." I saw how my mind mentalized a linear process of progress from imperfection to perfection, but in my teacher's Reality, creation unfolded instant by instant from perfection to perfection. In the spontaneous emergence of everything in life becoming itself by the will of Divine Love, creation and evolution were seen to be one and the same.

I learned to accept that I couldn't even know where I was on the path. How could I? Does the ant know where it is in relation to the entire garden? No. It knows only the little piece of ground it stands on at any given moment. I took guidance from my teacher's experience, written in *Power vs. Force*:

> People wonder, "How does one reach this state of awareness," but few follow the steps because they're so simple. First, the desire to reach that state was intense. Then began the discipline to act with constant and universal forgiveness and gentleness, without exception. One has to be compassionate toward everything, including one's own self and thoughts. Next came a willingness to hold desires in abeyance and surrender personal will at every moment. As each thought, feeling, desire, or deed was surrendered to God, the mind became progressively silent. At first, it released whole stories and paragraphs, then ideas and concepts. As one lets go of wanting to own these thoughts, they no longer reach such elaboration and begin to fragment while only half formed. Finally, it was possible to turn over the energy behind thought itself before it even became thought.
>
> The task of constant and unrelenting fixity of focus, allowing not even a moment of distraction from meditation, continued while doing ordinary activities. At first, this seemed very difficult, but as time went on, it became habitual, automatic, requiring less and less effort, and finally, it was effortless. The process is like a rocket leaving the earth. At first, it requires enormous power, then less and less as it leaves the Earth's gravitational field, and finally, it moves through space under its own momentum.

Suddenly, without warning, a shift in awareness occurred and the Presence was there, unmistakable and all-encompassing.[206]

Doc wanted to make sure I knew that spiritual states came of their own and not as a result of ego striving. One time I was standing with Susan in their kitchen, and he asked us, "How does Doc define Enlightenment?" (He often referred to himself in the third person, a style of language common for mystics, as the sense of self is universal and not personal.)

We had no answer. He said, "It is the recognition of the Divinity of the Self. You yourself are what you're looking for. All that exists is God. Nothing but God can exist." Another time, when I was giving lectures on mystics at a local church, he asked Susan to call me on the phone and he said, "I want to make sure you know that what the world calls enlightenment is a state, not a person. It is a condition. It is a spontaneous revelation. You're standing at the bus stop and suddenly there is the Realization...." He never called himself enlightened; he simply shared his inner experiences with those who listened. He knew I viewed enlightenment as something to work for, to succeed at, and so he often reiterated that it was a spontaneous gift of Grace.

Devotion meant to surrender all wants and expectations related to spiritual life. I had thought that just being near him would make me enlightened or put me in a perpetual state of bliss. Actually, being that close to the Fire was almost too difficult to bear. It brought up all my inner blocks to Love that needed to be burned off—jealousy, pride, anger, addiction, shame, etc. When I complained about a problem, Doc would quip, "You've earned the karmic right to process out this negativity."

# Putting Shame into the Fire

In order to merge with Love, I had to surrender all the blocks to Love, including self-rejection. "He who realizes his humanliness realizes his godliness," is a Sufi saying that summed up the challenge.

Being close to the fire of his love, deep-seated insecurities about my own humanness came to the surface. Mainly, it was the repressed pain and shame over my sexual orientation and love life. Given my rigid religious background, I had a split between the spiritual and the sexual. The two dimensions were polarized in my psyche as good and bad, godly and carnal, holy and sinful. Though I'd heard nothing negative about gay people in all the years of attending his seminars, I still held within my psyche a primal fear that no spiritual community would ever accept me. The old religious conditioning inside me was fearsome: Would I be cast out? Was I a second-class seeker, not as pure as others? Would I be told I had to be celibate, forced to choose between my love for a partner and my love for God?

I struggled with this conflict for over a year, even while I was going to Doc's house to interview him. He was the one place of Pure Love for me, and I was terrified of rejection. I hoped that my teacher would be as accepting of me as Swami Prabhavananda was of his Vedanta disciple Christopher Isherwood, a well-known writer in the mid-twentieth century, translator of the Bhagavad Gita, and author of a landmark biography of the great Hindu saint Ramakrishna. When Isherwood took his initiation with Swami Prabhavananda, it was at a time when homosexuals were arrested and subjected to shock treatments and other cruel measures. Isherwood had a deep longing for spiritual truth, and his journals show the struggle to align his sexual desire with his spiritual commitments. He was relieved that his Swami wasn't prudish and did not view homosexuality as a sin; he simply encouraged all disciples to transmute lust into love, equally for a lawfully wedded heterosexual couple as for Isherwood.[207] He did not require Isherwood to become celibate but rather challenged him to see his lover as Krishna himself. In this way, he would reach the highest form of love. But I'd also read the account by Andrew Harvey, brilliant visionary and translator of Rūmī, of his painful rejection by a guru after many years of devoted service to her. She told him that homosexuality was not acceptable and that he must leave his lover and marry a woman. That is, she demanded that he reject himself and his own heart. After reading his memoir, *Sun at Midnight: A Memoir of the Dark Night*, I was sick with dread—what if my teacher rejected me?[208]

I had no choice but to walk through the fear. Spiritually, it was crucial for me to come to a place of peace about sexuality, for I knew that sexual energy was an expression of kundalini, the life force within the spiritual centers that takes a person to God/Reality. In some traditions, sexual energy is said to constitute one fifth of the kundalini. In other words, it is a building block for spiritual realization. "The more sex-power the human being has, the easier he will reach God or Truth," said Bhai Sahib, Sufi master, to Irina Tweedie.[209] Bhai Sahib guided Tweedie to refine, not reject, the sexual energies. "A man who is impotent can never be a saint or a Yogi. Women too can be impotent. The Creative Energy of God which manifests itself in its lowest aspect as procreative instinct is the most powerful thing in human beings, men and women alike."[210]

I knew I couldn't simply repress, hide, or avoid this "sex-power." Keeping it locked in the lower chakras out of shame would block it from being used in the service of Love. Even those who are called to a celibate monastic life need to transform the sexual energy of desire into love; if repressed, then chaos reigns. My journey was to pull sexual energy up from the lower chakras (shame, guilt, fear, pride, desire) into the heart chakra (lovingness). I had to summon the courage to put this part of myself into the Light of my teacher's love.

I was tempted to take the "spiritual bypass" that is common among seekers.[211] "I'm over that, beyond that, above all that lower energy. I've already transcended that. I'm spiritual now, evolved beyond sexuality." But my teacher encouraged us to be ordinary, to own all of our humanity. "Know thyself" was a step before "surrender thyself." Otherwise, what is one really surrendering? "You have to own who you are in order to give yourself; you have to master the world before you can surrender it," he said. When I attended the monthly events, I noticed how my teacher advised people to be ordinary by getting a job, adopting a pet, cooking a meal for the family, or volunteering to help others. When young aspirants told him that they spent all day in meditation, his response was often blunt: "Go to school and get a job." Being spiritual didn't mean leaving the world. He said, "By loving your ordinary existence, you are loving God. To love all of life in all of its expressions, without exception, including yourself, is to love God himself."

Over time, as I came to trust that his love was unconditional, I felt that I could share this most hesitant part of myself. I knew if I held something back, it would only block the Grace that came through him, like a tarp over a piece of ground prevents the rain from watering that part of the garden. If it's not watered, it doesn't grow.

The news of my sexual orientation changed nothing between us—except that I felt totally relieved and free to be myself. He mirrored to me my innate wholeness. Though sexuality had been a big deal to me due to my religious background, he viewed it as a natural human expression, neither good nor bad in itself. Over the years, I knew several gay people who were in his orbit. His statement to me was, "If that's what you are, then you have to own it." Susan was also accepting. When someone sent an email to the office asking, "Where do gay people come from?" she responded, "The same place as you and me." One time I asked her, "Why do you think gay people are on the planet?" She replied, "To teach the rest of us about unconditional love."

Doc undid decades of dogma for me when he told a large audience, "Love is love. Our love for each other is not different than our love for God.... God loves us through our love for each other and all living things."

When I worked with him on his *Letting Go* book, it was a marvel to me how accepting he was of all of human life. Because his vision had declined with age, we did the edits verbally. I went over to his home and read through the manuscript with him many times. By that point, I thought I'd gotten to a place of comfort with the topic of sexuality, but the editing work revealed pockets of resistance in me, as I felt awkward when we worked on the section about sexuality. I still had the residue of a psychic split between spirit and flesh. He had no such split. In him there was neither aversion nor attachment. To him, sexuality was a clinical fact, a very ordinary human function—no big deal.

In one of his last public lectures, he gave his clinical research finding that "6.5 percent of both men and women are born homosexual. It's genetic. So, it's not a moral problem. It also occurs in the animal kingdom. 6.5 percent—no matter what culture or nationality." Some of the things that people in society "condemn as a moral problem," he said, "are biologic fate."[212] Even though I'd already been completely received by him as an individual, I could finally embrace the issue on a collective level that some people are "born that way." This opened the door to actualize what Sunlight had told me: "We have to love our self completely, because all of us are created by a loving Creator who loves all of creation."

Overall, Doc's teaching on sexuality was revolutionary to me because of its sheer simplicity. It was the same teaching he gave on all the things that human beings might say or do. What matters is the energy field, which is set by intention, and not the outer form. If we come from a place of love, this intention sanctifies whatever we do. If sexuality is driven by "gettingness" (craving) or "doingness" (performance), then there will be suffering. But when coming from love, sexuality is a joyous experience. It's not about getting something from the other but sharing the experience of oneness. It's not about "doing it right" but surrendering to the joy of the moment. He affirmed sexual intimacy as a beautiful experience when coming from the energy of love.[213] When energized by love, the sanctum of sexual intimacy parallels our surrender to the Beloved. All the veils of outer life can be let go and we stand naked as we really are. The relief is immense. Trust and safety are innate to love. There is no shame or fear. There is delight in being naked with another in total transparency. In the state of love, it's the heart that leads, not the mind with beliefs and rules. We don't go to a lover and say, "Let's make logic!" We go to a lover and say, "Let's make love" and we shed our clothes. Shedding the clothes of separateness makes possible the sharing of oneness.

In contrast, in the states of desire and pride—the typical scenario of popular sex culture—there is playing the game, strutting our stuff, pursuit, seduction, manipulation, conquest, possessiveness, getting it on, making them pay, love 'em and leave 'em. Desire is a firecracker that fizzles, while love is a fire that never burns out. Desire is about getting, while love is about being. Desire sees the outer; love sees the inner. Desire values how we look; love values who we are. Desire is based on appearances; love is based on essence.

The Karmapa said something similar: "If the relationship is founded on true and genuine love, it is authentic," he said. "But if a relationship is based only on desire and not on love, then whether it is a homosexual or heterosexual relationship, it still is not going to be very good."214

Experientially, the path of love required me to let go of religious and moral dogmas and to transcend both attachments and aversions related to sexuality. Identities and hang-ups had to go. I learned to be grateful for all the love relationships in my life. During the years I lived in Arizona, I had the gift of a partner I was spiritually aligned with. Our life together was devoted in service to our teacher. He and his wife embraced us as family. Their acceptance brought freedom and joy to an area of life that had been fraught with shame.

For other spiritual students, their shame was different. The list of self-rejections is endless. In whatever case, I learned that until devotees accept who they are, their human nature, and all that they have done and experienced, they will not experience their wholeness or be able to give their entirety to God. The ego itself had to be accepted. Doc told me:

View your ego as a little animal—a furry little pet. It's not 'evil' for wanting this or that. The ego can't help what it wants. It merely seeks its own survival as it understands it to be. Egocentrism is successful for survival in the animal world. And with the frontal cortex, now you have a thinking animal that uses intellect to dominate others through ideological views. You won't see anything on the nightly news that you don't see on Monkey Island at a zoo or in the wild. Rivalry for top dog, hurling feces at others, territorialism, clashing of antlers, only now it's expressed verbally through the intellect of the frontal cortex. If you see the ego as a furry little animal, you'll stop hating it. You can watch its greediness without joining in its greediness. Treat your ego with compassion and it calms down.

I learned to watch the ego drives in myself and others like a mother watches a child to make sure it doesn't get into trouble or bother others. Doc explained that the first emergence of love on the planet was "through the feminine, motherhood, love of the mammalian for its young."[215]

## AT THE FEET OF THE TEACHER

Love was emerging in my life as I nurtured new potentials. As much as was possible for me, I gave myself wholeheartedly to serving my teacher. My mind had little understanding of what transpired in the interactions with him. I didn't question it. This was remarkable for an academic, trained to be skeptical and to analyze concepts and presentations of information. I followed the guidance found in all spiritual traditions: If you are blessed to find a genuine teacher, then you trust absolutely.

People sometimes asked me "Did he give you any special teaching when you were with him?" My experience was that each student was given what they needed to fulfill the role they had. I applied the Buddhist precept "Refrain from taking what is not given to you," to spiritual teachings as well as to physical things. I didn't assume that what was given to others was meant for me or that what was given to me was meant for others. Doc advised me to be discriminating in sharing spiritual information. He knew my tendency to want to be helpful and to be a good neighbor, as he called it, so he warned me: "If a spiritual process is given to those who are not ready for it, it can be harmful." He quoted Jesus: "Do not cast your pearls before swine." When I was with Doc, I treasured everything he gave me and prayed not to want what was given to others. I learned the importance of living fully the light I was given and more would be given. If I pretended to have more than I had, then the inner light began to dim. I was careful not to take what wasn't given to me. One time I was given some of his hair (considered a first-order relic) to deliver to a well-known religious leader. I wanted to keep a strand for myself, but I refrained from taking it and simply delivered it as requested.

At times I suffered jealousy of those who appeared to get more of his attention than I, but I worked to follow his teaching not to compare myself to others: "Within the group there is great variation due to 'karmic ripeness'.... Therefore one cannot compare oneself to others or expect some fortuitous suddenness such as that which was offered to the well-known teacher Ramana Maharshi."[216] He said different levels of consciousness were simply different, not better or worse, and affirmed the spiritual law that all sincere seekers are given what they need when they are ready to receive it.

Being with Doc was to live on a *razor's edge*, as in the Vedas. If shadow motives—jealousy, self-importance, wanting something for oneself—were detected, as eventually they were, the student would feel a cut. Purity of motive was the only way to walk the razor's edge and not get cut.

I had an unconscious shadow side that needed to be special and recognized, so I got cut several times in everyday interactions with my teacher. One time, for instance, I was very excited to find a talking thermometer for him so he could push a button and hear the outdoor temperature. He liked it a lot and pushed the button often, but I was crestfallen when he daily gave credit to another person for finding this wonderful item. I caught myself wanting to correct him and say, "No, Doc, it was I who found it and gave it to you!" Then I saw how ridiculous it was to claim every good idea as my own while at the same time want to give credit to others for every bad idea! One day, standing in the kitchen with a mess on the counter, I said, "Doc, if so-and-so hadn't put this here, I wouldn't have spilled it!" He exaggerated my blaming attitude by saying, "Well, then, let's hang 'em!"

The razor's edge cuts egotism away. It was painful but necessary. There were times when I left Doc's house angry and hurt because he hadn't accorded me the specialness I'd wanted. He was a clean mirror in which every interaction reflected back my self-seeking motivations. Outward piety and moral perfectionism did not impress him. In fact, he often poked fun at my efforts to be a "goody two-shoes." He knew I had a strong need for social approval and to win the good opinion of others. For example, when I told Doc that I'd left a rental cabin much cleaner than I'd found it and had even taken off and scrubbed all the window screens—I was feeling prideful and hoped to impress him—he quipped, "Oh, what a good person you are!" I knew it wasn't a compliment, as I'd heard him say at a satsang, "A 'good person' is one thing; enlightenment is another." Of course, to a person who didn't care about cleanliness, he'd have said something else. He encouraged students who were lax to be more conscientious, and encouraged the rigid ones (like me) to be less so. In all things, the middle way.

Spiritual ambition gnawed in me. I found it hard not to hope for some spiritual reward or personal gain out of my efforts and dedication. I prayed to be freed of this because I knew that the ego taints everything it touches. It takes credit for what has been given by Grace, and the Light is taken from those who claim to be its source. It would be absurd for a light bulb to take credit for the light shining through it! Doc said I should expect the spiritual ego to come in and take credit for things, and told me to joke about it and not take myself so seriously. If not made light of, egotism lies hidden in the dark; things done in the dark draw darkness to them. I tried to keep my spiritual ego in the light by joking about its insatiable need to be superior, to know things, to take credit for things. The antidote to spiritual pride, Doc said, was simply to be grateful for what had been given to me.

Rarely did he give me a direct correction. Rather, he evolved me through his presence, humor, and silence. Sometimes when we sat together, I asked him a question and he ignored it. In the silence, the egotism of my question became obvious to me.

Ultimately, the teaching was not in his words but in his being. He was totally free and totally present with whatever and whoever was there. He embodied spontaneous and effortless grace. I made sure to record his words, but what I remember most is the actual experience of sitting there as he talked (or not) and how everything about him went deep into me. The words were immaterial compared to the quality of the atmosphere. It seemed to me he was in a constant state of surrender and prayer.

I learned a lot about love just watching him go about his daily life. When he fed the three kitties, he knew each one's happiness. Once while I sat with him the kitties went berserk over a toy that rotated with bouncing little balls at the end of long antennas. They pounced on the balls over and over again, dipping and diving over each other. We watched them with great amusement. Doc said, "Kitties don't think. They just are. That's how love is." I began to refer to these moments with my teacher as kitty satsangs. He was teaching me how to lighten up: "The kitty doesn't ask himself 'Do I enjoy playing with this ball?' Kitty just knocks it across the room and plays with it!" Doc was giving me the message "Just be natural, just be free, just be!" I was too serious about my spiritual practice, and now see it as an irony that we humans need spiritual practices to return to our real nature. Whereas the kitty just is, we have to "practice" being spontaneous, natural, free, present in the moment.

Through Kelsey his dog, Doc taught me the importance of discipline and caring for others. At 3 p.m. every day, he took the dog out with him to get fresh eggs from the Happy Eggery chicken house, built with his own hands. This routine delighted Kelsey, and Doc was committed to it even when he was in his eighties, frail, and in need of an arm to hang on to. After one walk out there, he told me, "I got through it by praying." I asked him what he prayed. "For knowledge of God's will and the power to carry it out."

Watching him talk about the day's events with Susan was instructive. While he and I were working on a project, Doc would always welcome her into his little office. There was none of the customary barrier between spouses—"Let me finish this," or "Don't interrupt me while I'm working." For him, hearing his wife and sharing her joy or concern was just as important as writing a book or doing a radio interview. His face would light up when she came to check on us. "Honey, I missed you while you were gone—this crazy lady (pointing to me) has been working me nonstop ever since you left! How was your trip into town?" He easily stopped our work mid-sentence to hear Susan's report of an errand or phone call. The love between them was palpable even in accounts of garage sales and grocery shopping. It was, as Doc liked to say, a facet of love called joie de vivre.

Doc never seemed bothered by the phenomena around him. Some days their house was like a grand central station. Broccoli the African Grey parrot singing, "Hi Ho! Hi Ho! It's off to work we go!" The handyman hammering. The gardener blowing. The phone ringing. Someone coming in to ask Doc to sign a box of books. Another asking him how to respond to an emailed question. Three cats playing. Kelsey herding the cats, then growling if they got near her bone. Doc didn't resist the vicissitudes of life. He saw them not as obstacles but as the unfoldment of life itself, inseparable from Divinity. I had the sense he lived to serve everyone around him because he saw the divine essence of all.

The energy that prevailed in their home was Divine Order. The everyday buzz of life was one thing, but if there was an energetic problem—snafus in communication, machinery not working, negative attitudes—he took care of it immediately, through prayer and self-clearing, smudging, and incense. Many times I witnessed him pray, "God I ask for a miracle for _____" and it would happen—the healing of an emotional pain or physical condition; the resolution of a relational conflict; the saving of an animal or tree; the recovery of a lost item. Once, the TV went haywire. Susan and I were pushing two or three different remote controls, unhooking and re-hooking the cables, pressing the reset button, etc. Nothing worked. We gave up. Then suddenly Doc said, "Okay, it's working." We turned it on and it worked. I asked him, "How did that happen?" He replied, "I prayed for Divine Order in the household." The same thing occurred the next day when the phone went dead and then suddenly was back to normal. Susan said, "Things like this happen all of the time." He didn't do such things in public, however, because he said it would captivate the "spiritual adolescent" of people and become an obstacle. He told me, "The spiritual ego of seekers is easily glamorized by the outer trappings: special clothing, secret codes, miraculous healings, ancient mysteries, performances, and pieties. These appeal to the spiritual adolescent, which likes to be special." Better to learn the Real than be wowed by magic tricks.

Out and about in the world, Doc embodied unconditional compassion. It was so ordinary, however, that most people wouldn't have noticed. One time, I was standing with him in a large circle of people in front of a church after the morning service. We were all listening to some bagpipers play a lively Irish tune. Several little girls were twirling and dancing in the middle of the circle as we cheered them on, clapping to the beat. Suddenly one girl tripped and fell to the ground. Instantly, Doc bent down, reaching out to her. He was the oldest and most feeble person in the crowd—nearly blind, leaning on a cane, yet he was the only one to make an instantaneous response. The rest of the audience, even the parents of the child, followed many seconds behind. A photo of the moment shows the crowd of people thinking about what just happened and what should be done. Most people think and then act. In contrast, the sage responds instantly. True compassion comes straight from the heart and acts swiftly, clearly, and without distinction. My teacher didn't know this little girl, but in that moment it looked as if she were the dearest person in his life.

Doc Hawkins, first responder to a little girl who fell while dancing to bagpipe music in front of St. Andrews Episcopal Church, Sedona, Arizona, 2010 (Fran Grace/courtesy of The Institute for Spiritual Research).

I noticed his effect on strangers. He purposefully avoided being seen as a miracle worker, yet I witnessed many moments where his energy field transfigured a situation. Once, we went to the Department of Motor Vehicles to renew a handicap placard for his car. Government offices are not known for their friendliness. At first, the clerk was in a sour mood: *Don't cross me—I'm having a bad day* written all over her face. She gave us the many reasons why we couldn't get the placard, culminating with the dreaded dead-end "And I can't locate your record in my computer. You'll have to go back to your doctor." I felt annoyed at the inanity, and maybe Doc did too, but I saw him shift, as if he were opening something up. Within five minutes, the woman was smiling as she handed him his new placard.

His was the most intimate yet impersonal love I've ever experienced. He gave effort to relate to us all as individuals because he knew we saw ourselves that way. With each human or animal in his life, he forged a meaningful connection according to our specific language of love. For his dog, he understood her need for a routine, treats, and comfort during thunderstorms. For a shy staff person born in Germany, he used basic words in German to help her feel at ease in the office. When he heard that a sixty-something neighbor got a cancer diagnosis, he went to see her and told her about the slower cancer growth rate for people over sixty. This meant a lot to her, coming from a physician. He related to people where they were.

As the years went by, living close to Doc, my heart was slowly polished. Every interaction was a subtle guidance as my perceptions were corrected through humor. He never criticized or gave advice. He merely shifted the way I was seeing something. One time, he and Susan came over to our house and I sat with him on the front porch. I was very proud of the view of an enormous rock formation called Thunder Mountain. People paid extra to live in a house that had this view. Just in the moment that I was thinking how special the view was because of the rock—and that the view was *mine*—he said, "Too bad they can't move that rock. It gets in the way of the view!" We laughed. Whenever I was holding something with pride—feeling enhanced by something of mine—his humor cut right through it. How absurd to applaud myself because of a rock! He always shifted my attention from the obvious to the subtle, from a thing to the space, from the content to the context, from the personal to the impersonal, from the "mine" to the Divine.

I came to learn that it's standard for a spiritual teacher to disconcert the mind of a disciple, never let it settle on anything. Habits of mind are like cement and the teacher's work is to make a crack in the cement so the light of the Higher Self can get through. Tweedie's Guru relentlessly threw her mind into confusion, upturning every belief system. He told her he was "hammering her head into her heart." The process was grueling and went on for years. Day in and day out, she heard, "Whatever can be understood with the mind is not a high state. Truth is in the heart." A friend who sat at Tweedie's feet in London explained how she learned to listen from an intuitive place beyond the mind:

> I found that listening beyond the mind is where I could get the hints. For instance, one time after telling a story, Mrs. Tweedie paused, looked off into the distance and said, 'Family jewelry, interesting thing.' I felt that this was for me, even though it made no sense at the time. Then quite a while later, my mother died. She had wanted me to have her pearls, but they were given to someone else. I could have gotten very upset over this and caused a ruckus, but I remembered Mrs. Tweedie's comment, 'family jewelry, interesting thing,' and those little words allowed me to let it go.[217]

It took me years to learn how to listen for subtle hints and register them from an empty space. I first had to disengage long-standing mental habits, especially the need to understand what I was hearing. "Understanding" was really just filing new information into old belief systems, and this had to go if I was going to hear things from the heart. Doc disconcerted my mental presumptions by coming out of left field with nonsensical comments or seeming inaccuracies. The absurdities functioned like curveballs thrown at the logical mind. For example, I was always very prompt and prided myself on punctuality. No matter how precisely I arrived to his house on time, he would say, "You're late again!" It did no good to defend myself, for promptness was not the point. Being right and insisting on my rightness—this was the point, and he always met my attempts with humor. As soon as I stopped defending my promptness, he stopped saying I was late. I was being trained to learn humility and to surrender lifelong perceptions and perfectionisms.

Another instance was when he would tell me, "I lectured in a hundred places. Exactly one hundred. Not ninety-nine. Not 101. Exactly one hundred." Some days he said it several times an hour. I'd be sitting there, thinking *How can you know that for sure? And anyway, you are wrong. You said it was a hundred places last week, and then you lectured yesterday in Phoenix, so now it would be 101.* Every time he said it, I felt angry. My ego mind wanted to argue and contest his calculation, call him wrong, correct him, but the soul knew that the point was not about facts but truth. His truth was a hundred, a number of completion. It was a training for me. Every day with him, I had to surrender a lifetime of academic conditioning, with the mental proclivity to argue a point, nitpick an inconsistency. Until a seeker can let go of inconsequential details, she will not be given anything greater. I surrendered my need to know. Doc taught me the path of "radical humility." He said, "Humility means you ask for Truth to be revealed instead of assuming that you already know it." Being with him was an infusion of Truth more than an explanation of it.

I first saw Swami Chidatmananda, a Hindu *acharya* (leader) from India, at a seminar given by my teacher. "You are so blessed to be ever in his service," Swami said. "It is only for the sake of uplifting so many people that such a Master arrives on the planet. Rarest of rare. To get even a glimpse of a Master like that is a fulfillment of life."

You might think Swamiji stood out to me for his orange robe, brown skin, and striking white beard, but this was not the case. It was his focused attention—sharp as a knife—that struck me. I said to myself: *Now here is true devotion.* His whole being expressed one-pointedness of mind, fixed on the Divine and nothing/no one else. I imagined that upon seeing Swamiji, God would say, "That one belongs to Me."

It wasn't that Swamiji acted like a devotee. Previously, I had noticed devotionalism of the outward kind. People arrived to the seminar at 3 a.m. to be first in line, to claim a seat closest to the teacher. They sat in public places, eyes closed, meditating; they swooned dramatically, blissed out. When I asked my teacher about such things, he said, "They have a picture in mind of what they think a spiritual person is supposed to act like, and then the ego produces it." Swamiji did none of this. His devotion was inward, private. He was in a state of constant inner meditation, so there was no need to sit and close his eyes in the middle of a crowd. Since he trusted the will of Divinity to put him exactly where he needed to be, there was no rush to be first in line. He was natural, efficient, respectful, joyous, and full of good humor.

Just a few weeks before Doc died, Swamiji gave me a lesson on "Devotional Love."

Swami Chidatmananda (courtesy of Chinmaya Mission).

*Chapter Twenty-Six*

# Devotional Love
## Encounter with Swami Chidatmananda

*Devotion to the people is devotion to the Supreme Self.*
—Swami Chinmayananda

## On a Higher Plane

Swamiji is steeped in the ancient scriptures of India. He has studied them in their original language, applied them through decades of daily practice, and taught them worldwide. His initiation into spiritual life came under the authority of his Guru, Swami Chinmayananda (d. 1993), whom he serves to this day. In 2001, he came upon the writings of my teacher, Dr. Hawkins, recognized their resonance with the scriptures of India, and made it a priority to be in his presence. He is devoted to the Supreme in whatever form It takes.

In July 2012, the Swami brought a small group from India to meet with Doc and Susan at their home. They were doctors, business professionals, mothers, and monks. Devotion means that no matter their station in outer life, they give their best effort to all of life's tasks, out of love for the Supreme, seeking no reward. They encapsulated what Swami Vivekananda had said at the 1893 Parliament: "to love for love's sake."

The visit was inspiring. Their questions came from the heart. They asked Doc how he maintained a loving state. He replied, "I sense the spirit in each person, and it's the spirit I love. I love because the spirit of God is in each living thing. Everything is part of God. By loving each other, we love God. And by loving God, we love each other. Each one of us is an expression of God. I say to God, Thank you for their devotion. Thank you for my life. I bless all living things in Thy name with gratitude. Amen." He gave thanks for their presence and love. At their request, he blessed them.

This meeting turned out to be the last meeting Doc had with a group. I interviewed Swamiji just a few days before Doc passed from this world. Swamiji's comments helped me to bear the loss of my teacher.

Since then, I've been with Swamiji many times. In October 2013, I traveled to Hyderabad, India, and visited the Swami's ashram and schools. I experienced the all-encompassing hospitality that devout Indians extend to visitors. My companion and I were met at the airport with two dozen red roses, and then taken to a meeting with delicious refreshments and admiring school officials who treated me like a dignitary. I was embarrassed to receive their honor and gifts, but did so out of love for my teacher, for I knew he was the object of their devotion. I did my best to reflect back their dearness and his love for them. Swamiji accepted me even though I was far from the ashram standard. Quietly, without a big to-do, coffee was served at breakfast. In true devotional love, which I experienced at the ashram, we are loved as we are, wherever we are on the path.

Swamiji is a busy man, engaged in the world. He exemplifies the teaching "Wear the world lightly, like a loose garment. Be in the world but not of it." He gives lectures and workshops at religious centers, businesses, health clinics, and universities. Twice a week he is on TV in India, teaching the Upanishads and other classic spiritual texts for a modern audience concerned about happiness, success, relationships, and ethics. He oversees eighty Chinmaya Mission centers, ten of which have monastic ashrams. The monks, male and female, do deep study of Vedic scriptures, receive spiritual training under his guidance, follow an Ayurvedic vegetarian diet, take a vow of celibacy, and are of service wherever they are placed. His disciples reflect well on him. They are genuinely warmhearted, dignified of spirit, and trustworthy. Anything you have that is most precious would be safe in their care.

Swamiji's message and manner help ordinary people who are looking for relief from stress and conflict. Though his life is set apart for Divine Service—monastic robe, sacred vows—one feels that he is one of us, that he understands our problems. When he speaks at the university or to politicians or CEOs or physicians, he doesn't quote in Sanskrit. He tells humorous stories from everyday life that shed light on the common blocks to health, success, and happiness. These are things that interest everyone. Who doesn't want to be healthy, successful, and happy? At the same time, his messages contain an invitation to the Higher Self, the soul's ultimate quest. One time he came to our university and gave a lecture on stress reduction. He recounted a story of his Guru, Swami Chinmayananda, and had the whole audience laughing at the ego while at the same time we got the important spiritual instruction to change our inner attitude.

> Once, it happened with my Guru, back in 1960s, that on his way from Bombay to Delhi, just before landing, the pilot announced, "Due to bad weather, they have asked us not to land right now, to keep going around in the skies for sixty minutes." The passengers reacted variedly to this situation. One said, "Oh, How can I get delayed? I have a very important business meeting and I cannot be late! If I am late, I will lose these prospects and my business will suffer. How can I accept this?" Another said, "I'm going to see my relatives for the first time in ten years. They are so eager to receive me. They've been waiting at the airport with enthusiasm. If I am so late, their

enthusiasm to see me will die down, and by the time
I get there, they will already be so bored they will not
care to see me!" Someone else asked, "Why does this
seem to happen only with me? Whenever I get on the
plane, it's always delayed. And whenever I go to receive
somebody who is flying, it is the reverse!" Someone
else said, "An astrologer told me that the planets are
in opposition to me—Mars, Saturn, Mercury—and
that's why this is happening." Another said, "Karma
is to be blamed."

On and on, the diverse passengers with their
various pressures and stressful responses. Then all
of them noticed that the Swami was quite engaged.
He was replying to letters. He even seemed happy
about the delay. They asked him, "How is it we are
so disturbed and you are not? How can you take the
situation so coolly?" He said, "Can we change the
situation? No. Is there anything we can do to control the time of the landing? No. When we cannot
change the situation, why would we allow the situation to paralyze us? Annoy us? Disturb us? Our best
option is to change the way we think about the situation. If we bring a change in our thinking, then our
stress level will immediately come down."

Swami speaks on a plain level with people, but he lives on a plane
higher than most. A characteristic of such teachers is that they can
bend time. Whereas most of us are in a war with time—"Never
enough time! I'm rushing to meet the deadline! Racing against
the clock!" Those aligned with Love have little time-related stress.
Their reality is "There's always enough time." They don't rush; they
don't delay. They take care of each thing as it arises, confident that
everything needful will be accomplished without strain. When the
ego steps aside, something more powerful is in the driver's seat. I've

never seen anyone arrive through Los Angeles traffic as swiftly as the Swami. As we've seen throughout this book, where there is purity of love and motive, the Red Sea parts.

The Swami is a lesson not only in giving devotion but also in receiving it. In May 2015 I was with him during his visit to a Hindu community in San Diego. Several families presented him with lovingly prepared food on a silver plate, a traditional way of serving food to the guru. They saw to his every need and comfort, presented gifts, and asked for his blessings on their lives. After his talk at the temple, he came to me and said, "I didn't know until now that I've been invited to dinner by two other families. We will go to see them on our way home. *To receive devotion is a gift to the giver.*" It was nearly 9 p.m. I wondered how he could have so much energy. We went by the two homes, visited, and ate. He received their gifts. I noticed that he didn't eat everything placed in front of him. He gave his presence but consumed little food. I, on the other hand, am a curious and eager eater, so I tried everything on the plate. I learned: We give a blessing to others by receiving their love, but we don't have to take in everything that's offered.

In August 2012, Swamiji was giving talks in Phoenix, Arizona. I visited him at the private home of a devout Hindu family. When I arrived, removed my shoes, and entered the home, I noticed the atmospheric silence. It was a typical suburban neighborhood with auto traffic, children playing, gardeners with blowers, but there was a stronger vibrational field of meditative silence that pulled me into its peace as soon as I entered. Beauty. Simplicity. Human warmth.

I told the Swami that I didn't expect my teacher to be here much longer.

# CONVERSATION WITH SWAMI CHIDATMANANDA

SC:   It is a most divine blessing to be in the physical presence of a Great Master. Even the objects, when they are touched by the Master, carry that vibration for a hundred years and longer. Every particle is divinized. Such a Master takes a physical manifestation only for our sake, to teach all of us. Otherwise we would not be able to know the total, nameless, formless Truth. When Truth manifests in form, it comes through the Master, and it makes it easier for us to know Truth. We are all fortunate to have been with Dr. Hawkins. And you are so blessed to be ever in his service. It is a great blessing. Knowing God, understanding God, and thinking of God is one thing; being with God in the presence of a Master is totally different. You are in the physical proximity and verbal communication. There is nothing like it. No other *sadhana* is required! No other spiritual practice is required.

Q: Just to be of service to my teacher is enough?

SC: Yes. Being in his presence there is upliftment, and that alone allows us to transcend.

## What is Devotion? Lessons from the Scriptures and Sages

SC: I am so fortunate that you are giving me an opportunity to talk to you about Love and Devotion. Now first, I would like to share some teachings on them, and then we can discuss.

(For the next fifteen minutes, the Swami spoke in a very dynamic way, not from his head but from his whole being, infused with the scriptures of India. When he spoke Sanskrit words, he went into a meditative state and his speech became chanting. It was more of a transmission than an explanation.)

I would like to start with a very nice statement made by my teacher, my Guru, Swami Chinmayananda, on love. "Love is a link that connects; a force that attracts; a fascination that seizes; a clasp that grasps!"[218] I find this to be relevant. When we express our love, we get connected with our Beloved—whomsoever the Beloved may be. Love is the connecting link that connects the lover with the Beloved. And love is not only the connection, it is also an attraction. Not an ordinary attraction; it is a force! Like the magnet attracts the iron pieces, it pulls! It is a force that attracts. Also, it is a fascination that seizes! We are totally seized by that love. And it is a clasp that grasps! So we are caught by it. We are held by it.

One of the great devotees of Bhakti Yoga (the Path of Devotion) is the Sage Narada. In the *Narada Bhakti Sutras* he says: "What is devotion? It is *sä tvasmin paramapremarüpä*. This devotion is of the nature of Supreme Love, not an ordinary love. In ordinary love, we expect things in return. We want some security or some assurance. We want some recognition or satisfaction. This love is not like that. It is of the nature of Supreme Love. And, very importantly, this love is directed toward God. Then, it is called Devotion."

In the ordinary mind, thoughts flow in various ways. The content of thought might be about all kinds of things. But Supreme Love is about love and only love. Thoughts are constantly flowing in love toward the Supreme Being. This is Devotion.

In that Supreme Love, there is another thing that is added, and it is called *Anyana Bhakti*,[219] which means Exclusive Devotion. There is no one else, nothing else, and nobody else in it. And that exclusive devotion is *total* love. Nothing else but love. Not a little bit of love. Not some more love. Not half love. *Total* love. That is what is called Anyana Bhakti. In other words, it is one-pointed or single-pointed devotion.

It is also said that this kind of total love, this Supreme Love for the Lord, is devotion to the Divine and is of the nature of "*amåtas-varüpä*"—Immortality.[220] The one who develops such a love actually attains Immortality, because that Love itself is Immortal. By the very fact that such a person is in this type of total, exclusive, and continuous love, he or she is already immortal.

It is said here that such a love has total attention on the Supreme. Normally, a human being divides attention among many things. Multitasking is everywhere. We have so many gadgets! When attention gets divided among various things, we may not be able to be fully present to one thing. Total presence in a single thing is rare. If total presence in one single thing is not there, there is no joy that can be felt. There is constant moving of attention—here is one thing, then another. Maybe one's work demands such an attention that is divided, and we may be skillful at it, but still, there is no total involvement or presence in any one thing. Attention is divided. Awareness is lost. Joy is not there. And here it says, "Love demands total involvement." In this Supreme Love, there is no fragmentation. Entire attention toward the Supreme brings the experience of Infinite Bliss. This is what the Narada Bhakti Sutra says. It isn't some transitory thrill or momentary high. Total love for the Supreme brings Immortality and Infinite Bliss.

Another thing to note: Whosoever he or she may be, the one who gains this Supreme Devotion is "siddhobhavati," meaning attains Perfection.[221] There is no more imperfection left in the devotee. The involvement with the imperfect instruments is not there, because one is not seeking sensory pleasures. One becomes Perfected in Love. And such a devotee is "tuñöobhavati." Bhavati means "becomes" and Tushti means "Extremely Satisfied." One becomes "Extremely Satisfied." No trace or iota of dissatisfaction is left in that individual. He or she is so totally contented, that there is no need for anything else, there is no thought about anything else. In our normal, everyday life, we gain satisfaction by fulfilling our desires, wishes, and wants. But such satisfaction is time-bound. It is temporary. We are satisfied and content for a brief period of time. After that, it disappears. Again, we go in quest for an object of our satisfaction. Then we have another little bit of satisfaction. But it is never a total satisfaction. When an individual is totally and completely satisfied, there is no need for any further satisfaction or pursuit. One never comes down to the level of dissatisfaction. This type of total satisfaction comes from Supreme Devotion, which is continuous, exclusive love.

Sri Krishna says in the *Bhagavatam*[222]—a text of many deeds, miracles, glories, and stories of devotees—"*mamänusmarata cittaà mayyeva praviléyate*," meaning: the mind that learns to constantly remember Me is the mind that is following Me. So the mind that learns to constantly remember Me comes to dissolve into Me. It dissolves into Me and revels in Me. What a wonderful thing! So whenever we are thinking of the world, the mind goes there and becomes involved in it. We gain a little bit of satisfaction. Then the mind will go somewhere else, thinking of something else.

But here, Sri Krishna says, the mind that learns to constantly remember Me comes to dissolve in Me. No other identification with the mind is possible because now the mind itself is dissolved. Identifying with the mind, creating a specialized identity that "I am the ego, I am this mind" is no more! Mind is dissolved, gone into that Supreme Being from whence the ultimate nature has come. Once the mind is dissolved, there are no impurities left. They revel in Him, in that Highest Bliss or Joy.

Having attained such a level of devotion where one is perfected, totally satisfied, with immortality, and the mind completely merged into the Lord, now such a person never has a need for anything else. No more desires. Why do we have desire? Because we want some satisfaction, some fulfillment, and to gain something we don't have. But here, he desires nothing. He cares for nothing. The attitude is "I don't care"—This is not an egotistic statement; it only means that he doesn't want anything anymore.

Also: "*na çocati*"—such a person never grieves.[223] The mind never goes into grief. And, "*na dveñöi*"—such a person never hates anybody. Hatred cannot find place or space in such a person because of the Supreme Love. And, then it is said, "*na ramate*"—such a person never wants to delight in anything other than this Love and Devotion. There is no interest in any other thought or desire or wish or want or emotion. Only Love and Devotion.

And he becomes "*na utsähé*." He or she finds no enthusiasm at all for any sensory enjoyment. He or she never comes down to seek joy with eyes, nose, tongue, ears, or organs—all related to form, taste, smell, touch. The person of Supreme Love never seeks anything at sensory level for gratification, because there is so much Joy available in that level of Love.

Then it is said, such a person at that level becomes "*matto bhavati*," that is, "Totally Intoxicated" with Love and Devotion. And that person is "*stabdho bhavati*"—such a devotee attains Total Silence. It is

like, one Master says: Suppose a person is singing the glories of God
constantly, and suppose a person is dancing for God, and it goes on
and on in ecstatic sound and whirling movement. Suddenly, when it
all stops, there is Silence. So total is the Silence that one is instantly
absorbed into It. He or she becomes "ātmārāmo bhavati"—revels only
in the Self.[224] There is no desire to revel in anything else. That individual self is connected with the Supreme Self and revels only in That.

Then another great Master Veda Vyasa, who has authored many
scriptures such as the Mahābhārata, and the Puranas, says that the
devotee is attached to God. He says, devotion means being in worship of the Lord with deep love and strong attachment. For them,
attachment to God is not like attachment with the senses. It is only
with God and nothing else.

Another great Master, Maharishi Garga, says: Devotion is a great
attachment to listening to the stories of the glories of God.[225]

Another great devotee, Sage Shandilya, says: "Devotion to God
that is not opposed to attachment to the Inner Self, is true devotion."[226] It is more knowledge-based: Self-knowledge. The Inner Self,
deep inside this body, mind, memory, and ego, is the luminous Self,
the shining Light of the Self. Getting connected to that Inner Self
means that one connects with God through the Inner Self. This
same Inner Self is the Supreme Self. God Himself is here available
as the Inner Self. Instead of getting attached to the body, mind, intellect, memory, and ego, the devotee gets attached to the Inner Self.
Attachment to the Inner Self is attachment to God.

Then Adi Sankara, a great Master of *Advaita* (Non-duality),
says: "Devotion is most effective for liberation." Although he spoke
most frequently of Non-duality, he said that if you want to attain liberation, devotion is an effective way.

Sage Narada, in the Sutras we discussed earlier, says: "Total dedication of ALL actions at the altar of the Lord" is Supreme Devotion.
The true devotee says, "At the altar, I surrender all of my actions to
the Lord." This includes all moments of forgetfulness of the Lord
and the excruciating pangs. Everything of one's experience is surrendered to the altar of the Lord; it is all dedicated to God. Even one's

thoughts are dedicated to God. "I give all unto God." That is Supreme Devotion.

## Krishna and the Gopis: Dancing with Joy

Then Sage Narada refers to a beautiful thing. You must have seen the pictures of Krishna and the Gopis dancing around?

Q:   Yes, I've seen images of the Gopis, milkmaids, and their dancing to the flute of Lord Krishna, Gopala, as a young cowherd. What does it mean?

SC:   The milkmaids, Gopis, give an example of Supreme Devotion. Krishna says, "Let go of all other duties and responsibilities that are associated with you in this life, and surrender unto Me alone."[227] The milkmaids had children, husband, responsibilities, and duties towards their parents and in-laws. It is not like a modern society. This was thousands of years ago. To think of going to attend to a meeting or meet someone, even a spiritual divine being, was not allowed for women. Sri Krishna started playing the flute at night, and the Gopis would hear that flute and go out to him. It was said that these milkmaids were previously great sages, *rishis*, who saw God only through knowledge. But they did not experience and see God through love and devotion. Hence their incarnation as Gopis was to experience that Supreme Love of God. The husbands saw that their wives were so involved with Lord Krishna, and they could not understand what the attraction was. He was an ordinary guy. Why would they be interested in him? The husbands were all feeling uneasy; they thought, "We would also like to experience it."

In the Bhagavad Gita, it is said: God is *Sat* (existence), *Chit* (knowledge-consciousness), *Ananda* (bliss); these are the three attributes of God. One could relate to God through any of these attributes. Rarest is relating to God through Ananda—Joy and Bliss. The world will never oppose anyone related to God through Existence and through Knowledge, but with Ananda, there is difficulty. Especially for women, to relate with God through Ananda, there might be some eroticism, some sensuality, some sexuality—this is how certain people might think. The Gopis' husbands perhaps thought this way. However, the One who created all the beauties in the world, who is able to manifest the most beautiful things in the world, how could such a Being fall for sensuality? He is the storehouse of all beauty. He alone is the most beautiful. He is not going to fall for sensory beauty.

These Gopis were fascinated with the uneducated cowherd, Krishna. This devotion was possible because they thought the dharma or righteous duty they had towards their children was not greater than their duty towards Sri Krishna. The duty they had towards their husbands was not equal to or greater than devotion to Krishna. This was the same for all of their duties, daily chores, taking care of elders, and so on. They saw devotion to Krishna as the ultimate. Children we have everywhere. Husbands we have everywhere. Elders and duties we have always. But this is the time when Sri Krishna is playing the flute. Everyone is sleeping—husbands, children, elders. He never calls anyone. He just plays the flute. The Gopis hear the music.

Lord Krishna plays the flute at night when everyone is in deep sleep. This means, everyone has gone unconscious. Who can get the signal and message of the Lord? Only one who is so alert, even in deep sleep. One who is not unconscious in sleep. The milkmaids are awake, even in deep sleep. They are alert. They alone could hear that Music. It is like the child who is tuned to the sound of the car instantly knows that the father is coming. These milkmaids are tuned to his flute at midnight. So they leave their bed and go out to him.

Krishna is manifesting there as Joy—*Ananda*. In knowledge, you can be serious. But, here, how is Ananda expressed? Dance! There is so much ecstasy and joy that you must dance. There is no control over it. A serious person cannot dance! Krishna is dancing. Everybody gets into the dance. They forget their bodies; they forget their minds. The only thing that is there is *raasalila*—dance in joy with the Supreme Being. Only the Supreme exists in the dance. The vibrating theatre of the universe—everything dances at the particle level. As long as he dances, creation continues. As long as micro-particles keep dancing, manifesting–non-manifesting, only then does life goes on. Sri Krishna connected with the Gopis through dance, that is, through Ananda—Joy. It was the pure, highest Joy where everybody became one! This Joy has great spiritual power.

In *Bhagavatam* there is a story of the (son of Vyasa) King Pariksit who was cursed to die in seven days. He was asking everybody, "How can I attain realization within seven days?" They told him, "Listen to the love and devotion of God, then you will realize within seven days." This King after hearing the glories said, "I can understand everything, but I cannot understand these milkmaids going to dance with the Lord, with no permission from husbands or elders." He was asked to see the reflection of the Sun in different water bodies like lakes, ponds, rivers etc. The source being the same, the reflections are different in shape, size, and color in different water bodies. Similarly, seeing the reflection of the Lord in different bodies, some are children, some husbands, some mothers-in-law, etc. The moment the reflection realizes that "I am not connected with this water body and I am actually connected with the Source Sun in the sky" it irresistibly gets drawn to merge into the original source. Similarly, as long as the knowledge has not dawned that "I am not connected with this body but I belong to that original source," I am involved in fulfilling my duties and responsibilities. The Gopis had realized this truth and they felt as though they were going back to that original Source by the playing of the flute. Their only thought was, "I have to merge into *That* which is my Supreme Goal of Life."

Q: I often feel a conflict between my duties in the world and my spiritual longing. But the Gopis simply follow the joy of their heart?

SC: The beauty of connecting to God in Ananda is rarely done. These Gopis get so much merged into the Lord that they don't see themselves as separate from Him. "Don't try to tell us about knowledge of God. We are so in love with God that our minds have merged into Him." When our mind is filled with Love of God, there is no space for anything else. We start to experience the vibration of love and come back feeling fulfilled.

The lives of Gopis are connected to the teachings of Sri Krishna. This is especially clear in the Bhagavad Gita, in the chapter allotted for the path of devotion, Bhakti Yoga. Bhagavan Krishna says, "What is this bhakti and why do you need to have bhakti?"[228]

First, He says, Fix your mind upon Me. Second, have the utmost faith. Superior faith, not ordinary faith. Great faith has five ingredients in it: 1) *knowledge* of the true nature of God and His glory, whoever that God may be; 2) *belief* in God; 3) *respect* for God; 4) *love* for God; and 5) *surrender* to God. When these five ingredients are there, it is total knowledge of His true nature and glory. *This is the highest, greatest faith.* Third, fix your mind on Me, with great faith, in constant devotion by meditating on Me. Those who fix their minds on Me, have the greatest faith, and who meditate on Me are considered to be the best yogis.

First, keeping Me as Supreme God. Second, dedicating *all* actions unto Me. No more actions are being done for the sake of one's own satisfaction or gratification. Third, meditate on Me with undivided devotion. Worship means to meditate upon Him in undivided devotion, surrendering the mind. Then, Krishna says, one can finally merge in the Lord and remain with the Lord.[229] How?

Fixing the mind on Me alone. Fixing the intellect on Me alone. Fixing the memory on Me alone. Fixing the so-called ego on Me alone. The four components of mind, intellect, memory and ego— fix them on Me alone. Alone. Thereafter, what will happen to you? You will dwell in Me only. Mind fixed on Me, intellect fixed on Me.... Where are you now? You are *in* Me. If you are in Me, then you *are* Me. Finished. That is the beauty given by God. Do not have any doubt about such things. Don't have doubt about how to reach God, how to dwell in God. It is simple: mind, intellect, memory, ego all fixed on Me, and then you will dwell in Me.[230]

## Qualities of the Devotee

Then, it is said, there are the qualities of the people who attain this level. The world can understand such people only by their qualities, by knowing their external mannerisms and behavior. Otherwise our limited mind cannot know the unlimited Truth. What are the qualities of the devotee who has attained the state of that Supreme Devotion with the Lord?

**Friendliness:** This is friendliness towards all beings. It is irrespective of caste, color, creed, religion, etc. They don't have any division or any barrier in their friendliness. As a friend, you are just open to all. We can tell anything to a friend. In friendship, there is no restriction. People who don't share things with their family members will share them with their friends. People who don't share things with their life partners will share them with their friends. To be a friend is to be completely open. Accessibility is there, without reservation. No compulsions or inhibitions are there. And so it says, such a person is friendly with all beings. Not just human beings, but also with birds, animals, insects, plants, grass, everything.

**Compassion:** The compassion flows toward everyone and everything around.

**Equanimity:** Such a person treats everybody as equal. There is no "higher" or "lower," no superior or inferior, and no question of any division at all, as all beings are equal. Everything is seen as equal, and everybody is seen as equal.

**Forgiveness:** Such a person forgives everybody. There is no question of the other's shortcomings, character defects, limitations, and lower aspects. These do not bother the one who dwells in God. Forgiveness is unconditional. Everybody is recognized as in their true nature, beyond their shortcomings. They are not defined by their defects or limitations. Total forgiveness, no matter what.

**Contentment:** The person who has attained Supreme Love and Devotion is totally contented. Full of contentment. The heart is filled, and the mind is filled. No trace of discontentment. No trace of any want or wish.

**Self-control:** Such a person is always in control, meaning they are always aware. They do not let themselves be controlled by a desire, an emotion, a feeling, a tendency, or an impression.

**Self-knowledge:** They are full of knowledge about the self and have deep-rootedness in that knowledge. Somebody may have self-knowledge intellectually, somebody may have a glimpse of self-knowledge momentarily, but they are not firmly rooted in self-knowledge. In the state of supreme love and devotion, the self-knowledge is complete and firmly rooted.

**Devotion and Gentleness:** Devotion pours out of them.

**Total purity:** Absolutely everything connected with them is pure. Everything you see in them is pure and purity. Words, actions, intentions, and movements—all is pure.

**Efficiency:** They are so efficient that anything they take up just happens. They are skillful in everything they do. It is majestic even to look at them and watch how they function, how they move, how they sit, how they talk, and how they do anything. They are full of efficiency and grace in everything they do.

**Neutrality:** They are neutral doers of everything. They are not inclined toward any particular thing.

These are the very beautiful qualities of the person of Supreme Devotion. In addition, we can note the qualities that they do not have, which are the lower-level things such as Dr. Hawkins describes as negative energy fields on his Map of Consciousness.

First, in the Bhagavad Gita, Krishna himself says of such persons that they have no hatred. They do not hate anyone.

Second, they do not have the notion of "mine," as in "This is mine; that is not mine." They have no conflict between mine and not mine. The moment I say, "This is mine" or "This is not mine," I distance from what is not mine and I am attached to what is mine.[231]

Third, they do not have the notion of "I" or "I-ness." This "I" is the limited, small self (ego).

Fourth, they have no anxiety. They are not anxious for anything.

Fifth, they do not have over-elation.

Sixth, they are not intolerant toward anything.

Seventh, they have no fear.

Eighth, dependency is not there. They do not depend on anything or anyone for any reason. Normally, human beings depend on something outside of themselves for gratification, satisfaction, and wish fulfillment.

Ninth, they have no selfish action. There is no selfishness in action.

Tenth, they do not have grief.

Eleventh, they do not have desire. They are free of all pairs of opposites, such as: honor or dishonor, comfort or discomfort, profit or loss. They are not affected by these things.

This is the state of those who have attained the highest level of Supreme Love. For an ordinary devotee, if they have total access to the will of God, whatever happens in their life is the will of God. God alone wills everything. Anything that I think I am achieving, gaining, acquiring, and improving, that also is offered unto God. It is said to the ordinary devotee to have a personal Deity, of whichever God or religion, and contemplate that chosen Deity. Meditate upon the total, cosmic form of the God. And then you will attain to the absolute imperishable nature of that God.

Now we are free to discuss.

## Living Examples of a Spiritual Master

Q:   Swamiji, thank you. I hope and pray to become what is described in those scriptures.

SC:   We all hope and pray that by God's blessings and the Master's grace upon us that we can really be in that state of devotion. I see all of these things in the work of Dr. Hawkins in the path he described as "Devotional Non-duality," only it is said in a different way. It came out of him so naturally! There is no difference between what he has experienced and discussed and what these great sages and saints of India said. Absolutely, he has tasted that highest Truth, so he gives it to us in a more modern, receivable, and agreeable way.

Q:    Do you see him as having the qualities of a devotee in Supreme Love, as outlined in the Hindu scriptures?

SC:    Oh! He is beyond the qualities! There is no doubt about it. He is There. He is not anyone ordinary. It is only for the sake of uplifting so many people that such a Master arrives on the planet. Rarest of rare. To get even a glimpse of a Master like that is a fulfillment of life. To sit and talk and get blessed by such a Master, nobody can explain the significance of it. It is taught in our spiritual tradition that anybody who realizes God and attains realization, it is considered as God. One who attains that higher Supreme Consciousness is not different from the Supreme Consciousness and is one with It.

My Guru, Swami Chinmayananda, is like that. And his Guru, Tapovan Maharaj, was a great realized Master. He lived in the Himalayas. He was full of love for God. He would see trees and plants and animals and go immediately into *Samadhi*. He would see the snowfall and go into Samadhi. When such a Master is here, what else do we need? That is why I appreciate your service to Dr. Hawkins. Who will ever get such a chance to do this service? Very rarely does such a great Master come. Many times, we were blessed to be in his presence. To have heard his teachings and to have had his loving glance from his beautiful and divine eyes, and the Grace that flows through those eyes is enough.

## Presence of the Guru in Life and After Death

Q:    Swamiji, were you drawn early in life to the path of devotion?

SC:    Certainly, because my parents were connected with my Guru Swami Chinmayananda. My mother's grandmother was a person who went out in search of Truth, into the mountains; after a few years, she came back and started to teach people about spiritual life. She could not teach her daughter, who was not interested. But her granddaughter (my mother) was very interested in spiritual things, and so she taught her about meditation. They influenced me a lot. Eventually, I got connected with this great Master and saw his unconditional love for everyone. I saw that selflessness which keeps on serving and never expects anything in return. Even though I was the only son to my parents, I was totally drawn to this life. He gave me permission, and my parents allowed me to take up a life of spiritual service. I was drawn at a very young age but could only commit myself after graduation of law studies at the age of twenty-four. Since then, I have been totally involved with Swami Chinmayananda and Chinmaya Mission. Swami Chinmayananda left his mortal body in 1993.

Q:   Is the presence of your Guru still with you?

SC:   Yes. I feel His presence. His guidance is and will always be there. A Master's guidance is such that, at any point in time, when I need some clarification, it comes. I feel that the personal deity is not a mere photograph or image, but it is a living presence which responds and guides. I have not attained that level of Self-realization. I am very open about that. But my Master told me to follow the path and he will decide. "Don't be concerned about Realization," he said. "Your only concern is to practice and to serve." So I am going ahead in that way, leaving it all to His Will. He is definitely guiding. Only with guidance from great masters is our path possible.

## Devotion in Everyday Life

Q:   Readers of this book are mostly not monastic and they may not be religious. How does devotional love for the Supreme relate to everyday family life, work, society, and all of the usual commitments?

SC:   Ah, yes. When there is love for anything that we do, there is total absorption of mind in that. When the mind is totally present in whatever we do, then whatever we do flows with *excellence*. Whatever we set our mind upon, there is that total presence of mind and love, so one starts enjoying what one does. When one starts enjoying what one does, then naturally the love and joy within the person, whether business or other kinds of work, family-related service, everyone around that person will be touched by the excellence of their work. And they feel touched by their love. When other people see the finished goods of such a focused mind, love, and attention, they will be uplifted and attracted. It is not a mere object that is produced, but it is the touch of that something above and beyond. Even a businessman, an artist, any kind of working person, or a housewife can excel in this way by being totally present in whatever they do.

The second thing is what Swami Chinmayananda said, which is in his pledge given to the people daily: "Devotion to the people is devotion to the Supreme Self." How beautiful it is. You need not worry that you are devoted to people, because that devotion is also to the Supreme Self. If we start having that full love, which is not different from devotion, to our family members, our "near and dear," we will create such a bond of love that everyone will feel satisfied and contented in receiving that love and they will also automatically reciprocate in love without demanding that you give it. When they are getting so much, they will automatically want to give.

A third thing that we have seen is that whenever we hold our love back to ourselves, there is no satisfaction. We are restricting something. We feel uneasy. When we allow the love to flow, then life is uplifting and enjoyable. There is a free flow of energy in every part of life. We all have qualities that are not so great, and if we focus upon the negative qualities, it is difficult to express our love. Who doesn't have imperfections? Until one reaches absolute perfection by becoming one with Supreme Consciousness, we have our negative qualities. So let us just not focus on them, let us sideline them and not give importance to them or identify with them, not be involved with them. We can relate to people without focusing on negative qualities in them or in us. That is where I also see what Dr. Hawkins said,

"I love the God in the other." My connection is with the God in the other, and I am in love with That.

Q:  So how can I apply this principle of loving the Divine in another person when they say or do something that angers me and I have an instinct to fight back, take revenge?

SC:  In the moment, yes, one feels that instinct. But then immediately we want to surrender that and let go of it. Not deny it, but not give it importance. The more we give importance to it, the more burdensome it becomes in our head. Why carry the unnecessary weight? We do not have to carry the weight and feel crushed by it or under it. Let us just let it go and be in the flow of love and be happy. It is joyous to give love. It is my privilege to give love! Whether I understand what happened or why it happened or not, I have the joy of giving love. Otherwise, there is retaliation, revenge, and this never brings true happiness or growth. Even though it may come up in our involvement with the world, from the innermost tendencies of the mind, one should be able to consciously look at these reactions and pray to God to take them away and surrender them.

## Transcending Sensory Attachments

Q:  You mention that a person who is devoted has transcended sensory attachments. Most of the people I know—including myself— have sensory enjoyments we're attached to: affection, favorite cuisine, travel, movies, home, etc. We want to be absorbed in God, but we're not fully there yet. College students in my Meditation course say that things run through their mind during meditation: cars, alcohol, drugs, sex, ice cream, video games, etc. What is a first step to be free of this?

SC:  If they start experiencing something more *inside* that gives a little peace, then they have started. Suppose the Name of the Divine is taken. That Name of the Divine carries the power of that Divinity. It carries the essence of the Divine. When a Name, which is given in the various scriptures, is taken and repeated inside, slowly the vibration, power, energy, and grace of the Divine starts flowing. Through the Name it is created, and through that channel it starts flowing. Then, slowly, the change in a person starts to happen.

Q:   So the power of a Divine Name, repeated within oneself, gradually lessens the attachment to physical pleasures. This is the Jesus Prayer or the Sufi zikr. I heard that Gandhi always had the Name of God *Rama* going inside of himself.

SC:   Also, another way to awaken out of sensory attachment is to know about the great, evolved masters and their ways of functioning in the world. Or, just to merely listen to an inspiring story that is being told. Reading something good is a way to begin. For example, one can read the teachings of a highly evolved spiritual master or the sacred scriptures. When one starts to be involved with these writings, then automatically the reading starts to beautify a person.

It is said in one of the Master's teachings that someone comes into the compound of an individual and says, "I want to stay for a while in your compound. May I rest here?" "How will you rest?" "I have an umbrella. I will fix the umbrella and I will rest under it." He is allowed to come and rest under his umbrella. After some time, he says to the man who allowed him entrance, "This whole house belongs to me! Everything is mine!" So, it is said, If you allow the Name of God to enter like that, it will ask for only a small space inside; but, eventually, it will say, "Everything is mine!" It will remove everything that is not Divine. All that belongs to the lower self is removed, dissolved. One who is devoted may still be outwardly involved with life and material things, but he or she doesn't feel *pulled* by sensory attachments. They fulfill their household and social obligations, while inwardly their whole mind and heart is with God.

Also there are various selfless activities that can assist this transformation. Try to help somebody who is undergoing a lot of pain and trouble in life. Go and help that person, be a friend to them. In the process of helping that person selflessly, I discover something beautiful within myself. If I help another, it sinks into me deeply.

Q: Do these principles apply also to physical health? For example, you are giving a talk at the Mayo Clinic to medical professionals.

SC: Yes, they asked me to give a talk on stress management. How to relax. How to not give importance to notions in the mind; to understand that the world and worldly situations can influence us only in accordance with the thoughts in the mind. Suppose an event happens in the world outside. The event reflects in my mind as a thought. Once I identify with the thought, I am drowned in it and the world affects me. Otherwise, the world cannot touch me. The world appears in my mind in the form of thought, happiness or unhappiness... If it is thought in the form of unhappiness, I may feel misery, anxiety, stress, tension, fear, and anger. As long as I am alert and conscious enough to recognize that the world has no independent identity other than being a thought in my mind, then I can deal with the thought and become stress free. I can do breathing, meditation, yoga, japa, scriptural reading—these techniques help to feel stress-free.

It all turns on how I choose to deal with the situation. Swamiji used to say, "What comes to us is destiny. But what we do with what happens to us is self-effort." Therefore, with self-effort and God's grace, we can lessen the impact of negative destiny. We can uplift ourselves by God's grace and rise above the situation by choosing to look at it in a different way. It is the same as Dr. Hawkins has taught us in his book, *Healing and Recovery*. Dr. Hawkins is full of that Joy. Where there is Supreme Devotion, there is Supreme Joy and healing in all things. And even meeting you is very rare because you are divinized by his service. It is all God's will that it happened. Otherwise it would not have happened.

Q: What do you teach in the Chinmaya Mission?

SC: The values from the Hindu scriptures. What our teacher, Swamiji, taught is that, once the intellect is impressed upon with such values, then it will guide the mind. The mind, when influenced by values, will guide the body. When an individual is value-based, he or she will become a better individual. A Christian will become a better Christian, a Muslim a better Muslim, a Hindu a better Hindu. Service to country is service to God. Serving other people is service to God. Serving in love is the greatest thing that can happen. It is building a temple of Divinity in the heart of the people. I get to learn and I get to share. That's all it is. I feel it's only a process of my evolution, which can be helped by this type of service. I have yet to be Self-realized. In this process my Guru told me, "Just do what is taught to you," and then he will decide.

## When a Spiritual Master's Body Dies

Q: I have a more personal question, about Doc's physical death and the death of any Master. How to cope?

SC: It is said in the scriptures, for such a *jivanmukta*, which means the one who is liberated while living in a body, he has no identification with any of these instruments of mind, body, intellect, etc. He is beyond the body. He is reveling in the Self, which is beyond time, space and objectivity. His nature is That. To others, for people like you and me who are not in that state, it appears as if there is a change that is underway. But this is only appearance. Because the Master is not different from Consciousness, the body undergoes change but not he in his essence. He is One with that Supreme Consciousness and Divinity. A Master undergoes all these things because the body has some destiny. But he in his essence is beyond destiny. Great Masters have certain physical problems because of natural aging or service to others. Otherwise, Dr. Hawkins healed everything. At his age, the body slowly decays. Everybody is the same in this regard. But the Inner Self is there. Even after he departs from the body, whenever we ask, his presence will be there to help us and guide us. He always surrounds us. In his Divinity, he is never attached with appearance nor bound by it. He knows that the body is an appearance, and he knows how many times he has taken up a body and left it. But our love for him is different. It's not easy to let go of such a Master for he is not an ordinary being. It rarely happens in creation. I wish and pray that Dr. Hawkins continues to be here for us as long as God extends it, with our prayers. He is the rarest of the rarest, so if he stays longer it is a great blessing for more people.

Q: He says that he has never been in a physical body that lived this long. A few of us are serving him because of his old age, and we have the opportunity to be close to him and be blessed through that service.

SC: That occurrence is only to uplift the people around him. Otherwise people may take lifetimes to get to that level. Just by serving him, so much negative is cancelled and you take a leap to a higher level. Just by serving his presence, you are uplifted. That is the reason such Masters come down. They descend only to help us ascend.

Q: The last few days he is not in the body. He seems everywhere in the room.

SC: These are the rare moments. Does he know the time of his death?

Q: That is something beyond my understanding. He says, "I can go at any time. It is God alone who knows."

SC: It is left to God. He is totally There.

Q: He is totally surrendered. He says, "Whatever is, IS God's will." And he is always praying silently within.

SC: He has made it clear that prayer is important. If you pray, situations will change, and your approach will change. The response from Divinity will change the things around you.

Q: I watch his total surrender. The body is in distress, but he doesn't struggle against the situation. Neither is he passively resigned, as he is willing to do whatever is needed for the health and longevity of his body. It's hard to explain—there is surrender but not giving up. I cry for myself because, for me, all the Love of the Universe is localized in that little form we call "Doc."

SC:   If Love is not localized, then we cannot contact it. How would we know it? It is only God who makes contact by localizing His Love.

Q:   Were you with your teacher when his body died?

SC:   Yes, I was there. I had many opportunities to be with him and travel with him. I attended his teachings at the ashram in the Himalayas. He conducted lectures for forty days at a stretch. That was the beginning point. Then I saw how glorious the Masters are, wherever they are, and to whatever religion they belong. Once you have tasted that beauty in one Master, that unconditional love, that presence and the glow of the Supreme, in walking, talking, you see it on others. It just flows. Once I saw it and tasted it, there was nothing else like it. God manifests Himself as the great Masters. Every second is of value to be in that presence. I underwent these experiences when my own Guru left the body in San Diego. It was displayed for several days. Their energy starts spreading around to all places. That was the first time that I could see such things. Photographs and paintings showed the different colors of auras all around. Later, I read in a Tibetan book that the auras emanate from Great Masters. There was crying and separation, because that love is localized in the body that died. Slowly, it took time. We did his sixteen-day ceremony at Himalayas.

The Master is not confined in the body. His real form is inside of us. And if you meditate, it will appear at any time to you. Later, I began to understand what my Guru himself used to say, "When you want to contact me after my departure from the body, close your eyes and I am in your heart." I started to feel that. Then I started seeing other Masters also—where Divinity alone flows. Dr. Hawkins is so rare. Every second is valuable. Last time, when we requested to see him, I only wanted one second, one moment. But he was so kind that he met us and talked. He allowed us to prostrate, and he blessed us. This is a once-in-a-lifetime chance. I sent the photos immediately to my parents in India. My father reads all of Dr. Hawkins's books. My mother watches the DVDs. Even though she doesn't understand the language, she knows him as a Great Master. I always have his books with me. It's a rare thing in creation that he put everything on a scale, the Map of Consciousness. Nobody has done that until now. God has brought him to do that for all of humanity. You can understand everything in the world just by looking at the Map of Consciousness.

To have a relationship with a Master is superb. We see how they are selfless, how they don't want for anything, except to shower love. I have come across a couple of them in this life. All of the inner qualities are the same. Different levels they might be, I cannot know. I can only prostrate and seek their blessings and their grace. Just one glance is enough. The scriptures say that when Great Masters leave the body, to be there is a great service and offering, and it happens rarely.

Q:   I believe that to be true.
      (*Silence.*)
      I wanted to come to your satsang tonight.

SC:   No need. When you have seen God himself, we are dust particles at his feet. You have seen God. This is just a dust particle (pointing to himself). Go and stay with him every second.

Q:   I hear you, Swamiji. I will do that. Thank you.

I left the Swami and returned to my teacher's house. My only desire was to be at his feet.

Author with her teacher at a Christmas party,
answering his questions, 2010
(courtesy of The Institute for Spiritual Research).

# Chapter Twenty-Seven

## Surrendering to the Light

I memorized this Sufi prayer: "I do not ask to see. I do not ask to know. I ask only to be used." It helped me walk through the darkness of not knowing. One night, I had a dream suggesting that the Light was guiding me even in times of darkness:

> I am walking through a narrow dark tunnel underneath Chartres Cathedral. In the darkness, I see only one light. It is a torch of Fire held up in front of me as I follow behind my teacher and his wife through the narrow passageway. I am not afraid, for I am in very good hands. I will follow this Fire wherever it goes.

I have followed the Light through many dark tunnels. The "torch of Fire" in that dream was experienced in real life at a candlelight Christmas Eve service, two years before Doc died. I was sitting next to his wife and he was on her other side, next to the aisle. It was evening. All was dark in the church except for a single flame held by the priest who then lit the candles of the acolytes. One of the acolytes came to our aisle and lit the candle held by my teacher, who turned to his wife to light her candle, and then she lit mine, as the congregation softly sang, "Silent Night, Holy Night." I stared a long time at his hands holding the votive flame. It was as if he held Christ's Love for the whole world in his hands. I thought, "I will always remember this moment—it is burned into my memory." I dedicated myself to honor the Flame of Love he passed on to me, no matter where it took me.

## "Love is a Closed Circle"

I saw Doc often the last few years of his life—in all kinds of circumstances, with all kinds of people—and never did I see him take anything for himself. He was in service to the Divine as it was expressed through whatever and whomever was in front of him. He *allowed* people to express their devotion and to give to him because it served *their* evolution.

One time, a large group of Buddhists came all the way from South Korea just to be with him for two hours, and each person went up to him and received a blessing. The next day, I asked him, "What's the benefit of expressing devotion to the teacher?" He said, "By surrendering to the teacher, you increase the likelihood of becoming that to which you have given yourself." I took from his answer that each of us is the outcome of whatever we have said yes to.

Doc was empty. I struggled with wanting *someone* or *something* to bow down to. When someone asked for his blessing, he gave it, but there was no visible lineage, no ritual ceremonies, and no sacred objects. My inner struggle appeared in a dream:

> The Karmapa will speak in a grand hall at the university. The atmosphere is expectant; it will be a grand affair. The organizers are buzzing around, doing the final touches, wanting it to be just so. We're waiting for the Karmapa to arrive and walk down the aisle in a formal procession. But he's late.
>
> I go outside to look for him. Unbelievably, he is a very large black puppy! He's running up and down the hills in playful, adventurous fashion. When I call to him, he runs over to me, wagging his tail, jumping up on me, licking me. It's a real lovefest. I manage to

get him into my car, thinking I can drive him to the event hall where people are waiting for him—but no!—he jumps out of the car and runs off. Clearly, he won't let me box him in!

I go back into the event hall. I see several Buddhist academics huddled worshipfully around someone. I think it must be the Karmapa, but it's not. It's a sick, anemic-looking man. His body is diseased from a lifestyle of vanity. I'm shocked that they're all totally enamored of him. I think: *How could they possibly think this is the Karmapa? Why would they worship a sick, vain man? Are they so taken with their own idea of what the Karmapa looks like that they completely miss the real essence of the Karmapa?!*

The dream suggests that I was beginning to realize that Buddha-nature is in the naturalness and joy of everyday life. What expresses this more than a tail-wagging pup? In the dream, this Being is so large and boundless that I can't control him. He is black, the color of the "void"—the timeless empty space, free of distinctions, formless and vast. In the dream, I recognized the essence of the Buddha. Yet the part of me (Buddhist academics) that still identified with outer effects was attached to worshipping the intellect (vain man) and grand displays of piety (procession, pomp).

The dream gave me an experience of Buddha-nature as the "is-ness" of life: silent, natural, loving. Doc confirmed this one day when he and I were watching a documentary on Zen Buddhism. When it was over, he said: "They gave us everything but the essence of it! We got the history, beliefs, practices, architecture, landscaping, and chants of Zen but not the essence of Zen. The trappings—gongs, roshis, rice bowls, speaking Japanese—are not the essence. The truth of Zen is in the silence. It is impenetrable by words. The Truth is a prevailing energy field of Love which pervades all things and which in its own essence is silent."

Doc knew I had a playful side, and he made up a nickname for me. He came to refer to me as "Fran-Fran," which instigated a series of jokes between us:

Doc: "Fran-Fran."

Fran: "Doc-Doc."

Doc: "Knock-knock."

Fran: "Who's there?"

Doc: "It's not a 'who' but a 'what.'"

Even as he connected to me as a person, a "who," his humor cut the illusion of personhood. He said, "You are not a 'who' but a 'what.'" He recommended his students ask themselves, in continual contemplation, "What am I?"

That "what" is Awareness itself, the basis of the realization of the Self. As we surrender who we think we are, we come to the "what," the substrate of existence. Letting go of identities and personas, beliefs and attachments, what is left? Formless essence. Silent Awareness. As time passed, I was shedding "who." Letting go of identities, self-definitions. One day it dawned on me: I'm not a professor, though I work as one. I'm not a devotee, though I serve as one. I'm not a woman, though I live as one. I'm not a "me," though I function as one. "What" replaces "who." Love dissolves every "who" I try to hang on to. The river loses its name when it flows into the Sea.

Yet the vastness was unsettling. When I looked at him, his eyes looked back at me without the customary veil—totally transparent, unguarded, with no hesitation. There was no "person" looking back at me. The atmosphere was empty of personhood but infused with Presence. "When I look in other people's eyes, there is only one Self," he said. I could barely hold his gaze for fear of dissolving into a nameless state. What I most deeply longed for—to surrender to Love—was also what frightened me the most.

Near the end of his life, I was sitting with him at their cabin in the woods. We were watching deer and elk grazing outside the window. The family dog lay at our feet, content. Susan had gone to visit her elderly mother. I noticed all of the books he wrote lined in a row on a bookshelf. I asked him, "What's it like to know you wrote so many books?" He said, "I don't see the books as mine, and have no pride or possession about them. It wasn't the personal self that wrote the books. God was looking around for a mind that wasn't thinking. I was just a channel, a space that was empty. People see a body and a person, and they think that the person wrote the books. But that wasn't the case. It's like a violin—it can't play itself, it has to be played." Long silence. And then he said, chuckling, "I stopped thinking years ago. I don't need to think. It's like a saw... too much noise."

Behind closed doors, I witnessed his humility and a depth of surrender that surpassed comprehension. At times, he was on his knees. Advanced beings are lightning rods for the negativity on the planet. For example, in the months before his final public lecture, which was on "Love," he seemed to go through an inner excruciation of all that was opposite to love. "When you commit to love, it brings up the opposite," he said. I became aware of the darkness in the world: malevolence, cruelty, denial of Truth, hatred, betrayal, envy, distortion—all that is hostile to love. By means I don't fully understand, it seemed that his work was to bear an intense battle within his consciousness on behalf of the world. It nearly broke his body. I imagined that the last lecture might turn out to be a funeral instead of a lecture. If not for Susan's loving care, I think his body would have disintegrated.

I witnessed Doc's preparation for that last lecture. His preparation wasn't what public speakers or educators generally do. It wasn't mental; there was no thinking through it, no rehearsal. Rather, he *became* the topic. He was more of a space than a person—a space of infinite potential. He asked me to read to him from the sections in his books about Love. When I read, he closed his eyes and listened. An atmosphere of pristine receptivity settled over the room. I sensed his total and complete attention. I haven't the capacity to know what was going on for him in those moments, but I sensed his unwavering dedication to his students. Even on the days that he was in physical pain and needed to lie down, he still wanted me to read to him. He said he wanted to "refamiliarize" himself with the energy field that people were expecting to learn about at the lecture. I don't think his students understood the sacrifice this entailed. Having left behind a limitation, who wants to go back to it? Only out of great compassion does a teacher attune himself again to an energy field he transcended long ago. Each time I read to him, I was aware of what seemed to be a sacrifice he was making for us.

In the months before his Love lecture, I made a film for him out of photographs I'd taken around his home and his teaching events through the years. It was purely an expression of devotional love, as I have no professional skills in photography or video creation. He and Susan valued the heart behind it and decided to show it at the beginning of his Love lecture. He said, "It captures the style and feel of the whole thing. It will allow people to feel like they've been with me."[232]

"Gloria in Excelsis Deo!" Doc began the Love lecture with this exclamation as he had every other lecture. It was his way of reminding us to honor the Divine and not the speaker. Those of us who witnessed Doc backstage knew of his profound surrender just before he went onstage. In one instant, he relinquished his weeks of preparation and turned the lecture over to Divine Grace. He became, he said, "a conduit." Thirty minutes prior, a friend may have brought him to the back entrance in a wheelchair, but now we marveled at how such a frail frame of a man (in his eighties) was suddenly dancing with his cane onstage.

Because of Doc's poor eyesight, I read his prepared points at the lecture, and the points sparked extemporaneous dialogue between him and Susan onstage. Susan was the Shakti to his Shiva. By this, I mean the two cosmic energies as described in the ancient writing *Soundarya Lahari* ("Ocean of Beauty"). If it hadn't been for Susan and the creative energy (Shakti) she embodied, Doc would have remained totally still, totally silent. Her energy, he told me, was "the fulcrum" that activated him to write and speak. One day I mentioned this to her, and she said, "There was no other way. It was his destiny.

I loved him and this meant I had to share him." Few partners would be willing to share their lovemate with the rest of the world. Through dialoguing with her at the last lecture, his teaching was responsive to the needs of the gathering. At the end—tears and longing, people hung on to the edge of the stage as his wheelchair rolled out. He was nearly collapsed. Susan closed the lecture by encouraging us to live the teachings we'd been given.

Even at the last, as Doc's body weakened, I saw that his life was devoted to bearing and alleviating the suffering of the world. The depth of his surrender to Divinity was unfathomable and total. Devotees projected various divine titles onto him, but he always pointed them toward whatever Divinity they followed—Jesus, Buddha, Krishna, etc.—and before Whom he himself was emptied. He told me many times, "It's the teacher who serves the student, not the other way around."

Before he passed away, he finished his commitments in the world—final books and video-recorded dialogues with Susan on topics related to everyday life. I worked with him on his official revision of *Power vs. Force* and wrote the new foreword for the very book that had brought me to him many years earlier. We finished the edits on his last book, *Letting Go: The Pathway to Surrender*. It arrived from the publisher the week after he passed away and became a top seller on Amazon; it was practical. I opened to the chapter on grief and stayed there for a season or two.

As he prepared to leave this world, I prepared to remain here without him. A few weeks before he died, I had a dream of his death. Doc's health was improving, but the dream let me know the time was at hand. For several months, he had been preparing us. "I'm ready to go at any time." "Dissolving back into the Self." "The work here is done. There is nothing more to say." Shortly after, he had a fall that began his physical decline and gave time for those around him to let go. I initiated what turned out to be many years of Jungian analysis; this helped me handle the process of losing him and cope with the ensuing life changes. Dreamwork is central to Jungian psychology, so I learned to work with dreams.[233] As Doc's body weakened, I was having dreams of objects and movements going counterclockwise.

> Tibetan *tingshas* are circling counterclockwise on the ceiling above me as I lie in bed. They're speeding up, faster and faster and faster. Suddenly they plummet next to me on the bed with great force. I'm relieved they don't crush me. Then I hear footsteps. Someone is coming. I'm afraid. The door opens. It's a woman I don't know. She has come to take me downstairs, into a place I don't know.

The dream suggested that I was being drawn by a deeper descent into the unconscious psyche, where the Self awaits. Soon afterward, in a state of meditation, I heard, "The projection on him has to die." I had placed all of my inner gold onto the teacher; had projected God onto him. He carried it with grace, but he'd never asked for it. The time had come to uncover the source of love *within*. One week before Doc passed, I had a mandala dream that signaled the innate wholeness that would eventually be pieced together from the raw materials he'd given me:

> I am assembling a mandala on the ground with pieces of stone and wood of all different shapes and sizes. The mandala will be about a foot wide and tall—twelve inches in diameter. A man to my left is encouraging me. I've never done this before—made a mandala out of raw material—and he is encouraging me to go ahead and do a 'draft' here on the ground. It's understood I'll rebuild it later, more permanently, in my own house. I like touching the pieces. I like the feel of the stone and wood.

Following Doc's death, I've had to do the work he always said was necessary: to find within my own self the wholeness I admired in him. Love by definition is authentic. It doesn't allow imitation of others, since each heart carries its own bond with the Beloved, and this bond longs to be lived. By analogy, each flower in the garden has its inborn destiny.

Doc passed away on September 19, 2012, during the Jewish Days of Awe. He was a Universal Spirit. He recalled lifetimes as a slave, a pirate, a Christian crusader, a blacksmith, a temple dancer. He recalled dying by the Ganges many times as a Hindu ascetic. He knew the esoteric imprint of the Sufi whirling dervish. He recounted lifetimes as a Buddhist monk. This lifetime, he was born into an Episcopalian family and fulfilled the mystical teaching of Christ, "The Kingdom of God is within you."

Many people told us of experiences of his presence before, during, and after his death. The Teacher is an Ever-Living Presence and Eternal Truth.

Doc appeared to me in dreams right after his death, suggesting that I had to give up the attachment to what he was *not*—his physical attributes—in order to realize the truth of what he *is*, a Universal Spirit. In the dream, Doc had come back to life and had guided me to a crossroads. I sat weeping in the center, the place where four roads intersected. The paved road to the right went to his house and his remains. To the left was a dusty path to the unknown. I knew I had to go left, into the unknown, and "become" the teachings he had given me. Going left meant a descent into my own depths to uncover the essence, the eternal part of myself, which is not different from the state he inhabited. It's the "what" of existence, the "suchness," the Self, the same as Love.

This was not happy news to me. I had expected to live in that small town forever, right around the corner from Doc's home, his wife, his animals, and his relics. A whole lifestyle and anticipated future had been built on the projection of Self onto my teacher and being in his "inner circle." In my spiritual ambition, I had seen myself as having a special role there. But Love is a Fire that burns all personal wants. It was extremely painful to have my identity as a special devotee dismantled. Even my attachment to holy things and places had to go. Yes, the energy of his Realization is in the relics; however, to imagine that it was *only* there was to hang on to an attachment and not live the whole of the Truth he taught me: "Love is present everywhere."

I ended up in the place I least expected—back in California, living an ordinary life of work and family. Adopting a dog, teaching college students, greeting a neighbor, tending to grandchildren... In the years since my teacher's death, life has given me an experience of his teaching: "Just being ordinary in itself is an expression of Divinity." It's not what I wanted, but it's certainly what I needed. Whenever I fretted that I had no time to write this book, I heard his voice inside of me, *The path is more important than the task. You have to BE the book.*

The Light is everywhere and animates all things. It's in the affection of a lovemate, the laughter of a grandchild, the wagging of a dog's tail, the eyes of a horse, the earnest question of a college student, the softness of an elderly neighbor, the blooming of an orchid in the kitchen window. "The commonplace and God are not distinct," my teacher told me. I had believed that the Light was mainly in sacred things and holy people. I had split the world into secular and sacred. In the years after his death, Love has unified the two. The supposed duality of secular and sacred dissolves into the sheer being-ness of everyday life. What is more sacred than the sunrise? What is holier than partners caring for each other through good times and bad, every day, come what may? What is more devoted than to rise each morning and live another day when the way seems unclear, God feels far away, and darkness looms?

Even the situations we might call tragic turned out to be holy encounters with Love. I will mention one here—the death of parents. Through such real-life experiences, Doc's teachings on love are incarnated.

When my father was nearing ninety, and my mother was suffering from Parkinson's, my two brothers and I moved them from Florida to

Mississippi, into a condominium near the brother and his wife who are medical professionals. I'm thankful that we didn't fall into the pit of resentment that often occurs among siblings in this type of situation. On one hand, there can be resentment on the part of the sibling who carries the weight of caring for older parents, day in and day out. On the other hand, the other children might feel less loved because there is a favored child. One might feel used and the others rejected. All could feel justified in their feelings. Fortunately, my brothers and their partners are fine and generous people, and we were able to love our parents without competing for their love.

My father died within the year of the move. Miraculously, given my decades of anger toward him, he and I were at peace with each other. At the Moon Cabin, I had thrown my log of resentment into the fire and let go of needing him to be someone else. I had worked to own the shadow sides of myself that I'd always projected onto him— alcoholic, authoritarian, stubborn know-it-all—and then I could love my father rather than hate him. I came to understand that he had given me all the love that he *could* have given. My teacher had taught, "Everyone is always doing the best he can at any given moment."

I talked to Dad on the phone the day before he died. He could barely speak, but I heard him listening. It was his soul listening, not his mind. The mind listens for facts, and the soul listens for love. "Thank you, Dad. You gave me everything I needed from you."

Mother lived another eight years. It was a journey none of us would have chosen, but it was a great lesson in the truth that love doesn't depend on mental or physical abilities. Due to Parkinson's and several strokes, she lost all physical functioning and left-brain cognition. She had no memory, little capacity to speak, and no connection to time of day or season. Someone observing would have said, "How tragic. She's just a vegetable." I found the opposite to be true. To see only the outer layer of an invalid with dementia—*that* would have been tragic. Rather, she took us on a journey into the farther reaches of love, and it remains one of the holiest experiences of my life.

I felt I owed it to Mom to presume that there was valor in her suffering. Yes, there was the "distressing disguise," as Mother Teresa called the physical condition of people in misery from famine, illness, disability, or loneliness. But there was also Mom's inner essence, and this became more and more vivid. I saw her bravery to endure loss of control and surrender to the total care of others, and in this way, she became my teacher. Mom was surrounded by loving care from my brother and his wife and several caregivers. It can be so difficult to trust the love of others. It's the ultimate test of loving—the giving over of ourselves to the care of others when we have nothing to give but our helplessness. In a state of helplessness, the ego's resistance melts and we open to being loved as we are, naked and with nothing to give. It would have negated the soul's journey to view her condition only as tragic when it was truly an "inner triumph," as Viktor Frankl described.

Of course, our family had normal human feelings of loss and sadness, and it certainly *felt* tragic to us. Seeing one's mother deteriorate beyond recognition is heartbreaking. We went through stages of grief. After one visit, several years before her death, I cried and cried to my brothers, "She's not Mom anymore." Indeed, *that* mother wasn't with us anymore. How then was I to relate to the person she was becoming? This is always the challenge—how to love each other even as our outer being changes.

I had always assumed that illness was unfortunate and the sooner we got over it the better. In Mom's case, however, I saw that illness was an avenue of love. When I met with Betty Eadie, she told me that some souls actually choose to endure conditions of illness, dementia, and disability in order to help those around them to learn unconditional love. This resonated with me. My mother's illness helped many people, perhaps especially her caregivers and their families, who felt grateful for the meaningful work and financial peace of mind. They were with her twenty-four hours a day for the last several years. One of them had just lost her job when the local factory shut down, and then she started to work for Mom. This caregiver, a mother of three young children, had been diagnosed with breast cancer; she never stopped telling us how thankful she was for her work with Mom. The world is an interplay of circumstances that are interconnected and purposeful. Illness gives us an opportunity to grow in patience, perseverance, and compassion.

Mom's condition also brought the opportunity to observe a process I'd learned about from my teacher—in cases of senility, Alzheimer's, or progressive severe disability, "the aware aspect of the spirit departs and begins to locate in the spiritual dimensions.... mental consciousness is no longer dominant."[234] The person is leaving the world in stages, perhaps visiting other realms, and thus there is a gradual loss of cognitive memory and orientation to earthly clock time. Their words may sound like meaningless babble, but they are actually reporting experiences from another realm. My mother often spoke the names of her relatives who had passed, as if she were with them. Her eyes would sometimes be glassy, and she seemed to be in another realm, which she called heaven. In one of those states, she suddenly said to me: "I want to go home. I hope you understand. When I hear your laugh, I'll know it's you—into the ages. If you need me, I will come. Your dad and I love you so much and always have. I'm here with him and those I love. I look forward to it—seeing you and your friends. There are some things I'll be able to say there that I can't say here."

She was highly responsive to being loved, and she was easy to connect with through music, so I sang to her instead of talking. The last time I saw her, I sang all the words I wanted to tell her. Her body had shrunk to nothing, her limbs so stiff that she had to be lifted in and out of bed. She couldn't see very well, yet the inner being knows when it is loved. I sat close to her in the hospital bed, caressed her face and hands, and sang some of her favorite hymns, such as *Amazing Grace*. Her response was instantaneous. Her physical agitation calmed and she was riveted back to the room.

Love in the form of total oneness melted the barrier between us. The room felt imbued with angelic love, by which I mean a quality of tenderness that is exquisite. In those moments, it was as if a veil had been lifted and we were in a timeless dimension, akin to the Light I had experienced at age fifteen. It was an atmosphere of Loving Presence. Mom was very alert on the inside. The Light that shone through her eyes was entrancing. I wanted to lose myself in her eyes. She who had rejected my experience of the Light when I was fifteen now shone with the same Light. As I sang, she kept saying, "Peace, Peace, Peace."

"I'm glad you're here," she said after a while. And then touching my ring finger, she asked, "Are you married?"

I said, "Yes, Mom, I'm very happy." I wasn't married in the conventional way that she was asking about, but it didn't matter. She just wanted to know that I was happy and loved, and I could certainly say yes to that. She put her palm on my head, as if blessing me. I received it as such. Gestures of love from a dying parent are precious in whatever way they are offered.

"Do you understand?" she asked me.

I said, "Yes, Mother, I understand...."

"I'm so tired... I want to go to heaven."

Five months later, my brother called me and said Mom wasn't eating anything. That evening, I felt her presence. She had come to say goodbye. The next morning, my brother called. "Right after we got to her bedside, she took her last breath."

My teacher spoke of physical death as an experience of exquisite beauty and freedom: "When you leave the body, what you take with you is what you *are*. Your experience is what you've been willing to know and to own about yourself. All that you *had* is forgotten. There's no memory of money, possessions, powerhouses, and what you *did*. In death, all you have is what you *are*." The Love is magnificent, he said, "beyond all words to describe it."[235]

Betty J. Eadie encountered that magnificent Love in her near-death experience. At thirty-one, mother of seven children, she went into a Seattle hospital for routine surgery. When her body hemorrhaged to the point of death, her spirit traveled to the other side, "what the world calls heaven" she said. Betty was given knowledge about how the universe works, the purpose of earthly life, and the way to happiness and wholeness. She put her learning into *Embraced by*

*the Light,* a book that became a longstanding bestseller. She saw that every simple act of kindness that helps another soul—even a smile—ripples out to countless people and places. A single change of heart has the power to change the world.

Betty J. Eadie (courtesy of Betty J. Eadie).

# Chapter Twenty-Eight

# LOVE IS FOREVER

## Encounter with Betty J. Eadie

*Religions can be helpful to people,*
*but they are not perfect.*

*There is truly only one way to God,*
*and that is through the pathway of Love.*

—BETTY EADIE

## EMBRACED BY THE LIGHT

At age four, Betty was taken to a boarding school for Native American children on the Rosebud Reservation, in South Dakota.[236] They told her she was "the worst of the lot—a heathen and a sinner" because her mother was full-blooded Lakota Sioux and her father was Irish. It was a degrading environment. Betty told me,

> I was stripped of everything I had a belief in or knowledge of. I was only four, but I knew the importance as Native people to wear our hair long. And I did. All

the Native Americans, male and female, wore their hair long. It was part of our spirituality that kept us close to God our Creator. But as soon as we got to the boarding school, they cut our hair up to our ears and then deloused us. We didn't have lice, but they forced the spray upon us anyway. It was very demeaning. Their treatment of us stripped us of our spiritual roots and injected fear, shame, guilt and judgment.

"Doomed to hell, a heathen and a sinner"—that's what Betty's childhood poured into her, and that's what she believed about herself. "I couldn't figure out what kind of a God would send a little four-year-old to hell." As a child, she learned to despise the Lakota part of herself. "When I took a bath, I used to look at my brown skin with shame and try to wash it off." As a teen, her own Lakota mother told her, "Stay away from Native boys. I want you to marry 'white'. Otherwise you will never make it in this world." Betty married "white."

When she was thirty-one, Betty had a near-death experience (NDE) that changed everything in the world for her. She was alone in her hospital room following a routine hysterectomy. At 9:30 p.m., she hemorrhaged. "I felt myself bleeding to death, like every last drop of blood was being drained from me. Death was coming up from my feet, and I was too weak to reach the switch that called a nurse for help."

Suddenly she found herself outside of her body, looking down at it. She realized that her essence was not a body of flesh but a spirit. "My spirit came up from my body effortlessly. I turned around, looked down, and saw my body lying there on the bed. I never imagined you could see a spirit, much less be above your own body. But, my death wasn't scary—no more painful than if I were to take off this dress and drop it on the floor." For the next four hours of clock time, she had what is regarded as the most detailed NDE ever recorded. Raymond Moody, M.D., author of *Life After Life* and the leading pioneer of

NDE studies, views Eadie's as the most comprehensive and profound NDE ever told.

The first place Betty visited in her spirit body was her home. She saw her husband, Joe, reading the newspaper in his chair while her children were going wild with a pillow fight, feathers flying everywhere. She thought to her husband: *You promised to put the kids in bed and here you sit, reading the paper!* But he couldn't see or hear her. As much as she loved her family, she felt a greater pull to return to her body in the hospital.

Betty returned to her hospital room and heard beautiful chimes. "And then I felt an energy like a whirlwind, or a tornado, it was a tunnel effect that sucked me up into it. The tunnel was so black I couldn't see anything, but I felt bathed in warm liquid love." She felt like she was being purified and cleansed by unconditional love. "I could have stayed there for eternities."

Then she saw a pinpoint of Light come down, as though it were searching for her in the darkness. "It came to me like a finger pointing—'Okay we're ready for *her.*'" Her spirit was drawn to the Light, which became brighter and brighter as she came near to it. "It drew me and I wanted to go. I was going faster and faster and faster, a speed that I cannot describe."

As she approached the Light, she saw that the Light was actually the figure of a man. "Around him was the most radiant white Light. It flowed and sparkled. It was Beautiful. It was Alive. It was Aware. It was Living Light. The Light radiated a quality of Pure Love surpassing anything on Earth. Then—*I know who He is. I KNOW who he is!* And I ran to him like a child runs to someone they've loved forever. His arms opened wide, and he drew me to him." She weeps as she remembers his embrace. "That was and still is a very profound moment in my life! I felt I was finally *Home* and *The Light* was Jesus." She couldn't see his exact physical features clearly because of the brightness of his radiant Light. "However, I *knew* his essence, and I knew he was my loving brother Jesus and I called him Jesus. I wept as I told him, 'I never want to leave you again—ever!'"

Betty was shocked to be embraced by him and to receive his love. She had been taught to have a negative view of herself and did not feel worthy of him. "I never really knew that God loved me. I was raised to feel condemned by God, to believe I was a 'heathen and a sinner,' yet here in this incredibly beautiful place he was embracing me. I remembered that I had known him for eons, and that I had always had his love."

She cried to Jesus, "Why did you send me there? I will never go back again—I won't go back again!" She recounted her miseries and oppressions to him. She was resentful about her life. "I had a chip on my shoulder as I told him all of my hardships on Earth. Native American. Irish. Why? Taken away from my parents at age four. Why? Sent to Indian boarding school. Poverty. Abuse. Why? He said, 'I know and you know. You chose it. Your life on Earth is according to Your Father's Will, and it has strengthened you to serve your purpose, your mission on Earth." Betty couldn't believe what she was hearing. "I did? He knows?!" she asked.

Jesus told her, "You chose your DNA, Irish and Native American, and that combination has given you the inner strength that you needed. You chose your perfect cellular memories from generations of family, all that would make you the perfect Betty on Earth to do what you have to do while you're there." He explained the purpose of life on Earth: "You go there to learn about love. How to love and how to acquire to love. Your Spirit growth depends upon as many of the attributes of God as you are capable of. Everyone is challenged to do this, however, in different ways."

She said, "What about all the things I did that were not very good?" Jesus said, "They *were* good. You learned from them, didn't you? That is what earthly life is all about. That is also why you cannot judge a single soul. You do not know their purpose on Earth, nor what they are capable of handling. They are being stretched too. You do not know why they chose that course of study."

During her NDE, Betty was downloaded with storehouses of knowledge but not through a mental process. The Light transmitted knowledge instantly as a permeation of her being. She understood the word "omniscience" for the first time. She saw blueprints for healing people and the planet, and she saw the underlying structures and energies of the universe. "All healing comes from within, so does all misery."

She saw that Indigenous Peoples have a vital role to play in the world. "The Creator placed a sacred knowledge in the cellular memory of Native Peoples." They are spiritually attuned and trained to work with sacred ways; they respect and care for life, give thanks to the Creator, walk in a sacred manner, and bring a "saving balance" to the Earth.

She saw that each particle has intelligence. There are many worlds and planes of existence. Reincarnation occurs, but not in the way we usually understand it—most people don't have repeated lives on Earth but in other worlds created by God. We have ancestors' memories inside us as a form of past-life knowledge.

Energies are either positive or negative, and we have the power to choose one or the other and thereby create the life and world we live in. To choose love, generosity, and kindness brings the greatest joy. She explains: "What you give returns to you. Whatever you put out there comes back to you—love, anger… the process is like a ripple effect. What goes around comes around. If you're not busy taking, you can receive. If your prayers are to heal others, you are healed."

In a life review, Betty saw the ripple effect of every thought, word, and action in her life. Even the smallest gesture caused a domino effect that impacted countless people and places. Seeing the effect of her temper and lack of compassion, the chain of hurt became too much for her and she couldn't bear to view any more. Jesus and those with him held her in total mercy. "Do not judge yourself so harshly," Jesus said. She realized then that the only judgment was her own self-judgment. She told me, "What I learned in my NDE was very different from what I had heard in the churches I belonged to. God's Love is Infinite. It is only our belief systems that can block it."

Earthly life is like a school, she explained to me. Our mistakes are not failures, but lessons we learn and knowledge we gain and internalize because of them. We come to Earth at different levels of spiritual awareness, choose a "course of study," and we are given the experiences we need to learn the lessons in that curriculum. Only through experience is knowledge internalized and "known." All of our experiences are opportunities for growth and knowledge, more so than any book of study. "What you internalize becomes part of your spiritual essence. Experience is the only way you internalize anything. We are here on Earth to gain wisdom that can only be gained through personal experience. Life is the best teacher."

Betty told two experiences from her NDE that deeply impacted me. The first took place in a garden area. She noticed that the Light did not come from "out there," and so there were no shadows like on Earth. Instead, Light came from within. Each flower, tree, flowing water, and being was lit up from the inside. "Everything was alive, in praise of its life and Creator, responsive to love. The grass was aware of my love of grasses as a Native American child as I walked on the prairie. The grass grew up to that perfect point on my calves. As I walked faster, I could feel the grass loving to massage the back of my leg where I loved to feel it. The grass was alive, and it could be in any way it needed to be for the sake of its love for me, and the love I felt for it."

When Betty went to a waterfall, she saw that every drop of water was praising God. "When I saw each droplet praising God with its life, its love, and its beauty, it was then that I understood that each one of us praises and blesses God by our very being, our essence." Hearing this, I remembered Grandmother Mona's teaching: "Speak to the water, it's alive! It's your relative."

Roses symbolize love, and Betty had a revelational encounter with one. As she looked deeply into it, the rose grew right before her eyes. As soon as she felt a desire to know it more intimately, she was brought inside of it and made able to penetrate its deepest parts. She heard a symphony of splendor as each petal, each part of the rose, sang its joyous praise of God. And there were thousands of other roses joining in the grand chorus to celebrate a joy unspeakable. And then—she not only saw a rose, heard a rose, felt a rose, she became and *was* a part of the rose. "We are all one!" she lit up with joy as she described the ecstasy of this moment.

"I learned too, that as you walk and talk, you emit tone and a vibration. Thus people and even animals are aware of who you are without actually seeing you first. I learned that it is important to do all things with grace, avoiding emotions of anger and chaos in every movement. Our energy affects all other energy."

The second experience was in the societal realm—"a drunken bum." Betty said, "I was so judgmental back then. Of course I would be—look at how I had been judged. I was a person of low self-esteem, low self-worth. In order to feel better about myself, I put others down. Isn't that what we all do?" Her escorts pulled back a veil to show her a typical scene on Earth: a city street with a drunk. "What do you see, Betty?"

"I see a drunken ole bum lying in his vomit."

Then the guides looked at her with a grin: "Now let's see what he really looks like in spirit." They took him out of his physical body and Betty saw his spirit, a magnificent being of Light! "I was mortified. My judgment insulted me." She explained: "We each have an essence, an inner Light that radiates out a certain circumference. On Earth, we don't see this inner Light, but in heaven you cannot hide it; it is who and what you are. The drunken bum's light was brilliant and radiated purer love than my own. In comparison, my light was a pitiful little three watts, like a nightlight, and made me shudder in embarrassment."

Betty asked her guides, "How can this be?" They told her that the drunken man was actually a great being who came to Earth for one purpose—he is going to make eye contact with an attorney who walks that street. Because of that spirit contact, the attorney will do a lot of good for alcoholics. She learned that the two men were soul friends who had made a covenant with each other to do this earthly work. But, she told me laughingly, "We do not usually remember our mission. Otherwise, Jesus said, we would get it done just to get out of here, rather than in its perfect timing! Everything under the Sun has its perfect timing."

The NDE impressed Betty with one core message: "Above all else, love one another." This is how she ends her book and all of her talks. "'Love one another' is the message Jesus wanted me to share with the world."

It took Betty almost twenty years to share this message. She had a hard time when she came back because that realm of unconditional love has no parallel on Earth. Even the deepest earthly love, she said, cannot compare. It was love in its purest form—infinite, totally unconditional, all-forgiving, overflowing, ever-giving, without beginning, without end. Adjusting to "normal" life after her NDE was not easy. She longed for the vibrant spectrum of colors, the oneness, the melting love and ecstatic joy of heaven. It took her many years to integrate the new knowledge and capabilities gained from the NDE into her body, mind, psychology, spirituality, and family life.

In 1992, she was ready to fulfill her task by publishing a book to share her experience. *Embraced by the Light* was an overnight success. It was #1 on *The New York Times* Bestseller List for 78 weeks. Even three years later, it remained on the *Times* Bestseller List when she published her second book, *The Awakening Heart*, which also landed on the list. Betty became a celebrity—interviewed on all the major networks, featured in *People* and *Time-Life* magazines, making headlines as she traveled around the country to speak to audiences as large as 15,000. World leaders wrote her letters of gratitude. Ritz Carlton and Waldorf Astoria owners invited her to stay. The upperclass places that had thrown her out as an impoverished Indian child now welcomed her.

But Betty's book didn't fit easily into existing frameworks. Even bookstores weren't sure where to stock it. On one hand, Christians complained that the book was "too new-age" in its affirmation of diverse paths, mercy, love, and forgiveness. Rightwing Christians published critical reviews and heckled Betty in public. Other readers said her book was "too Christian." This dilemma resolved quickly when *Embraced by the Light* became a bestseller featured at the front of bookstores in its own display.

Music legend Prince fell in love with Betty's book and made it mandatory reading for all of his employees. She told me, "Prince wanted me to go on tour with him, talk onstage, and wanted to buy *Embraced by the Light* for everyone at his concert." But Betty didn't know who Prince was. "I didn't know about pop culture and celebrities." When he came to one of her talks in Minnesota, he invited her to his studio in Paisley Park. They became instant friends. Prince told her about his difficulties. As she was leaving, they hugged and then laughed because they were the same height and both wearing four-inch heels! Betty told me how her ignorance allowed her to be natural: "I was able to sit with famous people and not be intimidated by them, just like you and I are sitting. I wasn't intimidated by them. When I went on *Oprah*, I didn't know she had the most popular show in the world. What I saw then and see now, is that we are all God's children. God created us all, no one greater than the other. Why would you be afraid of your spirit brother or sister? That's how I saw each celebrity and grew to love them."

Now in her seventies, Betty continues to touch the lives of millions. Her books have been translated into more than forty languages, and her podcast is downloaded in almost every country in the world. A movie about her life is in the works. These successes haven't gone to her head. When I met her, I noted her humility, simplicity, humor, wisdom, and naturalness. There was no attempt to please, persuade, promote, or impress. On the outside, she appears an ordinary mother and grandmother, but from the inside, Light radiates around and through her. It's palpable and far-reaching. She laughs easily at herself. She loves people in the measure they need and can receive. She points them to their inner truth. She told one audience, a local chapter of the International Association of Near-Death Studies (IANDS): "Do not listen to everyone. Do not even listen to me unless you're prone to. Listen to your heart. Let it resonate in here (points to her heart center) before you believe anything or anybody. Listen to your heart because that is where God speaks to you daily."

I saw her speak at three different venues, each with its own mix of people. One was at a Hindu *mandir* in a diverse neighborhood in Berkeley, another at a Unity church in a mostly white, upper-class area. She was the same genuine spirit in both settings, greeting everyone warmly. Someone commented, "This is the kind of loving atmosphere people are hoping for when they go to church." The NDE infused Betty with an intelligence and power of love that people recognize as healing and they want to be near it.

I learned a lot from watching how she interacted with people. Love, clearly, is different from mere niceness. In one instance, we were standing outside of a restaurant, observing a young man in the parking lot asking people for money. When he came over to us, I was ready to give him a dollar, but Betty's energy zipped up and she said, "No." After he walked away, I asked her, "Why didn't you give him anything?" She said, "He was looking for a victim. I didn't want to make him worse by enabling his negative tendencies. Love is not blind, it sees more deeply." The next day, I was walking with her on a sidewalk and a young woman with tattoos came up to her. I thought: *Betty will rebuff her like she did the young man yesterday.* But Betty embraced her and listened closely to her story. The young woman was a survivor of ritual abuse and *Embraced by the Light* had healed and comforted her. She had been praying to meet Betty, and wept as she described what she had been through. "I knew you'd see me as God sees me. It means the world to meet you. I pass out your book as much as I can. I had to close it once because rays of light were pouring out. Last night, I woke up and saw you in front of my bed in your Native dress. You handed me your book *The Ripple Effect.*" Betty held her for a long time. She told me, "She's breaking a chain of abuse in her family. The ripple effect is enormous."

Betty discerns the hearts of people. If their heart is sincere, she holds nothing back. If they have ulterior or negative motives, the door closes. "Love does not cater to negativity," she said. I realized that I had put up with a lot of negativity in my life, thinking it was loving when really it was my own dependency.

"Brothers and Sisters in Spirit"—this is how Betty greeted her audiences in northern California, very much like the greeting of Swami Vivekananda at the first Parliament of the World's Religions in 1893: "Sisters and Brothers of America."

Betty's mother was full-blooded *Sicangu* Lakota *Oyate*.[237] The greeting of the Lakota people is *mitakuye oyasin*, meaning, "We are all related" or "all my relations." Betty says it is a prayer that "conveys the heartfelt interconnectedness underlying all living things, and honors the Creator by acknowledging the harmony he intends for all his creations." When she says, "Brothers and Sisters in Spirit," she offers a prayer that runs deep in her veins and in the spirit of our land.

"We are all brothers and sisters." A Hindu monk from India and a Christian mother of eight from the Rosebud Sioux Tribe of South Dakota each came to the same realization, a century apart. Love awakens the hearts of whoever is ready, no matter race, religion, gender, or station in life. When the heart opens, the power of love comes through and enlightens the world with the message of our oneness. It's similar to sunlight. When we open the blinds, light fills the room, but most of us keep the blinds in place. We may think we know a lot—our sophisticated ideologies, doctrines, and philosophies—but we're in the dark about the Reality of Love. According to Betty Eadie and Swami Vivekananda, our belief systems are what blind and bind us.

Betty told me that many of our beliefs are buried in the subconscious and we have to uncover the lies "poured into us" by often well-meaning people. She told the audience: "We are empty vessels at birth, and whatever is poured into you about yourself, is what you come to believe you are. You accepted untruths, just as you do truths. You learn to become what you are told about yourself." Examples of the lies we carry inside of ourselves (and mete out to others) are: "You should be ashamed of yourself"; "You deserve punishment"; "You have to earn love"; "Unless you're perfect, you can't be loved"; "You can't trust love"; "Life is unfair." As we talked, I realized that some of those twisted beliefs still lived in me.

# CONVERSATION WITH BETTY J. EADIE

Betty was one of the first on my list of people to interview, but it took years because of her many commitments. A family situation brought her to northern California and she was scheduled to give three talks at public venues. When I asked again for an interview, her kind assistant told me that Betty would call my cell phone if a space opened up. Not holding my breath, I drove the ten hours anyway, knowing it would be a blessing simply to see and hear her. The day after her second event, the phone rang. Betty asked me to meet her at a home-style restaurant. We entered into a timeless space, absorbed in our sharing. I felt known in my essence, the greatest gift we can give someone. Three hours went by like ten minutes.

## Mission and Purpose of Life on Earth

Q: You were shown we all have a mission. What do you think yours is?

BJE: To bring to those who are open to hear it, the most powerful message of God's unconditional and eternal love for all. I was given experiences of this truth, and knew I had to share it. Love is supreme. And God is Love. The only way to be like God is to love as He loves, unconditionally. Without love, we are not like him at all. We are here to grow in love for every person.

Q: You said in your talk that we don't really know what our mission is, or that of other people.

BJE: I don't think we are meant to know. I believe our missions will come as a surprise to each one of us. We could be here just to reach one other soul about how to love. I'm reaching a lot of people just trying to get to that one person! We need to refrain from judgment of how each person lives, because we do not know what their purpose is, their mission. Those who appear rough on the outside might be an angel in disguise on the inside, like a baby with birth defects teaches a family about love. Our purposes are not always grand or grandiose. Besides for our own growth, our purposes are usually for one another. Some can fulfill their connections in silence. I was shown this in heaven, that everyone and everything has a field of energy that surrounds them. We all have this light, this energy. When it compresses, we say, "I'm depressed." The way to get your energy up is by sharing your light with other people. Life is never just about you. It is almost always about others. If you're not sharing your light, you break the flow of life, and make it difficult to receive more. If you are open to give, you are open to receive. If you do not pass on the light you have been given, then you do not receive any more. Same thing is true of finances. People do not like to let go of what they have. However, it is in the giving that you will receive. Very simply taught in the law of tithing. But unless you internalize this, the knowledge is of no good.

## Going Beyond Belief Systems

Q:   You and others say that the main reason for an earthly life is to learn about love.

BJE:   Yes. However, our belief systems can limit us. To those entrenched in traditional beliefs that teach anything other than LOVE, I would say, "Forget about bragging that you are a nonbeliever, neither label your faith with obscure, mystifying, unintelligible beliefs that do not include life's only healing energy of love. Stay open to love's possibilities, for God is LOVE."

Q:   The same is true for a religious or spiritual person—not to cling to their beliefs?

BJE: Yes, when excluding love or current enlightenment about God—Absolutely! Look at all the changes that have happened in the world. They used to think the Earth was flat, and time and greater knowledge proved that to be wrong. It was once thought too that the Earth was the only living planet, and now we are learning otherwise. Medicine as well is advancing to include our DNA and cellular memory, which play a huge part in our ill-health and our healing. Times past, we did not have this knowledge; doctors and scientists never believed it to be true, and we trusted their knowledge. In 1992, I wrote about this in my book. It was highly criticized but it has since come to fruition. I have learned that there is nothing absolute except for the fact that there is a God, a Heavenly Supreme Being, or Creator.

Beliefs are often established through tradition, not truth. Did you see a movie titled *The Village*?[238] It speaks volumes about traditions and the comfort people find in them. In the movie, people isolated themselves in the middle of a forest and built a wall around themselves. The children grew up under the teaching that there were monsters that surrounded the outside walls of the village— that they would attack them and kill them should they go beyond its boundary. Then one day, someone tested that teaching and ventured out to discover a city, though narrowly escaping a trap set by the village. Returning to the village he shared his newfound truth how different life was in the city, how nothing threatened like they'd been taught by the Village. Since this truth would destroy their teachings, a plan was set by the Village Leaders to withhold truth and continue in their ways. They didn't see the value of Truth and did not want to lose control over those of their flock, so they continued in their myth. Many religions do the same, some knowingly and some unknowingly. They are able to continue because of their egos and the traditional teachings of fear.

Q: How did your NDE change your view of reality and your beliefs?

BJE: The experience transformed my fears from past religious teachings. I had become what you might call a wounded soul from them. At four years old, I was taken from my home and placed into a Catholic Indian boarding school where I was told I was going to hell. What saved me at that age, shortly after being taken to that boarding school, was that I became very ill. I caught double pneumonia and whooping cough, and I heard the doctor tell a nurse that I died. I had my first NDE, though I did not know it as such back then. I do not remember much from it except that God held me in his arms and loved me. I clung to those feelings of love for years. Eventually I forgot the experience, but I always had His Love in my essence to receive and to give. Looking back, I know it saved me from the horrors of boarding school.

When I went to Cochrane, Ontario, at the invitation of the Mushkegowuk Tribal Council, as a speaker at their Residential School Healing Conference, I spent an entire day counseling individuals, listening to the harm done to them—raped, beaten, all in the name of God, which is absolutely devastating to any spirit. Since we give out what we have to give, many of the men I counseled confessed they raped their daughters and often beat their wives. What tore my heart at this conference were the men. They felt beaten down, torn and depressed, and were ashamed to tell me what they'd done due to their alcoholism. I coaxed it out of them, because if you do not acknowledge your mistakes or what you have done in shame, it can remain a gnawing dark secret that can last for a lifetime. Telling someone (confessing your sins) gets that secret out of your subconscious, where it's doing the damage. When you bury your feelings, they take root. They do not die. Over time the deed might fade, but the root never does. It actually grows to become stronger. The roots of sinful deeds feed on denial; they enhance shame and guilt. The longer they are buried, more deeply rooted they become, and then when they sprout and surface, they often take on various forms and identities. You may wonder: *Where did that thought or action come from?* To understand, you have to go to the root cause. Before my NDE, I didn't know this. During my NDE, I was given greater knowledge of the spirit. After coming back, I wanted to do something with this knowledge. I knew a wounded spirit had to be reached to be healed. I went to school to become a clinical hypnotherapist, to reach and heal the spirit that holds the root of the cause.

## Integrating Our Profound Experiences

Q: In your book *The Awakening Heart* you describe how hard it was for you to be here in the world after the NDE. Emotionally you struggled; physically you had adjustments. There was a high-intensity energy in your body; so intense it would set off electrical equipment. It's as if you experienced a huge "download" into your system that took years to "install" into your life here.

BJE: It took years to adjust and to put my experience into words. How do you put to words an experience that is Sacred? The description of the Deity, of heaven, of angels, warring angels, guardian angels, the many worlds, the people who exist in those worlds, their loving knowledge of us, and how they carefully watch over us? How to put that into words in a way that people can understand? It's hard to put something that you feel and believe is so sacred out there, knowing it might be trampled on by the unbelieving.

Q: I felt angry to learn that people attacked you and your experience. And religious people were some of the worst—their hateful signs and attacks.

BJE: When I first told my husband that I had to write the book, he said, "You do not know where you are putting yourself! People will be upset, and even angry!" I listened, but searched my heart and finally told him, "I have to write it. I told Jesus I would." And in time, *Embraced by the Light* was downloaded, like in the movie *The Matrix* when the woman got into a helicopter and needed to know how to fly it, she opened herself up to the knowledge and it was downloaded into her. I understood how that is possible and experienced the downloading of my book. I learned that we still have sacred knowledge of Heaven within us, just waiting for us to discover it.

Q:   Last night, you pointed to your heart center and said, "It's all in here." The readers of this book may wonder, "If it's in me, how do I experience it? How do I connect to the love within?"

BJE:   You have to begin with desire for it. Desire comes before hope, and hope before faith. At least that was the case for me. I can only tell you how I established it in me. I didn't trust religion. Just about every church I had joined said they were the one and only true church. I thought: *I'll play it safe and just join them all!* And I did. I studied what they believed, and learned that a lot of them were really off base from what I thought a loving God should be. I found that some of them use their teachings of fear of God and guilt over past mistakes to control people. I continued my search, going from one to another to find the right church to raise my kids in. As a mother I needed to feel that I had done the best I could for them. Then, at age thirty-one, I had the magnificent NDE that broadened my perspective and sent me back to Earth with a knowledge I couldn't deny. The understanding I received of God was downloaded not only to my brain but in my heart and soul! From that moment—[*weeping*] I'm sorry to cry, that was and still is a profound moment for me—I am compelled by His Love. People say, "How did you take your book to unaccepting, angry people?" I was very, very shy, but he gave me strength as well as the words to use and speak.

## Healing

Q:   Looking at you now—confident, composed, fearless—it's hard to believe you were timid.

BJE:   I have grown. There is little doubt that before my NDE I suffered at some level the indignities of low self-esteem, low self-worth, and just about low-everything. I often felt I was at the bottom of the totem pole because of those feelings. Back then, Indian children were kept ignorant, distant from all worldly goods, understandings and aspirations. When I came back from the NDE, I had this new inner strength that lifted me and drove me—compelled me to share what I experienced. And yet I didn't understand it all myself. I had no pastor or priest that I could go to and discuss my experience with. I prayed about it, over and over. My prayers were always answered, and that's another blessing. In the NDE, I was taught a blueprint for healing and wholeness, and I learned to follow that blueprint. I thought: *Once I achieve this deep healing in myself, I will know that it's something I can share with all my heart to help other people.* That learning curve took nineteen years for my book *Embraced by the Light* to be published. All the knowledge I acquired had to be internalized through experience and my own inner healing.

Q:   When you first came back from the NDE, you had many struggles. You gained a lot of weight, had severe depression, and then developed panic and agoraphobia. How did you heal from these things?

BJE:   It took baby steps to heal, especially with the agoraphobia, it was a little bit at a time. Many people suffer this problem—fear and panic attacks when going outside into open spaces. I talked myself through it. I would say, "Okay, What's the worst thing that can happen to me if I walk out that door?" And of course it was about death—"I could go out there and be killed by a car." Well, I'd already done that, I died and loved it! I just needed my body and mind to let go of a false thought or emotion of fear. I knew I could train my body and mind, so I put them to the task by walking out the door and going around the block. Baby steps. It wasn't easy. Halfway around the block, I would hurry back home. Over time, I broadened the distance, further and further until I was walking seven miles a day. The miles strengthened my body while my determination and resilience brought my body and mind into harmony. I gained confidence. Then I needed to address the yearnings of my spirit. Compared to heaven, the world was awful. I longed for the love I had experienced on the other side. As much as my husband loved me—and his love was wonderful—his love paled in comparison to what I had experienced and it was not enough for me. It was not the same quality of love as in my NDE. It just couldn't be. I tried to explain that to him, and he would say, "You know I love you with all my heart." I knew he loved me, but he didn't understand that he really didn't love me with all his heart and that his love is just not at the same level of love as in Heaven. I couldn't explain this to him, or for that matter the entire NDE, at least not at that time. I couldn't discuss the whole thing in depth with anyone.

The first person I shared my NDE with, in full, was my best friend. She came to the hospital the day after I had the experience. I said, "I have to tell you what happened to me." She held my hand and I poured my heart out, telling her everything. And here's the strangest thing: My friend had been drinking that day, she told me later, and could not remember a thing I told her! I believe it was God's perfect plan to protect me, my spirit was just that tender. I was able to release all that had happened to me and yet had she been sober, it would have been too much for her to absorb. She just sat there patting my hand all the way through, so I thought she got it, but she didn't get anything! She said later, "I'm glad I was drunk and didn't remember what you told me. It would've blown me away." Her pattern of belief at the time would not have allowed her to accept anything of what I told her.

Q: You said last night in your talk, "God uses what *is*." Maybe our imperfections, like alcoholism, serve a purpose we can't see?

BJE: Exactly. No one is perfect. My friend was drunk that day, but I needed a friend and she was there for me. When I started to share it with my husband, raised Southern Baptist, he just sat there; his eyes got wide, and he said, "You best not share this with very many people." That shut me up. So there I was, all alone, and I had to share it with someone! It was more than I could bear, holding it all inside. It created an energy in me that needed to get out, and my friend helped me by being there. As soon as I recovered from the surgery, I tape-recorded my experience. Although every cell in my body recalled it, I wanted to leave its details for my children in case I should die again soon.

Q: You also found a way to share your gifts of healing with people by training in clinical hypnotherapy.

BJE: Yes, during the NDE, I learned about healing the body by use of the mind and spirit. I went back to school and studied psychology. To be honest, I was bored in school. I had learned so much more in my NDE about psychology than what was presented academically. I went on to learn about mind integration, how to take the part of you that is off base or off course and integrate it with the stronger parts. Not rid yourself of it, because every part is necessary for the total. Some therapists would have you get rid of the part that is off base, while integration of it is best. For example, people say, "I got rid of my wounded child, I made my inner child grow up." Why? That's the part of us that makes us delightful and fun. Don't get rid of *anything,* just integrate and harmonize it. If it is working against you, give it a different job.

Q: So true healing involves the integration of all parts of ourselves, not rejecting anything?

BJE: Yes. And celebrate the fact that you are in touch with that part of yourself. Most people are not in touch with what is inside of them, because they are afraid of what they might find. Yet if they just realize there are no absolutes except for the existence of God, that would be freeing. There is no reason to feel afraid or ashamed of who we are. We have amazing power inside of us. If we can think of it, conceive it, then we can become it or have it. It is ours. When you internalize something, it then becomes a part of your essence. We are electromagnetic physical beings, and therefore as we expand and as we attract more light, our knowledge expands to receive more, and the more we receive the greater we grow in essence. Then all you have to do is open up your heart and your mind to receive the full glory of God.

Q: Betty, I have a hitch in my own healing process—a skin condition. You said in your talk if a problem or dis-ease isn't cleared on the spiritual level, then the physical and mental levels cannot be cleared. I've experienced the truth of this many times over, healing from various things, but the skin problem hasn't improved, and for twenty years I've pondered the spiritual root of it. I wonder if it is a reaping of what I have sown. I was very judgmental of others, telling them they do not belong, they were sinners, outside of God's mercy. On my skin, it's as if I wear a garment of guilt about that, as in the phrase "spots on the soul," a badge of the pain I've caused others, a visible reminder of my guilt, like some people get a tattoo to remind them of something.

BJE:   Perhaps it's a self-punishment. And it's okay with you because you think you deserve it.

Q:   That's very disturbing. Could a healing occur if I were to let go of the belief that I deserve punishment?

BJE:   Let me tell you a story. After the NDE and becoming a clinical hypnotherapist and mind-integration therapist, I was able by the grace of God to rent an office in a medical building. As soon as the other tenants found out I was into hypnosis, they complained—they were doctors and dentists and had a bias against hypnotherapy. I told the leasing manager, "I'll give a first session for free to any of them who comes, and that they personally experience what I do, then they can decide about my lease." I was encouraged when a doctor brought his daughter. She was in her twenties, covered with boils from head to toe. He had taken her to dermatologists, doctors galore, but she only got worse. He asked me, "How do you do it?" "I go to the spirit." He responded, "Oh, you're into new age and healing the inner child?" I answered, "No, the inner child is reacting to the spirit. I go deeper to the spirit." His face looked puzzled. "I don't understand, but we'll give it a whirl. I've tried everything else." His daughter, sitting across from me, said, "I've been to every doctor. I don't see how you can help me." I asked her, "Is this something you want to try?" Looking at the red boils on her arm, she said, "Yes but how are you going to do this?" I said, "Let's go straight into hypnotherapy and we'll find out, and if at any moment you're uncomfortable, let me know." I was amazed at how quickly she went into hypnosis and accepted the depths to her spirit. Her problem was that she'd had a beautiful cat when she left home for college. The cat died, and her parents had it cremated—all without telling her anything about it because they knew it would devastate her. When she came home and expected to be greeted by her cat, they told her the cat had died and they gave her the remains. Under hypnosis, she began screaming, "I didn't get a chance to say goodbye to my cat! It just makes me boiling mad!" And there it was—the boils on her skin. The next session, I had her go back in and say goodbye to her cat in the way that made her comfortable. Her own mind and spirit knew exactly what she needed. She held it on her lap, petted it and cried like a baby. The next session, her boils had already started to clear. I didn't mention it to her and she didn't say anything about it, but her dad did. "Betty, this is a miracle." A couple weeks later, he called to say the boils were gone and to congratulate me. I told him, "It's a miracle created by your daughter. I just guided her to it."

Q: That's an amazing story. So you just guided her to the inner truth of her spirit and then her skin healed?

BJE: If you do not get to the spirit, there will not be a healing. It goes back to "feelings buried alive never die." One question I always ask my clients who are under hypnosis is, "This condition is serving you. If so, in what way?" This particular young woman said it was serving her because she was boiling mad and could not release her anger. She had no way to express it because these were her loving parents, so she just created the boils. And then I ask, "Are you ready to release it?" In her case, she said, "Oh, yes, it has served its purpose." With the evidence of those boils that could not be healed, she was paying her dad back big-time—all the money to dermatologists and other doctors. That is how the subconscious mind works. Payback or reward, however you look at it, it serves. Under hypnosis, you ask, "How is it serving?" That is when I discover whether they are capable of letting it go or if it is still needed to help them.

Q: Could it be also that our illness or condition serves to help others evolve? I've always thought this was the case with my mother's dementia. It served those around her.

BJE: Yes, in fact, illnesses are almost always about someone else, but it can also be about self-punishment. People are really into punishing themselves. I think you suffer from that.

## Love is More Powerful than Negativity

Q: Speaking of punishment, is there a hell?

BJE: The one you make or the one you believe in. When you die, you take your belief system with you. If you believe you need to go to hell, God is so wonderful that he will not destroy your belief systems, he will let you go there. Hell is not really a place, it's a condition. In my NDE I asked about hell. Hell was my greatest concern. I had been told I was going straight to hell, a heathen and a sinner. There was no question about that. However, Jesus' response to my question about hell put it in perspective for me. He said, "As a good mother, would you throw any of your children into hell, a pit of fire, into outer darkness?" Of course I would not, and I am just a human being with a lot of faults, yet even I would not do that. God's love is greater than mine and He will not cast anyone into hell—but there is more that I learned: If you die and think you have to go to hell, that is self-punishment and you'll live it for a time until you let go of that false conception and you call out for Jesus Christ. You'll read that in Howard Storm's book. He tells how he went to hell and called out to Jesus even though he was an atheist. Angels swooped down and got him out of hell. Was it a real hell or was it the hell he created? It was the hell he created. I always tell people, when you die, don't fear the light. Then there's the case of Berkeley's famed paleontologist, Professor Charles Camp. He found the first dinosaur here in California. Atheist to the core who did radio programs with Christian ministers. He argued with them about life after death and he insisted, "When you die, you're dead, that's it." Well imagine his surprise when he had four NDEs and met God. He said, "I'm so sorry. I wasted my life telling everyone that you don't exist." God said, "You did a good job at what you were supposed to do. You got those religious leaders to think more deeply about things."

Q:    What did you learn about religion in your NDE?

BJE:    God loves us unconditionally, and Christ is a messenger of love. People misinterpret or simply do not get what his mission was and is. It is not that we go back to God through him, but that we follow his message of Love and return to God through the path of Love that Jesus set an example of. It is God's will that there are many religions, because people are at different levels of spirit growth when arriving here. Religions can be helpful to people, but they are not perfect and cannot be perfect because they are tainted by the hands and minds of mankind. There is truly only one way to God, and that is through the pathway of Love. Many Christians do not believe or perhaps do not understand what Jesus said in the Bible, that he came here to take away the sins of the world, to do away with the law of Moses. Some churches tell us we are sinners going to hell. What did Jesus say? "On my death, I take with me the sins of the world." His never-ending guidance and recommendation concerning prudent future action is "Come follow me!" Yet few trust his words—that we are free to follow him and we are *his*. Some cling to the idea of sin and sinners out of fear of God and of course believing that other people are worse sinners than they are! Do not get me wrong. I understand there are some who choose to disbelieve and follow a path to destruction. It's all about choice.

Q:    If we create our own hell by buying into negativity, what are negativities to avoid?

BJE:    There are things I learned that do not fit with what is popular to believe, but I will share some of what I know. Gluttony of anything is a "sin"—guilt over past mistakes, anger, grief, food, spiritual gluttony, hopelessness, greed. Rap music can destroy the rhythm of the heart. Cursing is destructive. We are to bless with our words, not curse. We are to protect what we see with our eyes, as they act as recorders to all they see. What not to view relates also to pornography—once your eyes capture a negative image you will not be rid of it. Pornography turns your sexual response off over time because of brain malfunction. I tell people, "If you watch pornography, break from it as soon as possible!" It is also very dangerous to play around with the unseen. There is danger in the paranormal because you are dealing with energies. Black magic exists…. It can pull the spirit down quickly. Nothing comes between God and us except what we place there. Suicide might be a momentary fix but it does not relieve the eternal pain you will face in your life review. You can better deal with your problems here on Earth.

Q: What do you recommend as a path?

BJE: The path of love. Stay with love and with loving people. Pure Love is the only healing energy there is, so stay on the side of Love at all times. Align yourself with Pure Love, even though it seems almost nonexistent here on Earth because of flaws in our thinking. No matter what it is, if it does not have love in it, it is NOT of God. If a person or group condemns other people and faiths, get up and go, because that is not of God—it is not love. God is Pure Love. The Kingdom of God is right here in the heart (points to her heart). You do not need to belong to a church; however, it is good to belong to a group of like-minded spiritual friends. Still, if your faith in God is not growing, then find a place and group where you are growing in love.

## Balance of Masculine and Feminine Energies

Q: When you came back from the NDE, you reclaimed your Lakota roots. You say when you wear your Native American dress it gives you an aura of strength and protects you.

BJE: The first time I wore my Native dress was on a stage in New York, and since then I almost always wear it when I speak. It makes me feel proud of my Native heritage, honor for my people and the sacred knowledge they hold. When I walk onstage there is often a hush in the room. The Native dress speaks of simplicity and respect to the spirit, attributes quite often forgotten. Its long fringe draws energy from the Earth and communicates respect for The Creator. It also reminds me to be humble. Native Americans deliberately leave in flaws to what they make as reminders that man is not perfect, only The Creator is. Wearing the dress I feel to be reverent and respectful, it actually protects me—from me! One time I'll never forget: We arrived to an event where at least a hundred hecklers gathered. Police had been called, their anger and protest signs made evident their cause. The police surrounded my car and said, "Mrs. Eadie, you're gonna have to take the back door." I thought of my childhood days and said, "No, I'm not." Without thinking any further, I went to the front door with two police officers in front of me and several following behind. I'd gone in the back door my whole life as a Native American, and I wasn't going to do it again. The protestors were menacing, they got right up in our faces with their signs. I wanted so badly to say all the worst things in the world to the people yelling in my face. Here they were professed Christians and behaving like that. I prayed, "Dear Lord, please keep me from opening my mouth." I thought of my imperfection and felt to reach down and touch that part of my dress, the flaw, and it brought a calm and a peace—a reminder. When I have that dress on it's like having that cloak of inner authority and love for my heritage, and it protects me and what we stand for. I have great love and feelings for all God's children, but on this day, I was brought to remember just how human I am. To walk through that crowd of hecklers required a masculine strength and courage. Even the police officers commented about it. "Have you no fear of anything? Those people were vicious. They recently shot and killed a minister and a doctor, all about abortion. Hatred is insane—killing people whom they say are killing others." I was confused. I am not pro-abortion. I am pro-education of what follows women that choose abortion.

Q:   Is it important to have a balance of masculine and feminine in ourselves and in the world?

BJE:   Yes. My NDE made me more balanced, so I am both very feminine and very masculine. I used to be very shy, very timid. Now I'm not afraid of anything. I know nothing will come against me and succeed. When you know the battle has already been won, you have no fear. It was difficult for my husband to get used to me because now I am more solid, outspoken and firm. I say what I mean and I mean what I say, or so they say. I am not fearful or challenged by people, male or female, whereas before, I used to be intimidated. Not now. One time I was walking into an event to speak, and this great big hand grabbed me. It was a big, tall man. He squeezed my hand tight and he told me I was going to go to hell for writing my book. I just stared at him, wondering what awful thing brought him to become a bully. My brothers taught me an old trick of bending a finger and it forces them to let go. I did it to him all the while not changing the look on my face. He let go with a shocked look on his face. I said very slowly, "Do not ever do that to me again."

When sent back to Earth, I was told a change would be put in place in me. My visit in Heaven where I received and responded to "extra spirituality" would now require me to have an "extra dose of humanness." I did not understand what they meant by humanness until I found myself living it. I seem to struggle with more faults and flaws now with that extra humanness than I ever did when they left me alone. I needed the humanness to balance the extra dose of spirituality, and I understand that now. After my NDE, I began to joke more, take light of situations, and be a little crazy. I wanted to be more like Jesus, and while there I learned that humor is a part of God's nature.

In each of us we have the precise dose that we need of the masculine and feminine qualities to serve the purpose of God. No one else can determine what the right dose is for you or for me; we are given the right balance for what we need to do. Whenever there's an imbalance on the Earth, God will increase this or that to provide a perfect balance. We have people who are what we have determined to be gay. To condemn them is wrong, because they add the perfect balance to what is missing in our world today. Gay men and women have very unusual combinations of masculine and feminine. But because of condemnation they often want to commit suicide. Feminine energy is gifted with certain traits and an extra dose of spirituality. Women are basically the nurturers of the Earth, but some have lost touch with that and do not want to be bothered with children.

Q:   Yes, I rejected my feminine side and took a very masculine route with dogmatic religion that silenced women, and devalued feelings and the heart. I also went an academic professional track. All that cut me off from my nature, heart and soul. Then, in my early thirties, I fell in love with a woman, and my life as I'd known it fell apart. You might say I fell in love with the lost feminine side of myself. It was healing, reconnected me to my heart. I had suffered from a panic disorder for years, and it healed overnight. I had been very homophobic, telling gay people they were going to hell. I got to live through the demeaning judgment I had meted out to them.

BJE:   Exactly. You had to live through it so *you* could heal from the inside out. You had to lose your judgmental attitude to understand that you can love within the same sex. So often I have met with people who have finally decided to come out of the closet and share their truer feelings, which are often so painful that they consider suicide. My dear friend Will, who is gay—I wrote about him in *The Awakening Heart*—is still struggling with it. I think every circumstance in life will grow you. It goes back to mind integration: Acceptance of something will bring understanding of it, but if you reject feelings, then there will be conflict and this is a destroyer. Anything you are conflicted about can eventually harm you. This may be the reason for your skin issue. Back when you taught others with dogma, your subconscious mind may have noted your harm to them. The belief that you wounded them would hurt you deeply.

Q:   (*Weeping.*) It was horrible to do that to others, castigate them for how they loved, the most precious thing about them, and I really do feel so sorry for the way I preached and condemned.

BJE:   Yes, condemning sends out a terrible message that may live a long time, and now you punish yourself and it pains you. That pain will continue to be manifest until you really forgive yourself. Ignorance is forgivable. Your intentions were pure. You *didn't know*.

## Ripple Effect

Q:    The doctrine I preached was what I'd learned from my culture, my family, my church leaders, everyone around me. It was a ripple effect of falsehood.

BJE:    We are what has been poured into us. And it really is as simple as pouring that out and saying as you pour, "This is rubbish. This is what other people put into me, but it's not who I am on the inside! I want/need to be ME." And that's it. And then just be YOU. If you really think about it, no one really cares about you because they are too busy thinking of themselves, not about you. What they see in you and don't like is generally something they recognize consciously or subconsciously in themselves.

Q:    And I lost pretty much everything except two dear friends who loved me even though they didn't understand me.

BJE:    So actually you gained true friends, which is rare, as people often base their friendships on what you do for them or how you are with them.

Q:    You say that even small kindnesses are significant in the ripple effect—how our words, thoughts, and actions are like stones thrown in a lake and make ripples.

BJE:    The little stones are better in creating a lasting ripple than a big clunking rock that makes a grand splash and goes straight to the bottom. The little ones skip lightly across and touch many places on the water, creating multiple ripples.

Q:   What's an example of a small kindness that ripples?

BJE:   Whenever you see others who are ill or cranky, say a prayer for them. They need it. The reason they are that way is because of their pain. Trust me, it's never about you. They may be angry and pick on you because you are there and they need an outlet, but it's never about you; it's about how they feel. You can stop and say, "Can I do something for you? Are you all right? Why are you upset?" Most people are just thirsting to find someone who can understand.

Q:   And—to be clear—being kind and loving doesn't mean to ignore problems, does it? I noted how you rebuffed the guy hitting people up for money.

BJE:   Yes I did. Look at the story of Jesus Christ when he went to the temple and saw the people using it to make money. He threw them out. He didn't say or think, "Well, I'm not going to judge these people for doing this." He didn't say, "They are in my temple just doing what they know how to do best, hawking holy things." He took action to eliminate them and their negativity from that sacred environment. People will say, "What about turning the other cheek"? To me, turning the other cheek means to turn around and get out of there, not say, "Here, hit me on this side as well."

Q:   What would you like to say to the readers of this book?

BJE:   I always end everything with the same sentence that I was given to bring back: "Above all, Love one another and everything else will be fine."

"Love one another" is the biblical teaching of Jesus. It was engraved on the tomb of Mother Teresa in Calcutta. It was also the teaching given to Howard Storm during his NDE. When I met with Betty Eadie, she told me to look him up, so I did.

Howard was an atheist professor who had a near-death experience while waiting for emergency surgery. He was thirty-eight, a graduate of University of California at Berkeley, chair of his department, and he thought he knew everything. He was arrogant, hostile to religion, and critical of others. The NDE changed all that. When he left his body, he initially found himself in a realm he called hell, with beings so crippled by pain and void of hope that their only interest was to torment others. They didn't annihilate others; they preferred to feed off their everlasting anguish. People wound up in this hellish place by rejecting love. In great despair, even though he was atheist, Howard called out to Jesus for help because he remembered a line from a song he'd learned as a child: "Jesus loves me, this I know." Instantly, a Light came to rescue him from the dark pit. He entered a realm of Love in which the spectrum of colors amazed him. On Earth, as a painter, he'd only ever seen three primary colors, but in this spiritual realm he saw eighty primary colors, spectacular in their vibrancy. That realm and all that happened to him there was more real than anything he'd ever experienced on Earth.

In his life review, Howard saw the truth of his interactions with people—on the surface he appeared to be a good person, but underneath he was manipulative, bitter, and indifferent. As a child, he was coldhearted toward his father for working long hours; when this angered his father, Howard rejected him as a villain and spent his life resenting him. Though he played the part of a compassionate professor, he was really bored by college students who came by his office with their personal problems; his heart was closed to them. One of his only triumphs of love was when, as a child, he silently embraced his sister one night as she cried. It was hard for him to see his lack of caring and how he'd missed the whole point of living. The "light beings" (his words) who guided him through this experience assured him of total forgiveness. Their lovingness melted his heart to the point that he weeps whenever he talks about the experience. He says that Love is real and available to anyone who calls out for it.

When Jesus told him he'd have to return to the world, Howard pleaded to stay in the realm of Love, but to no avail. Then he volunteered to use his artistic gifts to build a big and beautiful shrine for Jesus, but Jesus said, "I'd rather you didn't. You've spent so much of your life hiding out in the studio, avoiding people.... I don't really care about shrines. People like to build shrines. I understand that. It makes them feel good, but it does absolutely nothing for me or for God."

Howard asked, "Then what's your idea of what I would do?"

Jesus said, "Love the person you're with."

"No problem," said Howard, "Now, what do you want me to *do*?"

Jesus: "I just told you—love the person you're with."

Howard: "Yeah, but after I do that, what do you really want me to do?"

Jesus: "That is what I want you to do: Love the person you're with."

Howard: "That's simple enough, it's easy. I can do that."

Jesus: "Oh, really? Well, that's what I want you to do. That's enough."

Howard: "How is it enough?"

Jesus: "If you do that, you'll change the world."

Howard: "You want me to change the world?"

Jesus: "Exactly. That's why I put you in the world in the first place."

Howard: "A lot of people have tried to change the world, and they usually turn out really bad: Hitler and Stalin and Mao Tse Tung all wanted to change the world, and they made it worse. If I try to change the world, isn't it possible that I could make a lot of terrible mistakes and make the world a worse place?"

Jesus: "The way I want you to change the world is by loving the person you're with."

Howard: "Wait a minute, that's a contradiction. You want me to change the world but you just want me to love the person I'm with?"

Jesus: "Yes. If you love the person you're with, then they'll go out and love the person they're with, and *they'll* go out and love the person they're with, and it will be like a chain reaction, and love will conquer the world. That's God's Big Plan."

Howard: "It's not going to work."

Jesus: "Why won't it work?"

Howard: "Even if you had a million people, I don't think it's going to happen."

Jesus: "There're more than a million people in the plan."

Howard: "Well, from what I know of the world, you don't have enough."

Jesus: "Actually, we have all the angels in the plan."

Howard: "I'll do it, but I just don't see much hope for it."

Jesus: "You don't know enough to see how it's going to happen."

After his NDE, Howard left his academic career, became a Christian pastor, and wrote the book *My Descent into Death*.[239] Howard gave me permission to pass along that dialogue from his experience. He said, "I've tried to be part of that program. Personally, I have no big plan other than to be loving. The only problem is that I thought it would be easy, but it turns out to be the hardest thing I've ever done."

In their NDEs, Betty, Howard, and countless others have encountered Divine Love in its pure form of all-forgiving, unconditional foreverness. When touched by the power of love, in whatever way it occurs, a person is never the same, and this is the gift we are all capable of giving the world through our kindnesses and friendship by loving the person we're with, at any given time. By loving the other, we love ourself. This is what my teacher taught me:

> Everyone has the opportunity to contribute to harmony and beauty by kindness to others and thereby support the human spirit. That which is given freely to life flows back to us because we are equally part of that life. Like ripples on the water, every gift returns to the giver. What we affirm in others, we actually affirm in ourselves.[240]

# EPILOGUE

The love I had gone in search of and found in the presence of my teacher had been in my life all along—a mother's love, the play of creatures in the backyard, the kindness of a stranger, the wind blowing through trees, the patience of a partner, the joy of friends laughing. It was even in the pain of life—illness, loss, dementia, heartache, divorce, rejection, death. Whatever our pain, this can also be our path. The pearl found in the shell begins as an irritant. Sometimes we don't get rid of an irritant—it just works on us until one day we realize it has become a pearl.

> The life the path
> in pain or joy,
> a solitary pilgrim
> lights the way.
>
> Each step emerges
> from the stillness
> and falls back
> into the silence,
>
> casting no shadow
> and leaving no footprint,
> creating universes
> outside of time.

Moving in and through
with grace and ease,
a solitary pilgrim
along the way:

the path my life
in pain and joy.

—Elizabeth M. Cheatham

Just as I was finishing this book, I dreamt that my teacher was walking alongside me, even when I didn't remember that he was there:

I am on a journey to find Doc. I received a letter telling me where he was. Before arriving there, I get out at a rest stop. I am walking on the sidewalk and suddenly see that Doc is walking alongside me.

I travel on, still looking for Doc, not remembering that I'd seen him on the sidewalk. I arrive at the place where I was told he would be. I'm in a large meeting room with a hundred people. I see Doc out of the corner of my eye. He's walking around the periphery of the room and passes by, in back of where I'm sitting. I'm aware that he knows everything about me as if he is inside of me.

Again, I forget that I've seen him, and I go to the information desk and ask to see Dr. Hawkins. The woman behind the desk says, "Oh, yes, I just saw him in the garden." I'm taken beyond any building to a beautiful park with a path that goes for many miles in the pure, lush green. I'm captivated by the beauty and quietude. I have the feeling of coming Home. I don't see Doc in his physical form, but I know I am meeting him, finally, in his formless truth, the essence of my own Self.

The dream suggests that the journey of this book is complete. When Doc died, I thought I'd lost him. The heartache felt unbearable. It was very lonely, and no one understood the exact nature of my grief. Doc had been the one place of Pure Love on the planet for me. In the years after his death, this book took me on a journey to learn about the power of love in its many expressions. Each encounter illumined an aspect of love that he had taught me, and each became a steppingstone to a deeper realization. The love Doc emanated is everywhere, walking beside me, within me, and all around me. How could I have ever thought otherwise? In the dream, the verdant pathway stretches for miles and miles, beyond what I can see. After a lifetime of searching, I stand in the realization of what he told me at the beginning: "You yourself are what you're looking for."

This ending dream takes us back to the one described in the preface, which occurred five days after my teacher's death and presaged the journey of this book. In that dream, I was looking for my teacher's house in a misty verdant realm with a river running through it. I didn't know how to find his house. The only person I could see in the mist was an old woman—the ageless feminine wisdom—and she directed me to walk across steppingstones over the river. And then I saw it—the unpaved road that led to my teacher's house. That dream ended with: *It's the feeling of being on my own journey now, poised on the path that leads to Love.*

In Sufi teaching, "Love is a closed circle" with no beginning and no end. My teacher's love was complete and total at the very start, yet I had to make a journey around the entire circle, only to discover that he had always been inside me. By "he," of course, I mean the Self in all—the same Light that infused me with its Love at fifteen. Each encounter described in this book brightened that Light, and now I see it. This is the journey of every traveler on the path of love—going in search of what we already are. If we are fortunate, we meet those wise ones who do not take our Light but brighten it, for they know how to stoke the inner flame.

Without love, nothing would exist. Love enables life to regenerate itself, for love is the substance of life. Anything done with love, no matter how small, ripples out as a blessing to all. When hearts open, the power of love radiates into the world and relieves the suffering of masses. It reveals solutions to pressing problems. It heals longstanding divides.

As soon as love is chosen, a golden way is paved.

# ENDNOTES

1   My teacher is Dr. David R. Hawkins (1927–2012).

2   David R. Hawkins, *Power vs. Force*, Author's Official Revised Edition (Sedona, AZ: Veritas Publishing, [1995] 2012), 127–28.

3   See his sermon "Loving Your Enemies," written while he was in jail in Montgomery for his nonviolent civil disobedience during the bus boycott, delivered at the Dexter Avenue Baptist Church in Montgomery in 1957. For a collection of King's sermons on love, see *A Gift of Love*, revised edition (Boston: Beacon Press, 2012).

4   Alice Walker, *Anything We Love Can Be Saved: A Writer's Activism*, reprint edition (Ballantine, 1998).

5   Azza Karam, "Religion: Between 'Power' and 'Force,'" January 3, 2018, Inter Press Service. Karam is Senior Advisor UNFPA; Coordinator, UN Interagency Task Force on Religion. http://www.ipsnews.net/2018/01/religion-power-force/

6   Hawkins, *Power vs. Force*, video (Sedona: Veritas Publishing, 1995).

7   Riane Eisler, *The Chalice and The Blade: Our History, Our Future* (San Francisco: HarperCollins, 1987).

8   Hawkins, *Power vs. Force*, 153–54.

9   David R. Hawkins, *I: Reality and Subjectivity* (Sedona, Arizona: Veritas Publishing, 2003), 219.

10  So as not to violate copyright, I have paraphrased. Readers are encouraged to study *Power vs. Force* on their own. Note: All references to calibrated levels of people and places were verified by Dr. Hawkins himself in 2010. There is not a single calibration in this book that was not verified by him in person.

11  Hawkins, *I*, 219.

12  David R. Hawkins, *The Eye of the I: From Which Nothing is Hidden* (Sedona: Veritas Publishing, 2002), 69.

13  David R. Hawkins, *Transcending the Levels of Consciousness: The Stairway to Enlightenment* (Sedona, AZ: Veritas Publishing, 2006), 256.

14  David R. Hawkins, *Letting Go: The Pathway of Surrender* (Sedona, AZ: Veritas Publishing, 2012), 186.

15  Hawkins, *I*, 419. Hawkins's theory of brain changes corresponds well to some of the recent findings by neuroscientists and cognitive psychologists. See, for example, Richard Davidson, "Towards a Biology of Positive Affect and Compassion," in *Visions of Compassion*, ed. Richard Davidson and Anne Harrington (New York: Oxford University Press, 2002), 107–30.

16  One version of the story is told in Ravindra Nath, *Living with the Eternal Truth: From the Lineage of the Golden Sufis* (Nevada City, CA: Pelican Pond, 2017).

17  *The Practice of the Presence of God and The Spiritual Maxims* (Mineola, NY: Dover publications [1895] 2005).

18  *Science of the Heart: Exploring the Role of the Heart in Human Performance* (HeartMath Institute, 2001).

19  Quoted in *Travelling the Path of Love: Sayings of Sufi Masters*, ed. Llewellyn Vaughan-Lee (Inverness, CA: The Golden Sufi Center, 1995), 115.

20  See article by Llewellyn Vaughan-Lee, "*Adab*: Sufi Etiquette in the Outer and Inner Worlds," *Sufi: Journal of Mystical Philosophy and Practice* (December 2013).

21  Llewellyn Vaughan-Lee, *Love is a Fire: The Sufi's Mystical Journey Home* (The Golden Sufi Center, 2000), 22.

22  Llewellyn Vaughan-Lee, audio, Qualities Necessary for the Path, "Non-Being, Part 2" (The Golden Sufi Center, 1996).

23  Llewellyn Vaughan-Lee, DVD, Where the Two Seas Meet, "The One Quality Needed for the Path" (The Golden Sufi Center, 2009).

24 Anonymous, told to author, May 2018.

25 Llewellyn Vaughan-Lee, *The Face Before I Was Born*, 2nd Edition (The Golden Sufi Center [1997], 2009).

26 Vaughan-Lee, *Love is a Fire*, 24.

27 Llewellyn Vaughan-Lee, *The Return of the Feminine and the World Soul*, 2nd Edition (The Golden Sufi Center, [2009], 2017). Hilary Hart, *Body of Wisdom: Women's Spiritual Power and How It Serves* (Winchester, UK: O-Books, 2012).

28 See his books, *Spiritual Ecology: The Cry of the Earth*, Revised Edition (The Golden Sufi Center, [2013], 2016); Llewellyn Vaughan-Lee and Hilary Hart, *Spiritual Ecology: Ten Practices to Awaken the Sacred in Everyday Life* (The Golden Sufi Center, 2017).

29 Anat Vaughan-Lee, "Making the Way for the Feminine," transcription of Closing Reflection given at the Global Peace Initiative for Women, Jaipur, India, 2008, archived at www.workingwithoneness.org.

30 Llewellyn and Anat are featured in a film on the feminine, *As She Is*, directed by Megan McFeely (2015).

31 For a lovely book on the common essence of Sufi and Christian practice, see Llewellyn Vaughan-Lee, *Prayer of the Heart in Christian and Sufi Mysticism* (The Golden Sufi Center, 2012). The foreword is written by Cynthia Bourgeault who, following in the steps of her teacher, Father Thomas Keating, has done much to bring the heart of the Christian contemplative tradition to Westerners.

32 Hawkins, *Power vs. Force*, 211–12.

33 Dante Alighieri, *Vita Nuova*, I, translated with an introduction and notes by Mark Musa (Oxford University Press, 1992), 3.

34 *Vita Nuova*, II, 4.

35 *Vita Nuova*, XVI, 30.

36 Robert Johnson, *Inner Gold* (Kihei, Hawaii: Koa Books, 2008), 55–6.

37 Unless otherwise noted, all quotes of Mother Teresa referenced in this chapter fall under the auspices of this copyright statement: "The writings of Mother Teresa of Calcutta © by the Mother Teresa Center,

exclusive licensee throughout the world of the Missionaries of Charity for the works of Mother Teresa. Used with permission."

38  Karma Lekshe Tsomo, "Mother Teresa and the Bodhisattva Ideal: A Buddhist View," *Claritas: Journal of Dialogue & Culture*, Vol. 1, No.1 (March 2012), 96–105.

39  Mother Teresa letter to Dr. David R. Hawkins, August 23, 1991, shared with me by his wife, Susan J. Hawkins, also archived in Mother Teresa Center.

40  Bradley James, talk given at Holy Name of Jesus Catholic Community, Redlands, California, March 19, 2015. His words are used with permission.

41  Told in St. Peter's Square, September 3, 2016.

42  There are several excellent depictions of Mother Teresa's life, such as: Kathryn Spink, *Mother Teresa: An Authorized Biography*, Revised and Updated (San Francisco: HarperCollins [1998], 2011); Mother Teresa and the Missionaries of Charity, *Works of Love are Works of Peace*, a photographic record by Michael Collopy (San Francisco: Ignatius, 1996); Mother Teresa, *Come Be My Light: The Private Writings of the 'Saint of Calcutta,'* edited with commentary by Brian Kolodiejchuk, M.C. (New York: Doubleday, 2007); Mother Teresa, *A Call to Mercy: Hearts to Love, Hands to Serve*, ed. with introduction by Brian Kolodiejchuk, M.C. (New York: Image Books, 2016).

43  *Mother Teresa*, documentary film directed and produced by Ann and Jeanette Petrie (New York: Petrie Productions, 1986).

44  Martin Rosales, interview with author, May 24, 2013.

45  Fr. William Petrie, "Reflections of My Time Spent with St. Teresa of Calcutta by Fr. William Petrie." http://www.sscc-usa.org/?post_type=wpv_sermon&p=27666

46  Bradley James, talk given at Holy Name of Jesus Catholic Community, Redlands, California, March 19, 2015, cited with permission. Interestingly, independent from Bradley, Dr. David Hawkins found that Mother Teresa's energy field and that of the moment of elevation during Eucharistic mass were indeed the same, in the 700s on the Map of Consciousness®, an energy field of such self-giving Love that it has the power to transfigure physicality and circumstances. Other

examples of the energy fields in the 700s, according to Hawkins, are St. Teresa of Avila, Meister Eckhart, *Cloud of Unknowing*, Ramana Maharshi, Dogen, Shankara, Gandhi, Chartres Cathedral, and many scriptures such as the Heart Sutra.

47 David R. Hawkins, Interview with author, June 24, 2010.

48 Used with permission from the students. All quotes are from the most recent Compassion courses in Spring 2017 and 2018 at the University of Redlands. Hundreds of students have taken the course since it was first taught in 2004.

49 Petrie Productions created two films, *Mother Teresa* (1986) and *Mother Teresa: The Legacy* (2004). See http://petrieproductions.com. When I spoke briefly with Jeanette Petrie on the phone in 2010, she said, "Intuitively we knew it was a good idea to document the words and actions of a living saint." *Mother Teresa* is in a class by itself.

50 David C. McClelland, "Some Reflections on the Two Psychologies of Love," *Journal of Personality* 54 (1986) 2: 334–53.

51 Mother Teresa speaking in the film *Mother Teresa*, by Petrie Productions.

52 Anonymous participant, told to author, May 20, 2018.

53 David R. Hawkins, *Devotional Nonduality: Discovery of the Presence of God* (Sedona: Veritas, 2006), 77.

54 Ethel Spector Person, M.D., "Preface to the Reprint Edition," *Dreams of Love and Fateful Encounters: The Power of Romantic Passion*, first published in 1988, American Psychiatric Publishing (APPI), ix.

55 Viktor E. Frankl, *Man's Search for Meaning* (Boston: Beacon Press, 2006), 37. All quotes from Viktor Frankl used with permission of the Viktor Frankl Estate, 1 Mariannengasse, A-1090, Vienna, Austria, EU.

56 Printed in Frankl, *Man's Search for Meaning*, special edition with selected letters, speeches and essays, translated by Helen Pisano (Boston: Beacon Press, 2014).

57 Frankl recounts these experiences in *Man's Search for Meaning*, 26–27, 37–40; *Recollections: An Autobiography* (Cambridge, MA: Basic Books, [1995], 2000), 87–92.

58 Frankl, *Recollections*, 59.

59 Viktor E. Frankl, *The Will to Meaning*, Expanded Edition (New York, Plume, [1969], 2014), xvii.

60 Frankl, *Man's Search*, 48.

61 Frankl, *Recollections*, 82–83.

62 Frankl, *Man's Search*, 15.

63 Frankl, *Recollections*, 94–98.

64 Haddon Klingberg, *When Life Calls Out to Us: The Love and Lifework of Viktor and Elly Frankl* (New York: Doubleday, 2001), 151.

65 Missionary of Charity Sister C., who trained under Mother Teresa in Calcutta, personal correspondence with the author, May 16, 2016. Interestingly, Frankl's grandson, Alex, told me that Elly Frankl confirms that Mother Teresa and Frankl spoke by phone several times. Klingberg, Frankl's biographer, p. 333, says that Mother Teresa nominated Frankl for the Nobel Peace Prize.

66 Frankl, *Man's Search*, 112.

67 Viktor E. Frankl, *The Doctor and The Soul*, Third Expanded Edition (New York: Vintage Books, 1986), 132–3. Originally published in 1946 (German), first English edition 1955.

68 Frankl, *Doctor and Soul*, 150–51.

69 Frankl, *Man's Search*, 111.

70 Frankl, *Recollections*, 111.

71 Frankl, *Doctor and Soul*, xxvii.

72 Frankl, *Man's Search*, 65–66.

73 Frankl, *Man's Search for Meaning*, Preface to 1992 edition, xiv. Nietzsche quote, 76.

74 Klingberg, *Life Calls Out*, 275.

75 Ibid., 275.

76 Ibid., 312.

77 Frankl, *Will to Meaning*, 43–44.

78    Stanley Milgram, "Behavioral Study of Obedience," *The Journal of Abnormal and Social Psychology*, Vol. 67, No. 4, 1963.

79    All quotes of Porete in this chapter come from Marguerite Porete, *The Mirror of Simple Souls*, translated and introduced by Ellen L. Babinsky (Paulist Press, 1993).

80    The story of the two Sabbaths is told in Yitzhak Buxbaum, *Light and Fire of the Baal Shem Tov* (2006), 93–96.

81    Hawkins, *I*, 109.

82    There are several books on Huston Smith's life: Dana Sawyer, *Huston Smith: Wisdomkeeper* (Louisville, KY: Fons Vitae, 2014); *Tales of Wonder: Adventures Chasing the Divine, An Autobiography* by Huston Smith, with Jeffery Paine (SF: Harper One, 2009); *Live Rejoicing!* by Huston Smith with Phil Cousineau (Novato, CA: New World Library, 2012).

83    Frankl, *Will to Meaning*, 64.

84    Spiritual Summit Conference, 1968, sponsored by the Temple of Understanding.

85    René Descartes, *Meditations on the First Philosophy in Which the Existence of God and the Distinction between Mind and Body are Demonstrated*, Great Books of the Western World, Vol. 31 (Chicago: University of Chicago Press, 1952), 79.

86    My heartfelt gratitude to Sister Joanna of Sinai, who served as translator and interpreter for Father Pavlos and offered generously of her time and expertise in editing this chapter.

87    According to Orthodox understanding of the underlying theological issues.

88    See Sister Joanna's article on the monastery, which gives a beautiful description of the history, theology, and practice of the Sinai tradition, *The Ladder of Heavenly Unity*, *Parabola* 41:4 (Winter 2016–17).

89    A note from Sister Joanna: "Although the most commonly found translation is 'a' sinner, the correct translation, which some texts reflect, is clearly 'the' sinner. As, in order for prayer to be effective, it must arise from a humble heart, the humble person considers himself not one of the crowd of sinners but the first amongst all, indeed, the only one.

Father Pavlos has pointed out, however, that it is acceptable to say 'a' sinner if easier, as long as one understands this point."

90 The Sinai monks' black bread is baked in small rolls, which, due to the dry desert atmosphere, become notoriously hard within a few hours of leaving the oven.

91 *Nepsis* is an important aspect of practice in Orthodox Christianity. Jesus Christ spoke of it in the Gospel of Luke 12:37: "Blessed are those servants whom the Lord when He comes shall find watching." A state of abiding attention, it is considered to be a mark of sanctity.

92 *Mysteries of the Jesus Prayer*, produced by Norris J. Chumley (Magnetic Arts Production, 2010).

93 Quoted by Llewellyn Vaughan-Lee, interview with author.

94 Hilary Hart, *The Unknown She* (The Golden Sufi Center, 2003), xiv.

95 See also her chapter about her gay friend Will: "The Courage to Live," in her second book, *The Awakening Heart: My Continuing Journey to Love* (New York: Pocket Books, 1996).

96 The truncating effect of homophobia on one's spiritual life is described by Diane Eller-Boyko in this open access article: "Longing for the Feminine: Reflections on Love, Sexual Orientation, Individuation and the Soul," *Psychological Perspectives: A Quarterly Journal in Jungian Thought*, 60:3 (Dec 2017) 289–316.

97 The estimated number of LGBT people based on population research published by the World Psychiatric Association in 2016 was 250 million; however, the data do not include the LGBT individuals who decline to identify themselves due to fear of death or other negative consequences. The harm done by rigid religious views is more severe than most people realize. The common statement, "You can be gay but don't act on it," has an unrecognized destructive effect, such that many attempt suicide. Most humans long for love, connection, and family life; sexual expression is one of nature's ways, created by the Creator, to draw us into close-knit bonds. A family bond facilitates our survival and happiness. Frankl's dictum applies here: Never to require of others an heroism that we are ourselves do not or cannot do. Forced chastity ("don't act on it") requires a stricture that not many people in history have ever achieved, even when chosen voluntarily for monastic

or priestly purposes. It is not a viable solution; it sets up almost certain failure followed often by cruel dynamics of shame and despair. The most humane approach, following the Golden Rule, is to respect people's freedom to love each other in accordance with their natural orientation. This is the place I've come to after witnessing the suffering of gay persons caused by rejections of their natural need for affection, sexual expression, and love.

98    Helen Luke, *Such Stuff As Dreams Are Made On* (Morning Light Press, 1999), 36.

99    In his speech to mark the fiftieth anniversary of Hitler's invasion, Frankl began: "I must ask of you to expect no words of hatred from me.... I refuse to call people collectively guilty." How, he wondered, is attributing collective guilt to the Nazis different from the Nazis' own "so-called 'kin liability'"? See his "Memorial Speech to Mark the Fiftieth Anniversary of Hitler's Invasion, March 10, 1988, Rathausplatz, Vienna," printed in *Man's Search for Meaning*, special edition with selected letters, speeches and essays, translated by Helen Pisano (Boston: Beacon Press, [1950], 2014), 177.

100    My Anishinaabe colleague Larry Gross, whose office is next to mine, says in his book that stories are integral to education in Native American communities. In his book, *Anishinaabe Ways of Knowing and Being* (Surrey, England: Ashgate, 2014), he says stories are "written on the land of the people and also written on the hearts of the people" (157). Stories develop "heartstrings" in us (164).

101    For an excellent book about the Grandmothers, see Carol Schaefer, *Grandmothers Counsel the World* (Boston: Trumpeter, 2006).

102    Jeneane Prevatt of The Center for Sacred Studies in Sonora, Calif., who goes by the name Jyoti. She continues as their "ambassador."

103    *As She Is*, directed by Megan McFeely, 2015.

104    Hawkins, *Truth vs. Falsehood: How to Tell the Difference* (Toronto: Axial Publishing, 2005), 352–53.

105    For background, see Gross, *Anishinaabe Ways of Knowing and Being*, 67–69.

106    Anonymous, shared with author July 2014.

107 The current anti-tobacco dogma suppresses alternative research propositions, such as the finding that cancer from smoking may stem from pesticides used in manufacturing tobacco and not the use of tobacco itself. Also, one gram of vitamin C daily prevents cell damage from smoking. Hawkins, *Power vs. Force*, 141.

108 Llewellyn Vaughan-Lee, audio, "Changing the Story," Mercy Center retreat (The Golden Sufi Center, 2013).

109 Vaughan-Lee, *Spiritual Ecology*, i.

110 Eadie, *The Awakening Heart*, 208–12.

111 See letter from Grandmother Beatrice in the *National Catholic Reporter* (April 2009). The "Roman Pontifex," written by Pope Nicholas V to King Alfonso V of Portugal in 1455, gave the king authority "to invade, search out, capture, vanquish, and subdue all Saracens and pagans whatsoever, and other enemies of Christ wheresoever placed," and to take all of their possessions and goods and "to reduce their persons to perpetual slavery...."

112 Hawkins, *I*, 397.

113 Gandhi, audio recording of his article "God Is," *Young India* (November 10, 1928), made on October 20, 1931, available at: http://gandhiserve.org/information/listen_to_gandhi/lec_1_on_god/augven_spiritual_message.html

114 Hawkins, *Power vs. Force*, 381.

115 Ibid., 382–85.

116 Vaughan-Lee, audio, "The Magic of Creation and the Sword of the Creator" (The Golden Sufi Center, 2006).

117 Hawkins, *I*, 18.

118 Hawkins, *Power vs. Force*, video (Sedona: Veritas Publishing, 1995).

119 Hawkins, *The Eye of the I*, 91.

120 Ibid., 250–51.

121 Vaughan-Lee, audio, "Teacher, Without a Face, Without a Name, Part 1." (The Golden Sufi Center, 1992).

122  *Shankara's Crest-Jewel of Discrimination*, translated with an introduction by Swami Prabhavananda and Christopher Isherwood (Hollywood: Vedanta Press, 1947), 33.

123  His Holiness the Dalai Lama, *Dzogchen: Heart Essence of the Great Perfection* (Boulder, CO: Snow Lion), 34.

124  Quoted in Llewellyn Vaughan-Lee, editor, *Travelling on the Path of Love*, 35.

125  "This is Samsara: An Interview with Tenzin Palmo" by Bethany Senkyu Saltman, MRO, Mountains and Rivers Order, *Mountain Record*, n.d., n.p. http://archive.is/IYE8i

126  For a detailed account of Palmo's years in the cave, see Vicki Mackenzie, *Cave in the Snow: A Western Woman's Quest for Enlightenment* (London: Bloomsbury Publishing, 2009).

127  Mackenzie, *Cave in the Snow*, 124–25.

128  All quotes from the Karmapa found at the official website, http://kagyuoffice.org/

129  H.H. the 17th Karmapa, public talk at Hunter College, New York City, July 29, 2011, transcript available at this webpage: http://kagyuoffice.org/his-holiness-the-karmapa-speaks-on-compassion-and-the-nature-of-mind-on-the-eve-of-his-departure-to-india/

130  Hawkins, *Transcending the Levels of Consciousness*, 41.

131  Jetsunma Tenzin Palmo, "Lighten Up," *Lion's Roar*, February 7, 2011.

132  Hawkins, *The Eye of the I*, 116.

133  Hawkins, *I*, 197. The full quote: "The 'hatred of sin' is still just hatred, and because it is still just hatred, it is not morally superior. The 'hatred of sin' creates the absurdity of an error's condemning an error."

134  *Being* (Redwood Valley, CA: Earth Books, 1988). The book effulged from her inner Self at the time of the Harmonic Convergence, as "the new world of love you long for."

135  For Wilson's personal account, see *Bill W.: My First 40 Years* (Center City, MN: Hazelden, 2000), 145–46.

136  Hawkins, *The Eye of the I*, 204.

137 Hawkins, *I*, 219.

138 Copyright Dedan Gills, originally published as "A Hymn to Unity and Patience" in *Sufism: An Inquiry*, Vol. 16, No 1, 69.

139 In *Native American Wisdom* with photographs by Edward S. Curtis (Running Press, 1993).

140 Copyright Dedan Gills.

141 Hawkins, *Power vs. Force*, 150–1.

142 Hawkins, *Truth vs. Falsehood*, 324.

143 David R. Hawkins, "How to Instantly Tell Truth from Falsehood," lecture given for Shift in Action, Institute for Noetic Sciences.

144 Reincarnation has been the subject of scientific research. A summary of it is given in Marjorie Hines Woollacott, *Infinite Awareness: The Awakening of a Scientific Mind* (Rowman and Littlefield, 2015.)

145 Hawkins, *I*, 222.

146 Cheryl Simone and Sadhguru Vasudev, *Midnights with the Mystic* (Newburyport, MA: Hampton Road Publishing, 2008).

147 Sadhguru's life, teachings and experiences are covered in numerous books. See: Sadhguru, *Inner Engineering: A Yogi's Guide to Joy* (New York: Speigel and Grau, 2016); Sadhguru, *Encounter the Enlightened: Conversations with the Master* (New Delhi: Wisdom Tree, 2003); Sadhguru, *Mystic's Musings* (Coimbatore, India: Isha Foundation, 2003); Sadhguru, *Essential Wisdom from a Spiritual Master* (Mumbai, India: Jaico Publishers, 2008); Arundhathi Subramaniam, *Sadhguru: More Than a Life* (New Delhi, India: Penguin Ananda, 2010).

148 See Sadhguru, *Ambience of Love*, DVD (Coimbatore, India: Isha Foundation).

149 See Shekhar with Sadhguru, *Love, a Chemical Hijack*, DVD (Coimbatore, India: Isha Foundation, n.d.).

150 For example, the book edited by Simmer-Brown and Grace, *Meditation and the Classroom*, (Albany, NY: State University of New York Press, 2011). There are at least thirty publications (that I'm aware of) about our program.

151   For example: C. Ko, F. Grace, G. Chavez, S. Grimley, E. Dalrymple, L. Olson. "Effect of Seminar on Compassion on Student Mindfulness, Self-Compassion and Well-being: Randomized Controlled Study." *The Journal of American College Health* (March 2018).

152   Thanks to Dr. Karen Derris in our Department of Religious Studies who arranged this visit related to the work she has done to co-edit two books by the Karmapa, which came out of her college students' conversations with him in India: *The Heart is Noble* (2013) and *Interconnected* (2017).

153   Hawkins, *Power vs. Force*, 150–51; Hawkins, *The Eye of the I*, 204.

154   H.H. the 17th Karmapa, public address to the University of Redlands, March 23, 2015.

155   For example, these books give an introduction to the practice: His Holiness the 17th Karmapa, Ogyen Trinley Dorje, *Traveling the Path of Compassion* (Woodstock, New York: Densal, 2009); His Holiness the Dalai Lama, with Howard C. Cutler, *The Art of Happiness* (New York: Riverhead Books, 2009).

156   The Karmapa, Ogyen Trinley Dorje, *Interconnected: Embracing Life in Our Global Society*, ed. Karen Derris and Damchö Diana Finnegan, transl. Damchö Diana Finnegan (Somerville, MA: Wisdom Publications, 2017).

157   Heartfelt gratitude to Damchö Diana Finnegan, Karen Derris, members of the Karmapa's Office of Administration, and all who helped make possible my encounters with His Holiness in India and at the University of Redlands.

158   Nisha J. Manek, MD, FRCP (UK) and William A. Tiller, PhD, "WHITE PAPER XXV: The Sacred Buddha Relic Tour: For the Benefit of All Beings," Presented at the Annual "Toward A Science of Consciousness," University of Arizona Center for Consciousness Studies, Tucson, Arizona, April 9, 2012. Nisha J. Manek, MD, "Symmetry States of the Physical Space: An Expanded Reference Frame for Understanding Human Consciousness," *The Journal of Alternative and Complementary Medicine*, Vol. 18, No. 2, 2012, 1–10.

159   Louis Sahagun, "The Dalai Lama Has It, But What Is 'It'?" *The Los Angeles Times*, December 9, 2006.

160  See Paul Ekman, *Emotional Awareness: A Conversation Between the Dalai Lama and Paul Ekman, Ph.D.* (New York: Henry Holt, 2008), especially 231–33.

161  Karmapa, *Interconnected*. This book is based on conversations with students from the University of Redlands and co-edited by professor Karen Derris. See also my interview with Dr. Derris about this book on Heart Matters radio show, KDAWG Station, Redlands, California, February 23, 2018. Other books of the Karmapa's compassion teachings: *Compassion Now!* (Woodstock: KTD Publication, 2004); *The Heart is Noble*, co-edited by Karen Derris and Damchö Diana Finnegan (Boston: Shambhala, 2013).

162  For background and early accomplishments of the 17th Karmapa, see Michele Martin, *Music in the Sky: The Life, Art and Teachings of the 17th Karmapa, Ogyen Trinley Dorje* (Boulder: Snow Lion, 2003).

163  Thanks to Venerable Damchö Diana Finnegan for her expert work as an interpreter and translator.

164  Mandela, Interview with Oprah Winfrey, O *Magazine*, April 2001.

165  Quotes for the five points in this section taken from Nelson Mandela, *Long Walk to Freedom*, 622.

166  Mandela, Interview with Oprah Winfrey, O Magazine, April 2001.

167  Mandela, *Long Walk*, 624.

168  Address by President Nelson Mandela at the Golden Doves of Peace Award Ceremony, 7 June 1994, on website of Nelson Mandela Foundation.

169  Ibid.

170  Quoted in Rachel Ramirez, "Ethics Week: Linda Biehl speaks about forgiveness after her daughter's murder," *The Beacon*, University of Portland (February 22, 2017).

171  Marina Cantacuzino, The Forgiveness Project, interview published online on March 29, 2010. http://theforgivenessproject.com/

172  Ibid.

173  A concise summary of experiments and theoretical framework is presented in William A. Tiller, "Knowledge, Intention and Matter,"

*Oxford Handbook of the Psychology of Religion and Spirituality*, edited by Lisa Miller, (Oxford University Press, reprint edition, 2013).

174  Manek and Tiller, "WHITE PAPER XXV: The Sacred Buddha Relic Tour: For the Benefit of All Beings"; Manek, MD, "Symmetry States of the Physical Space."

175  William A. Tiller, *Psychoenergetic Science: A Second Copernican-Scale Revolution* (Walnut Creek, CA: Pavior), 2007, 89.

176  Hawkins, Interview with Yun Kyung Huh of Dahn Meditation Center, Korea. September 1996. Transcript in *Dialogues on Consciousness and Spirituality* (Sedona: Veritas Publishing, 1997).

177  Jill Bolte-Taylor, *My Stroke of Insight: A Brain Scientist's Personal Journey* (New York: Viking Press, 2008), 41. For an illuminating verbal account, see her interview with Oprah Winfrey, "Interviews: Parts I–IV," Soul Series, May 2008.

178  Bolte-Taylor, *Stroke of Insight*, 71.

179  Ibid., 49.

180  Ibid., 67.

181  Ibid., 74–75.

182  Ibid., 171.

183  Eben Alexander, *Proof of Heaven: A Neurosurgeon's Journey in the Afterlife* (New York: Simon & Schuster, 2012), 71.

184  Joseph McMoneagle, *Memoirs of a Psychic Spy: The Remarkable Life of U.S. Government Remote Viewer 001*, Charlottesville, Hampton Roads publishing company, 2002, xi.

185  For his written account, see McMoneagle, *Memoirs of a Psychic Spy*, 49.

186  David Nicol, *Subtle Activism: The Inner Dimension of Social and Planetary Transformation* (Albany, New York: SUNY Press, 2016).

187  Hawkins, *Power vs. Force*, gives the foundation for his groundbreaking work. The appendix includes an explanation of the muscle-testing method (clinical kinesiology). Note: the Author's Official Revised Edition (Veritas Publishing, 2012) is the most accurate and

reliable edition of this book. Pupillary response is another mechanism of testing intention, seen in the pilot study "Nonlinear Pupillary Response" done by Carol Davis, M.D., https://pupillaryresponses.wordpress.com/

188 Irina Tweedie, *Daughter of Fire: A Diary of a Spiritual Training with a Sufi Master* (Inverness, CA: The Golden Sufi Center, [1986] 2006), 517.

189 Ibid., x.

190 C. G. Jung writes of the dangers of the "disciple/devotee" archetype in his essay "The Relations of the Ego and the Unconscious," pointing to the inflation of the ego that sees itself either as a prophet or as a follower of *the* truth and *the great master*. On the surface, the disciple bows in pious submission, but the dynamic is often a result of unconscious superiority and fosters infantile regression. C. G. Jung, "Two Essays on Analytical Psychology," in *Portable Jung*, ed. Joseph Campbell, transl. R. F. C. Hull (New York, NY: Viking, 1971), 120–21.

191 Tweedie, *Daughter of Fire*, 533.

192 Vaughan-Lee, *Fragments of a Love Story: Reflections on the Life of a Mystic* (Inverness, CA: The Golden Sufi Center, 2011), 91.

193 *Me and Rūmī: The Autobiography of Shams-I Tabrizi*, transl. William C. Chittick, (Louisville, KY: Fons Vitae, 2004).

194 Tweedie, *Daughter of Fire*, 524.

195 Hawkins, *I*, xvi.

196 Recounted in Vaughan-Lee, *Circle of Love*, 25.

197 Anonymous, shared with author June 5, 2018.

198 Hawkins, *Eye of the I*, 37.

199 John Friesen, "Dog Ends Gunman's Plan for Shooting," *Toronto Globe and Mail*, 6/24/04. The gunman had five guns and 6,000 rounds of ammunition.

200 Hawkins, *The Eye of the I*, 88.

201 Hawkins, *The Eye of the I*, 225.

202  Hawkins, "The Power of Devotion," audio CD (Sedona, AZ: Veritas Publishing, n.d.).

203  Hawkins, *I*, 12.

204  Ibid.

205  Tweedie, *Daughter of Fire*, 287-8.

206  Hawkins, *Power vs. Force*, 391–2.

207  Christopher Isherwood, *My Guru and His Disciple* (Farrar, Straus and Giroux, 1980).

208  Andrew Harvey, *Sun at Midnight: A Memoir of the Dark Night* (Tarcher, 2002).

209  *Daughter of Fire*, 497.

210  Ibid., 149.

211  "Spiritual bypass" discussed in John Welwood, *Toward a Psychology of Awakening* (Boston: Shambhala, 2002).

212  David R. Hawkins, "Spiritual Life in Today's World," October 16, 2010, Mingus High, Cottonwood, Ariz. This was a radical statement coming from someone who had been trained in the 1950s by Lionel Ovesey, influential Freudian researcher. In line with prevailing views at the time, Ovesey's research depicted homosexuality as a disorder, curable through Freudian psychoanalysis and what was termed conversion or reparative therapy. As scientific research on the matter has progressed, The American Pyschiatric Association removed homosexuality from the list of mental illnesses in 1973, and the World Psychiatric Association did the same in 2016, making strong statements on the harm of conversion therapy and the often-brutal treatment of LGBT persons.

213  Hawkins, "Sexuality" CD audio.

214  Zaynab Zanam, "Karmapa visits Princeton, discusses women's rights, social activism, environment," *Daily Princetonian* (April 1, 2015), "A Buddhist Perspective: Gender, the Environment and Activism," delivered at Princeton University Chapel.

215  Hawkins, "The Power of Devotion."

[216] Hawkins, *I*, 20.

[217] Anonymous, told to author June 5, 2018.

[218] Sri Adi Sankara, *Narada Bhakti Sutra*, with commentary by Swami Chinmayananda (Langhorne, PA: Chinmaya Publications, 2013). Refers to sutra (verse) 2.

[219] Holy Gita, with commentary by Swami Chinmayananda (Langhorne, PA: Chinmaya Publications, 1996). Chapter 9, verse 22.

[220] *Narada Bhakti Sutra*, sutra 3.

[221] *Narada Bhakti Sutra*, sutra 4.

[222] *Srimad Bhagavata Mahapurana*, transl. C. L. Goswami and M. A. Shastri (Gorakhpur, India: Gita Press, 2006)

[223] *Narada Bhakti Sutra*, sutra 5.

[224] *Narada Bhakti Sutra*, sutra 6.

[225] *Narada Bhakti Sutra*, sutra 17.

[226] *Narada Bhakti Sutra*, sutra 18.

[227] Gita, chapter 18, verse 66.

[228] Gita, chapter 12, verse 2.

[229] Gita, chapter 11, verse 55.

[230] Gita, chapter 12, verse 8.

[231] Gita, chapter 12, verse 15.

[232] "Love is the Ultimate Law of the Universe," DVD created and produced by Fran Grace (Sedona: Institute for Spiritual Research, 2011).

[233] Working with dreams is practiced in many spiritual traditions—for example, Tibetan Buddhist, Indigenous, Jewish, and Sufi paths. The Naqshbandiyya-Mujaddidiyya Sufi path has been a principal source of guidance and group practice for me. See Llewellyn Vaughan-Lee, *Catching the Thread: Sufism, Dreamwork, and Jungian Psychology* (The Golden Sufi Center, 1998) and *In the Company of Friends: Dreamwork within a Sufi Group* (The Golden Sufi Center, 1994).

[234] Hawkins, *I*, 268-9. Dr. Hawkins also states that, just as the non-physical consciousness often leaves before the physical body dies, the

spirit or soul "does not enter the embryo until the third month of gestation.… If the embryo aborts or dies in utero, the soul has to find another viable embryo in which to incarnate." This statement is independently confirmed by Llewellyn Vaughan-Lee—the soul enters the human embryo at three months.

235 Hawkins, "Death and Dying" CD, (Sedona, AZ: Veritas Publishing, n.d.).

236 All quotes in this chapter are from Betty Eadie's presentations that I heard in northern California, March 2016, or from my extended interview with her. You are encouraged to read her books for yourself, as nothing can replace firsthand accounts: *Embraced by the Light, The Awakening Heart, The Ripple Effect*. She has recorded audiobooks, and her voice enhances the transmission of her knowledge and love to the listener.

237 Sicangu Lakota Oyate, also known as the Rosebud Sioux Tribe, is one of seven Lakota tribes that constitute one of the seven council fires of the Great Sioux Nation.

238 *The Village*, film produced by M. Night Shyamalan, 2004.

239 Howard Storm, *My Descent into Death* (Harmony, 2005). David Sunfellow posted the dialogue at http://encounters-with-jesus.org/love-the-person-youre-with/. I quote it here with permission from Howard Storm.

240 Hawkins, *The Eye of the I*, 69–70.

# BIBLIOGRAPHY

*Alcoholics Anonymous.* Fourth edition. New York: Alcoholics Anonymous World Services, Inc., 2001.

Alexander, Eben. *Proof of Heaven: A Neurosurgeon's Journey in the Afterlife.* New York: Simon & Schuster, 2012.

Alighieri, Dante. *Vita Nuova.* Translated with an introduction and notes by Mark Musa. New York: Oxford University Press, 1992.

_____. *Divine Comedy.* Translated by Allen Mandelbaum. New York: Knopf, 1995.

Al-Ghazzali. *On Knowing Yourself and God.* Translation by Muhammad Nur Abdus Salam. Chicago: Great Books of the Islamic World, 2002.

Arabi, Ibn. *A Prayer for Spiritual Elevation and Protection.* Translation by Suha Taji-Farouki. Oxford: Anqa Publishing, 2006.

Farid Ud-Din Attar. *Conference of the Birds.* Translation and introduction by Afkham Darbandi and Dick Davis. London: Penguin, 1984.

Au, Wilkie and Noreen Cannon. *Urgings of the Heart.* Mahwah, NJ: Paulist Press, 1995.

Avila, St. Teresa of. *Interior Castle.* Translated by E. Allison Peers. New York: Image Books, [1961] 2004.

Beckwith, Rev. Michael. *Spiritual Liberation.* New York: Atria Books, 2009.

Biehl, Linda. Interview with Marina Cantacuzino. The Forgiveness Project. Published online on March 29, 2010. http://theforgivenessproject.com.

Bourgeault, Cynthia. Foreword. In *Prayer of the Heart in Christian and Sufi Mysticism* by Llewellyn Vaughan-Lee. The Golden Sufi Center, 2012.

Bolte-Taylor, Jill. *My Stroke of Insight: A Brain Scientist's Personal Journey.* New York: Viking Press, 2008.

_____. "Interviews: Parts I–IV." SoulSunday series with Oprah Winfrey, May 2008.

Brunton, Paul. *A Search in Secret India.* London: Rider, 1934.

Burckhardt, Titus. *Chartres and the Birth of the Cathedral.* Bloomington: World Wisdom, 2010.

Buxbaum, Yitzhak. *Light and Fire of the Baal Shem Tov.* New York: Continuum, 2006.

Capra, Fritjof. *The Tao of Physics,* Fourth edition. Boston: Shambhala, [1975] 2000.

Cheatham, Elizabeth M. *A Gift from Eternity.* Scottsdale, Arizona: Heartsong Press, 1996.

Chittick, William C. *Ibn' Arabi: Heir to the Prophets.* Oxford: One World, 2005.

Chumley, Norris J. *Mysteries of the Jesus Prayer.* Film produced by Norris J. Chumley. Magnetic Arts Production, 2010.

Climacus, St. John. *The Ladder of Divine Ascent.* Translated by Colm Luibheid and Normal Russell. Malwah, NJ: Paulist Press, 1982.

Curry, Bishop Michael. "Sermon at the Royal Wedding of Prince Harry and Meghan Markle." May 19, 2018.

Dalai Lama, H.H. the 14th, Tenzin Gyatso. *Dzogchen: Heart Essence of the Great Perfection*. Boulder, CO: Snow Lion.

_____. *My Land, My People: The Original Autobiography of His Holiness the Dalai Lama*. New York: Warner Books, [1962] 1997.

Dalai Lama, H.H. with Howard C. Cutler. *The Art of Happiness*. New York: Riverhead Books, 2009.

Davidson, Richard and Anne Harrington, editors. *Visions of Compassion*. New York: Oxford University Press, 2002.

Davis, Carol, M.D. "Nonlinear Pupillary Response," https://pupillaryre-sponses.wordpress.com/.

Davis, Laura. *I Thought We'd Never Speak Again*. New York: Harper Collins, 2002.

Descartes, René. *Meditations on First Philosophy in Which the Existence of God and the Distinction between Mind and Body are Demonstrated*. Great Books of the Western World, Vol. 31. Chicago: University of Chicago Press, 1952.

Eadie, Betty J. *Embraced by the Light*. Reprint edition. New York: Bantam, 2004.

_____. *The Awakening Heart: My Continuing Journey to Love*. New York: Simon & Schuster, 1996.

_____. *The Ripple Effect*. Seattle: Onjinjinkta Publishing, 1999.

Easwaren, Eknath. *Gandhi the Man: The Story of His Transformation*. Tomales, California: Nilgiri Press, 1997.

Eden, Donna. *Energy Medicine*. New York: Penguin, 1998.

*Edie & Thea: A Very Long Engagement*. Film directed by Susan Muska and Grea Olafsdottir. 2009.

Eisler, Riane. *The Chalice and The Blade: Our History, Our Future.* San Francisco: HarperCollins, 1987.

Ekman, Paul. *Emotional Awareness: A Conversation Between the Dalai Lama and Paul Ekman, Ph.D.* New York: Henry Holt, 2008.

Eller-Boyko, Diane and Fran Grace. "Longing for the Feminine: Reflections on Love, Sexual Orientation, Individuation and the Soul." *Psychological Perspectives: A Quarterly Journal in Jungian Thought,* December, 2017.

Estes, Clarissa Pinkola. *Women Who Run with the Wolves.* New York: Ballantine, 1992.

Frankl, Viktor E. *Man's Search for Meaning.* Boston: Beacon Press, [1959] 2006.

_____. *Recollections: An Autobiography.* Cambridge, MA: Basic Books, [1995], 2000.

_____. *The Will to Meaning.* Expanded edition. New York: Plume, [1969], 2014.

_____. *The Doctor and The Soul.* Third expanded edition. New York: Vintage Books, [1955] 1986.

Friesen, John. "Dog Ends Gunman's Plan for Shooting." *Toronto Globe and Mail,* July 24, 2004.

Gandhi, Mahatma. *The Story of My Experiments with Truth.* Translated by Mahadev Desai. Madison, WI: Demco Media, 2004.

Gills, Dedan. "A Hymn to Unity and Patience." *Sufism: An Inquiry,* October 30, 2012.

Gills, Dedan and Belvie Rooks. *I Give You the Springtime of My Blushing Heart: A Poetic Love Song.* Inner Pathway Publishing, 2019.

*Gospel of Ramakrishna*. Originally recorded by M., disciple of the Master. Translated by Swami Nikhilananda. Fifth printing. New York: Ramakrishna-Vivekananda Center, [1942] 1988.

Grace, Fran. *Carry A. Nation: Retelling the Life*. Bloomington, IN: Indiana University Press, 2001.

_____. "Unconditional Love: Applications of a Timeless Teaching." *International Journal of Philosophy and Theology*, December 2017.

_____. "Beyond Reason: The Certitude of the Mystic from Al-Hallaj to David R. Hawkins." *International Journal of Humanities and Social Science*, September 2011.

_____. "Spirituality within Higher Education." In *Spirituality and Deep Connectedness: Views on Being Fully Human*, edited by Michael Brannigan. New York City: Rowman & Littlefield, 2018.

_____. "A Semester Within." In *Learning Journeys with the Labyrinth: Creating Reflective Space in Higher Education*, edited by Jan Sellers and Bernard Moss. New York: Palgrave MacMillan, 2015.

_____. "The Power of Meditation in College Learning." In *Embodied Pathways to Wisdom and Social Transformation*, edited by Jing Lin, Edward Brantmeier, Rebecca Oxford. (Charlotte, NC: Information Age Publishing, 2013.

_____. "New Foreword." In *Power vs. Force*, by David R. Hawkins. Author's Official Revised Edition. Sedona, AZ: Veritas Publishing, 2012.

_____. "Foreword." In *Letting Go: The Pathway of Surrender*, by David R. Hawkins. Sedona, AZ: Veritas Publishing, 2012.

_____. "The 'Map of Consciousness': A New Paradigm for Mysticism and Healing." In *Perceiving the Divine through the Human Body*, edited by June McDaniel and Thomas Cattoi. New York: Palgrave MacMillan, 2011.

_____. "From Content, to Context, to Contemplation: One Professor's Journey." In *Meditation and the Classroom*, edited by Judith Simmer-Brown and Fran Grace. Albany, NY: State University Press of New York, 2011.

_____. "Meditation in the Classroom: What Do the Students Say They Learn?" In *Meditation and the Classroom*, edited by Judith Simmer-Brown and Fran Grace. Albany, NY: State University Press of New York, 2011.

_____. "Viktor Frankl and the Search for Meaning." *Parabola*, Winter 2017.

_____. "Learning is a Path not a Goal: Contemplative Pedagogy – Its Principles and Practices." *Teaching Theology and Religion*, April 2011.

_____. "Contemplative Pedagogy: FAQs." With Thomas Coburn, Anne Carolyn Klein, Louis Komjathy, Harold Roth, and Judith Simmer-Brown. *Teaching Theology and Religion*, April 2011.

_____. Guest Editor, "Spirituality in Higher Education: Problems, Practices, and Programs." *Journal of Religion and Education*, Summer 2009.

_____. "A Pedagogy of Reverence." *Journal of Religion and Education*, Summer 2009.

_____. *Love is the Ultimate Law of the Universe*. Film created and produced by Fran Grace in gratitude and devotion for her teacher, Dr. David R. Hawkins. DVD. Sedona, AZ: Institute for Spiritual Research, 2011.

Gross, Larry. *Anishinaabe Ways of Knowing and Being*. Surrey, England: Ashgate, 2014.

Hart, Hilary. *The Unknown She*. Inverness, CA: The Golden Sufi Center, 2003.

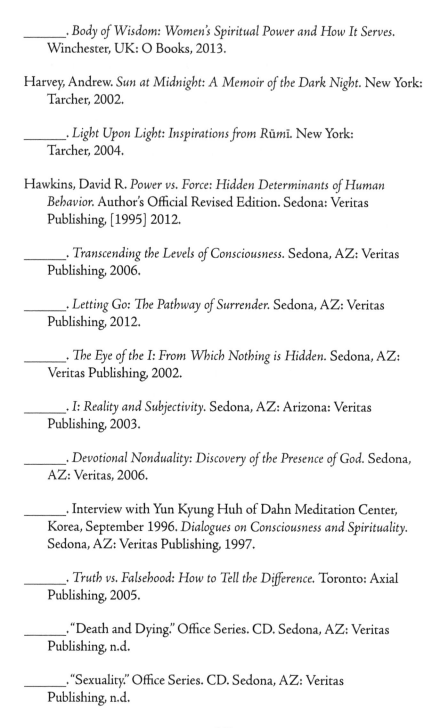

_____. *Body of Wisdom: Women's Spiritual Power and How It Serves.* Winchester, UK: O Books, 2013.

Harvey, Andrew. *Sun at Midnight: A Memoir of the Dark Night.* New York: Tarcher, 2002.

_____. *Light Upon Light: Inspirations from Rūmī.* New York: Tarcher, 2004.

Hawkins, David R. *Power vs. Force: Hidden Determinants of Human Behavior.* Author's Official Revised Edition. Sedona: Veritas Publishing, [1995] 2012.

_____. *Transcending the Levels of Consciousness.* Sedona, AZ: Veritas Publishing, 2006.

_____. *Letting Go: The Pathway of Surrender.* Sedona, AZ: Veritas Publishing, 2012.

_____. *The Eye of the I: From Which Nothing is Hidden.* Sedona, AZ: Veritas Publishing, 2002.

_____. *I: Reality and Subjectivity.* Sedona, AZ: Arizona: Veritas Publishing, 2003.

_____. *Devotional Nonduality: Discovery of the Presence of God.* Sedona, AZ: Veritas, 2006.

_____. Interview with Yun Kyung Huh of Dahn Meditation Center, Korea, September 1996. *Dialogues on Consciousness and Spirituality.* Sedona, AZ: Veritas Publishing, 1997.

_____. *Truth vs. Falsehood: How to Tell the Difference.* Toronto: Axial Publishing, 2005.

_____. "Death and Dying." Office Series. CD. Sedona, AZ: Veritas Publishing, n.d.

_____. "Sexuality." Office Series. CD. Sedona, AZ: Veritas Publishing, n.d.

_____."The Power of Devotion." CD. Sedona, AZ: Veritas Publishing, n.d.

_____."How To Instantly Tell Truth from Falsehood." CD. Lecture at the Institute for Noetic Sciences. Sedona, AZ: Veritas Publishing, n.d.

HeartMath Institute. *Science of the Heart: Exploring the Role of the Heart in Human Performance*. San Jose, CA: HeartMath Institute, 2001.

Holy Bible. George Lamsa's translation from the Aramaic of the Peshitta. San Francisco: Harper Collins, 1933.

Holy Gita. With commentary by Swami Chinmayananda. Langhorne, PA: Chinmaya Publications, 1996.

Isherwood, Christopher. *My Guru and His Disciple*. New York: Farrar, Straus, Giroux, 1980.

_____. *Ramakrishna and His Disciples*. Hollywood: Vedanta Press, 1965.

James, Bradley."Gift of Love: Music to the Words and Prayers of Mother Teresa." CD Album. Only Little Things Music, 2001.

Johnson, Robert. *Inner Gold*. Kihei, Hawaii: Koa Books, 2008.

Jung, C. G. *Memories, Dreams, Reflections*. New York: Vintage Books, [1961]1989.

_____."Two Essays on Analytical Psychology." In *Portable Jung*, edited by Joseph Campbell, translated by R. C. Hull. New York: Viking, 1971.

_____. *The Collected Works of C. G. Jung*. Translated by H. Read, M. Fordham, G. Adler, & W. McGuire, Eds., & R. F. C. Hull. Bollingen Series XX. Princeton, NJ: Princeton University Press.

Vol. 6. *Psychological Types*. (1921/1976)

Vol. 7. *Two Essays in Analytical Psychology*. (1917/1966)

Vol. 10. *Civilization in Transition.* (1928/1970)

Vol. 12. *Psychology and Alchemy.* (1944/1968)

Karam, Azza. "Religion Between 'Power' and 'Force.'" Inter Press Service, January 3, 2018.

Karmapa, H. H. the 17th, Ogyen Trinley Dorje. *Interconnected: Embracing Life in Our Global Society.* Edited by Karen Derris and Damchö Diana Finnegan, translated by Damchö Diana Finnegan. Somerville, MA: Wisdom Publications, 2017.

_____. *Traveling the Path of Compassion.* Woodstock, NY: Densal, 2009.

_____. *Compassion Now!* Woodstock, NY: KTD Publication, 2004

_____. *The Heart is Noble.* Edited by Karen Derris and Damchö Diana Finnegan, translated by Damchö Diana Finnegan. Boston: Shambhala, 2013.

Keating, Thomas. *Open Mind, Open Heart.* 20th edition. New York: Continuum, 2006.

King, Martin Luther, Jr. *A Gift of Love: Sermons from Strength to Love and Other Preachings.* Revised edition. Boston: Beacon Press, 2012.

Klingberg, Haddon. *When Life Calls Out to Us: The Love and Lifework of Viktor and Elly Frankl.* New York: Doubleday, 2001.

Ko, Celine, and, F. Grace, G. Chavez, S. Grimley, E. Dalrymple, L. Olson. "Effect of Seminar on Compassion on Student Mindfulness, Self-Compassion and Well-being: Randomized Controlled Study." *The Journal of American College Health,* March 2018.

Krishna, Gopi. *Kundalini: Evolutionary Energy in Man.* Boston: Shambhala, 1997.

Kübler-Ross, Elisabeth. *Wheel of Life: A Memoir of Living and Dying.* New York: Simon & Schuster, 1997.

Ladner, Lorne. *The Lost Art of Compassion*. San Francisco: Harper Collins, 2004.

Lane-Spollen, Eugene. *Under the Guise of Spring: The Message Hidden in Botticelli's Primavera*. London: Shepheard-Walwyn Publishers, 2014.

Lawrence, Brother. *The Practice of the Presence of God and The Spiritual Maxims*. Mineola, NY: Dover publications [1895] 2005.

Lings, Martin. *Sufi Poems: A Mediaeval Anthology*. Compiled and translated by Martin Lings. Cambridge, UK: Islamic Texts Society, 2005.

Luke, Helen. *Such Stuff As Dreams Are Made On: The Autobiography and Journals of Helen M. Luke*. Morning Light Press, 1999.

Mackenzie, Vicki. *Cave in the Snow: A Western Woman's Quest for Enlightenment*. London: Bloomsbury Publishing, 2009.

McClelland, David C. "Some Reflections on the Two Psychologies of Love." *Journal of Personality*, 1986.

McFeely, Megan. *As She Is*. Documentary film directed by Megan McFeely. DVD. 2015.

McMoneagle, Joseph. *Memoirs of a Psychic Spy: The Remarkable Life of U.S. Government Remote Viewer 001*. Charlottesville: Hampton Roads Publishing Company, 2002.

Mandela, Nelson. *Long Walk to Freedom*. New York: Little, Brown and Company, 1994.

_____. Interview with Oprah Winfrey. *O Magazine*, April 2001.

Manek, Nisha J. and William A. Tiller. "White Paper XXV: The Sacred Buddha Relic Tour: For the Benefit of All Beings." Presented at the Annual Meeting, Toward A Science of Consciousness, held at the University of Arizona Center for Consciousness Studies, Tucson, Arizona, April 9, 2012.

Manek, Nisha J. *Thursdays with Tiller*. Sedona, Arizona: Sojourn Publishing, 2019.

_____. "Symmetry States of the Physical Space: An Expanded Reference Frame for Understanding Human Consciousness." *The Journal of Alternative and Complementary Medicine*, 2012.

Martin, Michele. *Music in the Sky: The Life, Art and Teachings of the 17th Karmapa, Ogyen Trinley Dorje*. Boulder: Snow Lion, 2003.

Merton, Thomas. *Thomas Merton Reader*. Edited by Thomas P. McDonnell. New York: Image Books, 1974.

Milgram, Stanley. "Behavioral Study of Obedience." *The Journal of Abnormal and Social Psychology*, 1963.

Mills, Roy. *The Soul's Remembrance*. Seattle, WA: Onjinjinkta Publishing, 1999.

Mother Teresa. *Works of Love are Works of Peace*. A photographic record by Michael Collopy. San Francisco: Ignatius, 1996.

_____. *Come Be My Light: The Private Writings of the 'Saint of Calcutta.'* Edited with commentary by Brian Kolodiejchuk, M.C. New York: Doubleday, 2007.

_____. *A Call to Mercy: Hearts to Love, Hands to Serve*. Edited with introduction by Brian Kolodiejchuk, M.C. New York: Image Books, 2016.

Muktananda, Swami. *Meditate: Happiness Lies Within*. South Fallsburg, New York: SYDA Foundation, 1980.

Nasr, Seyyed Hossein. *The Garden of Truth: The Vision and Promise of Sufism, Islam's Mystical Tradition*. San Francisco: Harper Collins, 2007.

Nath, Ravindra. *Living with the Eternal Truth: From the Lineage of the Golden Sufis*. Nevada City, CA: Pelican Pond, 2017.

*Native American Wisdom*. With photographs by Edward S. Curtis. Running Press, 1993.

Nicol, David. *Subtle Activism: The Inner Dimension of Social and Planetary Transformation*. Albany, New York: SUNY Press, 2016.

Oliver, Mary. *Why I Wake Early: New Poems*. Boston: Beacon Press, 2004.

Palmo, Jetsunma Tenzin. *Reflections on a Mountain Lake: Teachings on Practical Buddhism*. Ithaca, NY: Snow Lion, 2002.

_____. *Into the Heart of Life*. Ithaca, New York: Snow Lion, 2011.

_____. "Lighten Up." *Lion's Roar*, February 7, 2011.

Person, Ethel Spector. *Dreams of Love and Fateful Encounters: The Power of Romantic Passion*. New York: American Psychiatric Publishing (APPI), 1988.

Petrie, Ann and Jeanette. *Mother Teresa*. Documentary film directed and produced by Ann and Jeanette Petrie. DVD. New York: Petrie Productions, 1986.

Petrie, Fr. William. "Reflections of My Time Spent with St. Teresa of Calcutta by Fr. William Petrie." http://www.sscc-usa. org/?post_type=wpv_sermon&p=27666

Plato. *The Republic*. Translated by Desmond Lee. Second edition. New York: Penguin Books, 1974.

Porete, Marguerite. *The Mirror of Simple Souls*. Translated and introduced by Ellen L. Babinsky. Mahwah, NJ: Paulist Press, 1993.

Prabhavananda, Swami. *The Sermon on the Mount according to Vedanta*. New York: New American Library, 1963.

Ramirez, Rachel. "Ethics Week: Linda Biehl Speaks About Forgiveness After Her Daughter's Murder." *The Beacon*, University of Portland, February 22, 2017.

Remen, Rachel Naomi. *Kitchen Table Wisdom*. New York: Riverhead, 1996.

Rohr, Richard, "Creation as the Body of God." In *Spiritual Ecology* edited by Llewellyn Vaughan-Lee. The Golden Sufi Center, 2016.

Rūmī, Jalāl ad-Dīn. *The Masnavi*. Book One. Translated by Jawid Mojaddedi. Oxford: Oxford University Press, 2008.

_____. *Rūmī: Fragments, Ecstasies*. Translated by Daniel Liebert. Omega Publications, 1999.

Sadhguru Jaggi Vasudev. *Inner Engineering: A Yogi's Guide to Joy*. New York: Speigel and Grau, 2016.

_____. *Encounter the Enlightened: Conversations with the Master*. New Delhi: Wisdom Tree, 2003.

_____. *Mystic's Musings*. Coimbatore, India: Isha Foundation, 2003.

_____. *Essential Wisdom from a Spiritual Master*. Mumbai, India: Jaico Publishers, 2008.

Sahagun, Louis. "The Dalai Lama Has It, But What Is 'It'?" *Los Angeles Times*, December 9, 2006.

Saltman, Bethany Senkyu, MRO. "This is Samsara: An Interview with Tenzin Palmo." Mountains and Rivers Order, Mountain Record, n.d., n.p. http://archive.is/IYE8i

Sankara, Sri Adi. *Narada Bhakti Sutra*, with commentary by Swami Chinmayananda. Langhorne, PA: Chinmaya Publications, 2013.

_____. *Crest-Jewel of Discrimination*. Translated with an introduction by Swami Prabhavananda and Christopher Isherwood. Hollywood: Vedanta Press, 1947.

Sannella, Lee. *The Kundalini Experience*. Lower Lake, CA: Integral Publishing, 1992.

Sawyer, Dana. *Huston Smith: Wisdomkeeper*. Louisville, KY: Fons Vitae, 2014.

Schaefer, Carol. *Grandmothers Counsel the World*. Boston: Trumpeter, 2006.

*Secret of the Golden Flower: A Chinese Book of Life*. Translated by Richard Wilhelm with commentary by C. G. Jung. New York: Harcourt and Brace, [1931]1962.

Shah, Idries. *Tales of the Dervishes*. New York: Penguin, 1993.

Sheldrake, Rupert. *Morphic Resonance: The Nature of Formative Causation*, 4th edition. Park Street Press, 2009.

Tabrīzī, Shams-i. *Me and Rūmī: The Autobiography of Shams-i Tabrizi*. Translated by William C. Chittick. Louisville, KY: Fons Vitae, 2004.

Simmer-Brown, Judith and Fran Grace. *Meditation and the Classroom*. Albany, NY: State University of New York Press, 2011.

Simone, Cheryl and Sadhguru Vasudev. *Midnights with the Mystic*. Newburyport, MA: Hampton Road Publishing, 2008.

Sinai, Sister Joanna of. "The Ladder of Heavenly Unity." *Parabola* 41:4, Winter 2016–2017.

Smith, Huston. *The World's Religions*. San Francisco: Harper, [1961]1991.

_____. *Tales of Wonder: Adventures Chasing the Divine, An Autobiography*, with Jeffery Paine. San Francisco: Harper One, 2009.

_____. *And Live Rejoicing!* with Phil Cousineau. Novato, CA: New World Library, 2012.

Spink, Kathryn. *Mother Teresa: An Authorized Biography*. Revised and updated. San Francisco: HarperCollins [1998], 2011.

*Srimad Bhagavata Mahapurana*. Translated by C. L. Goswami and M. A. Shastri. Gorakhpur, India: Gita Press, 2006.

Storm, Howard. *My Descent Into Death*. New York: Harmony Books, 2005.

Subramaniam, Arundhathi. *Sadhguru: More Than a Life*. New Delhi, India: Penguin Ananda, 2010.

Sunlight. *Being*. Redwood Valley, CA: Earth Books, 1988.

Tiller, William A. *Psychoenergetic Science: A Second Copernican-Scale Revolution*. Walnut Creek, CA: Pavior, 2007.

_____. *Conscious Acts of Creation: The Emergence of a New Physics*. With W.E. Dibble, Jr., and M.J. Kohane. Walnut Creek, CA: Pavior Publishing, 2001.

_____. *Science and Human Transformation: Subtle Energies, Intentionalities and Consciousness*. Walnut Creek, CA: Pavior Publishing 1997.

_____. "Knowledge, Intention and Matter." In *Oxford Handbook of the Psychology of Religion and Spirituality*, edited by Lisa Miller. Reprint edition. Oxford: Oxford University Press, 2013.

Tsomo, Karma Lekshe. "Mother Teresa and the Bodhisattva Ideal: A Buddhist View." *Claritas: Journal of Dialogue & Culture*, March 2012.

Tweedie, Irina. *Daughter of Fire: A Diary of a Spiritual Training with a Sufi Master*. Inverness, CA: The Golden Sufi Center, [1986] 2006.

Tzu, Lao. *Tao Te Ching*. Translated by Stephen Addis and Standley Lombardo. Indianapolis, IN: Hackett Publishing, 1993.

Upanishads. With commentary by Sankaracarya, translated by Swami Gambhirananda. Two volumes. Kolkata, India: Advaita Ashrama, 1958.

Vivekananda, Swami. *Pathways to Joy*. Edited by Dave DeLuca. Maui: Inner Ocean Publishing, 2003.

Vaughan-Lee, Anat. "Making the Way for the Feminine." Transcription of Closing Reflection given at the Global Peace Initiative for Women, Jaipur, India, 2008. Archived at www.workingwithoneness.org

Vaughan-Lee, Llewellyn. *Catching the Thread: Sufism, Dreamwork, and Jungian Psychology.* Inverness, CA: The Golden Sufi Center, 1998.

_____. *In the Company of Friends: Dreamwork within a Sufi Group.* Inverness, CA: The Golden Sufi Center, 1994.

_____. *Prayer of the Heart in Christian and Sufi Mysticism.* Inverness, CA: The Golden Sufi Center, 2012

_____. "Adab: Sufi Etiquette in the Outer and Inner Worlds." *Sufi: Journal of Mystical Philosophy and Practice,* December 2013.

_____. *The Face Before I Was Born.* Second edition. Inverness, CA: The Golden Sufi Center, [1997], 2009.

_____. *Love is a Fire: The Sufi's Mystical Journey Home.* Inverness, CA: The Golden Sufi Center, 2000.

_____. *Fragments of a Love Story: Reflections on the Life of a Mystic.* Inverness, CA: The Golden Sufi Center, 2011.

_____. *The Return of the Feminine and the World Soul.* Second edition. Inverness, CA: The Golden Sufi Center, [2009], 2017.

Vaughan-Lee, Llewellyn, editor. *Travelling on the Path of Love: Sayings of Sufi Masters.* Inverness, CA: The Golden Sufi Center, 1995.

_____. *Spiritual Ecology: The Cry of the Earth.* Revised Edition. Inverness, CA: The Golden Sufi Center, [2013], 2016.

Vaughan-Lee, Llewellyn and Hilary Hart. *Spiritual Ecology: Ten Practices to Awaken the Sacred in Everyday Life.* Inverness, CA: The Golden Sufi Center, 2017.

von Bingen, Hildegard. *Scivias.* Translated by Mother Columba Hart & J. Bishop. Mahwah, NH: Paulist Press, 1990.

Walker, Alice. *Anything We Love Can Be Saved: A Writer's Activism*. Reprint edition. New York: Ballantine, 1998.

Ware, Bishop Kallistos. *The Inner Kingdom*. Crestwood, New York: Vladimir's Seminary Press, 2000.

Welwood, John. *Toward a Psychology of Awakening*. Boston: Shambhala, 2002.

Wilson, Bill. *Bill W.: My First 40 Years*. Center City, MN: Hazelden, 2000.

Woollacott, Marjorie Hines. *Infinite Awareness: The Awakening of a Scientific Mind*. Rowman and Littlefield, 2015.

Yogananda, Paramahansa. *Autobiography of a Yogi*. 13th edition. Los Angeles: Self-Realization Fellowship, 1998.

Zanam, Zaynab. "Karmapa Visits Princeton, Discusses Women's Rights, Social Activism, Environment." *Daily Princetonian*, April 1, 2015.

# Interviewees for *The Power of Love*

In 2010, this book was conceived with the guidance of my teacher, Dr. David R. Hawkins, who verified the energy fields of the people interviewed herein. This section includes their biographical profiles, the occasion of the interviews, and information for private donations to their organizations.

Our original list included others whom, for various reasons, I was unable to interview. I recommend them to the reader for study and inspiration on the topic of love: Rev. Michael Beckwith, Rabbi Phillip Berg, Jill Bolte-Taylor, His Holiness the 14th Dalai Lama, Andrew Harvey, Fr. Thomas Keating, Nelson Mandela, Seyyed Hossein Nasr, Mary Oliver, Pope Francis, Bishop Kallistos Ware, and Oprah Winfrey.

**Swami Chidatmananda** is a spiritual teacher whose core teaching emphasizes the oneness (non-duality) of all beings. Swamiji travels across the globe delivering lectures that are profound yet simple enough for a novice. Swamiji's humility and pleasant demeanor make him very approachable to people from all walks of life who seek relief, whether from ordinary issues or the deeply held misperceptions that cause immense stress and suffering. His creative and scientific presentations unearth the ancient philosophies of India for modern and rational minds, thereby transforming them for the better. An element of humor is seen in his style that smooths and simplifies the subject and has a healing effect on the audience. He gives regular discourses on spiritual topics and the scriptures of

India for Indian television. Swamiji's topics, such as "Art of Healing," "Beyond Suffering," "Learning through Relationships," and "The Greatness of Mind" address humanity's core problems. His spiritual sessions for political leaders on "Achieving Success with Values" are acclaimed. He is the author of the popular Telugu book *Learning through Relationships* and *The Greatness of the Mind* in English. His lectures and guided meditations are available on CD through the Chinmaya Mission. Swamiji is a Law graduate from Osmania University. Inspired by Pujya Gurudev Swami Chinmayananda ji, he joined Sandeepany Sadhanalaya in Mumbai in 1989 under the tutelage of Swami Purushottamananda ji. In 1993 he was initiated into brahmacharya deeksha by Pujya Gurudev and posted as the Acharya of the mission center at Hyderabad. He was initiated into sanyasa deeksha by Swami Tejomayananda ji, in 1999. He is presently Acharya (Teacher in Charge) of Chinmaya Mission Hyderabad and Regional Head of Andhra Pradesh, India.

I have known Swamiji for many years, attended several of his talks in the U.S., traveled to visit him in Hyderabad, India, and conducted an extensive interview with him in 2012.

Donation Information:
Chinmaya Seva Trust
214/1 Kundanbagh
Begumpet, Hyderabad 500016, India
http://chinmayakailas.com/donation

**Betty J. Eadie** is the author of *Embraced by the Light*, which broke records in publishing as the first book from a small press written by an unknown author that stayed at #1 on *The New York Times* Bestseller List for 78 weeks. The book recounted her near-death experience (NDE), considered by leaders in the field to be singular in its details and depth. Kimberly Clark-Sharp, current president of the Seattle Chapter of the International Association of Near-Death

Studies, found Eadie's account the most detailed and spellbinding she'd come across. Raymond Moody, M.D., author of *Life After Life*, viewed Eadie's as the most comprehensive and profound NDE ever recorded. Betty's second book, *The Awakening Heart*, was also a bestseller; her third book is *The Ripple Effect*. She became an overnight celebrity, invited by all the major TV networks to share her experience. Her books have been translated into forty languages and continue to have a profound effect on a wide variety of readers, bringing hope and love where none existed. She founded her own publishing company, Onjinjinkta Press, to make available the unique account of Roy Mills's pre-birth memories in *The Soul's Remembrance*.

Born to a full-blooded Lakota Sioux mother in Valentine, Nebraska, Betty spent her early childhood on the Rosebud Reservation in South Dakota. In the wake of her NDE, she returned to her Native American spiritual roots, studied psychology, and completed her training in clinical hypnotherapy. She opened a practice to help people heal from trauma and other difficulties through mind integration. Mother of eight, grandmother and great-grandmother of many, she continues to share her knowledge and healing wisdom with countless people through inspiring podcasts and presentations. A film is being made about her life. Betty is the spiritual advisor for The Indigenous Institute, a non-profit organization founded by Jeff Eadie, with this mission: "To provide aspiring education that will assist Indigenous Peoples in achieving their Creator-given potential while enriching their lives." The vision is "thriving, hopeful, healthy, and sovereign Indigenous Peoples and Nations living their traditional way of life."

I have used *Embraced by the Light* in my college class on Mysticism for many years. In 2016, I had the chance to join Betty for her visit to northern California where I attended her public presentations and conducted an extensive interview with her.

Donation Information:
The Indigenous Institute
https://www.theindigenousinstitute.org

Viktor Frankl, M.D., Ph.D. (1905–1997) is the author of the classic Holocaust memoir *Man's Search for Meaning*, listed as one of the "ten most influential books in America" according to a survey conducted by the Book of the Month Club and the Library of Congress. It is a standard text in American colleges and used around the world. Frankl founded a school of psychotherapy called Logotherapy/ Existential Analysis. His approach of "healing through meaning" is regarded as the "Third Viennese School of Psychotherapy" (the other two founded by Sigmund Freud and Alfred Adler). Frankl published the first book about logotherapy after his liberation from the Nazi concentration camps, first in German in 1946 and later in English in 1955 under the title *The Doctor and The Soul*. Frankl's thirty-nine books have appeared in forty-four languages. He served as professor of neurology and psychiatry at the University of Vienna Medical school. For twenty-five years, 1946–1971, he was head of the Vienna Neurological Polyclinic. For four decades, Dr. Frankl made hundreds of lecture tours worldwide. His wife, Elly Frankl, traveled with him. He received honorary degrees from twenty-nine universities in Europe, the Americas, Africa, and Asia. In addition to professorships at Harvard, Stanford, and other American universities, he served as Distinguished Professor of Logotherapy at the U.S. International University in San Diego, California. He received numerous awards, including the Oskar Pfister Award of the American Psychiatric Association.

Alexander Vesely is an award-winning filmmaker. He was born in Vienna, Austria, in 1974, and is Viktor Frankl's only grandson. Alex's talent was noted at an early age, as soon as he discovered the value of filmmaking while watching home movies. Some of his earliest video footage was taken of his grandfather, who bought Alex his first video camera. He trained and worked as a psychotherapist, and this psychological depth is apparent in his films. Vesely has directed many short films, commercials, and documentaries, but is most proud of *Viktor & I*, which won several prestigious film awards in the United States, including the Diamond Award for the Best Documentary at the California Film Awards. Another film, *Wizard of the Desert*, is about the American psychiatrist and medical hypnotist Milton Erikson, whose life's work began at a young age. Paralyzed by polio and expected to die, Erikson discovered inner mechanisms of mind to reactivate healthy body function. This film has received rave reviews. Alex is working on a new documentary entitled *Pioneer of Meaning*.

**Mary Cimiluca,** the representative for the Frankl family and CEO of Noetic Films, Inc., is an entrepreneur, professional speaker, and radio talk show host. For thirty years she has incubated, developed, and managed several small businesses. She serves on the Advisory Council for the Statue of Responsibility, a monument project envisioned by Viktor Frankl. Throughout her life, she had several encounters with Frankl; however, it wasn't until Mary met Alexander Vesely in 2008, after surviving serial life challenges, that she grasped the "meaning" of those encounters. Her passion has shifted to helping others uncover the meaning in their own lives. She has now launched an unexpected career in film production, learning from some of the best teachers in Hollywood, including Suzanne Lyons, past President of Women in Film International and the Hollywood Film Institute. In 2010, Mary Cimiluca joined with Alex Vesely to establish Noetic Films, Inc. to produce and distribute films with depth, meaning, and substance. She is the producer for *Viktor & I* and *Wizard of the Desert*, which opened in Anaheim, California, to a sold-out crowd of 1,675 fans. Her unique expertise and out-of-box approaches resulted in full funding for both documentaries. Where others see obstacles, Mary sees possibilities.

I have used Frankl's writings in my college teaching for thirty years. His book is a textbook for my course on Compassion. I interviewed Alex and Mary in 2015.

Donation Information:
Mary Cimiluca, Producer
Noetic Films, Inc.
25501 Crown Valley Pkwy., Suite 103
Ladera Ranch, CA 92694
www.viktorandimovie.com

**David R. "Doc" Hawkins, M.D., Ph.D. (1927–2012)** grew up in Wisconsin and served in the United States Navy before he became a physician, author, lecturer, researcher of consciousness, and spiritual teacher. As Medical Director of the North Nassau Mental Health Center (1956–1980) and Director of Research at Brunswick Hospital on Long Island (1968–1979), he had the largest practice in New York State. In 1973, he coauthored *Orthomolecular Psychiatry* with double Nobel Laureate chemist Linus Pauling, and interviewed on numerous national TV broadcasts. In midlife, an unexpected and shattering realization of the Oneness of All Existence transformed Dr. Hawkins's life. It took thirty years for him to articulate the experience in a way that would be meaningful to others. In 1995, at age sixty-eight, he published *Power vs. Force*, introducing his now well-known Map of Consciousness.® The book has been translated into twenty-five languages, with over a million copies sold, and has evoked praise from such notables as Mother Teresa. Twelve other books followed, as did lectures at the Oxford Forum and Westminster Abbey, as well as at many universities. Documentary films, magazines, and radio interviews (e.g., *Oprah Radio*) have featured "Doc" and his work. His numerous awards include: the Huxley Award for the "Inestimable Contribution to the Alleviation of Human Suffering," the Physicians Recognition Award by the American Medical Association, 50-Year Distinguished Life Fellow by the American Psychiatric Association, the Orthomolecular Medicine Hall of Fame, and a nomination for the Templeton Prize. For recognition of his contributions to humanity, Dr. Hawkins was knighted in 1996, and in 2000, a large community of Buddhists in Seoul, South Korea, bestowed upon him the designation "Tae Ryoung Sun Kak Tosa" (Teacher of Enlightenment). At age eighty-four, Dr. Hawkins gave his final public lecture, on the topic of "Love," to an audience of 1,700 people spanning many nationalities and religious backgrounds.

**Susan J. Hawkins** is the "fulcrum," Doc said, that made possible the sharing of his knowledge and presence in the world. Blessed with keen intuition, she offered crucial insights and companionship, and he was never onstage without her. She joined him in several video-recorded dialogues on practical topics such as "Improving Your Relationships" and "Live Your Life Like a Prayer." Susan is an avid gardener and animal lover. She is president of the foundation started by her late husband, The Institute for Spiritual Research.

Dr. Hawkins is my spiritual teacher. While I lived around the corner from his home, I saw him frequently during the last years of his life, edited two of his books, and conducted many hours of interviews for a book about his life.

Donation Information:
The Institute for Spiritual Research, Inc.
P.O. Box 3516
Sedona, AZ 86340
https://veritaspub.com/donations/

**The International Council of the 13 Indigenous Grandmothers** is a global alliance of Indigenous Grandmothers to bring prayer, education, and healing for Mother Earth, all of her inhabitants, and for the next seven generations to come. Since their beginning in 2004, they have traveled around the world to gather in ceremony and conduct healing rituals for women, water, reconciliation, Indigenous communities, and other concerns. Coming from the four corners and many continents of the world, each of them is a leader in her own tribe and community. They have received many awards for their humanitarian efforts, such as the International Pfeffer Peace Award, Humanity4Water Compassion Award, and the Partnership for Global Justice Award. They are featured in a documentary film, *For the Next Seven Generations: The Grandmothers Speak*, as well as in a book by Carol Schaefer, *Grandmothers Counsel the World*.

Original Thirteen Indigenous Grandmothers: Margaret Behan Arapaho, Cheyenne of Montana, USA; Rita Pitka Blumenstein, Yup'ik from Alaska, USA; Aama Bombo (Buddhi Maya Lama), Tamang from Nepal; Julieta Casimiro, Mazatec from Huautla de Jimenez, Mexico; Flordemayo, Mayan from the Highlands of Central America and New Mexico; Maria Alice Campos Freire from the Amazonian Rainforest, Brazil; Bernadette Rebienot, Omyene of Gabon, Africa; Tsering Dolma Gyaltong from Tibet; Beatrice Long Visitor Holy Dance, Oglala Lakota from the Black Hills of South Dakota, USA; Rita Long Visitor Holy Dance, Oglala Lakota from the Black Hills, South Dakota, USA; Agnes Baker Pilgrim, Takelma Siletz of Grants Pass, Oregon, USA; Mona Polacca, Havasupai-Hopi-Tewa from Arizona, USA; Clara Shinobu Iura of the Amazonian Rainforest, Brazil.

**Grandmother Mona Polacca** is a Havasupai-Hopi-Tewa Elder who lives in Arizona and is an envoy of peace throughout the world, bringing a basic call to consciousness about the fundamental elements of life: water, fire, earth, and air. As a spiritual leader of her people and participant in interfaith alliances, she is a member of the World Council of Religious and Spiritual Leaders, and is recognized for her international work in the areas of human rights and water rights. She is President/CEO of the Turtle Island Project, a nonprofit organization, founded in 1986, that blends Indigenous wisdom with Western science for healing and health. According to Native American tradition, the whole world is referred to as "Turtle Island." Grandmother Mona says, "The turtle is a good symbol for change. It is deliberate. When it is threatened, it finds its strength by going inward. And when it is ready to go forward, it sticks its neck out. That is a good way for us to think about healing." Since age nineteen, Grandmother Mona has worked in her Native community in the field of social work, especially addiction recovery. She has her master's degree in Social Work. She has been leading "Women's Healing Journeys," a weekend gathering and sweat lodge, for thirty years.

I met the Grandmothers at their Gathering in 2014 in the Black Hills, South Dakota, sacred land of the Lakota; and in Arizona in 2016, I had an extensive interview with Havasupai-Hopi-Tewa Grandmother Mona Polacca.

Donation Information:
International Council of the Thirteen Indigenous Grandmothers
http://www.grandmotherscouncil.org/donate
Turtle Island Project
http://www.turtleislandproject.com/index.html

**His Holiness the 17th Gyalwang Karmapa,** Ogyen Trinley Dorje, is the head of the 900-year-old Karma Kagyu Lineage and guide to millions of Buddhists worldwide. Born in 1985 to a nomad family in Tibet, he lived in rural life until age seven, when he was recognized as the reincarnation of the 16th Karmapa and was returned to the Tsurphu Monastery in Tibet, historical seat of the Karmapas. Over 20,000 devotees witnessed this event. Once enthroned at Tsurphu, His Holiness began studies in Buddhist sciences of mind, rituals, and sacred arts, and began the fulfillment of his leadership role by giving audiences and bestowing empowerments. However, since many of the teachers in his lineage were not in Tibet, and receiving the oral transmission of the lineage teachings was necessary for his role, he embarked on a long and harrowing journey to India by horseback, foot, helicopter, and train. Arriving in 2000 to Dharamsala, he was welcomed by Tenzin Gyatso, His Holiness the 14th Dalai Lama. A year later, he received refugee status from the government of India, where he has been a guest ever since. In India, His Holiness grants audiences to thousands of visitors every year at Gyuto Monastery. He also leads Buddhist retreats that draw thousands, bestows empowerments, participates in conferences on the environment and other world issues, and has made several trips to the United States and Canada. His Holiness is recognized as a meditation master and scholar of Buddhism, as well as a gifted painter, poet, songwriter, and playwright. He is an environmental activist and global spiritual leader who is also interested in technology, women's well-being, and animal welfare. In this way, the 17th Gyalwang Karmapa is bringing the Karmapa lineage's activities to bear on the pressing issues of the 21st century—with the compassion and wisdom of a living Buddha. He is the author of many books of Buddhist teaching. Two of them, *The Heart is Noble* and *Interconnected*, are based on dialogues with college students from the University of Redlands who spent several weeks with him in India, showing his interest to engage Buddhist teaching with the questions of the next generations.

In 2013, I interviewed His Holiness at Gyuto Monastery, his home base in Sidbhari, India. In 2015, he visited the University of Redlands for several days to renew friendship with students and the co-editor of his books, Dr. Karen Derris. The Karmapa spent ninety minutes in dialogue with the Meditation Room program for which I serve as steward.

Donation Information:
Gyuto Tantric Monastery
P.O. Sidhbari-176 057
Dharamshala, District Kangra (H.P.) INDIA

**Mother Teresa (St. Teresa of Kolkata (1910–1997)** and the Missionaries of Charity. Mother Teresa left her home in Albania at age eighteen to join the Sisters of Loreto. Three years later, in 1931, she went to Calcutta, India, to teach at St. Mary's school for girls. She made her Final Profession of Vows in 1937, and became principal of the school in 1944. On September 10, 1946 ("Inspiration Day"), she received what she called her "call within a call," an inner dictation from Jesus to leave the convent and serve the "poorest of the poor." Four years later, church leaders gave her permission to form a new society called Missionaries of Charity. In a pioneering work of living among the poorest of the poor, the Missionaries of Charity established homes for the dying, the elderly, lepers, and orphans. Mother Teresa was given numerous awards and honorary degrees, including the Nobel Peace Prize in 1979. Within thirty-one years of the start of her mission in 1948, her one-to-one-person method had reached millions, and the white sari with blue border had become a universal symbol of compassion. When she died in 1997, the Missionaries of Charity were spread throughout the world: 4,000 members, 610 foundations in 123 countries, over a million lay workers on all seven continents. In 2016, the Catholic Church canonized her as St. Teresa of Kolkata. The Missionaries of Charity have continued her legacy of loving selfless service, making their home among the poorest of the poor.

For twenty years I have worked in the legacy of Mother Teresa's love, using her biography in my Compassion course, visiting the Motherhouse in Calcutta, her convent in Rome with its Home for the Poor, and the Mother Teresa Center in Mexico. In 2015, we hosted a large exhibit of her life at our university. In 2016, I was invited to attend her canonization in Rome, Italy. Over the years, I've interviewed people who worked closely with her.

Donation Information:
Mother Teresa Center
524 West Calle Primera, Suite #1005N
San Ysidro, CA 92173 USA

**Jetsunma Tenzin Palmo,** nee Diane Perry, was born in London, England, went to India at age twenty, and became one of the first Western women to be ordained a Tibetan Buddhist nun and the first to carry out the traditional meditation retreat in a Himalayan cave, which she did for twelve years under the direction of her Guru, His Eminence the 8th Khamtrul Rinpoche. Her life story and experience became widely known through the book *Cave in the Snow*, published in 1998 by Vicki MacKenzie. Palmo faced entrenched bias from male monks who viewed her quest for enlightenment as hopeless because she was a female. She stayed the course, advocating for full ordination for nuns and their access to Buddhist training. On direction of her lama, she founded a nunnery, Dongyu Gatsal Ling Nunnery ("Garden of the Authentic Lineage"), located in the region of the Dalai Lama's residence in Dharamsala and close to Tashi Jong, monastic home to many great Buddhist adepts and teachers. The DGL nunnery gives a rare opportunity to women for traditional training in Buddhist practice, philosophy, and spiritual excellence. The nunnery completed its temple in 2013, a traditional religious space and the first to feature sacred feminine imagery drawn from Buddhist iconography. Palmo is the chief administrator and visionary of the nunnery, and speaks worldwide on issues of women's concerns, Buddhist practice, and peace in troubled times.

Having studied her books and admired her courage for many years, I interviewed Jetsunma Tenzin Palmo at her nunnery in India, in 2013.

Donation Information
(Sponsorship of a nun costs $360 per year)
Dongyu Gatsal Ling Nunnery
Village Lower Mutt
PO Padhiarkhar, Via Taragarh
Distt. Kangra HP 176081 India
www.tenzinpalmo.com

**Father Pavlos of Sinai,** born in 1939, has spent many decades as an ascetic priestmonk of the Greek Orthodox Church, immersed in the hesychast tradition of the Sinai desert. A graduate of the School of

Theology at the University of Athens, he settled at St. Catherine's Monastery, the oldest Christian monastery in continuous operation, situated on the holy ground of the Burning Bush at the "God-trodden Mountain of Sinai" in Egypt. The sixth-century monastery is home to the second largest collection of ancient manuscripts in the world, as well as its most important collection of Byzantine icons. Revered as an icon of the ageless tradition he represents, Father Pavlos spoke extensively throughout the United States during visits from 2010–12, where his message of simplicity and the monastery's example of peaceful coexistence with Bedouin neighbors struck a chord in times of chaos and inter-religious conflict. He is steeped in the rhythm of prayer and liturgy of the ancient Orthodox tradition, while his presence conveys the inner peace that radiates only from the depths of intimacy with God. He is featured in the film *Mysteries of the Jesus Prayer*.

In 2011, I participated in his visit to Southern California, heard him speak several times, and interviewed him at that time.

Donation Information:
Friends of Mount Sinai Monastery
PO Box 231953
Encinitas, CA 92023-1953 USA
http://www.mountsinaimonastery.org/support/

**Belvie Rooks and Dedan Gills** are the founders of Growing a Global Heart, a vision that inspires the ceremonial planting of millions of memorial trees to honor the forgotten souls of our past—victims of urban violence, the Underground Railroad, and the Trans-Atlantic Slave Route in West Africa—as part of a process of collective healing and a solution to climate change. The Growing a Global Heart motto is: "Healing the wounds of the past—in the present—while creating a sustainable future." This project brings communities together to plant trees throughout the world in honor of the millions of lives lost in acts of violence, and to seed new hope for humanity and the earth.

"To plant a tree is to plant hope." They have engaged in memorial tree planting projects along the Trans-Atlantic Slave Route in West Africa, the Underground Railroad in the US and Canada and also for victims of urban violence. Both Belvie and Dedan have essays in *Global Chorus, 365 Voices on the Future of the Planet*, an anthology that includes Nelson Mandela, Maya Angelou, the Dalai Lama, Jane Goodall, and others.

**Belvie Rooks** is a writer, educator and human rights activist whose work weaves together the worlds of spirituality, feminism, ecology, and social justice. As an educator she was a member of the founding faculty of the College of Social Justice at the State University of New York (SUNY) Old Westbury. She has been a board member of the Institute for Noetic Sciences (IONS), Bioneers, and the Ella Baker Center for Human Rights. Her published works have appeared in many publications and anthologies including: *Sacred Poems and Prayers in Praise of Life; The Same River Twice: Honoring the Difficult*, edited by Alice Walker; *My Soul is a Witness: African American Women's Spirituality; Life Notes: Personal Writings by Black Women; Birthing God: Women's Experiences of the Divine; Moonrise: The Power of Women Leading from the Heart; Ecological and Social Healing: Multicultural Women's Voices.* She is also an American Book Award winner as senior editor of *Paris Connections: African American Artists in Paris.*

**Dedan Gills** (**1945–2015**) described himself as a "soulutionary." He was a poet and active member for eight years in one of the first urban intentional environmental communities in the country— the L.A. Eco-Village. Certified in Permaculture, he was a founding member of the L.A. Permaculture Guild. His poems have appeared in the *International Sufi Association Journal.* Born in Watts, California, Dedan was instrumental in the formation of the Black Student Alliance movement in Southern California and for a time was a member of the Black Panther Party. The demise of the Black Liberation movement was followed by years of despair while trying to find his activist footing on a different ground. He became an unrelenting advocate for human rights and Mother Earth. Dedan worked to integrate principles of permaculture design, sustainability, environmental awareness, and the greening of the inner spirit for healing and recovery. He gave tirelessly to groups of people abandoned by mainstream culture—the homeless and those suffering from addiction and incarceration. He touched many souls while actively and simultaneously addressing their physical, material, and emotional wounds. As he was known to say, "Things come and go, but the soul is eternal. When souls embrace, it is like a kiss that lasts forever!"

I met Belvie and Dedan at a small café in northern California. They have twice spoken at University of Redlands, and I interviewed them extensively in 2014.

Donation Information:
Growing a Global Heart
PO Box 51
Elk, CA 95432 USA
http://growingaglobalheart.weebly.com
https://www.facebook.com/growingaglobalheart/

**Huston Smith, Ph.D.** (**1919–2016**) was born in China to Methodist missionary parents. He graduated from the University of Chicago and began his long career as a professor and scholar in religious studies, following the path of both the mind and the heart. He taught in many places, but had his longest tenure as Thomas J. Watson Professor of Religion and Distinguished Adjunct Professor of Philosophy at Syracuse University. He is best known for his best-selling book, *The World's Religions*, with over 3 million sold and still a classic text in universities and general study in religion. As a young professor at Washington University, he televised popular lectures on religion for NET, the pre-runner to PBS. Those early educational broadcasts are credited with introducing the American public to the fascinating study of world religions. In 1964, while in India, Smith "discovered" the Tibetan monks' unique multiphonal chanting with its audible overtones, brought it to MIT for analysis, and the result was a "landmark" find in musicology, according to *The Journal of Ethnomusicology*. Bill Moyers, a leading PBS figure, devoted an entire TV series to Smith's life and work, *The Wisdom of Faith with Huston Smith*. Smith's own film documentaries on Hinduism, Tibetan Buddhism, and Sufism all won awards in international film festivals. His book, *Why Religion Matters: The Fate of the Human Spirit in an Age of Disbelief*, won the Wilbur Award for the best book on religion. He was recognized for his contributions to humanity with awards such as the Courage of Conscience Award from the Peace Abbey. Smith published at least fourteen books in his illuminated career, including *Cleansing the Doors of Perception: The Religious Significance of Entheogenic Plants and Chemicals*, *The Soul of Christianity*, *Tales of Wonder: Adventures Chasing the Divine*, and *Live Rejoicing!*. Though he remained a Christian throughout his life, his personal quest took him deep into the practice of Vedanta, Sufism, Zen Buddhism, and Judaism. After his experiments with entheogenic substances, he was an advocate before the U.S. Congress for religious usage of peyote on behalf of the Native American Church.

I've used Huston Smith's books in my classes for thirty years, and have long admired his scholarship and his open-minded quest for Truth. I met with him at his home in 2011 for an interview. He was ninety-two.

**William A. Tiller, Ph.D.,** is a fellow of the American Academy for the Advancement of Science, and Professor Emeritus of Stanford University's Department of Materials Science. He has worked as a scientist for fifty years in two parallel tracks, each highly regarded in its own right. In his professional track, that of conventional science, he has published over 450 papers, three books, and several patents. He became a world-class expert in the area of crystallization, with books on the topic published by Cambridge University Press. After nine years as an advisory physicist with Westinghouse

Research Laboratories, he was invited to join the faculty of Stanford University's Department of Materials Science as a professor with tenure. He retired from his academic position after thirty-four years. In his avocational track, which began early in his career at Stanford, Tiller pioneered serious experimental and theoretical study of the field of psychoenergetics, which he predicts will become an integral part of tomorrow's physics. In this new area, he has published an additional 150+ articles and four seminal books: *Science and Human Transformation: Subtle Energies, Intentionalities and Consciousness; Conscious Acts of Creation: Emergence of a New Physics; Some Science Adventures with Real Magic;* and *Psychoenergetic Science: A Second Copernican-Scale Revolution.* His website, tiller.org, offers free downloadable White Papers that give the history, descriptions, theories, mathematics, and outcomes of his cutting-edge experiments into what he sees as a multidimensional universe. His research demonstrates the critical role of human consciousness in shaping our environment, health, and psychology—in other words, human intention has a definitive influence in the world.

**Jean Tiller** met Bill when she was twelve and he was thirteen. They didn't see each other for another five years. They dated and then married when she was twenty-one and he was twenty-two. Since then, for nearly seventy years, Jean has been his partner in all things, in life, parenting, spiritual search, and research. With her extraordinary gifts of intuition, emotional intelligence, and meditation skill, she has been a crucial collaborator in Tiller's experiments.

I participated in lab group discussions with Tiller's assistants, and in 2013 conducted an extensive interview with Bill and Jean in their home.

Donation Information:
The WAT Foundation for Human Intention Applications
Box 760
Pine, Arizona 85544-0760
https://www.tillerresearch.org

**Sadhguru Jaggi Vasudev** is a yogi, mystic, and visionary. Named one of India's fifty most influential people, Sadhguru's work has touched the lives of millions worldwide through his transformational programs. He has a unique ability to make the ancient yogic sciences relevant to contemporary minds. His approach does not espouse any belief system, but offers methods for self-transformation that are both proven and powerful. An internationally renowned speaker and author of *The New York Times* bestseller *Inner Engineering, A Yogi's Guide to Joy*, Sadhguru has been an influential voice at major global forums including the United Nations, the World Economic Forum, and the World Presidents' Organization, addressing issues as diverse as socioeconomic development, leadership, and spirituality. He has been invited to speak at leading educational institutions, including Oxford, London Business School, IMD, Stanford, Harvard, Yale, Wharton, and MIT. In February 2017, Sadhguru was the recipient of the Padma Vibhushan Award from the Government of India, the second-highest civilian award, accorded annually for exceptional and distinguished service. Sadhguru established Isha Foundation, a nonprofit, volunteer-run organization operating in more than 300 centers and supported by over 9 million volunteers worldwide. Through powerful yoga programs for inner transformation and inspiring social outreach initiatives, Isha Foundation has created a massive movement dedicated to addressing all aspects of human well-being. Sadhguru has also initiated several projects for social revitalization, education, and the environment through which millions have been given the means to overcome poverty, improve their quality of life, and achieve community-based, sustainable development. In 2017, Sadhguru initiated Rally For Rivers, a nationwide campaign aiming to implement sustainable and long-term policy changes to revitalize India's severely depleted rivers, which found great support among India's leadership and the people, with more than 165 million participating in the movement.

I interviewed Sadhguru at a satsang in 2013, and have been with him for four of his events.

Donation Information:
Isha Foundation
Attn: Finance team
951 Isha Lane
McMinnville, TN 37110

In the U.S.: https://isha.sadhguru.org/us/en/donation
In India: https://isha.sadhguru.org/in/en/donation

**Llewellyn Vaughan-Lee, Ph.D.,** is a Sufi teacher in the Naqshbandiyya-Mujaddidiyya Sufi Order. Born in London in 1953, he has followed the Naqshbandi Sufi path since he was nineteen. In 1991, he became the successor of Irina Tweedie who brought this particular Indian branch of Sufism to the West and is the author of *Daughter of Fire: A Diary of a Spiritual Training with a Sufi Master.* Vaughan-Lee then moved to northern California and founded The Golden Sufi Center. Author of more than twenty books and several articles, his initial series of writings provided a detailed exploration of the stages of spiritual and psychological transformation experienced on the Sufi path, with a particular focus on the use of dreamwork as inner guidance on the journey. In 2000 his writing and teaching centered on spiritual responsibility in our present time of transition, the awakening global consciousness of oneness, and spiritual ecology (see workingwithoneness.org). He was featured in the TV series *Global Spirit*, interviewed by Oprah Winfrey for her *SuperSoul Sunday* series, and has been interviewed on radio shows relating to Sufism, global consciousness, spiritual ecology, and subtle activism. His recently published book, *For Love of the Real* (foreword by the 14th Dalai Lama) is regarded as a completion of over twenty-five years of his writing and teaching, as it draws together many of the threads of his work, which began with his 1993 book *The Bond with*

*the Beloved*. As a mystic and sheikh, Llewellyn has made a vital contribution to Sufism by articulating the ancient principles of the path for the modern psyche, presented in his books on Sufism as well as in twenty-five years' worth of teachings and interviews, as available in the audio archive https://goldensufi.org.

**Anat Vaughan-Lee** is an artist and has belonged to the Naqshbandiyya-Mujaddidiyya Sufi Order since 1973. For many years she has been working with groups and dreamwork in the Sufi tradition, which encourages the deep feminine way of inner listening. In 2003, she was a delegate to first Global Peace Initiative for Women at the Palais des Nations (UN), in Geneva. She alsogave a presentation at "Making Way for the Feminine," a gathering of women spiritual leaders held in Jaipur, India, in 2008. Recognizing the need and urgency of the moment for the re-emergence of the feminine, she compiled and edited the writings of her husband, Llewellyn Vaughan-Lee, on the subject of the sacred feminine, which has emerged as the book *The Return of the Feminine and the World Soul*.

Following my extended interview with Llewellyn and Anat at their home in 2011, I've been in their presence many times, and this path became a principal source of guidance.

Donation Information:
The Treasurer
The Golden Sufi Center
PO Box 456
Point Reyes Station, CA 94956-0456 USA
https://goldensufi.org/donations.html

# INDEX

Buddha: and energy field levels, xliv, xlvii; "heirs to our own karma," 291; and loving kindness, 30, 283; and paths to God, 530; "put no head before your own," 297, 491; surrender of, 524–25

Buddha-nature, 253, 257, 282, 298, 520, 583

Buddhism: and Four Immeasurables, 399; and full ordination for nuns, 278–79; and Hawkins's Map of Consciousness, xlv, 262; and "hungry ghosts," 235; and Karmapa, 395–96; and loving-kindness practice, 253, 282; Mahayana Buddhism, xliv, 281–82; model for love in, 285; relics of, 395–96, 397–98, 398, 432; and *tonglen* practice, liii, 290–91, 383, 443; *See also* Palmo, Jetsunma Tenzin; His Holiness the 17th Karmapa

Burning Bush (biblical), 173–74

business world, power of love in, 406–7

butterflies as symbols of spiritual transformation, 216

caffeine, attachment to, 353–54

Cal-Earth Institute, *370*

Camp, Charles, 619

cancer, 230, 548

capacity to love, increasing, lv, 5, 27, 70, 204, 400, 427, 507–8, 527

Capra, Fritjof, 434

carbon footprints, 328

caringness, 512–13, 522

Casimiro, Julieta, 222, 226

caste system in India, 68, 79–80

catalysts of love, 4–5

Cathedral of Santa Maria del Fiore, 44–45

Catholicism, 49–50, 163–64, 166–67, 245, 286. *See also* Teresa, Mother

*Cave in the Snow* (Mackenzie), 277, 281, 338

caves, symbolism of, 203

Cayce, Edgar, 452, 470

*Celestial Hierarchy* (Dionysius the Areopagite), 45, 48

*The Chalice and The Blade* (Eisler), xxxiv

change, catalysts that force, 196, 199

"change of heart" vs. "change of mind," 392

changing the world, lii, 297–312, 302, 371, 373, 375, 389, 428, 477, 510, 628

Cheatham, Elizabeth M., 3, 631–32

Chidatmananda, Swami, 552, 553–79, 671: ashram of, 554–55; and author's trip to India, 554; on being in presence of a Master, 550, 557–58; on choosing one's attitudes, 555–56; on devotion, 558–66; devotional life of, 550–51, 570–71; on everyday expressions of devotion, 571–73; on five ingredients of great faith, 566; guru of, xxxi, 553, 570–71; on Hawkins as spiritual Master, 550, 553–54, 569–70; on Hawkins's books, 259; and Hawkins's Map of Consciousness, 568; interview with, 557–79; on Krishna and the dancing Gopis, 563–66; on physical deaths of Masters, 576–79; on qualities of devotees, 566–69; on sensory attachments, 573–76

"Child of the Middle Passage" (Gills), 335, 341

children: with autism, 466–68; death of a child, 425–26; of God, everyone loved as, 69, 605, 619, 622; Indigenous Grandmothers on, 222, 227, 238, 243, 248; innocence and kindness of, 238, 239; loving all children as one's own, 318, 392, 519; parenting of, 189, 238, 511; sold into slavery, 324–25; women choosing to not have, 624

Chinmaya Mission, 575–76, 672

Chinmayananda, Swami, 553, 555–56, 558, 570, 572, 578, 672

Chödrön, Pema, 253

Christianity: and author's encounter with the Light, 10, 11; and blind obedience to the church, 49, 122–23; Eadie on, 613, 620; Eucharist in, 433, 529; on Jesus as "way and the truth and the life," 529–30; and labyrinth walking, 262; literalist perspectives in, 11, 199; mystics of, 24, 72, 126, 164, 531; and religious life of author, 11–12, 38, 39–44 (*see also* Episcopal Church; *the* church); *See also* Pavlos of Sinai, Father; Smith, Huston; Teresa, Mother

Christmas Eve candlelight service, 581–82

*the* church: author's attendance of, 12, 50; and author's marriage, 89–90, 125, 131–32, 133, 134, 193; and author's relationship with Christianity, 528–29; and "Declaration for Women's Inclusion," 300; and the Divine Feminine, 85; exclusion practiced by, 121, 122, 134; fundamentalist doctrine of, 11–12, 40, 42, 199, 299; gender roles in, 12, 125–26, 132, 135, 195–96, 198–99; and LGBT persons, 207; love of God for members of, 433; and missionary work of author in Florence, Italy, 43–44, 49–50; and panic attacks of author, 12–13, 47, 194; perspectives on nude bodies, 46; perspectives on sexuality, 40, 89; and undergraduate education of author, 39–43

Cimiluca, Mary, 94, 675: author's meeting with, 92, 106–21; background of, 113–14; as Frankl family representative, 113; and Frankl's *Man's Search for Meaning*, 113–14; and logotherapy, 119; and mental health, 113–14, 115, 119; recollections of Frankl, 107; and *Viktor & I* (film), 106, 109, 110, 114–15

circles, symbolism of, 227–28

civil rights movement, 333–34

Civil Rights Trail, 331–32

Climacus, Saint John, 175, 181, 183

climate change, 321

*The Cloud of Unknowing* (anonymous), 164, 165

Coffeen Nature Preserve, 260

Coherence: development of inner, 431, 457, 469; and Earth's magnetic field, liv; effected with intention, 446, 463; effected with music, 437; of energies related to love and compassion, liv, 397–99, 431–32; facilitated by present company, 477; and "zones of healing," 397–98, 446

*Come Be My Light* (Kolodiejchuk), 75

commercialism, 233–34, 382

commitment, 527

communication as communion, 159

compassion: and activism, 318; for addiction, drug and alcohol, 304–5; adversity's strengthening of, 402; attention as foundation of, 384–85; of Au, 168; being in presence of master of, 397; capacity for, as precious jewel, 411; and examining motivations for behaviors, 379; and free will, 457; of Hawkins, 267, 269, 304, 343, 489, 498, 531, 534, 546–48, 547, 586; and *Homo spiritus*, 476; and Indigenous Grandmothers, 227; and Karmapa, 318, 393, 396, 400–401, 402–3, 409–11; and karmic perspective, 280, 343–44; as lesson from one's enemies, 280, 312; and Mahayana Buddhism, 281–82; Mother Teresa, exemplar of, 54, 71; as one of Four Immeasurables, 399, 410; for ourselves, 210, 283, 379–80, 400, 514;

practice of, xliii, xlix, 30, 55, 56, 76–78, 227, 290, 378, 400–401, 515, 531, 534, 593; and qualities of devotees, 567; and right-brain consciousness, 438; and *tonglen* practice, 290–91, 381–83

Compassion course at University of Redlands, 376, 376–92: ages of participants, 386; community service in, 377–78, 388–89; Courtney, story of, 387–88; and examining motivations for behaviors, 379; exemplars for, 377, 389; and hardship, 389; and levels of suffering, 385–86; meditation instruction in, 374–75, 378–79; and seeds of greatness in students, 427–28; on self compassion, 379–80; struggles shared in, 386–88; and *tonglen* practice, 381–83

compulsions, surrender of, 354

Confederate soldiers and Confederacy, 214–15, 316, 317, 329–31, 333

conflict, diffusing, 245–46, 508, 547–48

conscience, Frankl on, 119–20

consciousness: and the brain, xxxiv, l, liii–lv, 202, 226, 259, 358, 434–36; collective, l, li, 22, 208, 328, 371, 375, 427, 475, 510; cosmic, 440; and Descartes, 450; effect of great works of art, music, and architecture on, xliv; feminine consciousness, 22, 49, 201–3, 225–28, 234, 338; Hawkins's Map of Consciousness, xxxvii–xlvi, 261–62, 390–92, 470–71, 474–75, 516; and *Homo spiritus*, l, 475; and humanity's fork in the road, 375; interconnected, l, 242, 247, 311, 337, 375, 428, 440, 517, 592; Mandela's transformation of, 420–24; M-fields in, 428; non physical, 437, 439, 576, 598–99; shifts in, xvi, li, lii, 234, 257, 259, 298, 328, 332, 371, 420, 469, 473; Supreme, 570–72, 576; Tiller on, 474–75; *turiya* (fourth state of consciousness), 165

consumerism, xl, 224, 382

contemplative practices, 165, 286–87. *See also* meditation and contemplative practice; prayer

Copernicus, Nicolaus, 456

corporate community of Christ, 185

courage, xxxvii, xxxviii, xli, xlviii, 140, 208, 261, 391, 429, 434, 622

Cousineau, Phil, 142

Creation: and Creator, 23; and the four elements, 242–43, 248; sacredness of, 22–23, 202, 234, 519–20

*Eyes on the Prize* (documentary), 331

faith, xxx, 566

falling in love, 88–91, 205, 285, 364

*fanā* (annihilation), 20

fear: choosing love over, 208; of death/dying, 505, 522; and Hawkins's Map of Consciousness, xxxvii, xl, xlv, xlviii, 390; letting go of, 339–40, 537

the feminine, 21–22, 85, 202, 204, 225–28

feminism: and deferential behavioral patterns of author, 198–99; feminist awakening of author, 195–99; and reading feminist theology, 197–98; of seminary professors, 126–27, 195; viewed as threat to moral order, 299

fidelity, 505

fire as foundational element, 242–43, 248

first responders, 383

Flordemayo, 222

Florence, Italy: art and architecture of, 44–47; Cathedral of Santa Maria del Fiore, 44–45; missionary work in, 38, 43–44, 49–50; Ponte Vecchio, 47, 49; and spiritual renaissance of author, 44–46, 87

force (vs. power), xxxiv, xxxv–xxxvi, xxxviii, 121, 261–62, 436

forgiveness: for acts of violence, 413–14; and Enlightenment, 534; Frankl on, 98, 116–17, 214; Hawkins on, 344, 516–18, 534; 17th Karmapa on, 413–14; and karmic perspective, 344; as lesson from one's enemies, 312; and loving difficult/negative people, 516–17; of oneself, 515, 624–25; Polacca on forgiving our mother, 244; and qualities of devotees, 567; Smith on, 153; and South Africa's Truth and Reconciliation Commission, 425–26, 430; and Storm's near-death experience, 627

formative context, 322, 326

four elements of life, 242–44, 248

Four Immeasurables, 399, 410

Francis, Pope, xlviii, 64, 245, 671

Francis of Assisi, Saint, xliv, 286, 477

Frankl, Viktor, 94, 95–123, 674: and Compassion course at University of Redlands, 377; compassion for members of Nazi Party, 98, 117,

214, 517–18; on conscience, 119–20; contemplation of suicide, 101, 112; critics of, 116–17, 120, 214; death and gravesite of, 110, 113; on decency, 120, 121–22; on dignity of the spirit, 39; *The Doctor and The Soul*, 99–101, 102; and Elly (second wife), 102, 103, 110–13, 309; energy fields of, xliv, 263, 517–18; focusing on "best version" of others, 108, 116, 117; and Holocaust, 39, 104, 117–18, 475; and logotherapy, 97, 99–101, 103, 109–10, 111, 116–19, 475; on love as path to meaning, 206, 592; on love as ultimate goal, 92; *Man's Search for Meaning*, xliv, 39, 92, 101, 105–6, 110, 113, 117–18; and Maslow's "hierarchy of needs," 118; on Milgram Experiment, 121; on Mother Teresa/Hitler in us all, 117, 340; in Nazi-controlled Austria, 98–99; on Nazism and Holocaust, 104, 517–18; on passive suicides, 105–6; personal interactions of, 107–9; as prisoner in Nazi concentration camp, 95–96, 99, 103, 104, 120; professional life, 97–98, 103, 674; on recollections' ability change inner state, 443; religious life/perspectives of, 101, 109; on scientific reductionism, 104, 475; on suffering (meaning in), 100, 104–6, 115, 592; on teaching values, 145; and Tilly (first wife), 96, 99, 100–101, 102, 110, 112, 119–20, 443

free will, 342, 457

Freire, Maria Alice Campos, 222, 224, 231

Freud, Sigmund, 254

friendliness, xlii, 393, 567

friendship: befriending oneself, 283–84; and Compassion course at University of Redlands, 377, 389; and "friends for life," 113–14; for lifetimes, 279; powerful effect of, 180, 387, 399, 497, 499, 510, 621, 625; "soul friends," 280, 603; with/among women, 80, 195, 199–204, 497, 615

Frost, Robert, 208

Galatea and Pygmalion, 86, 87

Gandhi, Mohandas K.: and caste system in India, 68; and Compassion course at University of Redlands, 377, 389; energy fields of, xlvii, 263, 477; first courtroom address of, 200; on nature of God, 254; power of, xxxiii, xxxiv, 436; and power of love, 261, 392, 477; and repetition of God's name, 574; and soul force, liii

Garga, Maharishi, 562

gay population. *See* LGBT persons

697

Havasupai, 242

Hawkins, David R. ("Doc"), *250*, 251–73, *496*, 497–525, *501*, *580*, 676–77: on *agape* love, 519, 522; on animals, 507–8, 527–28; animals of, 493–94, 507, 544–45; atheism of, 256; in author's dreams, xix–xx, xxii, 581, 587, 589, 632–33; author's early encounters with, xix, 252, 254–55, 263–65, 493; on author's experience with the Light, 494; author's forewords to books of, 587, 715; author's home near, xix, xxi–xxii, 477, 481–82; author's inward prostration to, 267–68; author's kneeling before, 268–69, *270*, 271; author's lifetime-transcending relationship with, 280, 492; as author's "mirror" (self-awareness), 298, 543; author's recognition of, 280; and author's relationship with Christianity, 528–29; and author's sexual orientation, 536–39; author's testing of, 488–92; author's training from, 494, 527–35, 541–51, 582–87; background of, 256, 499–500; on being one's best, 510, 521–22; on books and writing, 585; on Buddha's surrender, 524–25; and Chidatmananda, 550–51, 553–54, 568, 569–70; and Christmas Eve candlelight service, 581–82; on compassion for oneself, 514; compassion of, 546–48, 547; on death/dying, 505, 522–23; death of, xix, xxii, *501*, 554, 576–79, 587–89, 633; on devotion, 297–98, 527–28, 551; on devotional relationships of teachers and students, 501–5, 582; directive given to author on teaching, 371, 492, 528–29; on Divine Order, 545–46; on ego/egocentrism, 540–41; encounters with Infinite Presence/Love, 255–57, 522–23; on endeavors done out of love, 508–10; on Enlightenment, 257, 297, 505, 516, 533–35; Episcopal Church membership of, 531; and existential vacuum experienced by author, 252–53; on exploitation perpetrated by teachers, 504; *The Eye of the I: From Which Nothing is Hidden*, 259; on fear, 339; on fidelity, 505; on fringe sects, 503–4; giving up attachment to, xxii, 633–34; on group in pursuit of Truth, 505; *Healing and Recovery*, 575; on hidden forms of love, 509–10; on his responsibilities to students, 293, 491, 504, 582, 587; on *Homo spiritus*, l, 475; on illusion of identity/personhood, 584; on importance of teachers, 530–31; interviews with, 234, 494, 501–25, 527–28, 530, 533, 535, 583, 585; *I: Reality and Subjectivity*, 259; on Jesus as "way and the truth and the life," 529–30; on karma, 342–45, 504, 511, 512, 535, 542; and the Karmapa, 405; lectures of, 498, 500, 502, 550, 585–87; *Letting Go*, xxxix, 538–39, 587, 715; as liberated being and living Master,

266, 569–70, 576–77; on love as ultimate law of the universe, l, 229, 345, 522; on love in everyday life, 506–10, 512–14, 521, 590; on love's power to counterbalance negativity, xlvii, 510–11; love transmitted by, xxix–xxx, 267, 297, 433, 494, 547, 557–58, 570; on loving difficult/negative people, 514–19; on loving "God in the other," 572–73; on loving oneself, 513, 515–16, 524; Map of Consciousness, xxxvi, xxxvii–xlvi, 259, 262–63, 391–92, 471, 507, 568; marital partnership of, 309, 545, 586–87; on meditation practice, 477; on Mother Teresa's inner suffering, 73–74; as mystic, 498–99, 531; on Native American rituals, 228–29, 233–34; on nature of God, 520, 531; on old age, 523–24; ordinary appearance of, 264, 489; *Orthomolecular Psychiatry* (Pauling and Hawkins), 500; others' perceptions of, 265–66; personality of, 265; on physical presence of teaching function, 490; on power of love to effect change, 508–11; on pragmatic value of love, 513; on prayer, 228–29, 512, 546; on purpose of many incarnations, 343; realization of the Oneness of All Existence, 256–57, 500; on religions, 518, 531; on role and limits of reason, xlii, xlvi, 448–50; as scientist, 436–37; on seeing the divine in everything, 519–22; on Self of students and teachers, xx, 298, 502–3, 633; on sharing a spiritual teaching with others, danger of, 511–12, 542; on spiritual communities, 518; on spiritual drivenness, 504–5; on starting where you are, 298, 299; on struggles and suffering, 256, 511; surrender of, 585, 586; "Tae Ryoung Sun Kak Tosa" (Teacher of Enlightenment), 501; teaching methods of, 266, 544–45, 548; Tiller on, 470–71; on timelessness of love, 255, 257, 522–23; on Unconditional Love, 519–21; as Universal Spirit, xxii, 531, 589; on various forms of Love, 506; "When the clouds are removed, the sun shines forth," 5, 257, 263, 379; on world peace, 510–11; "You yourself are what you're looking for," 251, 337, 535, 633; on Zen, 583; *See also Power vs. Force*

Hawkins, Susan, *501*, 677: on Doc as mystic, 498–99; Doc's devotion to, 523; on Doc's respect for trees, 493; energy of, 586–87; and home energy, 546; and homosexuality, 538; and lectures of Doc, 500, 586; on the Light, 497–98; marital partnership of, 309, 545, 586–87

Healing: capacity of love for, xxxviii, xlvi–xlviii, 53, 71, 194, 206, 262, 389, 427, 435, 444; Eadie on, 613–19; effected with intention, 461–68; and Indigenous Grandmothers, 230–34; and mission of Growing a Global Heart, 326–29, 333–34;

teacher's capacity for, 33–34, 433; and the wounds from ending relationships, 210–11

*Healing and Recovery* (Hawkins), 575

health and self care, 510, 575, 616–19

heart, power of, liii–lv, 34, 207, 236, 318, 388, 399, 423, 442, 607

heart *chakra*, xlvi, xlix, 537

HeartMath Institute, liii–liv

"heart of hearts," 18, 24, 122, 272, 499

Heart Sutra, xliv

hell, 619, 620, 627

hidden forms of love, 35, 74, 509–10

"hierarchy of needs" (Maslow), 118

Higher Selves, people living close to, 136

Hildegard, Saint, 255

Hinduism, xlv, 262, 502, 575–76. *See also* Chidatmananda, Swami

His Eminence the 8th Khamtrul Rinpoche, 275–76

His Holiness the 12th Gyalwang Drukpa, 278

His Holiness the 16th Karmapa, 395, 405

His Holiness the 17th Karmapa, xvii, xxx, 395–417, 679–80: on activists, 318; on adversity, 402; age of, 403; artistic expressions of, 415–16; author's dreams of, 402–3, 582–83; author's encounters with, 372, 403–6, 417; on empathy, 400, 407–8, 409–10, 417; on enemies, 412–14; energy fields of, xlvii, 263; on Four Immeasurables, 410; on full ordination for nuns, 278–79; on homosexual relationships, 540; on inclusive love, 399–402; on increasing love and compassion, 409–11; on innate goodwill for others, 399; *Interconnected*, 401; on interdependent existences, 414–16; interview with, 406–17; on jewel in every heart, 411; on love for all beings, 412–14; on meditation, 381, 383–84; peace and compassion of, 402–3; on power of love in the world, 406–9; on recollecting of kindnesses, liii, 401; and red string, 82; on relationships that transcend lifetimes, 279; on romantic love, 416–17, 540; on self compassion, 380; time spent at Univ. of Redlands, 372, 383, 392–93, *394*, *401*, 401–2, 403; on "watering down" of spiritual practice, 372–73

Holocaust, xvii, 104, 117–18, 120–21, 475

holy places, 286

homophobia, 206–7, 311

homosexuality, 206–7, 536–40, 624. *See also* LGBT persons

*Homo spiritus*, l, 474–75

hope, saying yes to, 429

hopelessness, 166, 184, 186–87, 620

Hopi, 224–25, 228–29, 230, 375

Hopkins, Gerard Manley, 28

Houston, Jean, 328

Humility: and avoiding judgmentalism, 184–85; as characteristic of interviewees, 62, 97, 116, 234, 424, 585, 605; and forgiveness, 517; importance of, 177, 234, 237, 305; learned at feet of teacher, 549–50

humor, xxx, 59, 222, 232, 280–81, 283, 391, 454, 494, 544, 549, 584

"hungry ghosts," 235

Huxley, Aldous, 149

identity, xvi, xliv, 92, 360, 434, 561, 584, 589

ignorance, xxxiii, 29, 30, 130, 209, 310, 342, 361, 515, 625

illness, spiritual dynamics of, xxxix, 105, 156, 230, 265, 591–93, 616–19

imperfection as gateway for Grace, xxiv

impotency, 537

India: author's trip to, xxxiii, 280–81, 403–4, 487, 554; *See also* Chidatmananda, Swami; His Holiness the 17th Karmapa; Sahib, Bhai; Teresa, Mother

Indigenous Grandmothers, *218*, 219–48, 377–79, 677-79: "all my relations" emphasis of (interconnectedness), xxxii, 216, 220, 225, 241–42, 243, 247, 248; around the world, 234–36; and Compassion course at Univ. of Redlands, 375; Councils held in circles, 227–28; and healing/sacred medicine, 230–34; integrated masculine/feminine consciousness in, 227; and living in alignment, 246–47; mission statement, 219, 222; nature of message, 221–22, 224; original thirteen Grandmothers, 222–23; origins of, 223; prayers

700

variety of methods for, 383–84; weeding analogy for, 253

memories from our ancestors, 601

Merton, Thomas, 157–58, 159

*Metamorphosis* (Ovid), 86

Michelangelo, 45

*Midnights with the Mystic* (Simone and Vasudev), 350

Milgram, Stanley, 121

Milgram Experiment, 121

Miller, Suzy, 463

miracles, 517, 546, 618

Miraculous Medal, 82–83

*The Mirror of Simple Souls* (Porete), 126

Missionaries of Charity, 53–83, 681: and Canonization of Mother Teresa, 57–59; and caste system in India, 79–80; conditions faced by sisters, 65–66, 78–79; and Diana, Princess of Wales, 80; and Frankl's *Man's Search for Meaning*, 101; and Home for the Poor, 63–64; international expansion of ministries, 71; and lepers ministry, 69–70, 80; lovingkindness of, 59, 63, 64–65, 66, 74; official recognition of, 68; prayer practiced daily by, 58; and relic of Mother Teresa, 57; serving the poorest poor, 67–70, 79; smiling of sisters, 59, 65–66; trust placed in God's providence, 59, 65–66; vow of poverty, 60–62, 64–66, 79; in Yemen, 65–66

missionary work in Florence, Italy, 38, 43–44, 49–50

mistakes, purpose of, xxiii–lv, 503–5, 602, 609, 615

*mitakuye oyasin*, xxxii, 248, 607

Mohawks, 332

Monroe, Robert, 437

Monroe Institute of Virginia, 437–39

Moody, Raymond, 598–99

Moon Cabin, 312, 336, 337–46, 591

moral superiority, author's struggles with, 40–42, 50, 138, 210, 299–301, 355–56

morphogenetic fields (M-field), 428

Moses (biblical), xlvii, 173–74, 181

Moses, Janet and Bob, 331

Mother Earth, 22, 203, 222, 224–25, 241, 243, 315, 355, 375, 381

Mothers: and healing mother wounds, 225; love for all children, 284, 317–18, 519; love for her own children, sacrificial nature of, 285, 288, 509, 541, 619; making peace with, 203, 225

*Mother Teresa* (documentary), 78

"Mother Teresa Effect," 79

motivations for behaviors, examining, 379

Mount Sinai, 171–74, 176–78

Mount St. Mary, 164

Muggeridge, Malcolm, 71

music, xliii, xliv, 415–16

*My Descent into Death* (Storm), 629

*My Land, My People: The Original Autobiography of His Holiness the Dalai Lama of Tibet* (Dalai Lama), 105

"Mysteries of the Jesus Prayer" (film), 186

mystics and mysticism: Catholic mystics, 164, 167, 352; caveat of, 489; and Christian religion, 531; daily life as/with, 498–99, 535, 544–46, 585; and doctrine of love, 126; encountered in seminary, 126; and Gothic and Renaissance architecture, 45; Hawkins, 498–99, 531 (*see also* Hawkins, David R.); and Hawkins's Map of Consciousness, xxxviii, xliv, xlv; and Hawkins's publications, 259; and Mother Teresa, 67, 72, 73; mystic experiences of scientists, 434, 436, 437; response of the church to, xv, 12, 25, 166, 531; and Sadhguru, 351, 358; and Smith, 147, 148, 152; in *Song of Songs*, 25; suffering of, 29; and surrender to love, 25, 26, 28, 29, 126, 130, 484, 487; and *theosis* (mystical union with God), 173; and *unio mystica*, xiv, 167, 305, 500; Vaughan-Lee, 20 (*see also* Vaughan-Lee, Llewellyn); *See also* Sufism

Najm al-Dîn Kubrâ, 15

nakedness, 45–46, 202, 539–40

Naqshband, Baha ad-Din, 19

Naqshbandiyya-Mujaddidiyya lineage of Sufis, 19

Narada, Sage, 559, 562, 563

*Narada Bhakti Sutras* (Narada), 559, 560

narcissism, 383, 519

Nasr, Seyyed Hussein, 671

Nation, Carry A., 137–40, 304

Native American Church, 148

Native Americans: artwork of (with intentional flaw), xxiv, 622; chiefs and medicine men and women, xlvii; and Eadie's Lakota heritage, 597–98, 611, 621–22; forcible conversion of, by Catholic Church, 245; and healing/sacred medicine, 230–34; and "original instructions," 228, 242, 248, 375; past sufferings of, 244; on prayer, 221, 228–30; role of (as spiritual leaders), 601; and sacredness of life, 147–48, 237, 248; and Snake Dance of the Hopi, 228–29; spiritual principles of, 235, 237, 240–41, 598, 621; storyteller sculpture, 221; and sweat lodges, 233–34, 262; *See also* Indigenous Grandmothers

Nature: life and death in, 260–61; rhythms of, 204

Nazis and Nazism: and Frankl's compassion/nonjudgment, 98, 117, 214; and guards' acts of mercy, 100; and Holocaust, xvii, 103, 104, 117–18, 120–21; parallels with Milgram Experiment, 121

near-death experiences: of Camp (atheist), 619; of Eadie, 280, 594, 598–604, 606, 610–12, 613–15, 619–20, 622; and Hawkins's Map of Consciousness, xliii–xliv; of Johnson, 4; of McMoneagle, 439; Smith on, 152–53; of Storm, 619, 626–29

Needleman, Jacob, 103

Negativity: and advanced beings, 585; and Bolte-Taylor's recovery experience, 436; Eadie on, 601, 606–7; handling negative people, 116, 119, 515, 573, 606; and Hawkins's *Power vs. Force*, xxxv, xxxvii–xliii, xlvi, 261; Jesus on, 518; karmic views of, 280, 290–91, 342–45, 535, 575; love's power to counterbalance, xlvi–xlvii, 236, 261, 619–21; negated by loving thoughts, 510, 572, 575, 601

neutrality, xli, 391, 568

Nhat Hanh, Thich, 403

Nietzsche, Frederic, 106

nihilism, 104, 475

Nilus of Sinai, Saint, 183

Nirvana, 435, 512

Noetic Films, Inc., 106, 114, 675–76

noetic knowledge, 8–9, 148

Nofemela, Easy, 425–26

nonattachment, xxii, 288, 515, 523, 539

nonbelievers, 609

non-harming (*ahimsa*), 303

non-possessiveness, 240–41

nonviolence, 311

Nûn, Dhû'l, 27

nuns, 278–79. *See also* Missionaries of Charity; Palmo, Jetsunma Tenzin

oceans, symbolism of, 201, 260, 482–83

old age, 523–24

Oliver, Mary, 311, 377, 384, 671

OM chants, 262

*On Death and Dying* (Kübler-Ross), 440

Oneness: author's awareness of, 7–8, 44, 203, 261, 345–46, 355, 593; as essential aspect of love, xvii; and existential loneliness, 385; Hawkins on, 257, 346, 517; Karmapa on, 414–15; and perspectives of Gills and Rooks, 318, 326; as Reality, 147, 149, 203, 231, 331, 354, 434, 435; Sunlight on, 310–11, 337; Tiller on, 472; and Vasudev's Isha Foundation, 354–55; Vaughan-Lee on, xiv, xvii, 23, 35

openheartedness, 268, 316, 430

oppression, 310–11, 390, 421

"Original Instructions," l, 228, 242, 248, 375

*Orthomolecular Psychiatry* (Pauling and Hawkins), 500

Palmo, Jetsunma Tenzin, 274, 275–94, 681–82: on attachments, 284–85, 288; biography about, 277, 281, 338; on change starting from within, 427; on contemplative practices, 286–87; on devotional love of teachers/gurus, 291–94; enlightenment pursued by, 276, 279; on experiences in endless lifetimes, 343–44; and Jetsunma title, 278; on language of love, 282; on loving children, 318; on loving-kindness, 282–84; meditation practice of, 277; monastery life of, 276, 278; nunnery established by, 277–78, 293; ordained as a nun, 276; on radiation of love, 286; recognition of Guru, 273, 292–93; relationship with Guru, 275–76, 279; retreat in Himalayas, 276–77, 281–82; on romantic love, 284–85; on suffering/difficulties, 289–91; on thought pollution, 286, 287–88; and *tonglen* of mother, 381; unconditional love of mother, 288–89; and weeding analogy for meditation, 253

palm raised, as portrayed in works of art, xliv

panic disorder of author, 12–13, 47, 194, 198, 252, 624. *See also* anxiety

parents of author, 105, 203, 590–94

Parliament of the World's Religions, xxviii, xxxi, xxxiii, lv, 266, 529, 554, 607

past life regression, 492

Paul, Saint, 28, 128, 179, 185

Pavlos of Sinai, Father, *170*, 171–90, 682–83: on agape love, 180–81; on Americans, 175, 182; on authentic love/love in action, 176–80; on Bedouin neighbors, 172–73, 179–80; on corporate community of Christ vs. individual spirituality, 185; education of, 186; on evil, 184; on God as love, 180, 185, 188; on hopelessness, 184, 186–87; on inner peace, 164; on Jesus Prayer, 178–79, 185–86; on judging others, 175, 181–82, 184–85, 187–89; on jury duty, 186; on life as monk in the desert, 172, 174–75; on love, three stages, 185; on loving those who hate you, 178–79; on *nepsis* (vigilance, watchfulness), 184–85; and refuge in Sinai desert, 88; on rejection of God (atheism), 188; relatability of, 176; and respect for other traditions, lv, 172–73; student workers acknowledged by, 189–90; on writings of ascetics at Sinai, 183

Peace: as the fruit of loving, 55, 63; and Hawkins's Map of Consciousness, xxxvii, xliv; inner peace leads to outer peace, 164, 172, 204, 291, 373, 375, 389; of 17th Karmapa, 402–3; and limitations of activism, 300, 310–11, 316, 318, 422; love as a work of, 53; making peace with mothers/Mother Earth, liii, 203, 224–25; with oneself, 136, 153, 204, 264, 354, 443, 514, 537; spiritual experience of, 7, 155, 255, 435, 440, 443

Peck, Marilyn, 211–13

*The Perennial Philosophy* (Huxley), 149

perfectionism, 41, 543, 549

Perry, Diane. *See* Palmo, Jetsunma Tenzin

Persian weavers, xxiv

Persons, Ethel, 90

Peter, Saint, 168, 193

Petrie, Ann, 78

Petrie, Jeanette, 78

Petrie, William, 70

peyote, 148

phobias of author, 47. *See also* anxiety; panic disorder of author; public speaking phobia of author

Pierpoint, Richard, 333

Pilgrim, Agnes Baker, 223, 225–26, 227

Pio, Padre, xliv, 263

pity, 56, 408

Plato, 235, 256

Polacca, Mona, *236*, 678–79: addiction recovery work of, 237–38; on connection with the Sacred, 228; on creation and the four elements, 242–44, 248; on healing mother wounds, 225; on humanity's fork in the road, 375; on interconnectedness, 241–42, 243, 247, 303; on living in alignment, 246–47; on making peace with mothers/Mother Earth, liii, 203, 224–25; name of, 237; on non-possessiveness, 240–41; on origins of Indigenous Grandmothers, 223; on power of prayer, 228, 229–30, 245–47; on practicing kindness, 238–40; on recognizing one's sacred beginnings, 237, 399, 441; on significance of small fires, 220; on small groups with Spiritual center, 235–36; on speaking to the living water, 602; on spiritual transformation symbolized by butterflies, 216; and talk at Wellesley College, 222

polarization, xxxv, 138, 261, 299, 310, 375–76, 391, 530, 536

Porete, Marguerite: depths of devotion of, 126, 131, 166; energy fields of, xlvii; on finding Him everywhere, 262; and Hawkins's Map of Consciousness, xliv; on lost vs. sad souls of religious people, 127–28, 130; on love, the power and necessity of, 126, 128, 130

pornography, 620–21

positive, focusing on what is, xliii, 116, 139, 424, 572, 601

positivity, benefit of, 248, 261, 286, 400, 436, 445–46, 510

possessiveness, 240–41, 523

poverty, 78, 290, 427, 600

power: of the circle, 228; and Divinity, xvi, 27–28, 254–55, 257, 338, 573–74; inner nature of, xxv, xxxiii, 221, 261, 294, 436, 616; like an electromagnetic field, xlviii; opposite of force, xxxiii–xxxviii, xli, 121, 261–62, 436; *See also* healing; heart, power of; love

*Power vs. Force* (Hawkins): about, xxxiv–xxxv, 259, 490, 500, 676; author's first encounter with, 254–59; author's work on revised edition of, 587; on compassion and universal forgiveness, 534; on counterbalancing effect of the power of love, xlvi, xlix; on energy fields, 261, 436; and Hawkins's encounters with Infinite Presence, 257; and Hawkins's Map of Consciousness, xxxvii–xlv, xlvii–xlix, 259, 262; on how to reach the ultimate state, 534; on the Light, 258; and Moon Cabin retreat, 337; Mother Teresa's blessing of, 55, 500; publication of, 490, 500; on spiritual practices' effects, 262; on Subtle Power, 430; on surrendering everything to God, 534

*The Practice of the Presence of God* (Lawrence), xliv, liii, 532

pragmatic value of love, 513

prayer: contemplative, 165; as expression of love, lv, 512, 601, 626; Hawkins on, 228–29, 256, 262, 344, 477, 509, 512; and Indigenous Grandmothers, 220, 221, 223, 224, 225–26, 228–30, 245, 246–47; the Jesus Prayer, liii, 164, 178–79, 185, 186, 384, 443, 574; life lived as a prayer, 44, 65, 384, 509, 544; and living in alignment, 246–47; of Mother Teresa for ceasefire, 79, 430; Native American teachings on, 221, 228, 607; Pavlos of Sinai on, 175–76, 178–79, 185–86; power to unite, 222; and ripple effect, 626; the *Shema Yisrael*, 100; Sufi prayer, 581

preservation, 244

pride, xxxvii, xli, xlviii, 391: and activism, 300–301, 318; in beliefs, 41, 50, 122, 130, 532; Hawkins free of, 585; and Hawkins's Map of Consciousness, xxxvii, xli, xlviii, 261, 391; and "knowing what's best for others," 301, 511; surrender of, 210, 269, 305, 483, 486, 532, 535, 537, 543, 544, 548–49

Prince, 605

Princeton Theological Seminary, *124*, 131–34, 137, 194–95

problem solving, 298

procreative instincts, 537

*Proof of Heaven* (Alexander), 437

prostration (surrender) at the feet of a master, 18, 60, 267, 292, 485–88, 541, 579

Protestant work ethic, 374, 524

Psyche (soul), 86–88, 132–33, 298, 301

*The Psychic Discoveries Behind the Iron Curtain* (Ostrander and Schroeder), 453

psychoenergetics, 450–51, 453–56

public speaking phobia of author, 125, 136, 196, 199–200: healing of, 140, 203

purpose (mission) of souls, 280, 608–9

Pygmalion and Galatea, 86, 87

*Pygmalion and Galatea* (Lagrenée), *84*

Pygmalion effect, 86–87, 116

qualities of love, xxx, 494

quantum mechanics, 455–56

Quran, xliv, 15, 384

Rābiʿa, xliv, xlvii

*rabita*, 19

racism: and apartheid of South Africa, lii, 417, 419–20, 421, 422, 423, 425, 427; discussed in Compassion course, 390–92; Gills on formative context of, 322; Westerners' resistance to karmic context of, 290

radiance: of goodness, 146, 397; of light, 27, 28, 34, 181, 435, 492, 599, 603, 605; of love and compassion, xxx, xlv, xlix, 67, 168, 262, 284, 286, 308, 351, 395, 494, 514, 522, 634; "we radiate what we are," 431, 471, 476

Ramakrishna, Sri, 145, 147, 255, 263

rape, spiritual, 504

rap music, 620

Reality, 147, 148, 149, 152, 203, 272, 305, 351, 352, 354, 360–61, 441, 522–23, 533

reason/rationality: bypassed by experiential knowledge, 356, 585, 601; and Hawkins's Map of Consciousness, xxxvii, xxxviii, xlii–xliii, xlvi, xlviii, 392; limitation of, xlvi, lii, 21, 127, 148, 165, 263,

714

# About the Author

Fran Grace is Professor of Religious Studies and founding Steward of the Meditation Program at the University of Redlands (California), where she has pioneered a contemplative and intergenerational approach to university education since 2004. Recognition for her teaching and research into spiritual life has included appearances on CSPAN and NPR, a Pew Fellowship from Yale University, a

**Fran Grace, 2018**
(Meggan Austin/courtesy of The Institute for Contemplative Life)

Luce Fellowship in Comparative Religion and Theology, and many teaching awards. After receiving her Ph.D. in 1997 from Princeton Theological Seminary, she wrote *Carry A. Nation: Retelling the Life,* which *Publisher's Weekly* named a "landmark" biography. In 2004, a life crisis opened a deeper interest in the existential and spiritual sides of life, and Fran then spent many years investigating the inner arts and sciences, expressed in such publications as *Meditation and the Classroom* (co-edited with Judith Simmer-Brown), *A Semester Within* (documentary film), and numerous articles. Her quest was enriched by an unexpected encounter with a teacher who introduced her to a path of inner freedom that respects the foundational teachings of all spiritual traditions. In 2008, she founded The Institute for Contemplative Life, a 501c3 nonprofit organization dedicated to the "inner pathway" common to all religions. Before her teacher's death i 2012, she edited and wrote the foreword to his widely popular boc *Letting Go: The Pathway of Surrender* by Dr. David R. Hawkins, wl taught her: "Love is both the means and the end."

# About Inner Pathway Publishing

Inner Pathway is the communications arm of the Institute for Contemplative Life, a 501(c)(3) nonprofit organization created in 2008. Our purpose is to present books and other materials to educate about and inspire the inner capacities of joy, unconditional love, peace, beauty, compassion, humor, and truth in a way that is of practical spiritual benefit in the present world. These inner capacities are the goal of every religion, yet religion is not required to access them. They lie within each person. The inner pathway is timeless and open to all, free of dogma, dues, or membership.

Contact Information:
www.innerpathway.com
info@innerpathway.com
877.478.7284
PO Box 1435
Redlands, CA 92373
USA

Additional Titles:
*I Give You the Springtime of My Blushing Heart:*
*A Poetic Love Song*
by Dedan Gills and Belvie Rooks

*A Semester Within*
by Fran Grace (documentary film)